ID699858

Handbook of Political Socialization

THE FREE PRESS SERIES ON POLITICAL BEHAVIOR
Stanley Allen Renshon, General Editor

Handbook of Political Socialization: Theory and Research
Stanley Allen Renshon

HANDBOOK OF POLITICAL SOCIALIZATION

Theory and Research

Edited by
Stanley Allen Renshon

THE FREE PRESS
A Division of Macmillan Publishing Co., Inc.
NEW YORK
Collier Macmillan Publishers
LONDON

Copyright © 1977 by The Free Press
A Division of Macmillan Publishing Co., Inc.

All rights reserved. No part of this book may be reproduced or
transmitted in any form or by any means, electronic or mechanical,
including photocopying, recording, or by any information storage and
retrieval system, without permission in writing from the Publisher.

The Free Press
A Division of Macmillan Publishing Co., Inc.
866 Third Avenue, New York, N.Y. 10022

Collier Macmillan Canada, Ltd.

Library of Congress Catalog Card Number: 76–55102

Printed in the United States of America

printing number

1 2 3 4 5 6 7 8 9 10

Library of Congress Cataloging in Publication Data

Main entry under title:

Handbook of political socialization.

    (The Free Press series on political behavior)
    Bibliography: p.
    Includes indexes.
    1. Political socialization--Addresses, essays,
lectures. I. Renshon, Stanley Allen.
JA76.H38   301.5'92   76-55102
ISBN 0-02-926340-9

Copyright Acknowledgments

Figures 2–3 and 2–4: From *Fortran Programming for the Behavioral
Sciences* by Donald J. Veldman, pp. 239, 240. Copyright © 1967 by
Holt, Rinehart and Winston, Inc. Reprinted by permission of Holt,
Rinehart and Winston.

Figure 8–3: From Theodore M. Newcomb, "An Approach to the Study
of Communicative Acts," *Psychological Review,* 60 (1953), Fig. 1,
p. 394. Copyright 1953 by the American Psychological Association.
Reprinted by permission of the APA and the author.

Table 10–2: From J. R. Nesselroade & P. B. Baltes, "Adolescent
Personality Development and Historical Change: 1970–1972," *Monographs of The Society for Research in Child Development,* 1974, *39,*
no. 154, Fig. 2, p. 4. Copyright © 1974 by The Society for Research
in Child Development, Inc.

306.2
H1912

Contents

v

10/27/78 Scholarly 19.95 - 17.34

169765

Part Three   Outcomes of the Political Socialization Process

Part Four   Possibilities

306.2
H191

Preface

The Handbook of Political Socialization: Theory and Research is the first of a projected series of handbooks on political behavior. Along with others currently in preparation, it is meant to address a basic subfield or conceptual focus within the discipline of political science. Each handbook will be concerned with four lines of inquiry. A primary concern will be delineation and explication of the boundaries of present inquiry, including major theories, concepts, and explanatory frameworks. Second, methodological techniques and assessment strategies relevant to validating alternative conceptual approaches will be examined. Third, each book will analyze current and past research as a basis for the fourth line of inquiry, that of establishing the most needed or promising roads for subsequent inquiry. It is hoped that, by covering each of these areas, the handbooks will prove helpful not only to those already familiar with the field but also to those beginning their explorations.

Scholarship is a collective enterprise, and this handbook is no exception. At the initial planning stage, a number of colleagues were most generous with their encouragement and I am most appreciative of Jeanne Knutson, Herbert Hyman, David Easton, Robert Hess, and Donald Searing in these matters. Several persons facilitated the handbook by virtue of their manual dexterity, not to mention their command of the fine points of the English language. The extensive typing requirements were well handled by Mrs. Dorothy Carmody and Mrs. Sylvia Hecht. A special word of thanks is due to Mrs. Elsie Friedman, whose considerable administrative and personal skills, combined with a warm and supportive temperament, have facilitated both the author and his work in numerous ways. Dennis Sullivan has worked hard all year on numerous aspects of this project and was especially helpful, as was Debbi Furman, in preparing the author index. I would like to extend my sincere appreciation to Lionel Dean for copy editing the manuscript and to Robert Harrington and Tita Gillespie of The Free Press for helpful guidance throughout production.

Bill Hanna played an important part in providing an intellectually stimulating and facilitative context. I should also like to give a special word of thanks to another colleague, Bill Bosworth. In a year of immense change his continued sensitivity to teaching, research, and writing schedules was most important. I am most appreciative of the continued encouragement and support I have received from both.

Last, but among the most important persons connected with this book, are the contributors. No editor could hope for a more considerate, flexible, and sagacious group. They have made the editing of this book not only intellectually exciting, but personally rewarding.

STANLEY A. RENSHON
New York City

About the Contributors

PAUL ALLEN BECK is an Associate Professor of Political Science at the University of Pittsburgh and the new Book Review Editor of the *American Political Science Review*. He has contributed articles on voting behavior, political parties, political socialization, and methodology to professional journals and is the co-author of a volume on political socialization in the American Political Science Association's SETUPS series. He is currently studying the impact of various types of elections on American political institutions and the public today.

STEVEN H. CHAFFEE is Vilas Research Professor in the School of Journalism and Mass Communication at the University of Wisconsin–Madison. A former journalist, he has done a wide variety of research on the role of mass media in adolescent socialization and in political processes. He is co-author of *Using the Mass Media* and editor of *Political Communication*.

NEAL E. CUTLER is Associate Professor of Political Science, and Laboratory Chief, Social Policy Laboratory, Andrus Gerontology Center, University of Southern California. His major research interests have focused on the analysis of ontogenetic and generational patterns of political attitudes and behavior—including studies in generational patterns of domestic and foreign policy attitudes, the analysis of the political behavior of older persons, and the application of demographic concepts to the study of politics.

JAMES CHOWNING DAVIES, Professor of Political Science at the University of Oregon, is the author of *Human Nature in Politics* and the editor of *When Men Rebel and Why*. He is currently at work on a study of political ideology.

DANIEL A. FRIEDMAN taught at Chamerade College and the University of Hawaii, and is presently serving as a consultant to the Institute for Religious and Social Change.

KENNETH J. GERGEN is Professor and Chairman of the Psychology Department at Swarthmore College. He is the author of *The Psychology of Behavior Exchange, The Concept of Self,* and articles in the fields of personality and social behavior. He has been a Guggenheim and Fulbright Fellow and has edited a number of volumes including *The Study of Policy Formation* (with R. Bauer).

MARILYN BROOKES HOSKIN is an Assistant Professor of Political Science at the State University of New York at Buffalo. Her research has centered on the political involvement of adolescents, and currently involves analysis of comparative data on American and German students.

RICHARD JOSLYN is an Assistant Professor at Temple University. His research and teaching interests include political socialization, public opinion, voting behavior, and political methodology.

HAROLD D. LASSWELL is Ford Foundation Professor Emeritus of Law and Social Sciences, Yale Law School, and co-chairman, Policy Sciences Center, New York City. He is principally concerned with the study of personality in social and political processes. His publications include *Psychopathology and Politics; Politics: Who Gets What, When, How; Power and Society; Power and Personality; The Sharing of Power in a Psychiatric Hospital* (with Robert Rubenstein); and *A Pre-View of Policy Sciences.*

JAMES A. NATHAN, a Foreign Service Officer for several years, has taught in Mexico and at Indiana University. Professor Nathan has published widely in foreign policy, international affairs, and international education. He has written articles for *World Politics, Military Affairs, The Washington Monthly, The Virginia Quarterly Review,* and other journals and is co-author of the book *United States Foreign Policy and World Order.* He is currently an Associate Professor at the University of Delaware.

JOHN J. PATRICK is Associate Professor of Education at Indiana University. His major interest is curriculum development in the social studies. He is the co-author of two innovative high school political science textbooks and of a textbook on methods of instruction for teachers. He has also written articles on curriculum development and instruction.

RICHARD C. REMY is Adjunct Associate Professor of Political Science and Director of the Citizenship Development Program at the Mershon Center, Ohio State University. He is the author of articles on political education and co-author of *International Learning and International Education in a Global Age.*

STANLEY ALLEN RENSHON is an Associate Professor of Political Science at Herbert H. Lehman College and The Graduate Center of the City University of New York. He is the author of *Psychological Needs and Political Behavior* and of a forthcoming volume, *Personality Theories and Political Analysis.* His current research focuses on the problems and prospects issues associated with the psychological assessment and monitoring of public officials.

ROBERTA S. SIGEL is Professor of Political Science at Douglass College, Rutgers University. She is the editor of *Learning About Politics,* and has authored articles in the fields of political socialization and political behavior.

SARA L. SILBIGER is a visiting Assistant Professor at Rutgers University, Newark. Her doctoral dissertation dealt with small groups and political organization. She is currently studying aspects of political learning among young school children.

ELIZABETH LÉONIE SIMPSON is Adjunct Associate Professor at the University of Southern California. She is the author of *Democracy's Stepchildren: A Study of Need and Belief* and of articles on political socialization and moral development. Her most recent book is *Humanistic Education: An Interpretation.*

HOWARD TOLLEY, JR., is Associate Professor of Political Science at Wilberforce University. He is the author of *Political Socialization to International Conflict* and an Associate Editor for national affairs for *Intellect* magazine. His recent research focuses on civil rights and criminal justice.

MATTHEW ULLMAN is a graduate student in Clinical Psychology at the University of Minnesota.

ROBERT WEISSBERG is an Associate Professor of Political Science at the University of Illinois, Urbana/Champaign. He is the author of *Political Learning, Political Choice and Democratic Citizenship,* and *Public Opinion and Popular Government,* and has published articles in the area of political learning and behavior.

PART ONE

INTRODUCTION

Assumptive Frameworks in Political Socialization Theory

Stanley Allen Renshon

By MANY STANDARDS the field of political socialization has enjoyed enormous success. There are numerous books, anthologies (Sigel, 1970; Schwartz & Schwartz, 1975), special journal issues (1977), professional panels and conferences, major overviews (Niemi, 1974) a bibliography of published and unpublished research that contains hundreds of items (Dennis, 1973b), and increasing coverage in introductory political science texts. As Dennis notes, "For a field that had been named and defined less than a decade before, this is a phenomenal rate of growth" (1973a, p. 439). Moreover, as the chapters in this volume amply demonstrate, this growth has been accompanied by real advances in our understanding of the processes by which political orientations develop.

Current professional concern is preceded, of course, by a long succession of political theorists and practitioners interested in the process by which the child develops into the citizen. Yet, for all of their concern and frequent insights, early observers were handicapped in several ways. First, they lacked the necessary specialized techniques for observation and analysis. Second, their "models of man" were relatively underdeveloped. As Allport points out in his discussion of the history of social-psychological thinking (1968), various "sovereign concepts" have been employed at different times to describe the "essential" characteristics of human nature. The multidetermined, contextual, and interactive view of human behavior, which is now more routinely assumed, is a fairly recent development in the analysis of political life. But these conceptual advances

I would like to thank Robert Weissberg for his comments on an earlier draft of this chapter.

should not be viewed apart from the changes in observational standpoints that accompanied and frequently preceded them. If Ariés (1965) and other observers of the history of childhood are correct, concern with the child as a unique creature and with childhood as a distinct period is a relatively recent observational standpoint.

Yet, given that these advances have only recently been the basis of systematic research, controversy over theory, concepts, and methods is neither unexpected nor undesirable. This introductory chapter will examine some basic points of departure in each of these areas. Throughout, my concern will be to analyze the assumptive frameworks within which political socialization theory and research have proceeded, pointing out, where appropriate, difficulties and alternative possibilities. The analysis is divided into two parts: (1) Basic Frameworks; and (2) The Process of Political Socialization. In the first, we shall briefly examine definitions, theoretical rationale, and methodological approaches in political socialization theory. In the second, we will examine more closely the models of man and conceptions of political learning and motivation that have characterized the field.

Part 1: Basic Frameworks

DEFINITIONS

Boundary difficulties are inherent in all classification attempts and the field of political socialization is no exception. According to Greenstein (1970), the term may refer to (1) any study of children, (2) the acquisition of prevailing norms, (3) political learning of any type, or (4) actual observations of socialization in any of the preceding senses. With such a wide set of inclusionary standards, divergences in "formal" definition are not unexpected.

Definitions of political socialization have been generally focused on either process or outcomes. Typical of the former are Easton and Dennis' definition of political socialization as "those developmental processes through which persons acquire political orientations" (1969, p. 7), or Dawson and Prewitt's as "the developmental process through which the citizen matures politically" (1969, p. 17). The second, more frequent approach has been to stress political socialization as molding the child to an a priori set of conventions, rather than considering the child as an active innovator and modifier of political learning during the socialization process. Approached from another standpoint, this is Piaget's distinction between accommodation and assimilation, the latter referring to the child's action upon and modification of environmental transmissions, and the former stressing the child's modification of himself to meet the demands of the environment. As one critic has noted, "Political socialization studies analyze the development of political consciousness wholly in terms of accommodation"

(Connell, 1972–1973, p. 176). Consider the following representative definitions by political socialization theorists:

> [Socialization refers to] the process by which a junior member of a group or institution is taught its values, attitudes and other behaviors (Hess & Torney, 1967, p. 7).

> Political socialization refers to the learning process by which the political norms and behaviors acceptable to an ongoing political system are transmitted from generation to generation (Sigel, 1965, p. 1).

> The importance of such a formation (of politics as learned behavior) to understanding the stability of political systems is self-evident—humans must learn their political behavior early and well and persist in it. Otherwise there would be no regularity perhaps even chaos (Hyman, 1959, p. 17).

Illustrations could be multiplied, but those covered are perhaps sufficient to highlight the understatement in Sears' observation that *"more often overlooked is an alternative* definition that emphasizes the *child's idiosyncratic personal* growth, in which the developing human gradually obtains his own personal identity which allows him to express himself and to seek to meet his own idiosyncratic needs and values in his own way" (1975, p. 95, first emphasis mine, second authors').

In discussing some of these and similar definitions, Easton makes the point that, whatever the particular terms used and however ambiguous they may be, all of these definitions share one implication, viz.:

> They suggest that somehow an adult generation is able to mold a rising generation into something like its own adult image. Theoretically this kind of conceptualization clearly implies that the outcome of socialization is to provide for the continuity of existing forms and actions, that is, to insure the stability both in the sense of consensus or order (as against chaos) and of consistency of the system over time (1968, p. 134).

What can one made of these definitional assumptions? It seems clear that definitions which stress accommodation are in danger of confusing the intended aim of the process with its actual outcomes. But does the emphasis on accommodation have any further theoretical implications? Some think not (see, e.g., Greenstein, 1970, p. 973). However, the point is by no means settled, and we will turn to the implications of alternative conceptualizations in the second section of this essay dealing with models of man.

THEORETICAL RATIONALE

Political socialization appears to be an area whose importance seems intuitively obvious, but one which has nonetheless proved resistant to empirical documentation. One rationale, according to Easton, is a view of political socialization as the study of antecedents; i.e., "Every political orientation has antecedents of some sort; hence there is no limit to the number of the subjects that may be adapted for research" (1968, p. 127). The specific orientations chosen were frequently a joint function of intrinsic interest and a focus on behaviors which had already come under scrutiny for adults. Easton goes on to note that there was "little theoretical guidance except for the assumption that these topics of interest to the study of adults may be equally relevant for children and that childhood learning may point the way forward to adult behavior" (pp. 127–218). Easton labels this rationale "non-theoretical" in spite of the fact that at least its latter segment forms the assumptive basis of many subsequent justifications for the field. Yet Easton does have a point insofar as this approach does not present a list of specific variables that should be studied along with an explication of the nature of their theoretical importance.

A second major justification is "that political socialization is an important factor, a key variable in the understanding of the political system" (Easton, 1968, p. 218). This approach forms the basis for Easton's (1968) *political theory of political socialization* (see also Easton & Dennis, 1969), "whose objective would be to demonstrate the relevance of socializing phenomena for the operations of political systems" (p. 126).

Of course, given this rationale, the key questions are, first, exactly what about the political system does political socialization help us to understand, and, second, what are the particular linkages by which these effects can be traced to political socialization. The major emphasis to date has been on the former question—not, as we shall see, without good reason.

At least two major effects of political socialization on political systems have been put forward. The first concentrates on the implications of political socialization for political behavior in general and role performance in particular. Illustrative is Greenstein's contention that "political learning has effects on later political behavior of the individual exposed and by extension to the political system" (1968, p. 555). The latter approach may be seen in Almond's observation that "if political socialization produces the basic attitudes in a society towards the political system . . . we can gain understanding of one of the essential conditions which effect the ways in which these roles are performed" (1960, p. 31). A second set of implications concerns the impact of socialization on change and stability in the political system. As Dennis and his colleagues note, "A chief reason why the political socialization process has recently come under such intense analytical study is the new recognition of its connection to the process of fundamental change and stability in the political system" (1971, p. 25).[1]

Each of the above rationales shares one basic assumption and thus a major

---

[1]In early studies, especially those utilizing a systems maintenance approach, the emphasis was clearly on the latter and not on the former. Easton (1968, pp. 131–144) has vigorously criticized this approach on numerous grounds, but he notes: "The major drawback of a theoretical perspective that emphasizes system maintenance is that research inspired by a concern for stability . . . must overlook a wide range of consequences that socialization has for political diversity, conflict and change" (p. 141). In order to avoid this "bias," Easton proposes that a concern for system "persistence" replace the concern for system "maintenance," one difference being that systems can change and still persist.

empirical difficulty; viz., they assume the process by which political socialization has an impact on individuals, which in turn has consequences for the political system. Perhaps the "simplest" linkages proposed are those which relate political learning to subsequent political behaviors. But these linkages present the empirical difficulty of connecting early political learning with either (or both) transtemporal or cross-domain behavior.

The former would require demonstration that early learning persisted through time to influence adult political behavior, whether specifically role connected or not. The latter requires demonstration of a linkage between political learning (usually conceived of in terms of norms or attitudes) and political behavior, even if the political learning has been fairly recent. The first linkage requires longitudinal observation which is not yet available in the field, while the intricacies of the second linkage are sufficiently complex to defy a one-to-one correspondence between learning and behavior under most circumstances.

Yet these difficulties, while considerable, pale before the extensive linkage requirements necessary to connect individual learning with systemic outcomes, such as "persistence" or "stability." Aside from operational problems with such concepts (see the Nathan and Remy chapter in this volume), knowledge regarding the aggregation of individual impacts is primitive at best. It is clear, for example, that some actors have more impact than others, that particular distributions of attitudes at any time point may not coincide with the operating assumptions or procedures of major institutional structures, and that there are a number of "multiplier" and "nonadditive" effects that must be taken into account. It is small wonder, given these enormous difficulties that the theoretical (much less the empirical) specification of individual learning-system outcome linkages has been slow in developing.

This should not be taken as a suggestion that such linkages do not exist. In all probability they do. But they will remain potential areas in which to demonstrate the importance of political socialization rather than presently satisfying rationales[2] until greater advances are made in dealing with the aggregation of individual impacts.

A NOTE ON "UNIVERSAL THEORY" IN POLITICAL SOCIALIZATION

Like many other areas in political science, political socialization has been heavily influenced by the behavioral movement. According to an early report (1944–1945) of the SSRC (quoted in Dahl, 1961, p. 765), one objective of the

[2]In discussing the importance of political socialization theory, it should be noted that several alternative justifications (other than system-level outcomes) have been put forward. Schonfeld has suggested two other possible points of interest in studying children (1971, p. 552). The first concerns the use of children "to tap the adult's normative image of politics and government." Here the assumption is that adult attempt to transmit idealized conceptions of political life which might be

new approach was to examine "the behavior of individuals in political situations . . . with the object of formulating and testing hypotheses concerning uniformities of behavior in different settings." This approach, the *nomothetic*, is typically contrasted with the *ideographic* approach, which seeks to understand human behavior in terms of the unique confluence of factors acting at a particular time/space juncture.

While both approaches are potentially compatible, political socialization has leaned rather heavily to date on the former. As Connell notes, "Political socialization studies . . . strain towards generalization and consistently suppress the immediacy and concreteness of the present situation; their ultimate search is for abstract cross-situational laws" (1972–1973, p. 186).

The search for cross-cultural, transhistorical generalizations is necessary for any deductive theories of political behavior since "without universal generalizations, deductive explanations are impossible" (Meehan, 1965, p. 100). Thus Easton and Dennis note, "Our primary objective is to expand the boundaries of general theory, not to add to a partial or special theory of democracy . . . (since) it is only incidentally that we present a case study of that class of systems" (1969, p. 69). Elsewhere, in discussing the adequateness of their sample, the same authors note that "there is little question that our sample imposes narrow limits *on any universal generalizations we might hope to obtain*" (p. 401, emphasis added).

What are the prospects for such a general theory of political socialization? Apparently, not very promising. Given that political socialization research has uncovered variations in who learns what, etc., based on such characteristics as sex, race, socioeconomic status, ethnic group affiliation, and political culture, the chances of discovering universal processes seem remote.

It may be that the search for universal laws in political socialization, like the search for the Holy Grail, is destined for ultimate failure; yet this does not preclude its contribution of advances in our understanding. As Argyle and Delin have thoughtfully suggested, "There *are* laws of socialization, but they are restricted in scope" (1965, p. 78, emphasis in original). These they term "non-universal laws of socialization," cautioning that "this is not to say that there is anything indeterminate about socialization since it is possible to specify the conditions under which any particular mechanism will operate" (pp. 73–79). Argyle and Delin's position seems to argue for the development of middle-range theories in political socialization[3] rather than the more inclusive global theories that others have attempted.

---

useful in tapping the range of possibilities that citizens see as characterizing the ideal political system. A related idea put forward by Greenstein is to study children as naïve cultural informants (1974, p. 721) in a variety of political areas. Second, Schonfeld suggests that "relations in the child's world that are analogous to political relations might be examined in an attempt to develop hypotheses to explain poorly understood aspects of political life" (p. 552).

[3]These middle range theories may be defined as those "that lie between the minor, but necessary working hypotheses that evolve in abundance during day-to-day research and all-inclusive systematic efforts to develop a unified theory that will explain all the observed uniformities of social behavior, social organization and social change" (Merton, 1968, p. 39).

There are two major drawbacks to global theories and the approach they represent. First, theoretical utility has frequently been discussed in terms of inclusiveness; i.e., the more observations (data) that can be subsumed under a particular theoretical rubric, the more useful it is said to be, to a point. Yet, as theories attempt to include more divergent observations, they tend to increase their level of generality and lose their empirical specificity. Thus, such concepts as "system stress," "diffuse support," and "system persistence" may help us to understand the general process of political socialization but may falter as specific guide to empirical linkages for particular groups, situations, or processes.

A second major difficulty with the search for general theory, as it is currently conducted, is that it tends to neglect the specific historical context within which current political socialization processes have developed. There is, of course, nothing in the behavioral approach which necessitates a neglect of historical processes. As early as 1951, Easton denied that "the political behavior orientation implies a rejection of historical knowledge"; in fact, he suggested, "historical knowledge is likely to be an essential supplement to contemporary observation of political behavior" (quoted in Dahl, 1961, p. 767). Yet, as Dahl admits in assessing the behavioral movement, "in his concern for analyzing what *is,* the behavioral political scientist has found it difficult to make use of what *has been*, i.e., with history . . . despite disclaimers and intentions to the contrary, there seems to be little room for doubt that the actual content of almost all of the studies that reflect the behavioral mood is a-historical in character" (1961, p. 771, emphasis in original). It is perhaps with this in mind that Dennis, in a recent discussion of potential advances in explanation in the field, thoughtfully notes, "We should pay attention to how explanatory factors vary under different geocultural and social conditions—especially across historical epochs" (1973, p. 495).[4]

METHODOLOGY IN POLITICAL SOCIALIZATION RESEARCH

In a field that has produced such an enormous amount of research, the attention paid to method has been small. Since theoretical advances are more likely when the assumptions and limitations of procedure are explicitly addressed, this neglect could prove damaging. The purpose of this section, therefore, is to bring together a number of diverse, frequently scattered observations regarding current techniques, procedures, and strategies as a framework within which to consider some alternatives and extensions.

The first and most obvious point to be made is that political socialization

---

[4]One possibility would be to focus on political beliefs within a population or individual as a function of the historical political traditions of a particular culture (for an illustration see Connell, 1971, pp. 234–237). Another would be to examine the agencies of political socialization as "dependent" rather than "independent" variables. Here the focus would be upon the socialization of political socialization agencies.

research has relied heavily on the survey questionnaire. As Fred Greenstein has aptly stated, "Political scientists interested in political socialization have been relentlessly monistic in their use of paper-and-pencil surveys, especially fixed-choice questionnaires in studying children" (1975, p. 137). Such a procedure has much to recommend it. It allows assessment of large groups of respondents to a wide range of "constant stimuli" and by utilizing forced-choice alternatives facilitates response categorization and thus data analysis and interpretation. Along with these advantages, however, there are several difficulties.

The use of fixed-choice questions is more appropriate when the universe of discourse in a particular area is already mapped out, and the meaning of differences among response alternatives well understood. In the absence of such knowledge, difficulties regarding the range and interpretation of responses are likely to ensue. Sometimes these difficulties show up in problems of response balancing; e.g., when Easton and Dennis ask children to rate the President (1969, p. 179), they give the following alternatives: "I like him (1) more than anyone, (2) more than most people, (3) more than many people, (4) more than some people, (5) more than a few people, and (6) less than almost anyone." Since five of the six alternatives are phrased in a positive way, if the child really dislikes the President he can indicate this only by selecting the last alternative (Kolson & Green, 1970, p. 529). Moreover, not only is the last option more extreme than most of the corresponding alternatives at the top, there is also some question as to what kinds of behavior would lead to its selection.

Research on the Australian prime minister by Connell (1971, pp. 55–57) suggests there are very important differences between child and adult understanding of what constitutes a "bad" political leader. Young children, according to Connell, inevitably defined a bad prime minister as one who had done something "grossly and unequivocally wrong—committing thefts or murders . . . causing an invasion of the country, etc." (1972–1973, p. 174). Connell concludes, "Given this understanding of the question, it is clear that the children will have no grounds for choosing the unfavorable end of the scale unless the man is publicly known to have committed disastrous and unlikely blunders" (1972–1973, p. 174).

The problem of shared meaning raised above is an important but frequently overlooked difficulty in political socialization. Much of the field's research on children is comparative in the sense that it examines them with specific reference to the behaviors of adults who are taken as the dominant models. Hess and Torney observe that one criterion for the selection of items in their original questionnaire was "the similarity of items to areas of behavior studied in adults" (1967, p. 269). Aside from the problem of differential salience and extensiveness of focus, research which proceeds on these grounds tends to assume that the meaning of such "items" is similar across age domains. In cross-culture research great attention is paid to problems of "equivalence," yet similar concern has not been evident in assessing the degree to which particular symbols and categories have equivalent meaning status or are appropriate with both adult and child respondents.

Sometimes, as in Connell's research, these questions are dealt with directly, but more frequently it is the paradoxical or contrary information which leads one to pause. In an early study, Greenstein (1965) found an extraordinarily high idealization of the President among his respondents (p. 31), yet when asked to choose an exemplar, only 3.3% chose the incumbent President (p. 138). Greenstein goes on to comment, "What we need . . . is evidence of the meaning to the child of choosing one or another kind of exemplar" (p. 149). Equally informative are differences in interpretation among researchers. There is growing agreement that "don't know" categories should be included in research on children (Kolson & Green, 1970, p. 529; Vaillancourt & Niemi, 1974, p. 131; Vaillancourt, 1973, p. 386), yet their interpretation in any particular circumstance appears variable. Kolson and Green (1970) argue that "don't know" is selected to reduce dissonance (p. 533, an interpretation shared by Sigel & Brookes, 1974, pp. 108–110), or as an act of evasion (p. 531). Marsh (1972, p. 257) appears to assume the equivalence of "I don't know" with "I don't care" as a response to questions regarding the difference between "Freedom," "Liberty," and "Equality." Dennis and his colleagues, surveying the vast number of "don't know" responses to their statement "Democracy is the best form of government," conclude that this suggests that "Democracy is not as salient as a general symbol for the type of regime that the British have as it is in other countries" (1968, p. 77). Finally, Arterton (1974, p. 279) equates a large number of "don't know" responses with a high degree of "confusion" in his respondents. My point is not that any particular interpretation is wrong, but simply that more inquiry into the assumed meaning of particular responses seems merited.

Meaning equivalence and question balance do not exhaust the difficulties of survey research in political socialization. Another problem concerns the inclusion of particular alternatives. The typical question on party preference asks the child to select from among Republican, Democrat, or Independent, the latter category assessed by including a "sometimes Democratic, sometimes Republican" alternative (Hess & Torney, 1967, p. 103). In most cases the present party structure is simply assumed. Yet when one group of children were given the following alternative: "I would be for some other party—please tell me what its name is _____," 5% of the white children and 9% of the black children wrote in a third-party choice (Vaillancourt & Niemi, 1974, p. 130). In a third wave of the same panel when third-party alternatives (e.g., Peace and Freedom party and American Independent party) were specifically given in a forced-choice format, 34% of the black children (no comparable data are presented for white children) selected a "minor party" (p. 133). Along with questions of party preference stability, the potentially different meaning of preference independence when changes periodically include third parties illustrates the potential impact of alternative inclusion and exclusion on substantive findings.

Along with problems of balancing and inclusion, response set among children also merits consideration. Response set refers to the tendency of a respondent to answer a set of survey or test items differently than he or she might have had the content of the questions been put in a different form (Cronbach, 1946, p. 476). In the only direct study of response set bias in political socialization, Kolson and Green (1970, p. 53) suggest three different dynamics. The first operates under conditions of uncertainty when the survey is perceived as a test and results in a tendency to gamble (guess). The second, "acquiescence set," refers to respondents who answer in a particular direction regardless of the content of the question (Couch & Keniston, 1960). The third, "agreement response set," the authors relate to agreement tendency when respondents are given authoritative statements.

The study involved alternatively worded questions about political and non-political objects. Each object to be rated (including a fictitious political leader, Thomas Walker) was presented in either a positive, negative, or neutral light by the question. Kolson and Green found that their respondents (fourth- to eighth-graders) did have a tendency to gamble in circumstances where they could not have had previous information (e.g., the fictitious candidate). In those areas where the respondent had the least information, the wording of the question (positive, negative, or neutral) had the most effect. Moreover, there were a high number of positive responses regardless of the direction of presentation. According to the authors, these data suggest that "apparently, there is a tendency for children . . . to respond in a positive direction once they have decided to gamble . . . a negative response is evidently conceived to be a very grave incrimination of the object in question" (1970, p. 536). This latter assessment fits quite well with Connell's observation regarding the meaning of bad political leaders. In sum, these results suggest caution in dealing with children's survey responses.

Theory and method are, of course, closely connected and nowhere is this connection more obvious than in the tendency to examine children in terms of adult models. In an early monograph, Greenstein suggested that "the political orientations which are most important in the behavior of adults arise earliest in the childhood learning sequence" (1965, p. 78). This focuses our attention not only on the relevance of early learning but on exactly what it is that constitutes the most important orientations for adult behavior.

Answers to this question can be related to current models of democracy. Weissberg (1974, pp. 176–182) distinguishes three: the electoral competition model, the representative model, and the participatory model. One gains some idea of the latitude covered by noting that the electoral competition model is built on "the basic idea that citizens have a right to choose their leaders" (p. 176), while "at the core of participatory democracy is the belief that *politics include all social* life. . . . Politics is thus not limited to government—it occurs in the home, in school, wherever else decisions are made affecting people's lives—and democracy is realized when citizens effectively control their own lives" (p. 179, emphasis added). Leaving aside the accuracy of either position, it is clear that each model will have very different implications for the range of behaviors and orientations examined. Many studies of children and politics, following the first or second model, have stressed party preference, orientations to those formally in office, political structures, and campaign-related behaviors.[5] Such a focus is neither erroneous nor unreasonable, especially at early stages of inquiry. However, it is likely that such orientations, while important, are by no means always crucial to understanding political stability, change, or persistence; nor do they constitute by themselves a sufficiently broad view of the political process.

A second, related difficulty with the child as small adult model has to do with the salience of politics, and more specifically those partisan orientations and issues presumed to be so important to adults. Converse found, that in 1956, between 26% and 29% of the adults surveyed appeared to have "non-attitudes" on an issue that had been fiercely debated among elites for three decades (1974, p. 651). Yet it appears that "non-attitudes" are related in part to salience,[6] for Converse notes, "I should make very clear that such events (indicators of non-attitudes) were rare to nonexistent when questions dealt with the immediate terms of the respondent's life" (p. 650). If this is the case for adults, there is little reason to think it inoperative for children. If attitude strength and belief system coherence increase as a function of salience, then the documented difficulties of "explaining" the variance in children's orientations may have less to do with the variables being utilized to explain and more to do with the lack of attitudes toward politics among children (Renshon, 1975a).

These issues are further complicated by the larger problem of children's realistic thinking. A number of observers have suggested that political explanations for children, when given, are sugar coated (Easton & Hess, 1962; Greenstein, 1965, pp. 45–46), and many of the questionnaires used to assess the child's political world seem to reflect this assumption. Consider the following question: "Would the President always want to help me if I needed it?" (Easton & Dennis, 1969, p. 179). The idea (or myth) of presidential or governmental responsiveness as a *personal* attentiveness to individuals in the mass public can be seen in a number of survey questions (e.g., Easton & Dennis, 1969, p. 185; Hess & Torney, 1967, p. 40; Sigel & Brookes, 1974, p. 121). As Connell asserts with typical provocativeness, "It is not so much the children's 'trust' that is being measured, as their ability to swallow rubbish" (1972–1973, p. 169).

One should not confuse the child's ability to reason with his ability to view the political system realistically. It is true that certain mental operation capacities arise only at particular stages of development, but this evidence does not obviate the capacity for political realism past a very early age. Evidence that children can and indeed do assess the political world is readily available: for example, Sigel

---

[5]For example, all three of the political behaviors of children examined in the Hess and Torney survey (1967, p. 296) specifically mention a political candidate. Regarding the attention paid to partisan orientations, one need only examine their relative emphasis in many assessment instruments to determine the importance given to them (see, e.g., Greenstein, 1965, pp. 173–179; Andrian, 1971, pp. 170–177).

[6]For further evidence that perceived salience increases the "constraint" of political belief systems among members of the mass public see Cobb (1973, p. 126) and the work cited by him in footnote nineteen of his essay.

(1965) found that black children responded more dramatically to President Kennedy's assassination than white children, a finding which she argues is not unexpected given the possibilities that blacks associated realistically with him.[7]

As one examines current assessment procedures in political socialization research at least three glaring omissions, aside from previously discussed difficulties, are discernible. The first concerns the lack of a major longitudinal study, begun with a sufficiently young age group, to trace the processes of political socialization. Dual (Jennings & Niemi, 1975) or multiwave (Sigel & Brookes, 1974) panel studies represent a great advance over the one-shot, cross-sectional design and can increase our understanding of particular developmental stages. However, as we approach the third decade of research in this area, the lack of a major longitudinal study is a cause for action as well as concern.

The second glaring omission concerns the use of observational techniques in both natural and experimental settings. As Adler and Harrington note (1970, p. 189), "There have been precious few observations of what is going on in any institutional setting, including the family, with regard to political socialization." And, as Orren and Peterson point out (1967, p. 390), "These circumstances raise considerable obstacles to empirical research on the dynamics of the socialization process." The obstacles are, of course, that much socialization goes on without either parent or child necessarily being aware of what is happening. This suggests the need for future political socialization research to become more involved in naturalistic observation in a variety of contexts.[8] This omission will most certainly require remedy if the study of "how" is to complement the study of "what" in the socialization process.

The third major omission concerns the detailed study of important political subgroups, of which two come immediately to mind. The first are political elites, both current and potential. If political leadership functions as a "multiplier of effects" for the linkages between individual learning and system impacts, the

---

[7]Another interesting bit of evidence comes from Greenstein's (1975) attempt to utilize a story completion technique to tap children's responses to authority. In one story the chief of state is presented as driving his (or her) own car at excessive speeds and being stopped by a policeman. The point of the story is to assess how a child views the political leader responding to being caught in this infraction, and what the child himself thinks of this situation. In all, 18% of the French children, 29% of the English children, and 8% of the American children challenged the assumptive basis of the story. By far the largest portion of the challenges related to expressed disbelief that the head of state would ever drive his own car, or be unattended by an escort. Such information cautions against the assumption that all children are removed by virtue of immaturity, inclination, or misinformation from making realistic assessments of and commentary upon a wide range of political life.

[8]There are available a variety of new techniques which greatly facilitate behavior analysis in varied settings. Key among these is the combination of modern videotape recording equipment and the development of powerful analytical tools for the analysis of communication at a variety of (verbal and nonverbal) levels. These include techniques for analyzing the organization of experience (Goffman, 1974), body communication (Birdwhistell, 1970), and proximic analysis (Scheflen, 1976). These may be utilized in conjunction with more traditional analyses of verbal communications such as content categories (Bales, 1953), hesitation rates, voice tone (Goldman-Eisler, 1968), etc. There apears to be no immediate reason why these (and other) techniques could not be useful to political socialization researchers in a number of areas, including unobtrusive measurement or direct observation.

paucity of research in this area can only be continued at great theoretical (and policy) cost. The second group which merits extensive attention are political "deviants." Despite all of the expressed concern with moving political socialization theory from its conservative emphasis on stability to a concern with change and persistence, the individual mechanisms by which this occurs have been given little empirical attention. The important role of the deviant merits specialized attention in this regard.

In other words, political socialization urgently requires sophisticated subgroup analysis which goes beyond demographic breakdowns. Sometimes this will require a change of focus. In other instances, it simply requires that advantage be taken of the "natural" groups that may be selected out in many surveys. A good illustration of the possibilities is provided by Sigel and Brookes in their specialized analysis of "changers," i.e., those who gave positive responses toward the government in 1966 but who by 1968 had become more critical (1974, pp. 118–119). Other possibilities will no doubt suggest themselves.

Difficulties with current techniques and procedures are responsible for the increasing recognition that a strategy of "multiple operationalism" (Dennis, 1973b) is a productive way to proceed in future research. Illustrative is the growing use of semiprojective and other techniques. Greenstein and Tarrow (1970), presented children from three countries with stories about political figures which the respondents were then asked to finish. Another variant developed by Knutson (1974) consists in showing the child a series of pictures with a range of political themes. Thus, the theme "legalized force" shows two persons in interaction, one of whom is dressed in uniform, while the theme "leaders and followers" is portrayed by a man surrounded by a group of semidistinct individuals, etc.

The advantage of these techniques is that they allow greater insight into the meaning of responses and are capable of assessing a wider range of politically relevant dispositions. One major drawback is the difficulty of coding, especially if systematic content analysis is attempted (e.g., Greenstein, 1975, p. 1384). Still, the decision to allow children to speak at length for themselves does reward the investigator with a wide range of important data, not all of which is supportive of that obtained by fixed-choice questions.[9]

The use of these "new" techniques does not exhaust the possibilities open to political socialization researchers; Wahlke and Lodge (1972) have demonstrated the utility of psychophysiological measurement of arousal to political stimuli.

---

[9] I have already noted the ubiquity of positive orientations toward authority found in early and many subsequent studies of the child's political world. However, Knutson (1974) found that children (in 1971, before Watergate) responding to the pictures depicting "authority" tended to see the authority figure as remote and judgmental. She concludes that

> authority, even from the viewpoints of young children, is not always seen as infallible or necessarily regarded with positive affect. The impersonality and indecisiveness that these children generally saw here contradict the compulsive positive affect for authority so frequently found in paper-and-pencil studies of socialization (p. 22).

Similar disjunctures using open-ended questions have been noted by Connell (1971, pp. 43–44).

This technique might be utilized with young adults and perhaps even younger children. It would then be possible to see to what extent affect toward political authorities could be validated with independent data sources. More interesting would be the attempt to combine this (and other methods) with experimental situations (Thorson & Thorson, 1974) in which the behavior of leaders was systematically varied. Videotaped political dramas with different themes and outcomes could easily be constructed for this purpose.

In considering the difficulties and possibilities that confront political socialization researchers, it is well to keep in mind that many of the difficulties we have raised are not unique to this field. Moreover, it seems unlikely that most of the techniques utilized will ever become the purified instruments of human observation that many critics appear to expect and some utilizers have sought. And while it is well to keep in mind the limits of survey and forced-choice methodology, it seems unlikely that these important research tools will soon become historical curiosities. The continuation and extension of systematic (empirical, not necessarily numerical) research cannot rest on exaggerated claims or expectations regarding technical research instruments alone. Difficulties in instrumentation can be minimized with care but not eliminated. Rather explicit attention to instrumentation and procedure, coupled with the careful examination of assumptions in pursuit of theory, appears to be the most fruitful road of future advance. It is to the latter that we turn in the following section.

Part 2: The Process of Political Socialization

MODELS OF MAN IN POLITICAL SOCIALIZATION THEORY

The emphasis on the individual was proclaimed early in the behavioral movement. According to Easton, "Behavioral research has . . . sought to elevate the human being to the center of attention" (1953, p. 203). However, it is not certain that these laudable theoretical intentions have been successfully implemented, at least in political socialization research. Baker notes:

> Conspicuous by their absence from political socialization studies are *people*—the person, the individual. Political behavioralism has been criticized for its emphasis upon the individual, but the validity of this assessment and criticism can be questioned (1971, pp. 591–592, emphasis in original).

One difficulty here is that aggregate analyses sometimes obscure or distort the very individual process they attempt to capture. As Knutson notes (1974, p. 9), "The analysis of socialization as an individual process requires assessment at the individual level." Yet, even apart from these possibilities, it is reasonable to ask not only *if* persons have been placed in the center stage, but *what kind* of persons. It is this latter question that will be our focus of concern.

What models of man have been most prevalent in political socialization research? The answer appears to be a passive, reactive model.[10] Previous observations (in the definition section) are conveniently recalled and summarized by Dennis' suggestion that "the major thrust of past research has been upon socialization and what society does for [one might add to] the individual" (1968, p. 107, brackets mine). Or, to put it another way, the individual "appears as a *tabula rasa,* on which society *imprints* its attitudes, values and behaviors" (Baker, 1971, p. 593, emphasis in original). In its most extreme form, the doctrine of *tabula rasa* suggests that "all human being are deemed to possess the same potentialities at birth; they become different persons owing to varied upbringing and training, and generally to varied circumstances in their lives" (Dobzhansky, 1973, p. 281).

The assumption of *tabula rasa* is pervasive in social science and socialization theory, even among those who criticize the latter on other grounds. Thus Rafky, in the midst of a phenomenological critique of current socialization theory, observes that "the child, initially a *tabula rasa,* is enculturated" (1973, p. 55). Nor must we search far to find the same assumptions in political socialization. Easton and Dennis note that "our data at least suggest this, (that) the political marks on the *tabula rasa* are entered early and continually refurbished thereafter" (Easton & Dennis, 1965, p. 43; see also Easton & Dennis, 1969, p. 137).

Paradoxically, the impact of environmentalism is so pervasive that its assumptions appear to have been accepted even among those political socialization theorists who have stressed the importance of individual personality characteristics rather than "agencies." Thus, Froman notes that socialization theorists would do well to study personality, which he conceptualizes as "the postulation of a set of variables having to do with the child's psychic makeup *which intervene between* the environment and his behavior" (1962, p. 305, emphasis added). In other words, environment → personality → political behavior. A similar model has been put forward by Greenstein, who notes that political socialization theorists should keep in mind that political behavior will be a joint function of "the situational stimuli and partly of the person's psychological dispositions.... *And the latter are learned or 'socialized'*" (1970, p. 973, emphasis added).

The difficulty with such models and with the assumptions that underlie them is not so much that they are patently erroneous but, rather, conceptually insufficient. If, as Dobzhansky has pointed out, the *tabula rasa* assumptions were com-

---

[10]Paradoxically, one contributor to this viewpoint in political socialization theory was Herbert Hyman. As Merelman points out:

> As a Sociologist it was natural for Hyman to think of political socialization primarily as one facet of social structure.... Not surprisingly, therefore, Hyman organized his book around findings related to the agencies related to socialization for he shared the assumptions of most sociologists that human development is almost exclusively a process by which the environment conceptualized in terms of social agencies, impresses itself upon the helpless, formless child (1972, p. 135).

pletely accurate, "people would be interchangeable. When brought up in a certain way they would be conditioned for any function or role in the social system . . . (but) the *tabula rasa* myth (cannot) withstand critical examination" (1973, p. 281). This suggests that a model of man useful for understanding political behavior in general and more specifically political socialization, will be advantaged by a reconsideration of the role of biological mechanisms in human development.

To illustrate the possibilities, we will examine the impact to two innate socially facilitated, but not socially derived, personal characteristics.[11] These two are activity levels and intelligence. To minimize possible misunderstandings, it should be emphasized that such a focus does not attempt to substitute one form of determinism for another (e.g., biological for environmental). In other words, biology *is not* destiny, but neither can it be safely ignored by political socialization theorists.

The model of individual temperament and political socialization to be suggested (but not fully explicated) is based on the following assumptions. First, there are a relatively small number of inherited dispositions. Second, these dispositions are important, but not solely determining for human behavior. Third, these dispositions are broad in scope and supportive of multiple "traits." Fourth, these characteristics are partially modifiable by environmental forces. Fifth, these characteristics not only are influenced by the environment, but in turn "structure" environmental possibilities; i.e., the relationship between innate characteristics and environment is interactive. These assumptions lead to a view of biologically based characteristics as setting the general parameters within which political learning proceeds, and outside of which political learning can take place only in unusual circumstances.

The first characteristic to be heuristically examined is level of activity which, simply put, refers to total energy output. Activity level affects vigor and tempo as well as activity style (Buss & Plomin, 1975, pp. 7, 31). What evidence is there that activity levels are inherited? Most of our information about heritability levels is obtained from studies of monozygotic (identical) and dizygotic (fraternal) twins as well as family studies. Generally, the greater the *MZ* interclass correlation compared to the *DZ*s, the greater the suggestion of high heritability (Loehlin, 1969). In order to merit consideration as an inherited characteristic, Buss and Plomin specify four additional criteria: (1) stability during childhood; (2) retention into maturity; (3) adaptive value; and (4) presence in animal forebears (p. 9). A complete review is not possible in the present context, and for an extended

---

[11]Much of the discussion of innate and acquired characteristics has been confounded by a restrictive definition of instinct (Yankelowitch & Barrett, 1970) which has been increasingly recognized as inadequate. Illustrative of the changes that have taken place in the concept's formulation is Hebb's observation: "The term 'instinctive' will be used to refer to behavior other than reflexes in which innate factors play a *predominant* role" (1949, p. 166).

More recent formulations have suggested the ways in which even individual genes are responsive to their environment, and gene pools responsive to variations in the larger social context (Beals & Kelso, 1975). For a fuller consideration of the role of instinct in personality theory and political analysis see Renshon (forthcoming).

treatment of the evidence in each area the reader is referred to Buss and Plomin (1975) and the references therein.

Allowing for differences in assessment instruments, research into the heritability of activity levels among twins has been extensive (Eysenck, 1956; Scarr, 1969; Willerman, 1973) and generally supportive (but see Vandenberg, 1967) of a large heritability factor. Moreover, studies of parents and children are also supportive. Willerman and Plomin (1973) report a correlation of .48 for mother-child activity levels, while Caldwell and Hersher (1964) report correlations of .40 between mothers and their children. Interestingly, these parent-child correlations appear to be unaffected by child-rearing practices (Plomin, 1974). These studies suggest that one "politically relevant" characteristic "transmitted" by the family may be activity levels. The question, of course, is to what extent activity levels are politically relevant.

Given the paucity of research dealing directly with activity levels and political behavior, what follows is speculative. Nonetheless, it is hoped that it will be suggestive. Consider in this context Barber's well-known typology of presidential character (1972). Barber contends that character "is the person's stance as he confronts experience" (p. 8). One of the two basic poles of character is an active-passive dimension which Barber asserts is "a *central feature* of *anyone's life*" (p. 12, emphasis added), and which he defines as the general tendency to act or be acted upon. He further notes that "in everyday life we sense quickly the general energy output of the people we deal with."

There is a significant overlap between Buss and Plomin's activity temperament and Barber's active-passive dimension. Thus, it is plausible that Barber's presidential typology contains biological as well as social-development types. One possible implication of a more biologically grounded analysis of Barber's typology concerns the problem of type transition, viz., whether, and under what circumstances, persons characterized under one rubric (e.g., active-positive) may change to another. Barber's model suggests that the four major presidential types are characterized by enduring orientations with supporting longitudinal syndromes.

Yet extended discontinuities in experience could lead to transitions. An "active-positive" who experienced a succession of political deprivations might reassess how he felt about his energy output in the political arena. Similarly, an "active-negative" who experienced continual and significant political satisfactions might become more "positive" about his energy output. The latter dynamic might have been operative for former President Nixon at the time he won the presidency, at least until Watergate began to unravel (Renshon, 1975b).

On the other hand, to the extent that activity levels are biologically rather than experientially based, we would expect fewer and less dramatic changes in the activity continuum in response to political experiences. We would not expect a leader who qualifies as a "passive" in Barber's typology to become an "active" because of a series of political rewards, nor would we expect an active to become passive in response to typical political deprivations. Since there are presently no longitudinal analyses of Barber's character types and certainly none which examine the typology from this perspective, the above must remain highly provisional. However, we are on firmer empirical ground when we examine the impact of the second illustrative factor, intelligence.

The nature and dynamics of human intelligence are matters of ongoing debate in the biosocial sciences (for a recent overview, see Cronin et al., 1975). One difficulty is whether there is a generalized reasoning (Guilford et al., 1962) or intelligence (Thurstone, 1938) factor, or whether intelligence is more adequately conceptualized as a set of multiple abilities which must be assessed in relation to particular problems. Guilford (1956, 1959) has discussed three facets of intelligence including (1) operations and processes (e.g., cognition, memory, convergent thinking, divergent thinking, and evaluation), (2) content (e.g., figural, symbolic, or semantic), and (3) content which results from the application of a particular operation (e.g., units, classes, relations, systems, transformations, and implications).

From the perspective of the controversies in this area, the analysis of the role of intelligence in the political socialization process is embryonic.[12] Yet those few studies following this line of research provide findings whose implications appear to merit further exploration. Hess and Torney (1967), using standard IQ scores, found that high-IQ children personalize the government less (p. 151), view the compliance system in less absolute terms, realizing that laws may be defective (p. 161), and are less likely to view the policeman as having wide knowledge, although this apparently does not extend to other figures such as the President (p. 163). Furthermore, high-IQ children generally have more reservations about the competence of the government (p. 168) and the President's fallibility (p. 169) and are more likely to accept the possibility of change in the governmental system (p. 181). This suggests that the ability to be critical about politics may be related in part to conceptual abilities. In the area of participation, high-IQ children were found to have a greater sense of political efficacy (p. 171), greater interest in politics (p. 174), and greater frequency of political discussions (p. 176), and were generally more politically participant (p. 186).

One of the difficulties with the Hess and Torney study is that no multivariate analysis is attempted, so that the independent effects of IQ and social class may

---

[12]In addition to the above complexities, the concept of intelligence has been marked by controversy over heritability and environmental facilitation. Critics and proponents agree that biological transmission plays a role in intelligence (Vandenberg, 1971), but such factors as nutrition (Corsin, 1972) and other of the multiple dynamics contained under the rubric "social class" also have an impact (Guilford, 1967, pp. 347–411). Additionally, there are increasingly sophisticated attempts to differentiate intelligence from such processes as creativity (Torrance, 1962). Thus, originality, flexibility, and elaboration can be empirically distinguished from response to tests of general intelligence (Guilford, 1968). Last, as one would expect given the above controversies, the measurement of intelligence has become a point of increasing contention (Goslin, 1963). At issue is not only whether what is being measured is really intelligence, but whether current assessment procedures are insensitive to variations in cultural experiences and assumptions.

be confounded.[13] In a subsequent study utilizing a sample of high school students, Harvey and Harvey (1970) found that high IQ was inversely related to degree of superpatriotism, anticommunism, and militarism, but was positively related to "Belief in the Bill of Rights." Economic liberalism was found to decline as IQ increased, while no relationship was uncovered between IQ and "Authoritarianism." High IQ was also found to be positively associated with a high sense of "Citizen Duty" and a high sense of the "Relevance of Government" but not, surprisingly, with a sense of political efficacy or political participation as found by White, Easton and Dennis, and Hess and Torney. The authors point out that the age of the respondents, the measurement of their dependent variable, and the time of assessment differ for these studies and may be the cause of the discrepant findings (p. 583).

Of equal importance here is the Harveys' attempt to use multiple regression models to test the relative impact of SES and intelligence. Utilizing three major models of impact, the authors examined 14 political variables and found that "from an analysis of the causal models, it can be argued that intelligence presents a much stronger and more clearly causal relationship to political behavior than SES" (p. 590). These findings would appear to suggest that intelligence has some impact on political orientations, that is independent of social experience as measured by SES. This does not suggest that experience cannot facilitate intelligence. Nor does it deal with the impact of intelligence on the process rather than the content of political learning. We will return to this possibility in the following section.

The role of biological factors in political socialization is an area fraught with both difficulty and promise. We have suggested some of the latter above, but the former should not be neglected. Aside from the current impossibility of empirically distinguishing the "exact amounts" of heredity and environment for any given factor, care must be taken not to confound contextual dynamics with biological invariants. Sometimes what appear to be universal (and thus at least potentially biologically regulated) responses turn out, upon further examination, to be a reflection of a particular temporal and cultural context.

For example, in discussing the widely found propensity for children to respond positively to political leaders, Merelman suggests:

> Similarly, the "benevolent leader" syndrome . . . may be explained partially by his inability to reason abstractly, to be self-conscious about his thinking, or to relate concrete judgment to general rules. Because the child reasons intuitively and syncratically, he reaches the personal application side of thought very rapidly. Reliance on a

---

[13]White (1968) attempted to bypass this difficulty by obtaining a multiple regression equation for each of the 47 schools in this sample and using T-tests on the partial regression coefficients that resulted. The variable with the largest number of significant partial correlations was then considered to be the best predictor (for a critique of this method, see Jackman, 1970). Using this procedure, White found intelligence to be the best predictor.

benevolent leader is both the outcome and the symbolic representation of a syncratic rather than analytical thought process (1969, p. 764).

In a subsequent examination of children's orientations to authority after Watergate, Arterton notes: "We would like to draw some conclusions as to whether these perceptions of the President as benevolent, infallible, protective and omnipotent *are part and parcel of the child's development process and therefore fairly impervious to influence* from contemporary events or whether they are dependent upon a state of 'politics as usual' " (1974, p. 271, emphasis added). Arterton's study and others (e.g., Jaros et al., 1968) appear to establish that the perception of benevolence is not an immutable biological "given" but, rather, quite responsive to changes in political circumstances.

Clearly, much careful research will be needed in this area to establish the biological and social parameters of politically relevant orientations and behaviors. Yet, in spite of the difficulties, the potential importance of these factors, coupled with the paucity of research attempting to link them directly to matters of political interest, suggests that the role of biologically transmitted individual differences (and universal processes) remains a significant frontier for future political socialization research.

THE PROCESS OF POLITICAL LEARNING

Few concepts are more crucial to political socialization theory than that of political learning. Yet, curiously, political learning continues to be a concept more frequently used than explicated. It is, moreover, one element of the political socialization process which has only infrequently been the object of systematic observation.

Examining current definitions of the field, it is difficult to recall the sense of urgency of Hyman's early lament about seeking "far and wide for any extended treatment of political behavior as learned behavior despite the fact that this is patently the case" (1959, p. 17). Currently, it is difficult to locate a definition or discussion of the field that does not mention "political learning." Yet empirical attention has not followed definitional concern. As Roberta Sigel cogently suggests, "Political socialization is a misnomer for what we study because we study what children have learned . . . not how they have learned it" (1966, p. 3).

As Cook and Scioli, in one of the few explicit examinations of the concept, note:

> When operating at the synthetic (i.e., factual) level of discourse any attempt to use the concept of political learning or "the political learning process" as a defining term or concept in a scientific explanation of political behavior is inappropriate. The main reason for this objection is the ambiguity resulting from the lack of a clearly explicated empirical referent for the concept of "the learning process". . . . Since psychol-

ogists differ with regard to the learning process, the unqualified utilization of the concept within political science is highly questionable (1972, pp. 950–951).

An analysis of political learning might profitably begin with the concept of learning. According to Sears and his colleagues, learning "is the changing of the person's potentialities for acting in the future" (1957, p. 447). Along similar lines, Cook and Scioli note "that learning as an intervening variable, is reducable in observational terms to the change in the probability of emitting a particular response associated with the reinforced practice of that response" (p. 956). Social learning, then, can be understood as a function of two variables, the reward and the schedule of reinforcement. The former refers to "any event which makes more probable a response which it precedes [as in classical conditioning] or follows [as in the case of operant conditioning] with some regularity" (Danziger, 1971, p. 31). The degree of reward regularity is referred to as the reinforcement schedule, which varies from continuous (positive or negative) to fixed-ratio reinforcement (a reward every n^{th} time).

The language of social learning theory generates high expectations regarding its usefulness for political socialization theory and research. Rotter, in urging political scientists to make more explicit use of social learning theory, notes: "For social learning theorists, behavior is determined by a number of principles that carefully tie together prior experiences and later behavior (and) . . . a number of other important principles, based on careful experimental research" (1975, p. 132). Illustrative is the law of effect which links the increased probability of emitting a response with a past reward for that response in a similar situation. The terms *law and principles* might appear at first glance to be problematic when applied to human behavior in complex settings, since the principles and laws of learning theory have been derived in large part from animals much lower on the phylogenetic scale than man, in laboratory environments which do not approach the complexity of the human context. Does this create a problem? Not according to Gerwitz (1969), who argues:

> Except that stimuli occurring in natural settings are likely to be more variable than stimuli in contrived laboratory experiments . . . there is nothing intrinsically special about stimuli provided by people or about social settings as contexts of learning. Thus the concept "social learning" simply defines a category of learning that involves stimuli provided by people, but that follows the same principles as non-social (e.g., animal) learning.

This assumption seems to have carried over to analyses of political learning. Merelman, in an early paper about social learning theory and political legitimacy, suggests that "the learning process by which lower animals are trained to make responses to stimuli may be taken as a paradigm for the development of political legitimacy" (1966, p. 549). Neither Merelman nor others who advocate increased attention to social learning theory are unaware that for humans the higher symbolic processes extend (if not significantly alter) the learning process.

For this reason attention must be paid not only to primary but also to secondary rewards which may be symbolic as well as tangible (Merelman, 1966, p. 560; Rohter, 1975, pp. 148–149; Cook & Scioli, 1972, p. 957). Yet these very extensions, made necessary by the characteristics of the human organism, make problematic the direct application of social learning theory to political learning.

One difficulty arises from the attempt to specify what constitutes a "reinforcement" or reward. If, as in operant conditioning theory, a reinforcement is anything that follows an act which increases its future likelihood, one is committed to a postbehavior definition, since it can only be shown that a particular intervention constitutes a reward after it has been shown to increase the likelihood of specific behaviors.[14] This presents the possibility that what may operate as a reward at one point in time may, because of satiation, fail to elicit behaviors at a subsequent point (Cook & Scioli, 1972, p. 958). Moreover, if one defines reinforcement broadly to include anything the person wants, needs, or values (Waldman, 1973), the possibility is raised that rewards may be individually, subculturally, or otherwise specific. Thus, a particular stimulus may prove to be a reward for one cultural or social group, a neutral stimuli for another, and a deprivation to still another.

Another difficulty concerns the sources and alternatives available for satisfying secondary symbolic rewards. In the laboratory, alternatives are more easily made inaccessible than in normal social contexts, and it should be recalled that Pavlov had to render his famous canine subject immobile before conditioning could successfully proceed. Even when the environment can be controlled, there are difficulties with experimenter effects (Rosenthal, 1966) and with specifying exactly what it was that served as the reward. And if this is difficult in the "controlled" laboratory environment, it is certain to be more so in natural settings in which "cues" are multiple and ambiguous, not singular and obvious. Indeed, in some cases it is the meaning attached to particular events which determines whether and to what extent they are considered rewarding, depriving, or extraneous.

There are a number of other difficulties with current conceptualizations of reward, some of which we can only note here. One problem is the specification of what types of learning are most likely to be governed by a straightforward accounting of specific rewards and punishments. The assumption that the same principles apply with equal accuracy across learning types is problematic. Second, there is the difficulty of specifying the impact of age on the efficacy of social learning principles. A "simple" schedule of reinforcements and punishments may be more efficacious at early ages, when the more complex cognitive

---

[14]As Postman (1947) has pointed out, there is the additional problem of circularity. Phrased as "anything that increases the probability of a response," one is led to a definition of the law of effect as "a reinforcer increases the likelihood of the recurrence of a response which it follows." Additionally, one is led to a definition of a reinforcer as "anything which increases the likelihood of the recurrence of a response which it follows." Clearly, to increase its empirical usefulness, it is necessary to define reinforcement independently of the recurrence of a response.

contents and capacities have not developed. This disjuncture between cognitive capacities at different ages points to one difficulty of drawing analogies between organisms at different points on the phylogenetic scale. While it may be true that persons calculate and act in politics on their general ratio of rewards and deprivations, they do so in the context of social comparison and legitimacy. Pigeons and rats, however (even those living in the rarefied atmosphere of Cambridge), do not look to their "peers" or reference groups as a source of either general or legitimate expectations.[15]

Not only might we expect operant conditioning to be more successful for some ages and types of learning, but we would suggest further that the efficacy of social learning principles will also vary by individual character attributes, both developmental and biological. Thus the same character traits that allow a person to withstand group pressure (high self-esteem, stubbornness, low need for social approval) would also operate to reduce the efficacy of many reinforcement schedules. Moreover, there is at least suggestive evidence that congenital biologically based dispositions of the kind discussed in the previous section also play a role in affecting the efficacy of social learning principles: e.g., Buss and Plomin (1975, chap. 5) document the evidence for a biological role in the existence and development of sociability, which is generally defined as the tendency to move either toward or away from persons. Differences in this tendency have been observed during the first year of life (Freedman, 1965) and in many other studies reviewed by the authors (see especially pp. 110–114, 116–117, 119).

As was the case with our discussion of activity levels, we will treat these findings as only suggestive, yet they do raise some interesting possibilities. Consider the impact of peers on political learning. According to Dawson and Prewitt, their effects can be powerful, since

> in primary groups even the very subtle forms of disapproval are effective as instruments for motivating or restricting behavior. Similarly, group praise and reinforcement can serve as an effective socializing mechanism. *The close personal ties mean that members are extremely sensitive to group pressures. This renders their rewards and punishments as extremely potent* socializing instruments (1969, p. 135, emphasis added).

Yet if Buss and Plomin are correct, one would expect that persons low in sociability, even given peer group membership, would be less desirous of and

---

[15]It might be argued that an adjustment of the reinforcers and their schedule is all that is required to rescue the generalizability of "principles of learning" for both groups. Yet as Merelman (1966, esp. pp. 553–558) has convincingly documented, the difficulties of dealing with multiple and complex higher order S-R chains involved in symbolic rewards and vicarious learning (Rohter, 1975, p. 138) in political life are enormous. They include attention to discontinuities between symbols and policies, connotative overflow, feedback requirements, the generation of new legitimacy symbols, the selection of proper symbolic sanction contexts, and the problem of the appropriateness of symbol weights to particular public policies. To these complexities one must add the necessity for governments to maintain continuity if the problems just raised are not to prove insurmountable. In short, the existence of symbolic learning generates complexities which make the literal application of principles derived from nonsymbolic thinking a difficult, if not dubious, enterprise.

169765

therefore less dependent upon the particular rewards that groups may provide in the socialization process.

Another biological parameter which must be addressed by social learning theory concerns the role of intelligence. In a previous section we suggested an impact on what is learned, yet the real importance of intelligence in the political socialization process may very well be not in the area of "what" but, rather, in "how." The possibilities are illustrated by a model of personality and political learning developed by Sniderman (1975) which includes three facilitating variables (exposure, comprehension, and reward value of acceptance) which lead to political learning (p. 125). It seems that at least one major component of the model, comprehension, is clearly related to intelligence. In a complex, changing environment, it takes a certain amount of cognitive capacity to understand just what the message is. Disjunctures between environmental complexity (which give rise to multiple and ambiguous "messages") and individual understanding capacities ensure slippage in the social learning process, and thus may be viewed as one dynamic underlying social change.

What is the impact of intelligence on political learning? According to Hess and Torney (1967), "High intelligence accelerates the acquisition of political attitudes" (p. 148). Moreover, as we already have noted, high-IQ children tend to see compliance in less absolute terms (p. 161), have more reservations about the competence of government (p. 168), and are more likely to accept change in the political system (p. 181).

As expected, high-IQ children are less likely to answer "don't know" to political inquiries, but there are other less obvious impacts. High-IQ children tend to shy away from making extreme statements with regard to political objects (White, 1966, p. 722), a tendency which may help to explain the results noted above. Presumably, high-IQ respondents would be less prone to "positive bias" and "agreement response set." The last point to be noted here concerns the stability of IQ and response stability as a function of intelligence. According to one critic of trait theories, "An individual's behavior across ability measures (e.g., including intelligence) tends to be fairly consistent and reasonably stable" (Mischel, 1968, p. 14). The implication is that intelligence will have important lifelong effects on political learning. Examining the impact of intelligence on political opinion stability, Vaillancourt found: "Responses of those in the high I.Q. group were as stable or more stable than those of the low I.Q. group for 45 of the sets of tau-b values" (1973, p. 380). This finding suggests that one way in which intelligence speeds up the political socialization process is by facilitating the stability of political orientations at an earlier period than might otherwise be the case.

These studies are of course only suggestive of the ways in which political learning is either facilitated or bounded by genetically based biological characteristics. Yet they do point to the limits of political learning conceived of solely in terms of stimulus-response and operant conditioning.

Two additional problems in current conceptions of political learning, the direction of effects and the motivational sources, also deserve extended comment. Inherent in a learning theory (S-R model) approach is the assumption of directionality which runs from the stimulus (environment) to the response (organism). Implicit in this model is the assumption that the organism is the object, not the initiator, of cues and that the success of learning is to be evaluated in large part by how well the organism succeeds in internalizing environmental givens.

The impact of these assumptions can be seen in the way in which political socialization research has conceptualized both implicitly and explicitly the relationship between "agencies" and individuals. The dominant model is agency → individuals. Thus we talk about persons being socialized by the family (and other agencies) as if the child were a passive recipient of every environmental cue. Implicit in this conceptualization is the assumption of cue homogeneity and continuity. The first suggests that the actors or structures emit the same messages, while the latter requires message continuity across time.

Research by Jennings and Niemi suggests that parental political homogeneity is typically quite high. In their nationally representative sample of high school seniors, seven tenths of the parents were homogeneous at least with regard to partisan preferences (1974, p. 54). Yet elsewhere, after reviewing a large array of political orientations, for which there were low to moderate levels of parent-child agreement, the authors conclude "that any model of socialization that rests on assumptions of pervasive parent *to* child value transmissions . . . is in need of serious modification" (1968, p. 183, emphasis added).

If the family were an invariant set of structures, relationships, and contexts, we would expect the rate of political homogeneity among siblings to be very high indeed. Yet Hess and Torney, in a comparison of sibling and randomly matched pairs of children, found that for 113 scaled items the proportion of significant correlations was only 12.6 for the siblings as compared to 2.7 for the randomly matched pairs. While siblings are clearly more homogeneous than random pairs, the rate is not overly impressive from the standpoint of the uniformity of agency effects model. Moreover, "for the total sibling group, only five correlations of .21 or above appeared" (1968, p. 113).

The Hess and Torney study also suggests doubt about the second assumption of the agency transmission model, viz., cue continuity over time. Siblings with a small age difference (two grades or less) had a higher proportion of significant associations (16.1) than did siblings separated by large age differences (10.7). These findings fit in with a well-developed literature in psychology on birth order and socialization whose implications for political learning have been reviewed elsewhere (Renshon, 1975c). Thus, first-born male children are subject to different environments (including parental expectations and skills) than subsequent siblings. While differences in the socialization experiences related to parental treatment would be expected to decrease the uniformity of the "family context," do parental political orientations remain stable over time? It seems not. Jennings and Niemi, in examining their sample from 1965 through 1973, found that changes had taken place among parents (and their children) on such important variables as political trust and cynicism, as well as on issues like civil rights (1975, pp. 1330–1334). It would thus appear that the child does not receive uniform or unambiguous signals from this important agency. Indeed, they may not receive any direct signals at all given Jennings and Niemi's finding that "parents by and large do not care what their children's partisan preferences are" (1974, p. 61). Moreover, correspondence should not be confused with similarity of meaning, even in the case of partisan preference. As Lane and Sears remind us, "It would be highly misleading . . . to say that no change has ensued between a man adopting his father's democratic political preference and voting for Al Smith in 1928, and *his* child's maintaining the familial tradition and voting for John Kennedy in 1960'' (1964, pp. 22–23).

Yet the issue of transmission direction goes beyond the continuity of agency cues. Uniformity of cues does increase parent-child correspondence (Jennings & Niemi, 1974, chap. 6), especially on partisanship (but on other characteristics also). But the child does not simply internalize cues, whether uniform or not. As Connell points out:

> Children do not simply reproduce the communications that reach them from the adult world. They work them over, detach them from their original contexts and assimilate them to a general conception of what government is about (1971, pp. 27–28).

In other words, models of political transmission appear to have heavily emphasized the "receptivity" of the child and the preponderance of the agent. Integrating the individual (whether in childhood or subsequently) as an active part of the political learning process is necessary to correct the imbalance. Yet, as Dreitzel points out, "Of course children cannot be understood as active and possibly controlling partners in an interaction process as long as their congenital dispositions are not taken into account" (1973, p. 15). As we have suggested earlier, these congenital dispositions impact not only on what is learned politically, but how it is learned. It is also likely that they are responsible for cueing different responses in parents (Bell, 1968) and, it should be added, in subsequent socialization agencies. The highly active or intelligent child (to use our two illustrations) simply experiences a different socialization trajectory than his passive or intellectually less gifted counterpart, at least in this society.

It should also be noted that individuals actively attempt (sometimes with success) to change the socialization agencies to which they are subject. Thus one might wish to look at the socialization of socialization agencies as well as the socialization of citizens. Illustrations that come to mind are school reform (see the chapter by Patrick in this volume) and attempts to ensure more "objective" television reporting. Along the same lines, one can suggest that changes in support for the Vietnam war among some adults were at least a partial function of parent-child interactions which did not conform to the dominant model of parental transmission.

A related difficulty in current political socialization models concerns the mechanisms of political learning. Jennings and Niemi stress the importance of observation and imitation while noting the importance of reinforcement learning

(1974, p. 18). Hess and Torney present four models of political learning; (1) accumulation, (2) interpersonal transfer, (3) identification, and (4) cognitive development. Aside from difficulties in motivation dynamics to be discussed shortly, two of the four models (accumulation, identification) explicitly assume a teacher → learner relationship. A third (interpersonal transfer) does so implicitly, since what the child has learned *from* other contexts is in the interpersonal transfer model generalized to other spheres. Only the fourth model assumes some interpretive activity on the child's part, but even this is limited since it only assumes that "it is not possible to teach a given concept to a child who has not reached an appropriate developmental level" (p. 25).

While social learning, reinforcement, and other derivative models may be useful for explaining much political learning, it would be mistaken to assume that they account for it all. If positive schedules of reinforcement were sufficient as well as necessary, practice would indeed make perfect, but this is clearly not the case. As White points out (1969, p. 54), increased praise (or other rewards) may increase a person's desire to solve a problem, but not necessarily his capacity to do so. While social learning theory has to date provided political socialization with its dominant models of political learning, there are arenas in which other models are necessary. Chief among these are learning contexts which require configurative and integrative skills, usefully examined under the rubric of "insight."

In some cases insight will be preceded by direct cues from external sources, which provide a new view of current, past, or future realities. The rearrangement of existing assumptions, by which the person "sees" his position in society as a result of current distributional arrangements, may be preceded by years of positive or negative rewards during which no such connections were made. The attempt to provide alternative explanations of the individual's current life situation is at the heart of recruitment attempts by many social and most revolutionary movements.[16]

In more typical political circumstances, the origin of insight lies not so much with external cues as with the individual's capacity to reexamine basic assumptions and arrive at unique syntheses required by the particular contexts. Illustrative is Rokeach's now classic study on open and closed belief systems (1960). Rokeach invented a problem which required subjects to reexamine their basic assumptions if a solution were to be found. Open-minded subjects were able to solve the problem more quickly, in the absence of authoritative information, than were closed-minded subjects, since their learning routines included the ability to reassess the apparent "givens."

In this connection it is instructive to note Torrance's definition of creativity as

> a process of becoming sensitive to problems, deficiencies, gaps in knowledge, missing elements, disharmonies, and so on; identifying the difficulty; searching for

---

[16]In extreme situations such as forced captivity, new views may be taught directly by a system of rewards or punishments, but the evidence is that while long-term effects are observable among those who have been subject to forced resocialization, they do not include continued commitment to the new world view, if the context is changed.

solutions, making guesses or formulating hypotheses about the deficiencies; testing and retesting the hypotheses and possibly modifying and retesting them (1966, p. 6).

It should be emphasized that creativity and insight do not rest merely on the application of routinized cognitive procedures. While both involve an orientation to problems and their solution, neither the process nor the outcome can be considered mechanical.

At the micro level, the acquisition of knowledge regarding formal political structures and procedures may be more amenable to social learning approaches than an understanding of the role of such structures and procedures in the context of larger social problems (e.g., the allocation of societal resources and their implications and alternatives). Additionally, the relative importance of insight in the political learning process will also be partially dependent on dynamics operative at the macro level; e.g., political contexts characterized by rapid and extensive social change would be likely to increase the importance of creative and insight learning modes. Correspondingly, such a context would decrease the efficacy of social learning approaches, to the extent that they emphasized the mastery of "previously successful" models or routinized approaches to novel contexts.

The above considerations suggest that concepts of political learning which rely exclusively, or even primarily, on assumptions of transmission *from* teacher *to* learner, neglect an important dimension of that process. Part of the importance of creativity and insight as learning modes lies in the implication that models of the political learning process must take seriously a view of the learner as creator and initiator as well as receptor. In short, a reconsideration of the direction of effects in the political socialization process would appear both necessary and helpful. Yet such a reconsideration cannot proceed very far without analysis of the motivational dynamics that underlie political (and other types of) learning.

POLITICAL LEARNING AND MOTIVATION

Every theory of learning is based on assumptions about motivation. To the extent that political socialization theory has borrowed conceptualizations of specific mechanisms from social learning theory, it has in the process obtained a set of assumptions about *why* as well as *how* people learn. Interestingly, while attention in the field has been focused on the lack of systematic analyses of the latter,[17] it is the former which is the real *terra incognita* of political socialization

---

[17]Sigel (1965, p. 4; see also Weissberg, 1974, pp. 15–16) discusses two broad types of political learning, incidental and deliberate. Dawson and Prewitt (1969, chap. 5) further divide the former category into interpersonal transference, apprenticeship and generalization. Under direct (or deliberate) learning, they consider four methods: imitation, anticipatory socialization, political education, and political experience. Hess and Torney (1967) discuss four models of political learning including accumulation, interpersonal transfer, identification, and cognitive development. Finally Jennings and

theory.[18] In the discussion that follows, our focus will be on two broad models of individual motivation and their implications for political socialization theory. The first, and until recently the most prevalent, has been labeled the compensation-reduction model. The second, arising from various strands of dissatisfaction with the first, is labeled the surplus-growth model.

Social learning theory is built upon a compensation-reduction model of motivation. While this model contains a number of tenets, three will be of direct concern here. The first involves the principle of maximized utility, the second involves the assumption of tension reduction as the key component of reward, while the third concerns the locus of rewards, whether intrinsic or extrinsic. In its most general form, utility refers to the propensity of persons to seek increases in gratification and decreases in deprivation. Given that form, the assumption is hardly controversial, but difficulties arise when assumptions of maximization are coupled with utilitarian calculations. The assumption of maximized utility, then, suggests that persons act not only to achieve a rough preponderance of rewards over deprivations but, in fact, always seek to maximize the highest rewards possible in any situation. Aside from the difficulties of reward specifications, already noted, persons may choose to satisfy rather than maximize particular values (Simon, 1957). Moreover, persons who are satisfiers on a particular value may under appropriate conditions become maximizers. Thus, while election to office in the United States typically requires 50% plus one of the votes cast, there are conditions (such as higher political ambitions) where the minimum number of votes needed to win could be dysfunctional for the winner's subsequent political pursuits.

The second assumption of the model involves the association of pleasure (reward) with decreases in tension. In the animal laboratory, from which the major tenets of social learning theory have been developed, avoidance has frequently appeared as a modal response in learning experiments. This has lead to the view that animals avoid novelty or anything else that might result in deprivations (increased tension). Nor is this assumption absent from discussion of political learning. Thus Schonfeld, in a discussion of the child's introduction to authority relationships, suggests, "Let us begin with an assumption upon which

---

Niemi (1974) discuss observation, reinforcement, and cognitive theories as approaches to the study of political learning.

Thus there seems to be no surfit of discussions of political learning although there is a paucity of research related to directly establishing the operation of particular types of learning in specific instances. What is missing from many such discussions is explicit recognition of the child as an active part of the learning process. It is this omission which forms the basis of our focus on "insight" as a learning mode.

[18]The psychology of motivation is an area of complex conceptual controversies and empirical discrepancies. An extensive treatment of the issues involved is not possible within the confines of the present context. An extended discussion of these issues within the framework of a consideration of personality theories and political analysis may be found elsewhere (Renshon, forthcoming, chap. 4). My purpose here is to call attention to and specify some of the implications for conceptualization of the political learning process.

most people can agree; people will try to avoid stress and, if possible, to reduce it'' (1971, p. 595). Perhaps, but this raises the questions of what is stressful to whom and why; and the evidence to date is far from conclusive.

While avoidance may be a modal laboratory response, it is by no means the only one. Thus, Dember (1956) ran rats through a modified T-maze, which contained locked glass doors at the arms, painted black and white respectively. On the second run through the maze, the glass doors were removed so that entry was possible, and one black arm was repainted white, so both arms were then color uniform. The question under consideration is whether there will be any difference in the rate at which different arms are selected when the rat reaches the choice point.

Several expectations are possible. "Spontaneous alternation" theory suggests that variety is sought in the sense that the alternative already selected on a previous run will produce satiation. Thus no differences are predicted by this model for the second set of runs in Dember's experiment, since the closed glass doors during the first run prevented entry into either side of the T-maze. Along similar lines, stimulus satiation theory would not predict variation in entry decisions based on color, since on the second run both arms of the maze are the same. Yet, if variety is sought, even by animals this low on the phyletic scale, there should be significant differences in entry selections, with rats choosing the door which has changed in color. And that is exactly what happened. On the second run, 17 out of 20 rats chose the arm of the maze where the color had been changed.

What does this experiment have to do with political learning? It strongly suggests that the empirical basis upon which "principles of learning" have been built in what appear to be well designed, carefully controlled experimental settings do not completely support the concept of reward solely as a tension-reduction dynamic. And to the extent that this is so, one can only further question the transferability of that assumption from the animal laboratory to human learning and behavior. Indeed, there is ample research evidence on the latter which suggests that increases, not decreases, in tension and stimulation are necessary for optimal functioning and learning (Sales, 1971; see also the work on sensory deprivation summarized in Solomon et al., 1961). Additionally, exploratory and variation-seeking behavior among persons is a well established finding in the social psychology laboratory and in field investigations (Maddi, 1961). These findings are important because novelty and change are generally considered to be tension-increasing phenomena.

The third tenet of the compensation-reduction model to be examined here concerns the locus of motivation. Among the issues are whether, to what extent, and under what circumstances rewards are intrinsic (internal locus) or extrinsic (external locus). A focus on the latter has, as already noted, been the perspective of social learning theory and is doubtless accurate for numerous political orientations and behaviors. Inherent in this tenet is the assumption that it is primarily social norms or the power of models to dispense social rewards and punishments that operates to facilitate motivation.

A useful illustration is the widespread association of the good-citizen role with political participation. To the extent that participation results in satisfaction of the good-citizen role, a case could be made for the externality of the motivational locus. However, there are several difficulties with this position. First, it assumes that the norm of active participation and good citizenship is, in large part, uniformly held. But evidence from a recent study of definitions of the good-citizen role found that a substantial minority (over one quarter) defined the good citizen without reference to any active participation (Jennings & Niemi, 1974, p. 272). Second, it assumes that the norm of activity is largely uniform in transmission. Yet a recent analysis of more than 30 years of research on the presentation of the good-citizen norm in schools and textbooks notes the prevalence of passivity as a civic virtue (Andrian, 1971). Moreover, it should be noted that there is at least some discrepancy in teaching children to be politically active, passively (i.e., by exhortation).

Some of the general difficulties we have discussed above in connection with the compensation-reduction model of motivation and learning will perhaps come into sharper focus when we examine the role of identification and imitation. Discussions of political learning in the political socialization process have heavily stressed the importance of both. Dawson and Prewitt note that "imitation . . . is the most extensive and persistent mode of social learning known to man" (1969, p. 73), whereas Jennings and Niemi, although they discuss other forms, nonetheless conclude, "The older psychological formulation which most reflects our thinking is that Bandura and his associates have come to call observational learning . . . principally modeling, but also matching, imitation, copying, contagion, cue-taking, and identification" (1974, p. 15).

Clearly, imitation has important implications for political learning. Dawson and Prewitt give as an illustration "the close correspondence in political outlooks found among peers and work associates (which) seem to indicate that imitation of some sort serves as a means of socialization within such relationships" (1969, p. 74). A similar line of argument is put forward by Cook and Scioli in a discussion of the efficacy of social learning theory for political socialization research. As an illustration, they note the Bennington study whose "findings posit a relationship between an individual and a specifiable element in the immediate environment of the individual (i.e., reference groups)" (p. 956). The authors then go on to analyze these overlapping identifications in terms of social reinforcement theory, and discuss with apparent approval

a conceptualization of the socialization process at Bennington congruent with the principle of selective reinforcement. Conformity to group norms results in group praise (positive reinforcement) and deviation from approved behavior results in group sanctions or the deprivation of group values (negative reinforcement).

Such formulations appear reasonable, but closer examination reveals two major difficulties. The first concerns self-selection, while the second involves the motivational mechanisms which underlie identification and imitation.

The first difficulty arises because, while imitation is no doubt ubiquitous, it is by no means indiscriminate. The Bennington study discussed above, as an illustration of the applicability of social learning theory to political socialization, is a case in point. More than two decades later, Newcomb studied continuity and regression in his Bennington sample and asked, (1973), "What seems to be the differences between those who and those who do not remain non-conservative?" The answer appears to be: "In sum, nearly all of the still non-conservative women mention either husbands or public activities (most commonly both) that have served to maintain previously non-conservative attitudes" (p. 420). To the extent that entrance into marriage (and the constellation of social and peer activities related to particular partner choices) is a function of personal preference rather than social pressure, the element of self-selection into particular peer and social groups must be taken into account. Newcomb makes a similar point when he remarks, "It would hardly seem to be a matter of chance that a set of men who are less conservative than is to be expected (on the basis of social demographics) are married to a set of women of whom just the same thing is true" (p. 418). In other words, the social power of the group which Cook and Scioli view as establishing the applicability of social learning theory to political socialization, might also be profitably viewed from the perspective of individual initiative and choice.

In analyzing (even indirectly) the individual motivational basis of identifications and imitation in the political learning process, theorists have relied on either social learning or psychoanalytic theories of motivation. While self-selection may be operative for peer and other associations later in life, is it observable at earlier stages of development, especially with regard to the family and political learning? After all, the child does not choose his family, and parents are the most frequently available models for observation, especially during the early years. Indeed, it does seem as if this is one illustration of the relative importance of various types of learning, at different stages of development. (In addition, the *what* will probably have very specific links with the *how* of political learning.) Yet the acceptance of the large role of imitative learning in certain contexts (in this case, the family) does not necessarily resolve all of the difficulties.

According to Rohter, "The general rule is that a previous history of being rewarded for imitative behavior increases the probability of imitation in the future" (1975, p. 139). Moreover, this process is especially important in the case of the family because "the child comes to copy diverse responses performed by his parent because he is consistently and potently reinforced for such behavior" (p. 140). However accurate this may be, as a general rule, according to research done by Jennings and Niemi, it seems unlikely to be helpful in the specific case of political socialization, because

> much of what passes for political socialization—especially in the home—*is low keyed and haphazard*. While socialization in this model may occasionally be effective as

that in the conscious direct and systematic mode, it tends to create a vacuum. . . . This is partly because the cues will be more *ad hoc* in nature, perhaps contradictory in direction *and infrequently reinforced* (1974, p. 330, emphasis added).

If parents do not either directly reinforce particular political orientations,[19] or apparently care very much about instilling them (within wide boundaries) then how is it that "similarity between parents and their children is vast" (Jennings & Niemi, 1974, p. 177)? One suggestion comes from Rohter's observation that the impact of models will be a partial function of the "homogeneity or heterogeneity of behaviors they display" (p. 140). Here learning theory fares much better in the empirical findings. Jennings and Niemi in a careful examination of continuity and discontinuity in cue presentation, note that "almost without exception, the child is more likely to reflect one parent's orientation when that orientation is also shared by the other parent" (p. 177). But such findings tell us more about when (in the sense of under what circumstances) than they do about why (in the sense of motivation).

Another explanation put forward to explain the why of identification in the political learning process is psychoanalytically oriented. In political socialization theory its most manifest form is the "vulnerability hypothesis." Hess' early formulation is worth noting at length:

> To the child authority is defined not only as superior but as exceedingly powerful. In comparison to his father and mother, he sees himself as relatively helpless. He is not only physically inferior, he is also dependent upon adults for the most elementary aspects of physical and emotional care. In short, he is weak, dependent and vulnerable. The response of the child to his feeling of vulnerability is to reassure himself that the authority figure is benign and that he will protect him rather than harm him. He sees authority figures as benign because it is too threatening to see them as malevolent. This tendency is a psychological technique for dealing with feelings of aggression toward authority. We propose then, that the child's image of political authority is designed to cope with his feelings of vulnerability and aggression with regard to superior power (1963, p. 542).

Three lines of evidence could be developed to support the psychoanalytic approach to motivational dynamics underlying identification as a mode of political learning. First, it could be demonstrated that children indeed do not give critical evaluations of political authority. A second approach would be to see to what degree high evaluations of political leaders are associated with high evaluations of fathers. The third approach would examine the impact of family authority patterns on orientations to authority. Presumably, the more punitive the parents (and thus the more threatening), the more similarity of views there ought to be.

None of these three lines of argument have been supported by empirical

---

[19]In fact, this statement must remain tentative since Jennings and Niemi do not rely on any direct observations of political learning in the family but, rather, a comparison "of parent and offspring response to the same question stimuli in an interview situation" (1975, p. 16).

research. The first line of support is compromised by the finding that children are not adverse to expressing hostility to political authorities, even given sociopolitical marginality. Jaros and his colleagues found this among poor rural white children: "There is no doubt that Appalachian children manifest far less favorable political affect (towards authority) than do their counterparts elsewhere" (1968). The objective sociopolitical circumstances (poverty, neglect, and hostility from authorities) of these respondents, according to psychoanalytical theory, would have resulted in just the opposite. Nor are children dependent upon marginal social position to express antipathy to political authority. Arterton (1974) found in the wake of Watergate that children were uniformly less favorable to the President with regard to his personal characteristics, although his power ratings remained virtually unaffected (pp. 275–276).

Second, empirical research has failed to establish an association between perceptions of the father and perceived benevolence of political authorities. In a direct examination of this possibility, Jaros (1967, p. 387) found "no relationship whatsoever . . . between children's anxiety levels and their propensity to attribute benevolence to the President." Moreover, Arterton, in his study of children's response to Watergate, found "no discernible differences . . . between ratings in 1962 and 1973 for 'your father' on any of the scales which measured significant changes in attitudes towards the President (data not shown)" (p. 286). The vulnerability model would have predicted that changes in affect toward the President would have been accompanied by changes in affect toward the father (or parents).

Last, empirical inquiry has failed to support the proposition that punitive emotional and physical child rearing would lead to an increase in parent-child correspondence. On the one hand, punitive emotional relationships should lead to an increase in parent-child correlations, since presumably they are threatening and would lead to greater use of identification as a defense. Correspondingly, the more authoritarian the family power relationships, the more agreement there should be for similar reasons. Yet, in examining parent-child correspondence in their nationwide sample, Jennings and Niemi (1968) found that neither proposition received empirical support. Affective closeness was unrelated to transmission patterns, while for the latter what patterns did emerge suggested a reverse of that predicted by the vulnerable model (e.g., more democratic families have greater correspondence). In short, "family interaction patterns are often unrelated to the flow of attitudes from parent to child" (1974, p. 81).

The failure to establish any of the three lines of evidence to support the psychoanalytic theory of the motivation underlying identification in political learning, while not necessarily fatal, is nonetheless damaging. Moreover, since learning theory and psychoanalytic theory share the assumption of gratification as essentially a reduction of tension, questions are raised about the former as well. What would an alternative to this model suggest for political learning?

At the beginning of the section we mentioned two models, one the compensation-reduction model, the other a surplus-growth model. One way of conveniently summarizing some differences between the two is by noting that in many ways they are mirror images. Thus, while the former stresses maximization of utility, the latter stresses the variations in patterned pursuit among multiple (and sometimes conflicting) values. Illustrative is Lasswell's distinction between the "political man" (1930) who organizes his energy in pursuit of maximization of a single value (power) and "democratic man" (1951) who flexibly pursues multiple values. On the second assumption, while the former equates gratification with tension decreases, the latter suggests that for some persons increases in tension will be sought and not avoided, especially if this results in increases in intrinsic rewards. Thus, the last point of difference to be examined here concerns the locus of causality. The compensation-reduction model stresses outside agencies and external factors as the source of rewards and thus motivation for (political) learning. The surplus-growth model does not deny the efficacy of external rewards, but additionally stresses the intrinsic motivation and satisfaction derived from mastery and gains in personal competence.

How would a surplus-growth model account for the motivational dynamics underlying identification as a process of political learning? Rather than emphasizing the child's need to reduce tension and cope with the anxieties generated by powerful authority figures, an alternative formulation would additionally focus on the child's exploratory behavior motivated in large part by a desire to increase his personal control and competence. The tension-reduction emphasis of the psychoanalytic model is based on extrapolations from situations which are not representative of the entire, or even typical, range of parent-child interactions. Thus, much emphasis is put on toilet training and the Oedipal conflicts as situational prototypes, but as White points out:

> It seems to me that the Oedipal prototype falls short as a general model for the phallic stage in just the way that toilet training failed for the anal stage. Once again Freud selected for his central image a hopeless situation, one where defeat for the child is inevitable ... if these were the true and determinative models it would be quite a problem to explain the survival of any sense of initiative (1960, p. 125).

These situations represent socialization to the broad limits of personal control and choice, but it is important to emphasize that many more parent-child interactions develop around themes of increasing and extending the child's personal control and competence. Certainly, increases in mastery produce delight and other rewards, but the point is that they do so for *both* the child and his parents, not for the latter alone. It has been repeatedly observed that children are more likely to engage in behavior which brings about some "result," than that which is not followed by anything which can be directly related to the effort. In these cases it is easy to suggest that the result is the "reward," but this does raise the question of why a result which is connected with the child's initiated action should be more rewarding than one which is not. The answer proposed here is that such behaviors are intrinsically rewarding to a person because control over relevant aspects of the individual's life space is a basic and crucial human need.[20]

It might be argued, of course, that needs for personal control serve a tension-reduction function, and this is no doubt partially accurate. But to view the need primarily in this way collapses the distinction between approach and avoidance. If novel mastery situations were indeed highly threatening, and mastered only to reduce that tension, one would expect avoidance as a predominant response, not engagement.

Clearly, the history of successful mastery attempts will have an important impact on subsequent undertakings here. Early, conspicuous or consistent failure can certainly lead to increases in anxiety regarding mastery. In this case, mastery attempts will be limited in both scope and resource commitment, until an area of control emerges. This may involve "narrowing" or some other technique by which the scope of the mastery context is reduced until it becomes manageable. But unless there are overwhelming circumstances, low feelings of personal control do not result in cessation of attempts at mastery, as one would predict if tension reduction were the paramount concern: e.g., in a study of university undergraduates, I found that low levels of feelings of personal control were actually associated with increased political participation (1975c).

According to the competency-based model then, identification between parent and child is certainly not solely, and perhaps not even primarily, a defense against anxiety. Rather, it is the competence and mastery (both real and perceived) of the parents, coupled with the need for personal control by the child, which provides a strong motivational underpinning to the identification process. At first, it is likely that the "perceived" competence of the parents in the many areas that the child has yet to master provides a firm basis for identification, yet as the child grows and becomes aware of the larger social context within which mastery and personal control both take place and are evaluated, changes in the strength and range of identifications are possible.

The implication of changes in expectations of personal control in the political arena may be seen in Greenstein's suggestion: "One suspects that, since by the sixth, seventh and eighth grades children are well aware of status differences, the lower class child has begun to develop a sense of his own (and his parents') inadequacy in coping with the abstract, the verbal, and the remote—including the symbols of the world of politics" (1965, pp. 104–105). Yet there is more to this reality appraisal than intellectual incapacity, for Hess and Torney found that ratings of fathers showed marked social class differences. Children from lower class families rated their fathers as less able to make others do what they tell them than did upper-status children. As the authors go on to note, "This may result from the child's knowledge about his father's occupational role—an awareness that middle- and upper-class jobs carry more prestige and power" (1968, p. 116).

---

[20]An extended consideration of the evidentiary lines for this argument have been developed elsewhere (Renshon, 1974, pp. 43–58).

As we noted before, the child is neither unknowledgeable about, nor unresponsive to, "reality" considerations.

The broad social class differences noted above are illustrative of the ways in which macrosocietal considerations may affect the definition and range of capacities that underlie feelings of personal control. But it must be stressed that as early as these impacts may be felt and perceived, there are many areas in which the parents are considered competent, simply by virtue of having adult skills. This, coupled with the additional need gratification given by many parents (food, clothing, emotional warmth, praise) (see the chapter by Davies in this volume), suggests why parental competencies (and not simply those of any adult) serve as one important motivational basis of the identification process.

What are some general implications of a surplus-growth model of motivation for the study of political learning? The first point is that the political learning process can be usefully conceptualized from the point of view of the individual's needs and skills, as well as from the requirements of the socializers. From this perspective the individual becomes a crucial, not a residual, component of the learning process. A corollary point is that rewards cannot be productively considered apart from the needs and wants that they are presumed to satisfy. Certain rewards may have short-term utility as a facilitator of political learning, but they may also entail long-term deficiencies. Thus, the child may indeed "learn" that a good citizen is essentially passive and quiescent and receive the appropriate symbolic and tangible rewards for doing so; but this satisfaction will be short lived in the face of any necessity to intervene in the political process to further feelings of personal control.

A third point relates to the relative importance of intrinsic and extrinsic rewards. While no one can doubt that the latter play an important role in facilitating political learning, learning itself can frequently be its own reward. This will be especially likely when there is acquisition of new understandings and capacities which facilitate increases in feelings of personal control and other needs. A fourth point concerns limits on learning and their implications for political life. To return to previous illustrations, ranges of intellectual capacity appear to have an impact not only on what is learned, but also on how. Additionally, individual activity levels may influence the propensity to engage in political activity aside from considerations of the good-citizen role or its facilitation (or lack thereof) by particular structural or procedural arrangements. This is one reason why current debates about "participatory democracy" will profit by keeping in mind that frequent and consistent political participation may be dependent upon individual biological dynamics as well as upon abstract models of citizen obligation acquired during the socialization process.

· A last point concerns efforts to conceptualize the adequacy of political socialization. This has not been a major concern of political socialization theorists, in part because of the behavioral emphasis on description rather than prescription. Yet prescription may play a role in model building. Illustrative is Levy's suggestion that "there is adequate socialization in a society if there is a sufficient number of adequately socialized individuals for the structural prerequisites of a society to operate" (Levy, 1954, p. 187). As Easton points out, conceived of in this manner, "socialization loses its neutral character as a term referring to a process that may have positive, negative or indifferent consequences for the society and generally carries a positive connotation for the fulfillment of the postulated functions" (1968, p. 135). The adequacy and implications of conceptualizing political socialization as a neutral process will be the focus of more extensive treatment at the conclusion of this chapter. At this point we simply note that, even when care is taken to emphasize alternative outcomes in the context of the norms of particular societies, difficulties ensue. Thus Sigel notes: "While the definition of a well functioning member will vary with the political system—from obedient passive subject in one system to (an) active participating citizen in another—a well functioning citizen is one who accepts (internalizes) society's political norms and who will then transmit them to future generations" (1965, p. 2). Even in this carefully phrased statement, the perspective is clearly that of "societal requisite."

A surplus-growth model of individual motivation and political learning would suggest an alternative perspective and begin not with societal but with individual requirements. Such a perspective would attempt to establish a firm empirical foundation for the analysis and understanding of citizen character and motivation. It would then proceed to analyze not only what the socialization of citizens implies for the functioning of political systems but, additionally, what the functioning of political systems implies for the mode (and range) of citizen character development.

Conclusion

Since the phenomena with which political socialization theory deals are both cross-cultural and transhistorical, it seems unlikely that failure to satisfactorily resolve some of its theoretical or empirical difficulties will lessen its importance as a focus of political analysis. The process by which the child develops into the citizen (of whatever polity) and its implications for the political system have been recognized, even by its critics, as a crucial dimension of the relevance of the field. Thus Connell notes:

> Questionnaire surveys of the political ideas of school children were by no means new in the 1950's. If one looks at American journals of psychology and education from the late 20's on, one can find dozens of surveys, mostly of high school students, but sometimes of primary, using political opinion items and attitude scales. What was new was neither the technique (admittedly improved) nor the subject matter (admittedly extended). What was new in the political socialization studies was that the people giving the tests were political scientists who always had in mind some political pay-off, and who were looking for links between the patterns they traced in childhood

and features of the political system. The constant attempt to make this linkage is what decisively distinguishes political socialization studies from the social-psychological fumblings that preceded it, and is what entitles it to serious regard (1972–1973, p. 167).

Given these considerations, it is somewhat surprising that the political nature of political socialization has not received more extensive attention. Part of the problem has been that, in the attempt to conceptualize the process in neutral terms, its political nature has been obscured. The major thrust of this approach has been to suggest that because no particular outcome for the political system is suggested, in terms of either change or stability, political socialization theory is not biased. Easton and Dennis, in proposing to examine the process rather than the outcomes of political socialization, note:

> What a child becomes or what happens to an adult over time may be in large part a product of longitudinal patterns gradually altered through various kinds of autonomous experiences. We need not prejudge the matter by incorporating it into our definition of socialization itself (1969, p. 12).

We have already noted Easton's criticism of functional approaches to socialization, and his turn to a systems perspective as an antidote. From this perspective Easton and Dennis argue, "Systems analysis does not possess a built-in conservative bias . . . (since) our theoretical posture does not allow us to predict in advance whether the particular content and method of socialization will, in fact, enable some kind of political system to continue" (1969, p. 66). Yet, while the theory may be neutral, it remains to be seen whether the same is accurate for the process.

Illustrative is the list of broad outcomes of the political socialization process suggested by Easton and Dennis (p. 66). The authors clearly state that their concern is a general theory of political socialization and not a more specific theory of socialization and democracy. Yet it is important to examine their general points within the context of democratic political theory because

> it is a curious feature of political socialization literature that politics is treated as the effect of the process, but hardly ever as its cause. Investigators rarely ask hard political questions about who benefits, who controls, and who attempts to control the processes they study (Connell, 1972–1973, p. 181).

As political socialization moves into its third decade of empirical research, these appear to be questions at least worth asking. In the absence of specific attention, they will nonetheless retain importance as the findings of political socialization are brought into the policy arena.

What, then, are the specific political implications of the general theoretical points made by Easton and Dennis. First, they note that political socialization is "a major kind of response by which political systems may seek to avoid stress on its essential variables." How is this accomplished? First, by ensuring that the political decisions are accepted as binding. Yet it must be recalled that at least one aspect of democratic political process is the continued ability to question and (attempt to) change the current political agenda. Moreover, while it may be true that "authority is more stable when obeyed automatically" (Greenstein, 1968, p. 551), there is a tradition within democratic political theory which argues for examination of the obligations of political compliance. Also, recent research in moral development theory (see the chapter by Friedman in this volume) suggests that higher levels of moral development will not be characterized by automatic compliance. One could, in addition, question not whether but, rather, to what extent automatic compliance is consonant with the theory of democratic character and citizenship.

A second way in which socialization helps to limit stress on the political system is by limiting "the volume and variety of demands," thus preventing "the communications networks from being overburdened to the point of collapse." One can imagine a variety of ways by which this could be accomplished. Demands could be simply minimized by force, but this approach runs the risk of increasing politicized frustration and thus the likelihood of political instability. A less stressful point of departure is to mitigate demands by either making them illegitimate or nonpolitical. The former relies on the ability to authoritatively define "excessiveness," while the latter requires that no connections be made between particular individual needs and governmental responsibility. The role of political socialization in both of these processes has been little analyzed. Yet their importance is well captured in Weissberg's (1974, pp. 58–60) observation regarding the implications of current political socialization procedures in the United States:

> If politics involves a choice of alternatives among different ways of organizing and governing political life, and each individual begins with the full range of choices before him, we can readily see that by adolescence most Americans have narrowed down the range of political alternatives. . . . There is nothing inherent about this process, but as we have seen, the socialization process in the United States does a thorough job. The political consequences of these choices are enormous. . . . The fact is that most young Americans, with little or no consideration of the alternatives or analysis of the evidence, make important decisions on their political community, authority roles, and descriptions of this system.

At first glance, these observations appear to conflict rather directly with Jennings and Niemi's observation that "it is not much of an exaggeration to say that parents socialize their children despite themselves" (1974, p. 61). The authors are referring here to their finding that in the American family political socialization is pretty much a laissez faire process. Yet it is only so with certain boundaries. Thus, the authors also note:

> We hasten to add that the lack of deliberate efforts to direct the socialization of youth in partisan directions does not mean that such efforts are lacking on all political and social matters. Parents are concerned about their children's attitudes regarding basic societal rules, such as obeying the law and being loyal to one's country. . . . An additional qualification (is that) parents may be totally indifferent about their chil-

dren's political views—so long as they do not become _____ (Socialists, Communists, John Birchers, Ku Klux Klansmen, SDSers, pacifists, etc.). (1974, p. 62)

The implication of the above observation is that while the theories used to analyze the political socialization process may indeed be neutral regarding outcomes, the process itself—in particular, political context—is decidedly not. This dimension of the political socialization process certainly merits more extensive analysis than it has been given to date. It also leads to an alternate conception of a political theory of political socialization. Rather than focusing primarily on the implications of political socialization for the functioning of the political system, it would in addition focus on the impact of political processes on political socialization. Put in another way, this perspective would examine the reciprocal processes involved in assessing the impact of who gets what, when, and how on who learns what and so forth.

Such a focus makes no provision for excluding consideration of the larger systemic effects of political socialization; it simply adapts a different strategy of ascertaining the way in which the impacts are aggregated. Rather than beginning with societal requirements and examining any particular socialization process in terms of them, this approach begins conceptually with the individual person and attempts to see how current distributional arrangements, coupled with individual capacities and needs, impact upon who learns what from whom; when, how, and with what effects and implications.

It is likely that such an approach to a political theory of political socialization will entail at least as many and perhaps more difficulties as has the system's perspective. These should not be overlooked. It will require, among other things, attention to differentiating needs and wants, as well as a theoretical framework by which personality needs, social experiences, and resultant political beliefs and assumptions can be systemically linked. Furthermore, it will require extensive attention to the linkages between character, political beliefs, and political behavior both toward and within political institutions. The attention to institutions will strike some as a regression to a focus against which the behavioral movement rose in protest. Yet a return to the study of institutions may function as an important vehicle for understanding the process by which individual socialization outcomes are translated into systemic effects seems potentially profitable.

Clearly the two approaches (individual and systemic) are different sides of the same coin; they are complementary, not mutually exclusive. Moreover, successful outcomes for either approach are correctly viewed as long-range possibilities, rather than immediate prospects.

Yet to the extent that either succeeds in empirically establishing the reciprocal linkages between individual political outcomes (who gets what, etc.) and political socialization (who learns what, etc.), political analysts will have developed two not necessarily incompatible justifications for the field. The first, of course, would be a justification in terms of the importance of the outcomes to the political system, whether in terms of stability, persistence, or whatever. The second justification, having established this link, would be the ability to move from the "contemplative" to the "manipulative" mode, or from political analysis to political intervention. This will no doubt prove to be a difficult and controversial transition, and one that many political analysts will find uncomfortable. Yet there can be little doubt of the movement of political socialization theory out of the narrower confines of academic research into the broader arena of public policy. At a minimum, such a transition will require an explicit confrontation with personal and social values. Yet, even given apparently useful theory and laudable values, the outcomes will not always be in accord with intentions. Nonetheless, it seems well to recall here that empirical analyses do have important normative implications, and these should not be overlooked. Socialization research will not profit by completely divorcing values from political analysis, nor is objectivity necessarily a terminal goal. Rather, it seems beneficial to recall Harold Lasswell's injunction that "objectivity is put where it belongs, which is in the service of goal values" (1948, p. 122).

Postscript

In the preceding discussions, we have touched upon a number of basic issues and assumptions in current political socialization research. Our presumption has been that it is useful to examine not only the superstructure of empirical findings, but the theoretical foundations upon which they are built. We have, at various points, suggested some alternative models of the political socialization process, not with the assumption that they will displace current models, but, rather, that their perspective will prove a useful addition to subsequent theoretical and empirical undertakings. As Martin Landau has wisely noted in this regard: "Much of the conflict over the use of models is superfluous. The choice is not between models and no-models, but between a critical consciousness of their use and uncritical acceptance" (1961, p. 353).

2

Methodological Appropriateness
in Political Socialization Research

Robert Weissberg and Richard Joslyn

THE STUDY OF POLITICAL SOCIALIZATION, like the study of politics more generally, has been growing methodologically more sophisticated. Contemporary socialization research employs a wide variety of data gathering techniques, complex multivariate statistics, as well as cross-national and longitudinal study designs. Nevertheless, despite rapid advances in method, our substantive knowledge of the socialization process has proceeded relatively slowly. Indeed, much of the previous standard wisdom on the subject has been called into question as a result of this new sophistication and, to date, no new body of positive findings has replaced the older knowledge. Whereas the literature was once replete with strong, virtually "self-evident" assertions about the crucial role of the family and the school in the political learning process, for example, contemporary claims on these matters are far more cautious and limited.

Part of the reason for this state of affairs is that socialization theory has not kept pace with methodological advances. Though their techniques may incorporate the latest research advances, most analysts are still more or less operating theoretically at a level no more developed than when Herbert Hyman wrote *Political Socialization* over 15 years ago. Thus, confusion cannot help but occur when a wide variety of techniques are generating a virtual avalanche of data not

The data and tabulations utilized in this chapter were made available in part by the Inter-University Consortium for Political Research. The data were originally collected by M. Kent Jennings. Neither the original collector of the data nor the consortium bear any responsibility for the analysis or interpretations presented here. The authors would like to thank E. Wood Kelley for his assistance.

sharing a common rigorous theoretical framework. However, it is also true that part of the lack of advancement in socialization research is methodological in character. This problem does not so much concern deficiencies in technique per se, but the appropriateness of certain techniques to particular theoretical assertions: i.e., underlying all techniques of analysis are assumptions about how the real world operates and these methodological assumptions need not be consistent with the analyst's theoretical assumptions. Hence, even if one uses perfectly acceptable "standard" techniques to test a very reasonable theory, the results can be very counterintuitive or haphazard unless theory and method are synchronized properly. It is our contention that this problem of inappropriateness of theory and method is common in socialization research and that existing data viewed from a different methodological perspective will yield fewer confusing and counterintuitive results.

We shall approach the problem of methodological appropriateness by examining some of the theoretical and data problems in two substantively important areas: (1) the transmission of political attitudes from parent to child; and (2) the existence of subcultural variations in political learning in the United States. Our endeavor is largely illustrative and, while we hope to make some substantive contribution, we shall emphasize the raising and clarification of problems. From time to time we shall draw on data from the Jennings 1965 study of high school seniors and their parents. We must emphasize that our selection of this data set is not an implicit criticism of Jennings' methods or findings. In fact, this is undoubtedly the best available socialization data set and thus highly amenable to reanalysis.

The Family's Transmission of Political Attitudes

Until quite recently it was customary to assert that, of all the agents of political learning, the family was of paramount importance. Writing in 1959, Herbert Hyman summarized the results of a dozen separate studies involving numerous types of data and samples which generally made a good case for family influence. Relying more on the research of anthropologists and sociologists, James C. Davies (1965) made perhaps the strongest claim when he asserted that "most of the individual's political personality—his tendencies to think and act politically in particular ways—have been determined at home, several years before he can take part in politics" (p. 11). Indeed, such assertions were considered virtually truisms beyond serious scholarly debate.

More recent analysis, however, has called into question much of the conventional wisdom on the impact of the family on political learning. R. W. Connell (1972), e.g., has raised several methodological questions about the research on which this wisdom rested. Among other things, many studies misconstrued agreement across generational lines with agreement between parent and child; other studies relied on children to take questionnaires home to their parents and this appears to have inflated measures of parent-child attitude agreement. Even more devastating than such methodological criticism has been the research conducted by Jennings and his associates (Jennings & Niemi, 1968) that reports generally weak correlations between parent and adolescent on a wide variety of political orientations. These low relationships have led Jennings to speculate that many attitudes previously viewed as family determined may in part have their origins in accident or historical happenstance (Jennings & Niemi, 1974, pp. 329–335).

Our contention is that neither the original conventional wisdom nor the various counterclaims are conclusive. Each set of claims may be correct, but many aspects of these arguments remain unproven despite some claims to the contrary. Specifically, we shall argue that (1) many of the analytical strategies employed in research on family impact are inappropriate theoretically and (2) the commonly employed measures in the study of family influence frequently bias the results toward very low relationships. We shall show that using methods based on different statistical assumptions and treating attitudinal data differently yields a theoretically sounder picture of the family's role in political socialization. Our analysis proceeds by first describing the predominant approach in studying the family's influence. This approach will then be criticized and some alternative will be presented and illustrated using the Jennings 1965 data.

THE BASIC MODEL OF PARENTAL INFLUENCE

The typical research design for measuring the family's influence involves the administration of similar attitudinal questions to both parents and children. Perhaps the ideal would be longitudinal data for both parents and child for, say, 30 years, but even if this were possible, it would not represent a basic theoretical departure from the current approach. The types of questions asked vary from study to study with variables such as partisan identification, political cynicism, attitudes toward democratic values, participatory orientations, and attitudes toward minorities the most common. Scores on these measures for parent-child pairs are then correlated using such statistics as taub, gamma, or the product-moment correlation. Large correlations are treated as evidence of parent-child agreement and this agreement in turn is treated as evidence of successful "transmission" or parental "influence" in learning. Recent research by Tedin (1974) has raised the issue of parent-child agreement being a consequence of common social identity (e.g., sharing a racial identity), but the introduction of such third variables represents a statistical elaboration of this transmission model, not an alternative conceptualization.

THEORETICAL PROBLEM

On the basis of common-sense notions of family life, research by sociologists, and a vast body of psychological theory, this dominant approach to transmission is open to serious question. In the first place, it may be the case that even if parents are completely successful in controlling the socialization of their offspring, they may not *want* to replicate their own values, and thus parent-child dissimilarities may mask successful transmission. We could readily imagine, for example, politically aware blacks consciously rearing their children to a different set of political values than they themselves hold. A comparable process occurred, no doubt, in the case of immigrants wanting their children to grow up as assimilated Americans. Research by Bronfenbrenner (1965), e.g., suggests that parents' views on child rearing can be changed—by books such as Spock's *Baby and Child Care*—so discontinuities can appear where parents maintain complete control. Perhaps the most persuasive evidence of this phenomenon is Inkeles' (1955) study of child-rearing values in pre- and postrevolutionary Russia. Inkeles finds that in response to dramatic political change parents place less stress on their own traditional values and more emphasis on the newer Soviet values. All in all, given the rapid change of the contemporary world, it would appear unrealistic to expect parents to want to replicate perfectly their own political values and beliefs.

A second general theoretical problem involves the question of what identical responses to the identical stimuli by parent and child would look like. As Kagan (1969), in his discussion of continuity of human characteristics from childhood to adulthood, makes clear, things which look alike may not be identical and identical appearing responses may in fact be quite different. Though Kagan's analysis focuses on two measures on the same person at different times and for psychological traits, it is clear that his argument is applicable to comparisons of the responses of children and adults at one point in time and for political orientations as well. Essentially, Kagan distinguishes among three forms (or "faces") of continuity. First, there is *complete continuity*, by which is meant stability in both the underlying psychological process and in the manifest response. A second form is *genotypic continuity*, i.e., the basic psychological response remains stable but the particular manifestations of this characteristic change. Kagan illustrates this type of continuity with the case of a child with a strong case of anxiety over parental rejection which at age 6 manifests itself in refusal to attend school, but at age 12 appears as excessive obedience to parental authority. Finally, there is what Kagan calls the "fool's gold" of continuity, the *behavioral phenotype*. Here the behavior (or attitude) remains constant but the causes of the behavior change over time. Crying in childhood versus crying as an adult is a conspicuous illustration of false continuity.

It is clear that, of the three forms of continuity, political scientists examining the family's transmission of attitudes have sought evidence for the existence of complete continuity almost exclusively (even at the expense of ignoring the possibility of fool's gold continuity). To be sure, this might be the theoretically correct choice for the type of variables analyzed and for the populations sampled, but such a contention has not even been openly discussed, let alone proven. Kagan suggests three conditions under which complete continuity is likely to occur. Translating these from one individual statement over time to simultaneous comparisons between parent and child, these conditions are: (1) childhood measures occur sometimes after puberty when change is slowing down; (2) the genotypic construct is operative in both parents and children; and (3) overt responses are not suppressed or inhibited by social or age-related norms. Perhaps only the first of these conditions is satisfied by current political socialization research. However, the evidence on the other requirements is almost nonexistent. It is entirely possible that certain underlying political dispositions that develop during adulthood are simply not present during childhood in the same form so that searching for identical parent-child responses to identical questions is meaningless. That children will give responses to questions designed to measure basic political orientations is not, of course, proof that children have developed these political dispositions. While measurement validity is always a concern, it is clearly of special concern when making child-parent comparisons (especially when young children are involved) yet very slight attention has been given this problem of validity.[1]

Political scientists have also been inattentive to the possibility of powerful social norms inhibiting or modifying complete continuity. Kagan's (1962, 1969) own longitudinal analyses of aggressiveness clearly demonstrate that traits can appear both in childhood and in early adulthood, but the form of this behavior is dependent upon environmental constraints. Specifically, Kagan found that aggressive male children tended to remain aggressive into early adulthood (complete continuity). Aggressive young females, however, perhaps due to social strictures against female aggressiveness, became less overtly aggressive but instead manifested high academic motivation, independence, and "masculine" interests in early adulthood. In other words, the phenotype trait—aggressiveness—varied from complete continuity to phenotype continuity depending on intervening social norms. Given what we know about age-related norms of obedience toward parental authority and peer group pressure (particularly during adolescence), it is obvious that even if parent and child were following the identical pattern of political development, manifestations of identity could very well be temporarily obscured by age and social position pressures. We could imagine, e.g., a parent and child having the identical ethnocentric attitudes

---

[1]One exception to this insensitivity to validity problems is Easton and Dennis' analysis of sense of political efficacy among children in grades 3 through 8. Validity is established for a sense of political efficacy scale by factor analyzing several questions and, when the political efficacy questions load highly in the same dimension, this is taken as evidence that the underlying "sense of political efficacy" exists in the minds of the respondents. See David Easton and Jack Dennis, "The Child's Acquisition of Regime Norms: Political Efficacy," *American Political Science Review* 61 (1967), pp. 25–38. It should be noted, however, that factor analysis is open to question as a means of proving validity and several studies of sense of political efficacy among adults raises substantial questions of validity. (E.g., see George I. Balch, "Multiple Indicators in Survey Research: The Concept 'Sense of Political Efficacy,'" *Political Methodology* 1 (1974), pp. 1–44.) On the validity of certain measures of childhood attitudes more generally, see Kenneth L. Kolson and Justin J. Green, "Response Set Bias and Political Socialization Research," in *Political Attitudes and Public Opinion*, ed. Dan D. Nimmo and Charles M. Bonjean (New York: McKay, 1972), pp. 203–214.

but differing in their responses to survey questions if, say, the parent worked in an environment encouraging such ethnocentrism while the child attended a progressive school that emphasized more liberal values. Under such conditions, phenotype continuity for the child might emerge as hostility between teacher and child but school pressures would for the moment repress complete continuity.

Even if we put aside the problem of environmental traits inhibiting the emergence of identical parent-child responses, there still remains the difficulty of deciding when childhood data are "really" the same as adulthood data. This difficulty is equally due to inexactness in existing theories of individual political development and problems of measurement equivalence. Regarding the theoretical problems, considerable longitudinal research (Bloom, 1964; Knutson, forthcoming) on a variety of characteristics suggests a *general* pattern like the one depicted in Figure 2–1. In words, this figure says simply that within certain environmental limits the closer one gets to adulthood the more one becomes like an adult. Such a statement appears obvious, but its implications for child-parent comparison are rarely explicitly stated. Specifically, this means that even a child who eventually will be identical to an adult will not be like that adult until

Figure 2-1. General Development Pattern for Attitudes

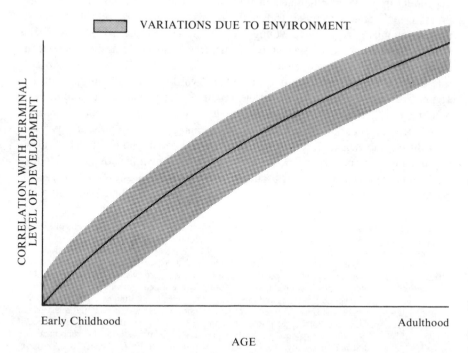

Source. Adapted from Benjamin S. Bloom, *Stability and Change in Human Characteristics* (New York: John Wiley, 1964), p. vii.

adulthood. Thus, to search for close similarity (as opposed to different positions on the same developmental path) between, say, a 10-year-old and a 35-year-old is to bias the results toward very modest relationships at best.

A number of solutions to this problem are possible. The most practical one is to measure preadult characteristics as close to the end of the developmental process as possible. Though this short-range strategy does not allow one to make empirical statements about agreement between parents and young children, it is assumed that if agreement does not exist just prior to the end of development, it is very unlikely to have existed at an earlier time. This is part of the reasoning employed by Jennings and his associates in choosing high school seniors in order to measure child-parent similarity.[2] The weakness of this solution, obviously, is that it assumes that political phenomena will follow pretty much the same pattern as, say, physical development, achievement motivation, IQ, and certain personality characteristics: i.e., political development largely ceases in late adolescence or early adulthood. Needless to say, such an assumption is open to serious theoretical and empirical question. Such might be the case in areas of political learning such as national loyalty and regime support, but it is less clear that orientations such as political cynicism or party identification cease development in late adolescence.

The ideal solution to incorporating developmental change into measures of agreement requires that we know the precise pattern of development for the particular political orientation under study. Once this were known, the hypothesis that parents and children held the same attitude could be stated in a precise way that incorporated the particular developmental changes in the life-cycle. In effect, this amounts to little more than a statistical correction for age and, in a more sophisticated version, a correction for parent-child environmental experiences. It is evident, however, that political scientists (and psychologists) are a long way from such knowledge. The developmental curve in Figure 2–1 is merely a free hand approximation of many differing patterns only barely dignifiable as an empirically based general trend. What this means, thus, is that lacking a developmental correction factor we can never be sure that parent-child differences on a variable are not really indicative of "true" identity, or vice versa.

Moreover, even were we able to develop a corrective factor for important variables, we would still face the more practical problem of devising equivalent measures for populations that differ considerably in their cognitive development, vocabulary, and awareness of social norms about appropriate responses to certain types of sensitive issues. It is well known, e.g., that young children interpret many political concepts quite literally, are prone to accept what are by adult

---

[2]Jennings and Niemi (1968, p. 171) also assume that because high school seniors will soon be leaving their parents, parental influence will soon end. Thus, if influence does not occur now (or previously), it will not be felt in the future. Obviously, the reasoning is open to further discussion since social influence can certainly operate without physical proximity. A simple illustration would be partisan voting—an adult vote may be "determined" by one's parents through the earlier transmission of partisan identification.

standards extreme positions, and are unable to perceive important distinctions. Hence, a set of questions appropriate for adults is likely to be inappropriate for children, and the opposite is equally true. This is the virtually identical problem faced in cross-national research where one can never be quite sure that sentences mean the same in different languages. The common solution is to interview "young adults" who have already mastered the adult vocabulary and can make adult-like distinctions. This is certainly an acceptable practice, but as the only solution to this problem it is of no help whatsoever with preadolescent political learning. If preadolescent-parent political similarity is an important question (and we think it is), decisions must be made in equivalences between very different appearing questions.

In light of all these theoretical and measurement issues, it is clear that the usual research tactic to seek evidence comparable to complete continuity is open to serious question. Complete continuity for the variables usually employed and for the populations usually sampled *may* be theoretically appropriate and practical, but such a contention remains undemonstrated (or rarely even stated explicitly). Perhaps the principal advantage of the parent-child agreement equals successful transmission model is that it is eminently simple to operationalize. Obviously, however, this model of successful transmission is merely one of many possibilities and the work of psychologists such as Kagan suggests that its use may be quite limited. It is also obvious that further elaboration of transmission models requires better theories of individual political development. As it now stands, we are unable to say what childhood attitudes or behavior will be more or less like adulthood attitudes or behavior and until we can make such statements child-parent comparisons are not much more than guesses. In short, children may or may not be just what their parents want them to be politically, but the dominant model describing this control cannot provide us with a comprehensive answer.

A final theoretical problem of the standard parent-child transmission model concerns what we mean when we employ terms like "transmit" or "influence." The prevailing assumption is that pairwise intergeneration identity on a political issue is evidence of transmission. Certainly the argument is plausible, but it is far from being self-evident. If we were dealing with adults sharing the same attitude, we would be unlikely to attribute this consensus to the influence of one on the other unless additional data were available. Obviously, the problems raised here are similar to the general issues involved in measuring concepts like "power" and influence that have perplexed so many political scientists and philosophers. We can avoid these theoretical and operational difficulties by redefining analysis solely in questions of parent-child agreement. This is what in fact is done by most analysts though terms like transmit are still used. Unfortunately, however, this simplification robs the analysis of its substantive value. The important information for questions of political stability, insulation of political attitudes from extrafamily manipulation, and other research questions leading us to examine parent-child attitudes depends on the establishment of influence relationships and the existence of mere issue agreement is only incidental. Clearly, then, even if we could formulate rules for establishing true parent-child issue agreement, these rules would be meaningless unless we could also make clear and measure what we mean by terms like "family influence" on political learning.

MEASUREMENT PROBLEMS: VARIANCE

Whether we accept the existence of identical issue positions between parent and child as evidence of successful family transmission or somehow correct for environmental and developmental differences, the conventional method of demonstrating correspondence entails the use of various measures of statistical association. With the exception of partisan identification, where the common practice is to use percentage agreement between parent and child, parent-offspring attitudes are correlated, and a strong statistical relationship is taken as evidence of effective transmission. Though researchers have employed a variety of scales and measures—e.g., tau-b, gamma, phi, product-moment correlation, and others—for our general purpose the differences between these statistics, though important in special circumstances, are outweighed by certain basic similarities and common substantive implications.

This decision to compare parent-child attitudes by measures of statistical association has important, though far from obvious, substantive consequences for the things we can say about parent-child correspondence. This importance derives from the elementary condition that, for measures of association to be meaningful, variation must exist on both the independent and dependent variables. Statistically speaking, one cannot explain a constant or use a constant to explain. If one were to use constants, the correlation would have to be zero, since no variation could be accounted for nor could it covary with anything. In terms of regression analysis, e.g., the existence of a constant independent variable would not permit the computation of a best-fit regression equation since all solutions would yield equal results (zero variance in the dependent variable would yield a correlation of zero). For this reason, then, research using these statistical techniques must focus on nonconsensual phenomena.[3]

Translated into concrete terms, this means that if we had a society (or subculture) in which virtually everyone held the same values and attitudes, the statistical assessment of the relationship among these values or attitudes would yield highly misleading results. With nothing to statistically explain, all statistical measures would be either incalculable or zero and this would be interpreted as complete independence despite the fact that all variables were perfectly related. If some variation did exist—and it almost certainly would—it is probable that it

---

[3]Jennings and Niemi (1974, p. 285) are aware of the problem of analyzing highly consensual attitudes, but avoid it by focusing on nonconsensual components of the political culture. They note that on issues such as political assassination or the value of laws parent-child continuity is almost always assured.

would be due to factors such as data collection error or question ambiguity rather than true variance and thus would be randomly distributed. Of course, given a sufficient number of variables and random factors and a large enough sample, one would find at least a few statistically "significant" relationships.

To avoid zero relations or relationships due to random factors, research must focus on only those phenomena distributed in an analyzable way, i.e., variables which show substantial individual differences (Horst, 1966, pp. 159–161). It is also clear that there is little new knowledge to be gained from asking questions for which the distributions, because of extreme modality, are known in advance. The almost trite quality of such analysis is illustrated by some of the early Gallup polls in which adults were asked whether they favored a state religion in America or the use of aristocratic titles. In both instances it came as no surprise that over 90% rejected these proposals (Cantril, 1951, pp. 868–869). To the extent that "obvious" distributions such as these among adults are theoretically uninteresting, the problems associated with analyzing highly modal distributions are largely hypothetical.

However, when we come to measuring parent-child attitude correspondence, the problems associated with relationships between highly modal distributions become more relevant. The reason is simple: It is highly plausible that the family's principal influence may be in the domain of highly consensual attitudes and behaviors. At least in the United States, such dispositions as national identity, acceptance of the legitimacy of political authority, reverence for such concepts as "democracy," and many core features of the political culture are *likely* to be transmitted from one generation to the next via the family. Hence, in the extreme case, if every parent were an equally loyal American and every parent succeeded in making his child into a carbon copy of himself, the statistical association between parent-child disposition would be zero. Perhaps for this reason we find that many discussions of the family's influence on highly consensual issues assert this influence rather than offer numerical indicators. Such verbal assertions are not, of course, adequate substitutes for quantitative empirical relationships.

In actual socialization research this problem of insufficient variation is handled in several ways. The easiest solution is to focus exclusively on nonconsensual attitudes. One would merely employ previously tested questions on which variations in response have been found to ensure that one's measures are capable of explaining or being explained. The same result can also be accomplished by selecting issues that have little or no meaning to respondents. Under such circumstances random answering will guarantee a range in the distribution (in the language of scale construction, one wants items that "discriminate" among individuals). Finally, variance can be introduced by drawing finer and finer distinctions between response categories: e.g., a question like "Do you want to be an American?" can readily be made into a multiple choice question with alternatives such as "I am very proud to be an American," "I usually like being an American," etc. We should emphasize that the practice of creating a more normal distribution out of a highly modal distribution is fully in accord with accepted methodological procedures.

Unfortunately, however, the probable net result of these decisions is either to give a misleadingly low indication of transmission or else to avoid theoretically important variables. As Philip Converse (1964) has suggested, and as reliability coefficients on many standard attitude items confirm, to focus on opinions about many contemporary issues, i.e., issues that statistically discriminate, is to focus on issues characterized by a considerable amount of instability at the individual level. Of course, the existence of a significant amount of instability biases correlations downward. At a more theoretical level, the avoidance of consensual issues by using only items that "discriminate" excludes some of the politically most meaningful variables from analysis. It is indefensible to argue that issues everyone agrees on are less important politically than those questions generating extensive disagreement. In addition, the drawing of finer and finer distinctions need not necessarily contribute to greater precision. On such basic issues as national identity, political legitimacy, and various other core beliefs, a lack of conscious thought on these matters might make finely drawn distinctions irrelevant to most citizens and thus are responded to in the expected pattern.

The severity of this problem of limited variation becomes even more apparent when we examine what happens when we analyzed highly modal variables. Imagine, e.g., that we were interested in a dichotomous variable on which 80% of the parents and their children gave the same answer. Table 2–1 depicts various possible joint distributions and the strength of various commonly employed measures of association. What is perhaps most important to observe in these hypothetical data is that under the condition of random association (Table 2–1a), 68% of the parent-child agreement is already "explained." In other words, given the marginal distributions, 68% (64% agree-agree, 4% disagree-disagree) agreement would occur by chance alone.[4] Thus, even if 68% of all parents were *in fact* parent and child would be 0.0. It should be apparent, then, that low correlations do not show that parents have "failed" to perpetuate their own attitudes.

It is also important to observe that under these conditions of high consensus the effective range in variation is quite limited by the marginals and thus a relatively small shift will greatly affect the magnitude of the different measures of associations. For example, a comparison of tables 2–1b and 2–1c shows that a shift of 5 people in each row (or column) almost doubles the size of the product-moment correlation, tau b, and phi; yet another similar shift will result in a correlation of 1.00 (Table 2–1d). If we examine what happens when 90% of both parents and children share the same attitude (Table 2–2), these tendencies are magnified

[4]The effects of marginal distribution on the possible size of correlation coefficients is discussed more generally in John B. Carroll, "The Nature of Data, or How to Choose a Correlation Coefficient," *Psychometrika* 26 (1961), pp. 347–372. Perhaps we should emphasize that a "random" association is strictly a statistical notion and does not indicate that phenomena are empirically unrelated. Merely because issue agreement between parent and child can be predicted by a random statistical model does not mean that this agreement is uncaused or in some sense nonexistent.

Table 2.1. Hypothetical Relationships between Dichotomous Variables among Parent-Child Pairs with 80–20 Division

Table 2.1a. (Random Association[a])

		CHILD	
		Yes	No
Parent	Yes	64	16
	No	16	4
		80	20

$$r = 0.0$$

Table 2.1b.

		CHILD	
		Yes	No
Parent	Yes	70	10
	No	10	10
		80	20

$$r = .375$$
$$\text{tau b} = .375$$
$$\text{gamma} = .75$$
$$\text{phi} = .3438$$

Table 2.1c.

		CHILD	
		Yes	No
Parent	Yes	75	5
	No	5	15
		80	20

$$r = .6875$$
$$\text{tau b} = .6875$$
$$\text{gamma} = .9565$$
$$\text{phi} = .6563$$

Table 2.1d. (Perfect Association)

		CHILD	
		Yes	No
Parent	Yes	80	0
	No	0	20
		80	20

$$r = 1.00$$

Table 2.1e.

		CHILD	
		Yes	No
Parent	Yes	60	20
	No	20	0
		80	20

$$r = -.25$$
$$\text{tau b} = -.25$$
$$\text{gamma} = -1.000$$
$$\text{phi} = .2188$$

[a]Random association was established by multiplying the marginals for each cell.

even greater. Observe that a shift of 3 people can increase the correlation from 0.0 to .33 (tables 2–2a, 2–2b). On the other hand, a shift of 2 people in a different direction (tables 2–2a, 2–2f) changes a 0.0 relationship into a −.11 association.

When we stop to consider all the data generation problems associated with survey research—particularly research on pairs of respondents with different cognitive capacities, vocabularies, and frames of reference—we can see that the

Table 2.2. Hypothetical Relationships between Dichotomous Variables among Parent-Child Pairs with 90–10 Division

Table 2.2a. (Random Association)		CHILD		Table 2.2b.		CHILD	
		Yes	No			Yes	No
Parent	Yes	81	9	Parent	Yes	84	6
	No	9	1		No	6	4
		90	10			90	10

$$r = 0.0$$

Table 2.2b.:
$$r = .33$$
$$\text{tau } b = .33$$
$$\text{gamma} = .8065$$
$$\text{phi} = .2778$$

Table 2.2c.		CHILD		Table 2.2d. (Perfect Association)		CHILD	
		Yes	No			Yes	No
Parent	Yes	87	3	Parent	Yes	90	0
	No	3	7		No	0	10
		90	10			90	10

Table 2.2c.:
$$r = .6667$$
$$\text{tau } b = .6667$$
$$\text{gamma} = .9709$$
$$\text{phi} = .6111$$

Table 2.2d.:
$$r = 1.00$$

Table 2.2e.

		CHILD	
		Yes	No
Parent	Yes	80	10
	No	10	0
		90	10

$$r = -.1111$$
$$\text{tau } b = -.1111$$
$$\text{gamma} = -1.000$$
$$\text{phi} = .0556$$

picture we get of the transmission process of highly consensual attitudes is easily affected by extraneous factors. In light of these problems, it is no wonder that many analysts are deeply perplexed over the paradox of considerable intergenerational continuity in overall distributions on questions while the correlations between parents and children are moderate to low (Jennings & Niemi, 1968). Our explanation of this odd state of affairs is that considerable parent-child agreement is "explained" by random association and that going beyond the random baseline is difficult, given all the typical data collection problems. In other words, even if all parents and children agreed, a few question misinterpretations and the like would destroy a large proportion of the variation still left to explain beyond the random baseline so correlations (i.e., the measure of nonrandom covariation) will necessarily be low to moderate.

To see how deceptive the usual measures of association can be in showing parent-child agreement, let us examine some of the typical data presented by Jennings and Niemi. Table 2–3 shows the marginal distribution, the tau-b's, and the proportion of parents and students who give the same response on each of five policy preferences. On the whole, Jennings and Niemi interpret these data as showing only moderate to poor evidence of family transmission. Their disappointing findings lead to a further search for higher correlations through subdividing respondents by race, region, and salience of issues in order to find better evidence of transmission. The focus on the low tau b's completely obscures, however, the fact that on the average slightly over two thirds of children and parents give the same response to each question. Hence, if we were to define "successful" transmission as parent-child identity in at least two thirds of the cases, we have strong evidence of transmission (though most of it would be explained by random association).

MEASUREMENT PROBLEMS: COVARIATION

Thus far, when discussing the statistical relationship between parent and child attitudes, we have spoken in terms of some form of correlation coefficient. Though different researchers using data with different scale properties have employed a variety of measures, virtually all of these correlation type measures have a common property of particular relevance to our analysis: they are measures of covariation. For example, a strong positive product-moment relationship between, say, parental liberalism and offspring liberalism means (strictly) that as parental liberalism increases, child liberalism also increases, and that one is a fairly good predictor of the other. The relationship, whether with interval or ordinal scales, is one of two (or more) phenomena moving together at a certain rate (the slope of the regression line); the relationship *does not* depict how close two phenomena are to each other. Under special circumstances (e.g., where the mean differences are known) some measures like the Pearson product-moment correlation can be translated into an indicator of proximity, but such information is not automatically conveyed by an r, tau-b, gamma, and the like.

This property of correlational measures does not pose any inherent problems for socialization research. What causes the problem is the disjunction between the exact way theoretical propositions are stated and the measures used in the actual data analysis. Specifically, propositions about parent-child agreement are almost always formulated in terms of proximity, e.g., parents and children hold

Table 2.3. Parent-Child Distributions and Agreement on 5 Policy Issues (Jennings & Niemi data)

QUESTION		DISTRIBUTION			TAU B	% PRECISE
		Favor	*Depends*	*Oppose*	*Agreement*	
Prayer in public schools	Students	67%	4%	29%		
	Parents	80	5	16	.29	69
Federal role in school desegregation	Students	71	10	20		
	Parents	59	13	28	.34	64
Stay in United Nations	Students	87	9	4		
	Parents	86	9	5	.11	79
Allow speeches against churches	Students	86	*	14		
	Parents	72	*	27	.08	69
Elected Communist can hold office	Students	36	1	63		
	Parents	28	*	71	.13	61

Source. Jennings and Niemi, *The Political Character of Adolescence,* 1974, pp. 65, 79.
*Less than .5%.

the same attitude, but are then tested employing a covariation statistical model. Obviously, there is no theoretical reason why propositions about family influence cannot be put in covariation language where correlation coefficients would be theoretically appropriate.[5] Our contention is that to formulate a theoretical relationship one way and then test it inappropriately can lead to misleading substantive conclusions.

To see how results can be completely misleading let us consider some hypothetical examples. Tables 2–4a and 2–4b depict two possible joint distributions on a five-point scale for both parents and children. In Table 2–4a each child is precisely two scale positions away from his or her parent and thus the two scales covary perfectly, i.e., the correlation is 1.00. On the other hand, the data in Table 2–4b show no systematic covariation between parent and child scale positions so the correlation will be 0.0. However, if one examines the similarity of parent-child pairs, it is apparent that many more children are closer to their

[5]Flacks in his study of student radicals reports a pattern of child-pattern agreement consistent with a correlation model: i.e., relatively liberal parents in their generation had children relatively liberal in their generation though parents and offspring differed on these issues. See Richard Flacks, "The Revolt of the Advantaged: An Exploration of the Roots of Student Protest," *Journal of Social Issues* 23 (1967), pp. 52–75.

Table 2.4.   Hypothetical Distribution of Parents and Children on 5-Point Scales

		(a) Perfect Covariation					(b) Random Association				
		PARENTS					PARENTS				
		Low		High			Low		High		
Children	Low	0	0	33	0	0	0	0	0	0	0
		0	0	0	34	0	0	11	11	11	0
		0	0	0	0	33	0	11	12	11	0
		0	0	0	0	0	0	11	11	11	0
	High	0	0	0	0	0	0	0	0	0	0

parents in Table 2–4b than in the case of perfect covariation in Table 2–4a. The actual distance between parent-child pairs in both tables is as follows:

DISTANCE IN SCALE POSITIONS BETWEEN CHILD AND PARENT	TABLE 2.4a.	TABLE 2.4b.
0	0%	34%
1	0	44
2	100	22
3	0	0
4	0	0
	100%	100%

In other words, in Table 2–4a no parent and child agree precisely compared to 34% of the cases in Table 2–4b. Moreover, in Table 2–4b, 78% of the children were within a single scale score of their parents in contrast to 0% in Table 2–4a.

This problem with interpreting correlations as measures of proximity (and vice versa) is further illustrated by the hypothetical data in Figure 2–2. Let us imagine that both parents and children were distributed, say, along a liberal-conservative dimension. Let us also imagine that all parents are generally successful in passing on their ideological values, but due to a variety of factors— e.g., adolescent rebellion, children's misperception of parental position, measurement error, etc.—few children are exactly like their parents with some children a little more liberal than their parents and others slightly more conservative, but these deviations are nonsystematic. This is the pattern in Figure 2–2a. Compare this pattern of close proximity with a moderate amount of nonsystematic variation with the pattern in Figure 2–2b where parents and children differ substantially but the variation is perfectly ordered (and thus the correlation is 1.00). Again, it is quite apparent that a measure of covariation can be very deceiving as an indicator of child-parent correspondence when the correspondence is stated in terms of similarity of opinion.

Figure 2-2. Hypothetical Child-Parent Distributions on Liberal-Conservative Scales

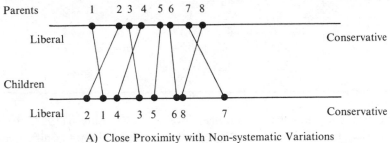

A) Close Proximity with Non-systematic Variations

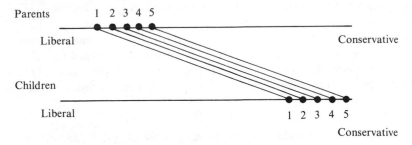

B) Low Proximity with Systematic Variations

If we are going to state transmission propositions in terms of proximity, it is clear that we need a different type of statistic than the commonly employed measures of association. Several measures of proximity have been developed by statisticians, sociologists, and psychologists and could readily be used; e.g., the intraclass correlation (r_i) is merely the Pearsonian correlation between $2N$ pairs of observations and the second N, the values of X_2 replacing X_1, and vice versa.[6] Thus, if one had three pairs of observations for two variables, e.g.,

$$
\begin{array}{cc}
X_1 & X_2 \\
2 & 1 \\
4 & 3 \\
6 & 5 \\
\end{array}
$$

[6]The intraclass correlation is discussed in greater detail in R. A. Fisher, *Statistical Methods for Research Workers*, 7th ed. (Edinburgh: Oliver & Boyd, 1939), pp. 216–232. For purposes of simplified computation, the intraclass correlation can be defined as follows:

$$r_i = \frac{[(S_1^2 + S_1 - S_2)^2]r - (\bar{X}_1 - \bar{X}_2)^2/2}{(S_1^2 + S_2^2) + (\bar{X}_1 - \bar{X}_2)^2/2}$$

where $\bar{X}_1$ and $\bar{X}_2$ are the mean of X_1 and X_2, S_1 and S_2 the standard deviations, and r the Pearson correlation between X_1 and X_2.

the intraclass correlation (r_i) would simply be the Pearson correlation between pairs:

X_1	X_2
2	1
4	3
6	5
1	2
3	4
5	6

This intraclass correlation has been further developed by Robinson (1957, 1959). This measure, the Coefficient of Agreement (A) is essentially the differences between the variances of two variables divided by the maximum variance possible. In two-variable relationships it is identical to $r(i)$ but A has the advantage for retaining the same limits over multiple variable relationships whereas $r(i)$ does not.

A third commonly employed measure of proximity, and one also closely related to the intraclass correlation, is the multidimensional distance formula (D) developed by Osgood, Suci, and Tannenbaum (1967).[7] This measure has been used extensively in the analysis of semantic differential scales and is defined as:

$$Dil = \sqrt{\underset{j}{\Sigma dil^2}}$$

where Dil is the linear distance between scale scores i and 1, and dil is the algebraic difference between the coordinates of i and 1 on the same scale, j. For our purposes, i and 1 would be parent and child scores on the same scale, j. D could be employed for several different types of comparisons. We could, e.g., compute the D for a single parent-child pair across difference scales, or the mean D from several parent-child pairs can be calculated on a single scale. Though D has been explored at great length by statisticians and is obviously relevant to future socialization research, it does suffer from the problem of not yielding an easily interpretable number. Of course, many commonly explored statistics are not intuitively interpretable, but since our purpose here is largely illustrative, we shall use a proximity measure whose meaning is more self-evident. Specifically, let us use the average distance scores to compare proximity with covariation models of association. This measure, which we shall denote with d (as opposed to D) is defined as follows:

$$d = \frac{\Sigma (i - 1)}{jn}$$

where i and 1 are scale positions, $(i - 1)$ the algebraic value of the scale positions for two individuals (or two scales for the same individual), and N is the number of pairs of cases (or number of scales in the case of a single individual) on

---

[7]Other approaches to the measurement of distance are offered in Lee J. Cronbach and Goldine C. Glesa, "Assessing Similarity between Profiles," *Psychological Bulletin* 50 (1953), pp. 456–473.

measure j. To make it clear how d operates, let us consider the hypothetical data in Table 2–5. Perfect agreement between parent and child occurs in the main diagonal, with each successive diagonal representing an increase of 1 unit of distance between parent and child. Simply adding the number of cases for each distance yields:

0 distance between pair	40 cases
1 unit distance	28 cases
2 units distance	26 cases
3 units distance	4 cases
4 units distance	2 cases

The total distance $(i - 1)$ is the total of number of units times number of cases (e.g., 26 cases 2 units apart equals a distance of 52). In this example the total distance is 100 units and, since there are 100 cases, the average distance, or d, is 1.00. In other words, in these hypothetical data, the average parent-child pair is 1.00 units apart from each other although the correlation is 0.0.

As in the case of D, d requires that scale intervals are equal, scales being related have the same number of intervals, and scales are independent. Of these requirements, the one requiring scales to be of equal number of intervals is particularly difficult to satisfy since measures in political socialization research typically vary in their number of intervals. Thus, a d of 1.00 would mean something very different for a 3-point scale than for a 7-point scale. The simplest solution, given the prior existence of different scales, is to standardize d by dividing by the scale range. This statistic, d/r, varies between 0 and 1.[8] Table 2–6 presents some of the Jennings data on parent-child agreement in four scales with d, d/r, and the tau-b correlates.

Table 2.5. Hypothetical Distribution of Parents and Children on 5-Point Scales

		PARENTS				
		1	*2*	*3*	*4*	*5*
	1	1	1	6	1	1
	2	1	1	6	1	1
Children	*3*	6	6	36	6	6
	4	1	1	6	1	1
	5	1	1	6	1	1
		10	10	60	10	10

$$r = 0.0$$

[8]The advantage of incorporating a scale's range into the proximity measure is illustrated by partisan identification. As a 7-point variable, the distance (d) between parent and child is 1.30; as a 5-point scale, it is .85; as a 3-point scale, .48. The respective d/r's are .19, .17, .16.

Table 2.6. Parent-Student Distance on Various Political Scales

| | PARENT-STUDENT DISTANCES | | | | | | | | | |
POLITICAL ATTITUDE	0	1	2	3	4	5	6	d	d/r	TAU B
Party identification (N = 1,852)	32.9	33.9	16.9	7.7	5.3	2.8	.7	1.302	.186	.47
Ideological sophistication (N = 1,867)	29.7	27.8	16.2	16.1	10.2			1.500	.300	.16
Political trust (N = 1,874)	21.8	32.5	22.1	14.3	6.6	2.7		1.592	.265	.12
Cosmopolitanism (N = 1,380)	18.8	34.0	22.3	13.5	13.5	4.0	1.1	1.704	.243	.17

Source. Student-Parent Socialization Study, made available by the Inter-Unversity Consortium for Political Research.

Except in the instance of parent-child partisan identification, the correlations in Table 2–6 suggest a picture of weak transmission. However, analysis of the closeness of parents and children suggests a stronger case for transmission (assuming, of course, that identity of attitudes equals transmission). In all four scales a majority of the student-parent pairs are within 1 scale position of each other. Note, e.g., that the association of .16 in the case of ideological sophistication would suggest low success in predicting child scores from parent scores, yet in fact 57.5% of children are within 1 scale position of their parents. Both the *d* and the *d/r* reflect this clustering of parents and children around the same positions, i.e., the average parent and student pair are less than .3 of the scale range apart on all 4 items. To be sure, party identification still remains the best case of parent-child similarity, but it certainly does not exist in sharp contrast to these other areas of political learning.

MEASUREMENT PROBLEMS: STABILITY

In common with research on political attitudes generally, analyses of parent-child correspondence treat an attitude as a discrete point on some continuum or scale. This point can be very large as in a dichotomized scale or highly refined as in a 100-point rating scale. It is readily acknowledged that the point generated by the measuring instrument may be only an approximation of the "true" attitude, but the point is nevertheless believed to exist in some platonic sense. If respondents should all choose one scale position or indicate their acceptance of several response categories, within a short period of time the requirements of a "good" attitude scale are not satisfied and the concept under study is either abandoned or new measures are developed.

Though this notion of "attitude" possesses many advantages, particularly in conjunction with common statistical techniques, results from several socialization studies have raised important questions about the utility of making point-to-point comparisons. In particular, test-retest correlations and reliability coefficients on many commonly employed items suggest considerable response instability of many preadult attitudes: e.g., in an appendix to a government report version of their eight-city study, Hess and Torney (1965, appendices C.01, C.02, C.03) report test-retest correlations in the range of .3 to .5 for many of the questions that figures prominently in their analysis. The number of children giving the identical response is also low, frequently less than 50% and very rarely above 70%. Similarly, Vaillancourt (1973, 1974), in her panel study with three interviews in six months among children age 9–15, reports low response stability on a variety of questions on political interest: image of the President, level of political participation, and partisan identification. Such instability makes establishing parent-child agreement a hit-or-miss affair. If we define influence as parent-child agreement, and assume that both parent and child can give any 3 of 5 responses to a given question at any one time, the odds of precise agreement are obviously low (.33) even if such agreement in fact exists.

The problem of stability is made even more perplexing when we realize that, even if we had perfectly reliable and accurate indicators, the basic character of the phenomena under study can generate unstable appearing responses. The most obvious reason is the process of childhood development. We *expect* children to change their opinions as they encounter new information, develop new intellectual capacities, and become more like adults. The experience of being interviewed or completing a questionnaire can itself be part of this process. It is even possible that sudden, random-like opinion shifts may be perfectly consistent with some (yet unknown) orderly developmental pattern. Hence, to judge childhood attitude stability in terms of unchanging responses to the identical question may be unrealistic and theoretically inappropriate. The response sequence "I don't know," "I always trust the President," "I usually trust the President," and "I don't know" could be an age-related manifestation of an underlying, highly stable disposition.

A closely related problem is that parents—whether randomly or systematically—also are prone to political attitude change. As Converse's (1964) research makes clear, considerable individual volatility of response exists on many policy issues despite aggregate stability. Thus, even if parents' attitudes determined children's attitudes, we might very well have a situation not only of childhood attitude instability, but substantial parent-child issue divergence as children lag behind the latest parental shift. Another possibility would be that a child determined to follow politically in, say, his father's footsteps may adopt a political position representing some fluctuating average of paternal over-time issue stands, and this average need not be just like any one particular issue stand. The complexity is multiplied by the fact that mothers and fathers can disagree on issues and, if the child adopted a position somewhere between his or her parents, we would again find a lack of precise point-to-point agreement despite the possible existence of strong parental constraints on their children's political learning.

In light of all these considerations of childhood attitude volatility, unclear developmental patterns, adulthood opinion instability, and shifting parental disagreements, it should be no surprise that instances of precise parent-child agreement on attitude scale positions are less common than previously believed. Indeed, it is quite likely that at least some instances of parent-child agreement that we do find are due to chance. Moreover, it is also apparent that many of these factors encouraging volatility are enduring political or psychological conditions, and vast improvements in existing measurement techniques and strategies are unlikely to solve these problems. We cannot, for example, expect parents to hold more stable opinions or for mothers and fathers to disagree less politically. In short, more reliable attitude scales are not the answer since the phenomena under study are themselves characterized by change and development.

What this does suggest is that we must consider alternative ways of viewing attitudes and parent-child agreement. Unless we modify—not merely "improve"—the existing approach it seems clear that unreliable measures and low correspondence are going to be the rule regardless of whether or not parents do successfully transmit attitudes to their offspring. What we shall propose instead is that the transmission process not be judged in terms of point-to-point agreement but, rather, on the basis of parental success in inculcating their children with *acceptable ranges* of attitudes. Of course, "acceptable" can vary across family, across attitude, and over time and thus must be determined empirically, but adding the complication to our analysis is certainly preferable to assuming that point-to-point correspondence is desirable or possible for all parents on all issues. In effect, we assume that parents will stop exerting influence when their children are "close enough" to what they consider the "right" political views at a particular age and the repression of objectional opinions is probably more important than achieving mirror images.

Since we have not gathered our own data and thus must rely on data based on the point-to-point approach to parent-child agreement, our analysis here can only be illustrative. Specifically, we shall (1) briefly describe an approach to the study of attitudes that reduces some of the measurement and theoretical problems associated with point-to-point comparisons; (2) present illustrative data on parent-child political agreement incorporating some aspects of acceptable ranges of agreement and disagreement notions of attitudes; and (3) elaborate some of the measurement and theoretical problems associated with the alternative approach. Again, we should add that our purpose is to suggest new possibilities and not to criticize existing research as wrong.

Our basic conception of attitude here is the one developed by Muzafer Sherif and his associates (Sherif, Sherif, & Nebergall, 1965). This approach (sometimes labeled the "social judgmental" approach) defines attitude as an individual's stand on some object, issue, persons, institutions, and the like. This attitude is inferred from an overt behavior (e.g., an answer to a question) and is evaluative in nature, i.e., the individual "likes" or "dislikes" objects or in some other way reacts with a degree of emotion. Unlike the attitude as a point on a scale perspective, this approach conceives of an attitude as a continuum of possible responses with some possibilities highly acceptable, others obnoxious, and yet others to which the individual is indifferent. The end points of the continuum are set by the linguistic categories available to the individual and the availability of positions within a given society: e.g., a nineteenth-century survey of attitudes on racial equality would obviously find few people holding opinions of the merits of integrated schools or affirmative action.

The latitudes of acceptance, rejection, and indifference on a given issue can vary enormously by individual. One person might accept only a single narrow issue position and reject all other alternatives as intolerable. A second person could very well accept half of all possible issue positions on the same scale and be indifferent to all the others. It is assumed that the meaning of difference between positions is entirely determined by each individual. Hence, while one respondent might view, say, socialism and communism as indistinguishable, another might draw a firm line between the two. Generally, we expect to find that as personal commitment and involvement on an issue increase, the range of acceptance decreases, the range of rejections increases, and indifference shrinks to zero. This implies that where personal commitment is weak people can choose a large number of specific issue positions, all of which reflect their underlying attitude with no single position necessarily representing the one and only "best" position.

This conception of attitude would then treat "instability" of responses as an indicator of range latitude. Hence, rather than interpret, say, successive responses of "very liberal" and "somewhat liberal" as instability of an underlying attitude, we would instead conclude that the individual probably possesses a wider range of acceptance than someone who will endorse only a single position. We must emphasize that the data generated from attitude as point scales cannot be automatically translated into ranges of acceptance or indifference though test-retest reliability measures on such scales can be suggestive for aggregate estimations. To determine such ranges, the respondent must sort out all the various alternatives into categories ranging from most to least preferred, not merely choose a single alternative as the only acceptable preference. In this approach instability would be defined as a shifting of range limits, not selecting different alternatives all within the range as acceptable or objectionable.

Using this attitude-as-range approach we could establish parent-child correspondence in a number of ways. The most obvious is the overlap between ranges of acceptance: e.g., a parent and child would be considered to hold the same partisan attitude even if one might choose "strong Democrat" and the other "weak Democrat" provided that the difference between "strong" and "weak" were viewed as virtually inconsequential. In addition, a common range of rejections could be an indicator of parent-offspring agreement (e.g., "It doesn't make any difference what you are so long as you're not a Republican"). A third possibility is similarity in the width of ranges. Although a parent and child may both endorse a position, they can still vary in the latitudes of acceptance, rejection, and indifference and thus, in a sense, really possess different attitudes despite point-to-point agreement. The opposite can also be argued: the existence of identical latitudes, especially where the range of acceptance is narrow, indicates a similiarity in political perspective despite divergences in most preferred issue positions.

As we have said, the utilization of this approach to attitudes requires the collection of different types of data than now generated, not merely "better" measures. Nevertheless, we can use some of Jennings' data in a way roughly consistent with this attitude as ranges conception or illustrative purposes. We shall do this in two ways. First, we shall examine parent-child agreement in ratings of religious groups within different denominations. Our argument is that, on issues of family importance like one's own religion, the range of acceptable family deviation is far narrower than for evaluations of different religious groups. Ideally, we would need a direct indicator of the importance of religious identification in the home; but it seems safe to assume that most parents are concerned

Table 2.7.   Parent-Child Differences among Jews in Ratings of Jews, Catholics, and Protestants

	Jews Rating	Jews Rating	Jews Rating
Differences	*Jews*	*Catholics*	*Protestants*
0–10	47.4	27.3	24.0
11–20	28.2	16.9	29.3
21–30	2.6	15.6	10.7
31–40	6.4	18.2	14.7
41–50	14.1	18.2	20.0
50+	1.3	3.8	1.3
	100.0%	100.0%	100.0%
N =	78	77	75

that offspring share their perspective or at least the family's own religion. The second illustration concerns partisan identification. Our basic argument here is that the baseline for comparing parent-child correspondence is not precise agreement but, rather, the extent to which parent-offspring variation is cotermi-nous. Instead of expecting children to follow a shifting preference exactly, we think it more reasonable that correspondence be evaluated in terms of remaining within the range of these shifts.

Tables 2–7 and 2–8 present parent-child differences in ratings of religious groups according to family denomination. Jennings and Niemi (1968), in their analysis of these ratings data, suggest that pairwise agreement is moderate at best despite intergenerational similarity of mean scores (the overall product-moment correlations for ratings of Jews was .22 and .36 for Catholics). In contrast to this conclusion of at best moderate agreement, the data when arranged in this fashion offer more evidence suggesting successful transmission. Note, for example, that

Table 2.8.   Parent-Child Differences among Catholics on Ratings of Catholics, Jews, and Protestants

	Catholics Rating	Catholics Rating	Catholics Rating
Differences	*Catholics*	*Jews*	*Protestants*
0–10	49.3	34.6	33.9
11–20	33.3	25.9	32.4
21–30	6.9	13.5	15.8
31–40	5.7	13.5	10.0
41–50	4.3	7.5	7.7
50+	.5	5.0	.2
	100.0%	100.0%	100.0%
N =	438	437	442

almost half of Jewish and Catholic children are 10 or less points away from their parents in ratings of their own religion. If we interpret even a 20;point difference as "not all that important" in most families, the degree of parent-offspring correspondence is even more impressive for ratings of fellow believers. The patterns in tables 2–7 and 2–8 are by no means surprising and fit quite well with our intuitive notions of variations of acceptable religion-related attitudes within families. What is surprising, perhaps, is the expectation that parents would try to establish precise agreement between themselves and their children on evaluations of groups probably quite distant from family life. On such distant issues perhaps only the most striking deviations would be viewed as deviant with even a 30- or 40-point difference being "close enough for all practical purposes."

A second illustration of the advantages of conceiving of an attitude in terms of a range concerns the handling of over-time variability. Specifically, if parental attitude is in a constant state of flux, it is somewhat unreasonable to expect a child to follow precisely each new shift. Instead, the appropriate question would be the extent to which the child stayed within the bounds of parental variation. An answer to this question requires longitudinal data for both parents and offspring, and while Jennings has collected these data they are unavailable for our analysis. In lieu of such data, we shall substitute data from the 1956–1958–1960 SRC panel study which gives us a rough idea of attitude change in two- and four-year intervals. Such data offer some idea of the baseline against which we can evaluate parent-child correspondence.

Table 2–9 depicts partisan identification turnover for 1956–1958–1960 together with parent-child agreement in 1965 (party ID is here treated as a five-point scale of Strong and Weak Democrat, Strong and Weak Republican, and Independent). Note that the panel data shows that only about 60% of adults exhibit precise continuity for these time spans. Put somewhat differently, about 40% of the children of these adults would not have been exposed to a perfectly stable stimulus on which to base their own partisan loyalty. If such adult shifts were typical in 1965, then the figure of 39.9% precise parent-offspring agree-

Table 2.9. Over-Time Stability and Parent-Child Agreement by Partisan Identification

DISTANCES	OVER-TIME STABILITY			PARENT-CHILD AGREEMENT
	1956–1958	*1956–1960*	*1958–1960*	
0	60.6%	57.4%	61.6%	39.9%
1	31.4	33.3	31.8	39.4
2	6.6	7.9	5.3	17.4
3	.8	1.0	1.0	2.8
4	.8	.6	.4	.7
d	.502	.545	.470	.854
d/r	.100	.109	.094	.171

Source.   Student-Parent Socialization Study, SRC Panel Study.

ment is not as low as it first might appear given the difficulty of many children knowing exactly where their parents stood. Moreover, it is clear from these data that both adult shifts and parent-child differences of more than one position— e.g., from a Strong Democrat to an Independent—are relatively rare. Thus, at least in the aggregate, we find considerable stability in partisanship, but it appears to be the stability of constrained movement, not zero change.

Though treating attitudes as ranges of responses solves the problem of low stability of more common measures and makes intuitive sense when dealing with developmental processes, this perspective is not without its drawbacks. In terms of the array of statistical measures readily available to researchers, the social judgmental approach is unwieldy. Instead of each respondent having a single number representing his or her attitude, much more information per individual is required, i.e., the ranges of acceptance, rejection, and indifference. Also, the information will vary across individuals and summary measures such as the mean can be highly misleading as a best guess for describing individual patterns if only because there is so much more to be summarized. No doubt statistics appropriate to this conception of attitude can be developed, but their current absence makes analysis complex and perhaps even uninviting.

At a more theoretical level, we may have a situation where due to the low salience of many political issues the ranges of acceptance may be so wide that demonstrating complete parent-child dissimilarity is virtually impossible. Combining many different responses into a single, much wider response almost guarantees that some overlap of acceptance between parents and offspring will occur. We can very well imagine, for example, virtually all Americans—children and adults alike—overlapping substantially in their acceptance of positive statements about nationalism, the virtue of the constitutional order, and abstract support for democratic values so analysis merely concludes that all parents and their children are exposed to the general political consensus and that children cannot help but be similar to their parents. Converse (1974) raises another problem in this attitude-as-range approach when he suggests that, where ranges of acceptance are very broad, it may be misleading to even speak of an individual holding an attitude. And if we could not distinguish a ''nonattitude'' from a very broad acceptance range, our analysis of transmission obviously has problems.

THE INFLUENCE OF THE FAMILY: A CONCLUDING NOTE

Since our basic purpose was to raise and occasionally illustrate certain issues, we cannot here settle some of the controversies about the family's role in the socialization process. Nor have we dealt with all the issues that need to be resolved before we can make well grounded assertions on the subject. We have, for example, ignored such questions as analyzing parental interaction, the measurement of family authority ''structure,'' and the possibility of preadults influencing the political learning of their parents, to mention only a few areas needing more theoretical and methodological attention.

What we have done, however, is to show that existing searches for answers have either approached the problem in an overly simplistic fashion or wieh inappropriate measurement strategies. The theoretical problems in particular are most troublesome since it is difficult to develop new techniques of data gathering and analysis unless it is clear what is to be analyzed. We have argued that three tasks are among the most important on the theory building agenda: (1) incorporating into analyses some notion of parental objectives in the socialization process instead of assuming the desire for precise replication; (2) unraveling the developmental processes in attitude formation so we can better distinguish intergenerational continuity; and (3) formulating more precise indicators of family "transmission" or "influence" than mere parent-offspring issue agreement. These are not easy problems to resolve, but our knowledge in these areas must be substantially improved if we want to offer well grounded assertions about the family and the socialization process.

At the more methodological level, we have shown that many of the common approaches to data analysis are either inappropriate to the assertions being tested or yield misleading results. This is particularly true where parent-child attitude distributions are highly modal and theories are stated in terms of proximity but tested in terms of covariation. These problems are not unique to the study of political socialization, but they are especially important when examining the family's role since many relevant orientations are highly consensual and the important question is one of similarities, not just statistical association between nearly identical attitude scales. We have also argued that, given the low stability of indicators that conceive of an attitude as a discrete point, it makes both theoretical and methodological sense to think of attitudes in terms of ranges of acceptance, rejection, and indifference. Fortunately, the methodological problems we have described are relatively easier to solve than the theoretical problems just mentioned though important questions are still unresolved.

The major substantive finding of our analysis is that more pairwise intergenerational continuity exists on certain political attitudes than is suggested by the analyses of Jennings and Niemi. Partisan identification still remains the best example of parent-child correspondence, but it certainly is not true that this is an exception in a sea of dissimilarities. Of course, as we have argued, it is not perfectly clear what such similarities mean. Such similarities *may* be proof of parental influence or they *may* be evidence of strong extrafamily pressure for political homogeneity. Regardless of what they may indicate, however, we must recognize these similarities instead of dismissing them as nonexistent because most of them would occur by chance alone.

Subcultural Variations in Political Socialization

The study of subgroup variations in political learning, like the analysis of the family's impact, has been among the most popular areas of research. Early studies such as those by Greenstein (1961) and Hess (Hess & Torney, 1968) and his associates emphasized sex and social class–related differences. More recent studies have considerably widened the scope of our attention. Greenberg (1970), Lyons (1970), and others have focused on racial differences in beliefs about government and the political process. Jaros, Hirsch, and Fleron (1968) raised some basic questions about the uniformity of the socialization process in their research on Appalachian whites. Particularly within the last few years, analysts have sought out distinctive groups such as Chicanos (Garcia, 1973), the Amish (Jaros et al., 1974), Mennonites (Leatherman, 1962), and others well beyond the mainstream of American politics.

Each of these many subcultural studies has had its own particular set of research questions. Analyses based on some of the more "exotic" groups such as Appalachians or the Amish have commonly sought to test propositions about political learning not readily testable within the general population. Jaros (1968, 1974), for example, found Appalachia to be an area in which variations in attitudes toward political authority and family structure allowed analyses not possible among children in the dominant culture. In other instances, especially with regard to sex- and race-related differences, research derives from a policy concern over the unequal distribution of political costs and benefits among social groups. Perhaps the foremost concern permeating research on subcultural differences, however, is the extent to which distinctive cultural or ethnic groups are fully integrated into what might be called the mainstream political culture. Given the potential explosiveness of political conflict where society is divided along sharp communal lines, it is no wonder that many researchers have focused on, say, whether blacks and whites relate to the government and political authority in the same ways.

Though many studies share an underlying concern for communal differences, rarely is it clear what is meant by statements such as "blacks and whites are different from each other politically." Several opposing meanings can be implied by such a statement, and each meaning would lead to different types of empirical analysis. Perhaps the simplest, and operationally the most common, meaning is that on a particular indicator the distribution for blacks is unlike that for whites; e.g., on a question like "Is government honest?" if 75% of whites answered "Yes" compared to 60% of blacks, we would usually conclude that blacks differed from whites though we might note that most blacks and whites hold the same opinion. For such statements the unit of analysis is the group, and even if we have several similar questions yielding the same marginal distributions, such confirmation by itself does not allow us to make statements about the particular orientations of *individual* blacks and whites.[9]

A second notion of subcultural political difference focuses on response patterns involving several variables. Whereas the first notion of group difference

---

[9]The relationship between individual attributes and collective characteristics is even more complex than indicated here. For a more complete discussion of the problem, see Paul F. Lazarsfeld and Herbert Menzel, "On the Relations between Individual and Collective Properties," in Amitai Etzioni (ed.), *Complex Organizations* (New York: Holt, Rinehart & Winston, 1961), pp. 422–440.

described an aggregate difference one measure at a time, here the focus is on individual configurations of multiple items. This second conception of group difference is probably what most analysts have in mind when they speak about cross-national differences in political culture: e.g., the claim that Americans and Germans are different politically implies far more than separate percentage differences on an array of questions. More likely, we mean that Americans and Germans diverge in the way they structure political phenomena. This second notion of difference can perhaps best be described as a difference in Weltanschauung whereas the first difference is a mere disagreement over specific issues. Even if Americans and Germans had the same marginal distributions on numerous questions, we would probably not claim that individual Americans were just like individual Germans since many individual differences are consistent with the same overall response distributions.

Our argument here is somewhat analogous to perceptual disagreements over Gestalt-type patterns. Consider, for example, the familiar drawing which can be seen as either a vase or as two faces. The first notion of difference we discussed is equivalent to two people both seeing, say, a face but disagreeing over whether the face was attractive or ugly. On the other hand, our second notion of difference corresponds to one person seeing the faces, the other perceiving the vase. In the case of answers to survey questions, this would be the equivalent of two people whose responses were always opposite versus two people whose response patterns were completely independent. In the first instance, the patterns of one person can be predicted from the patterns of the other despite complete substantive disagreement; in the second instance, the response patterns are different despite some response overlap.

It should be clear that these two distinctive notions of "politically different" imply very different sorts of political conflicts. Differences of the first type abound in all societies and may or may not be indicators of fundamental communal division. Indeed, according to the first criteria of difference, it is unlikely that even two subsamples (or groups) in a politically homogeneous society will be alike since by chance alone the marginal distributions on some measures will diverge. On the other hand, differences of the second kind do suggest a basis for deeper communal or subcultural political conflicts. Here the conflict is not only over different issues or contrary beliefs, but also involves participants who may have difficulty understanding the perspectives of their opponents. Under these conditions we might expect disagreements on what issues belong together, what was the context of a problem, or what really affected what. Social groups might very well have to relate politically to each other as if they were separate nations bargaining over an international treaty where in the absence of a common framework everything had to be decided in great detail.

The study of political socialization across different social groups has implicitly emphasized the second meaning of political difference: i.e., children from distinctive racial or ethnic groups are asked questions on various topics to measure the existence of a distinctive political perspective. In contrast to the study of public opinion among adults where, say, racial differences on an issue is an important datum in itself, comparable differences among black and white children are not of prime analytical importance. Rather, if such issue-by-issue differences are large and consistent, they are taken as being indicative of a more basic cultural divergence. Typically, the percentage distributions on four or five questions about the virtues of the government, the character of the president, and the goodness of the system generally are divided by social groups and, when the predicted item-by-item differences occur, most researchers have concluded that significant subcultural political socialization patterns exist within the dominant political culture.

Obviously the typical approach is appropriate to the first type of political difference we considered though the argument is phrased in terms of the second type of difference. Blacks and whites may be profoundly dissimilar in the ways they conceptualize political phenomena, but this item-by-item percentage distribution is the inappropriate method for establishing the relationship. What we need is another approach to finding subcultural variations in political learning, an approach more sensitive toward *patterns* of response to political stimuli than the overlap of content in these responses. We shall proceed as follows. First, again using data from the 1965 Jennings study, we shall examine the distinction between subcultural political differences based on aggregate item-by-item analyses versus analysis based on individual response patterns. Second, we shall briefly consider some alternative methods for going beyond gross item-by-item comparison to measure overall differences in political socialization. Finally, we shall illustrate some of these methods by examining race and social class differences using data drawn from the student-parent socialization study.

AGGREGATE ITEM-BY-ITEM VERSUS INDIVIDUAL PATTERN COMPARISONS

To see the differences between conclusions drawn from group data as opposed to data on individual patterns of response, let us examine racial differences in beliefs about governments. Table 2–10 presents three commonly employed questions about the government divided by race. This format is typical in most studies dealing with subcultural differences in socialization. The "standard" interpretation of these data would probably be that blacks tend to be less positive toward the government than are whites. On all these questions fewer blacks than whites give the most positive response, though this difference is small on the question of government paying attention to public opinion. Literally, this interpretation of the data means that on any given indicator there is a greater likelihood that a negative response will be offered by a black. However, because the results from each question are presented separately, we cannot make any

Table 2.10.   Racial Differences in Beliefs about Government, Aggregate Item-by-Item Percentage Differences

QUESTION	RACE	
	White	*Black*
1. How much attention do you feel that government pays to what people think?		
(1) Good deal	46.3%	42.3%
(3) Some	43.7	45.8
(5) Not much	10.0	11.9
2. How much of the time do you think you can trust the government in Washington to do what is right?		
(1) About always	43.0%	31.9%
(3) Most of the time	49.7	52.9
(5) Some of the time	7.3	15.2
3. Do you feel that almost all of the people running the government are smart people who usually know what they are doing		
(1) Know what they are doing	85.5%	78.3%
(3) Other, depends	1.1	.5
(5) Don't know what they are doing	13.4	21.3

Source.   Student Parent Socialization Study.

statements about the existence of a distinctive black or white response pattern. Statistically, any number of highly divergent individual patterns would be consistent with these overall marginal distributions.

Table 2–11 presents the data from Table 2–10 recalculated according to the response patterns offered by *individual* blacks and whites. When we examine the various combinations of response patterns within each racial group, we see that except where the pattern is very rare for both races there exists no distinctive black or white response patterns. Both whites and blacks tend to cluster in certain response sets such as the 111, 311, 131, or 331 patterns. A few patterns—e.g., 113—are somewhat more common in one group than in the other, but this finding is certainly no evidence that blacks or whites hold distinctive political perspectives. Moreover, while the impression given by Table 2–10 was that blacks tended to be more negative toward the government, a close inspection of the date in Table 2–11 shows relatively few blacks who give more than one negative answer to these questions. In fact, 7.5% of the black respondents give two or more "5" (negative) responses compared to 6.1% of the whites for a net difference of 1.4%.

Though the technique illustrated in Table 2–11 is clearly more methodologically and theoretically appropriate for answering the question of basic differences in political socialization than the conventional approach depicted in Table 2–10,

Table 2.11. Racial Differences in Beliefs about Government, Individual Response Patterns

RESPONSE PATTERN[a]	RACE	
	White	*Black*
111	23.7%	16.2%
311	14.5	7.6
511	1.9	3.0
131	17.8	14.1
331	19.9	22.7
531	3.8	4.5
151	.8	4.0
351	2.1	5.6
551	1.0	.5
113	.1	0
313	.1	0
133	.3	.5
333	.3	0
533	.1	0
153	.1	0
353	.1	0
553	.1	0
115	1.5	2.0
315	1.3	3.0
515	.3	0
135	1.6	4.0
335	4.1	4.5
535	1.6	2.5
155	.5	2.0
355	1.5	2.0
555	1.1	1.0

Source. Student Parent Socialization Study.
[a]The numbers in the response pattern refer to the numbers to the left of the responses in Table 2.10.

this technique is limited. The use of these questions may be satisfactory for purposes of illustration, but a more thorough analysis of this problem will certainly require many more variables. Even the addition of a few more variables would, however, made for an overly complex, unparsimonious form of analysis (particularly where variables had numerous response categories). Furthermore, this type of approach makes systematic comparisons across different groups highly unwieldy. Research on subcultural variations should be able to tell us not only whether a socially distinctive group is also politically distinctive, but how several distinctive groups compare with each other in terms of diverging from the dominant political culture. This goal requires a more parsimonious approach to the data than the one depicted in Table 2–11. In short, our purpose here has been to show that the usual way of depicting subcultural differences is inappropriate to the theoretical purpose underlying the research. Our next task is to consider a more appropriate and useful model to analyze variations in basic socialization patterns.

MEASURING SUBCULTURAL SOCIALIZATION

Our basic assumption is that the goal of research is not only to determine whether distinctive groups differ in the context of their responses, but also in the structure of these responses. The existence of distinctive group response patterns, regardless of agreement or disagreement on the content of responses, is taken as evidence of a basic difference in political socialization. How are such differences in structure to be measured? While there are several statistical techniques that one way or the other deal with "structure," an appropriate method for our purposes would in addition meet several other requirements.

First, as we have previously suggested, this technique should be capable of handling numerous variables simultaneously. To claim, for instance, that blacks and whites are "different" politically requires far more than, say, comparisons on three or four indicators. Thus, some form of multivariate analysis is necessary. A second requirement is that group differences could be summarized without extreme loss of important information and be interpretable in some way consistent with conventional statistical usage, e.g., as a proportional reduction of error. As we have seen, merely reporting the percentage distributions for all possible response patterns is highly unparsimonious. Reducing such data into measures of association and then comparing correlation matrices across groups provides some improvement, but even here the quantity of data makes reasonably precise, succinct comparisons difficult. A third requirement concerns the types of comparisons to be made. Ideally, we should be able to show not only whether, say, blacks differ from whites but also whether this difference is greater than the difference between whites and Chicanos. This capacity could also be applied to cross-time comparisons with the same group or even such comparisons between different groups. Finally, there are practical considerations of both data and computation. It would be especially helpful for such a technique to make use of existing types of data—e.g., Likert scale questions, and readily available and simple computational routines.

The method to be suggested here to satisfy these requirements is an extension of factor analysis developed by Kaiser, Veldman, and others (Veldman, 1967).[10] Essentially, this method requires the generation of orthogonal factor structures with the identical variables for each group. Though inspection of these separate factor structures by itself would provide a rough idea of structure similarity, this would not only be unwieldy but imprecise since the computation of the factor

[10]This technique is also consistent with Tannenbaum and McLeod's theoretical discussion of how group differences in socialization might best be measured. See Percy H. Tannenbaum and Jack M. McLeod, "On the Measurement of Socialization," *Public Opinion Quarterly* 31 (1967), pp. 27–37.

structure typically maximizes explained variance and such maximizations in each structure may obscure more fundamental similarities. What is necessary, then, is to equate the origins and factor-vector orientations of the two structures and determine the overall degree of structure similarity. In the case of RELATE, a routine developed by Veldman, this is accomplished by generating a transformation matrix from a matrix of cosines which moves one structure into maximum proximity with the other. After factor reorientation, a matrix of cosines for all pairs of factors is computed with the diagonal element of this matrix indicating the similarity of the two-factor structures.

To illustrate the logic of this type of analysis let us examine the simplified example presented by Veldman. Consider the following factor loadings:

VARIABLES	GROUP A		GROUP B	
	I	II	I	II
1	.72	−.55	−.15	.93
2	.51	.17	−.52	.44
3	.60	.32	−.70	.15
4	.34	.34	−.71	.18
5	.45	.31	−.58	.29
6	.28	.29	−.64	.04

At first glance, it appears that the basic factoral structure in Group A is quite unlike the structure in Group B. Nevertheless, the overall factor structure in both groups is quite similar. To see this similarity, let us first view these factor loadings as vectors in common space (Figure 2–3). Careful scrutiny of Figure 2–3 will indicate a close similarity between the configurations of vectors for groups A and B. This similarity is strikingly confirmed when the structure for Group B is rotated to maximize factor contiguity (Figure 2–4). In fact the correlation (cosines) between Factor I for both groups is −.62 while for Factor II the correlation is .79. In short, both groups possess a similar pattern of underlying response dimensions despite the initial appearance of dissimilarity.

It should be clear that this approach to establishing group difference satisfies the previously enumerated requirements. It can handle large numbers of variables in a parsimonious way and provide summary statistics whose meaning is readily interpretable. This approach also allows the precise intergroup comparisons of socialization. Thus, we are no longer limited to rough approximations based on visual inspection of data but can now make precise statements about the size of group differences simultaneously across a number of separate entities—e.g., ethnic, racial, economic, generational groupings. In addition, there is the obvious application of measuring the same group of parents and children over time to describe how children begin to perceive the world in an adult-like way. Perhaps most important, however, this method is based on comparisons of *patterns* of response and hence is theoretically more appropriate to establishing subcultural

Figure 2-3. Test Vectors of Structures A and B in a Common Factor Space

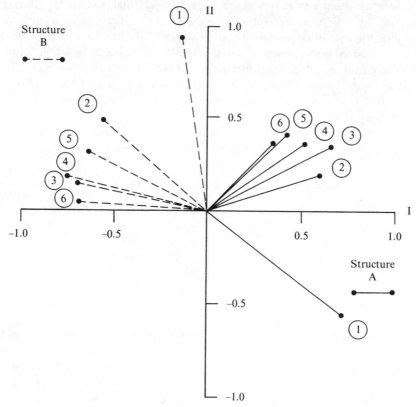

Source: Veldman, *Fortran Programming for the Behavioral Sciences,* pp. 239-40.

searchers have used some of these same questions for similar purposes.[11] Obviously, the issue of which indicators are most relevant for such purposes is crucial, but since our goal is largely illustrative we shall make do with the available data.

Because the statistical procedures previously described would require a relatively advanced knowledge of computer programming, we shall use instead the

[11]The questions are: Should a speech be allowed opposing churches? Should a communist be allowed to hold public office? Voting is the only means of control. Government is beyond understanding. Goverment is interested in public opinion. Are government people crooked? Does government waste money? Do you trust government to do right?; Are government people smart?; feeling thermometers for labor unions, Southerners, Catholics, Big Business, Jews, Whites, Protestants, Negroes; Should schools begin with prayer?; Should federal government integrate schools?; Should the U.S. stay in the UN?; and partisan identification.

Figure 2-4. Test Vectors of Original Structure A and Structure B After Rotation to Maximize Test-Vector Contiguity

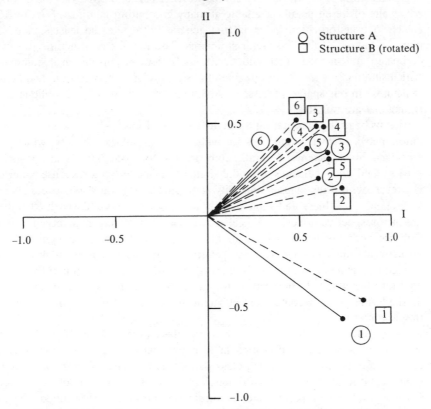

Source: Veldman, *Fortran Programming for the Behavioral Sciences,* pp. 239-40.

searchers have used some of these same questions for similar purposes.[11] Obviously, the issue of which indicators are most relevant for such purposes is crucial, but since our goal is largely illustrative we shall make do with the available data.

Because the statistical procedures previously described would require a relatively advanced knowledge of computer programming, we shall use instead the

[11]The questions are: Should a speech be allowed opposing churches? Should a communist be allowed to hold public office? Voting is the only means of control. Government is beyond understanding. Goverment is interested in public opinion. Are government people crooked? Does government waste money? Do you trust government to do right?; Are government people smart?; feeling thermometers for labor unions, Southerners, Catholics, Big Business, Jews, Whites, Protestants, Negroes; Should schools begin with prayer?; Should federal government integrate schools?; Should the U.S. stay in the UN?; and partisan identification.

FCOMP program from the OSIRIS package of computer programs. Logically and statistically, FCOMP is very similar to RELATE and possesses the obvious advantage of being readily available at many computing facilities.[12] As in RE-LATE, a transformation index is first generated to give the least squared fit between factors of the two factor structures. The two factor structures are then compared and, among other statistics, a coefficient of correlation is computed which summarizes the overall degree of correspondence between the two factor structures. In our analysis the factor structures are orthogonal, but oblique configurations are possible.

Let us begin by considering racial differences. Table 2–12 presents the correlation matrix of factor structures for white students, black students, white parents, and black parents. Overall, comparisons for both parents and students across racial lines indicate substantial similarity of underlying response patterns. However, within the overall similarity some interesting variations occur. Note, for example, that black and white parents are somewhat more like each other than are their respective offspring. It is also true that black teenagers diverge far more from their parents than do white children. In fact, white parents and children are virtually identical in their response patterns (a finding consistent with the data offered in our treatment of family transmission of attitudes). Though these data confirm strong racial similarities, they also suggest the possibility that basic dissimilarities may become more apparent in subsequent generations if present trends continue.

The pattern of relationships for social class (Table 2–13) also shows an absence of sharp group divisions in response patterns. Indeed, middle-class children are as close to working-class parents as they are to their own parents (and the same holds true for working-class students and middle-class parents). Once again, the high parent-student correlations provide further support for the continuity of political perspectives suggested in our previous analyses. These data also suggest that racial differences are more significant than social class differences though further analysis is obviously required on this question (work-

Table 2.12.   Factor Structure Correlation, by Race and Generation

	BLACK STUDENTS	WHITE PARENTS	BLACK PARENTS
White students	.71	.96	.78
Black students		.73	.71
White parents			.79
Black parents			—

Source.   Student Parent Socialization Study.

[12] A more complete description of this program can be found in *Osiris III: System and Program Description* (Ann Arbor: Center for Political Studies, 1973), pp. 627–636, and in *Osiris III: Formulas and Statistical References,* pp. 73–76.

Table 2.13.   Factor Structure Correlation, by Social Class[a] and Generation

	MIDDLE-CLASS STUDENTS	WORKING-CLASS PARENTS	MIDDLE-CLASS PARENTS
Working-class students	.86	.88	.84
Middle-class students		.84	.85
Working-class parents			.89
Middle-class parents			—

Source.   Student Parent Socialization Study.
[a]Social class is measured by parents' perception of their class.

ing- and middle-class attitude structures have a correlation of .86 compared to .71 for black and white students).

GROUP DIFFERENCES: A CONCLUDING NOTE

It should be clear that our analysis has only scratched the surface of what we mean when we make assertions about different socialization patterns among blacks, Chicanos, or other groups. As in the analysis of family influence on learning, the most important and perplexing issues are theoretical in nature. Most researchers (ourselves included) have been quite casual in selecting what indicators are most appropriate as measures of "basic" political orientations dividing subpopulations. Though questions like "Is the President a good person?" intuitively seem important, the choice of questions like this one does not seem to be rooted in any particular theory of communal conflict, intergroup hostility, or even associated behavioral consequence. It is obvious that since group differences in at least some indicators are a virtual certainty, given a large enough question pool, demonstrations of differences per se are meaningless unless they are within an explicit, politically important context.

Even if specific questions are hypothesized as theoretically important, the level of analysis still remains to be settled. Are we most interested in the uniqueness of individuals, all of whom happen to have distinguishable racial or social class characteristics? Or, on the other hand, is the group itself the unit of analysis with individual-level characteristics largely irrelevant? No doubt, a strong case can be made for either perspective or some combination of the two, depending on the basic questions under study. Unfortunately, however, not only is neither argument openly discussed in terms of some larger political theory of communal conflict, but analysts frequently seem oblivious to the argument itself.

In terms of the statistical analysis of group differences, it is evident that our illustration of comparisons of factor structures is only one of a multitude of possibilities. As we argued at the beginning of this chapter, underlying all statistical procedures are assumptions of how phenomena are ordered, and hypotheses with different assumptions about differences in group socialization patterns will naturally require other statistical procedures. If, for example, the group itself and not the individual were the unit of analysis, statistics such as the standard deviation, degree of overlap between distributions, and the like would be more appropriate than within group correlations and factor analyses.[13] Even if our conception of "group difference" were accepted as most appropriate, several other multivariate techniques sensitive to structure are readily available and should be used, if only to determine the consistency of findings across different procedures.

Conclusions

We began by noting that, despite increasing methodological sophistication in the study of political socialization, results only infrequently have been adding up to a body of consistent, well grounded knowledge. Much contemporary research raises as many problems as it solves or leaves them to "future research." Continuity of knowledge exists only at the most general level (frequently as "tendencies"), if it exists at all. Hopefully, our analysis can improve this situation in the areas of family influence on learning and subpopulation variations in socialization. Our basic stricture is simple: propositions about the socialization process must be stated precisely and then tested with the appropriate data and statistical procedures. No one could possibly disagree with this assertion and every researcher will surely claim to abide by it. Nevertheless, the evidence seems clear that ad hoc theorizing and inappropriate methodology are fairly common and contribute substantially to the confusion in the field.

---

[13]See, e.g., James S. Coleman, *Introduction to Mathematical Sociology* (New York: Free Press, 1964), pp. 398–404, for illustrations of this approach.

3

Comparative Political Socialization:
A Theoretical Perspective

James A. Nathan and Richard C. Remy*

THIS CHAPTER REVIEWS AND DISCUSSES comparative political socialization research. This research compares the political socialization process of two or more political systems. Political systems are geopolitical and/or analytic *constructs* of human political behavior. Nations are political systems. Schools, unions, trade associations, political parties, and the like may also be viewed as political systems (Denhardt, 1971; Gillespie & Patrick, 1974). They, like nations, are social units possessing authority structures that allocate scarce values such as health, welfare, wealth, power, and rectitude (Easton, 1965; Eckstein, 1973; LaNoue & Adler, 1968). Systems, as a unit of analysis, may also include geographically larger areas than single nation-states. Aggregations of states, transnational organizations (such as the multinational firm or the Common Market), can be viewed as political systems (Alger, 1972; Nye, 1972). Further, in the study of international politics, global political interactions are often seen as constituting an international "system" analytically comparable to political systems at "lower" or "smaller" levels of organization (Kaplan, 1957; Weltman, 1973).

The study of political learning relevant to these political systems is generally called political socialization. Research on comparative political socialization is characterized by a relatively small number of studies. The antecedents of this research sought to illuminate the relationship between individual personality development and national culture. The bulk of contemporary comparative political socialization research uses survey analysis techniques and conceptual

*With William Kiley.

frameworks drawn from political science to arrive at descriptions of the attitudes of preadults in different national political systems. Thus, typically, the political orientations of individuals, say, from England and the United States, have been studied to yield some generalization about the process of socialization in these political systems. A few studies have sought to compare the socialization of individuals toward the different political systems of which they are members, such as local, state, national, and the international system.

In this essay we first examine the evolution of comparative political socialization research. We shall then review some of the findings of this research. Finally, we will suggest some new research directions and techniques.

The Ideology of Comparative Political Socialization Research

SYSTEMS AND SYSTEMS MAINTENANCE: THE EASTON AND DENNIS CONTRIBUTION

Research on comparative political socialization began with the emergence of interest in the socialization process itself among political scientists. A fundamental assumption underlying this research is that political socialization is a functional process common to all national political systems. A functional process is an activity which aids a system to maintain itself. There are other processes which aid systems to maintain themselves. They, like socialization, are commonly labeled inputs of a political system. Generally, among scholars who study socialization and comparative political systems, the process of socialization is considered to be one of the most important for systemic survival. As Almond (1960) explains:

> All political systems tend to perpetuate their cultures and structures through time and ... they do this by means of the socializing influences of the primary and secondary structures through which the young of the society pass in the process of maturation (p. 27).

The relevance of socialization for "system maintenance" has recently been critically elaborated by Easton and Dennis in *Children in the Political System* (1969). This study is the fullest expression to date of the systems approach in political socialization and is based upon a sample of nearly 12,000 white second-through eighth-grade children in urban public schools in four regions of the United States. To Easton and Dennis, previous political socialization research has been locked into an interpretation of the system's metaphor which has carried it in a "system-maintaining, stability-emphasizing direction" (p. 27). How change occurs, whether or not diversity within a system may perpetuate itself "do not appear to be significant or central questions" (p. 36) in political socialization research, according to the authors.[1]

Easton and Dennis' concern with the system maintenance bias of systems theory is not novel. There has been a considerable body of commentary criticizing general systems theory and its attendant vocabulary of structures, functions, equilibrium, and stasis for fixating upon system preservation. Lockwood (1969), in discussing Parsons, e.g., argues that in systems analysis it is necessary

> to single out relatively stable points of reference, or "structural" aspects of the system under consideration, and then to study the processes whereby such structures are maintained. This is the meaning of the "structural-functional" approach to social system analysis. Since the social system is a system of action, and its structural aspects are the relatively stable inter-actions of individuals around common norms, the dynamic processes with which the sociologist is concerned are those which function to maintain social structures, or, in other words, those processes whereby individuals come to be motivated to act in conformity with normative standards (p. 283).

As an alternative to this misplaced emphasis on "system-maintenance," Easton and Dennis have advanced a theory of "system-persistence." The three principal components of this formulation and their relationship can be expressed in the simple formula: system persistence equals system maintenance plus change. In *Children and the Political System,* Easton and Dennis (1969) attempt to relate the political socialization process to these three components and in so doing free socialization research from its exclusive focus on system maintenance.

The model of a political system on which their "systems-persistence" theory rests is derived from Easton's earlier efforts to construct a general theory of politics based on a systems metaphor. The political system is seen as a "vast conversion process through which the inputs of demands and supports are transformed by various structures and processes into outputs, that is into authoritative decisions and actions" (p. 48).

Political socialization is linked to systems change through the notion of "system stress": i.e., political systems may experience stress on their "essential variables" in terms of insufficient compliance with their outputs, excessive input demands, and/or insufficient input of support, diffuse or specific. Within this framework, political socialization is seen as a kind of response by which a system may seek to avoid such stress.

Unfortunately, the data presented in *Children and the Political System* are essentially independent of the theoretical argument relating political socialization to system change developed in the first three chapters of the book. The questions which bear the brunt of the analysis deal with various roles in the authority

---

[1]It should be noted that Easton and Dennis are careful to argue that there is nothing in the logic of systems analysis which prohibits the political socialization researcher from analyzing the linkage between political socialization and system change. Thus they note, "It bears repetition that systems analysis does not possess a *built-in* conservative bias" (p. 66).

structure, particularly those of the policeman and the President. Essentially, these questions are aimed at assessing how much children know about objects of political authority (cognition), how much they like them (affect), and how important they are to them (salience). There is nothing in the nature of these types of questions which is specifically designed to illuminate processes of change or conflict.

What Easton and Dennis find, rather, is that the children in their sample developed quite early and maintained highly positive, supportive images of major political roles (the structure of authority) in the American system. More specifically, they find children like the President and believe in his dependability, benevolence, trustworthiness, and reliability. The overall tendency, then, in primary socialization toward the "structure of authority" is toward "political stability." It should be noted, however, that the principal questions utilized in *Children in the Political System* were not originally designed to illuminate change, and that they do not do so when change is considered should not be surprising.

At best, then, the authors link political socialization to systems maintenance through the structure of authority and do not deal with change, which in the thrust of their analysis becomes what is left over after system maintenance is accounted for. If system persistence equals system maintenance plus change and the authors are unable to link political socialization to change empirically, then what is the relationship between political socialization and systems persistence? The answer to this question depends upon fathoming just what is really meant by system persistence.

In the Easton and Dennis formulation,

> a political system persists when two conditions prevail: where its members are regularly able to allocate valued things, that is, make decisions; where they are able to get these allocations accepted as authoritative by most members most of the time (p. 49).

These two conditions are the "essential variables," the crucial life processes of "any political system." Unfortunately, by equating the life processes of a political system with the authoritative allocation of values, Easton and Dennis equate Easton's definition of politics with the persistence of political systems.

This formulation of persistence impels the authors to argue:

> In the society called the United States a political system has persisted over the centuries through the very fact that it has been able to change itself, radically, from a relatively decentralized federal system without extensive popular participation at its founding to one with a relatively high degree of political centralization and universal adult suffrage (p. 49).

Easton and Dennis' very abstract notion of a political system includes both the America of 1790 and 1970 since there was an authoritative allocation of values in the America of 1790 and the America of 1970. What has happened to the concept of change in this formulation? Was the American political system of

1790 the same as the American political system of 1970? Or was the czarist political system in Russia prior to 1917 the same as the Bolshevik system of 1925? Similarly, was the political system of France prior to 1789 the same as the political system of France after 1789? What has "persisted," according to Easton and Dennis, are the essential variables or central life processes of the system-allocative structures and processes in general. In this sense of persistence, a political system could not possibly fail to exist other than in the case of the destruction of the population. For, as long as there are human organisms in any semblance of social interaction, Easton and Dennis' definition of system persistence as the authoritative allocation of values still applies.

Thus, change appears swallowed up in a theory which is pitched at a sufficiently high level of abstraction that it loses empirical referents and hence can explain everything. Therefore, what most students of politics would normally call change is not system level change in the Easton and Dennis scheme. Questions of atomic war, civil liberties, changes from dictatorship to democracy, revolution, and the like are not directly relevant to the fact that political activity has occurred "over the centuries" in the same geographic location.

If one studies political socialization toward those "structures" which are related to the biological survival of an organism (and states and systems in this sense are hardly ever extinguished—one has to think about Carthage) then this persistence does not hinge upon the specific internal process for allocating values. Rather, persistence occurs simply when values are allocated. Then, one may ask, why study the development of children's attitudes toward the system at all? The relationship of political socialization to political change has been swallowed up in a vast abstraction. For, by admission and logical necessity, Easton and Dennis formulate a "political theory of political socialization" which sees as essentially peripheral the study of political socialization toward types of political orientations that could have implications for change with any sort of empirical referents. In so doing, they leave unanswered the question of the relationship of political socialization to change. Thus, they do not provide an alternative conception of the political socialization process which remedies the bias toward the status quo in the literature of which they are so critical. Their formulation of political socialization has no apparent connection with change beyond an assertion.[2]

Easton and Dennis' elegant attempt at reformulating the systems metaphor which underlies socialization research runs straight into a problem common to structural-functional approaches. In a sense, as Walter Buckley (1969) has pointed out, this kind of analysis

> represents the modern version of [a] biological model. [But] whereas mature organisms . . . cannot change their given structure beyond very narrow limits and still remain viable[,] this capacity is precisely what distinguished sociocultural sys-

[2]For an elaboration of this argument see Remy (1972). For other views of the Easton framework see Reading (1972) and Thorson (1970).

tems. . . . In effect, the specification of conditions essential for the persistence of any society . . . can tell us little about the particular structures it will develop to satisfy them, granted that persisting societies are meeting the requirements at or beyond the minimum level, the function concept itself provides no criteria for judging the widely varying levels and structural procedure *within* [emphasis in original] the system (pp. 14–16).

Our interest in Easton and Dennis' effort stems from the fact that it is an important attempt to reformulate the systems metaphor in a way which lays a base for a political theory of political socialization. Our skepticism about their success in relating political socialization to systems persistence in a meaningful way should not obscure their positive contributions. The problems inherent in Easton and Dennis' systems approach to socialization research are reflected in the research reviewed here. A primary difficulty is the complexity of the "answers" required when asking questions from a systems perspective. Systems analysis provides a helpful but abstract framework which offers few clues as to how complex phenomena, such as national integration, political attitudes, and "agents" of political learning are interrelated. Data generated by comparative socialization research informed by this systems metaphor tends to be massive yet little differentiated. Knowledge accumulated in such research has generally not been especially useful, therefore, in making general statements of interest about specific systems or specific statements about general systems. The ability to make a number of detailed, explicit, consensually shared, parsimonious statements about the nature of political systems still eludes political scientists.

Extant Research in Comparative Political Socialization

Since the concept of political socialization commonly refers to the induction of individuals into the prevailing political culture, it has naturally drawn researchers' attention to political learning about national political life and away from political learning relevant to other levels of political life. Thus, we will first consider *cross-national* research which has comparatively examined political socialization in different national political systems. Then we will consider a *cross-system level* approach to comparative political socialization research.

COMPARING POLITICAL SOCIALIZATION IN DIFFERENT NATIONAL SYSTEMS: BEFORE THE CIVIC CULTURE

Recent research on political socialization toward different national political systems was preceded by the contributions of scholars who concerned themselves with the formation of national character. Speculations on the roots of variances between nations are, of course, as old as recorded history. For centuries, scholars have sought to clarify the development of the "personality" of nations. The onset of the Second World War promoted the expansion of research which attempted to assess cultures alien to the American political system. Accurately describing the nature of the personality of nations became an urgent policy necessity under the press of war and the pressure of America's global preeminence and responsibility in the postwar environment. During the Second World War, studies of the childhood sources of the Nazi and Japanese character were found in works like Ruth Benedict's *The Chrysanthemum and the Sword: Patterns of Japanese Culture* (1946); Erich Fromm's *Escape from Freedom* (1941), Bertram Schaffner's *Fatherland: A Study of Authoritarianism in the German Family* (1948), and Margaret Mead and Rhoda Metraux's *The Study of Culture at a Distance* (1963).[3]

The effort to find the roots of national difference was accelerated in the mid-fifties by two events. First, there was a "non-aggression pact" between anthropologists and sociologists—each recognizing, after a long tendentious dispute, the validity of the other's vocabulary regarding the nature of culture and society. This allowed for greater interdisciplinary cooperation between those social sciences accustomed to crossnational research. Second, the advance of a comparative method was also prompted by a reinvigorated interest in exploring crossnational differences by political scientists. To no small extent, policy considerations continued to promote the expansion of research in this area. As Gabriel Almond (1956) explained:

> In the first place, American interests have broadened to include the many areas outside of Western Europe—Asia, the Middle East, Africa, and Latin America. Secondly, as our international interests have expanded and become more urgent, our requirements in knowledge have become more exacting. We can no longer view political crises in France with detached curiosity or view countries such as Indo-China and Indonesia as interesting political pathologies (p. 391).

It was Almond (1956) who creatively used established notions from sociology and anthropology to suggest that comparisons of different political systems would be aided by the concept of "political culture." This was a novel construct in the literature of social science. This concept established the critical linguistic convenience for the comparison of political systems which would avoid the "oversimplifications" of the national culture literature.

> Every political system is embedded in a particular pattern of orientations to political action. I have found it useful to refer to this as the *political culture*. There are two points to be made regarding the concept of political culture. First, it does not coincide with a given political system or society. Patterns of orientation to politics may, and usually do, extend beyond the boundaries of political systems. The second point is that political culture is not the same thing as the general culture, although it is related to it (Almond, 1956, p. 396).

[3]For excellent reviews of these various efforts see Brodersen (1957), DeVos (1968), DeVos and Hippler (1969), and Inkeles and Levinson (1969).

THE CIVIC CULTURE AND AFTER

The first sustained use of this notion of political culture was to appear some years later in Almond and Verba's *The Civic Culture* (1960). This landmark research sought to clarify the origins of support for democratic political systems. In *The Civic Culture,* Almond and Verba saw political socialization as involving the transmission of the political culture of a political system from one generation to another. The political culture was

> the political system as internalized in the cognition, feelings, and evaluations of its population. People are inducted into it just as they are socialized into non-political roles and social systems (p. 14).

The Civic Culture was a departure from the classic national character descriptions, if only that it lent the weight of survey evidence to observations previously made by others. Thus, although criticized for its ethnocentrism and methodological weaknesses, *The Civic Culture* marked what might be termed the "modern" era of comparative political socialization research. Since political socialization was considered one of the primary functions in the structural-functional model of Almond and Verba, *The Civic Culture* sought to offer an account of how childhood orientations in the United States, United Kingdom, Germany, Italy, and Mexico developed.

In examining the agents of socialization, Almond and Verba's purpose was to test the impact of nonpolitical authority experiences on political socialization. The authors felt that the most important socialization institutions were the family and the school; however, they also included the effect of job participation in their analysis. As a measure of participation, each respondent was asked three questions with respect to decision making in the family, school, and job: (1) How much influence would they have in decisions? (2) Were they free to protest decisions? (3) Did they actually protest?

Almond and Verba found participation within the family followed an identifiable pattern—United States, United Kingdom, high; Germany in the middle; and Italy and Mexico at the bottom. However, there was a sharp distinction between the United States and the other countries with respect to participation in school, with the United States displaying the highest rate of participation. Job participation followed the same pattern as the family. The authors concluded, "In general, respondents in the two nations where frequency of political participation seems to be highest (United States, United Kingdom) also report most frequent participation in non-political decisions" (p. 345).

In testing the impact of participation on civic competence, Almond and Verba found some connection between democracy in the family and democratic behavior in politics. However, this relationship was very complex and muted by intervening variables, primarily age and education. Participation in school discussions was positively related to civic competence in all countries except Italy. Further, there was a clear connection between teaching and attitudes toward civic competence, with civic competence appearing to be dependent on the content of the teaching.

Almond and Verba concluded that nonpolitical experiences had a cumulative effect on civic competence: e.g., the effect of participation in the family "added" to job participation had a greater impact on civic competence than participation in the family alone. They also acknowledged the probable importance of the impact of the structure of the political system on the development of civic competence.

One of Almond and Verba's major assumptions was that democratic institutions depend on democratic substructures, and this has been a recurring theme throughout the socialization literature. Thus, *The Civic Culture* helped considerably to narrow, perhaps prematurely, the focus of research on socializing agents to nongovernmental authority structures such as the family, school, job, or peer group. Most of the crossnational research that followed has also used survey data and concentrated on the relationship between political attitudes and one or another of the agents of socialization pointed out by Almond and Verba.

Since other research at the time of *The Civic Culture* found crossnational differences in Western European cultures with regard to partisan orientations (Davis & Verba, 1960; Campbell & Valen, 1961), the next step was to attempt to locate agencies "responsible" for these differences. Thus, in more recent years numerous investigators have attempted to expand the scope of crossnational research, as well as to investigate what socialization agencies may be related to partisan orientations. Dennis and McCrone (1970) sought to discover what factors lead to a "rising or falling level of mass commitment to the partisan institution," in Britain, France, West Germany, Italy, Belgium, and Holland. The authors found "a generally consistent pattern of growth of partisan feeling well before voting age in all of these countries" (p. 131). The British appear to be the earliest to take on a partisan political identification and the French the latest, with the Italians resembling the French.

To what extent is children's attainment of party identification related to parental transmission? Dennis and McCrone reported:

> French parents to a low degree reproduce their political preferences in their children, and such partisan images as are reproduced early are not as likely to be parentally reinforced as the child grows older. In Britain and Germany, by contrast, wider influence of parents is indicated and the influence becomes extended as children get older (p. 132).

Pinner (1972) further investigated Almond and Verba's (1963) finding that civic cooperation grew out of such experiences as an individual's participation in family or school decisions. Thus, Pinner attempts "to show a relationship between parental overprotection and negative orientations toward political processes and institutions" (p. 98). Using data from Belgian, French, and Dutch university students, Pinner found that Belgian and French young people felt less capable of handling the environment beyond the family circle than did the Dutch students. He concluded that political distrust is positively related to family over-protection and that political disaffection shows a similar, although less strong, relationship.

Elder (1968), using the five-nation data of *The Civic Culture* study and an eclectic collection of other data sources, attempted to assess secular trends in parent-youth relationships since 1900. Elder concluded, in reaffirmation of *The Civic Culture* findings,

> that the greatest increase in the prevalence of democratic parent-youth relations oc-curred in the three urban nations followed by Italy and then Mexico. Forces promoting social change generally emanate from urban centers where technology, education and communications systems are most developed. Thus, one probable source of change toward democratic family patterns would be the urbanization of a society: the move-ment of rural families to the city and the influence of urban-industrial areas on the hinterland (pp. 219–220).

Elder's findings are predictable in light of *The Civic Culture*. However, secondary analysis is rare in political science and Elder's study is a welcome exercise, for most comparative socialization research has tended to be autistic; i.e., it has not sought to replicate the research of others. Rather, researchers have sought conceptual breakthroughs by generating "new data" about previously uninvestigated political systems. As a result, cumulative inquiry has been inhibited.

THE ORIGINS OF REGIME SUPPORT

In a sense, all socialization studies are about "regime support." This is the case because socialization is usually taken to mean "the inculcation of ideas, symbols, and disciplines that are part of the general culture.... [P]roper so-cialization ... is essential to that social unity on which political institutions must rest" (Sutton, 1965, pp. 51–52). But most scholars, by studying agents of socialization or congruence between different socialization agencies, do not explicitly ask the question, "How is regime support related to political learn-ing?" This has, however, long been the explicit concern of Easton and his associate Dennis.

Dennis, Lindberg, McCrone, and Stiefbold (1968) sought to measure general support for major themes of democracy among 8- to 15-year-olds in the United States, Great Britain, Italy, and Germany. These themes were: participant de-mocracy as measured by political efficacy questions; liberal democracy as mea-sured by tolerance of minority dissent survey items; and pluralist democracy operationalized by support for a competitive party system. Clearly, this research is related to the interests of *The Civic Culture* and could have made an effort to corroborate that research and, if possible, give it further elaboration. The ques-tions, however, were not really comparable to those used in *The Civic Culture*, but instead were extensions of the 1962 survey undertaken in the United States by Easton, Hess, Torney, and Dennis (Hess & Torney, 1967; Easton & Dennis, 1969).

In each of the four nations Dennis and his colleagues surveyed, it was found that, increasingly with age, students displayed a willingness to endorse the idea that "democracy is the best form of government." However, British support consistently lagged behind the other three countries.

The authors also expected to find that the efficacy levels in the different countries would mirror the ratings of civic competence found in *The Civic Culture*. The results, however, were such that they defied meaningful comparisons. The authors did find that levels of support for dissent at the oldest age group (15 years) were greatest in Great Britain and lowest in Germany. But the developmental trends appeared upward in Great Britain, the United States, and Italy, while the German pattern was mixed. With regard to support for a competitive party system, the authors noted:

> Age trends in party system support... generally go up in all four countries.... However, the United States is the only one of the four that shares both a consistent trend upward in pro-party system support and a decline in sentiment against the party system (p. 51).

There was also a tendency in the German sample to support a one-party system. This led the authors to conclude that Germans may prefer expert and objective means of solving conflict rather than allowing the solution to emerge from party competition. The Italian results suggested that political parties are seen as necessary but often harmful. The English also exhibited mixed feelings. In summary, the youth of these nations moved progressively to a set of orientations more favorable to their respective party systems.

In investigating the roots of support for the British political system, Dennis and another group of associates (1971) noted the "special character of English political learning prior to adulthood and how much learning relates to problems of stability and change in the British Political System" (p. 27). The authors uncovered what they considered to be rather striking findings. First, less than half the respondents at each age level (8–10, 11–13, 14–17) agreed with the statement that Britain is the best country in the world and nearly 25% at each level strongly disagreed.

With respect to affective orientations toward government, between 40% and 50% of the respondents thought that government was not necessary and almost 30% thought government did more harm than good. When asked the frequency of error by government, only 35% of the British students responded in the "rarely" or "never" category while comparable percentages for Americans, Germans, and Italians were 66%, 44%, and 60%. To the authors the results raised serious questions as to the viability of the British political system.

> However firm our beliefs and how much traditional wisdom gives us to understand that the British system is stable, we may nonetheless profit by calling into question

such cherished assumptions. Britain has indeed enjoyed remarkable progress and steady evolution of her political order. The bedrock of this happy constancy has been formed in a homogeneous political culture and wide public regard for strong government. Can the continuity of this system be maintained in the indefinite, or even into the relatively near, future?

The "frailty of system-legitimization" of "Young Albion," as the authors put it, may, however, not be as woeful a condition as they indicate. To imply that British "loyalty and secure sense of national identity" is "not so firm" as it might once have been (p. 31) is to deny the British the capacity to assess their objective situation as a people relative to others in global society. Clearly, Britain is not what it used to be. To expect that British youth believe that times have not changed is benighted, and perhaps a bit insulting. The implication of this attitude is that a society must live with illusions or fall by virtue of having faced unblinkingly an unfortunate state of affairs.

Moreover, as Professor Budge (1971) commented:

One of the reasons why, on the moral level, we approve of democracy is the freedom it provides for internal criticism and discussion. Why then on the empirical side should such criticism be regarded as undermining a democratic regime? On the contrary its absence may be more dangerous. There is also a danger—since we do intend to make use of empirical conclusions in our moral recommendations—that if legitimate criticism is used empirically as an indicator of disaffection, we may try to suppress or avoid it when making policy recommendations. In the end this tendency could sharpen conflict rather than promote healthy adjustment (p. 390).

Using questions and the American data from the Easton-Dennis, Hess-Torney effort of the 1960s, Abramson and Inglehart (1970) attempted to ascertain systemic support amongst samples of 8- to 17-year-olds in the Netherlands, France, the United States, and Great Britain. Noting that young Americans see the President as the benevolent contact point of the political system, the authors ask: "Does this pattern hold true in other political systems with other types of chiefs of state?" Since "most stable democracies are monarchies," they assert, the "monarch . . . may . . . be a key of legitimacy" because monarchical authority resembles parental authority. A monarch, like a parent, has lifetime tenure. Like a parent, a monarch attains position according to rules of kinship. The monarch reaches office without the possibly confusing and anxiety-producing conflicts which surround the selection of elected chiefs of state. The monarch may also be highly visible to children. The more colorful and concrete pageantry of politics—the part that would be most striking to young children—tends to center on the monarch. Thus, Abramson and Inglehart hypothesize, a child tends to transfer positive affect from parent to monarch and thence to the political system as a whole.

The authors were unable to use the English data to examine trust levels but in all three European nations it was found that the prime minister was not the functional equivalent of the monarch or the American President in terms of children's affective orientations. The prime minister is seen as powerful but not especially benevolent. For the prime minister is seen as a largely partisan representative of a "more abstract concept . . . the two-party system, democracy (or [the] rule of law)." Presumably, Holland is more stable than France, in part because it has a monarchical symbol of authority that the French system does not possess.

By and large, research on political socialization in developed countries has labored in one of two related fields. Either this research has reanalyzed the questions and at times the data of *The Civic Culture,* or it has structured inquiry around questions that relate childhood orientation to authority to the stability of political systems.[4] Studies which are informed by the theoretical concerns of *The Civic Culture* are more interested with identifying those mixes of orientation within a population which might contribute to "modernity" or a "participant political culture." On the other hand, those studies informed by the research questions first elaborated by Hess and Easton and Greenstein are more directed toward divining the relationship between attitudes about leadership and the structure of the political system. However, toiling in fields with similar research designs and with even the same goals in mind should not be taken as an indication of a cumulative enterprise which would help elaborate the original research statement. For most of the work in cross-national political socialization has been fragmentary. It has rarely sought to retest original hypotheses—whether they stem from the work of Almond and Verba or studies which concern themselves with the interface between psychological orientations toward authority and the structure of political systems.

NEW TECHNIQUES OF CROSS-NATIONAL SOCIALIZATION RESEARCH

An interesting development in cross-national socialization research has been the use, by a handful of researchers, of a semiprojective research methodology rather than a survey approach. Thus far, this technique has been restricted to studies on Western Europe and the United States. Greenstein (1970a, 1973, 1975) and Greenstein and Tarrow (1969, 1970a, 1970b) have used this method to look at 10- to 12-year-old French, British, and American children's images of government and politics.

[4]An exception is Inglehart's (1967) study of French, West German, Dutch, and British adolescents' orientations toward political integration. Inglehart found that European youth had different, more favorable attitudes toward increasing integration than did older generations of European elites. He predicted integration would advance as the young generation became a majority of the voting population in Common Market countries and attributed this commitment to European integration to "differences in the early socialization of different age categories."

Principal findings indicate the level of political information in France is in sharp contrast to that of the United States and Great Britain. In the United States and Britain virtually all the children knew who the president or prime minister was and about half could give fairly detailed descriptions of the role. In France, while almost all could name the president, only 13% could give the sort of detailed descriptions received from the English and American samples. Greenstein concludes that this data supports previous studies indicating that subtle social divisions in France are based on mass political apathy and indifference rather than on consciously sensed ideological cleavage in the electorate.

With regard to affective orientations, only 50% of the United States sample showed positive affect toward the president, with 50% in the neutral category. In Britain the queen was mostly seen in a favorable light while the prime minister was given a neutral rating. In France all political figures received a neutral rating. The British view of the prime minister was richly articulated in spite of the absence of a formal curriculum in civic education. Americans, on the other hand, tended to focus on the president's international role and did not have the breadth in description characteristic of British children.

Gallatin and Adelson (1970, 1971) have also used a semiprojective technique. In two studies utilizing a sample of American, British, and German 10- to 18-year-olds, the authors focused on traditional questions in political philosophy, particularly the relationship of public goods to individual rights and legal guarantees of individual freedom. Students in all three countries displayed an emerging sociocentric orientation in late adolescence. With regard to such socially desirable objects as vaccinations and education, older children gave much more sophisticated, community-oriented reasons for providing the services and were much more likely to recommend harsh treatment for the recalcitrant than were younger children.

In the examination of legal guarantees of individual freedom, Gallatin and Adelson analyzed the students' evaluation of two potentially intrusive laws (a suggestion that men over 45 be required to have a yearly medical checkup and that people be required to paint their houses at least once every five years) by asking students to state whether or not individual freedoms ought to enjoy certain legal safeguards. Older subjects were both more aware that the proposed laws might constitute an invasion of privacy and more interested in obtaining legal guarantees of individual liberties, even in the event of an emergency. As in the examination of public goods, the developmental results were most striking. The authors take their results as evidence that certain cognitive orientations, such as ideologies, form later in adolescence.

Gallatin and Adelson's research does yield some difference in the "national ideology" of the teenagers they interviewed. The Germans showed "a docile, dependent, almost child-like attitude toward government authority." The American children scored highest on "Benthamite" calculations of what would be the greatest good for the greatest number, at the same time allowing for volunteer compliance and the opportunity to depart from the public good as long as the public welfare is not endangered. The British children did not stress the individual's obligation to the community. Rather, they saw the government as a disinterested referee, setting down and enforcing the rules of the game. By and large, these national differences are congruent with the observations of *The Civic Culture*.

Thus, while Gallatin and Adelson introduce no new variables or startling findings, they, like Greenstein and Tarrow, offer a new perspective. As Greenstein and Tarrow (1969) point out, the problems inherent in forced response survey items are likely to increase in severity in a crossnational setting. Children and adolescents' open-ended responses to questions involving subject matter with which they are likely to be familiar, or at least have an opinion, provide an alternative to forced-choice survey questions.

The subject matter of Urie Bronfenbrenner's research presents another new perspective in the literature of political socialization. Bronfenbrenner, as an exchange scientist at the Institute of Psychology in Moscow in 1963–1964, was able to test the hypothesis that

> in the Soviet Union, in contrast to America or England, children are less likely to experience peer pressure as conflicting with adult values and hence can identify more strongly with adult standards for behavior (1967, p. 199).

To Bronfenbrenner, American peer group relations, especially in the school, tend to reinforce the anomic capitalist and competitive values of the society as a whole, while the Soviet system stresses group achievement, cooperative inquiry, and group discipline, thus reflecting the communist ethic of the Soviet system.

In his study of peer groups, Bronfenbrenner (1967) concluded that United States children would be more likely to engage in antisocial behavior under the influence of peers than if alone or with adults, while in the Soviet Union peer groups reinforce compliance with norms. This results from the fact that from a very early age the Soviet peer group becomes a significant other that helps control the young person. Bronfenbrenner also discusses the widespread use of education techniques developed by Anton S. Makarenko, which stress character education as the primary purpose of schools and rely on the peer group as the major socializing agent.

Unlike Soviet society where the peer group is coopted as a socializing force and influenced heavily by adult society, American peer groups are autonomous. To a large extent, they develop their own behavior norms and are a primary example of what Bronfenbrenner sees as an increasing segregation by age in the United States. Given the part played by peer groups in Soviet socialization, one might expect to find that American parents are closer to their children. However, Bronfenbrenner's observations failed to support this conclusion (1967).

Like the Coleman Report (1968), Bronfenbrenner reached the conclusion that the most important factor in student academic achievement was the characteristics of other children attending the same school and, perhaps even more important, the characteristics of the children in the same classroom. These findings tend to be confirmed by Langton's (1967) study of Jamaican and American student peer groups. Langton found in Jamaica that lower-class students whose friends are all from the lower class are likely to hold political attitudes characteristic of the lower class, but that lower-class students in "heterogeneous class peer groups" which include higher class students, are likely to support higher

DEVELOPING COUNTRIES IN COMPARATIVE POLITICAL SOCIALIZATION STUDIES

As the discussion to this point indicates, comparative political socialization research has been primarily a Euro-American enterprise. Very few studies have focused upon developing nations, even though the function of political socialization within developing nations may be different from the function served by socialization in developed nations. For, despite the basic premises of structural-functional analysis, it may not always be possible to locate meaningful, functionally equivalent structures within developing and developed nations.

Structural-functional explanations assume that a principal function (goal) of all systems is that they seek to survive, adapt, or somehow perpetuate themselves (Davis, 1959; Almond & Powell, 1966). Thus, it is only possible to compare structures for achieving this function if the function (goal) is found in all the systems being compared. However, examination of "system behavior" and the behavior of politically active elements within the emerging nations gives us uneven evidence for concluding that the goals of these systems are necessarily stability, adaption, or preservation as we think of those functions in the context of western developed nations. The "system goals" of these nations may, in fact, be to build in a capability for adaptation to rapid systemic change. If this is the case, the role of political socialization could be entirely different (Sklar, 1967).

Nevertheless, the argument for examining other political systems, given political socialization's focus on regime stability and on democratic norms, is compelling. If research is limited to only the systematic processes of developed nations, then we can say little conclusively about the relation of these processes to system stability or persistence until the developed systems under investigation conclusively change in their stability or persistence. On the other hand, "developing" societies are changing by definition. In the abstract, at least, we might be able to observe developing systems in order to find an indication of how the process of socialization interacts with regime change so as to more fully elaborate the functional process of political socialization, a process acknowledged to be common to all political systems.

With this in mind, we will consider the few studies which have comparatively examined political socialization in developing and nonwestern nations. In 1967 Koff and Von der Muhll studied Kenyan and Tanzanian primary and secondary school students. One of the basic suppositions of this study was that "the schools of East Africa form the principal means through which the socialization of East Africans proceeds" (p. 18).[5]

Students in both countries reported they had learned most about being good citizens from teachers, rather than from parents and relatives, or from government leaders and religious leaders. While the students rated mass media as their primary source of information with teachers second, much of the exposure to mass media—newspapers and radio—was found to take place in school. Students in both countries also reported that the most important purpose of the school was to teach students to be good citizens.

Students were asked to pick attributes of a good citizen. Obedience to authority was the most frequently mentioned attribute in both countries. For primary pupils education was seen as the mark of a good citizen, but the relationship dropped off significantly for secondary school students. Working hard and interest in government shared about the same level of importance for older students. Though the political leadership in each country had wished to preserve tradition, the students clearly rated developmental and modernizing problems as more important than preserving tradition and customs. The authors concluded that citizens of Kenya and Tanzania would in the future be

> citizens for whom hard work counts for more than political activism, for whom traditions have lost their hold without being replaced by political ideology, for whom educational advantage has not led to a demand for privilege, for whom strong support for the existing political regimes is mixed with a disposition towards critical appraisals of individual performance in political roles (p. 51).

In an analysis of data from the United States, Chile, Puerto Rico, Australia, and Japan, Hess (1963) examined children's perception of political authority figures. The children were asked to rate their president or prime minister by answering questions that were eventually grouped into three attitude scales: benevolence, honesty, and competence. Respondents were grouped into three age groups (7–9, 10–12, 13+) and changes measured in the three attitude scales across age groups.

Hess concluded that children's early attitudes toward political authority figures arise from psychological needs as well as from the definitions of authority that come to them from experience. In one of the first expositions on this relationship between authority needs and political order he wrote:

> The child's concept of authority figures is derived from [H]is experience with his own parents, children's books, television and comics and the superior position of such persons as well as the respect they receive is evident. To the child, authority is defined not only as superior but as exceedingly powerful. In comparison with his father and his mother, he sees himself as relatively helpless. He is not only physically inferior,

---

[5]The authors do, however, note that the majority of East Africans in these age groups do not attend school.

he is also dependent upon adults for the most elementary aspects of physical and emotional care. In short, he is weak, dependent and vulnerable.

The response of the child to this feeling of vulnerability is to reassure himself that the authority figure is benign and that he will protect the child rather than harm him. He sees authority figures as benign because it is too threatening to see them malevolent. This tendency (which also applies to his view of parents) is a psychological technique for dealing with the feelings of powerlessness, and perhaps with his own feelings of aggression toward authority. We propose, then, that the child's image of political authority is designed to cope with his feeling of vulnerability and of aggression with regard to superior power (p. 549).

Reading (1972) used the Easton-Hess questions to compare the political socialization of fourth grade through secondary students in the United States and Colombia. Interestingly, whereas Americans showed increasingly with age a more favorable disposition toward their country, the Colombian sample evidenced just the opposite trend. When asked to write essays about government or country, the Colombia children's answers were negative, even derogatory— varying from laments about the quality of life to the quality of Spanish. Such answers, Reading points out, are not at all congruent with the kind of responses Greenstein (1965) found in his study of American fourth through eighth graders.

Congruent with the findings of Jaros (1968) and Arterton (1974, 1975), Reading suggested there is no inherent need in children to view political authority benevolently. To Reading, the process of developing supportive regime norms "may have to be reinforced (or perhaps even initiated) by the agency of socialization itself" (p. 376). Reading's data further suggested that it was social and religio-moral aspects of Colombia and not political ones which most impressed students; e.g., when asked, "which things about Colombia impress you most," 75% of the Colombian students included, "Colombia is a Catholic country." No other response category was above 48%.

In a study in Chile and Peru, Goldrich (1970) examined the effects of political organization and political situations on the political socialization of adults by interviewing individuals in four urban squatter settlements. Goldrich found that "the least physically developed, the least legally established, and socioeconomically lowest of the settlements . . . is by far the most politicized" (p. 51). Hypothesizing that the difference between the high and low groups could be party organization, Goldrich controlled for that variable and found in all cases that the nonaffiliated are least politicized and the affiliated the most. Goldrich draws the conclusion that adults, previously inexperienced and uninvolved in politics, learn to engage in and sustain complex political demand making under certain circumstances: (1) a sense of acute need; (2) a perception of strategy of action adequate to meeting needs; and (3) the availability of an organization to channel the action. He concludes:

We have tended to look at the process of political socialization in too unstructured a fashion, the primary model being one of gradual learning. . . . But increasingly numerous revolutionary cases call attention to the extra-ordinary amount of mass political socialization of adults, as well as children, through organizations designed to produce new men by channeling their behavior (p. 73).

A suggestive anthropological study of the roots of political authority was undertaken by LeVine (1972) who has examined undifferentiated, primitive societies where the family or kin system is almost coterminous with the political system. In examining two stateless societies with segmentary lineage systems, the Nuer and the Gusii, he found marked contrast. The Nuer were reluctant to accept authority roles, while the Gusii welcomed such positions. The Nuer emphasized personal independence and accepted direction from others with extreme reluctance while Gusii had no such difficulty in displaying deference to those of higher status. LeVine suggests these experiences can be attributed to

> socialization into the authority structure of the family [which] leaves [individuals] with values and role expectations . . . adoptive in socio-political units above [nuclear] family level. Because of the convention between the early family environment of the child and the political system, it is reasonable to expect differences in the early learning experiences of typical individuals in Gusii and Nuer societies (p. 69).

Thus, LeVine concludes, the individual's attitudes toward authority are a function of early relationships with parents. Gusii fathers are disciplinarians while Nuer fathers are warm and playful. Gusii families emphasize sibling cooperation and adult adjudication of childhood disputes. The Nuer, on the other hand, set a high value on individual independence, self-assertion, and aggressive achievement.

LeVine hypothesizes that parent-child-sibling relations can be seen as a "model" of the authority system of the wider society in stateless political systems, but in more complex societies such simple congruences are less likely. As social stratification, differentiation, and multigovernmental level integration occur in a given society, primary socialization will have less impact on the political system. This implies that factory, school, and "systemic" outputs are the important agents of political socialization. Thus, childhood socialization in the family is but one of a plethora of processes and, if one is to understand the process completely, perhaps the analytic unit might necessarily have to be shifted from the individual to the political system itself if inquiry is to profitably proceed.

COMPARING NATIONAL SYSTEMS WITH POLITICAL SYSTEMS AT OTHER LEVELS OF SOCIAL ORGANIZATION

We have examined several kinds of cross-national socialization studies. First, those which deal with developed societies—chiefly, those limited to the original theoretical/empirical studies of Almond and Verba or Hess, Easton, and Greenstein. Second, we have surveyed studies that use "projective" or nonsurvey techniques to elucidate some of the richness of orientations toward various aspects of political culture. In addition, we have looked at the limited extant research using two or more national samples taken from the Third World.

It should be emphasized, however, that this literature compares only national political systems. It does not compare subnational socialization to national political socialization. Nor does it compare supranational socialization to national socialization or subnational socialization. In other words, designs using various systemic levels of analysis have, for the most part, not been utilized. This is not to discount the impact or importance of purely national political socialization. Systemic differences in China and the United States may be related to differences in the political learning of American or Chinese children. Yet children are members of many different political systems at the same time (Guetzkow, 1955; Jennings, 1967; Remy et al., 1975). Much like a cobweb, these systems overlap and interpenetrate but are distinguishable (Burton, 1972). Just as in the Middle Ages when individuals were subjects of local fiefdoms, larger kingdoms, and the Holy Roman Empire, so today individuals are simultaneously members of a multiplicity of overlapping and interpenetrating political systems. The typical American is thus a member of the international political system, the American national political system, and a variety of state and local level political systems.

Children are exposed to the notion that there are different and distinguishable levels of politics and government in a variety of ways. In the elementary grades the social studies curriculum is frequently compartmentalized into segments dealing with community helpers and neighborhood life, the political history of the United States and world geography and history. At the high school level, separate courses on such topics as local or state politics, national government and world affairs further elaborate the idea of the individual's membership in several political systems. Each of these systems has the potential for affecting the individual's life in different but often related ways. Outside of school, for both children and adults, the mass media regularly "sorts" the barrage of stimuli from the political environment into such categories as community affairs, local and state news, national news, and world news.

We should, therefore, also expect systemic differences in political systems at other levels of social organization to be related to preadult learning about these systems. Research that would proceed along this path would be predicated on two assumptions:

1. Systems such as national, local, and international systems are cases within a population of analytically comparable systems.

2. Political socialization is a process common to all levels of political systems.

Comparative cross-system level research examines similarities and differences in the political socialization process of the various political systems individuals confront. Both cross-system level and cross-national comparative socialization research view the political characteristics of different political systems as related to the political socialization process toward these systems. The idea is simply that "different political systems by virtue of their structure, their laws, and their distribution of authority impel people to develop specific political attitudes and behavior" (Sigel, 1970, p. 491). The notion that political structure can affect political socialization is not, of course, new. In fact, Sigel (1970) reminds us that "at one time it had been thought, perhaps somewhat naively, that alternations in governmental structure would almost *ipso facto* engender new political behaviors" (p. 491).

Political systems with different structural characteristics may offer preadults different stimuli for political learning. Such stimuli are mediated through agents of socialization like the family or schools, or intrude directly into the preadults' world as in television coverage of a presidential speech or a street scene involving a policeman. Differences in the direct and indirect stimuli offered by political systems with varying structural characteristics may hold important consequences for the developmental staging of the learning process, the imagery of the system that preadults develop, and the nature and strength of the attitudes and behavior patterns they acquire in regard to the system.

Easton and Dennis (1969), e.g., note that the very nature of the socialization process requires that there be "structural linkages" or "contact points" between the political system and the child. In *Children and the Political System,* they found the structure of the American political system to be such that through the presidency it offered contact points or stimuli for young children which affected both the developmental sequence of the socialization process and the imagery of the system children developed. They concluded:

> In systems where authority objects are less capable of losing their abstract character—where they are less amenable to being personalized, to being made highly visible and salient, or where the collectivity of authorities cannot readily be typified by a few strategic individuals or types or roles—we would expect the child to establish contact with the system less readily, more clumsily and abstractly, and probably at a later, less impressionable age (p. 324).

James Rosenau (1967) has also suggested that the structural characteristics of political systems influence the behavior of individuals within those systems. While Easton and Dennis do not delineate the possible categories of variables around which propositions linking political structure and political learning might be constructed, Rosenau links the nature of domestic and international political phenomena to motivational and role variables among individuals. In essence, he argues, it appears that the "structure of the two areas" elicits different motivations and touches different roles among adults with respect to political issues found within their national and international political systems (p. 29).

The difference between cross-national and cross-system level comparative socialization research is that cross-system level research compares learning about national political systems to learning about political systems at other levels of organization: e.g., a research question of interest in this area is how American youth relate to local, state, national, and international political systems.[6]

One study of this type was undertaken by Jennings (1967). By constructing a "cosmopolitan scale," Jennings placed a national probability sample of American high school seniors on a continuum in terms of their focus on the different political systems (local, state, national, and international) of which they were members. In so doing, he argued:

> There is an understandable tendency in political studies to focus on one system at a time, as in community studies or in national participation studies. In so doing some of the richness and complexity of how man relates to his political environment is sacrificed. Although it is conceivable that man confronts and relates to each political system (or subsystem) in identical ways, this seems most unlikely, given the institutional and behavioral varieties accompanying the different systems of which he is a member (p. 292).

The twelfth graders surveyed evidenced a greater level of interest in national and international affairs than in state and local level affairs. Nearly one fifth of the students ordered their interest in direct correspondence to the step-like geopolitical dimension of international, national, state, and local. In the aggregate, Jennings found that "the students lean much more toward the larger systems and higher levels than toward smaller systems and lower levels, more toward cosmopolitan rather than a provincial orientation" (p. 296).

Remy and Nathan (1974) used a national elite sample of 1,811 American high school seniors to compare political socialization toward the American national political system with political socialization toward the international system. The independent variable was the difference in the characteristics of the national and international system operationalized as the presence or absence of institutions of centralized political authority within each system. The dependent variable consisted of students' attitudes toward political phenomena associated with these two systemic levels as measured by the students' levels of optimism or pessimism in respect to the future of each system.

Specifically, the authors examined the hypothesis that students would display a more pessimistic orientation toward the future of a political system characterized by the lack of a centralized government (the international system) than toward the future of a political system characterized by the presence of government (their national system). To examine this hypothesis the authors constructed an optimism/pessimism scale. The respondents were asked to evaluate a series of 10 predictions about the future of their national political system and 10 predic-

---

[6]One study which bears a prima facie resemblance to others in this section is the study of Appalachian children by Jaros and his colleagues (1968). Jaros compares the political socialization of Appalachian children with that of children from other areas. If Appalachia constituted a political system, it could be considered a comparative study of political socialization in different systems. While Appalachia does possess some distinctive geopolitical characteristics, it does not exhibit an authority structure which allocates values.

tions about the future of international society. Optimism/pessimism scale scores from 0 (pessimistic) to 100 (optimistic) were created. The national mean for the sample was found to be 62.6 while the international mean was 48.3. These results supported the hypothesis that students viewed the future of international society with relatively more pessimism than the future of national society.

Both the Jennings and Remy and Nathan studies used a single sample of Americans to adduce preadults' orientations toward political systems at different levels of social organization. Comparing one sample of preadult orientations toward different levels of political systems appears to have a distinct methodological advantage. Such an approach builds in controls for factors which are usually confounding where more than one research population is used: e.g., if the research population were from two nations, say, Uruguay and the United States, and the research question were orientations toward authority at various levels of social organization, then intervening factors such as family structure, peer group interaction, and the like might make generalizations difficult. Analyzing one sample of preadults' orientations toward multiple levels of political systems helps to minimize problems of this type and provides a better opportunity to isolate the effect of the structural variations within the political system under study.

Finally, we may note that while political scientists usually concern themselves with governmental structure of one sort or another, an additional unexplored research alternative is the examination of both governmental and nongovernmental political systems across different national settings. Thus, one might study the political socialization that occurs toward school political systems in the Soviet Union and in the United States (Bronfenbrenner, 1970). In addition, one might contrast the political socialization which occurs in the American business firm with the socialization which occurs in an Israeli kibbutz, viewing both as political systems. In doing such a comparison, one would examine the extent to which the hierarchically and competitively structured business firm socialized its members differently than the communalistic ethic of kibbutz socialized its members. Further, one could probe the evolution of individual's orientations toward authority in each of these political systems. Such comparative study could help further illuminate the relationship between political structure and political learning.

Other Research Considerations in Comparative Socialization Research

What conclusions can be drawn from the existing research on comparative political socialization? Contrary to any impression which might be given by this review, it would be potentially very misleading for us to make specific inferences about political socialization patterns across the various nations represented in the studies reviewed here. Most of the existing research has labored in the same vineyard as Almond and Verba's *The Civic Culture* and this research owes a great intellectual debt to that landmark research. However, such a debt should not be mistaken for scientific elaboration. The research reviewed here is generally fragmentary and has used unduly varying samples of respondents, different research instruments, and a range of data analytic techniques to elicit previous work in different systemic settings.

It should be pointed out that the concept of political socialization has directed researchers' attention toward certain aspects of political learning and away from others. It has focused attention on that part of political learning related to the acquisition of the knowledge, attitudes, values, and skills necessary for the persistence of the ongoing political system. In so doing, it holds promise of helping political scientists to better understand an important facet of the human condition: viz., the regularities of human politics through time and space. However, the concept of political socialization has directed researchers' attention away from investigating political learning which is unorthodox and does not conform to the prevailing political culture. As a result, the current research we have surveyed here does not appear very useful in helping us to understand how and why political systems change, and how and why some individuals do not acquire political orientations acceptable to the political system of their society.

As we have seen, Easton and Dennis sought unsuccessfully to deal with this gravitation toward consensus. Yet, practically, the effect of adopting the socialization systems' perspective in national and crossnational research has been to focus comparative socialization research on what Litt (1969) has described as "citizen experience with the ballot box" (p. 1294). This ballot box approach is reflected in the dominant concern of most researchers with the development of young people's orientations toward various aspects of electoral politics, especially orientations toward political parties, voting, and officeholders and other regime incumbents. While Goldrich's study of squatter settlements in Latin America is somewhat of an exception, experiences with defiance, the policeman's mace, and processes of discontinuity and conflict have largely fallen outside the boundary of comparative research to date.

It is probably not surprising that American social scientists would use familiar conceptual "tools" to assess systems which are relatively uninvestigated or unfamiliar. Yet it is certainly an open question as to the significance of electoral politics in the political life of nonwestern and developing systems. Indeed, there is even considerable disagreement among political scientists as to the importance of the role of electoral politics in the United States today. Similarly, electoral politics as conventionally defined may play little or no role in the life of political systems at other levels (such as the international political system) which could be the subject of comparative political socialization research.

This point is worth expanding. The existing political socialization research on Americans assumes that the political experiences of preadults are circumscribed by the phenomena and institutions of the adult political world, such as the mayor, the President, voting, the Congress, political parties, and the like. This assumption has made its way into the comparative research we have reviewed. This research has helped clarify what and when children learn from their encounters with aspects of the adult political system as this intrudes into their world—whether in a deliberate lesson by a socializing agent, in a TV program, or in a street encounter involving a policeman. Current research, however, sheds light on only one portion of the totality of political learning. It is the portion accounted for by stimuli from the adult political world. But the world from which children are learning also encompasses the political phenomena that arise from children's daily interpersonal experiences with peers and adults.

In our view, then, the "political world" of preadults consists of two "dimensions." The first involves preadults' awareness of and attitudes toward such things as governmental authorities and political parties. In addition, it includes preadults' fleeting encounters with the physically and psychologically distant world of "adult politics," such as exposure to political news on television, overheard adult conversations about matters like elections, explicit instruction by adults (e.g., "we are Democrats"), and experiences with "political figures" such as policemen.

The second dimension consists of the politics and governance of preadults' everyday life. This is the political world children encounter in the course of their relations with parents, teachers, other school personnel, peers, older children, and a wide variety of adults in neighborhood and community settings. In their daily experience, children deal with phenomena and problems that political scientists consider to be fundamental ingredients of political life. These include leadership and followership, cooperation and conflict, influence and power, authority and legitimacy, rules and compliance.

There is a sizable literature in psychology, education, and sociology from which we know a good deal about the phenomena that characterize children's interpersonal world; about children's cognitive, social, and behavioral capacities; and about their processes of learning and development. This literature contains insights and findings that seem full of political relevance. These can serve as a rich source of ideas for the gathering of data and the identification of variables. They do not, however, shed direct light on the question of political learning that results from children's encounters with the political dimensions of their everyday world because they do not approach this world with a political question in mind.

In short, neither students of politics nor students of children have so far provided knowledge about the political content of the interpersonal world of children's daily experience or about the political learning that results from living in and adapting to this world. If we are to extend and deepen our understanding of the development of political values, beliefs, and behavior, then this gap in our knowledge of political learning should be remedied.

To remedy this gap, new and imaginative research designs and data collection techniques are needed. Comparative research to date has generally used survey techniques and questions adopted from studies of adults. Few studies have sought to measure children's political skills and abilities and most studies have been descriptive rather than explanatory.

There is a need for conceptual/theoretical development; for a concern with *how* the child develops politically. There is a need to investigate forms of political learning appropriate to the age level being observed rather than being superficially similar to adult attitudes of which they might be precursors. There is a need for a multimethod approach to gathering data (such as ethnographic techniques) rather than relying solely upon survey research techniques. New knowledge generated by research on the politics of children's everyday life can help deepen our understanding of how humans develop politically. Further, such knowledge can have practical application in school contexts.

Is a Political Theory of Political Socialization Possible?

We have suggested some new modes of comparative political socialization research because they may have the potential to facilitate movement toward the development of what Easton and Dennis (1969) have called a "political theory of political socialization." Easton and Dennis have distinguished three types of possible theories about socialization. The first type, they explain, would be a "general theory of socialization" capable of describing and explaining at the most general level "the way in which socialization occurs, regardless of subject area" (p. 18). The second type, a "theory of political socialization," would be designed to understand "the way in which socialization occurs in the political sphere" (p. 18). The last type of theory Easton and Dennis call a political theory of political socialization. Its objective, they note, "would be to demonstrate the *relevance* of socializing phenomena for the operations of political systems" (p. 18). The thrust of this third type of theory should be to explore the position of socializing processes in the operation of "any and all kinds of political systems" (p. 19).

Thus, a theory of children's political learning of value to political scientists would have to, in essence, combine the second and third types of theories of socialization Easton and Dennis describe. Treating children's learning as a process of political socialization into the political culture of political systems requires the development of two sets of interrelated propositions. The first of these would link children's socialization to the structure and configuration of the political system under study. These propositions would be concerned with the extent to which the particular characteristics of political phenomena in the system under study influence the socialization toward these phenomena. The second set of propositions would link children's socialization to the operation and functioning of the systems which we wish to examine. These propositions would be concerned with the relationship of socialization in one system to the overall state of and operation of that system and to such systemic phenomena as modernization, conflict, and decision making.

Unfortunately, the first half of the embryonic theory under discussion here has not really been developed in the literature on political socialization. As we noted earlier, Easton and Dennis (1969) do consider the relationship between the structure of political systems and the orientations individuals develop toward these systems. However, their discussion is limited primarily to interpretive considerations of how the peculiar configuration of the American political system facilitates children's early learning about the system through a process of "personalization." While their work in this area is highly suggestive, Easton and Dennis do not delineate other possible categories of variables around which propositions linking children's political learning to the structure of the political system could be built. The discovery and categorization of individual variables such as personality, class, or an individual's position and role in the political system and structural phenomena such as arbitrary or democratic authority patterns, and the interrelationship between these two classes of variables is the next operational step in the evolution of a fully developed political theory of political socialization. The examination of analytically comparable political systems within and between nations will, undoubtedly, be a useful methodological addition to the elaboration of such a theory.

PART TWO

THE ROLE OF AGENTS
THROUGH THE LIFE CYCLE

4

The Role of Agents in Political Socialization

Paul Allen Beck

POLITICAL SOCIALIZATION RESEARCH has been characterized by two general perspectives. The first perspective, which I shall call the teaching perspective, conceives of political socialization as the process through which political orientations are taught. The second, or learning perspective, emphasizes the individual's own learning activities and development and relegates teaching per se to a secondary, though not unimportant, role. The teaching perspective implies that the individual is taught all of his political views—an assumption the learning perspective would emphatically deny.

One of the principal topics of political socialization research has been the role of the agents of socialization. An emphasis on the agents derives directly from the dominance of the teaching perspective in the field. Indeed, that the name of the field of study is "political socialization" reflects the dominance of this perspective.

> For example, to call the whole process "political socialization" would seem to imply more initiative on the part of the socializer than of the socialized. By contrast, to refer to the process as 'political learning' probably places more emphasis on the role of learner vis-à-vis the teacher (Dennis, 1968, p. 107).

To socialize, after all, is to teach something to someone. A preponderant concern with socialization rather than with individual learning, then, has elevated the question of the role of agents to center stage.

The dominance of the teaching perspective may be traced to two primary sources. On the one hand, it reflects the overriding concern of the political scientist with macrolevel phenomena—the operations of political systems—and stability and change in political patterns over time. It is through its "agents" that the political system inculcates in new members the norms of political life—both traditional norms and new, revolutionary ones. In particular, those who have sought to explain why certain political patterns, such as democracy, persist from generation to generation are led inevitably to a consideration of the role of the agents of political socialization. No less importance has been assigned to the agents by those scholars who have studied the attempts of revolutionary regimes to solidify their positions. In both cases, the questions of who writes on the empty political slate with which the individual begins and what is written are critical.

The dominance of the teaching perspective and its corollary emphasis on the agents may be attributed also to the generative influence of the field's earliest contributors. Two of the eight chapters in Hyman's (1959) seminal review of literature on the learning of political orientations are devoted to the impact of the agents. The first broad-gauged empirical studies, those of Greenstein (1965) and the researchers at the University of Chicago (especially Hess & Torney, 1967), likewise gave considerable attention to the role of the agents. The efforts of these researchers contributed immeasurably to the subsequent development of the young field, magnifying for those who followed the importance of the agents. Imagine the difference, e.g., if Merelman's (1966, 1969, 1971a) research on the stages of cognitive development had been the first political science work on the child's political world.

The task of this chapter is to assess the state of research on this important topic of political socialization—the role of the agents. Since other chapters in this volume treat the more important agents in detail, I shall make no attempt to provide an exhaustive review of research. Rather, I shall restrict my focus to the empirical research designed to answer directly the question of the influence of each agent on individuals' political views. While this focus will not be confined to American studies, the paucity of empirical research on this question in other societies places limits on the extent to which this review may be generalized beyond the United States.

Some Preliminary Considerations

A preliminary consideration of some basic theoretical, methodological, and epistemological issues in the study of agental influence will simplify the review of research which follows.

THEORETICAL CONSIDERATIONS

The search for answers to the question of agent influence is complicated by substantial variations in the processes of socialization from individual to individual and from society to society. One common method of coping with such variation is to move to a higher level of abstraction, absorbing variability by organizing specifics along some common abstract dimension. One set of abstract guidelines which will prove useful in studying agent influence are the three preconditions for influence—exposure, communication, and receptivity.

The first precondition for the successful teaching of political views is exposure. The learner must come into contact with the teacher before socialization can be said to have taken place. Exposure to the most familiar agents of socialization—parents, peers, and school—in the United States, and probably other western societies as well, is sketched roughly in Figure 4–1. The horizontal dimension in this figure is the age of the individual. The vertical dimension is the percentage of all contact which is with a particular agent. Figure 4–1 shows that exposure varies considerably with agent and age. Understanding of the influence of various agents, including many not entered in Figure 4–1, could be enhanced substantially by the empirical specification of exposure curves. Furthermore,

Figure 4-1. "Rough" Estimates of Exposure to Agents

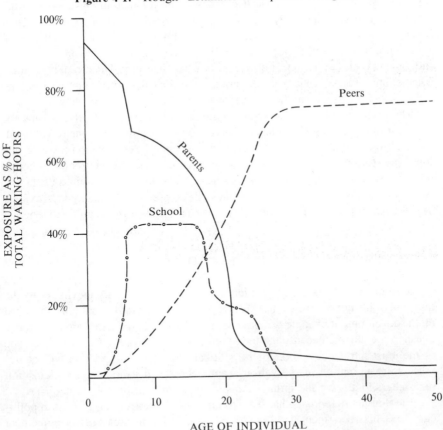

differences in the socialization process from one society or subculture to another may be explained by differential degrees of exposure to various agents, especially between modern and traditional societies.

While conducive to influence, exposure does not ensure influence. A second precondition—communications between agent and learner which have political content—must be considered as well. Where communications with political content do take place, some cues are more politically relevant than others. But, because even communications which have no manifest political content may influence the development of political orientations, the task of measurement along the communication dimension is difficult.

Even exposure and communication together do not guarantee agental influence. A third precondition must be considered: the receptivity of the learner to communications which come from a particular source. There are two aspects of receptivity which are important here. The first is the nature of the relationship between source and receiver. Strong emotional ties between these two certainly enhance receptivity. A second aspect of receptivity is the timing of the communication. Many socialization researchers have assumed that early learning is the most important learning because it is retained the longest and because it structures later learning. Recently, the validity of these assumptions has been challenged by several scholars (March, 1971; Searing et al., 1973). An alternative assumption is that, since specifically political behavior is not demanded of most individuals until adulthood, it may well be adult learning which molds political orientations. This question of the timing of critical learning must be resolved before socialization researchers can answer fully the question of agent influence.

These three factors—exposure, communication, and receptivity—are the preconditions for agental influence. Failure to satisfy any one of them will result in the absence of influence from that particular agent. Socialization research is a long way from precise measurement of any one of these preconditions, although the empirical identification of exposure curves may be within our reach. Nonetheless, a general awareness of these three preconditions should provide a useful backdrop as we move on to examine empirical evidence of influence.

METHODOLOGICAL CONSIDERATIONS

A study of the agents of political socialization brings us inevitably to the question of influence. How much influence has another individual (an agent) had on the development of some person's political views? Satisfactory answers to this question are elusive because the measurement of influence has proven to be one of the most intractable problems in political research. This section will be devoted to examination of the various approaches used by political socialization researchers to answer the influence question and the problems peculiar to each.

The dominant approach has been to infer influence from agreement in political views between agent and learner. Several different measures of agreement have been used. A common one has been simply the percentage of agents and learners who agree on a particular orientation. The virtue of this measure is that when we say 60% of parents and their children agree on party identification, we mean nothing less than a full 60% identify with the same party. A principal weakness of this measure is that percentage agreement can be affected by the fineness with which we have coded any particular variable; e.g., one would expect higher agreement on a three-category party identification variable than on the conventional seven-category version.

This problem may be solved in two different fashions. On the one hand, the percentage agreement measure may be standardized by subtracting from it the level of agreement expected by chance alone so that it is comparable across variables with different numbers of code categories (Beck, Dobson, & Bruner, 1975). The common approach, on the other hand, has been to utilize correlation coefficients as the measures of agreement. They have several advantages. Standardization and, thus, ready comparability across different variables is one. Another is that they add a new dimension to the meaning of agreement: they take into account the extent of disagreement—i.e., extreme disagreement in political views has a greater deflationary effect on the correlation coefficient than does only mild disagreement.

This advantage of the correlation coefficient is in turn eroded by a severe disadvantage, spelled out at length in the Weissberg and Joslyn chapter of this volume. As a measure of covariation, the correlation coefficient will show perfect association when there is no exact agreement in attitudes as long as the agent and the learner occupy the same positions along an attitudinal continuum relative to their peers. Perhaps one could argue that this is really an advantage—that reproduction of the same relative positioning is all one can expect from socialization in a changing society. But no one has used this justification of the correlation coefficient, and the Weissberg and Joslyn charge raises serious methodological questions about much of the research on the agents of political socialization. It remains to be seen how damaging this charge will be in substantive terms. Furthermore, there are problems with all alternative measures of agreement. Criticisms of the correlation coefficient seem destined to open even more, instead of closing, the debate over measuring influence.

The most valid use of the various measures of association comes in situations where there are independent observations of the political views of both agent and learner. These measures have also been used where the data are gathered from only one of the participants in the socialization process, typically by using the learner's perceptions of the agent's political views. A number of studies of agental influence depend on just this empirical base. Not only do these studies suffer from the problems already discussed, but they are flawed by a substantial bias toward higher agreement. Niemi (1974, pp. 45–77) has shown that the use of an individual's perceptions of the current views of significant others inflates agreement by at least 10%. This inflation surely increases when the respondent is called upon to recollect the political views an agent had some years before—e.g., the political views of parents when the respondent was a child. Because this problem of bias is a severe one and its magnitude has not yet been determined for a wide variety of orientations, studies using perceptual measures yield questionable results and will be ignored in this review.

Agental influences also have been measured in a few studies by comparing the aggregate distributions of the agent and learner. The more similar the two distributions are to one another, the more agental influence is inferred (Hess & Torney, 1967, pp. 120–132). The problems with the other measures are small in comparison to the pitfalls of these aggregate correspondences. Essentially, the aggregate measures lead researchers to commit the error of ecological inference—assuming that aggregate agreement is the result of individual agreement between agent and learner. Such an assumption is patently invalid in socialization research. Jennings and Niemi (1974, p. 214) have found, e.g., that aggregate agreement is higher between students and their social studies teachers than between students and their parents, but that the reverse is true at the individual level. Comparisons of aggregate distributions provide us with no evidence of agental influence. They too should be ignored as irrelevant to the question, and I shall do so in their review.

Up to this point, we have considered the problems involved in measuring agreement between agent and recipient. Our real interest, though, lies in the determination of agental influence. Agreement was the focus of attention only because it is the most common, and perhaps the only feasible, approach to answering the influence question. Yet, for the reasons spelled out below, inferring influence from agreement is a step fraught with danger.

First, agreement is not a necessary condition for influence. In the case of rebellion, e.g., the learner perceives the views of the agent accurately but adopts opposite views. Influence has surely taken place, for the agent has caused the learner to do something he would not have done otherwise. Yet this case would generate maximum disagreement using the conventional measures. Given this problem, it is fortunate for the measurement of influence through agreement that political rebellion seems rare in the United States (Lane, 1959; Middleton & Putney, 1963; Keniston, 1960, 1968). A second limit on the necessity of agreement for influence is that, where many agents are operating simultaneously, the influence of one cannot be expected to produce perfect agreement between that agent and the recipient. Again, influence will have taken place which is not reflected in the agreement scores.

It should be equally clear that agreement is not a sufficient condition for influence. Where the learner has not been exposed to an agent, agreement in political views would not be taken as evidence of agental influence. Even where exposure has taken place, agreement may derive from sources other than the agent. Both "agent" and "recipient" may have learned the same thing from some third party, or they may agree simply by chance. Another possibility is that several agents with similar views have contributed in unequal amounts to the views of the learner. Agreement is also not influence because it does not specify the direction of causality, while influence does. Perhaps this is best seen in the case of political interaction between husband and wife. If their views become more similar over time, who is the agent and who is the learner? Without additional information about previous views, this question cannot be resolved (Beck & Jennings, 1975).

Demonstrating influence is among the thorniest problems in any scientific research. It is best solved through the use of laboratory experiments in which exogenous forces can be controlled and the direction of influence manipulated. Unfortunately for social science research, yet fortunately for humans, these designs cannot be used in socialization research. Only in rare instances does "nature" provide quasi-experiments by isolating the interaction between a single agent and a learner or by bringing together agents who disagree. Thus, the fate of socialization research is that it must attempt to answer questions of agental influence under unfavorable conditions. This fact of life should not dim the ardor of socialization researchers. The question they are attempting to answer is an important one, worthy of considerable study. But the problems of measuring influence must make them cautious in drawing inferences about the role of agents in the socialization process.

EPISTEMOLOGICAL CONSIDERATIONS

Among the factors which shape the development of a field of study are the initial expectations of scholars concerning what they will find when they conduct empirical research. These expectations set the stage for research. They suggest the most important areas of inquiry, the kinds of hypotheses which should be framed, and sometimes even the data which should be used to test these hypotheses. Initial expectations also determine the weight which will be attached to subsequent research findings. One piece of confirmatory evidence will usually be accorded more attention than one piece of disconfirmatory evidence. Scholars seem to be satisfied when their expectations are confirmed, but they often search for methodological and other flaws in any study which fails to support these expectations.[1]

Initial expectations have played a particularly important role in shaping empirical research on the agents. These expectations have been derived from two basic assumptions about the process of political socialization. Searing et al.

---

[1]Within reason, this approach to empirical research is a sound one. Expectations formed by scholars should not be thought of as mere guesses. Rather, they are usually founded on a theoretical and assumptional base which has deductive coherence and, in many cases, corroboration in other fields of study. Furthermore, expectations and the theories from which they are derived are necessary to give data substantive meaning. Continual disconfirmation of expectations, though, should lead scholars to a reexamination of expectations and their theoretical and assumptional base. That scholars resist such reexaminations under these conditions attests to their needs, as human beings, for regularity and consistency. Reexaminations come more commonly from generational turnover in scholars, with the youngest generations free to discard the notions of their elders (Kuhn, 1962).

(1973) have named them the primacy principle (what is learned first is retained the longest) and the structuring principle (what is learned first molds later learning). The primacy and structuring principles draw attention to agents of early political learning, particularly parents. These agents are expected to be the most important of all. Peer groups and other agents which appear later in life or even in adulthood are not expected to be very important in the socialization process. As a result, most research has focused on the agents to which the child is first exposed: his parents and, to a lesser extent, the school.

Other important consequences derive from a concentration on early learning. First, the agents of early learning, especially the parents, are expected to have tremendous influence on the political views of children. Thus, the initial expectation was that parent-child agreement on political views should be very high. Second, it has been assumed to make little difference when child and parent political views are compared—children should show considerable resemblance to their parents at any age. Finally, political socialization has at least implicitly been thought of as completed in childhood, except where it involves training for specialized political roles, leaving little room for the effects of direct political experience.

Only recently have the two assumptions which underlie most political socialization research been challenged (March, 1971; Searing et al., 1973). It is hardly coincidental that this challenge came at a time when scholars' expectations were increasingly going unfulfilled in empirical research, as shall become apparent in the following review of principal research findings. It is too early to assess the full effects of either the direct or indirect challenge to the assumptional base of socialization research. They signal at least a turning point in the study of the agents of socialization—away from an almost single-minded concentration on early learning and its agents and toward a focus on learning throughout the life cycle.

With these theoretical, methodological, and epistemological considerations as a background, we can now turn to a consideration of empirical research on the agents of socialization. Most of our attention shall be focused on the three agents which have received the most study—parents, schools, and peers. These agents, and others, will first be considered separately and then what is known about their relative effects will be reviewed. Finally, the conclusion will be devoted to a general summary of the role of agents in political socialization and to some suggestions about the directions in which research should proceed in the future.

Parents as Agents of Political Socialization

An examination of the impact of the various agents of political socialization should begin with the parents—almost universally expected to be the primary agents. In part, this expectation is based upon the highly favorable position of the parents in terms of the three preconditions for influence. No other agents enjoy such a cumulative edge in exposure, communication, and receptivity. In no small part, this expectation is also based upon the conclusion from Hyman's (1959) seminal review of the early socialization literature: "Foremost among agencies of socialization into politics is the family" (p. 51).

This conclusion reflects the influence of initial expectations in shaping research results. Elsewhere in his book, Hyman is more cautious:

> These and other studies establish very clearly a family correspondence in views that are relevant to matters of political orientation. . . . While positive, the moderate magnitude of the correlations, however, leads to the formulation that parents are only one of the many agents of such socialization and that their influence is not that great (pp. 52–55).

The expectation of parental primacy probably led Hyman to override his qualifications in assessing the influence of parents. This expectation, furthermore, seems to have induced readers of Hyman's survey to pay more attention to his less cautious depiction of the parental role.

Not only does the weight of his evidence belie Hyman's strong statement about the role of the parents, except where partisanship is concerned, but the empirical base of his work is so weak that additional caution is surely in order. Few studies of parental influence had been conducted in time for Hyman's review, and the studies he was able to review did not lend themselves to easy cumulation. First, in no more than 3 of the 12 studies of parent-child agreement had the same political orientations been used. Second, the time frame of these studies was wide. Seven had been conducted prior to the Second World War, and the remainder were conducted in the late forties and early fifties. It is dangerous to generalize from studies with such a wide time frame, especially where this frame encompasses periods of substantial political change.

Third, all of the studies surveyed by Hyman are based on highly specific samples. Seven of them involved college students at one college or university, and no study could be generalized to a cross-section of American youth. Finally, in many of Hyman's studies, parental political views were determined through a questionnaire carried home by the child—a sure way to enhance agreement (Connell, 1972, pp. 325–326). Similar biases undermine a number of the additional studies cited by Hyman, because they depend upon perceived agreement.

A much clearer picture of parental influence is presented in the Jennings and Niemi (1968b, 1974) studies of a national sample of high school seniors and their parents. Party preference and candidate preference evince high rates of agreement. Association on the other orientations, though positive, is much less strong. These data paint a picture of weak parental influence, except where partisanship is concerned. As Jennings and Niemi (1968b) conclude:

> Any model of socialization which rests on assumptions of pervasive currents of parent-to-child value transmission of the types examined here is in serious need of

modification. Attitude objects in the concrete, salient, reinforced terrain of party identification lend support to the model. But this is the prime exception (p. 183).

Further challenge to the conventional wisdom of strong parental influence over children on political matters comes from Connell's (1972) inventory of research on agreement between parents and children. From the findings of over 40 studies conducted between 1932 and 1965, including the Jennings study, Connell concludes that "pair correspondence . . . is persistently present but persistently weak" (p. 327). By contrast, aggregate correspondence between parents and children is quite high. This leads Connell to infer that the parental role in the socialization process is not that of directly molding the child's political views but, rather, that of placing the child into a sociopolitical context which resembles that of the parents. The true agents of socialization are to be found in that context, not in the parents themselves. The major exception to these conclusions, as it has been in each case, is party identification.

In retrospect, the findings cited by Hyman, Jennings, and Connell seem to have a great deal in common. Each points to some agreement between parents and children in general, but surely not enough to guarantee parents a determinative role in the shaping of children's political views. Only partisanship, of all the orientations studied, consistently appears to be passed on with great success from parents to children. The disagreement between Hyman, on the one hand, and Connell and Jennings, on the other, comes in the inferences drawn from research findings. Roughly similar levels of parent-child agreement suggest strong parental influence to Hyman, though not without qualification, but suggest only a marginal parental sway to Jennings and Niemi and Connell. It is almost as if different expectations have allowed contradictory conclusions to be drawn from the same data. What was evidence for strong association to Hyman becomes, perhaps as a result of rising expectations fueled by Hyman's own work, evidence of only weak association to his successors.

The finding that, except for partisanship, only meager parental influence can be demonstrated may be surprising to even the most casual observer of child development. The parents, after all, occupy an enviable position for exerting influence. Especially in the early years of childhood, parents enjoy a virtual monopoly of exposure. Parents would also seem to be advantaged by the high degree of receptivity children accord to parental communications. This receptivity is based on strong bonds of affection between parent and child, the critical role parents play in satisfying children's needs, and the hierarchical nature of the family (Davies, 1965). While both exposure and receptivity may wane as the child matures and is exposed to other agents, the parents continue to enjoy great advantages in the socialization process along these two dimensions.

Of course, one reason for the failure to demonstrate greater parental influence may lie with the methodological problems involved in measuring influence. All of the studies reviewed so far have inferred the extent of influence from correlations between children and parents—a measure which has some serious deficiencies. Reliance on percentage agreement measures instead, though, has no effect on the substantive conclusions which have been drawn (Jennings & Niemi,

1974). Still, the possibility that extant measures underestimate parental influence must be entertained, although I am doubtful that the reason for the general finding of low parental influence is a methodological one. After all, measurement problems have not prevented the correlation for party identification from being substantial. Nor have they inhibited the agreement on religious preference from reaching very high levels in the Jennings data.

It seems more likely that the reason why parental influence is so small, given exposure and receptivity advantages, lies with the other dimension of socialization potential—communications with political content. Politics is rarely the subject of intense interest or discussion in most families. What discussion there is, furthermore, probably centers on more concrete political objects, such as parties and candidates, than on the more abstract considerations of policy or ideology. The impoverished views of politics which are exhibited in responses to survey questions by the great majority of adults (Converse, 1964) hardly suggest a high level of political discourse in the home. In short, the absence of political content from the life of the average American family must severely hamper the parental role in political socialization.[2] Indeed, there is some evidence that parents in the United States are largely indifferent about the political views of their children (Jennings & Niemi, 1974, pp. 61–62).

Two studies have found a relationship between the political content of communications and parent-child agreement. Jennings and Niemi (1968, pp. 180–183) examined parent-child correlations under a number of control conditions. Only the degree to which the parents discussed politics appeared to have any effect at all. For party identification and political cynicism, parent-child agreement grew with increases in discussion.

Drawing upon data from an Iowa City survey, Tedin (1974) suggests that the effects of differences in communication may be more comprehensive. When the salience to parents of *each* political view (in contrast to the general measure of salience) was measured, parent-child agreement on partisanship and policy issues grew as the salience of the matter increased. Additionally, agreement was enhanced by increases in the accuracy with which the children were able to identify parental political views. Both parental salience and perceptual accuracy undoubtedly reflect political content of communications. Salience brings about increased communication on a particular issue, while accurate perceptions result from greater communication (Jennings & Niemi, 1974, p. 49).

Another communication-related factor which contributes to the influence of the parent is the degree of consistency in parental views across a domain of similar political objects. Jennings and Niemi (1974, pp. 86–87) found, e.g., that the relationship between parents and students increased when other relevant attitudes of the parents were taken into account. This pattern was exhibited in all

[2]This view is endorsed in a 1971 study of children's attitudes toward the war in Vietnam (Tolley, 1973, pp. 112–118). For those children who indicated hearing their parents express firm convictions about the war, there is substantial agreement between child views and those the child perceives are harbored by his parents. But only half of the sample reported hearing parents express strong convictions for victory or withdrawal. For the remainder, parental influence is far less important.

three issue domains under examination—school integration, school prayer, and civic tolerance.

Parental consistency in communication of political views may be viewed in yet another way: in terms of the extent to which parents agree with one another in political views. The Jennings study contains personal interviews with both parents for 430 of the high school seniors, thus allowing analysis of the effects of consistency between mother and father. Based on this analysis, Jennings and Niemi (1974) conclude:

> Almost without exception the similarity between the student and a single parent... was exceeded by the similarity between the student and each parent when those parents saw eye to eye or behaved in congruent fashion. So pervasive was this pattern that it proved to be the strongest and most consistent of factors predicting parent-child similarity (p. 154).

The greatest impact of parental consistency comes where student-parent associations were already high.

Beyond this tendency for children to agree more with homogeneous parents, the Jennings data contain a faint trace of sex-related differences in transmission (Jennings & Niemi, 1974, p. 155). Girls are slightly more likely than boys to agree with mutually consistent parents. The feminine tendencies toward greater conformity to familial political views are greatest for the issue positions. Apparently the pressures for within-family conformity fall more heavily on girls than on boys.

One of the more interesting questions about parental influence which Jennings and his colleagues treat concerns the relative influence of mothers versus fathers. By examining the correlations of the child with each parent when the parents disagree, this question can be answered in at least a rudimentary fashion. The surprising finding here—at least to those who have believed the conventional wisdom that politics is the masculine domain—is that mothers seem to be more successful than fathers in passing on political orientations, particularly where political issues and feelings toward groups are concerned (Jennings & Niemi, 1974, p. 167).

Partisanship has consistently emerged as the political view most influenced by parents. Jennings and his colleagues have paid special attention to the differential impact of mothers and fathers (Jennings & Langton, 1969; Beck & Jennings, 1975). A slight maternal edge in partisan transmission to the high school seniors has been found, and indirect evidence on parental influence in earlier generations suggests that this maternal edge reflects a recent change in political sex roles—from politics as the masculine domain in previous generations to a more recent parity of the sexes in political influence. This trend is not unique to the United States. Butler and Stokes (1969, pp. 47–51) have reported its presence in Britain as well, using respondents' perceptions of parental partisanship. In Japan, by contrast, the traditional pattern of paternal dominance in politics remains intact (Kubota & Ward, 1970).

The increasing maternal influence on children's partisan orientations in Britain and the United States can be traced to changes along the communication dimension: as mothers have increased their interest in politics, and thus their tendencies to identify with political parties, their political influence over the children has grown. The same process is probably operating for other political orientations as well. Enhanced female politicization allows the mother to exploit her natural advantages in exposure and contact with the child. Yet, if the same societal changes which have politicized more females also take them out of the home with a frequency converging upon that of their husbands, the maternal exposure advantage may well be lessened, attenuating her growing advantage in political socialization.

With the discussions of variation in communication and parental agreement, we have come full circle in considering parental influence. We began with the expectation of substantial influence but little evidence. At the end, this expectation of substantial parental influence is raised again. What is different, of course, is that a considerable amount of empirical evidence has been weighed in between. This evidence has laid to rest the notion that substantial agreement exists between parents and their children on a wide variety of political orientations, although little evidence is available for some orientations. Yet the evidence also indicates potential for considerable parental influence where the parents share political views and where these views are communicated to the child. That neither of these favorable conditions can be taken for granted is a primary lesson of empirical research on the parental role. Perhaps only partisanship satisfies these conditions frequently enough to satisfy the expectations of parental primacy.

This picture of parental influence probably applies to other modern western societies in addition to the United States. There is good reason, though, not to generalize this picture either to more traditional societies or to societies in which the political authorities have extensive control over the activities of citizens. In the case of the former, the role of the parent in political socialization may be expected to be more pronounced. Children in traditional societies are much less exposed to nonfamilial agents of socialization, thus providing for greater continuity in political views from generation to generation. In the case of the latter, parental influence may be heavily circumscribed by direct competition from those agents of socialization, especially schools and peer organizations, controlled by the political authorities. The influence of parents in political socialization in western nations undoubtedly lies in between these extremes—while the parents no longer enjoy a near monopoly in the child's political learning, the consensual nature of the societies ensures a fair measure of compatibility in the political views of different agents of socialization.

Schools as Agents of Political Socialization

In most modern nations, schools also occupy a favorable position in terms of the preconditions for successful socialization. Except for the preschool years, they often rival the parents in exposure to the children. American children, e.g., spend a substantial portion of their waking hours in schools. College attendance extends this exposure into early adulthood for many. There is, additionally, identifiable political content in communications issued by the schools, particularly where the norms of citizenship are involved. Finally, schools generally enjoy a considerable advantage in the receptivity of children to their messages. Young children seem more receptive to influence attempts in general (Sears, 1975b). Furthermore, children come to schools expecting to be taught, as teaching and learning are the prescribed activities there.

Circumstantial evidence of the influence of schools in the United States may be found in the higher support for democratic norms (a principal focus of school socialization attempts) among better educated citizens. Yet this evidence and the favorable position of schools to the contrary, schools have not been accorded a very prominent role in political socialization research. Very little attention is devoted to them in Hyman's (1959) seminal review of the political socialization literature, and there has been little subsequent research focused directly on the influence of schools. The reasons for this, it seems to me, are twofold: First, the dominance of the parental primacy model in political socialization research has relegated schools to a secondary role, thus restricting research attention on this area. Second, severe methodological difficulties in demonstrating school influence have hampered researchers. Schools are institutions, not individuals, and the measures of agreement used to indicate parental influence are not appropriate. Only when the impact of individual teachers is assessed can such measures of agreement be relied upon. Furthermore, just as in the case of parents, virtually all young people are exposed to schools, thus rendering the reliable statistical technique of comparing control and experimental groups inoperative.

Research on the influence of schools falls into four categories. The first category is research on formal instruction and routines, which are unlikely to vary much from school to school, including such things as the curriculum, textbooks, and patriotic rituals. The second category is research focused on the contributions of teachers as individuals. While professional socialization discourages the expression of personal political views within the classroom, there is still considerable room for communications in the schools to be shaped by the personal views of particular teachers (Zeigler, 1967, pp. 93–119). The third category of research on school effects focuses on extracurricular activities. Finally, some researchers have concentrated on the peer group environment in the school, a subject which will be considered in the next section on peer groups.

No empirical studies attempt to assess the full impact of formal instruction and school routines. Several scholars have, however, singled out the civics courses in high school for special attention. In a study of three Boston communities, Litt (1963) compared political attitudes of students before they took a civics course with their attitudes after the course. Civics course graduates in all three communities were more likely to endorse the democratic creed and less likely to be politically chauvinistic than they had been prior to taking the course.

In terms of attitudes toward political participation and group conflict, as well as cognitions of the political process, however, the expected changes were found only in the upper-middle-class community. While some civics course effects were found, in summary they were neither comprehensive nor overwhelming.

A comparison of civics course graduates and nongraduates was undertaken by Langton and Jennings (1969) and Jennings, Langton, and Niemi (1974) for a national sample of high school seniors. Across a wide variety of political orientations, only negligible differences were found between the two groups. Quite the opposite picture appeared when blacks alone were examined: black students who had taken civics courses displayed greater political knowledge, political efficacy, and political tolerance. For blacks from less educated families, civics course exposure was also tied to increased politicization. The significant differences between civics course graduates and nongraduates for blacks, but not for whites, are interpreted as indicating that material presented in civics courses is new for most blacks but largely redundant for most whites. Similar findings are reported by Ehman (1969) on the effects of the social studies curriculum in Detroit and by Merelman (1971b, pp. 110–113) concerning the impact of school quality in some Los Angeles area schools. In each case, students deprived in their nonschool environments (blacks for Ehman, lower-class whites and blacks for Merelman) receive compensatory socialization from the school.

More attention has been paid to the impact of teachers as individuals. The strongest brief for substantial teacher influence is made by Hess and Torney (1967) based on a study of white school students in metropolitan areas of the United States: "The public school appears to be the most important and effective instrument of political socialization in the United States" (p. 101). Empirical support for this assertion is drawn from the lack of agreement in the political views of siblings, except where partisanship was concerned, and the convergence of the attitudes of students in each higher grade upon those of teachers.

Upon close scrutiny, though, this evidence does not warrant Hess and Torney's conclusion. The absence of widespread agreement between siblings does indeed challenge the parental primacy model. More direct evidence on parent-child agreement, surveyed above, points to the same conclusion. That parental influence is not pervasive, though, does not mean that school influence is perforce strong. Other agents of political socialization compete with schools for this honor, and their contributions must be assessed as well. Furthermore, the brunt of the evidence presented in the section on parental influence is that the influence process is too complicated to be tested by parent-child agreement, let alone agreement between siblings who themselves are at different stages of development. Finally, the convergence of aggregate teacher and aggregate student views as the students mature hardly demonstrates the influence of teachers or the school. The perils of ecological inference here are too obvious.

A more methodologically sound exploration of the impact of teachers has been conducted by Jennings, Ehman, and Niemi (1974). They compared the political views of individual high school seniors and their social studies teachers.

While such a matching ignores the variety of student-teacher contacts outside of the social studies, it does at least focus directly on the transmission of attitudes from agents assigned a political socialization role. The findings of this study cast considerable doubt on the proposition advanced by Hess and Torney. While the student marginal distributions are more like those of their teachers than those of their parents, the pattern of individual-level agreement is just the reverse. Teacher-student agreement is lower than parent-student agreement on all political orientations, and the parental edge over the teachers is usually substantial. The only indications of some teacher impact are the modest correlations between teacher and student on two school-related issues, school integration and prayers in school.

Given these data, the case for independent teacher influence is considerably weakened. Of course, such data touch only the surface of possible patterns of influence, leaving for further investigation a variety of important questions. The Jennings study focuses only on high school seniors, where contact with individual teachers is commonly limited much more than in the earlier grades in which a single teacher handles every subject. The matching of students with teachers also contains an artificial precision. Not only is it insensitive to the possible impact of one particular teacher and none of the others, but it may well understate the collective impact of all teachers. One must add to these qualifications the notion that correlation coefficients are not entirely satisfactory measures of influence, particularly in studying the kind of consensual attitudes most likely to be passed on by the school. Nonetheless, an empirically oriented social science must proceed on the basis of proof. Without convincing evidence of teacher impact (and the Hess & Torney study hardly provides such evidence), we cannot say that the teacher plays an important role in political socialization.

Comparatively little attention has been paid to the third type of school influence—the impact of extracurricular activities. Only one study, conducted by Ziblatt (1965) in an Oregon high school, has attempted to assess their impact directly. He found no relationship between high school students' levels of extracurricular activity and their attitudes toward politics, although there appeared to be an indirect relationship between the two through the intermediary, social trust. In addition, Almond and Verba (1963, pp. 352–363) found that opportunities to participate both formally and informally in school decisions led to greater confidence in one's own ability to exert influence in each of five nations, even though the relationships were not particularly strong. Again, a redundancy effect may be noted: the opportunity to participate in the school counts most for those with the least education. The Almond and Verba data do not bear directly on the realm of extracurricular activities. Yet they too show the effects of participation nurtured in the school.

This review of empirical research supports several conclusions about the role of schools in political socialization. First, it is most obvious that research designed to tap school influence is limited in contrast to that on the parents. One result of this is that we know virtually nothing about the impact of early education, where the influence of the school might be expected to be greatest. Where empirical research has been conducted, mostly null findings have resulted. Social studies teachers, civics courses, and extracurricular activities seem to have little impact on students' political views. The impact of civics courses and perhaps even participatory activities is constrained by the fact that the messages they contain have already been communicated to the students by other agents (or by earlier school experiences). Only where these messages are not redundant has the school been shown to exert some influence.

As was the case with parents, we must move to cross-national analysis to really appreciate the potential for school influence. The unsystematic nature of observations of the role of the school in other nations makes such comparative analysis only suggestive, hardly determinative. Wylie (1957, pp. 206–208) depicts the school in a small French town as an institution which attempts to inculcate certain political views through the curriculum but utterly fails to have an impact because of the counterinfluence of home, community, and even teachers. In the Soviet Union, by contrast, the schools are alleged to have played a critical role in socializing children to the norms of communism (Brzezinski & Huntington, 1963; Geiger, 1956). The Soviets were successful where the French authorities were not because they were able to isolate the parents and make them reluctant to pass on their own attitudes toward the regime.

School decentralization in the United States undoubtedly ensures that schools will not be used as coordinated instruments of socialization by national political authorities. There is suggestive evidence, though, that the schools are used in this fashion by the local community which controls them (Litt, 1963). Given the impact of the local community on American schools, it is hardly surprising that what evidence we have accumulated on the schools points to redundancy in cues, rather than competition with other agents. In conducting further research on the role of American schools in the political socialization process, it seems reasonable to expect wider confirmation of this finding.

Peers as Agents of Political Socialization

The third agent commonly identified as important in political socialization is the peer group—a term used to designate both age-homogeneous groups in general (the peer subculture) and age-homogeneous friendship groups in particular. Peer groups emerge in modern, universalistic societies. (Eisenstadt, 1956). In more traditional societies where particularistic kinship patterns predominate, peer groups do not typically form and cannot play much of a role in the political socialization process. Peer groups have been accorded a highly important position in American society, and a common theme of studies of postwar America has been the increasingly powerful sway such groups have exerted (Reisman, Glazer, & Denney, 1950; Coleman, 1961).

Like parents and schools, peer groups in American society occupy a favorable position for influencing the political views of individuals. Peer groups enjoy considerable exposure to the individual, and this exposure widens as he or the matures. Here the peer group stands in sharp contrast to parents and schools, whose exposure is greatest in the early years and wanes with maturation. Though differences in the exposure curves illustrate the important role which assumptions to about political learning play in conceptualizing influence. If the early years ship critical for political socialization, as the primacy and structuring principles ute pose, then parents and even schools will be looked to as the important as to a while the role of the peers will be played down. If important political socia be a tion takes place after the preadolescent years, then the role attributed to peers lege be more important. Of course, the timing of political socialization is large s as empirical question—albeit a difficult one to answer. It should be obvious by of that assumptions about the answer to this question have shaped the stud rent agental influence considerably. The dominance of the early learning hypoth vs. in particular, has relegated peers to a lesser position of "expected" influ era- than either parents or schools. to

The peer group, if the findings of Coleman (1961) and others ma am- generalized to the realm of politics, is also advantaged in terms of receptiv sian its communications. What is uncertain is the content of these peer commu cul- tions: to what extent does the peer group focus on political matters? In one s ions it may not matter what answer is given to this question. Peer groups typ nce form among individuals with common backgrounds, outlooks, and values. ion. political agreement is not a guiding force in the creation of most peer grou ntal may be a derivative of similarities along nonpolitical dimensions. Where flu- the case, the role of peers can at most be one only of reinforcement for previ learned political views.

For all of the attention paid to the importance of peer groups in the U States, it is surprising that so little research has been conducted on peer infl in political socialization. No greater testimony to the force of the early le assumption in socialization research could be gathered than from this clea parity between the inattention to peers as agents of political socialization a not attention paid to them elsewhere. A second reason for the inattention to cep- may be a methodological one: if peers usually replicate the political vie dern other agents, how can their influence be assessed adequately? eatest

This methodological problem has been overcome in one study of the pc three socialization influence of peers by focusing on situations in which peer ere is attitudes are likely to conflict with those of parents. Langton (1967) four ental working-class Jamaican children with predominantly middle-class f adopted many of the class-linked political views of their friends. Langton also assessed the impact of the wider peer culture on political views by dividing Jamaican schools into homogeneously working class and class heterogeneous. The former were found to reinforce working-class norms, while the latter reso- cialized working-class youths into middle-class political views except where economic matters were concerned. Langton reports a similar pattern for attitudes toward civil rights in Detroit schools. Additional evidence from the Langton study indicates that the two types of peer effect (friendship and peer culture) are additive in Jamaica: working-class students with middle-class friends in ogenous schools were least likely to retain working-class political views.[3]

ven more convincing evidence of peer group influence is provided in a of friendship groups by Sebert, Jennings, and Niemi (1974). Using metric data provided by all seniors in 13 of the schools in the Jennings , friendship groups were identified, and the agreement in five political between each respondent and his friends was determined. Substantial ment was found on all of the political orientations examined, with the st levels of agreement emerging with those whom the respondents them- had designated as best friends. An additional finding of interest is that girls substantially more likely to agree with their friends than were boys. This is other indication that girls are more sensitive to the views of those around

rhaps the classic illustration of the influence of the peer group in its er, age-homogeneous sense comes from the panel study of Bennington ge students conducted by Newcomb (1943) in the 1930s. The Bennington ence was shown to have a dramatic impact on student political views. Most students, especially those who had adjusted best to college life, became ideologically liberal over the course of their college years and, in the s, deserted the conservative dispositions of their families and social posi- While the liberal faculty at the school was surely a force behind these es, Newcomb attributed the principal influence to the peer group—what he he social environment of the school. Not only does this study demonstrate er groups can play a major role in the political socialization process, but it ghts the possibilities for political learning beyond childhood.

order to determine the lasting effects of the Bennington experience, New- et al. (1967) reinterviewed many members of the original panel 25 years In large part, the liberal attitudes inculcated long before had persisted. women continued to be far more liberal than others of the same conomic status. The survival of these liberal political views, like their was attributed to peer influence—both husband and friends. After college, nnington graduates had typically selected peers (especially husbands) who ted their political views. (Finifter, 1974, found a similar tendency among lican auto workers.) The importance of political considerations in this selec- ocess is illustrated by the fact that such liberal views were highly atypical

[3]These findings parallel the well known results of the Coleman Report (Coleman et al., 1966, p. 22). Where verbal achievement was concerned, the peer group climate of the school (i.e., the verbal achievement scores of classmates) was more important in explaining individual achievement levels than any other school-related factor. Working-class children were uplifted in achievement level in middle-class environments, but middle-class children's achievement levels were not depressed in working-class environments.

for the socioeconomic status of these women. The two Newcomb studies demonstrate clearly both the change-inducing and the reinforcing effects of peer group political views.

The scattered pieces of empirical evidence presented above may be assembled into a pattern of peer influence—both through friendship groups and throu[gh] the peer subculture. The dominant contribution of peer groups for adults seem[s] be to reinforce already formulated political views. The processes of friend[ship] selection, both purposively and inadvertently along political lines, contrib[ute] substantially to this end. At the same time, where the individual is exposed [to a] peer group with political views unlike his or her own, there appears to [be a] tendency for the peer group to be highly influential even as late as the col[lege] years. This exposure is undoubtedly rare even in a society as heterogeneou[s as] ours, because in the broader mosaic of heterogeneity lie many islan[ds of] homogeneity. When it does occur, however, exposure to peers with diffe[rent] political views than one's own can have a powerful effect on political view[s].

Additional insight into peer group influence may be gained from consid[era]tion of situations in other nations where peers have been used by authorities [to] reduce the role of parents in political socialization. The best documented ex[am]ple of this comes from the Soviet Union in the period following the Rus[sian] Revolution. Data on émigrés show how the creation of a proregime peer sub[cul]ture inhibited parental influence (Geiger, 1956). The experiences of other nati[ons] in which regimes have attempted to solidify their position lend further cred[ence] to the view that peers can be an important instrument of political socializat[ion]. This is not to suggest that peer groups are common antagonists of pare[ntal] political values—only that where they are, they may exert considerable in[flu]ence.

Other Agents of Political Socialization

The three agents considered above—parents, schools, and peers—d[o not] exhaust the list of potential agents of political socialization. Yet, with one e[xcep]tion, they are the only ones with near universal exposure to individuals in m[ost] societies. For this reason, it is understandable that they have received the gr[eatest] attention from political socialization researchers. As we move beyond these [three] "universal" agents, research efforts wane considerably, to the point that th[ere is] very little systematic empirical research upon which conclusions about ag[ent] influence can be based.

The one additional agent with virtually universal exposure in modern societies is the mass media. Few modern children are completely cut off from exposure to the media. The most prominent of the media in the United States is, of course, television. Elsewhere in this volume, Chaffee and Jackson-Beeck contend that television is the only medium to which young children are exposed, but that this monopoly on exposure is broken up by adolescence as the printed media become more important. The Jennings study shows that, by the senior year in high school, the printed media have emerged as important sources of political information (Jennings & Niemi, 1968a, pp. 450–452).

One principal question about the influence of the media in political socialization concerns the political content of their communications. There is substantial political content in newspaper stories and in presentation of the news and public affairs programming by television and radio. Few would dispute the point that considerable subjectivity is embedded in this news reporting. With this subjectivity comes the possibility of independent media influence. To consider the news reporting activities of the media as the only noteworthy political communications they contain is to ignore the subtle political messages contained in general entertainment programming, especially where television is concerned. These shows complement and in some cases serve as surrogates for real experiences and may have important effects on the formation of political views.

Another question about the influence of the media in political socialization concerns the receptivity of listeners or readers to their messages. Here, in contrast to considerations of political content of the communications, some empirical evidence can be assembled to provide an answer. Klapper (1960) has shown that receptivity to the media is highly selective, through both selective exposure and selective perception of communications. For this reason, he concludes that the media have little independent effect on political views of their audiences.

The brunt of the research evidence is that the impact of the media seems to be confined to increasing the level of information about the political world. In their before-and-after study of the effects of the media during the 1968 campaign in Wisconsin, Chaffee et al. (1970) found that media attention increased knowledge of the campaign but had no impact on campaign activity. A similar finding is reported in Tolley's (1973) study of children's attitudes toward the war in Vietnam: television was the most important source of information about the war but did not influence children's attitudes toward the war. In addition, respondents in the Hirsch (1971) study identified the media as their most important source of information about politics.

The effects of another institution—college—have received considerable attention in contrast to the media, undoubtedly because of the close proximity of college students and socialization researchers. College attendance has been found to increase liberalism, though there is movement in both directions, and to decrease attitudes associated with authoritarianism (Feldman & Newcomb, 1969, pp. 19–21, 30–32; Lane, 1968). These findings seem unaffected by background differences between college students and their noncollege peers and maturation, although most of the studies are not very careful about factoring out the compositional effects.

It is not entirely clear, however, which agent is responsible for these college "effects." Specific courses have been found to have no impact on participative orientations (Somit et al., 1958; Schick & Somit, 1963), and little attempt has been made to gauge the effects of the curriculum in general. There is little evidence of a direct faculty impact, even though faculty may be important in isolated cases. Rather, what influence faculty do exert seems to be filtered through the more pervasive college environment, particularly the peer group subculture. This, at least, is the interpretation in the Newcomb (1943, 1967) studies and the surveys of the literature conducted by Feldman and Newcomb (1969) and Lane (1968). The college environment facilitates sustained exposure to peers (particularly when the student lives on the campus). It is little wonder that peers should be considered so instrumental in the formation of the political views of college students. Yet attribution of influence to the peer subculture leaves the question of the source of the liberalism and nonauthoritarianism which characterizes the college peer subculture. With this question, but without any empirical research as a guideline, one is led back inevitably to the faculty and the curriculum.

One additional possible source of political views, the spouse, enjoys relatively wide exposure, although this exposure comes after childhood. In many cases husband and wife begin marriage with highly similar political views—more because of assortative mating on nonpolitical than on political characteristics. Where this initial similarity does not prevail, there is evidence of some change on the part of one and often both spouses. Traditionally, the wife has been thought to change more under these conditions than the husband, and an analysis of the parents of the high school seniors in the Jennings study supports this view (Beck & Jennings, 1975). These data show, additionally, that this is not a one-sided process, as some husbands appear to change as well. Only the lack of salience of politics will inhibit these tendencies toward political "balance" in partners' political views.

The remaining possible agents of socialization are not favored by the universal exposure of parents, schools, peers, and media or by the wide exposure enjoyed by college and spouse among adults. Among these remaining agents are the church, youth organizations such as Boy Scouts, siblings (who could also be classified as peers), and other adults for children, as well as the military and secondary organizations for adults. Even where there is exposure and the presumption of receptivity, there is considerable question about the political content of communications from these agents. Yet, even if these agents do not engage in manifest political socialization, the possibility of socialization with political consequences must be admitted. One need turn only to the role of the church in Northern Ireland's political conflicts or in modern Portugal and the role of formal youth organizations in Nazi Germany or in the Soviet Union to appreciate the conditions under which such agents may become important. Even in the western democracies, including the United States, many of these agents concentrate on the inculcation of values, thus contributing to political consensus and conflict.

In general, the uneven exposure of some of these "other" agents of political socialization restricts the amount of attention which will and can be devoted to them. This should not be taken as evidence that they are unimportant in particular cases—only that it is difficult to generalize about their importance. On the other hand, generalizations about the influence of the media, college, and spouse can be made without difficulty, and more research should be directed to that end. It is possible, though, that conceptualization of agental influence in terms of the three preconditions outlined earlier in this chapter will facilitate general theories of agental influence which can include all of the possible agents of socialization.

The Relative Influence of the Agents of Political Socialization

Empirical evidence on the influence of each of a number of agents of political socialization has been reviewed in the preceding pages. While this evidence allows some indirect comparisons of agental influence, it was not presented so as to facilitate direct comparison. The principal reason for this is that only a few studies are designed to allow direct comparisons of the influence of agents.

The major source of empirical evidence concerning the relative impact of various agents on political views is the 1965 national survey of high school seniors, their parents, peers, and social studies teachers conducted by Jennings. Jennings and Niemi (1974, pp. 211–217) have compared the influence of parents and teachers by contrasting parent-child and teacher-child correlations and employing partial correlations to "sort out" relative influences. As one would expect from the findings for each agent separately, parents exert far more influence than teachers, particularly where partisanship is concerned. Even in the realm of consensus values, presumably the domain of the schools, parent-student association exceeds teacher-student association.

The influence of friends compares more favorably with that of parents. Sebert, Jennings, and Niemi (1974) correlated the students' views on five political matters with those of parents and the seniors whom the respondent had designated as friends. For political efficacy and lowering the voting age to 18, the student-friend correlations exceeded those of the student and parent. For political trust, the student-parent correlations were slightly higher than those for students and friends. Only for party identification and vote preference was there a large parental advantage—providing further confirmation for the view that partisanship is the preserve of family influence.

One further line of inquiry pursued in the Jennings and Niemi volume concerns the effects of interagent agreement on the influence of agents (Sebert, Jennings, & Niemi, 1974, pp. 245–248; Ehman, Jennings, & Niemi, 1974, pp. 217–221). The dominant pattern is that interagent consensus in political views leads to heightened agreement between the student and all three agents—parents, teachers, and peers. Conversely, dissensus among agents depresses the student's similarity to each. This pattern is repeated without exception for peers and parents. It is often interrupted where teachers and parents are concerned: support for school prayers and school integration follow the general pattern, but party identification and partisan intensity do not. For the two partisan matters, the teachers are unable to add to the influence of the parents.

The correlations which underlie these results from the Jennings study, plus casual observations of the operation of American society, underscore the lack of conflict among agents of political socialization in this nation. Furthermore, on that orientation which possesses the highest potential for interagent conflict, partisanship, it seems likely that at least one agent (the school) withdraws from the field of competition and that conflict with other agents is minimized by strong tendencies for likes to associate with likes. Surely some of the success with which agents socialize newcomers to American society derives from the similarity of agental communications.

In societies characterized by greater intergenerational discontinuity, on the other hand, the potential for conflict among the agents is far more pronounced and, as a result, the socialization of the young probably is less successful overall. Thus, political views may tend to be less deeply embedded, more subject to change during adulthood, and perhaps even more ambivalent. In his study of the political socialization of the middle class in Egypt, e.g., Binder (1965) found the presence side by side of almost contradictory school and family socialization results and considerable ambivalence toward the political system.

There are no systematic studies of the relative effects of various agents under conditions of interagent conflict in other nations. Substantial impressionistic evidence indicates, though, that where the regime makes a strong push to counter parental influence, the predominance of the family in the political socialization process can be overcome (Brzezinski & Huntington, 1963; Geiger, 1956). Where the regime's attempts to inculcate certain political views through a centralized school system are unsuccessful, the likely reason is that the school is the only agent providing those communications. The key to agental influence under conditions of interagent conflict seems to be support or reinforcement from other agents. Political socialization of the young is undoubtedly more and more successful as the consensus among the agents emitting political communications grows.

Conclusions

> In many ways a child born into a system is like an immigrant into it. But where he differs is in the fact that he has never been socialized to any other kind of system. That is to say, he is being socialized politically for the first time rather than re-socialized as an immigrant (Easton & Dennis, 1965, p. 57).

As this new member of the system matures, he or she becomes increasingly cognizant of and involved in its political life. Tremendous political learning takes place, given the political *tabula rasa* with which the individual began. This learning starts very early. Meaningful cognitions of the political world are found as early as the second grade, probably the earliest opportunity for collecting data on political views. These cognitions become increasingly more sophisticated, and are joined by evaluative and affective orientations as the pace of political learning quickens through the grade school years. By adolescence, many of the individual's political views approach adult levels of development. Others are fleshed out during adolescence and even in adulthood, especially in its first years (Jennings & Niemi, 1968a). That considerable political learning takes place is undeniable. It is much more difficult to determine how.

This chapter has estimated the extent to which various agents have played an identifiable role in the political socialization process as teachers of political views. The parents demonstrate the greatest amount of influence, especially for partisanship. In general, though, parental influence has not proven as great as early students of political socialization expected it to be. It can be considerable (even beyond the area of partisan orientations) when the conditions are favorable—when parents agree, when the political orientations under consideration are salient to parents, and when the objects of orientation are relatively concrete. But the fact that these conditions are not often realized in American society attenuates substantially the influence of parents. The picture of parental influence which remains after careful weighing of the empirical evidence is one of considerable influence potential but only occasional realization of that potential. If nothing else, this suggests that political values are among the least important of the values American parents attempt to instill in their children.[4]

There are no other agents which can compete with the parents in their impact on a wide variety of political orientations. Peer groups appear to come the closest to matching parental potency. Their influence appears to grow as the individual matures, although this appearance may be deceiving due to the assortative processes of peer group formation. Judgment about the impact of peers must be suspended, however, until we know more about their influence across a wide variety of political orientations and contexts.

Research has failed to show that the school, either as an institution or in terms of the individual teachers within it, has much influence on the political learning of students. At most, it seems to be a source of complementary socialization for most Americans. Only for those whose political environment is "deprived" of political communications does the school offer new information and lessons, thereby serving as an important compensatory agent of socialization. This may account for the importance of the school in societies characterized by considerable dissonance between home and school. All in all, though, the dearth of empirical studies on the impact of schools sets severe constraints on generalizations about the role of this agent.

---

[4]Almond and Verba (1963, pp. 132–143) have shown that very few American parents care if their son or daughter marries someone of the opposite party. Surely the lack of concern on this more salient dimension of parental influence suggests even greater indifference about other political values. By contrast, parents in Italy were strongly opposed to interparty marriages for their children, a feeling which cannot help but permeate the political socialization process in that nation.

The impact of other agents of socialization is even less well documented than that of parents, schools, and peers. Only the mass media, whose impact seems to be limited to providing information, and the college environment, operating largely through the peer subculture, have been studied fairly systematically. Other agents have been neglected because either exposure to them is not widely distributed or the dominant assumptions in the study of political socialization have minimized their importance from the start. That they have been neglected does not diminish their potential as influential agents of political socialization.

Taken together, the findings reported in this chapter point to two conclusions about the agents of socialization. First, a great deal of research remains to be done before we can acquire an adequate understanding of their role in the political socialization process. Perhaps the only agent to which this injunction need not apply is the parents, who have benefited from initial expectations that they would prove to be the dominant agents of socialization. Of particular importance on this research agenda is research designed to assess the contributions of childhood agents to subsequent adult political views. This, after all, is the real test of influence. The second conclusion which may be drawn from the review in this chapter is that, even where agents have been shown to exercise influence, considerable variation remains to be explained in the political views of individuals—that is to say, the agents account for only a limited portion of political learning. The remainder of this chapter will be devoted to the implications of this second conclusion.

One reason why considerable variation remains to be explained in individuals' political views may be that the research methodologies adopted in the past are not appropriate for revealing real influence. Certainly the problems involved in measuring influence are serious enough to support a challenge of this sort. Other possibilities are that an individual's political views may represent the synthesis of the views of a number of agents, resembling none of them completely, and that there is such variation in the sources of influence from individual to individual that no general rule can capture adequately the influence process at work. Each of these reasons for low association has merit, as does the argument that measurement error may have attenuated the correlations considerably. Nonetheless, the fact that a variety of methodologies have been employed with little difference in conclusion should lead one to look beyond methodological reasons for the seeming weakness of the agents.

A second reason why considerable variance remains to be explained may be theoretical in nature. We may have searched for agental influence in the wrong places. Perhaps the agents have their most profound impact in the formulation of a deep-seated political *Weltansicht* and of a personality (Renshon, 1975). Alternatively, we may have searched for agental influence in the wrong fashion. Agents may consciously socialize learners to political views which the agents themselves do not hold. Both of these theoretical reasons for the absence of empirical evidence of agent potency have some merit, and research organized to probe them shows promise. Nevertheless, there seems to be little reason for expecting research along these lines to demonstrate strong agent influence where other research has not.

The most logical conclusion seems to be that agental influence explains only a part of political learning because the individual is capable of doing a substantial amount of learning on his own. Verba (1965) has expressed this view as follows:

> The study of political socialization has concentrated so heavily on pre-political experiences that it is often forgotten that much of what an individual believes about the political process is learned from observations of that process (p. 553).

Research on voting behavior, e.g., has demonstrated how changing political realities may lead to considerable changes in the partisan orientations of young adults during times of partisan realignment (Beck, 1974). Political learning by experience is surely not limited to adults. Recent research on the impact of Watergate on children (Arterton, 1974), earlier research on the impact of the Kennedy assassination (Wolfenstein & Kliman, 1965), and a recent panel study on attitudes toward government among Michigan school children (Sigel & Brookes, 1974) have shown quite convincingly the extent to which political events may permeate the child's world and affect his political thinking. While it is undeniable that the conventional agents of political socialization play some role in developing cognitions about these events, there is ample room for the child to internalize them in his own unique way.

With this observation, it is useful to return to the two perspectives on political learning outlined in the introduction to this chapter. The political socialization view has been pursued rigorously by political scientists, and a good deal is now known about agental contributions to the political learning of individuals. The political learning view has been far less popular and, as a result, the individual's own contributions to his political learning have been neglected. It seems obvious, then, that one new frontier in the study of the agents of political socialization is political learning without agents. This may involve examination of the effects of political events on children and adults, as well as assessment of the results of direct exposure to the most salient aspects of the political system. Only when the learner's own contributions to his learning are understood can the role of the agents of political socialization be properly assessed.

5

Political Socialization: From Womb to Childhood

James Chowning Davies

The Politically Crucial Pre- and Postnatal Environment

THIS CHAPTER'S BASIC ARGUMENT is that some of the tendencies of people to act that are politically most crucial are firmly established well before a child ever leaves home, and a few of them before it even leaves the womb. Easton and Hess say that "every piece of evidence indicates that the child's political world begins to take shape well before he even enters elementary school" (1962, p. 235). This chapter causally considers not only how children perceive the political world but also how they become predisposed to respond to that world—even children raised where there are no schools.

The earliest environmental forces operating on the child help establish lifelong patterns of person-to-person and person-to-society influence of every kind, including patterns of political influence. These latter are based on intimate influence relationships between child and mother and father. The individual's political power relationships are at work in all political interactions, within and without the family. The most crucial relationships are those affecting basic goals and ways of achieving goals as these apply to a large community, to the integrated big society of hundreds or thousands or millions of individuals. These relationships may seem to be small or private in some cases: an individual's or a family's decision to help build a well in the village to provide safe water for

Many people have variously helped, with their ideas, data, or editing, in the realization of this chapter. Most crucial was the help of Donald T. Cundy, Sarah Davies, Nancy S. Hoffman, David Krech, Bobbie Conlan Moore, Anne Parnaby, Stanley Renshon, David C. Schwartz, and Lynn K. Shephard.

drinking and abundant water for crops—or an individual's decision either to join the national army or to resist being drafted. Only if the power relationships have no significant effect outside the family or local community are they of no relevance here.

The relevant power relationships between the individual and others who are near and distant produce public choices and therefore establish public policy. These choices, these decisions, in the integrated big society now prevail over the multitude of choices which individuals make that at most affect only the local community. Indeed, broad public policy decisions often restrict individual choices that are seemingly altogether private. At some point in a nation's development, individuals who have been free to throw the family's sewage and garbage into the public street are forbidden to do such things. At some later point in a nation's development, individuals may be forbidden and then allowed to abort an unplanned, unwanted pregnancy.

People increasingly are unable to escape the sometimes protective, sometimes destructive long arm of the national government. People nevertheless continue to try to escape from making public policy decisions—and occasionally, perhaps increasingly, try to take part in making such decisions. In newly developing parts of the world that are still unintegrated internally, perhaps it all starts when children get immunized against bacterial disease—and when they get infected with the immunity-proof disease of "modern" desires. The choices now that are hard to make are those involving the areas of individual life that shall involve government action and the areas that shall remain private and immune from government action.

Predispositions established in the first few years of life relate to this issue of public and private areas, because children raised to expect the world to be overpowering are not as adults very capable of resisting efforts by government to invade any part of their lives. Neither are very powerless people very capable of demanding that government serve their interests also, rather than responding only to the demands of the powerful.

In India in 1975 it took the momentary destruction of all effective opposition and the imposition of harsh police measures against profiteering merchants to secure some degree of public control in support of an impoverished, even famished population of hundreds of millions. If the hundreds of millions were themselves able to wield significant political power, there would have been no need for action by the government of Indira Gandhi. And if any action by that government had been taken against a solidified nation of hundreds of millions, it would likely have failed.

Incursive action by the executive branch of the national government in the United States failed in 1974 when it was at last opposed by a nation of two hundred millions in the last stages of the Watergate affair. Two differences prevailed between India and the United States on these two occasions that were just one year apart: the general public in India was quite poor and powerless; in America it was prosperous and quite confident of its own power. The executive arm of government in India proposed action against a small group whose interests were not visibly supportive of the general public; the executive arm of government in America in the Watergate affair proposed action that was not visibly supportive of any policy other than the maintenance in power of the incumbent chief executive. The profound differences related to the degree of development of the two nations and of individuals within them. And the degree of individual development in any nation is, in critical degree, related to each individual's first six years of life.

The desire and ability to make fundamental public choices are not shared equally by people everywhere—even when they cannot escape the consequences of policy decisions made by others, notably by organized economic and political groups. The desire and ability involve exercising public influence and accepting the consequence of exercising that influence. Doing it is a large and sometimes palpably threatening act. It may cost a person his or her job or freedom or health or life—or all four in that order. A person may die ingloriously of starvation or languish alone in solitary prison confinement because he made a political choice that the established government would not permit.

Probably most people in the world do not and cannot yet accept political power and its responsibility. The forces inhibiting growth of the ability to exercise that power may start functioning before birth and become set during the first six years of life. While never irrevocably set, these forces underlie, for life, all later influences shaping the political behavior of human beings. When these early-internalized and childhood-fixed inhibitors are conjoined during adulthood with threats that reactivate early-established memories of similar threats, control of a people by an elite is easy and control of an elite by a people is very difficult, at least by those people who are power-inhibited in even the most advanced societies.

The major influencer is the family, either directly or as the proximal mediator of the distal influences which it transmits to the child from society outside the family (Davies, 1963, chaps. 5 & 6; 1965). But there are even prior influences that affect the bodily state and therefore the mental state of the individual during its fetal, neonatal, infantile, and early childhood epochs. All of these influences affect the desire and ability of the eventual adult to exercise political power. They are now considered here as they respectively relate to *whether* adults exercise that power and, if they do, *how*.

First of all, I will suggest some explanation for what is typically ignored: the very important political phenomenon that is called political apathy—and then is dropped from consideration. To understand politics in our era, we have to understand not only why people take part in politics but why they do not. Failing to consider the latter makes it impossible to understand politics as it develops in its earliest stages inside the heads of people who are themselves for the first time initiating their exercise of political power, whether as minority newcomers to an established polity or as the majority in a newly developing polity.

The Whether of Political Involvement

For virtually all people nearly all the time everywhere, there is no political activity. In primitive (that is, unintegrated, preexchange, preindustrial) societies, people have little concern for what happens outside the village or over the hill in the next valley or on the next island. What happens there does not affect them, and so there is no real need for political involvement. Indeed, even in advanced (that is, integrated industrial) societies, people spend only a small fraction of their time dealing with broad economic and social issues that do affect them. They do become increasingly involved spectators to political action, but they rarely feel called on to act—to vote, write letters, join political associations, go to meetings, join crowds, or help organize political influence. Most people do no more than vote, and only in national elections—in countries where they vote at all—and voting takes only a tiny fraction of their time.

However, when voting involves real choice and not mere ratification of already established rules or rulers, this tiny amount of time makes an enormous difference in how public policy decisions are made. This tiny amount of time limits the scope and establishes the general direction of elite-proposed public policy. The effort to make policy decisions and bear their consequences is so substantial that people in most of the world do not feel comfortable with even that amount of effort. They listen and talk with family and friends and then they indicate their decision privately and anonymously in a polling booth (if the rules allow it). Or, if in a crowd at a political gathering (if the rules do not prohibit public assembly), they protect their individual act of participating by losing themselves in the crowd, an anonymous multitude. (But police photographers are there and have individuals in sharp focus.) We are not here concerned with the rules of the political game as the elite establishes them. We are, first of all, concerned with whether people will choose to play it in light of their earliest influences, and second of all, with how these influences relate to how people obey, disobey, and change rules and rulers.

The most basic proposition may be stated thus:

A child who has been severely physically deprived throughout the first six years of life will very likely never become involved in any political decision making as an adult.

Physical deprivation, as we shall see, is by no means the only pertinent form of deprivation. So we can now specify and later explain the second most basic proposition:

A child who has been severely emotionally deprived throughout the first six years of life will very likely never become involved in any political decision making as an adult.

Both propositions are probabilistic, quantitative, nonabsolute statements, both internally and with respect to each other. Short of death, one cannot say that an adult who was severely *physically* deprived as a child will never become politically involved. In circumstances that encourage such involvement, in a generally advancing society, even an adult with a history of severe childhood *physical* deprivation may join a crowd that is burning the Bastille on 14 July 1789—or may vote in an election. Likewise, an adult who was severely *emotionally* deprived as a child may do the same things. Unfortunately, there is not yet any research that has systematically compared the political impact of physical and emotional deprivation. There is, however, some evidence that supports by inference the two basic propositions.

Nutrition and Hormones

Before presenting some evidence, we need to bear in mind some nonevidence. The most remarkable and neglectable fact about those who are 6 years old is that they have survived, whether with ease or with difficulty. This is remarkable because the death rate among children in unintegrated, preindustrial societies is high, and perhaps even a majority of them have had to struggle to survive infancy. This is neglectable because most people who can reflect about the conditions of survival have themselves survived with ease. The consequences of that first and elemental struggle—whether difficult or easy—persist in the brains of all individuals for their entire lives.

One of the most likely mental consequences of childhood malnourishment is an enduring, perhaps lifelong, tendency to be preoccupied with food, to keep oneself alive, and if possible to keep one's family members alive. As we shall see, it may also spill over into adult insecurity about many things other than food. This linkage between childhood influences and adult behavior involves ascertaining mental states that have been established before a child can verbally express itself and is therefore hard to demonstrate. It can, however, be inferred from research that has been done with adults who have volunteered to undergo experimental semistarvation.

At the University of Minnesota during the Second World War, 32 conscientious objectors volunteered to go on a half-normal diet of about 1,470 calories per day for a 24-week period, followed by a 12-week period of dietary rehabilitation (Keys et al., 1950). One of the rather typical subjects, called "Don" in the report (Brozek, 1953), experienced these physical changes in weight:

At start of 24-week semistarvation period	142 lb	65 kg
At end of 24-week semistarvation period	115	52
At end of 12-week rehabilitation period	120	54
21 weeks later (33 weeks after end of semistarvation period)	163	74

It is the mental changes that are most striking. "Don" was not only a conscientious objector but also, before the experiment, at age 25, a novice architect; unmarried but with a girlfriend to whom he was writing almost daily from Minneapolis. As a much involved member of the group of conscientious objectors in the experiment, he planned to do relief work abroad after the war. Then came semi-starvation. During the third week, his morale was high. Physically he tired easily but his mental energy and acumen were unimpaired and, unlike some others in the experiment, he was not always thinking about food. By the eighth week, he was dreaming about food. By the twelfth, that was all he thought about when he was awake. He developed aches and pains, with or without exercise. He became more restless and irritable. He found it hard to concentrate on anything. By the sixteenth week, he had frequent hunger pangs and headaches.

And, in the ominous and universal symptom of starvation, he became increasingly apathetic about everything save food. When his girlfriend came to see him during the eighteenth week, he found the visit to be a strain and he could not establish rapport with her. By the end of the semistarvation period, he had almost stopped writing his girl and had lost all interest in postwar relief work. He repeatedly expressed the hope that he would be placed in the one of four groups of experimental subjects that was to get the most abundant rehabilitation diet. As his elemental self-confidence began to dissolve, earlier in the experiment, he had said, ''I think it is a good idea to put strong checks on us.'' In short, in his hunger-derived but now pervasive anxiety, he wanted to divest himself of power.

During the rehabilitation period, ''Don'' became obsessed with the idea that he was not getting his fair share of food. He spent his time reading religious literature and had no desire to take part in any group activities. For a time his interest in relief work became active again, but he decided to work in the United States rather than overseas. He expressed greater awareness of the need to aid starving people everywhere, but he decided to get back to training for architecture and ''get started on his own.'' His concern for others, his self-esteem, and his self-confidence were radically, basically diminished by ''mere'' semistarvation. All this many-faceted involution and regression came not from being mentally bombarded by some dictatorship's torture, but quite simply from a diet that supported life but not vitality.

Semistarvation has been and continues to be the real way of life, for short or long periods, of millions of people. In the Nazi concentration camps, near the end of the 1939–1945 war, the daily food allowance was *reduced* from about 1,750 calories (300 more than in the Minnesota experiments) to about 1,050 calories and even to 800 (Richet, 1947; Lipscomb, 1947). These figures compare to a ''normal'' daily intake of about 2,700 to 3,000 calories for physically active people in a temperate climate.

There was severe famine in Holland during the winter of 1944–1945 when the Nazi occupation imposed a food blockade. Western Holland, which includes Amsterdam, The Hague, and Rotterdam, was hardest hit: caloric intake dropped as low as 700. Other parts of Holland enjoyed the abundance of 1,400 to 1,500 calories per day—half the normal amount (Stein et al., 1972). An entire nation became a dietary concentration camp. There was severe famine in Leningrad during the German siege of 1941–1944: about 20% of the 2.9 million besieged inhabitants died of cold or starvation (Pavlov, 1965, p. xiv). The famines of China and India in the early 20th century are legendary. And semistarvation remains a fact of life in much of the world in the late 20th century.

Our main concern here is not with the horror of starvation, which in so many ways demoralized and disempowered at least some experimental subjects in Minnesota and reduced large populations at least to nearly total preoccupation with staying alive during war-induced or catastrophe-induced famine. But it is ominous to note that the experience has caused some famished people to do the unthinkable, to eat from the bodies even of deceased family members (Khrushchev, 1970, pp. 234–235; Salisbury, 1970, pp. 546–547, 550–551) or literally to snatch food out of the mouths of the living (Turnbull, 1972, p. 161).

Our main concern is with the possible lifelong effects on adult political behavior of malnutrition in early childhood. On this specific and crucial question there is no direct research evidence. There is good gross evidence of a relationship between national nutrition levels and degree of economic, social, and political development (Davies, 1963, pp. 26–28; Stauffer, 1969). And there is good evidence that malnutrition-related diseases (like enteritis, diarrhea, pneumonia—and kwashiorkor, discussed below) are particularly lethal for children. These diseases are 3 times to 200 times as prevalent in primitive circumstances (e.g., in areas of Chile, Guatemala, and the Philippines) as such diseases are in advanced nations like Sweden and the United States (Stauffer, 1969, p. 373). One estimate is that 300 million of the 500 million preschool-age children (60%) in the world are mildly or severely underfed (Behar, 1968, p. 40). Perhaps more as consequence than cause, but quite surely as both consequence and cause, malnutrition stalks socioeconomic and political development like a lethal shadow. What happens to underfed infants now—even in nations that are generally advanced—is affecting the power relationships of adults to the big society among perhaps 60% of the world's population, *into the 21st century*.

The causes of political development remain a tangled knot from which it is not yet possible to lift out the strong threads of nutrition. An extensive analysis, based on abundant data gathered from 125,000 male army recruits in Holland, shows that there was no significant mental retardation or even lowered intelligence among those recruits who were gestated, born, or as infants raised during the 1944–1945 famine in Western Holland (Stein et al., 1972). However, the comparison group in the rest of Holland was not well fed but, as we have noted, semistarved. Nationwide, there was a considerable incidence of amenorrhea (which prevents conception) and a decline in live births. Nevertheless, the period of starvation was relatively brief and was followed by speedy and effective rehabilitation efforts. And the widespread popular knowledge in Holland of just what small children should eat makes the situation in that highly developed nation difficult to compare with the chronic crisis in the technically, socially, and politically least integrated areas of the least developed nations.

Research remains to be done on the political consequences of chronic childhood malnutrition, but physiological research provides some solid and ominous evidence of what happens to the prenatally, perinatally, and postnatally mal-nourished central nervous system. As the organ of behavior, the brain seems able to get nourishment at the expense of nearly all other parts of the body, but even it can be permanently damaged when malnourished, particularly before it has grown to its adult size and complexity.

One study of adult human starvation reported these losses in weight: fatty tissue, 97%; testes, 40%; skeletal muscle, 31%; heart, 3%; and brain, 3% (Parsons in Davies, 1963, p. 14n). A study of prenatal starvation involved experiments with guinea pigs that were fed a third of the normal diet during the last half of their pregnancy. Over half the fetuses were aborted or stillborn. Of those that did survive gestation, the average body weight was about half that of those whose mothers got a normal diet during pregnancy, but the brain weight was 85% of normal (Martin, 1973, p. 766). In experiments with newborn rats that were deliberately and drastically underfed for 24 days, body weights were a third of those not so starved, but the brain weights were 78% of normal (Cragg, 1972, p. 146).

Both the sequence (normal to subnormal or subnormal to normal nutrition) and the time of its occurrence are vital. In one experiment, rats that were healthy at birth were then undernourished for the first 21 days of life and thereafter fed normally. They suffered a permanent decrease from the normal number of cells in the brain, as well as in other organs. Those fed normally till their 22nd day but then underfed for 21 days suffered no decrease in other organs. Those underfed only for days 64–86 suffered no decrease from normal in number of cells in either brain or elsewhere (Winick & Noble in Winick, 1974, pp. 255–256).

In human beings, the brain contains about two thirds the adult number of cells at birth and nearly the complete number by the age of one year, when the brain has achieved about 80% of its adult weight. The period of most rapid brain cell growth during the crucial first year is from the 6th to 12th months. Among 19 children undernourished for more than 4 months out of their first year, "the intelligence or developmental quotients" at the age of about 4½ years were 30 points below a control group that was not undernourished (Martin, 1973, pp. 767–768).

There is even a good clue or two as to *why* dullness results from malnutrition during infancy. The number of *neurons* in the brains of rats that were starved in one of our just-mentioned experiments was about the same as among those not starved, but the number of *axons*—terminals through which one neuron is con-nected with others—was down 38%. This, in effect, plus retarded development of the brain's glia cells (the fatty cells which nourish the neurons), renders the brain much less able to make its normally intricate and discriminating responses to various stimuli, because there are fewer links between neurons. The perma-nently damaged brain cannot so easily make the choices appropriate to the healthy functioning and development of the organism.

The ominous implication of this research is that life in every human sense is permanently stunted for those who have experienced malnutrition in infancy. The ability to make political choices among them is quite surely nil. As we have noted, perhaps 300 million (some 60% of all preschool) humans have made a wrong first "choice," which becomes their last choice, that of being born to serve as the expendable nonlaboratory starvation testing material of a society undergoing development. During this epoch of population growth and of social and political change, when the elemental limiting factor is the ability to sustain life itself, these children are the sacrifice that humanity makes to establish these limits. Because of the nature of human beings, who contain organically the potential to demand and enjoy more out of life than mere survival, progress beyond survival is inevitable—except perhaps for those who have unnaturally suffered infantile brain damage because they did not get enough to eat. Is the political price exacted by malnourishment—being unable ever to make significant choices on issues of public policy, the price paid by malnourished infants throughout their short or long lives—also inevitable? Human nature is effectively unchangeable, but nurture is not nature. Lack of nurture can do almost irreparable damage: it can prevent the beyond-survival parts of human nature from ever emerging.

There are the beginnings of research on the politically relevant effects of chronic poor health. Among the general consequences are anxiety and depression, relating to an inability to handle stress; low self-esteem and high self-concern; social withdrawal and (in seeming paradox) dependency. We saw these phenomena in the Minnesota starvation experiments. More directly as to political portents, Schwartz has found, in a study of 2,000 urban high school students in the United States, that the 5% with poor health indeed were less involved both in student and (vicariously) in public politics and knew less about public issues than their healthier peers (Schwartz, 1973). Unfortunately, our knowledge of the political consequences of poor health remains at about the point Schwartz

There is more abundant knowledge about the second of the two basic propositions, the one on emotional deprivation. And there is at least one piece of research that reports on the combined effects of both physical and emotional deprivation in the disease known as kwashiorkor. Fortunately—because the continued effects are quite lethal—we have to put up with very imperfect analysis: the mortality rate was over 40% in the reported research in Uganda (Geber, 1973; Geber & Dean, 1955), and it is not easy to study those who are dead.

Kwashiorkor is the early childhood disease that in part is the result of a diet that is low in protein but high in carbohydrate. Its physical symptoms include edema (swelling), usually in the face and legs; weak and wasted muscles; depigmentation of hair, which becomes sparse and falls out easily; sometimes a flaky skin and ulcers; enlarged liver; anemia; diarrhea; and susceptibility to disease, notably tuberculosis. Its mental symptoms are misery, immobility, and the ominous, lethal apathy we noted in the Minnesota starvation experiments.

Kwashiorkor is a West African word translatable as "the weaning disease." It is prevalent in countries in the early stages of development, notably Africa and

Latin America. Nutritionally, it differs from marasmus, "the wasting disease," in that kwashiorkor results in part from severe protein deficiency, whereas marasmus results from overall deficiency, of protein and carbohydrate alike. Nutritionally, kwashiorkor relates to plenty of starch; marasmus to plenty of nothing. If prolonged, the latter means death from starvation. The former is more complex in its causes and consequences.

Kwashiorkor develops after traditional weaning, which in some parts of Uganda takes place very suddenly when the child is between 12 and 18 months old. From birth until weaning it gets not only a protein-rich diet from its mother's milk but also her almost continuous attention. The child eats, sleeps, plays with, and to a significant degree controls its ever present mother. At weaning time, all this constant interaction is suddenly interrupted. The child is then completely separated from its mother, sometimes by being put into another house, even in another village. The child may be put in the care of individuals it has never before seen. It is offered starchy food but is not forced to eat.

The consequences of abrupt weaning and separation are both physically and mentally disastrous. Suffering the loss of mother, who has given the infant both a rich diet in her milk and constant emotional support, and suffering the loss of the ability to control a nourishing and affectionate environment, the child must suddenly fend for itself, in a seemingly indifferent or even hostile environment. It develops a sense of its own impotence and of the environment's omnipotence. These victims of this situation who do survive must—even before they are 2 years old—recover from catastrophic physical and emotional deprivation at weaning time and recommence their growth. The deep trauma quite surely must affect their ability to make political choices as adults.

At this stage of social science we have studies of the immediate physical and mental consequences of kwashiorkor and do not have studies of adults, wherein those who had kwashiorkor and survived are compared with those who never experienced the disease. The 40% mortality rate reported in the Uganda study argues that the effects must be shattering. But people whose abrupt weaning is followed by separation from mother and by a starchy diet have survived for centuries. We do know that kwashiorkor occurs in the most traditional parts of countries in early stages of development. We do not know how much the disease retards the rate of development.

A large question that calls for massive research is this: what correlation is there between the mental effects of malnutrition, loss of emotional support, and sudden powerlessness in early childhood (in whatever combinations) and diminished ability in adulthood to make public choices? The question is indeed pertinent and the chain of consequences is indeed long between small children so deprived and adult political behavior. It will tempt some people to conclude that abrupt weaning is *the* cause of slow development, just as observing the practice of swaddling infants once led two writers to assert that swaddling is the cause of a whole range of behaviors of Russians (Gorer & Rickman, 1949).

(Male) Assertiveness and (Female) Nurturance

Before turning directly to a separate consideration of emotional deprivation, we have to deal with a couple of hormones. These are, generally speaking, produced within the body under the control of its genetic processes and so are beyond our preoccupation with various environmental influences. But the presence of varying amounts of at least two hormones in the fetus stems from the passage of these from the mother's bloodstream through the placenta. To explain the possible political consequences of this unusual prenatal environmental influence, we have to consider the behavioral effects of the balance between these two hormones, both of which are naturally present in at least all higher vertebrates, including both males and females.

These two hormones are the androgens and the estrogens. Boys and men have relatively more androgens than girls and women, who have relatively more estrogens than males. And the difference in balance has, as we shall see, much to do with differences in behavior between males and females. These hormonal differences are often neglected because, in perhaps all cultures, the socialization process establishes, by early childhood imprinting, many clearly defined differences in the ways males and females are supposed to behave. These role-expectation differences between males and females, often mistaken for natural differences, are cultural artifacts related to but distinct from another precocious environmental factor, the passage of sex hormones from the mother through the placenta to the fetus.

The determinants we are now considering are not cultural artifacts: they are environmental but also hormonal. Their effects are more akin to those of the *genetically* produced sex hormones and thus to genetically produced differences in behavior. That is, externally (exogenously) produced sex hormones have the same effects as those endogenously produced. Most of the effects of those hormones are intertwined with culturally induced sex-role demands, with the result that we lose sight of the difference between hormonal and cultural influences. But whether or not we approve on ideological grounds, there are some important differences between the ways men and women behave politically. Some of these differences derive, in a long causal chain, from differences in the balance of sex hormones. And some of the difference in balance is environmental, even though most of the difference is genetic.

Some experimental research will help explain the origins of these hormone-derived differences in behavior.

In one study, when pregnant monkeys were given an injection of testosterone (the principal androgen) during the middle of the gestation period (from the 39th to the 105th day of a 168-day pregnancy), female fetuses were permanently affected by this exogenous androgen. During the postnatal growth period (from 3½ to 15 months after birth), young females with this prenatal treatment were consistently more likely than untreated ones to act like males—to initiate play, to play rough, to chase other monkeys, and to make threatening gestures. They were, however, less likely than untreated *males* to do these things. The differences between the behavior of untreated males, testosterone-treated females, and untreated females diminished with maturation but maintained the same relative frequencies (Goy, 1970).

Hormonal treatment *after* birth has comparable effects, at least on female rats. When normally gestated female rats were injected shortly after birth with testosterone, as adults they fought with other like-injected female rats about ten times as much as did females that had not had the testosterone treatment. As in the case of our prenatally treated female monkeys, the postnatally treated female rats did not fight with each other as much as did normal male rats. When the testosterone-treated females were as adults given injections of progesterone (one of the estrogens) to make them more receptive to males, half of those that had had postnatal testosterone fought with their amorous male partners. In one case the female killed the male. None of the females that had not been given testosterone after birth fought with their male partners (Bronson & Desjardins, 1968).

Two generalizations about natural (i.e., noncultural) sex differences appear to be generally accepted by physiologists, by many psychologists, and perhaps implicitly by most nonscientists: males are more inclined to be assertive or even aggressive (i.e., assertive with the intent to do harm) than females; and females are more inclined to be nurturant than males. There is a considerable overlap, perhaps some of it due to cultural standards and some to the balance of the sex hormones in particular individuals. Even in "normal" populations, men act in ways that are associated with nurturance and other possibly female traits. Women do assert themselves, get angry, and even occasionally go to war and/or kill. Men do seek to be sought, show patience, and refuse to go to war and/or kill. Some women enter politics. Some men are at last free to stay home while their wives go out into the assertive, competitive world of paying jobs.

It nevertheless seems evident that men generally are more assertive than women, that women generally are more nurturant than men, and that there is a clear relationship between these differences and the amounts of androgens and estrogens in the circulatory system. Experiments with higher vertebrates, as we have seen, confirm the relationships between sex-hormone balance and animal behavior. Research among humans confirms at least the difference in sex-hormone balance. Judging by urine samples, men have about six times as much testosterone in their systems as women (Ganong, 1969, pp. 353–354) and women (relating to the time of monthly ovulation) have about 4 to 10 times as much estrogen as men (Ganong, 1969, p 364). Women after menopause have less estrogen in their systems than men have between the ages of 45 and 65 (Ganong, 1969, p. 363). Although the technology is available, evidently no collaborative research between physiologists and social scientists has established systematic correlations between sex-hormone levels and assertive-nonassertive and nurturant-nonnurturant behaviors of large numbers of people, particularly in their interactions in the big society. An increase in research and a decrease in rhetoric will improve and quantify our knowledge of sex differences that affect human behavior.

Meanwhile it is reasonable to hypothesize that the greater amount and the more assertive kinds of political involvement of men as compared with women are partly attributable to the higher androgen-to-estrogen ratio among men. Correlatively, it is reasonable to suppose that the lag in social and political development of women has not been altogether a cultural artifact. They have been naturally less assertive in addition to being culturally oppressed, in perhaps most societies, by men's (mostly cultural?) dominance. And the natural antecedent of this dominance is men's higher testosterone level. Legislation whose intent is to equalize the rights of women and men may actually diminish the effect of sex hormones and increase the effect of other common and innate characteristics of both men and women.

The Earliest Emotional Nurturance

Thus far we have had a look at perhaps the most neglected environmental influences, nutrition and (in certain circumstances) hormones, as these pertain to whether an individual will ever become a choice-making adult citizen. We have noted that malnutrition has a depoliticizing effect among famished adults and that it is often lethal in little children. We have noted in kwashiorkor the grievous immediate and possible later consequences of combined physical and emotional deprivation. We have noted that the sex hormones are basic determinants of the amount of assertiveness, aggressiveness, and nurturance that we higher vertebrates display toward each other.

Now we can more discretely abstract out those influences on human development that are emotional and thus more cleanly examine the second basic proposition: that a severely emotionally deprived child, like a malnourished child, is an unlikely prospect for making political choices as an adult.

First we will have a look at the disaster that overtakes a child raised without at least one adult to give it her (or conceivably his) nurturant attention and affection. Then we will consider experiments with monkeys that have explored the mother-infant relationship, in a depth not possible among humans. And finally we will look at two kinds of experiments that indicate the effects on the development of the brain of environments that are either exciting or just plain dull.

In extreme cases, the loss of a mother is lethal—in one study, it was found to be almost as lethal as kwashiorkor in Uganda in the 1950s. In a foundling home in the Western Hemisphere, an Austrian psychiatrist, René Spitz, studied the effects of maternal deprivation. Each of the nurses in the home had to care for 8 to 10 foundlings and so could give no one of the infants her undivided attention for very long (Spitz, 1965, pp. 277–278). By the end of the second year, and despite normal feeding and other bodily care, over a third of the 91 children were dead. Those that survived were either apathetic vegetables or were hyperexcitable—or oscillated between apathy and rage (Spitz, 1949, 1965). Among the symptoms that developed in these severely emotionally deprived children were "weepiness," insomnia, decreased body movement and facial rigidity, proneness to disease, loss of weight and appetite, withdrawal, and retrogression from normal development (Spitz, 1965, p. 282).

Quite independently in England, another psychiatrist commenced his research on parent-deprived children during the Second World War when children were evacuated from their homes in London during the bombing. John Bowlby found the same sorts of results of prolonged maternal deprivation that Spitz did. Before it is about a half-year old, a normal child raised in family circumstances where two or more older people are present is not very specifically attached to a particular adult and can tolerate absence from its mother quite well (Bowlby, 1969, p. 199). Thereafter, the degree of upset at separation from its own mother increases until about the age of 3. Then it diminishes: at the age of 5, children can tolerate Mother's absence without grievous upset (Bowlby, 1973, pp. 33–39). Although Bowlby dealt with mother absence, because mothers are the usual object of attachment, evidently it is the consistent attention of some one person rather than the attention of the mother that is crucial (Rutter, 1972, pp. 41–49).

Bowlby noted three stages of reaction to separation: outgoing protest, despair (which involves grief and mourning), and finally the in-turning defense of detachment (1969, pp. 27–28; 1973, pp. 26–27). The separated child at first screams to get his mother back, and finally he manifests his indifference by turning away from her when she does return. In perhaps most cases, when rejoined with his parents, he seems to try to punish his mother by showing strong attachment to his father (1973, p. 12).

The trauma of *privation* of affectionate contact, of never having affection from the time an infant begins to distinguish itself from its environment, is rare and probably very lethal, as suggested by Spitz's research in the semiprivation of a foundling home. The trauma of *de*privation, of loss of previously assured love (particularly between the ages of 6 months and 3 years [Bowlby, 1969, pp. 204–205]) is also rare but probably less lethal and to some degree reversible. Deprivation establishes a profound anxiety—even fear—of permanent loss of affection. One result is a possibly lifelong sense of isolation, both from those who are close and from those who are distant: in other words, a deep and lasting sense of interpersonal and social insecurity. Another is a possibly lifelong sense of impotence, of being totally controlled rather than of being able in some ways and degrees to serve one's own day-to-day welfare and to control one's own future.

The classic experiments of Harry Harlow with monkeys have probed further into the effects of loss of normal emotional nurture. Some newborn monkeys were reared with their mothers; others without mother but with age peers; others with a bare-wire mother surrogate covered with terry cloth. Still others were reared without even a surrogate, in total isolation, either in cages separated from even visual contact with other monkeys or in inverted-pyramid boxes within which they could move only a little and from which they could not escape.

To abbreviate the extensive findings (Harlow, 1958; Harlow & Harlow, 1962; Harlow & Suomi, 1970, 1971; and elsewhere), those reared from birth with age peers were close to normal (i.e., close to those raised by their own natural mothers) in their social interactions. Those reared with wire mothers became strange: some would sit apathetically in their cages, others would rage at passersby, others (like some of Spitz's foundlings) would alternate between these moods of extreme withdrawal and hostile interaction. Some, raging at themselves, would gnaw at their own flesh, even to the point of exposing bone. Those raised in total isolation rarely varied from a huddled position, sometimes with arm and hand encircling head as if to provide themselves with some love when the environment bereaved them of it. Those raised with a wire-cloth mother clung to her despite efforts to dislodge them with a sudden blast of compressed air or with spikes arranged to spring suddenly from mother's bosom. The more the blast of air or the spikes frightened the infant monkeys, the more tenaciously they clung to their ill-tempered, unpredictable fake mothers.

All of the abnormally raised monkeys, including those raised by their peers, had varying degrees of difficulty adapting to each others as adults, particularly in their sex life. When placed with normally raised monkeys, the (semi-)isolates were unsure of themselves and sometimes had to be rescued by the experimenters from savage attack by the normals which often, like other lower animals, attack the weak. Both male and female isolates were clumsy and ineffectual in their efforts to copulate, or they violently rejected the whole idea.

Using what he called a "rape rack" and the cooperation of some healthy primate studs, Harlow and associates got some of the reluctant females pregnant. Typically, they became monstrous mothers. Some of them rubbed the heads of their unwanted offspring against the bottom of the cage until they were grievously wounded. Some reluctant mothers bit through the skulls of their offspring and killed them. Yet the brutalized offspring preferred maternal hostility to maternal absence, and this incorrigible, indestructible need for contact cured some of the monstrous mothers.

All, in short, was in the long run not lost. Immature monkeys that had been socially deprived by some variation of the experiments proved to be effective therapists for their worse-stricken agemates and even to their elders. When unwanted infant monkeys clung desperately to their "motherless mothers," gradually some of the mothers became less rejecting and at last accepted their offspring. The infant cured the adult. In subsequent pregnancies, some of the formerly hostile mothers behaved quite normally toward their second- or later-born. In sum, love-deprived infant monkeys became unwitting, un-Freudian psychotherapists of each other and of love-deprived adults (Harlow & Suomi, 1970, 1971). But in any case the cure was slow. The "sins" of omission of affection were visited even unto the second generation, becoming sins of commission in the process.

The Harlow studies are of course not completed: there are not yet full data on the adult consequences of all variations of emotional privation and deprivation. But it is indeed very clear that the results of abnormal upbringing, bereft of "simple" contact with a live and warm mother, are catastrophic. In the words of the great pioneering psychologist, William James, "the great source of terror in infancy is solitude." There are certain organic characteristics in humans, primates, and, as we shall see, in even much lower forms of animal life that make intensive and continuing interaction with at least one significant conspecific critical for survival.[1]

The intense, primal need for continuous contact with others helps explain the use of isolation to break down political prisoners. It helps explain the intense attachment to Nazism among young people in Germany in the 1920s (Abel, 1938, pp. 152, 218, 246–247, 267). It also helps explain the passionate attachment of young people to antiregime movements in America in the 1960s, when parental rejection became a common (though not universal) factor in their transfer of emotional ties to political movements composed of young people who shared both ideals, interests, and often parental rejection. Lynette Fromme, who pointed a loaded pistol toward the President of the United States in Sacramento, California, in September 1975, had earlier said that she was thrown out of her home of origin by her father and then joined the frenetically close family of the killer, Charles Manson. As reported shortly after the September incident: "One night in 1967, a puffy-faced scraggly-haired girl of 17 sat on a sidewalk in Venice, California. She had always thought she was ugly and unloved, and she was crying. 'A man walked up,' she later recalled, 'and said,' "Your father kicked you out of the house." ' The man was Manson" (*Newsweek*, 15 September 1975, p. 18).

René Spitz has called infant feeding the "cradle of perception." It is more than that. Among humans and at least primates, nurturance both physical and emotional is the cradle of *all* behavior, of all fundamental habits, and of the most basic of the attitudes. The consequences of the primitive social contacts of infancy go deeper than even attitudes. They affect the very structure of the brain itself: they shape the cradle.

At least among laboratory rats, deprivation of normal social contact with other rats and with humans affects the development of brain tissue and even of enzymes involved in the process of passing signals from one neuron to another. In a long series of experiments, rats raised in normal contact with other rats, with laboratory technicians, and with the toys that rats like to play with were compared with those raised in darkened cages, with minimal handling by technicians, and with no toys. Postmortem examination revealed that those raised in an

---

[1]Allee, in his classic survey of the natural origins of group living, reports his experiments with the fatal effect of putting goldfish in water containing colloidal silver. All the goldfish died, but groups of ten goldfish survived nearly three times as long as isolated single ones. He found a comparable result among flatworms exposed together and singly to a fatal dose of ultraviolet radiation (Allee, 1958; pp. 32–33, 37–40).

emotionally and perceptually impoverished environment had smaller brains and different amounts of two enzymes (acetylcholinesterase and cholinesterase) involved in brain function than did rats raised in enriched environments (Krech, 1968; Quay et al., 1969). Parenthetically, laboratory rats raised in a more natural environment, with some freedom to explore the great "wild" world outside but adjoining the laboratory, had larger brains and higher neurotransmitter levels than the indulged but protected rats. This latter finding suggests that cerebral development as well as mental health require not just togetherness but also independence—i.e., emotional support *and* autonomy.

In discussing the establishment of emotional ties, we have not yet, except by implication, considered the critical nature of timing and sequence. We have noted but not dwelled on the inability of children to tolerate loss of mother or mother substitute before the age of 3 and the ability of *normally* raised 5-year-olds to stand some separation. The phenomenon we are now considering more directly is the need for certain things to happen during certain time periods if they are ever to be followed by other developmental processes (Delius, 1970, pp. 190–193). The rats, deprived in puppyhood of normal emotional and other stimulation, were *permanently* deficient in their central nervous and endocrine systems.

The critical nature of timing and sequence is overwhelmingly evident from the research in imprinting. Hess has defined it as the interaction between brain and environment "in which there is an extremely rapid attachment, during a specific critical period, of an innate behavior pattern to specific objects which thereafter become important elicitors of that behavior pattern" (Hess, 1973, p. 65). Imprinting that relates to food and other physical needs (that is, the establishment of the expectation of particular kinds of nourishment) probably begins at birth for all animals that have a distinct central control (i.e., central nervous and endocrine) system. To some degree, even worms have such a system and so are capable of learning.

Imprinting that relates to attachment (the establishment of emotional need-gratification patterns) begins a little later than physical need-gratification patterns. For baby chicks and ducklings, the critical time for the first attachment imprinting, which establishes what is the chick's or duckling's "mother," is from 13 to 16 hours after hatching. Before that period of mere hours, mother imprinting usually does note occur, and after that 4-hour period it occurs with less durability. At about 50 hours after hatching it is virtually extinct. During the critical period, chicks and ducklings can be imprinted to respond to a human or other stimulating object, as though the object were a normal mother hen or duck.

We have already noted Bowlby's report that in humans attachment to a particular mother begins at about 6 months. As with primates and humans, the attachment of young fowl becomes less intense as they mature: they can waddle alone. But in one experiment it was acutely reactivated when ducklings were electrically shocked. And in another, when ducklings were conditioned to summon a "mother" in the form of a feeding bottle that appeared when they pecked a key, their distress calls diminished—even before the bottle appeared (Hess, p. 111). Perhaps even young ducks and young humans share a desire to control. Pecking or crying that has been previously followed by the appearance of Mother gives the very young the sense that it has some measure of control and thereby gives it some sense of security.

What I have tried to do thus far is to indicate various ways in which physical and emotional deprivation during the first years of life can destroy or seriously diminish the ability of people as adults to take part in making choices in public policy, in making political choices. I have recounted field and laboratory research findings that pertain to these earliest, most enduring, and hardest-to-change influences. These first socializing influences work both ways, permanently strengthening or permanently weakening the very foundations of individuals' physical and mental ability to live and grow. If they establish a self-sustaining viable organism, it is resistant to all sorts of later influences that threaten its well-being and it is able to face the challenges of change and development. If on the other hand they establish a frail, barely viable organism, it is vulnerable to all later forces.

In Uganda in the 1960s a primitive mountain people was faced with a double disaster. As the nation of which they were a largely unwitting and unwilling part began to modernize, the central government moved this people off some of their normal hunting and foraging lands. Then a drought devastated their already arid and now shrunken territory. Unable to relocate any more and unable to sustain life off the land, they began figuratively to devour one another (Turnbull, 1972). They could not cope with a challenge not of their making: their society collapsed in a struggle of each person against every other person to survive. Their own culture did not train children (or adults) to engage in mutual support *except* in the context of a hunting and foraging society. When the land shrank from governmental action and dried up from drought, their mutual support changed to mutual exploitation and even killing.

In Holland and Leningrad during the Second World War, as we have noted, a similar famine struck, perhaps more suddenly even than among the Ugandan mountain people. The central cause of disaster—externally imposed deprivation of amounts of food below the minimum needed to support life—failed to break the hunger-weakened fabric of society. It failed partly because the Dutch and Russians were united rather than divided by their clearly visible enemy and partly because their modern technology facilitated their collaborative adaptation to a transitory deprivation which they quite deliberately shared. With vigorous and speedy outside help after the famine-causing blockade was ended, these afflicted people recovered quickly. If the mountain people whom Turnbull studied had been able to foresee an end of the drought and a beginning of vigorous governmental aid when it ended, perhaps there would not have been the almost total social disintegration that actually occurred. But the outside society was as indifferent to them as a people as they were to each other as individuals.

The broad implication of the research and evidence we have considered says nothing about the Indestructibility of Mankind. We can say that individuals, in groups of thousands and millions, are relatively fixed for life, in their collective ability or inability to meet all later challenges by things that happen to them during their first few years. We cannot say that *all* individuals in all circumstances who have enjoyed abundant physical and emotional nourishment in the first years will be able to meet all challenges. But we can infer, from the research we have examined, that without that nourishment, individuals will not be able to meet many challenges, whether relating to survival or to making political choices.

Phylogeny, Ontogeny, and Epigenesis

What I have said above may seem abstracted from and unrelated to ongoing political events. What, on the face of things, does a year-old Guatemalan, Chilean, or Ugandan child suffering from the weaning disease have to do with politics in these or any other countries? What even does famine have to do with politics? What do "motherless mother" monkeys that mangle or kill their young have to do with oligarchy, dictatorship, democracy, or any other political institution? And what do early childhood deprivations have to do with adult political behavior? Before you too quickly say "Everything" or "Nothing," let me indicate the context and the relevance of the research and ideas thus far discussed by explaining the political pertinence of three biological terms: phylogeny, ontogeny, and epigenesis.

Phylogeny is a grand term used to label that complex interaction of forces in the organism and in the environment that, over billions of years, have produced all the discrete, distinct forms of life that we now see about us every day. Phylogeny takes place within *species,* including Homo sapiens. The phylogenetic process, in all humans since the species became distinct in the perpetual and therefore continuing dialogue between our genes and our environment, has produced a species that organically has thus far been able to interact successfully with the new challenges that forever have faced it.

Ontogeny takes place within *individuals,* in the dialogue with the environment that commences at intrauterine conception and continues through life. *If* he or she does develop ontogenetically, each human being is—in terms of his or her potential—able successfully to interact with the challenges that face it throughout life, from conception to death.

Epigenesis is the process in which the ability to meet each successive challenge of growth depends on the prior successful meeting of earlier challenges. It is the relational process that says growth stage C can occur successfully only if growth stages B and A have occurred; that B can occur successfully only if A has first occurred; and that if A does not take place successfully, nothing else will ever happen to that organism. Nothing else will ever happen because maturation requires not only genes, endocrines, and neurons but also a nurturant environment. The initial A, with relation to all social interaction, is good nutrition. Without it, B, the elemental social interaction, does not successfully occur. And without these successful foundations, ultimately P, the phenomenon of political choice making, is very unlikely ever to occur. Epigenesis of a negative sort, the kind that destroys or diminishes later development, may accurately be called the Chinese bound-foot phenomenon.[2]

Using these biological abstractions to help explain both the processes and problems of earliest political socialization, we come out with this applicability of the research material on humans and other primates. Each modern, industrialized, integrated *polity* has—with whatever bumps and grinds, in stable and violent times—been compelled by the nature of Homo sapiens and by the necessity of successful interaction between man and environment to go through the process of political development *phylogenetically*. Each *individual* human, in order to become a choice-making political participant within societies that have undergone or are undergoing political development, has had to go through that process *ontogenetically*. Or he or she has not become a choice-maker: he or she is acted on but does not become a significant interactor. And that is precisely where most of the people in most of the world in our time are: they are almost exclusively acted upon, politically (and otherwise).

Ontogenetically, most humans remain politically and otherwise immature and unfulfilled, in phylogenetically underdeveloped societies. They are in that condition primarily not for failure of the individual's genetic material, which is sufficiently alike among all humans, whether they dwell in the most advanced or the most primitive societies. They are in that condition primarily because of the failure of established customs and institutions and the failure of political elites who try too suddenly to introduce new customs and institutions.

Both elites and institutions ignore epigenesis. They ignore the stage at which particular groups of individuals and the society as a whole are. Elites and institutions treat the immature and unresponsible as though they had optimum childhood nurturance and are fully developed—or they treat them like cattle, incapable of development. And so fundamental efforts to change, built on illusions and disillusions (that is, on weak foundations), collapse. The Russian Revolution of 1917 brought to power a Communist party that degenerated into a self-sustaining elite alienated from its public, which after centuries of monarchical dictatorship lacked the confidence to make decisions. After India achieved independence in 1947, its Congress party degenerated into a self-seeking economic elite that exploited a childhood-impoverished people, institutionalized corruption, and did little else. Meanwhile, the Indian general public remained so preoccupied with survival that it could not even form a national community as the basis for coherent and cohesive political decision making.

---

[2]For a theoretical linkage between stages of individual development and the development of political institutions from oligarchy through democracy to civilized anarchy, see Davies (1976).

A foolish 5-year-old child is puzzled or laughs at the inability of a 5-month-old child to feed itself, to walk, to change its own diaper. A foolish adult in a "developed" polity is puzzled or laughs or (perhaps worse) "bleeds" at the ineffectual maladroitness of people in those societies that he patronizes as "underdeveloped," as they make mistakes that were made in his polity hundreds and perhaps thousands of years before. A foolish adult in an "underdeveloped" polity denies that he is a contributing part of that polity's—that public's and his own—lack of political confidence and good judgment. As a "developed" leader, he calls out his agitators to stir "his masses" into supporting him—or he calls out the troops to quiet them.

Prescriptions for societies sickened by tradition do not often cure. Cookbooks for societies hungry to become immediately modern do not train the cooks or modernize societies. Within each (later) society (after the first ones that pioneered development over many centuries) and within each individual, development has to take place and take place epigenetically. Each society, each individual, must be nursed before it can feed itself, be supported before it can stand alone, become knit together before many of its collective acts and individual actors can become self-sustaining, self-propelled, autonomous.

All three of these growth processes—phylogeny, ontogeny, and epigenesis—start with each successive society's beginnings and each individual's conception in the womb. And so political socialization starts there, not in civics or any other classes in grade school. Most infants do not rise in their cribs and pledge allegiance to the flag, the party, or the leader. But most children before they ever *go* to school have developed a particular and a lasting sense of being secure or insecure about getting food, affection, and recognition. Most children, long before school starts for them, have learned to return in kind the last two of these (plus trust or mistrust) to those who have schooled them as to what they can expect from individuals and society. And these childhood established expectations about food, affection, and recognition profoundly influence political behavior in adulthood.

The Family, Autocratic and Equalitarian

After our attempt to put socialization into political context, phylogenetically and otherwise, we are now ready to turn the discussion, epigenetically built on what has been said up to now in this chapter, to the family—the place where physical and emotional needs are or should be earliest fulfilled, in normal epigenesis.

Differences in family style in industrialized, highly integrated societies reflect differences in cultural background of the parents plus differences in their current circumstances. That is, parents who have themselves been raised in families in which there was a rather clear-cut power hierarchy probably tend to raise their own children to defer to their elders and to obey them without asking why. Parents raised in more equalitarian circumstances tend to raise their children to exercise more equal power and to receive and give equal deference within the family. The autocratic pattern may be the dominant one in a large society organized primarily on hierarchical principles, as in land-based feudalities, kingdoms, and dictatorships. The equalitarian one may be more frequent in a society organized on democratic principles. But there is such a large overlap that it is not at all surprising that divergent patterns appear in such relatively democratic societies as America and Israel.

Whatever the pattern of power within it, the family persists. The usually three-generation *extended* family, both as an economic and as a socializing unit, has tended to disappear in industrialized, integrated societies—but not the nuclear family. Culturally inherited hierarchical tendencies of the extended family, bequeathed to the nuclear family, conflict with new realities. Power—usually father's power, but mother's power in fatherless families—diminishes because of the loss of the breadwinner's economically based control. When the father or mother can no longer say to the sons and daughters: "Do as I tell you or you won't eat," he or she loses influence. When the husband can no longer realistically say to the wife: "Do as I tell you or you won't eat," he loses influence. This economic nexus is probably, as Friedrich Engels said (1884, 1891, esp. the chapter on The Family), at the basis of intrafamily patriarchy.

And—even before the husband's and father's power in the nuclear family is diminished by economic integration—the three-generation and typically rural family begins to disintegrate in the face of loss of extended-family economic power. The eldest, who traditionally controlled the land till he died, loses his control over the land that the other family members traditionally worked. The Chinese revolution of 1949 is only a recent and dramatic case in which the eldest surviving male in the family, who had maintained his land-based or other economic power in the face of epochal economic and other changes in the big society, suddenly lost it.

However, durable and powerful forces continue to hold families together. The intense, innate desire of people to get, be, and stay together—the desire to interact and to receive and give affection—provides a perpetual genetic basis for maintenance of those family bonds that are based on *this* innate desire rather than on the innate desire simply to survive physically. The nuclear family, with or without children and with or without both parents, seems to be enduring as the residual social unit. We noted the depth of this desire to get, be, and stay together in Harlow's monkeys.

The common banality about the nuclear family—the smallest society within the big industrialized, integrated society—is that it serves as the transmitter of customs, values, and everything else that the big society has to offer or impose. The banality seems quite surely to be accurate, but it does not tell much. It neglects the constructive or destructive role of the family in basic personality formation and it neglects the fact that parents exercise discriminating and influential choices about what they transmit from the big society to the children. What I suggest here is that, having in considerable degree lost the economic nexus as an influence basis, parents in industrialized, integrated society can and indeed do sensibly depend for their influence on the affection that they give or fail to give to (and receive or fail to receive from) their children. Affectional ties are one of the *major* factors influencing even such big-society derivations as affiliation to political parties and movements (Cundy, 1975).

The great power of affectional ties means that the influence of the big society is likely to be weaker than that of the proximal individuals who serve as mediators for big social influences. The family, friends, and associates are always there; the big society and government are usually abstract, distant, and at least seemingly indifferent. Probably the only way the big society *could* override the family's political influence is to make individuals totally dependent for their material existence on obedience to the government's arbitrary demands. In this, governments would be relying on the overwhelming individual desire to survive, the only desire stronger than the desire to form and maintain society. Such conditions have thus far prevailed only among political prisoners, and the durability of brainwashing that involves physical deprivation is usually very brief (Lifton, 1961).

Now let us take a look at some research on the family. Two logically polar types of parental authority bear the commonly used labels "authoritarian" and "permissive." Authoritarian parents are described by those following Erich Fromm's (1941, chap. 6) concepts as seeking to impose an absolute standard of conduct based on higher authority, such as age-old custom, law or its enforcers, the omnipotent national leader, or a god—all of these authorities having an inescapable and final power to harm those who disobey or displease. Permissive parents are described as those who avoid control, serve as resources (in both material goods and experience) when asked by their children, and generally approve or excuse when their children follow whatever impulse or whatever strong desire. The criterion is not an external higher authority but the child itself. He or she is free to manipulate the environment and to work out his/her anxieties on it as he or she sees fit.

To these polar parental types of totally external (authoritarian) versus totally internal (permissive) control, Baumrind (1966) has added a third type: authoritative parents, who possess something akin to Fromm's "rational" rather than "inhibiting" authority (Fromm, 1941, pp. 164–166, 270). These parents do exercise control; they do not allow their children to destroy things or to injure other children (or adults). Their control is firm but neither harsh nor abrupt. Authoritative parents are those in Baumrind's category who are patient and reasonable in discouraging those actions of a child that harm it or others and in encouraging those that help it or others.

Baumrind argues that neither authoritarian nor permissive styles are altogether good or bad but that authoritative parenthood is better than either. Citing a Swedish study of 656 adolescents, she reports that parental authority with authoritative characteristics was accepted by the child because it reflected "rational concern for the child's welfare." But authority that involved domination or exploitation of the child was not accepted (Baumrind, 1966, p. 898). And, again like Fromm (1941, p. 161), she emphasizes the central role of affection in whatever may be the style or combination of styles of authority that parents employ. "The manipulation by the parent of the love relation," says Baumrind, "probably poses a greater threat to the child's ability to make a conscious choice than even the use of unqualified power assertion" (Baumrind, p. 904).

There is a classic study of child rearing that may have suffered neglect because it, like Baumrind's work, runs counter to some of the unquestioned permissive assumptions of the 1950s. Sears, Maccoby, and Levin (1957) studied about 375 mother-child dyads. The children were between the ages of 5 and 6. Slightly more than half (198) of the families were middle class and slightly less (174) were working class.

Child-parent interactions were the prime focus of their research, which sheds some light on the childhood antecedents of adult political action. Considering aggressive (that is, deliberately destructive or harmful) action to be the consequence of the frustration of other and innate desires, Sears et al. found that such action in children is related to the mother's anxiety about child rearing, to her own low self-esteem, and to her esteem for her husband (Sears et al., pp. 257–258). Such parents tend to punish aggression against themselves severely and to condone it when directed against other children, either within or outside the family. Anxious and low-esteem parents thus either (unpredictably) punish aggression or (unpredictably) overlook it, and sometimes they even encourage fighting (Sears et al., pp. 245–246, 266).

If Sears et al. are correctly describing one style of child rearing, then it may be that aggression as a reaction to tense and unstable circumstances within the family is directed outside the family. This pattern, once established, may lead in adulthood to the displacement of aggression onto socially acceptable targets. The big society and its government, as successors during adulthood to punitive and capricious parental authority during childhood, may sanction the displaced acting out of aggression against officially sanctioned targets. We know that Jews became such targets in Nazi Germany. We know that radical students became such targets in the United States in the 1960s. What we need to know is the kind of family power relationship that prevailed during the early childhood of those most ready to aggress against government-approved objects, in these and other developed and undeveloped countries.

Sears, Maccoby, and Levin also found a relationship between parents' acceptance or rejection of children and the latter's development of conscience—that is, of an internalized set of sanctions favoring certain kinds of action and condemning other kinds. Psychologically expressed, conscience usually depends on children's identification with their parents. Sears et al. found that these internalized controls are more successfully established when mothers reward desired acts by praise and punish undesired acts by temporarily isolating the child and withdrawing love than when they give material rewards for good behavior, withhold such rewards for bad behavior, or physically punish their children (Sears et al., pp. 586–587). And they found that it was not affection but rather rejection that *increases* a sense of dependency and *inhibits* the development of conscience in children. Only 18% of the 99 rejected children had a "high conscience," compared with 31% of the 218 accepted children (Sears et al., pp. 383–384).

These authors found rather distinct differences in ways of child rearing between working-class and middle-class families. Sears et al. found that, in comparison with middle-class mothers, working-class mothers tended more often to be severe in and to use shame as a technique in toilet training; to reject dependency "with a punishing attitude"; to be upset about precocious sex behavior; to be more punitive of aggressive behavior, particularly against parents but to allow it against those outside the family; to insist on good table manners; to express more concern about doing well in school but less expectation that their children would go to college; to use physical punishment and ridicule. However, on the most basic and central substance of the interaction between mother and child—affection—there were no significant class distinctions. Working-class mothers were about the same as middle-class mothers in expressing warmth toward their children and in breast feeding (Sears et al., pp. 427–432).

To oversimplify somewhat, middle- and working-class mothers differ thus, in the Sears study. Middle-class children were trained more to stand on their own feet, to make their own decisions, and to make them in the light of the effect they have on others and on themselves. In sum, middle-class upbringing tends to diminish dependency, to encourage self-expression, and to increase conscience—*and all these things by the time children have become 6 years old*.

At this point, a bit of speculation may help relate class differences in child rearing to stages in cultural development. In America some differences are probably a direct consequence of the cultural heritage of immigrant (or, if black, slave) families[3] whose entry into the big society has been through the working class. They come from cultures in which the power structure within the family, local community, and big society are congruent and emphatically hierarchical. The father is the head (or at least the bully) of the household. The landlord or slaveowner is the dominant local figure who dispenses favors and sanctions. The governing elite dominate the big society. Each of these bosses is responsible to his conscience, which, being based on his often weak identification with those whom he controls, is itself weak. He is not directly responsible to those whom he controls. Such a tradition is bound to be reflected in the ways children are trained to accept the power of their parents and others. This historical influence is likely to be stronger in the development of children than the cross-currents of shared deference and power which are part of the democratic ethos and which more

---

[3]On the profound and enduring trauma of enslavement in Africa and slavery in America, see Elkins (1968).

strongly influence the rearing of the grandchildren than the children of such immigrants.

However, not all authoritarian child rearing is the consequence of tradition. Much of it is situational—*and even functional to the situation*. The reality for poor and subordinated people is inherently frustrating. Those at society's bottom—the chronic outsiders (blacks and migrant workers in America, untouchables in India and Japan) and the recent arrivals (immigrants in America, "guest" workers in Northern Europe who come from Southern Europe, the Middle East, and North Africa)—are struggling to survive physically and to start getting integrated into a society that often simply and casually uses those at the bottom as if they were disposable diapers.

In times of stress in any group, conflict is succeeded by the movement of power toward those who are or pretend to be best suited to direct the activities of others. Power is taken over or granted to those who are not directly affected by the severe stress of survival and integration, because those (including children) who are or feel incompetent and impotent to make decisions nevertheless see the need for decisions to be made, for policy to be established and carried out. *Because of the mental consequences of poverty*—which are frustration and stress—poor people can rarely avoid having authoritarian power relationships with those they see as being superordinate *or* subordinate to them.

Prosperous people do not live in the same world that poor people inhabit and rarely control. When prosperous people are frightened (for example, during an era of rapid social change), they also tend to act in an authoritarian manner, *because of the mental consequences of fearing loss of property and power*—which are frustration and stress. In such circumstances (as in Germany in the 1920s and Spain in the 1930s) prosperous people even accept dictatorship. In wars, democracy is cast aside; in local disasters (like hurricane or flood), citizens obey police without much question. And poor parents just entering a complex and integrated society themselves conform to the demands and constraints of the big society—and make their children do likewise. It is either that or—at least so it is supposed—the chaotic pursuit of self-interest in a Hobbesian war of each against all.

Oscar Lewis (1959) and his collaborators have closely studied life styles among families in transition from rural poverty to the integrated, industrial society. Their research has abundantly indicated the present conditions that perpetuate the traditional hierarchical power relations prevailing in most rural Latin American areas. And, in his somber study of what he calls "the culture of poverty," Lewis (1965) describes the struggle of each against all that keeps poor people impoverished and isolated in slums, where their human life is marginal to their animal existence.

Autocratic, even authoritarian (in the sense that authoritarian lends a mystique to vertically oriented power structures), family relations and child rearing are thus very possibly a consequence not only of traditional but also of the current situation. The situational response to severe and chronic crisis of survival-and-integration may, even when it is authoritarian, be more rational than one in which every one within a family is free to serve his own ends regardless of how these affect the durability of that elemental social unit, the family, and that even more elemental unit, the individual, who needs what the family provides.

Authoritarianism appears to be more common among black people in America than among whites of comparable middle-class circumstances (Smith & Prothro, 1957). Authoritarianism among blacks may also be functionally responsive to the circumstances of blacks, both historically and in the contemporary world, where their status is like that of recently arrived immigrants. They must often survive together under strong control or perish as individuals and as a disintegrated group.

Baumrind (1972) has found authoritarianism to be related among some black children she studied to a superior ability to become tough, self-assertive, and self-sufficient. Situationally, this syndrome may be the best available in the crisis of transition from the isolated subsistence of black people to their acceptance as blacks by white people and from their individual impotence to their cohesive assertion of power. We have noted the strong emphasis on affection as a socializing agent, and we have noted that Sears et al. found working- and middle-class mothers to be alike in this basic factor. When comparing this with the really significant differences in *style* between equalitarian and autocratic (or authoritarian) child rearing, we need not forget the more fundamentally crucial substance of affection.

Now we can have a look at a different phenomenon. It is a kind of resultant of affection, identification, potentiation, and security about food, clothing, shelter, health, and physical safety. This phenomenon develops (or fails to develop) during early childhood in step with other basic orientations toward self and others that children acquire during their earliest years. This phenomenon, as Thomas Aquinas noted half a thousand years ago, is one without which no society can develop or endure. This phenomenon is interpersonal trust.

The Development of Trust

Trust between individuals is a basic component of all mutually fruitful interactions. As Erik Erikson (1963) perhaps first emphasized, it develops initially within the family. It is basic to the successful functioning of families; of other small groups like local communities; of large groups like trade unions and business corporations; and of polities composed of millions of individuals. It does not prevail to a high degree in many communities; they thereby are weakened and sometimes even destroyed. Mistrust between spouses contributes to the breakup of marriages. Mistrust between children and parents contributes to their one-sided or mutual exploitation. Mistrust between labor and management likewise leads to often cynical one-sided or mutual exploitation.

Mistrust in a large polity is, when severe, radically debilitating. The 1973–1974 Watergate crisis of the Nixon presidency was one of the most severe in two hundred years of American political life. A major ingredient in the crisis was mutual mistrust between rulers and ruled. Nixon mistrusted the intelligence and judgment of the general public. It came to distrust his honesty. Dictatorships (whether bureaucratic, as in the Soviet Union, or autocratic, as in the extreme case of Mussolini's Italy) have extensively used force and guile to control their populations. They have had less success, as Thomas Aquinas would have predicted, than if they had used less force and guile and more trust to elicit the cooperation of their citizens.

We may here define trust as the ability of an individual to rely on the word and the actions of others for fulfillment of his or her needs. It is an early result of *early* and *secure* physical and emotional nurturance because an individual has learned, in the family and from infancy onward, that such reliance is predictable and supportive. It is, along with affection—which is intricately involved in the learning of trust—at the foundation of all interaction that is nonarbitrary. And this interindividual trust—a necessary part of the foundation of a just society—is established well (or established badly) in early childhood.

Trust is a complex phenomenon. Its very earliest testing ground is in the interaction between mother and newborn child at first feeding. Probably very few mothers tease their really hungry babies by capriciously offering and then withdrawing milk. Probably more mothers display affection and hostility to their small children rather capriciously, in ways that bear no relation to anything the child has done—or no relation that is apparent to the child. This capriciousness elicits mistrust. If such early interactions are at once nonsupportive and unpredictable and unjustifiable, the child will become enduringly socialized to mistrust. He or she is learning to expect not to receive help—predictably, from others who are more powerful—and is therefore learning that help must be sought not as a matter of right but of privilege. The child trained to mistrust is being trained to live alone, in suspicious, hostile, and impotent egocentricity. He or she learns to survive by guile, force, and obsequiousness.

A basic consequence of training in mistrust is that the child develops deep doubt of its own ability to survive physically and emotionally at the same time that it is compelled to try to survive alone. It learns its own impotence and its own need constantly to use its mental resources to exploit customs, values, and people to its own immediate advantage. Mistrust thereby radically constrains the ability of each affected individual to collaborate with all others in the realization of the needs and expectations of each. At its most aggravated level, it makes deceit, force, flattery, and servile solicitude the only bases on which social and political collaboration can be effected. Heavily relied on in dictatorships, mistrust increases the already enormous effort of developing societies to effect change.

Unfortunately, little systematic research has been done on trust. Without knowledge of its functioning in social and political interaction, it is impossible to understand comprehensively how societies either initially form, endure, or finally disintegrate. And it has to be understood in its childhood origins, as Erikson (1963, pp. 247–251) indicated, to appreciate its long-range effects on the growth potential of political systems.

Jean Piaget, the Swiss developmental psychologist, has meticulously described and analyzed (1932) a quasipolitical process that, under certain circumstances, indigenously develops among children even before they enter adolescence. This process is rule-making for certain of their games. Piaget describes the stages in which children, at first accepting rules as given (by parents and other authority figures), later develop a sense of their own authority to make their own rules. They become autonomous democrats. Perhaps Piaget does not sufficiently consider how the matrix of the children's rule-making is the society of which their parents are an integral part and how a high degree of mutual trust is an integral part of the highly developed Swiss culture. But he does note that "the primary condition of the moral life" (the establishment of the rules and interacting in accordance with them) is "the need for reciprocal affection" (1965, p. 176). This reciprocal affection, whose roots are innate but require postnatal nurturance, is indeed part of the foundation for the moral political society, and without some morality there cannot be a political society. Without mutual trust, which so intimately relates to and derives from reciprocal affection, it seems probable that the children in Piaget's research, rather than help make and abide by rules, would very likely deny the group's authority. They would obey the rules only when they win the game. And so would end the group, and with it collective rule making and collective rule acceptance. Trust, in short, is a continuing mutual obligation. As it develops, starting in infancy, the polity can develop. As it dies, so dies the polity.

Summary

My basic thesis in this chapter has been that *lifelong* patterns of social and political interaction are established before a child ever leaves home. I have argued that if these patterns are set so as to stunt the individual's development, they will either prevent or seriously damage his or her ability to make political choices as an adult.

However, the opposite is equally the case. If facilitative patterns are established, the basis is laid for some kind of optimal development, of the sort Piaget studied. Children can very early develop a measure of self-confidence and social integration that establishes the group itself as the authoritative rule maker and the individual as the responsible participant in the rule-making process. In short, the earliest influences on children are fundamental for both the political growth and stagnation of a big polity.

I have said that physical and emotional deprivation is like the Chinese bound foot: if parents and other child mentors do not facilitate normal epigenesis, it will occur only in very distorted form. One politically crucial kind of distortion emerges from the findings of Spitz in the foundling home of motherless children and of Harlow in the primate laboratory of motherless monkeys. You will recall that many of the victims in both circumstances oscillated between near total withdrawal and an occasional raging out at the environment. One (not a universal) pattern of initial political involvement of a people just commencing development is just like that: most of the time they feel alone and impotent—and occasionally they lash out at their masters, the political elites, in what is opaquely labeled "blind" rage.

We have considered whether indeed children can become responsible political choice makers as adults if they have not developed the mutual affection, confidence, trust, and respect that are generated from birth in the most intimate everyday interactions within the family. And we have glimpsed the exciting phenomenon of indigenous rule-making as Piaget observed it, noting that the autochthonous process is itself the product of near optimal interaction between the innate growth processes generating within the organism and the environment that makes it possible to realize the political potential of individuals. There are no political genes in human chromosomes. But the potential for making political decisions and bearing the consequences of making them has innate, organic components. And it requires careful nurturance from birth—if we are to end the process of shaping individuals whose capacity for cooperative self-rule has been stunted for life, like a Chinese bound foot.

6

Peers and Political Socialization

Sara L. Silbiger

To ASSERT THAT ONE SPENDS a large portion of one's life with peers is quite analogous to the discovery that one is speaking prose. Giving a label to a long acknowledged condition, however, does not do much to stimulate further understanding. Both the effects of speaking prose and interacting with peers are far more widely assumed than analyzed. In the present chapter, we will address the latter realm, peers, and more specifically the effect of peers on the acquisition of enduring political characteristics.

The impact of socializing agents is reliant on at least one of three roles these agents play: as providers of learning cues—information and attitudes; as role models; and as manipulators of rewards and punishments. While the more frequently studied socializing agents such as parents and schools each have some unique claim over at least one of these roles at some time, no uniqueness can be claimed for peers. By the time that peers begin to play a meaningful part in the life of a child, they must interact with other socializing agents. This makes it difficult to ascertain just what the role of peers is in political socialization and has led many to assume that peers are primarily reinforcers of socialization acquired from nonpeer sources.

We have strikingly little direct evidence to address to the question of peer political socialization. From what is available, plus considerable indirect evidence which will be highlighted in the pages to follow, we draw the conclusion that at least in the American context peers possess no regular turf. Yet they may play important socializing roles under special circumstances—sometimes fortuitous, sometimes predictable. The circumstances fall into three general categories which organize the discussion below: (1) those in which traits of the learner are central variables; (2) those in which qualities of the influencing peer are central variables; and (3) those in which characteristics of the subject to be learned are central variables. In each of these categories we have elected to discuss a limited number of variables which appear to offer particular promise for expanding our understanding of the peer role in political socialization.

Traits of the Learner

Variations in an individual's susceptibility to interpersonal and particularly peer influence have been the subject of a considerable experimental literature. Rates of compliance to peers and others appear to vary with the personality, preexisting beliefs, and social or demographic position of the learner. Almost none of this research deals with political influence specifically, and we are cautious about assumptions of transferability. Of the three, demographic variables probably lend themselves most easily to interdisciplinary transfer, and it is on these that this section will focus.

AGE

Age can be expected to affect the role of peers in political socialization in at least four important areas: (1) who we are learning from; (2) what are the settings and relationships of peer interaction; (3) what do we already know; and (4) what are we currently learning. Since each of these is discussed in other sections of this chapter, the present discussion should serve as a summary, synthesis, and emphasis rather than as a source for detailed discussion.

The influence of peers in social learning sets in at the preschool level (Bandura & Huston, 1961; Bandura, Ross, & Ross, 1961) and has been found, for some purposes, to match or surpass parental influence by seventh grade (Bowerman & Kinch, 1959). While such influence may contribute to prepolitical dispositions, little peer interaction regarding directly political objects has been documented before high school years. In a study of 1,200 third- to eighth-grade children, only 11 at any age mentioned peers as most important sources of information about Watergate (Silbiger, 1975). Hirsch, whose subjects extended from fifth to twelfth grade found little support for the hypothesis that, with age, peers increase their role as political socializers as compared to parents (Hirsch, 1971, pp. 72–77). Allen and Newtson also conclude that age itself is not as important as situational variables which may alter with age (1972).

During school years it appears that peer influences interact with those of parents and school and are unique in determining political beliefs and practices, if at all, with regard to issues of particular salience to youth culture. While some earlier studies of youthful political attitudes seemed to distinguish a political rebellion against adult beliefs (Middleton & Putney, 1963) subsequent research, even among radical students, fails to support the idea of a great generation gap insulating youth from parental influence (Keniston, 1968; Tedin, 1974; Merelman, 1968).

While none of the quantitative literature is capable of documenting this assertion, it seems likely, as Keniston's interviews suggest, that in the era of youthful idealism and insecure identity, a particular peer may become an important role model or "inspiration" for ideological development and/or participation (1968, chap. 4). It is unlikely that such singular though critical experiences will be disclosed by standard questionnaire approaches, but a fuller documentation of the peer role at this stage would benefit from increased use of in-depth and even psychoanalytic techniques.

As one gains in security and stability of self-identification, he is more likely to seek rewards from himself (Brim's *I-me relationship*) rather than from any single "other" (Brim, 1966, pp. 12–13). Brim also suggests that maturation brings with it a vast amalgam of significant others who may serve as reference points to the individual (p. 17). These others, from present and past, from fiction and real life, "free the individual from purely immediate pressures and give a broad base for his actions" (Brim, 1966, pp. 12–13). Following this logic, it seems fair to conclude that, for most adults, peers will serve to reinforce and support already developed attitudes and will be sought out on this basis (e.g., Newcomb, 1961; Finifter, 1974). The peculiar irony of peer socialization emerges here. With age the individual becomes decreasingly dependent on formal agents of socialization such as school and family, and interacts more frequently and intensely with peers. Yet peers have little left to teach in a field which has largely been preempted by earlier socialization. Only for new attitude objects and novel role learning will individual peers be likely to retain their influential power.

SOCIAL CLASS

Class may mediate the socializing impact of peers in at least two important ways. First, it has been suggested that, at least for young people, parents of lower-class status may be discredited by their children as reliable sources of useful information, with consequently increased reliance on peers (Remmers & Radler, 1957; Langton, 1969). While the cross-class comparisons of Remmers and Radler and Langton support this hypothesis, Hirsch, focusing only on a homogeneous lower-class population of Appalachian youth, found little reliance on peers as sources of either political information or partisanship (1971). In a similar contrast, Langton found that mother-dominated families, more frequent in the lower class, would be less valued for political cues with peers, thereby attaining increased importance. Hirsch found that, in the absence of a father, children were more likely to turn to mothers but not peers for political cues. Given the conflict in these findings, it is probable that class alone is not having the critical impact on peer power. An intervening variable, the child's perceptions of the way his parent's class will affect him, does help to clarify the relationship (Langton, 1969).

A second dimension of social class and peer impact is relevant only in mixed-class settings. In his now famous and controversial study of educational achievement, Coleman (1966), like others before him (e.g., Harvey & Rutherford, 1960), concluded that lower-class children were socialized to middle-class norms in mixed-class settings, but that downward socialization was not likely to occur. Given subsequent research (Pettigrew, 1967), the latter part of this hypothesis has been subject to question. Langton's findings among Jamaican youth support the existence of the "upward" socialization phenomenon with regard to a variety of political attitudes (1969, pp. 133–134).

Social class may also be related to a number of other conditions which may affect peer socialization to politics, such as family structure, values, and child-rearing patterns. These class-related attributes contribute to the delineation of a subculture, and they will be discussed in the context of cultural variation.

SEX

Women are not generally more susceptible than men to peer influence as opposed to other forms of influence (Hirsch, 1971, p. 78) except in specialized settings (collective upbringing, Shouval et al., 1975; and marriage, see below, p. 179). However, when one focuses exclusively on the peer relationship, there is considerable evidence that women yield more to social pressure than men (Carrigan & Julian, 1966; Hollander, Julian, & Haaland, 1965; Staples & Walters, 1966; Asch, 1956; Sebert, Jennings, & Niemi, 1974; others cited in Sistrunk & McDavid, 1971, p. 200). Particularly in the light of cross-cultural confirmations of these findings (Bronfenbrenner, 1964; Shouval et al., 1975), it might appear that women are stronger in their affiliative needs and are, therefore, more sensitive to cues present in interpersonal situations.

On the other hand, there are other studies in which women have not been found to be more compliant than men (e.g., Allen & Levine, 1969). Building from such studies, Sistrunk and McDavid (1971) devised an interesting research design which varied the sex relevance of the tasks around which conformity was measured. They found that conformity levels of both sexes varied according to the relevance of the task to their sex: men conforming more frequently when the task was female, women more compliant when the task was male, and neither more compliant when the task was neutral. The political implications of this study would point back to a cultural explanation. As long as politics is defined as a male task, women can be expected to be more conformity oriented. Cultural redefinitions of the relationship between sex and politics could reduce this compliance considerably.

The Influencing Peers

The likelihood that peers will have at least a short-run impact on the socialization process also is altered by characteristics of the influencing parties, particularly with respect to the type and quality of their relationship to the learner.

ATTRACTIVENESS

Attractiveness of the peer group to the individual participant increases the likelihood that it will have a socializing impact and be successful both in imposing sanctions against deviants and warding off outside influences (Kiesler, Zanna, & De Salvo, 1966; summaries in Thibaut & Kelley, 1959; Cartwright & Zander, 1953; Grupp, 1971). In his study of the House Appropriations Committee, Fenno (1962) suggests that high committee attractiveness is an important factor in its ability to socialize its members. Grupp (1971) similarly explains the ability of John Birch Society members to withstand external cues as deriving from group attractiveness. According to Janis (1972), attractiveness and cohesion are also responsible for high conformity patterns in foreign policy decision-making groups.

ENDURANCE

Peers are found to have a greater influence on one another when their interaction is expected to be (or has been) enduring (Lewis, Langan, & Hollander, 1972). Commitment to an enduring pattern of interaction is found to have an effect on opinion change even when the group itself is low in attractiveness (Kiesler, Zanna, & De Salvo, 1966). While commitment, in the experimental literature, is usually considered as an anticipatory phenomenon (the subject has signed up for several meetings or has been told that he cannot change groups), field studies have also cited enduring group interaction as increasing the likelihood of change (Fenno, 1962; Newcomb, 1943).

SIZE

The impact of group size on rates of conformity has not been clearly demonstrated (Allen, 1965). One replication on the Asch-type situation found that conformity increased up to a group size of five members (Rosenberg, 1961) and then declined while another found that conformity dropped off above a membership of eight (Gerard, Wilhelmy, & Conolley, 1968). Other studies using more ambiguous stimuli found no relationship between group size and conformity (Goldberg, 1954; Kidd, 1957). Most recently, with differing techniques, Nordholm has found increase of conformity with increasing group size in an ambiguous situation (1975), although her design did not consider groups of more than five members.

HOMOGENEITY

The groups discussed above were homogeneous in relevant opinions. When a group contains discordant subgroups, the size of the subgroup may be the most important consideration. Godwin and Restle have found that conformity to the views of a subgroup increases as the size of the subgroup approaches a majority (1974). Asch found, however, that even a single deviant introduced into his experimental settings reduced distorted (confirming) judgments from 37% to 5.5% (1956).

Simply the presence or absence of subgroups within a primary group, without considerations of size, is seen as influential to political socialization. Subgroups create a cross-pressuring effect on the individual which may reduce his conformity to either view, as well as his interest and participation in politics (e.g., McClosky & Dahlgren, 1959).

While homogeneity of peer opinion may facilitate opinion holding and action, it does not necessarily insulate the group from outside considerations or increase the likelihood that extreme positions will be assumed. Myers and Beck (1974) conducted a study of Vietnam "hawks" and "doves," placing them in homogeneous and mixed discussion groups. They found, contrary to expectation, that homogeneous groups were not more likely to move to the extremes of their preexisting opinions but, rather, that both hawk and dove groups become more dovish through discussion. This finding may, however, suffer from experimental design. Real world groups with presumed higher attractiveness and endurance may well insulate and polarize (Grupp, 1971; Festinger, Reicken, & Schachter, 1956).

Along with the size and clustering of opinions in peer groups, another situational variable is the consensus orientation of the group. While some groups exchange ideas, others strive for agreement and impose sanctions for disagreement. Maitland and Goldman (1974) found that groups instructed to arrive at a common point of view were much more likely to do so than others which conducted open-ended discussions. Another study of parent versus peer influence on political opinion found that college students were more likely to adhere to peer views when they believed that those views were important to the peers and that sanctions for nonconformity would be imposed (Merelman, 1968). Similarly,

Janis suggests that the consensual strivings of foreign-policy-making groups induced conformity which was less likely to be characteristic of groups without this attribute (1972).

When the salience of group membership and identity is increased by inter-group competition or comparable environmental conditions, rates of conformity are also positively affected (Snyder & Monson, 1975). Deutsch and Gerard's Asch-type experiment compared groups of the Asch design with groups which had been told that a group prize was available for high performance. The subjects in the competitive situation made twice as many distorted judgments as those in control groups (1955). Bronfenbrenner relies heavily on the Deutsch and Gerard analysis in his explanation of the exceptional socializing power of student peer groups in the USSR (1970b).

Probably because of the ways in which they vary with respect to the conditions just discussed, one type of peer may be more influential than another. Although we have several studies which compare peers with other agents of socialization, we have almost none which compare different types of peers. Any peer relationship bears the seeds of possible influence, but only one, that between marital spouses, regularly realizes this potential.

SPOUSES

Early voting studies documented partisan agreements in up to 95% of marital pairs (Campbell, Gurin, & Miller, 1954, p. 203; Lazarsfeld, Berelson, & Gaudet, 1944). While these studies did not explore the dynamics and direction of influence, it was generally assumed that if the pairs had not originally agreed on partisanship, then the wife had probably conformed to her husband's preferences (e.g., Key, 1961, p. 299; Bone & Ranney, 1976, p. 26). This direction of influence is confirmed by Beck and Jennings (1975). High concordance regarding partisanship was also assumed to generalize to other areas of political opinion.

Some relief from this picture is provided in Newcomb's data on Bennington College graduates, reinterviewed 20 years after college in 1960 (Newcomb, Koenig, Flacks, & Warwick, 1967, pp. 54–61). Relying on the wife's report of her husband's politics, Newcomb found high voting agreement among spouses (91% in 1960) but also found that 42% of the couples studied had differed on at least one presidential election and that, with regard to partisanship, patterns of conformity were not a one-way street. Although his data regarding partisan history of both spouses were complete for only 68 couples, he found that 14 wives changed to agree with their husbands but 8 husbands changed to agree with their wives. Two wives changed away from their husbands and three couples maintained a continuing disagreement (1967).

There does not seem to be any doubt that, with regard to partisanship, marriage partners tend to strive toward consensus but, at least among college-educated women, it is not inevitable that conflict will be resolved on the basis of husband dominance.

Partisanship, unfortunately for the ease of our understanding of political socialization, may be a unique phenomenon. Because of the clarity and constancy of the partisan cue, it is apparently transmitted with greater ease than more subtle or ambiguous political dispositions. While Newcomb found generally that spouses were likely to be on the same end of an ideological continuum from liberal to conservative, most of his women respondents considered their husbands to be more conservative than themselves. It is likely that reliance on the wife's report of her husband's views exaggerates their agreement somewhat, for other studies of spouses find that attributed agreement is often higher than actual agreement (e.g., Levinger & Breedlove, 1966). It is also probable that in marriages where politics is of lower salience, convergence on issues more ambiguous than partisanship is likely to be lower than in the Bennington findings.

SCHOOL FRIENDS

The impact of primary and secondary school friends for most types of political learning is usually inadequate to countervail the influence of family. Langton suggests, with regard to efficacy at least, that peers may heighten dispositions founded in parental views (1969). Probably adolescent friends are most influential when they are of a higher social class influencing lower-class schoolmates, or where the topic of learning has particular relevance to the peer generation. Because in quantitative studies peer influence appears with considerably less frequency than parental influence, we have tended to discount its importance. The minority of students who are influenced by peers may, however, be an important political subgroup, more change oriented or politically active. We would do well to focus more research on this minority to understand who they are, how they are influenced, and toward what consequences for the political system.

The same argument also applies to the study of college peers. Despite all the special circumstances of college friendship, there is little evidence that the college experience molds large numbers of students into new directions of political thought through peer or other forms of influence. It is likely that here, too, the peer influence is typically unique and specialized, most amenable to discovery by interview and depth probings rather than simple quantitative comparisons for freshman-senior attitudes. Distinctive peer influence during college away from parental norms is probably greatest during periods of high campus politicization and when, as in the era studied by Newcomb (1943), considerable change is taking place in society outside the college walls.

FRIENDS, COLLEAGUES, AND NEIGHBORS

Adult peer environments may be expected to overlap and reinforce one another with respect to political dispositions. Where work groups and friends are not in agreement with one another on voting choices and partisanship, the individual's conformity to each may be reduced (Berelson et al., 1954; McClosky &

Dahlgren, 1959) by cross-pressuring effects, or the individual may seek out special reinforcement of his own views among like-minded colleagues (Finifter, 1974). While Almond and Verba cite the contribution of work groups to feelings of civic competence (1963), other studies suggest the likelihood that this effect would vary according to occupation with peers intensifying the norms characteristic of the particular occupation (see Sigel & Hoskin in this volume). Among his Bennington graduates, Newcomb found that postcollege friends and type of job were closely related to the retention or change of collegiate political dispositions (1967). Although not specifically peer group oriented, work by Fuchs (1968, pp. 63–68) and Lorinskas, Hawkins, and Edwards (1969) suggests the importance of neighbors in the retention or rejection of ethnic political orientations.

VOLUNTARY ASSOCIATIONS

Almost all the research which purports to assess voluntary group impact on members actually studies gross distinctions between members and nonmembers. Members of various groups are typically combined to acquire scores of member attitudes, without reference to the distinctive socialization of each group or the actual process of intragroup communication. As a result, the studies most often tap political dispositions of joiners rather than the actual effects of membership in a specified group. Studies vulnerable to this limitation include those dealing with school-age groups (Hess & Torney, 1967; Hirsch, 1971; Ziblatt, 1965) and adult groups (Seeman, 1966; summary in Milbrath, 1965). To distinguish between the joiner psyche and the impact of voluntary group peer interaction requires longitudinal examination of specific groups.

Objects of Learning

The intensity of peer impact on political socialization also varies according to several characteristics of the traits of information to be acquired. In this section we will first consider some general properties of the object of learning, and then discuss the particular areas of political learning in which peer influence has been examined.

NOVELTY

The novelty of an object of learning enhances the probability of peer influence on it, particularly among adults. Sears and McConohay make the point that responses to novel attitude objects are most likely to be predictable from one's

present environment as compared to longstanding objects (such as political parties) which reflect earlier socialization (1973, p. 44). Longstanding objects have
probably been influenced by family and school but, when one is removed by
adulthood from these early agents and is also confronted with novel circumstances, peer influence probably should increase. Brim points out the likelihood
that novel objects of learning will crop up in adulthood, particularly in complex
societies as a result of geographic, social, and economic mobility as well as rapid
technological and social change (1966, p. 19). Sears uses this logic to explain the
socialization of what he calls the "New Urban Black" in the context of analyzing
riot behavior (Sears & McConohay, 1973 pp. 46–48). It should also be relevant
to the learning of other unconventional and/or deviant political behavior as well
as to the shaping of attitudes toward new issues (e.g., ecology) and events.

Several major studies have suggested that the impact of peers, at least among
children and adolescents, is a function of the closeness of the attitude object to
the peer culture. Young people are likely to turn to parents for cues on matters
relevant to the assumption of future adult roles and to peers for more contemporary or generational concerns (Brittain, 1963; Kandel & Lesser, 1972; Sebert,
Jennings, & Niemi, 1974). These findings would imply that in the political realm
young people would turn to peers for cues regarding such issues as lowered
voting age, legalization of marijuana, and draft laws. While Sebert et al. (1974)
find concordance higher with peers than parents on the 18-year-old vote, Tedin's
parent-child focus casts some doubt on this conclusion (1974).

When the object of learning is information about a political event, Hill and
Bonjean (1964) have hypothesized that interpersonal and presumably peer
sources increase relative to media sources with the importance of the event.
Interpersonal communication played an enormous role in the dissemination of
information regarding the deaths of FDR and John Kennedy (87.4% and 57.1%,
respectively) but was much less important for other events such as the launching
of Explorer I (18%) and Alaskan Statehood (6%) (Hill and Bonjean, 1964, p.
339).

When the object of learning is an attitude, presence of controversy and
conflict (Ostlund, 1973) and personal involvement with the object (Eagley &
Manis, 1966) tend to increase susceptibility to interpersonal influence and attitude change. The role of peers in these situations may be to draw attention to the
conflict (in this case, between ideas in the subject's belief system) which the
subject may then resolve according to his own desired identity.

POLITICAL OBJECTS AND PEER INFLUENCE

The entrance of peer influence into the child's political learning is less a
function of the introduction of new objects of learning than it is of new suscep-
tibilities of the child to reward and punishment. As the child begins to expand his
interactions and emotions beyond his immediate family to other children, peers

may begin to supplement or complement adults in providing available models and in manipulating rewards and punishments. The consideration of peer learning during childhood and adolescence usually does less to distinguish particular objects of learning than to distinguish relative roles of parents, peers, and others toward the shaping of the same dispositions.

In early childhood peers play a contributing role in the development of patterns of cooperation and moral judgment (e.g., Kohlberg, 1969; Piaget, 1948; Riccards, 1973), and probably to early feelings of personal control. Harrington has suggested that when a group of children establish methods of using three swings in a playground, they are engaging in the allocation of scarce resources and are hence involved in peer-based political learning (1973).

Learning more explicitly focused on the political system does not appear to engage peer influence until high school and college years where it has been studied for its relative contribution to efficacy and trust (Langton, 1969; Sebert, Jennings, & Niemi, 1974; Ziblatt, 1965; Prewitt & Karns, 1968), partisanship, and voting decision (Sebert, Jennings, & Niemi, 1974; Hirsch, 1971; Newcomb, 1943; Merelman, 1968), political information (Langton, 1969; Hirsch, 1971), support for system and civil liberties (Langton, 1969; Hess & Torney [3rd–8th grade], 1968), specific issue positions (Sebert, Jennings, & Niemi, 1974), politicization, and participatory orientations (Langton, 1969; Hess & Torney, 1968; Hirsch, 1971).

Some authors, most notably James Coleman (1961), have treated the adolescent world as insulated and exclusive of parental influence. Most studies of adolescent opinion, however, find a shared role for parents and peers, with no political objects which are exclusively determined by peers, and a few which are strongly, though not exclusively, dominated by parents. Drawing from the citations above, it is safe to conclude that acquisition of partisan orientations among American youth is largely a domain of parental influence and parents are generally more influential than peers on questions of specific campaign and candidate preference. In the Sebert et al. study of U.S. high school seniors, efficacy is found to be more heavily determined by peers than by parents, but Langton's analysis of Jamaican high school students suggests a dominant role for parents in the range from low to medium efficacy scores, but an increased relevance of peers in the range of medium to high efficacy (1969, pp. 147–158). Since in the Sebert research efficacy and views on the 18-year-old vote are the only objects of peer dominance, the authors conclude that both are closer to generational concerns. Tedin, however, finds that even on questions of considerable generational relevance, parents have considerable influence so long as the adolescent has accurate perceptions of his parents' views (1974).

These conclusions complement some aspects of Langton's findings to suggest that degree of peer influence in adolescent political socialization is less a function of the object of learning itself, than of the presence or absence of parental cue giving. (Langton, 1969, found that students from maternal families turned to peers for political information more often then those from father-present families.)

Sebert et al. (1974) also found that concordance between peers is greatest when peers agree with parents, thus reducing the exclusive role of peers across all the attitude objects they consider.

The role of peers, over the same set of attitude objects, is increased as the physical proximity and emotional intensity of relationships with parents is reduced after high school or college. Yet even then, as long as the attitude object remains constant, it is likely that peers will do more to reinforce, intensify, and clarify dispositions acquired from other sources at other times than to have an independent influence (Dawson & Prewitt, 1969; Finifter, 1974). Studies of adult peer influence on socialization have considered some of the same enduring objects: party and voting preferences (Reicken, 1959; Berelson, Lazarsfeld, & McPhee, 1954; Campbell et al., 1960; Lazarsfeld, Berelson, & Gaudet, 1944; Beck & Jennings, 1975; Finifter, 1974; Campbell, Gurin, & Miller, 1954; McClosky & Dahlgren, 1959), politicization and participation (McClosky & Dahlgren, 1959), political interest and information (Seeman, 1966), political competence and control (Seeman, 1966; Almond & Verba, 1963). In addition, more novel objects of learning have a special place in the peer adult relationship.

New information, as well as opinions about such information, have long been considered a special domain of peer influence. A theory of the process by which interpersonal influence contributed to the distribution of information and opinion was constructed by Lazarsfeld, Berelson, and Gaudet (1944) and reevaluated by other research since (e.g., Berelson, Lazarsfeld, & McPhee, 1954; Katz & Lazarsfeld, 1955; Katz, 1957; Troldahl, 1966; Ostlund, 1973, and cites therein). The "two-step flow" theory hypothesized that most persons low in political interest would acquire political information secondhand through peer "opinion leaders" whose exposure and intake from the mass media was higher. Information and influence were expected to be transmitted simultaneously. Later studies, perhaps reflecting the pervasiveness of media today, find that information is more likely to be received directly from media than from interpersonal sources. Miller's study of the news of Franklin Roosevelt's death (1954) found that almost 90% of the population had heard of the event within an hour and of these over 85% had heard of it from interpersonal sources. However, the composite average of six studies of President Kennedy's death assembled by Ostlund (1973) attributed only 55% of the information to interpersonal sources. Only 5% reported learning of Johnson's decision not to seek reelection from nonmedia sources (Allen & Colfax, 1968) and 15% reported such sources in learning of McGovern's decision to drop Eagleton from his presidential slate (Ostlund, 1973).

Extensive communication among peers may be engendered by media information about an event and may result in efforts to influence others. In Ostlund's study of the McGovern decision, e.g., he found that 46% of his subjects attempted to influence someone with respect to this event but, strikingly, only 20% said they had changed their minds somewhat as a result of such discussions and only 3% claimed a greatly changed opinion (1973).

Troldahl suggests a modification of the two-step flow theory which sorts out the flow of information from that of influence (1966). Both leaders and followers are expected to get their original information from media sources, but followers will seek out opinion from peer leaders when the information is inconsistent with their own preexisting beliefs. Leaders, on the other hand, will either form opinions on their own or seek further advice from experts. Troldahl found only a very slight confirmation of his theory, and very little belief change attributable to interpersonal influence. His experimental design, however, focused on a highly technical and nonpolitical object, and might be worth reexamination with political focus.

In addition to supplying new information, adult peers are considered distinctive in their contribution to learning of specialized political roles, particularly in the realm of leadership. A number of studies which purport to study the socialization of legislators actually consider recruitment (e.g., Prewitt, 1965) rather than socialization within the legislative role. While the role of peers in the former situation is not distinctive, it is deemed to be considerable in the latter. Studies of state legislators (Wahlke et al., 1962; Barber, 1965; Price & Bell, 1970), U.S. senators (Matthews, 1960; Huitt, 1957, 1961), U.S. representatives (Fenno, 1962; Feillin, 1962; Manley, 1965), and Canadian legislators (Kornberg, 1964) attest with varying degrees of quantitative evidence to the existence of widely shared norms, enforced by both social and political rewards and punishments. Fenno demonstrates that the group norms (appropriations committee) are distinctive to their specialized role rather than attributable to recruitment patterns by comparing group members to other legislators with similar party and constituency base. More recently, Asher (1973) has found relatively little attitude change in his longitudinal study of members of the House of Representatives. One wonders whether legislators are being socialized by socialization studies, and no longer need their colleagues to do the job.

It is likely that peer socialization of specialized elites would be worth evaluating in many other settings. Huntington's study of the ICC, e.g., suggests the evolution among commission staff of a proindustry outlook (1952). The role of peer influence in bringing about such important policy outlooks in specialized government agencies is rarely explored. It is likely that, again because of the unique or novel quality of the role to be performed, peer socialization will again play an important role.

Cross-cultural Variations

The discussion so far has concentrated largely upon the part played by peers in American political socialization. The contours of peer impact are likely to be shaped, however, by cross-cultural variations. Of the many ways in which culture may mediate peer influence, we will consider three: (1) types of peer institutions; (2) rates of change, or constancy of political objects; and (3) attitudinal norms regarding relationships between child and parent and child and friends.

PEER INSTITUTIONS

The extent to which a culture deliberately harnesses and institutionalizes peer groups to perform socializing functions will obviously affect the peer role. Under adult guidance, the Soviet school classes described by Bronfenbrenner (1970a, 1970b) use intragroup pressure heightened by intergroup competition to teach adult values to children. The Chinese apparently rely on adult groups founded in the workplace or neighborhood to communicate political information and con-solidate loyalty (e.g., Lifton, 1968). In the United States, by contrast, despite the proliferation of voluntary associations among both youth and adults, peer politi-cal socialization is haphazard, possibly because, save in the case of marriage, it lacks an institutional framework.

RATES OF CHANGE

In our earlier consideration of objects of learning, it was suggested that novel objects for which early socialization and parental models left us unprepared were more likely to be the focus of later, peer-based socialization. It would seem logical, then, to expect that cultures experiencing rapid rates of social and politi-cal change would frequently provide novel attitude objects and consequent op-portunities for peer influence. The few studies available to address this hypothesis do indeed authenticate a part of the expectations—a comparatively low impact of parents on their children's political learning (Kuroda, 1965; sev-eral studies of French partisanship, e.g., Converse & Dupeux, 1962; Koff, Von der Muhll, & Prewitt, 1973). They do not offer any evidence that an increased role for peer-based learning is created under such conditions.

NORMS AND ATTITUDES

A final cultural variable to be considered is prevailing attitudinal norms regarding patterns of interpersonal communication and compliance. It is likely that parent-child communication regarding political themes varies according to culture, though again it is not clear that peers will pick up the slack. In the Converse and Dupeux study, e.g., it was discovered that most French adults simply did not know the party affiliations of their parents and indicated by their responses that the matter had never been discussed (1962). We have, as noted, no evidence that a norm of peer communication of these themes is present either.

The studies which do account for both parents and peers in the context of attitudinal norms are, unfortunately, not directly political. Kandel and Lesser found marked differences between Americans and Danish, with regard to their views about responsibility to parents, which may be used to explain the lower reliance of Danish students on parent as opposed to peer advice (1972, p. 15).

In Bronfenbrenner's comparison of Soviet and Swiss children in collective settings (1970b), he compared the manner in which children would handle an incident of rule breaking with their upbringer's standards for handling a comparable situation. He found Soviet children overwhelmingly endorsed their upbringer's preferences in selecting a mode of problem solving which relied on peer interaction (75%). Swiss children mirrored the ambivalence of their upbringers, but were more likely to turn to adult intervention as their problem-solving technique (Bronfenbrenner, 1970b, p. 79).

Similarly, in their comparison of Soviet and Israeli children, Shouval et al. (1975) discovered a unique finding absent in all other countries the Bronfenbrenner group has examined: Israeli children gave the most "moral" answers to a series of posited dilemmas when there was no pressure from either parents or peers. The authors again explain this phenomenon in terms of parental and teacher expectations. Somewhat paradoxically, the Israeli child is taught to conform to a standard of nonconformity (Shouval et al., 1975, p. 487), a highly valued norm in the Israeli culture.

Barry, Child, and Bacon (1959) and Berry (1967) hypothesize a relationship between a culture's training for compliance and its economic needs. Low food accumulation subsistence societies are expected to produce individualistic members, and high accumulation (and sharing) societies to produce compliant members. Using an Asch design, Berry confirmed these expectations comparing the Temne people of Sierra Leone and Baffin Island Eskimos.

Peer Research—Critique and Suggestions

Though more than a decade has passed since Roberta Sigel pointed out to political scientists the need to focus more on the process as opposed to the outcomes of political socialization (1966), the subject of peer socialization has benefited little from her warning. For the questions of what, why, and how we learn from peers, we have far more speculation than evidence. What evidence we have is based on research designs which frequently rest more on wish fulfillment than on logic.

The most convenient approach to demonstrate the existence of peer influence is simply to question a respondent regarding his own perceptions of the degree to which he finds himself influenced by friends (e.g., Ostlund, 1973). A close relative of this approach, also relying on respondent reports, is to posit for him various hypothetical situations and ask him what sources of advisement he would most value for each—generally, with a comparison of parents and schoolmates as the available options (e.g., Hirsch, 1971; Langton, 1969). The obvious limitation of this self-reporting approach is the failure actually to assess the concordance of the subject's views with those of either peers or parents. One may well be tapping norms ("I think my mother is the right source") rather than actual practices or consequent influence.

To make up for this deficiency, some scholars have attempted to add data about the beliefs of alleged peers as a point of comparison with those of the subject and, when concordance is discovered, to conclude that peer influence has been at work. The discovery of peer opinion, however, may prove a stumbling block to this methodology. Several studies have used aggregate scores of people who are expected to be like the subject's peers as the relevant point of comparison. Langton, e.g., to demonstrate that upper-class peers socialize lower-class students to upper-class norms, compared the views of his lower-class subjects who claimed membership in upper-class peer groups with those of the aggregate of upper-class respondents in his Jamaican sample (Langton, 1969). DiPalma and McClosky, while not explicitly referring to peers, also use this logic, calling people conformers when their views correspond to a majority of their national sample (1970). When an aggregate is used as a proxy for an actual peer group, tenuous assumptions are being made about the prevailing beliefs in the particular group in which the subject is engaged, as well as about the preexisting beliefs of the subject prior to his group membership.

A somewhat more ambitious research methodology is required to overcome these limitations, including delimitation of specific peer groups, and premembership belief assessment. Sebert, Jennings, and Niemi have addressed the former problem by the utilization of sociometric techniques to designate the specific individuals their student subjects claimed as close friends, averaging their opinions on a variety of dimensions and then correlating the group averages with the scores of the subject (Sebert, Jennings, & Niemi, 1974). In a less political orientation this approach has also been used effectively by Kandel and Lesser (1972) and by Coleman (1961), always in school situations. This technique, reaching out as it does to others beyond the subject for influence, is difficult to apply except within arbitrarily delimited settings such as schools, clubs, or places of employment. This limitation is not severe, however, in the case of young people whose friends are often drawn exclusively from the school situation.

While the sociometric technique overcomes the first problem cited, it fails to address the more difficult question of controls for preexisting conditions. Nor does it inherently defend against the spuriousness that may be introduced by parallelism, or the independent experience of similar influences accounting for the commonality of group beliefs without intragroup influence. Sebert et al. attempted to address the parallelism problem by controls for social status, academic standing, student leadership, and popularity, a useful undertaking which might well be extended to other extragroup variables. Newcomb's now classic study of Bennington students (1943) as well as its update 20 years later (1967) are examples of the rare opportunities the literature affords us for observing the results of a method in which pregroup exposure attitude measures are available. While the longitudinal character of Newcomb's analysis makes it unusual in the study of peer influence, in the original Bennington study he does not delineate actual peer groups but, rather, compares the views of the subject with those of the aggregate college culture. In the followup study, while asking respondents about their own friends, spouses, and colleagues, he relies primarily on the respondents' perceptions of peer opinion and its influence.

The difficulties of assembling the necessary data under conditions of sufficient control are considerable justification for the logical inferences which have been necessary in the field studies described. The experimental setting, however, has offered possibilities which may be useful in at least adding or subtracting weight from the field analyses. In these settings, the peer relationship is typically artificially created (as opposed to reliance on natural friendship pairs or groups) and can be controlled and manipulated to account for such difficult variables as preexisting views, personality traits of participants, processes and styles of interaction, and intensity of group-oriented commitment.

The methodological advantages of experimental manipulation are, of course, balanced against new problems that the experimental setting creates. The most obvious of these is the transferability of findings to the real world, which problem is frequently exacerbated by particular characteristics of the experimental design. First, in order to create his or her simulation of some real world situation or process, the researcher usually relies on sets of instructions to his subjects. Though rarely considered in the experimental literature, it is highly possible that the behavior subsequently observed by the researcher is a product of the subject's response to the authority of the researcher (often a professor in the institution where the subject is a student) rather than to the conditions the study was designed to create. Second, in order to control for external influences on the subject extraneous to the research design, the research often selects for observation the development of attitudes or behaviors for which there has been no previous influence or socialization (Bandura, 1969, p. 218). However, the more uncontaminated an attitude object is from the point of view of external influences and prior socialization, the less likely it is to be directly relevant to the political system. Since we have several studies which suggest that the relative importance of peers as sources of influence varies according to attitude object (e.g., Brittain, 1963; Sebert et al., 1974; Kandel & Lesser, 1972), it is logically hazardous to assume that processes observed in the laboratory and built around apolitical objects may be transferable to the real world and to political objects.

A third strained assumption in the experimental studies of peer-induced conformity is that subjects who do not conform to experimentally designed peer pressure are less affected by peers than those who do conform. In fact, nonconformers in the lab may be conforming to peers or others encountered elsewhere. The lab results may not be distinguishing conformers from nonconformers but, rather, those who conformed now from those who conformed earlier.

Finally, an almost universal distinction between the laboratory and field situation is found in the motivations for participation by the subject in the experiment. These motives, which may include financial incentives, course requirements, or desire for self-discovery may engage the subject in a simulated peer group in ways which are distinctive from "normal" group engagement.

In suggesting new directions and emphases for the study of peer socialization, part of the message lies in correcting assumptions in methods already in use. More important, however, is the redirecting of research priorities, a task which should bear its own message for methodology.

In the American context, the research frontier is the individual and the minority of persons who show up as peer influenced at various points in their political life cycle. Instead of the aggregate techniques we have been relying on in field studies, such persons should be understood through the use of extended interviews, longitudinal followup, and other intensive approaches. It may be (and it is certainly worth discovering) that while most people most of the time are not influenced by peers, the one time they are so influenced is with regard to a critical turning point or major commitment. Or, as we mentioned earlier, it may be that those who are peer influenced constitute a distinctive group whose outlook or composition has disproportionate potential for influence. Both of these possibilities are inadequately explored in the literature so far, and unlikely to be discerned in mass, quantitative research.

There is also an important research frontier worth exploring in the crossnational arena. Comparisons of cultures which do and do not deliberately institutionalize peer units of political socialization might prove valuable indeed. Does such institutionalization encourage or discourage social change? Are societies with institutionalized peer groups altered in their ability to absorb such change? Is the deliberate harnessing of peer influence a hallmark of dictatorial regimes? Or can this practice be used to enhance and encourage democratic political competition? We have spent too much time scrutinizing the same questions (whether and how much we are socialized by peers) and with the same, often inappropriate techniques. It is time to take the next step and ask some larger questions. When you are socialized by peers what, if anything, does it portend for the performance of a political system?

7

Political Socialization
and Political Education in Schools

John J. Patrick

WHEN CHILDREN READILY OBEY the commands of a policeman directing traffic in front of their school, pledge allegiance to the flag in their classroom, select a class president by majority vote, or profess preference for their political institutions as part of a civics lesson, they are conforming to their culture. The children's behavior can be linked to political socialization, the process for transmitting their society's political norms. In contrast, when youngsters systematically raise questions and examine alternative answers about modal values and traditions or appraise the gap between societal ideals and realities, they may be experiencing political education beyond socialization. In American schools, there has been tension between those who would view political education of the masses as primarily socialization to the status quo and those who would try to teach as many youngsters as possible to think for themselves.

In order to influence and perhaps improve political learning in American schools, one must try to comprehend and appraise conflicting ideas and practices of leading political educators. Toward this end, the following topics are discussed: (1) the scope of political education and socialization in American schools; (2) the political learning of American youth; (3) shortcomings of traditional political education in schools; (4) alternative innovations in political education; (5) assessments of innovative curricula; and (6) questions for researchers and curriculum developers about political education and socialization in schools.

The Scope of Political Education and Socialization in American Schools

Political education involves learning and instructing about politics and political actors. In particular, it is concerned with "the authoritative distribution of advantages among people" (Froman, 1962, p. 3). *Learning* is a relatively permanent change in competence that results from experience and which is not attributable to physical maturation. A person who has learned can do something new as a consequence of interaction with his environment (Gagne, 1965, p. 5). Instruction is the creation of conditions that facilitate learning. It involves manipulation of the learner's environment to induce changes in capability efficiently (Gagne & Briggs, 1974, pp. 122–123).

The school is an important setting for political education. Through experiences in schools, youngsters learn political attitudes, beliefs, and behaviors both formally and informally—both directly through instruction and indirectly through casual experiences or chance happenings. Formal courses in history, civics, and government are designed to teach political knowledge, attitudes, and skills. Patriotic holidays and rituals are used to teach respect and love for the nation. Rules of political participation are learned through classroom discussion, committee projects, student government, and school club activities. Schoolteachers and administrators teach much political learning informally by their styles of behavior, their classroom procedures, and their attitudes toward children.

DISTINGUISHING POLITICAL SOCIALIZATION AND POLITICAL EDUCATION

Political education in schools involves socialization to a lesser or greater extent, depending on the values of educators and those whom they serve. According to Roberta Sigel (1970, p. xii), "Political socialization refers to the process by which people learn to adopt the norms, values, attitudes, and behaviors accepted and practiced by the ongoing system. Such learning, however, involves much more than the acquisition of the appropriate knowledge of a society's political norms and more than the blind performance of appropriate political acts; it also assumes that the individual so makes these norms and behaviors his own—internalizes them—that to him they appear to be right, just, and moral." This definition has deep roots in sociology and social psychology (Brim, 1965, p. 3; Guskin, 1970, p. 98; Remy et al., 1975, pp. 5–10; Goslin, 1969, pp. 1–21). As socialization pertains to the individual's *conformity* to his society's culture, political socialization refers to the individual's acquisition of his society's political culture or norms for managing "the authoritative distribution of advantages and disadvantages.'' The end toward which this process functions is the development of individuals who accept the approved motives, habits, and values relevant to the political system of their society and who transmit these norms to future generations.

Notice the difference between the preceding conception of political socialization and the following definitions:

> Political socialization is all political learning, formal and informal, deliberate and unplanned (Greenstein, 1965, p. 551).

> Political socialization consists of those developmental processes through which persons acquire political orientations and patterns of behavior (Easton & Dennis, 1969, p. 7).

These definitions equate political socialization, political learning, and political education. All political learning and education, whether supportive or subversive of the status quo, is viewed as political socialization. However, we cannot examine precisely the conflicting forces of maintenance and change in schools when we apply the same concept, political socialization, to political education designed to keep things as they are and learning experiences geared to develop human capabilities to initiate and manage change.

To be a maximally useful guide to inquiry, our concept of political socialization should *not* be so broad as to blur important distinctions; rather, it should help us to see particular phenomena more sharply and insightfully and to relate them to other precisely ordered sets of data. Thus, it seems useful to conceive of *political socialization as a major facet of political education, which pertains to learning experiences aimed at shaping human potentialities to support the sociocultural order.*

Political education and socialization in schools may be nearly coterminous. Both formal and informal educational experience may be geared to maintaining traditions. However, the scope of political education in schools may be much broader than socialization. Learning experience may be designed to foster competence to think critically and independently, which could lead to rejection of established political beliefs and practices.

Bay, Pranger, and Entwistle argue that schools should emphasize broad political education rather than narrow political socialization. Bay (1972, pp. 90–91) says: ''As with all education, political science education must aim at liberating the student from the blinders of the conventional wisdom, from political totems and taboos, so that he may make the basic choice of how to live and of political ideals as an independent person with optimal critical powers.'' Pranger (1968, p. 44) says that, in contrast to political socialization, a broad political education emphasizes the ''artificiality of political order and the citizen as a creative actor within this order.'' Entwistle (1971, pp. 10–11) says that political education, in contrast to socialization, should help youngsters learn to question basic assumptions of their polity and to consider alternative answers.

The preceding distinctions between political education and socialization have implications for researchers as well as for practitioners in curriculum development and instructional design. Students of political socialization should be concerned primarily with questions about the maintenance of political systems, about the transmission of political orthodoxy. They should ask how individuals learn to confrom to the sociopolitical status quo so that political norms are observed and established political roles are performed.

In contrast, students of both political education and socialization in schools should have broader concerns. They should ask not merely how individuals learn to conform so that political orders endure; but they also should ask how individuals learn to create and to change political orders. Students of political education should be interested in the adjustment of society to fit the needs of individuals as well as the adjustment of individuals to fit the needs of society.

Researchers and curriculum developers concerned broadly about political education as well as socialization are interested in questions and hypotheses about instruction and learning—the means and ends of experiences in schools. For example, they are interested in questions about the political competencies individuals should acquire (objectives of instruction), the means to the acquisition of these competencies (instructional techniques), and likely consequences of attaining these competencies.

FOUR DIMENSIONS OF POLITICAL EDUCATION AND SOCIALIZATION IN SCHOOLS

Four main dimensions of instruction and learning can be constructed to facilitate inquiry about political education and socialization in schools: (1) knowledge, (2) intellectual skills, (3) participation skills, and (4) attitudes. The surest way to determine the values of curriculum developers in political education is to examine their instructional objectives and practices in terms of these four dimensions, since they reveal what and how they believe students ought to learn. An educator whose ends and means stress recall of many details about government institutions is revealing very different values from one whose objectives and practices stress analysis and evaluation of political decisions. A curriculum developer's ends and means indicate whether he values learning that is rather trivial and insignificant or profound and relevant, that discourages initiative and creativity or that enhances potential for independent, divergent thinking, that is geared to keep a society essentially as it is or that enables the initiation and management of needed social change.

A common goal of American political educators has been to promote democratic citizenship (Weisbord, 1970, p. 2). However, variation in the instructional objectives and techniques of curriculum developers suggests very different interpretations of this common goal. Examination of instructional objectives and practices in terms of the preceding four dimensions can highlight conflicting ideas about what and how students ought to learn through political education and socialization in schools. These four dimensions also can be used to guide appraisals of alternative curricula and the political learning of students which is associated with different approaches to instruction. A prerequisite to these kinds of inquiry is discussion of the meaning of the four main dimensions of political education and socialization in schools: (1) political knowledge, (2) intellectual skills, (3) political participation skills, and (4) political attitudes.

POLITICAL KNOWLEDGE

The knowledge objectives of curriculum developers in political education refer to concepts, information, and factual judgments about government and politics. Knowing the legal duties and responsibilities of the president, various patterns of voter behavior, and the relationships between socioeconomic status and political participation is an example of outcomes of instruction which fits this dimension of political education.

Political knowledge objectives are related to assumptions of political educators about the common goal of developing good citizenship. Political educators assume that knowledge is necessary to the exercise of influence. "Good" citizens possess strategic information and knowledge necessary to effective political action. Political educators also assume that knowledge is necessary to the observance of national loyalty. Good citizens know the glories of their political heritage and the precepts of patriotic behavior. The two facets of the good-citizenship goal—teaching knowledge for effective participation and for conformity to the "establishment"—can create tensions and conflicts among thoughtful educators and students.

INTELLECTUAL SKILLS

Instructional objectives and practices associated with intellectual skills refer to ability to describe, explain, and evaluate political phenomena. In particular, intellectual skill learning pertains to locating and using evidence to support or reject factual claims. Examples of intellectual skills pertinent to political life are abilities needed to appraise results of a public opinion poll reported in a newspaper, to evaluate the accuracy of arguments appearing in newspaper or television editorials, and to construct a set of defensible claims about political reality. Intellectual skill learning also involves making rational moral judgments and evaluating the moral judgments of others.

A political educator's beliefs about intellectual skill learning are tied to assumptions about the goal of developing good citizenship. Some political educators stress intellectual skill learning because they believe that ability to think independently is central to good citizenship (Cleary, 1971, p. 11).

Although American political educators generally pledge allegiance to the value of intellectual skill learning, many are extremely cautious implementors of their "pledge." Others fail to practice what they preach. They proclaim the importance of critical thinking and inquiry while teaching uncritical acceptance of their conceptions of the "American way of life." They apparently are frightened by the potential for change that could result from developing a nation of thinkers. Conflicting beliefs about how far one should proceed in teaching thinking skills is a continuing source of tension among political educators.

POLITICAL PARTICIPATION SKILLS

Instructional objectives and practices for participation skill learning pertain to abilities needed to interact smoothly with others to maintain a group, to cooperate with others to achieve a common goal, and to negotiate and bargain to influence and/or make decisions. The skilled political participant is able to advocate ideas, to organize resources, and to administer people and things.

Most proponents of participation skill learning want to blend this theme with knowledge and intellectual skill learning. They believe that students should learn knowledge about influence, skills of organizing and interpreting evidence about influence, and *skills of using influence to achieve political objectives*. A main assumption underlying participation skill learning is that the ultimate end of political education is not knowing, but doing (Entwistle, 1971, p. 103).

Although the common goal of education for citizenship in a democracy implies the learning of political participation skills, political educators have been content merely to preach about the virtues of civic action. Most have not tried to teach systematically the particular competencies necessary to implement this "virtue."

POLITICAL ATTITUDES

Attitudinal objectives pertain to "an internal state which affects an individual's choice of action toward some objective, person, or event" (Gagne & Briggs, 1974, p. 72). The focus of attitudinal objectives is on feelings of accepting or rejecting, of approaching or avoiding. The common goal of education for good citizenship is weighted heavily with affective concerns such as promoting interest in politics, tolerance of diversity, feelings of efficacy, feelings of trust in government, feelings of patriotism, support for law and order, etc.

Most American political educators derive their attitudinal objectives from classical democratic political theory. They wish to develop *democratic political orientations*. A democratic political orientation consists of beliefs and attitudes that support the potentially conflicting practices of majority rule and the protection of minority rights.

The principle of majority rule refers to the populist or participatory theme of democracy. It subsumes attitudes such as political interest and sense of political efficacy. The majority rule theme of democracy is not operable unless large numbers of citizens display high levels of political interest and political efficacy.

The protection of minority rights refers to the libertarian theme of democ-

racy. It implies political tolerance, the willingness to grant rights and opportunities even to unpopular minority groups. The libertarian theme of democracy is
the essential check upon absolute majority rule, which presumably leads to
dictatorship.

When using the democratic model to generate attitudinal goals, different
political educators have stressed different facets of the model. Some have highlighted the importance of conformity to majority rule, single-minded national
loyalty, and law and order while superficially proclaiming allegiance to tolerance
for diversity, open-mindedness, and constructive skepticism. In contrast, other
political educators have tended to stress the critical thinking, open-mindedness,
freedom of speech and thought facets of the democratic citizenship model. These
conflicting themes have been a source of contention among political educators in
schools.

The Political Learning of American Youth—Knowledge, Skills, Attitudes

The political learning of American youth can be assessed in terms of the four
main dimensions of political education: knowledge, intellectual skills, participation skills, and attitudes. What are the achievements of students in terms of each
of these categories? What do these findings suggest about the impact of political
education and socialization in schools on student learning?

LEARNING POLITICAL KNOWLEDGE

Findings about the political knowledge of three groups are reported below:
seventh and eighth graders, high school seniors, and adults. These findings are
suggestive of what students learn during their middle school and high school
years.

Middle school students (seventh and eighth graders) are very aware of political phenomena. The roots of this political awareness are firmly implanted in
early childhood (Easton & Dennis, 1969, pp. 73–285). The junior high school
student is aware of the functions of rules and government in ordering behavior
and maintaining social stability (Tapp, 1970, pp. 29–31).

Although middle school students indicate a basic awareness of politics and of
governmental structures, they tend to express basic misconceptions and ignorance of the political process in our country. For example, (1) they tend to have
an exaggerated belief in the efficacy of individuals to influence government; (2)
they tend to have unwarranted beliefs about the impact of the ballot on public
policy decision making; (3) they tend to hold unrealistic beliefs about equality of

political opportunity and influence; (4) they tend to indicate misunderstanding of conflict as a basic element of the political process; and (5) they tend to underestimate the utility of party politics and to overestimate the viability and values of the "rational independent" model of voter behavior.

Seventh and eighth graders tend to express an unrealistic "personal clout" theory of political participation, which is based on the incorrect assumption that each citizen, regardless of personal skill and social position, can have direct and potent influence on public officials. Seventh and eighth graders tend to believe that the average citizen has about as much influence upon lawmaking as rich people, newspapers, and big companies. Despite their strong expressions of personal political efficacy, most seventh and eighth graders are uninformed about how to affect public policy decisions (Hess & Torney, 1967, pp. 32–59).

Middle school students tend to have a "town meeting" view of public policy making, which is based on the unwarranted assumption that most public policy decisions are influenced directly by voting in public elections. Most seventh and eighth graders believe that their representatives in government consistenly and faithfully reflect the popular will (Hess & Torney, 1967, pp. 74–92).

Most middle school youth do not understand that conflicts, competitions, and compromises are essential to the political process in our country. They tend to view conflict and competition between Democrats and Republicans as unnecessarily disruptive and even dysfunctional. Although most preadolescents are ignorant of particular differences in political ideas and programs which distinguish the Democrat and Republican parties, they favor the minimization of these differences. Seventh and eighth graders tend to view criticism of public officials during political campaigns as a manifestation of undesirable divisiveness (Hess & Torney, 1967, pp. 72–94).

Seventh and eighth graders tend to express an unrealistic view of the capabilities of voters. They highly value the "rational independent" model of voter behavior, even though very few voters are capable of acting consistently in terms of this norm. They fail to comprehend the utility of political partisanship as a guide to voter choice and to political participation (Sears, 1969, pp. 439–442).

From 1969 to 1972, the Education Commission of the States conducted nationwide surveys of the political knowledge and attitudes of 13-year-olds and 17-year-olds. Following are major findings of this study about the knowledge dimension of political education.

Most 13-year-olds and 17-year-olds have knowledge of superficial features of American governmental institutions. Apparently this knowledge increases with age, since a larger proportion of 17-year-olds than 13-year-olds displayed it in this study. However, a *majority* of *both* the 13-year-olds and 17-year-olds responded correctly to most questions in this study about American governmental institutions. It appears that by the time they graduate from high school most adolescents know details about government such as that Congress is composed of two houses, that the power of public officials is limited by law, that certain public officials are elected to office while others are appointed, and that responsibilities for providing various public services are divided or shared by federal, state, and local governments (Education Commission of the States, 1970, p. 54).

Most American youngsters recognize the need for government and laws and can state at least one positive purpose served by law. Our youth appear to understand that the essential function of law is to regulate human relationships for the purpose of minimizing disorder and protecting the rights of individuals. Most American youngsters appear to recognize both the service and conflict resolution functions of government (Education Commission of the States, 1970, p. 54).

Both younger and older adolescents express ignorance of key public officials and political leaders. Although most American adolescents can name the President and vice president, they tend to be unable to name their senators, congressmen, or governor. Most do not know the names of national political leaders such as the Senate Majority Leader, the Speaker of the House, or the Secretary of State (Education Commission of the States, 1970, p. 54).

A majority of adolescents and young adults showed ignorance of these facts about American government and politics: (1) the U.S. Constitution contains statements about civil rights; (2) the principle of separation of Church and state is the basis for Supreme Court declarations of formal religious instruction in public schools as unconstitutional; and (3) the presidential candidate of each major party is formally nominated at a national convention (Education Commission of the States, 1973, pp. 19–27, 43–47).

Another way to look at the possible impact of public school political education is to examine surveys of the political knowledge of adults. Since a large majority of American adults have graduated from secondary schools, the long-term impact of formal political learning in schools can be assessed roughly through the findings of nationwide survey studies of the adult population.

A recent survey by Louis Harris and Associates (1973, pp. 72–78), done for the U.S. Senate Subcommittee on Intergovernmental Relations, demonstrates massive political ignorance among nationally representative samples of adults. Less than 40% profess to be well informed about government or current political events. Less than half of the respondents could name both of their senators or the representative to Congress from their district. Less than two thirds knew that Congress is comprised of the House of Representatives and the U.S. Senate. Twenty percent said Congress consisted of the House, the Senate, and the U.S. Supreme Court—this after all the textbook preachments about the three branches of government. Lou Harris' observation (1973, p. 77) about his survey is that "these results indicate substantial gaps in the public's knowledge of both the structure of government and also of many of the key individuals elected to high office."

An important objective of traditional high school government courses has been to transmit information about governmental institutions and politics. Although the traditional approaches have dominated the public schools, the impact of these courses in the political knowledge domain (as suggested by various survey studies) has been meager.

LEARNING SKILLS IN POLITICAL EDUCATION

In contrast to the political knowledge domain, there is a paucity of data about intellectual and participation skill learning associated with political education. However, these limited data suggest that American adolescents tend to lack ability to make intellectual moves necessary to higher level cognition.

Studies by Tapp and Lockwood indicate deficiencies in intellectual skills of many American adolescents. The Tapp studies show that the vast majority of adolescents demonstrate low-level cognitive capability when thinking about legal and moral issues (Tapp & Kohlberg, 1971, p. 84). Only 20% of a sample of older adolescents studied by Lockwood demonstrated high-level cognitive capability when thinking about public issues. Only 50% of this sample demonstrated achievement of Piaget's formal operations stage of cognitive capability (Kohlberg & Lockwood, 1972).

An evaluation study of an experimental high school course, *American Political Behavior,* revealed a considerable lack of intellectual skills among "control group" students, those participants in the study who experienced typical secondary school government courses (Patrick, 1972, pp. 173–175). Although the study was conducted in only nine communities, one can reasonably speculate that the dearth of intellectual skills of the control group students in these communities, which varied in location, size, and socioeconomic characteristics, is manifested by a large proportion of American adolescents. Control group students tended to be unable to organize and interpret information and to make critical judgments about statements and questions: e.g., they tended to be unable to distinguish factual and normative statements, to make critical judgments about sampling procedures, to interpret contingency tables, and to make critical judgments about questions.

The Education Commission of the States survey (1973, pp. 45–46, 59–63) indicated the likelihood of low-level participatory skill development. Less than half of this sample of 17-year-olds could identify as many as three ways that citizens can influence their government. Only 25% of these adolescents could mention four political participation techniques, and only 11% could list five techniques for exerting political influence. Presumably, this obvious lack of knowledge of political participation techniques reflects low-level participation skill. Less than half of the respondents could interpret and mark a sample ballot correctly. However, this same study did indicate that both 13-year-olds and 17-year-olds have high-level capacity to work cooperatively in small groups to complete an assigned task. Nearly all youngsters in the study were able to work successfully together to complete an assigned task without behaving in distracting or impeding ways.

Although political educators traditionally have acknowledged the importance of developing students' intellectual and participant skills, they have given little attention to teaching these skills. Thus, it is not surprising that traditional government and civics courses seemingly have had little impact on intellectual and participation skill learning.

Some political educators have questioned the capability of adolescents to make high-level cognitive moves. To what extent can youngsters attain particular intellectual skills?

Joseph Adelson and several associates have done crossnational studies, involving American, German, and British youth at four grade levels (fifth, seventh, ninth, and twelfth). These studies have indicated that children of different age groups have different capacities for political learning. Prior to age 13, most youngsters do not have the cognitive capacity to perform complex mental operations about political phenomena: e.g., preadolescents are unable to deeply comprehend highly abstract political concepts such as government, society, democracy, or freedom. Preadolescents focus on the tangible and the concrete; they tend to personalize institutions and events. Preadolescents do not have the cognitive capacity to build complex networks between bits of information and between concepts; they often know many details about politics or government but cannot integrate these data efficiently in terms of conceptual frameworks (Adelson, 1972, p. 1030).

According to the Adelson studies, the 13-year-old is at the threshold of ability to deal with political abstractions, to reason from premises, to extrapolate from what is known to what is probably true about the unknown, to speculate and to theorize, and to use the hypothetico-deductive method of formulating and testing hypotheses (Adelson & O'Neil, 1966, p. 306).

Fifteen-year-olds can think competently and consistently in terms of political abstractions. They can think conditionally and probabilistically (Adelson, 1971, p. 1021). Fifteen-year-olds show ability to project consequences and to specify probable outcomes of particular conditions; they can infer conclusions from premises and extrapolate generalization from data; they can relate concepts and propositions to construct theories. In short, what the 13-year-old does inconsistently and irregularly, the 15-year-old can do unhesitantly and unfalteringly (Adelson & O'Neil, 1966, p. 306).

According to the Adelson studies, the most extensive increase in capacity for political learning takes place between ages 11 and 13. During this period, there is a marked softening in the more absolutistic, either/or style of thinking associated with childhood. There is a demonstration of capability to reason probabilistically, to think in terms of the tendency propositions of social science. There is the beginning of capability to assess political actions in cost-benefit terms, to examine systematically the probable gains and losses associated with different political decisions or behaviors, and to make political decisions on the basis of cost-benefit calculations.

The studies of cognitive development and political learning suggest that high school students tend to have the capacity to achieve skills necessary to high-level thinking about politics. Perhaps the failure of most students to achieve these competencies is associated with deficiences in political education in schools.

LEARNING POLITICAL ATTITUDES

Teaching democratic political attitudes is supposed to be an important goal of traditional political educators. To what extent do American youth express *democratic political orientations?* What do findings about the learning of political attitudes suggest about the impact of political education and socialization in schools?

Political socialization researchers and public opinion pollsters have gathered data indicating that large numbers of American adolescents and adults have failed to develop strong attachments to the libertarian theme of classical democratic theory. *Most American adolescents learn very well to be supportive of their political system; they do manifest strongly attitudes supportive of maintaining law and order and of obedience to legitimate authorities.* However, they tend to believe that those with values and conceptions that are very different from their own should not have freedom of speech, the right to dissent openly from established sociopolitical patterns. They appear to believe that because a set of values is orthodox it must be right for all peoples and all social conditions.

Older youngsters are more likely than preadolescents to think critically about particular laws and authorities. However, they still display tendencies toward intolerance of particular types of dissent. Consider these findings of the Education Commission of the States survey (1970, p. 36; 1973, p. 33). Only 25% of the 13-year-old respondents would allow the expression of atheistic or agnostic beliefs on television. Less than half of the 17-year-olds in this sample would tolerate the public expression of these unorthodox beliefs. Only 3% of these 13-year-olds and 17% of the 17-year-olds specified freedom of speech as a reason to allow the expression of unorthodox beliefs on television. Thirty-eight percent of the 17-year-old respondents opposed or were undecided about allowing an atheist to hold public office. Only 55% of this sample of 13-year-olds believed that "it is all right for a person to tell other people if he thinks the Governor or President is doing a bad job and can give a reason why in terms of free speech." Respondents in this study tended to accept general statements about the rights of minorities. However, they also tended to reject the extension of this principle to particular cases. A recent study of children in grades five through nine, by Zellman and Sears (1971, pp. 109–136), found the same inconsistency between support for democratic abstractions and application of the principles to specific persons or events. Several studies of adults' political attitudes also have revealed contradictions between support for democratic beliefs in general and rejection of particular instances of these generalizations (Harris, 1973, pp. 278–279).

Most youngsters apparently do not experience instruction in schools which could lead to substantial political attitude learning. A major study of the mid-1960s based on a national probability sample of 1,669 twelfth graders from 97 high schools, indicated that students' political attitudes—such as civic tolerance, sense of political efficacy, political interest, desire to participate in politics, and political cynicism—were not related significantly to instruction in government courses (Langton & Jennings, 1968, pp. 852–867). However, when comparing white and black students, the researchers found that instruction was more likely to have an impact on the political attitudes of blacks than on the attitudes of whites. Lower-class blacks showed the greatest gains of any student group in sense of political efficacy, political interest, desire to participate in politics, and political knowledge. But, despite the impact of civics instructions on black students in this study, the blacks still lagged far behind most white students in their development of political attitudes deemed desirable by typical public school political educators.

A "redundancy hypothesis" was formulated to explain the differential impact of civics instruction on black and white students. It appeared that most black students, especially economically disadvantaged blacks, found new political information and ideas in their civics and government courses. Even if much of this subject matter is unrealistic and highly idealistic, it is fresh material for these blacks and thereby can have some impact on their thinking. By contrast, most white students found that their civics and government courses offered much information that already had been presented to them either through previous courses or through out-of-school experiences. These students were likely to "tune out" this instruction about government because it was redundant. The researchers concluded from this study that typical high school government courses, as they existed in the mid-1960s, were relatively impotent devices for influencing the development of political competency (Langton & Jennings, 1968, p. 867).

Shortcomings Associated with Modal Practices of Political Education and Socialization in Schools

Examination of widely used textbooks in civics and government reveals much about the quality of the political education to which students are exposed in schools. Appraisal of these instructional materials can yield valuable suggestions about shortcomings of students' political learning. Findings about the context of instruction—the conditions surrounding students and teachers—also suggest clues about limitations in students' political learning.

THE RELATIONSHIP OF MODAL INSTRUCTIONAL MATERIALS TO SHORTCOMINGS IN POLITICAL LEARNING

Evidence about the instructional objectives and practices of political educators can be derived from critical reviews and content analyses of textbooks and teachers' guides. The following discussion is based on five analyses of traditional textbooks done in the past 12 years (Massialas, 1967, pp. 167–197; Smith & Patrick, 1967, pp. 105–127; Shaver, 1965, pp. 226–257; Gillespie, 1975, pp. 381–408; APSA Committee on Pre-Collegiate Education, 1971).

THE POLITICAL KNOWLEDGE DOMAIN

Teachers' guides and textbooks of traditional political educators have paid "lip service" to knowing about effective political participation, individual rights and freedoms, and more equitable distributions of benefits across various social groups. However, the instruction provided in these materials has seemed to emphasize transmission of tradition at the expense of learning how to use the political system to maximize opportunities and rewards. Loyalty, duty, order, and obedience have seemed to be highlighted rather than ideas and information about how the political system works, how different individuals and groups might derive more benefits from it, and how it might be improved. Widely used traditional textbooks have presented ethical-legal norms as actual political behavior, thereby confusing what ought to be with what is. The sociocultural foundations of political behavior and the extralegal factors that influence public policy decisions and the functioning of government have been ignored. Conflicts about values and techniques of conflict resolutions—the controversies, contentions, and compromises which are essentials of politics—have been omitted or treated superficially.

A recent study of best-selling high school government textbooks reports only minor differences between the content of these books and the traditional texts of the 1960s. The author concluded that government textbooks treat most political science concepts inadequately (Gillespie, 1975, pp. 381–408).

THE SKILL LEARNING DOMAIN

The goals and objectives associated with skill learning in traditional textbooks have suggested support for critical thinking and effective participation. The contents of lesson plans in teachers' guides and of textbook chapters belie the authors' proclamations of support for teaching intellectual and participation skills. The textbooks of the 1960s provided meager instruction about how to think critically or to participate effectively. Instead of teaching students to cope with the controversy and conflict surrounding public issues, the textbooks tended to tell students what to believe and how to behave.

A recent content analysis of best-selling textbooks indicates that the political educators seem to be more interested in transmitting the "right" facts and values than in teaching skills necessary to independent thought and action. The author (Gillespie, 1975, pp. 381–408) concluded that the textbooks failed to teach skills of inquiry aptly.

THE POLITICAL ATTITUDE DOMAIN

While superficially proclaiming allegiance to tolerance for diversity, open-mindedness, constructive skepticism, and inquiry, the instructional materials of political educators have tended to highlight the importance of conformity to majority rule, the value of loyalty, and the need for law and order.

The traditional political educator has wanted the right attitudes and values to be learned so that youngsters will maintain their "democratic" heritage: e.g., some traditional textbooks have included lists of attitudes and values to be accepted without question. These lists have emphasized acceptance of norms and obedience to rules more than the protection of individual rights or the encouragement of critical thinking (Hartley & Vincent, 1974, pp. 15–16).

Assessment of modal instructional materials reveals a narrow emphasis on socialization—instruction for conformity to the status quo—rather than a broad emphasis on political education for independent thinking and action. To what extent is the "hidden curriculum," the context of instruction in schools, consistent with the content of modal instructional materials?

THE RELATIONSHIP OF THE HIDDEN CURRICULUM TO SHORTCOMINGS IN POLITICAL LEARNING

Political learning may be affected greatly by the *context of instruction*—the conditions of learning surrounding teachers and students. Investigators of the sociology of learning have referred to the context of instruction as the hidden curriculum, a potentially strong shaper of beliefs and attitudes which is usually unnoticed by teachers and students. In particular, the hidden curriculum may influence students' views of authority. The school environment represents the first and, for many years of young people's lives, the most salient form of external authority with which they have direct experience. The way in which teachers organize their classrooms, the extent to which students are allowed or encouraged to participate in decision making about school rules, the quality and quantity of informal group activities and committee work students engage in all influence the students' acquisition of knowledge, skills, and attitudes.

Numerous studies have concluded that the modal authority structure in American schools is more like a business corporation than a governmental organization (Sexton, 1967, pp. 65–75). Sociologists have described the typical authority pattern of schools as bureaucratic (Boocock, 1972, pp. 172–186).

There is a division of labor according to functions, strict definition of statuses and roles according to accepted rules, and a hierarchical, pyramidal pattern of authority based on strict definition of accepted rules.

At the top of the hierarchy is the principal and his or her assistants. Counselors and teachers occupy the middle positions and students, the majority group, are at the bottom of the role hierarchy. Students are the only group in the school who have no choice about being there until they attain the legal school-leaving age. Although major school decisions are supposed to be made to benefit the students, they usually have little or no say in these decisions.

A main feature of the bureaucratically organized school is a rather "closed educational climate." There is an obvious continuous concern with problems of discipline, of maintaining the established authority patterns.

Many researchers and commentators have concluded that teachers and administrators tend to be unduly preoccupied with maintaining authority over students, with "putting down the kids." Teachers are pressured by colleagues and administrators not to be "soft" on discipline. Thus, their behavior tends to encourage conformity, docility, dependence, and unquestioning obedience. On the whole, our schools have emphasized strict obedience to rules as opposed to participation in making rules and inquiry into the need for and purpose of rules (Guskin & Guskin, 1970, pp. 149–160).

The Hess and Torney (1967) nationwide study of political learning of children in grades one through eight supports the proposition that the educational climates in our classrooms and schools tend to be "closed." They reported that the teachers whom they studied tended to focus upon the importance of authority, obedience to law, and conformity to school regulations, and tended to disregard the importance of active participation. Political duties were stressed by teachers, and the rights and powers of citizens were underemphasized.

Some researchers and political educators (Dreeben, 1970, pp. 85–108) have argued that the prevailing authority structures in schools are suited to preparing most students to perform adult roles successfully, since these authority patterns tend to reflect many patterns found in the adult world. In addition, they contend that the modal school authority patterns are appropriate to the needs of school authorities and their clients. They maintain that schools are designed to teach performance of technical tasks, not to mobilize a populace to support a government. Thus, the argument that schools must be organized democratically to buttress a democratic society is nonsense. Rather, it is appropriate for those with expertise—school administrators and teachers—to impose their decisions on their clients as long as those decisions are made in the best interests of their clients.

In contrast to the preceding arguments, many political educators would rather focus on the relationships of instructional strategies and techniques to the educational environment. They have noted consistency between traditional instructional materials and the modal bureaucratic organizational structure of schools. Instructional materials which foster a passive learning style and lower-level cognition, such as the textbooks of traditional political educators, tend to fit the rather closed educational climates found in most schools. Sarane Boocock's review of research about the sociology of learning (1972, p. 151) indicates that "the conventional classroom role structure is not conducive to active involvement of most students in the learning process."

One can speculate that inadequacies in instructional materials and in contexts of instruction have been associated strongly with shortcomings in the political learning of students. Can instructional materials that are more adequately designed have a significant impact on the political learning of students? Can improvements in both instructional materials and contexts lead to significant improvements in students' political learning?

Innovative Practices in Political Education in Schools

Attempts have been made during the 1960s and 1970s to develop instructional materials which might have a substantial positive impact on the political learning of high school students. These curriculum reform efforts have been launched mostly through the federal funding of university-based curriculum development projects. What are the promising innovative practices of the curriculum development projects in the four dimensions of political education: knowledge, intellectual skills, participation skills, and attitudes?

NEW POLITICAL KNOWLEDGE THEMES

Sharp criticisms of traditional political knowledge themes was one of several pressures which contributed to the lauching of the curriculum reform movement of the 1960s. The funders of several political education projects wanted to prompt reform of political knowledge goals and objectives in three main ways. First, the projects were counted on to upgrade course content to narrow the gap between the findings of scholars and the substance of instruction. Conceptual frameworks of social scientists were to be used to help students organize and interpret political phenomena.

A second responsibility of the projects in the political knowledge domain was to make courses more realistic and interesting. The projects were expected to include controversial subjects and to relate course content to the experiences and concerns of students.

Third, the projects were expected to stress the learning of knowledge about how political systems work as a key to the achievement of political goals. A main assumption was that people who have more knowledge about their political world have more *potential* to participate effectively in it than do those who are ignorant.

The knowledge themes of the political education projects can be placed in three main categories: (1) knowledge based on social science conceptual frameworks; (2) knowledge relevant to the analysis of public issues or problems; and (3) knowledge related to the legal system. Different courses include practices which fit each category. However, a course is placed in a particular category to highlight the type of practices stressed in the course.

KNOWLEDGE BASED ON SOCIAL SCIENCE CONCEPTUAL FRAMEWORKS

American Political Behavior (APB) (Mehlinger & Patrick, 1972) and *Comparative Political Systems* (CPS) (Fenton et al., 1973) are examples of courses which stress knowledge based on related social science concepts pertinent to political phenomena. Both APB and CPS reflect the assumption that systematic concept learning is a key to deriving more meaning from experiences in the political world.

Both CPS and APB aim to teach students knowledge of governmental institution and political behavior. However, both CPS and APB emphasize the learning of generalizations about the political behavior of groups rather than details about institutions and legal documents. Both courses also aim to teach students to use concepts to compare political behavior and institutions of different groups. The focus of comparison in CPS is the United States versus the USSR. In contrast, the comparisons in APB pertain to different social, economic, and political groups within the United States.

KNOWLEDGE RELEVANT TO THE ANALYSIS OF PUBLIC ISSUES

The *Harvard Public Issues Project* (Oliver & Shaver, 1966) and The *Utah State University Analysis of Public Issues Project* (Shaver & Larkins, 1973) are examples of courses which feature knowledge relevant to the analysis of public issues. A main assumption of both the Harvard and Utah projects is that the basic aim of political education should be to teach analytical skills that enable one to think about and "know" public issues. Both programs assume that learning a *process* for analyzing public issues is more fundamental than gaining knowledge associated with academic disciplines. However, overall objectives are stated which have implications for the learning of political knowledge.

An overall objective of the Harvard project is to teach the analysis of public controversy in terms of three types of issues: prescriptive (what should be done), descriptive (the actual state of affairs), and analytic (the meaning of words, concepts, and problems). To achieve this objective, students must acquire information about the conditions of public controversy and knowledge of concepts needed to organize and interpret evidence relevant to public issues. An overall objective of the Utah project is to teach a framework for analyzing the *ought* question associated with public issues. To achieve this goal, students must be able to comprehend and apply concepts necessary to the analysis of public controversy. The student must learn to identify his values and to compare and contrast them with value patterns of various groups.

KNOWLEDGE RELATED TO THE LEGAL SYSTEM

The *Justice in Urban America* course (The Law in American Society Project, 1970) and *The American Legal System* (Summers et al., 1974) are examples of courses with knowledge based on the study of our legal system. A main assumption of both programs is that a main element of political education ought to be systematic study of the application of law to daily living. The project developers believe that, without knowledge of law, the citizen is disabled from coping effectively with many personal and public problems.

The overall knowledge objectives of these projects indicate an emphasis on knowing what law is, how it is related to social organization and human behavior, and how it can be used to deal with problems. The focus is on the functions of law in society, not on the details of laws. To achieve overall knowledge goals, students must learn various legal and social science concepts. They also are likely to learn much specific information relevant to course concepts and topics.

NEW INTELLECTUAL SKILLS THEMES

A main similarity of current innovative approaches to political education is strong emphasis on helping youngsters to think more effectively about the people, places, and events of their political world. One commonality of political education project materials is instructional practices that encourage students to be active seekers and users of knowledge rather than passive receivers of information. These materials require students to demonstrate ability to use particular concepts, information, and skills to analyze case studies, to play an educational game, to interpret data, to test hypotheses or theories, etc. Students are expected to learn skills of using knowledge to make decisions and solve problems. The desired ultimate goal is to develop skills necessary to independent thinking and learning—to create capacity for learning how to learn.

A basic assumption is that learning intellectual skills is a key to increasing ability to perceive and cope with one's political world. In addition, those who have competence to appraise and to inquire are supposed to have *more potential* for effective political action than do those who lack these skills.

Intellectual skill themes of the political education projects can be placed into two main categories: (1) emphasis on skills of empirical inquiry; and (2) emphasis on skills of normative analysis of public issues and/or legal issues and problems. *Each of the programs reviewed here gives attention to skills of empiri-*

cal inquiry and normative analysis. The categorical distinctions are based on the greater emphasis given to one or the other of these dimensions of skill learning.

EMPHASIS ON SKILLS OF EMPIRICAL INQUIRY

American Political Behavior and *Comparative Political Systems* are examples of courses that emphasize skills of empirical inquiry. These skills enable learners to marshal evidence to make warranted judgments about political reality. The aim is to teach skills that enable systematic, independent learning about the political world.

The overall objective of the CPS course (Fenton et al., 1973) is to help students become independent thinkers. Toward this end, the CPS course stresses learning skills of formulating and testing hypotheses that can help students to more fully understand their political world.

The developers of both CPS and APB assume that knowledge and intellectual skills must be learned concurrently: e.g., when students learn skills of using concepts to organize information, they also learn knowledge of the concepts—definitions and information which fits the definitions. When students learn skills of formulating and testing hypotheses, they also learn knowledge of concepts used to build the hypotheses and information used as evidence to support or confirm the hypotheses.

The developers of both CPS and APB assume that concept learning and related intellectual skill learning is broadly transferable. Intellectual skills learned while solving a particular problem can be applied, or transferred, to the solution of new related problems. The CPS and APB developers assume that learning which is broadly transferable equips one to cope with change, an obvious constant of our society.

EMPHASIS ON SKILLS OF NORMATIVE ANALYSIS

The *Harvard Public Issues Project* and the *Utah State University Analysis of Public Issues Project* emphasize skills required for normative analysis of public issues. A *public issue* is a problem or value dilemma that has concerned people persistently throughout history and across societies. Normative analysis involves learning to formulate and use criteria to make value judgments.

The developers of the Harvard and Utah State projects assume that public issues involve questions about right or wrong. Our values determine our responses to these issues. Thus, political education ought to focus on skills of value clarification and ethical value judgment. Students should learn how to clarify, judge, and make decisions about policy positions on public issues.

The law-related courses, such as *Justice in Urban America* and *The American Legal System*, feature normative analysis of legal issues and problems. The course developers believe that students should learn to identify legal issues, to apply knowledge of law to the clarification of these issues, and to evaluate and/or make decisions about these issues in terms of criteria that reflect moral, social, and legalistic considerations.

Both *The American Legal System* and *Justice in Urban America* are filled with lessons that require students to acquire and apply skills needed to judge decisions of others and to make their own decisions about legal issues. Both projects hope to help students learn to use skills of legal reasoning to solve their own problems and to cope with the law-related problems of their communities.

EMPHASIS ON SKILLS OF MORAL REASONING

Recently some political educators have expressed dissatisfaction with the relativistic approach to values education inherent in the normative analysis of issues methodologies. Lawrence Kohlberg (1975, p. 673) believes that we should do more than merely help students to become more rational and self-aware when making value judgments.

Kohlberg's overall goal of instruction is to help students acquire the high-level reasoning skills of the highest stage of Jean Piaget's cognitive development model. Kohlberg (1975, p. 671) assumes that "advanced moral reasoning depends upon advanced logical reasoning; a person's logical stage puts a certain ceiling on the moral stage he can attain."

In brief, the Piaget model, upon which Kohlberg bases his work, posits several hierarchical stages of cognitive development through which individuals move as they mature. As the individual matures from infancy to adulthood, he gradually acquires the cognitive capacity to more effectively process information, to transfer experience into knowledge (Piaget, 1968).

Lawrence Kohlberg has devised a moral development model, with three levels and six stages (two stages per level), which corresponds roughly to the stages in Piaget's model. His goal of instruction is to facilitate movement of students to the next stage of their cognitive-moral development as posited by his model (Tapp & Kohlberg, 1971, p. 69).

Kohlberg (1975, p. 674) believes that "moral and civic education are much the same thing. . . . Civic or political education means the stimulation of development of more advanced patterns of reasoning about political and social decisions and their implementation in action. These patterns are patterns of moral reasoning. Our studies show that reasoning and decision-making about political decisions are directly derivative of broader patterns of moral reasoning and decision-making."

Edwin Fenton and colleagues have created lessons in moral reasoning, in terms of Kohlberg's ideas, to fit the *Comparative Political Systems* course. The Fenton group has created "moral dilemma" lessons aimed at teaching students to appraise the reasoning basic to alternative responses to moral conflicts.

A moral dilemma is a description of a difficult choice about what is right or wrong. A well-designed moral dilemma should "present a real conflict for the central character; it should include a number of moral issues for consideration; and it should generate differences of opinion among students about the appropriate responses to the situation" (Galbraith & Jones, 1975, p. 18). The developers assume that practice in appraising moral dilemmas, in terms of the various criteria associated with the different stages of Kohlberg's model, can facilitate development of higher level moral reasoning skills.

NEW PARTICIPATION SKILL THEMES

Attention to the participation skill dimension of political education is a reaction to the heavy academic emphasis of the curriculum reform movement of the 1960s. While endorsing improvements in political knowledge and intellectual skill learning themes wrought by the curriculum reform movement, some educators believed these reforms had not gone far enough. Thus, they proposed the extension of these reforms to include the learning of participation skills through experiences outside the classroom.

Advocates of participation skill learning assume that the good citizen is competent to act in the political arena. To Fred Newmann (1975, pp. 41–75), the overall goal of political education should be to increase ability to exercise influence in public affairs. Newmann says that educational goals calling for political action are meaningless without related objectives for the learning of competencies necessary to effective participation. In order to exert influence in public affairs, one must acquire competencies in political knowledge, intellectual skills, and participation skills. However, the emphasis should be on learning how to use knowledge and skill to influence public policy. Learning to define, describe, explain, and evaluate—to know and think about political reality—should not be ends in themselves. Rather, students should be taught to seek applications of their knowledge and skills in the political arena.

Newmann argues that only the politically competent person has the potential to make meaningful decisions about when and how to participate. Thus, political education should be a means to more widely distribute competencies so that vastly more people can have the opportunity to exert influence in public affairs if they choose to do so.

Newmann proposes extensive reform of social studies curricula to focus on teaching knowledge and skills for community action (1975, pp. 76–108). Instruction would interlace knowledge and skill learning in the classroom with practical applications in the community outside the classroom. These community applications might involve exploratory research about social processes that can be applied to the exercise of influence in public affairs. They also might involve volunteer service activities such as performing duties in a day care center or in a home for the elderly. However, the major focus of learning through participation in the community would be on social action projects, which involve participants in trying to change the policies and practices of private or public institutions in their community.

Through experience in the community, students would demonstrate their abilities to use knowledge and skills to cope with ongoing community problems. These practical experiences also would extend their knowledge and skills far beyond what could be learned in the classroom.

Newmann's proposals were generated partially from experience in designing and field testing a learning through community action course, *The Community Issues Program*. This program was piloted in 1969–1971 in high schools in Madison, Wisconsin (1975, pp. 109–110).

The *Comparing Political Experiences Project* (CPE) at Indiana University also emphasizes the values of learning political participation skills through integration of academic learning in the classroom and practical applications of knowledge and skills outside the classroom. In common with Newmann, the CPE developers aim to facilitate the attainment of political competencies needed to participate effectively in political life. Development of these competencies is supposed to enhance both individuals and their groups. A main participation skill objective of the CPE course is that students are able to recognize, evaluate, and perform a variety of roles played in a political group (Gillespie & Patrick, 1974, p. 7).

The proposals to stress political participation skill learning through community action are too recent to have spawned extensive curriculum development to test basic hypotheses about learning and instruction and community acceptance of this approach. Thus, the significane and potential impact of this emerging theme in political education is still in doubt.

NEW POLITICAL ATTITUDE THEMES

The political education projects of the 1960s tended to stress the critical thinking, open-mindedness, freedom of speech, and thought facets of the democratic model when formulating attitudinal goals. The project developers assumed that good citizenship requires acceptance of scientific method as the means for warranting factual claims and of normative analysis as the means of warranting value claims. They tended to be opposed to any form of instruction for exact, absolutistic attitudinal and knowledge outcomes whether in support of the status quo or in behalf of the development of some kind of utopian sociopolitical order.

Recently, prominent political educators have formulated overall goals which appear to have broader applications than the democratic citizenship model does for the formulation of attitudinal objectives. These goals may encompass main aspects of the democratic citizenship model, but they are not tied to one political ideology associated with particular socioeconomic conditions.

Lawrence Kohlberg and Christian Bay have formulated overall goals of political education which seem to preclude both the rigidity of teaching for specific, unchanging attitudinal outcomes (the aim of some democratic citizenship advocates) and the extreme ethical neutrality or relativism of those who stress to extremes the open-mindedness, political tolerance facets of democratic theory. In contrast, they have argued for the development of particular sets of attitudes that seem consistent with their desire to facilitate the fullest development of human potentiality. They have ends toward which they want students to grow, but these ends are not static. Rather, they reflect the dynamic variability of human potentialities.

Kohlberg's moral development model is an attempt to describe lower and higher levels of attainable human capabilities. The highest level of the model represents both Kohlberg's hypotheses about what most people might become and what they ought to become as thinking, valuing beings. A world filled with people exhibiting "postconventional" moral reasoning skills would, in Kohlberg's view, be a much better world. Thus Kohlberg, Fenton, and others advocate instruction for moral development in order to facilitate the fullest development of human capability for behavior in ways that would bring about a more just and satisfying society. However, they do not formulate the exact qualities of the good society, which remains emergent and subject to continual modification and growth.

Christian Bay (1972, p. 89) says that the fundamental goal of both political action and political education should be promotion of *some* conception of a more just society: "that is a society committed to optimal security and freedom for all human beings, on the premise of the equal and infinite worth of every human life." He warns against teaching students to accept any fixed formulation of the good sociopolitical order. Bay argues that we should teach our students to value the application of their knowledge and thinking skills to the creation of a more just society. Thus, he believes that a basic attitudinal goal of political education should be to teach students to desire to do all they can "to make truth serve justice." However, Bay warns against the temptation to sacrifice truth for justice. This temptation is stronger for those with fixed conceptions of the good polity than it is for those with more open, exploratory, dynamic conceptions of what is needed to promote justice and human dignity.

The preceding review has highlighted various innovative ideas and practices in political education. What has been the impact of these new curricula on students' political learning and on political education in schools?

Assessments of Innovative Curricula

Most of the political education projects' instructional materials have been available to the masses of high school students only since the early 1970s. Thus, data about the political knowledge, skills, and attitudes of survey studies are not applicable to assessments of the impact of the projects' materials on political learning. The long-range impact of these instructional materials on masses of students and on educational practices in schools remains to be demonstrated. At this time, one is restricted to the projects' evaluation studies and published appraisals by external reviewers to assess their impact on students and on the political education community.

Funders and clients have expected curriculum developers to conduct field tests and expert reviews of their instructional materials. In response to these expectations, all the political education projects conducted formative evaluation studies involving critical reviews of instructional materials by consultants and field tests in various kinds of schools.

Curriculum developers in the political education projects have practiced evaluation quite variously. The quality of their studies is uneven. However, each project did gather data and report findings that enable reasonable speculations about the worth of alternative objectives and instructional procedures.

KNOWLEDGE LEARNING ASSOCIATED WITH INNOVATIVE CURRICULA

What do evaluation studies suggest about the political knowledge dimension of the project materials? In the main, the instructional materials of the political education projects were associated with significant gains in political knowledge in terms of project objectives. Students of the *Justice in Urban America* course did tend to learn knowledge of key legal and social science concepts in the course (Wick, 1972). Likewise, students of the CPS and APB courses tended to learn the major concepts of these programs. In contrast to the APB students, the control group students in the project evaluation study were relatively ignorant of certain aspects of the behavior of voters, the recruitment of political leaders, the relationships of socioeconomic status to political behavior, the conflict and compromise inherent in the political process, and the role behavior of congressmen (Patrick, 1972).

Control group students were relatively naïve about recruitment to political leadership positions, about the inequality in political occupational opportunity that afflicts certain groups in our society. It is a fact of American political life that individuals with particular social characteristics are more likely than others to attain positions of political leadership. However, most control group students were unaware of this reality. Control group students tended to be ignorant of the relationship of socioeconomic status to political behavior: e.g., they tended to believe that "all individuals in our country can have an equal opportunity to influence the decisions of government officials." Furthermore, control group students tended to be ignorant of variation in political influence associated with higher or lower prestige occupations. The control group students were much less likely than experimental group students to know about the power of committee chairmen relative to other congressmen, the specialization of a congressman's job reflected in particular committee assignments, and the pressures on congressmen to compromise, to make deals with their colleagues.

SKILL LEARNING ASSOCIATED WITH INNOVATIVE CURRICULA

What do evaluation studies suggest about the skill dimension of the political education project materials? The findings about the impact of project materials on intellectual skill learning are quite mixed. The APB course did appear to affect the development of particular skills such as ability to interpret contingency tables, to distinguish factual and value judgments, and to appraise contrasting sampling procedures and questionnaire items. However, the impact of APB on intellectual skill learning was far less than on political knowledge learning (Patrick, 1972).

The CPS course had a significant impact on development of social science inquiry skills, a particular area of emphasis in this course (Social Science Education Consortium Staff, 1972, p. 736). However, this course did not have a significant effect in developing "the generalized skills measured by standardized tests." Nonetheless, a Social Science Education Consortium (SSEC) evaluation of the CPS course concluded that "their focus on developing inquiry skills and clarifying values provides students with learning which can be generalized to their personal environment."

The *Harvard Public Issues Project* (SSEC Staff, 1972, p. 750) reported very mixed findings about student gains in intellectual skill learning. Highly intelligent students seem to show substantial gains in learning skills of normative analysis. However, in their final project report, the developers suspend judgment about "whether it is possible to teach average high school students to carry on intelligent discussions about social issues."

Other evaluation studies of instruction designed to develop skills of normative analysis have yielded more positive findings: e.g., Kohlberg and Lockwood (1972, p. 19) studied the impact of the "Harvard" materials and moral dilemmas used in terms of Kohlberg's ideas. They found that this type of instruction, when it features "Socratic" classroom discussion leadership by teachers, can raise significantly the intellectual capability of adolescents. Kohlberg and Tapp reported (1971, pp. 86–87) that instructional materials and procedures which stress conflict resolution, problem solving, decision-making exercises, and role playing are likely to have a significant impact on legal and moral conceptualization and judgment.

ATTITUDE LEARNING ASSOCIATED WITH INNOVATIVE CURRICULA

What do evaluation studies suggest about the political attitude dimension of the project materials? For the most part, the project evaluation studies report little or no impact on attitudinal learning.

Some projects did not conduct evaluation studies about the learning of political attitudes. For example, the CPS developers stated (Adelson & Crosby, 1971, p. 173) that they were "unable to develop any means of assessing the impact of the curriculum on the attitudes and values of the students. Whether or not experimental students have a more articulated, more clarified and better justified value system than control students remains a mystery. Whether they show a significantly greater preference for assertions based upon scientific inquiry than control students is unknown."

Other projects (Patrick, 1972, pp. 177–179) attempted to assess political attitude learning while hypothesizing that there would be no measurable short-run effects. This hypothesis is consistent with numerous studies about the direct impact of instruction on social and political attitudes. The APB evaluation study reported findings consistent with this view of the relationship of instruction in one course and attitudinal learning. The APB course seems to have had no impact on the democratic political orientations of students (Patrick, 1972, p. 178).

Some projects reported (SSEC Staff, 1972, p. 755) increases in positive student attitudes about particular subject matter. For instance, students of the *Justice in Urban America* course seemed to develop "positive attitudes toward law and its functions within society." Most APB students (73% of those in the final field test) reported that they would "recommend that other students take this course." They also tended to report that, compared to other social studies courses they had experienced, APB was "more interesting" (Engle et al., 1972, pp. 77–78). A small-scale assessment by the Social Science Education Consortium (Turner & Haley, 1975) suggests that users tend to be satisfied with the project courses.

USING THE HIDDEN CURRICULUM TO IMPROVE POLITICAL LEARNING

The evaluation studies of the political education projects suggest that most of these instructional materials are associated with large gains by students in specific political knowledge. These materials seem to have a much weaker, but still important, impact on intellectual skill learning. There appears to be little relationship between these instructional materials and direct, short-run changes in political attitudes. Can the context of instruction, the hidden curriculum, be used to improve student learning of political attitudes and skills?

There is limited evidence about the relationship of political learning to the hidden curriculum. However, the available data suggest that the hidden curriculum is an important condition of learning which can be modified to improve student development of skills and attitudes.

An important weakness of most innovative political education programs has been insufficient attention to the instructional context. This neglect has probably resulted in severe inconsistencies between formal learning achieved through academic experiences and informal learning associated with the hidden curriculum. These inconsistencies can lead to the blunting or subversion of formal learning and to negative unintended outcomes.

When innovative instructional materials are adopted by a school with a "closed" educational climate, there is a very awkward fit between the manifest and hidden curricula of the school. The most keenly designed instructional materials may be blunted and distorted if used within an inappropriate context. A study (Biber & Minuchin, 1970, pp. 27–52) of the relationships of instructional innovations and educational climates concluded that "the effectiveness of innovations is, in the last analysis, dependent upon the total climate of the school. The use of new techniques will be conditioned by the dominant ideas and values of the institution as well as the motivation and competence of the teacher. A fertile method for stimulating problem-thinking and question-asking, for example, can wither on the vine in an atmosphere where the teachers rely on predefined structured organization and predictable sequences."

A rather "open" educational climate is necessary to proper implementation of instructional materials featuring active learning and higher level cognition. In an open educational climate, teachers and students feel free to ask controversial questions and to arrive at unorthodox answers, if they can validate these answers. To promote creative and productive intellectual moves, teachers help students to feel that they can explore and take chances and that the consequences for faulty decisions will not be unduly severe. If students make poor judgments, they are able to find out as soon as possible why they erred and what they must do to overcome their deficiencies. They are not so threatened by the possibility of making mistakes that they will not risk innovative responses which might extend their learning in unanticipated ways (Guskin & Guskin, 1970, p. 47).

An open educational climate does not preclude the teacher's leadership or authority in the classroom. Teachers need not concentrate so much on respecting students' rights and meeting students' emotional needs that they abdicate their responsibilities as authoritative leaders. Rather, within a supportive open educational climate, teachers should lead them to acquire the wherewithal to meet their challenges (Smith, 1968, pp. 309–310).

Studies of the sociology of learning support the value of a relatively open educational climate: e.g., Boocock's review of research (1972, p. 151) indicates that "a teaching style combining low authoritarianism with moderate to high task orientation and expressiveness seems to maximize the total range of positive effects (from learning gains to student morale to classroom orderliness)." Other reviews of research in educational sociology conclude that teachers who dominate the classroom in a dictatorial, or authoritarian, manner stifle the learning of higher level intellectual skills while encouraging highly specific, concrete responses (Harvey et al., 1970, pp. 122–133). Furthermore, excessively dominating, authoritarian role performance is likely to lessen the possibility that students will develop cooperative, creative, and self-directive behavior. In contrast, teachers who are respectful of student rights and feelings, who establish relationships of mutual trust that encourage speculation and innovation, and who are attentive to the emotional needs of students are more likely to contribute substantially to the development of desirable intellectual and social learning such as skills in divergent thinking and human relations (Banks, 1972, pp. 181–182).

Lawrence Kohlberg (1970, p. 122) argues that there is a strong relationship between the hidden curriculum and instruction for the development of moral reasoning skills. A "closed educational climate" would preclude the careful examination of moral dilemmas and consideration of various resolutions to basic moral issues. However, Kohlberg warns against the excesses of permissiveness in reacting against modal authority patterns in American schools. He advocates a middle ground between authoritarianism and permissiveness which is symbolized by the *disciplined*, independent thinking and learning associated with high-level cognitive and moral reasoning.

Kohlberg's argument is buttressed by a recent study about educational climates and moral judgment. The researchers (Biber & Minuchin, 1970, p. 43) found that a more "open educational climate" (of the type advocated by Kohlberg) is associated with development of students' moral reasoning "toward a higher, more advanced stage of moral judgment." A more traditional, closed climate is associated with lower-level moral judgment. Students in these schools tended to refer inflexibly to the rules and regulations of school authorities when making moral judgments.

Several studies suggest that the climate of the classroom can be manipulated to influence the development of political attitudes: e.g., a crossnational study involving adult respondents from five nations indicated a positive relationship between classroom climate and the development of a sense of political competence. Respondents from three of the nations in the study—the United States, Great Britain, and Mexico—who remembered participation in open classroom discussions about politics had a higher sense of political competence. A lower sense of political competence was expressed by adults who remembered no such classroom opportunities (Almond & Verba, 1963, pp. 352–360).

A study of high school youth in the Detroit metropolitan area (Ehman, 1969, pp. 559–580) indicated a positive relationship between classroom climate, instruction about issues, and the development of particular political attitudes. Social studies instruction dealing with controversial topics in a closed classroom climate tended to contribute to high political cynicism and low sense of citizen duty, sense of political efficacy, and desire to participate in politics. Instruction in an open classroom climate—where students felt free to raise questions, to critically appraise the ideas of the teacher and of one another, and to study and discuss controversial topics—was related to the development of certain good-citizenship qualities, such as high sense of political efficacy, low political cynicism, and high sense of citizen duty.

Glidewell and associates (1966, p. 232) report that when teachers share decision-making power in classrooms with students the effect has been to: (1) stimulate more pupil-to-pupil interactions; (2) reduce interpersonal conflicts and anxieties; (3) increase mutual esteem, rapport, and self-esteem; (4) induce a wider dispersion and flexibility of peer social power as manifested by a greater tolerance for divergent opinions in the initial phases of decision making and a greater convergence of opinion in the later phases of decision making; and (5) increase moral responsibility, self-inflicted work, independence of opinion, and responsibility in implementing accepted assignments.

Questions for Researchers and Curriculum Developers About Political Education and Socialization in Schools

The preceding discussion of political education and socialization in schools raises important questions related to the main concerns of researchers and curriculum developers. Researchers in political education and socialization in schools are concerned about who learns what knowledge, skills, and attitudes, how they learn them, when, and with what consequences. Their ultimate goal is to know more and more about the impact of schooling on students' political learning. Curriculum developers in political education are concerned about what should be their objectives of instruction and how to design instruction in schools to maximize students' achievement of these objectives. Their ultimate goal is to *develop* more efficient instructional materials and procedures for the greatest number of students.

The main concerns of researchers and curriculum developers interlace. Research-based knowledge about political learning in schools can guide curriculum developers in formulating and implementing proposals about how to improve instruction. The development of innovative curricula can offer opportunities to researchers to explore facets of political education and socialization which usually are not within their purview. The activities of both researchers and curriculum developers can be facilitated by increasing awareness among both groups of the other's perspectives and practices. A great need in the development of curricula in political education is more and better evidence about political learning of various groups of students and about the impact of various curricula on learning. Researchers in political education and socialization might fill this need more adequately if they become more aware of what curriculum developers are doing. Curriculum developers might tap the findings of researchers more adequately if they become more aware of their studies and findings.

Researchers and curriculum developers have a common stake in exploring answers to the following kinds of questions suggested by preceding parts of this chapter: (1) questions associated with the four-dimensional perspective on political education presented on pages 193–196; (2) questions associated with the quality of various curricula; (3) questions associated with the hidden curriculum as a major facet of political learning in schools.

QUESTIONS ASSOCIATED WITH THE FOUR DIMENSIONS OF POLITICAL EDUCATION

The four dimensions of political education—knowledge, intellectual skills, participation skills, and attitudes—are used by curriculum developers to guide analyses of instructional objectives and techniques. These dimensions can serve political socialization researchers by broadening the scope of their inquiries. Most political socialization researchers use some kind of survey design to study political attitudes. Studies of political knowledge tend to be superficial and the skills dimensions are not included: e.g., the Langton-Jennings study of the impact of the civics curriculum on political learning (1968, pp. 852–867) focused on political attitude learning. Inquiry about the knowledge dimension consisted of a six-item test (Langton-Jennings, 1970, p. 92). "Respondents were asked to identify (1) the number of years a U.S. Senator serves, (2) the country Marshal Tito leads, (3) the number of members in the U.S. Supreme Court, (4) the name of the governor of their state, (5) the nation that during World War II had a great number of concentration camps for Jews, and (6) whether President Franklin Roosevelt was a Republican or a Democrat." This is hardly a substantial indicator of students' political knowledge. This study did not include inquiry about students' learning of intellectual and participation skills.

Our knowledge of the political learning of American youth would be enhanced greatly by substantial survey studies of participation skills, knowledge, and intellectual skills. *What participation skills do various groups of American youth tend to manifest? What intellectual skills associated with reflective thinking about politics are demonstrated by different groups of American youth? What political knowledge (broadly conceived) do various groups of American youngsters tend to have?*

The Education Commission of the States (1970, 1973), through the National Assessment of Educational Progress surveys, has made a small start toward substantial inquiry about students' performances in terms of the four dimensions of political education. These studies need to be expanded and the skills dimensions of these studies need to be made more substantial. More researchers need to conduct survey studies in terms of all four dimensions of political education in order to construct a fuller picture of the political learning of American youth. Substantial data about student learning in terms of all four dimensions of political education could provide curriculum developers with solid grounds for making judgments about the learning needs of different groups of students.

QUESTIONS ASSOCIATED WITH THE QUALITY OF VARIOUS CURRICULA

During the past 15 years, there has been extensive development of new political education curricula. However, there have been few research and evaluation studies of these curricula. Political socialization researchers could enrich knowledge in their field and contribute substantially to the improvement of political education in schools by conducting inquiries about the impact of various curricula (reviewed on pages 213–219) on student learning.

How do different curricula affect students' learning of political knowledge, skills, and attitudes? Are some curricula more suited to particular social groups than to other groups? What can curriculum developers do to accelerate and enhance the acquisition of political knowledge, skills, or attitudes among different groups of students?

Data relevant to these kinds of questions would represent an ample contribution to knowledge about how students learn political knowledge, skills, and attitudes. At present this kind of evidence is very thin. Curriculum developers could use this evidence to build an empirical base from which to propose and implement reforms in curriculum and instruction. Too often intuition and reliance on authority have dominated curriculum development efforts, since there have been few systematic research and evaluation studies upon which one could rely. Solid findings about the varying quality of different curricula could help political educators to make their curriculum reform proposals more congruent with reality and more likely to succeed in attaining desired outcomes.

QUESTIONS ASSOCIATED WITH THE HIDDEN CURRICULUM

Political educators have become very aware of the hidden curriculum as an important factor of learning (see pages 204–206). Curriculum developers, however, have paid scant attention to how to use the hidden curriculum to facilitate learning. Very little knowledge has been found about how the context of instruction affects teaching and learning. Thus, political education and socialization researchers could make significant contributions to both knowledge and practice by conducting studies of the relationship between various facets of the hidden curriculum and students' political learning.

How do various facets of the hidden curriculum affect students' learning of political knowledge, skills, and attitudes? How can the climate of instruction in the classroom be manipulated to facilitate political learning? How can the organizational structure of schools be modified to facilitate political learning?

Current findings pertinent to these questions are few and the data base is shallow: e.g., manipulating teaching style and the sociopolitical climate in which instruction occurs seems to be a promising means for facilitating the development of political learning. Giving students the opportunity to openly discuss controversial topics and to inquire freely about conflict and conflict resolution could lead to the development of higher level intellectual and participatory skills and particular democratic political attitudes (see pages 206–213). However, these findings are based on very few studies of uneven quality. Replications and extensions of these studies are needed in order to provide curriculum developers with sufficient evidence to propose and implement new and powerful means to use the hidden curriculum as an important factor of political learning in schools.

Researchers in political education and socialization should become more informed about what curriculum developers do to improve political learning in schools. This awareness might prompt them to conduct studies which extend beyond the scope of their usual concerns. These studies could yield data which would contribute to a more complete picture of the political education and socialization of youth. Curriculum developers in political education also need to become more informed about what researchers have done and might do so that they can take advantage of their studies when trying to improve instruction and learning in schools. Hopefully, increased awareness of one another's work among researchers and curriculum developers might contribute significantly to knowledge and improved practices in political education and socialization in schools.

8

Mass Communication in Political Socialization

Steven H. Chaffee, with Marilyn Jackson-Beeck, Jean Durall, and Donna Wilson

STUDENTS OF THE SOCIAL PSYCHOLOGY OF POLITICAL BEHAVIOR often confess confusion over the role that is to be attributed to the mass media of communication. While all agree that the process of socialization to politics is very different in the absence of mass media, there is little agreement regarding that process where media influences are involved. It is clear that exposure to, and some absorption of, information and opinion of a political nature enters a developing child's life via the media well before there is much opportunity for overt political behavior. This is particularly likely to be the case where television news is available and, indeed, almost forcibly intruding into the youngster's daily life with information that is neither sought nor of much immediate usefulness. As Connell (1971) puts it, children of the TV era "develop an extensive acquaintance with the phenomenal surface of politics" although few even in adolescence "have any accurate grasp of the real balance of political and social forces." This vicarious experiencing of forms of behavior that overtly resemble political activity is difficult to disentangle conceptually or empirically from learned political behavior itself.

Support for preparation of this chapter came partly from the Wisconsin Alumni Research Foundation through the Research Committee of the Graduate School of the University of Wisconsin, Madison, and from the Vilas Trust Estate, through unrestricted grants to the first author. Among those offering helpful comments on an earlier version were Professors M. Kent Jennings and F. Gerald Kline of the University of Michigan, and Sidney Kraus of Cleveland State University. The authors also thank Professor Jennings for making available data from the CPS panel study prior to its archiving for general use in secondary analyses, and Professor Kraus for providing a prepublication draft of his literature review.

Six Alternative Models

One common resolution of this theoretical difficulty has been to treat measures of attention to media public affairs content as one of many dependent variables in political socialization research, alongside such other indicators of politicization as the development of party identification, images of authority figures, perceived efficacy, social responsibility, and so forth. This has been the approach of a number of investigators who have incorporated one or a few "media use" items into their survey questionnaires because media inputs are so obviously related to socialization process *somehow* (e.g., Greenstein, 1965; Easton & Dennis, 1969).

A different assumption, more common among specialists in communication research than in political science, has been that the media stand in a causal relationship to other indicators of socialization, and accordingly to treat media exposure as an independent variable in research. This "media effects" model coincides with popular thinking, in which rather strong and direct influences are attributed to the mass media (e.g., Schiller, 1970). The entire field of media content study, and the analysis of propaganda devices, presupposes major effects of politically tendentious material that reaches a large audience via media channels. Empirical demonstration of media influence at the social-psychological level, however, has been more difficult to achieve (Hovland, 1954; Weiss, 1969). There is evidence of media effects on the child's political knowledge (Chaffee, Ward, & Tipton, 1970; Conway, Stevens, & Smith, 1975), though, and at least one major review considers direct effects the most viable model (Kraus & Davis, 1976).

A contrasting third image, and the one that is most entrenched in the synthesizing literature on mass communication, is the "limited effects" model popularized originally by Klapper (1960). In this rendering, the person is committed to a particular line of political behavior, and this precedes and controls communication inputs from the mass media; consequently, one sees and hears only that portion of available media offerings that is congenial to attitudinal "predispositions" that have already been built up. At one level, this is undeniable; it is clear that early learning structures the child's acquisition of later information and the evaluative meanings he will attach to it. But to extend this principle infinitely as a means of explaining away the mass media will not do either. The very concept of socialization assumes that there must be, for each domain of cognitive or behavioral acquisition, some zero point at which the person has no preparation for the information the media are conveying to him. Partisan identification, e.g., accounts for a great deal of variance in the way adult citizens respond to media reports of controversial events; it is less powerful as a buffer among younger adults (Chaffee & Becker, 1975), and presumably becomes progressively less so with yet younger persons—who are less likely to hold strong partisan affiliations. The acceptance of the limited effects model as a comprehensive principle for dismissing the mass media as a causal factor in political socialization (e.g., Dawson & Prewitt, 1969) is as gross an over-simplification as an unbounded enthusiasm for the massive direct-effects image would be. The very young child probably has only a few limited principles by which to organize the information conveyed via the media; much of it will be lost because of this, and much of the rest will have rather strong influences. With maturation, the degree of prior structure increases and the extent of potential media influence correspondingly decreases. The limited effects model, which is based on research with highly partisan adults, should not be generalized uncritically to situations where socialization is the central question.

There are at least three other general models of the relationship between mass communication and political socialization that deserve our consideration here; all involve those two concepts plus a third variable which we can refer to for convenience as X. One three-variable model is that of indirect influence, in which variable X intervenes between media exposure and political behavior. This variable X becomes the explanation for different persons responding to the same media stimuli in different ways. Two general classes of concepts are frequently nominated for the role of variable X: intervening attitudes (cf. "predispositions" above) and intervening interpersonal communication. The latter is the keystone of the "two-step flow" model of media effects (Katz & Lazarsfeld, 1955). This concept is often integrated into a broad limited effects interpretation by assuming that one's interpersonal discussion partners are selected to support already developed political predispositions, to an even greater extent than is one's media fare. (Again, any such predispositional account seems logically unrelated to questions of socialization to politics, but the prevalence of the limited-effects model in academic writings on the media is too great to ignore; it will have to be treated as an empirical question.)

A fifth organizing image is that of contingent causation. Factor X is treated as a condition or orientation that may be present or absent; when it is present, media content leads directly to the acquisition of political information, affect, or behaviors, but when it is not present there will be no such effect. A few examples should suffice to give the flavor of some of the contingent conditions that have been suggested in various programs of research. McCombs and Weaver (1973) have shown that there is a high correlation between media content and a citizen's perception of the important problems of the day, but only among those persons who indicate a high "need for orientation" in their media use; they replicated this finding in a period dominated by news of the Watergate scandals (Weaver, McCombs, & Spellman, 1975). Rothschild and Ray (1973) demonstrated that repetitive political advertisements had little or no impact on voters in major elections, but did make some difference in voting for lesser offices. McLeod, Becker, and Byrnes (1974) found that voters who were exposed heavily to a number of media sources expressed views on important issues that most resembled those of the one medium on which they said they depended most heavily for their news. Contingent orientations either to politics or to media, then, appear to control "media influence" at least under some conditions.

A sixth and final possibility is that any statistical association between mass media use and political behavior might be a spurious artifact of a common antecedent: i.e., variable X might be an integrated pattern of, say, parental behavior or community constraints, which would lead the child to acquire media use habits and political interests that have overlapping characteristics—even though there is no direct causal linkage between the two latter sets of behaviors. To take a farfetched example, a worldwide sample survey would doubtless produce a correlation between watching television and preference for democratic political institutions; but this could be explained simply as the result of the historical fact that television has yet to be introduced into many nations and that these tend not to follow democratic principles of political organization.

Relevant Research

Unfortunately, almost all of the research on which the foregoing alternative inferences about mass communication and political behavior are based has dealt with adult citizens rather than with youngsters who are in the process of socialization. Of course, one might reasonably take the view that political socialization is a lifelong process, so that studies of any period in the life cycle would be relevant to the question. Again unfortunately, neither aging nor even the passage of time has been an important design feature in research linking mass media to political behavior. We will begin here by examining such evidence as exists on political socialization as it is ordinarily defined—i.e., on the role of the media in the development of political cognitions, affect, and behavior in children and young adults.

Because only a small published literature exists on the topic, we have for purposes of this chapter performed a number of secondary analyses on two existing bodies of panel data. One is a sample of some 1,200 secondary school students in five Wisconsin cities, who completed separate questionnaires in May and November of 1968; this will be called the "Five Cities panel" here.[1] The second is a national sample of 1,348 young people who were interviewed when they were high school seniors in 1965 and again in 1973, as part of a study at the Center for Political Studies (CPS) at the University of Michigan, headed by M.

[1]The full sampling procedure is described in Chaffee et al. (1970). Five cities were selected on the basis of socioeconomic and political diversity, in the Milwaukee suburban and Fox River Valley regions of Wisconsin. In April 1968, some 8,000 7th- and 10th-grade students completed questionnaires in school. Samples were drawn to provide approximately equal numbers for each sex, grade level, and community; in the fall, one parent of each of the sampled students was interviewed during the election campaign, and the students (now in 8th and 11th grades) completed a second questionnaire in November following the national election.

Kent Jennings; this sample will be referred to as the "CPS panel."[2] Some contrasts between these two data sources are worth noting. One is of adolescents (7th through 11th graders) measured at points six months apart in a presidential election year in the heart of the Vietnam war era; the other is of young adults measured at points eight years apart in nonelection years outside the period of major controversy over the war. This means that there will be many questions on which the two panels cannot be compared; but to the extent that they yield similar inferences, we can assume that those conclusions are relatively robust in the face of episodic and historical changes in the political milieu.

A recent survey of the literature by Kraus and Davis (1976) turned up only a handful of empirical studies relating mass media use to political socialization. One of these (Chaffee et al., 1970) is based on the Five Cities panel data that we will be examining below. The conclusions of these studies can be summarized as follows:

1. *The mass media constitute the principal source of political information for young people.* This finding has been rather consistent where it has been empirically tested, and meanwhile has frequently been assumed by other writers. It is most clearly demonstrated in the data of Chaffee et al. (1970), who partialed out other possible contaminating variables in a time-lagged panel analysis of the Five Cities sample. Supportive correlational evidence can also be found in Johnson (1973), Hollander (1971), Dominick (1972), and Conway et al. (1975); the latter study included a particularly rich variety of knowledge measures. One investigator has dubbed the media "the new 'parent' " in recognition of the dominance of media over primary group sources of political learning (Hollander, 1971). Children who pay close attention to news via the media are also more likely to discuss public affairs in the home (Roberts, Pingree, & Hawkins, 1975).

2. *The dominant mass media in political learning are newspapers and television; the relative contributions of these two media vary with the age and socioeconomic status of the sample.* In grade school, television is the principal source (Dominick, 1972; Conway et al., 1975), if only because few children have adopted newspaper use to any significant extent. In adolescence, newspapers become important too, and television use dwindles—although attention to TV news and public affairs programming increases. Television is the dominant medium of the poor, both urban (Dervin & Greenberg, 1971) and rural (Johnson, 1973). In preadolescence, *any* use of either medium provides some exposure to politically relevant information; later, however, there is a clear differentiation between those who pay specific attention to public affairs content and those who rely on the media primarily for entertainment, with the latter group slipping behind in comparative level of political knowledge (Chaffee et al., 1970). In the

[2]The CPS panel design is most completely described in Jennings and Niemi (1974). It began with a representative national sample of high school seniors in 1965; 1,119 of the original sample of 1,669 youths were reinterviewed in 1973, and another 230 responded to mailed questionnaires. Only those for whom data at both points in time are available are included in the analyses in this chapter.

Five Cities sample, which was designed to include a wide variety of socioeconomic levels and both liberal and conservative communities, the relative contribution of newspapers was only slightly higher than that of television among both junior and senior high students. Conway et al. (1975) found with a sample of fourth, fifth, and sixth graders that television news viewing was a stronger correlate of the degree of partisan identification, and of most indicators of knowledge, than was newspaper reading.

3. *Young people attribute to the mass media considerable influence on their political opinions, in addition to informative power.* Kraus and Lee (1976) listed 15 political topics and 18 possible sources of attitudinal influence on them, in a survey of New Hampshire high school seniors. The students ranked the media as the most important influence for 10 topics, second for 4 topics, and third on the remaining topic. Similarly, in the Five Cities study, Chaffee et al. (1970) listed two topics and four sources; the media were rated as the most important source of opinion influence in comparison with parents, friends, and teachers, by a wide margin—although the difference was not as great as in the ratings of informative power of these same sources. Conway et al. (1975) could find little evidence of unidirectional partisan influences of the media. Among children who watched TV news with some regularity, 31% said they identified with the Republican party and 30% with the Democrats; the corresponding figures for newspaper readers were 28% and 30%, respectively. The main impact of both media seems to lie in the sizable reduction of "don't know" responses to political attitude questions. The issue of media influence on overt political activity by young people, such as campaigning for a candidate, remains unresolved. Chaffee et al. (1970) tested specifically for time-lagged influences of media exposure on campaigning and concluded that the modest synchronous correlation that exists is spurious, evidently an artifact of some more general common antecedent rather than indicating any causal connection. Using part of the same data base but applying a path-analytic test instead of the time-lagged test, however, Jackson-Beeck and Chaffee (1975) found evidence that would permit limited acceptance of a media-activity effects hypothesis. A portion of this evidence is described later in this chapter (see Figure 8–4).

4. *Intergenerational differences in public affairs media use persist into adulthood; the child does not adopt the political-media norms of the parent.* Although there are some (generally low) correlations between children and their parents in both media use (Chaffee, McLeod, & Atkin, 1971) and political attributes (Jennings & Niemi, 1974), the dominant inference in both areas has been that parental influence is quite limited. On the basis of the 1965 wave of the CPS panel study, Jennings and Niemi (1968) originally inferred that "usage of the mass media for political news rises substantially after high school" because the parents were considerably above their children in this respect. The 1973 wave proved this conclusion incorrect, however, at least insofar as newspaper usage was concerned. The children (now grown into adulthood) had increased their television news usage; but the newspaper "generation gap" remained strong

enough to suggest that it is one "socialization effect" of contemporary times that will continue to manifest itself in the political community as successive cohorts of citizens reach adulthood in coming years (Jennings & Niemi, 1975).

The foregoing is obviously less than an imposing research literature. The studies are few and mostly limited in scope. The inferences they yield, while interesting and contrary at least to some popular misconceptions, are scarcely of the "gee whiz" variety. Kraus and Davis (1976) attribute the lack of a more extensive history of empirical research to disciplinary myopia. They point out, e.g., that the questionnaire for the first major national study of political socialization, designed by a team of leading political scientists and developmental psychologists (Hess & Torney, 1967; Easton & Dennis, 1969), included only one item on the mass media: "I have read about a candidate in newspapers or magazines." This questionnaire was administered in 1961–1962, when children were spending at least as much time watching *television* as going to school, according to mass communication surveys.

A similar complaint could be lodged against the latter body of studies; the overwhelming emphasis has been on cataloguing the types of programs children spend the most time watching or say they enjoy the most (e.g., Schramm, Lyle, & Parker, 1961), or on investigating the effects of specific entertainment program elements on such behavioral outcomes as aggression and to a lesser extent helping, altruism, or prosocial acts. The political effects of entertainment programming have been almost entirely neglected to date (Kraus & Davis, 1976), although Chaffee et al. (1970) show some evidence that junior high school students gain political information from TV entertainment exposure. Media researchers have long concerned themselves with political content and voting behavior, but have curiously worked around the edges of political socialization questions, focusing instead on adults and on episodic news events and election campaigns. One writer who is equally at home in the separate fields of political socialization and mass communication is Hyman (1959, 1963, 1973–1974). He has addressed the relationship between these two domains, but only from a humanistic and intercultural perspective with an eye toward possible future research.

Whatever the reasons for the relative empirical neglect of the topic previously, it seems to be a research area whose time has arrived. It is, in fact, ranked third in priority for future research by a panel of specialists in the study of children and television (Comstock & Lindsey, 1975). Studies of other influences on political socialization have not been as fruitful as had been expected, and they point to a need for fresh approaches (Jennings & Niemi, 1974). Studies of political communication patterns of adults have fit better with the limited effects model than media effects scholars would prefer. And at least a few groundbreaking studies have demonstrated that there is potentially a lot to be discovered. The remainder of this chapter will explore some possible directions for future research, primarily in the light of secondary analyses of data from some of the studies we have cited above.

Problematics of the Research

Before proceeding to analyses and discussion in which communication and political behavior are treated as unambiguous, palpable entities, we should pause to note that of course they are not. Billions of concrete bits of human behavior occur each day. To make sense of it, to provide some conceptual ordering of our observations of the things people do, we must necessarily abstract a few attributes of complex social activities and locate them in relation to one another in some sort of theoretical scheme. Our task is not eased by the fact that both of our central concepts here, communication and political behavior, share certain attributes that render them somewhat inaccessible to empirical study.

1. RELATIONAL NATURE

Neither communication nor political behavior can be observed in the actions of a single individual; instead, both are relational in nature, i.e., they are concepts that refer to relationships between persons. Communication is a transaction of shared meanings between persons, and political behavior involves the structuring of power relationships among persons. This forces the investigator, who normally interviews or otherwise observes only one person at a time, either to attempt to impose some common context on the individuals under study, or to make unchecked *ceteris paribus* assumptions about the immediate social environment of the behavior observed.

2. SYSTEM CONTEXT

Neither communication nor political behavior can be understood as isolated events, even of a social-relational nature. Rather, they make sense only in the context of institutionalized social systems, such as the person's language, culture, and community. This imposes a degree of specificity and relativism in theorizing that is at odds with the social scientist's drives toward generality and parsimony. Statements about, say, "party identification" or "media credibility" derived from studies in the United States would not be replicable in a system such as the Soviet Union where both political acts and the mass media function under distinctly different constraints.

3. MOTIVATIONAL AMBIGUITY

Even to the extent that political and communicatory acts can be defined and identified in the everyday world of human behavior, it will be the rare instance where an investigator who thinks in social-psychological terms can be certain that these behaviors are in some way brought about by specific variable factors that operate *within* the individual. A person may read a newspaper to learn the day's news—or simply because that is what he does every morning as part of his breakfast routine. A citizen may vote for a Republican candidate for county clerk because she approves of that party's positions—or simply because she is voting (as is her duty), and she checks the first name she finds listed on the ballot. When the same overt behavior can be ascribed to many potential causes, there is an inescapable ambiguity that precludes the drawing of certain and universal conclusions of the order of those in physics, or even in laboratory psychology.

Placed in the setting of studying "socialization," these problematics become even more vexing. We would prefer that the question could be boiled down to one of tracing through the person's life cycle various parameters of communication and their relationships to major varieties of political behavior. Unfortunately for scientific certitude, none of the external real world factors that give meaning to either political or communicatory acts can be relied upon to "hold still" over any extended period of time. Political and media systems are constantly undergoing historical change; these evolutions are only partially related to one another, and to other elements of the sociocultural context in which they occur. To some extent they are functionally autonomous, as in the case of media systems when new technologies are introduced into a society; the ubiquity of television in the United States, e.g., leads to behaviors and theoretical questions that simply did not exist prior to the advent of that medium, and still do not where TV has not yet been made available to people.

It is not enough to have noted these difficulties inherent in the kind of studies we are considering here. They are limitations not only on the research, but on the inferences that are drawn therefrom; i.e., we cannot assume that a conclusion from one study will be generalizable to other situations. On the other hand, it would be unreasonable to assume that no inference has any theoretical generality beyond the circumstances of a specific study. It will be incumbent on us, then, to consider those inferences that are supported by some research, and those hypotheses that appear worthy of empirical test, in terms of their potential applicability to new conditions and sociopolitical settings.

Exploring the Media-Socialization Relationship

The first empirical question most investigators would ask once they begin considering the possible role of media factors in political socialization is the extent to which there are simple correlations between a young person's level of media use and various behavioral indicators of politicization. Table 8–1, which is based on the CPS national panel data, displays the separate and joint contributions of indices of print and electronic media use measures, to a variety of indicators of socialization. It should be noted again that the 1965 wave of this study consisted of high school seniors; in the 1973 wave, then, these same

Table 8.1. Standardized Political Behavior Measures, by Media Public Affairs Use, High School to Young Adult

		LOW USE OF PRINT MEDIA		HIGH USE OF PRINT MEDIA	
		Low Electronic Media Use	High Electronic Media Use	Low Electronic Media Use	High Electronic Media Use
Political knowledge	1965	−.26	−.27	+.26	+.17
	1973	−.09	−.09	+.18	.00
Political activity	1965	−.19	−.07	+.07	+.21
	1973	−.40	−.20	+.21	+.36
Discussion of political affairs	1965	−.40	−.17	+.15	+.45
	1973	−.31	−.13	+.20	+.36
Attention paid to public affairs	1965	−.51	−.17	+.24	+.48
	1973	−.49	−.06	+.15	+.21
Strength of party ID	1965	.00	+.10	−.05	−.03
	1973	−.01	−.10	+.01	+.07
Trust in political system	1965	−.05	−.02	+.03	+.04
	1973	+.05	+.11	−.08	−.03
Perceived political efficacy	1965	−.17	−.27	+.23	+.10
	1973	−.17	−.06	+.09	+.13
N	1965	(403)	(216)	(442)	(287)
	1973	(376)	(265)	(340)	(367)

Note. Cell entries are standard scores, calculated as deviations of each cell mean from the overall mean for each row, and setting the row standard deviation at unity. The measures correspond by year, in that the 1965 media use measures predict 1965 political behavior measures, and the 1973 media use measures predict 1973 political behavior. Data are from the CPS panel; 1965 represents the senior year in high school. Standard scores can be compared from one row to another of this table, since the peculiar measurement properties of each measure (mean and standard deviation) have been statistically controlled via the standardizing procedure.

respondents had entered young adulthood, and were emerging from an era in which the mass media had brought many potentially politicizing events into their lives—an era of war, racism, and campus strife in which young adults often took the lead in political activism. The cell entries in Table 8–1 are standard scores, which permit us to make direct comparisons among the many political behavior measures; this is a statistical device that we will use frequently, because we are primarily interested in examining the general "shape" of the data rather than in testing particular hypotheses.[3] Comparisons from one line to another in Table 8–1 are statistically appropriate to make, and will give the reader an idea of the relative strength of relationships between media use and the various dependent variables.

The four columns of Table 8–1 represent, respectively, those who reported low use of both types of media; high electronic users; high print users; and those who ranked high on both measures. (Each media use scale was cut at the median for this analysis.) The dependent variables are mostly self-explanatory to those familiar with political behavior research.[4]

Political knowledge is clearly associated with heavy use of print media, but not with electronic media; indeed, among those who are high print users, the addition of high electronic media consumption is associated with *lower* knowledge scores. These patterns hold for both waves of the panel survey, but it is clear that the knowledge-print association is weaker in the 1973 wave, when the respondents were in their mid-twenties, than it was in 1965 when they were still in high school. We will examine this relationship in more detail later (see Figure 8–2).

The next three indicators of politicization can be considered as a group; they are conceptually similar, representing motivated behaviors, and they exhibit similar relationships with media use in Table 8–1. All three—political activity, discussion of politics, and attention paid to public affairs—are positively correlated with use of print and (to a lesser extent) electronic media in both waves of the survey. (The association is strongest in the case of the "Attention paid" measure, but this is almost tautological given that the media are for many people the primary method of paying attention to public affairs.) The weakest of the correlations is with the 1965 "activity" measure, which referred to on-campus "school politics." In the 1973 wave, real world politicking was the referent for the activity measure, and its correlations with uses of both media are quite strong in Table 8–1.

---

[3]Conversion of raw data into standard scores deprives the reader of the mean scores and standard deviations on the original measures. In most cases this is a trivial loss, however, since the scales themselves have little intrinsic or standardized meaning, being instead relative measures of the strength of feeling expressed by the person in response to an arbitrarily labeled set of alternatives (e.g., "very much, pretty much, not very much, not at all").

[4]Measures such as "political trust" and "perceived efficacy" are derived from a long series of studies reported by the Institute for Social Research at the University of Michigan. Readers unfamiliar with the conceptualization and validation of these scales may wish to consult Jennings and Niemi (1974) and earlier works in the political behavior series such as Campbell, Converse, Miller, and Stokes (1960).

The final three indices in Table 8–1 refer to various types of affect regarding politics, rather than to actual behavior. None of them is strongly related to either type of media use; there appears to be no consistent correlation of either party identification strength, or of trust in the political system, with media exposure; perceived efficacy is mainly associated with electronic media in the early (high school) wave of the study.

The overall pattern suggested in Table 8–1, then, is that attention to the mass media is part of a complex of high political activity that includes knowledge, discussion, and some sense of efficacy, and that this general pattern tends to sustain itself through the young adult years with some minor variations. Despite occasional complaints about the media as part of "the Establishment" in the era when this survey was conducted, it does not appear that affect either toward a political party or toward the system in general was statistically tied to the young person's media orientation. This contrasts with the Conway et al. (1975) finding of a strong correlation between news media exposure and degree of partisan identification, among fourth to sixth graders. The "partisanizing" effect of the media seems to dissipate with increasing maturity, as does the "informational" effect.

Evidence to support this general inference is available from the Five Cities study of adolescents as well. Table 8–2 summarizes the strength of relationships between students' ratings of the media and of personal information sources, with several indicators of media and political behavior. The entries in Table 8–2 indicate the direction and strength of the correlation coefficients between each pair of measures, for the two grade levels in the sample. High ratings of the media as sources of information and opinion regarding current events are strongly associated with both political knowledge and campaign activity. (As a validity check on the "source" measures, we may also take some comfort in the fact that the media information/opinion rankings are strongly correlated with the behavioral measures of newspaper and TV public affairs consumption, but un-correlated with measures of entertainment consumption in those media.)

The remainder of Table 8–2 shows only a few correlations of any appreciable significance. There is a strong association between watching TV entertainment programs and relying on teachers as one's sources of information. In the junior high age cohort, those who say their parents are a major source of current events information are also quite likely to watch a lot of public affairs programming on television. Finally, and most important for our purposes, heavy reliance on interpersonal sources outside the home—teachers and friends—is strongly associated with *low* levels of political knowledge. This pattern holds for both grade levels. Campaign activity is not correlated with any of the three interpersonal sources.

Again, then, Table 8–2 like Table 8–1 supports the general conclusion that media use and high levels of knowledgeable political activism among young people are statistically correlated. Given this clear replication of the main inference from the two studies, and some indication that it is specific—i.e., such

Table 8.2. Correlations between Ratings of 4 Sources of Current Events Information and Opinions, and Selected Measures of Media Use and Political Behavior

		SOURCE OF CURRENT EVENTS INFORMATION/OPINION			
BEHAVIORAL MEASURE		Parents	Friends	Teachers	Media
Newspaper public affairs reading	JrHi	++	0	0	+++
	SrHi	0	+	0	+++
Newspaper entertainment reading	JrHi	0	0	0	0
	SrHi	0	0	0	0
Television public affairs viewing	JrHi	+++	0	0	+++
	SrHi	0	+	0	+++
Television entertainment viewing	JrHi	0	+	++	0
	SrHi	+	0	+++	0
Political knowledge	JrHi	0	--	--	+++
	SrHi	0	--	--	+++
Campaign activity	JrHi	0	0	0	+++
	SrHi	0	0	0	+++

Note. Cell entries indicate direction and level of significance of correlation between rating of source listed in column with behavioral measure listed in row. A zero (0) indicates a nonsignificant correlation. One sign (− or +) indicates a negative or positive correlation at the .05 level, two signs (−− or ++) at the .01 level, and three signs (−−− or +++) at the .001 level. Data are from the November 1968 wave of the Five Cities study, with N = 641 for the junior high group and N = 651 for the senior high students. Figures on which these indicators are based can be found in Chaffee et al. (1970), although the information in this table is derived from a slightly different analysis, in which missing data have been deleted entirely.

235

extraneous factors as media entertainment use and interpersonal communication sources are not part of this intercorrelated complex of variables—we can turn our attention to questions of causation.

Causal Relations Between Media Use and Political Behavior

Since both the Five Cities study and the CPS survey are panel studies, they lend themselves to time-lagged correlational analysis. They are different in several respects, not the least of which is the duration of the time lag between the two waves of interviews in the longitudinal design: 6 months in one case, 8 years in the other. Such differences can lend strength to any inferences that survive tests of both sets of data. Cross-lagged panel correlation is a methodology that is still developing, having been given a major boost by the introduction of a baseline measure for assessing time-lagged data by Rozelle and Campbell (1969). We present here some raw correlation coefficients from which different readers might wish to calculate different interpretive statistics. The general logic of the method is to assume that, if media use "causes" knowledge gain, the correlation between Time 1 media and Time 2 knowledge should exceed the reverse time-lagged correlation. There is considerable methodological controversy, however, regarding the appropriate "control" statistics for testing and interpreting the media-to-knowledge coefficients.[5]

Figures 8–1 and 8–2 show the full set of correlations over time between two measures—public affairs reading and political knowledge—that are common to the two studies. The Five Cities data appear in Figure 8–1, with separate entries for the two age cohorts; the CPS data are in Figure 8–2. Several statements seem in order from these results. One is that the person's relative level of political knowledge in comparison with others in his cohort is much more stable over the short run (Figure 8–1) than over an extended number of years (Figure 8–2). Second, in the short-run study of adolescents it appears that public affairs reading at Time 1 predicts political knowledge at Time 2, whereas in the long-term study of young adults the time-lagged predictive relationship between these two var-

---

[5]The controversy over the cross-lagged method is complicated by the problem of measurement unreliability. The correlation between measures of the same variable at different times is affected by two separate components, real change in the variable over time and random error of measurement. In the typical study, measurement error is not assessed separately, so it is impossible to determine the extent to which a low correlation can be attributed to real change. Derivatively, a low time-lagged correlation between two variables might be mainly reduced by measurement error, which tends to be large in social science. The baseline estimate of Rozelle and Campbell (1969) provides a method of assessing whether a time-lagged correlation exceeds the level that would be expected if there were no causal connection between the two variables over the time span of a study. But, generally speaking, where there is considerable measurement error, the application of the baseline approach to causal inference tends to be somewhat conservative in that the estimate of the strength of the causal link will be fairly low. Many methodologists prefer to handle this type of data via path analysis, which has the added advantage of incorporating more than two variables into the total causal model.

Figure 8-1. Time-lagged Correlations Between Public Affairs Reading and Political Knowledge, During the 1968 Campaign

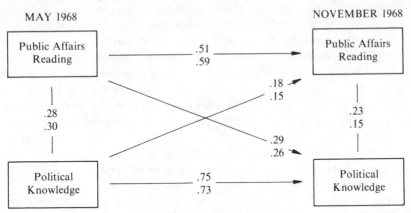

Data entries are Pearson correlations for junior high (N=615) and senior high (N=644) samples; junior high is shown above, seniors below. Data are from the Five Cities study. The public affairs reading measure is based on newspapers only. For additional data on related measures see Chaffee et al. (1970).

iables is reversed. Finally, one can also see in Figure 8–2 that the within-time correlation between these two measures decays in young adulthood, a finding we also noted in a different form in Table 8–1, and which we mentioned earlier in summarizing the research literature.

Without displaying other time-lagged analyses in full, we can summarize what they show. In the Five Cities study, the results for attention to public affairs

Figure 8-2. Time-lagged Correlations Between Public Affairs Reading and Political Knowledge, for Young Adults Over Eight-Year Period

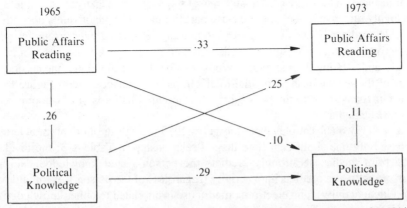

Data entries are Pearson correlations (N=1348). Data are from the CPS panel of 1965 high school seniors. The public affairs reading measure is based on newspapers and magazines.

media content is about the same as in Figure 8–1, when television viewing is substituted for reading. This is not true in the CPS panel data, however; there the time-lagged correlation between television public affairs viewing and political knowledge is zero or slightly negative. When measures of political activity are substituted for knowledge as the index of political behavior, the time-lagged correlations in both studies do not lend any support to an inference that there is a causal or predictive relationship over time: i.e., activity levels neither predict nor are predicted by media use levels (print or electronic) over either long or short periods of time. Knowledge is predicted well over time by media use (both print and electronic) in adolescence, but weakly (and only by print media) in young adulthood. In general, then, the media do approximately what they are designed to do—convey political information. Television is important earlier than is the newspaper—and its importance also declines at an earlier age. Political activity does not appear to be directly involved in these relationships.

Those inferences have been drawn on the basis of large and heterogeneous samples of young people. Verba and Nie (1972), however, have demonstrated the usefulness of considering different varieties of political behavior, instead of assuming that a single description would account for the political development of all persons. In this vein, we have in Table 8–3 broken the CPS panel into four groups, based on their 1973 scores on the knowledge and activity measures. These two measures are employed here because they represent key elements in the development of citizenship competence and participation; in nondemocratic polities, other indicators might be more relevant. The four groups in Table 8–3 can be thought of generally as four different types of citizens who have emerged in young adulthood. We can examine them separately, to assess the extent to which media inputs have influenced their development into differential patterns of political participation. Since we are assuming for the moment that the knowledge and activity measures are the criterion variables (outcomes) of differential socialization processes, we will also assume that the media use measures are the prior or independent variables in any causal sequence. The analysis of Table 8–3 is a highly unconventional one, because partitioning a sample on one's dependent variables ordinarily has the effect of attenuating seriously their correlation with predictive variables. Consequently, if the relationships were linear we would be greatly understating their strength. We have already examined the linear components of these relationships for the total sample in connection with Figure 8–2. Now our focus shifts to the possibility of differential patterns of development of political behavior.

For the two subsamples that emerge in 1973 as high in political knowledge, there is only one significant time-lagged relationship in Table 8–3: the level of 1965 print media use strongly predicts the person's later knowledge. Neither form of media use predicts high activity (regardless of the person's eventual level of political activity), and electronic media use is unrelated to either knowledge or activity outcomes. These findings contrast rather clearly with those for the two low-knowledge subsamples in Table 8–3. For them, the principal correlations are

Table 8.3. 1965 Media Use to 1973 Political Behavior Lagged Correlations, within 1973 Political Behavior Categories

1965 Media Use Variable	High Knowledge, Low Activity, 1973 (N = 327)		High Knowledge, High Activity, 1973 (N = 252)	
	Dependent Variable		*Dependent Variable*	
	KNOWLEDGE	ACTIVITY	KNOWLEDGE	ACTIVITY
Print	.18***	.01	.24***	.11
Electronic	−.02	.01	−.05	.05
	Low Knowledge, Low Activity, 1973 (N = 557)		Low Knowledge, High Activity, 1973 (N = 212)	
Print	−.11**	.24***	−.02	.23***
Electronic	.01	.10*	−.06	−.01

Note. Cell entries indicate time-lagged Pearson r between the 1973 dependent variable indicated in the column heading and the 1965 media use variable represented in the row, within each group. Asterisks indicate significance levels (* means $p < .05$, ** means $p < .01$, *** means $p < .001$). Data are from the CPS panel.

those linking 1965 print media exposure to 1973 levels of activity. There are two additional significant correlations in Table 8–3 that occur only in the most apolitical subsample, i.e., those who are below the norm for their agemates in both knowledge and activity by 1973. First, there is a slight correlation between earlier levels of electronic media use and later activity; coupled with the stronger correlation of print with activity, this invites the conclusion that the mass media serve somewhat to encourage political activity only among those who are otherwise disinclined toward politics. The other noteworthy item in Table 8–3 is the negative correlation between print exposure and political knowledge in the subsample that is low in both knowledge and activity. This is the only sample, across all the studies we have reviewed, in which a negative correlation between these two variables has been found. The reversal of the usual pattern in this subsample of politically inert young adults makes it clear that a single causal model of the role of media in political socialization will not suffice for all kinds of persons.

Political knowledge and activity levels are themselves somewhat correlated measures (as inspection of the cell Ns in Table 8–3 indicates). The four quadrants of Table 8–3 can be looked upon as emerging patterns of political culture in the total cohort of 1965 high school seniors; we might, then, infer that the direction in which the young adult grows, in terms of these indices of politicization, would be determined by his prior adolescent orientation to the print media much more than by electronic sources. There is no indication within this limited data set, of course, of the additional variables that would explain why some people are stimulated by print to reach high levels of *knowledge,* while other print-stimulated persons instead become politically *active* without necessarily knowing a great deal about politics.

Interactions with Other Variables: Education and Interpersonal Communication

To this point we have established a presumptive case for the importance of mass communication as a factor in political socialization, linked to acquisition of political knowledge and to the development of political activity patterns and certain forms of political affect. The suspicion must arise that other factors common to these two sets of variables might account for the statistical relationships between them. In this section we will examine two classes of variables that most observers assume are important in political socialization, and that are also related to patterns of media use. These are the extent to which the person attends institutions of higher learning, and the character of his interpersonal communication inputs within primary groups.

Table 8–4 shows the direct relationships between these two sets of variables and indices of use of the mass media for public affairs information. (The data are standard scores, calculated from the CPS panel data.) It is quite obvious that

Table 8.4.   Standardized Media Use Levels, by College Attendance and Political Discussion

	EDUCATION		POLITICAL DISCUSSION	
	No College (N = 492)	*Some College* (N = 856)	*Low* (N = 665)	*High* (N = 1000)
Public Affairs Use of Medium				
Magazines	−.92	+.68	−.77	+.64
Newspapers	−.43	+.33	−.72	+.59
Television	−.15	+.10	−.62	+.51
Radio	−.22	+.18	−.45	+.38

Note.   Cell entries are standard scores, calculated as deviations of each cell mean from the overall mean, and setting the overall standard deviation for each measure at unity. Data are 1973 media use measures from the CPS panel of 1965 high school seniors.

there are very strong positive correlations in all cases; the entries in Table 8–4 are all significantly different by pairs within rows. The effect of attending college is most marked on print media public affairs consumption, especially magazines; it is weakest in the case of television. The relationship between interpersonal political discussion and media public affairs use is also stronger for the print media, although the intermedia differences are not so great.

With those basic relationships documented, we can return to time-lagged analyses. Table 8–5 shows the strength of relationships between 1965 media use measures and 1973 political behavior indices, within levels of educational attainment. There the CPS sample is split into three groups—those who completed their education with high school, those who attended college for a year or two, and those who went even further in college. This partialing exercise appears on the whole to make little difference. Regardless of the level of higher education, the person's 1965 attention to electronic media makes no positive contribution to later levels of either political knowledge or activity; if anything, it depresses the knowledge level of the most educated group. On the other hand, print media use while a high school senior predicts both knowledge and activity gains positively in most cases. The effect (if the relationship is indeed causal) is stronger on activity for those who drop out of school within a year or two of high school, and stronger on knowledge for those who continue on in college beyond the first two years. Here again, then, we have evidence of differential processes of political socialization in which the role of the mass media varies for persons who are undergoing different socializing experiences in other spheres. And here again it appears that the print media are considerably more consequential in the years of young adulthood than are the electronic media—of which television is of course the main component.

Interpersonal discussion is a variable that has been firmly established as a motivating factor in information seeking (Chaffee & McLeod, 1973; Tipton,

Table 8.5. 1965 Media Use to 1973 Political Behavior Lagged Correlations, within Educational Attainment Levels

1965 Media Use Variable	No College (N = 492) Dependent Variable		1–2 yrs. College (N = 432) Dependent Variable		3+ yrs. College (N = 424) Dependent Variable	
	KNOWLEDGE	ACTIVITY	KNOWLEDGE	ACTIVITY	KNOWLEDGE	ACTIVITY
Print	.10*	.18***	−.01	.20***	.16***	.12*
Electronic	.00	.08	.03	.06	−.11*	.07

Note. Cell entries indicate time-lagged Pearson *r* between the 1973 dependent variable indicated in the column heading and the 1965 media use variable in the row, within each educational level. Asterisks indicate significance levels (* means *p* < .05, ** means *p* < .01, *** means *p* < .001). Data are from the CPS panel.

1970; Atkin, 1972). The uniformly strong relationships between interpersonal political discussion and media use in Table 8–4 render an attempt at differential analysis between media (in the fashion of Table 8–5) moot. Instead, let us turn to a more theoretically based analysis, focused on one major locus of habitual patterns of interpersonal discussion—the family. While our analysis will focus peculiarly on the young person's family of origin, there is evidence within the body of research to which we will refer that the dimensions of communication examined here are common to all institutionalized interpersonal communication systems. The family is a logical system to select for detailed analysis because almost all young people belong to one, and because it is the setting in which they have spent most of their time in the formative years. It is appropriate for consideration largely because it has been shown to be related both to mass media use patterns (Chaffee et al., 1971), and to indicators of political socialization (Chaffee et al., 1973). Mass communication and political behavior variables are related somewhat differently to one another in different types of family communication systems (Jackson-Beeck & Chaffee, 1975).

It has long been established that families vary enormously in the ways in which they raise children, e.g., in the degree of parental "protectiveness" re-

Figure 8-3. Fourfold Typology of Family Communication Structure, in Terms of Newcomb's A-B-X Model

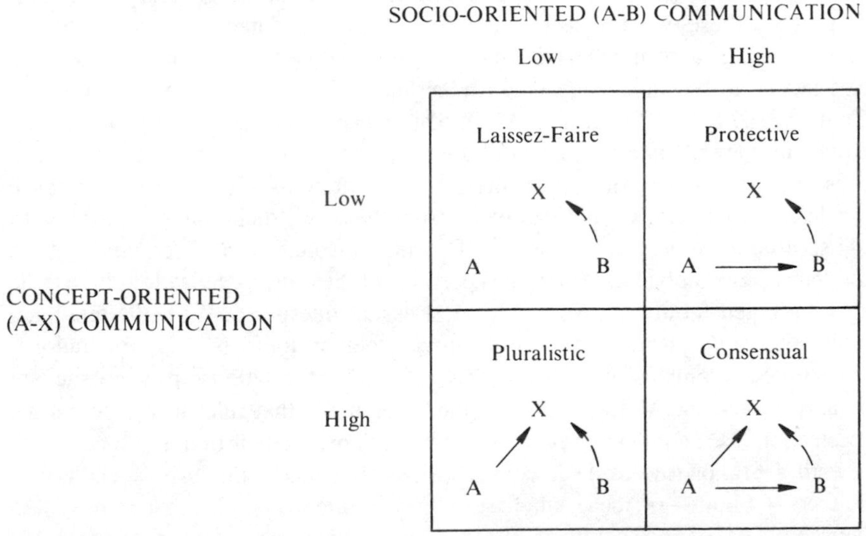

This figure is adapted from McLeod and Chaffee (1972). The A-B-X model is from Newcomb (1953). A is the child, B is the parent(s), and X represents topics of communication from the world outside the home. Solid-line arrows represent the cognitive orientations that the child learns as a consequence of the family's communication norms. Broken-line arrows represent the parents' orientations to extra-familial topics.

garding the child. Pinner's (1965) survey of Belgian, French, and Dutch youth demonstrated that the overprotected were less likely than others to trust political institutions and figures; they were also more disaffected, regardless of nationality. Lane (1965) and Jennings and Niemi (1974) also suggest that subtle norms of communication and interpersonal relationships within the family are basic for predicting political socialization processes.

Following this line of reasoning, family determinants of political socialization have been studied in a series of sample surveys of young people and their parents. One consistent finding has been that a unidimensional model does not adequately describe families' political communication behavior (Chaffee et al., 1973). Instead, families have been differentiated in terms of the relative emphasis they place on two types of cognitive orientations, which these investigators have called "socio-oriented" and "concept-oriented." The first of these is identified as an emphasis on maintenance of hierarchical personal relationships. The child is encouraged to defer to adults, to avoid interpersonal conflicts, and in general to place social harmony ahead of other criteria of personal relationships. In the concept-oriented setting, by contrast, emphasis is on self-expression and free discussion of controversial political and religious topics. The child is encouraged to weigh evidence and to come to independent opinions on current issues in the news.

While it might seem intuitively that the socio- and concept-oriented parent-child relationships should fall at opposite ends of a single general continuum, empirically these two dimensions turn out to be uncorrelated with one another; in surveys using large numbers of items, factor analyses consistently show these two factors to be statistically independent and internally consistent (McLeod & Chaffee, 1972; Chaffee et al., 1973). This means that there are approximately equal numbers of families that exhibit each possible combination of the relative presence (or absence) of each of these two orientations. The investigators have labeled the four family types that result from these two dichotomies according to the scheme illustrated in Figure 8–3. The interpersonal $A-B-X$ communication model of Newcomb (1953) underlies portions of the conceptualization, in that the socio-oriented family is assumed to be stressing interpersonal $(A-B)$ relations, while the concept-oriented family stresses person-topic $(A-X)$ orientations. Whereas Newcomb assumed that both $A-B$ and $A-X$ relationships were relevant to all persons, the McLeod-Chaffee model assumes that relevance is a learned orientation; i.e., some youngsters might learn to orient their thinking specifically toward $A-B$, or toward $A-X$ considerations, but others might be socialized to neither—or both—of these emphases. This implies, among other things, that Newcomb's (1953) principle of a "strain toward symmetry" will not be found in all families; it will be limited to those where both $A-B$ and $A-X$ relations are defined as equally relevant, so that conflicts between them cannot be resolved simply. The symmetry concept is one of a number of homeostatic or balance theories that flourished in social psychology in the 1950s and early 1960s, but have not proven as generally applicable as had been thought. See Festinger (1957), Osgood and Tannenbaum (1955), Heider (1946), and Zajonc (1960) for other varieties of balance theory, and Freedman and Sears (1965) and Bem (1970) for examples of the empirical bases for the current recession of this type of proposition.

The conceptual differences among these four types of families are worth noting, since they imply some important possible patterns of variation in political socialization. *Laissez-faire* children are thought to be virtually undirected, in regard to political socialization. There is an absence of "coorientation" between parent and child (see Figure 8–3). McLeod and Chaffee (1972) note that the socialization process for this group is less specific than for any of the other three.

In the *protective* family, the structural goal is obedience and social harmony. Conceptual matters, signified by an $A–X$ structure, are a lesser concern. Confronted with controversy, college students from such families have been highly persuasible (Stone & Chaffee, 1970), a finding clearly relevant to political behavior. It would seem that a lack of political knowledge and counterarguments contributes to an impressionable response to politics among children from protective homes.

Structural relations in the family indicate that the *pluralistic* child is faced with goals opposite from the protectives: $A–B$ (social) constraints are minimal, while open communication and discussion $(A–X)$ are valued. Independent seeking and processing of political information would seem to be a result, along with the political competence described by Chaffee et al. (1973).

For the child from the *consensual* home, conflicting goals and constraints might cause fragmentation in the political socialization process. These children are encouraged to be interested in ideas, but not to disturb the family with debate. Avoidance of conflictual aspects of politics might be the result, as would simple imitation of the parents' opinions and activities. In either case, some amount of political competence seems assured, but little active advocacy.

On a general level, McLeod and Chaffee's (1972) inference that parental constraints on the child's interpersonal communication can influence the process of political socialization has been supported. Using the same analytic framework as Chaffee et al., Sheinkopf (1973) reports significant differences in "anticipatory socialization" among children from the four family communication types. Specifically, children from pluralistic and consensual homes were prepared to encounter more future civic responsibility than were those from protective or laissez-faire home environments; the level of obligation they felt to work in political campaigns, to write to politicians and newspapers, and to support causes at age 25 was higher than those of protectives or laissez-faires.

Without presenting at great length the voluminous data from this body of research, we illustrate some of the main findings from it in Table 8–6. Here the four family types of Figure 8–3 are arrayed from left to right in approximately ascending order in terms of their likelihood of producing youngsters one would

Table 8.6. Standardized Measures of Media Use, Political Behavior, and Structural Factors, within Family Communication Pattern Type and Grade Level in Adolescence

		Low CONCEPT-ORIENTED FCP		High CONCEPT-ORIENTED FCP	
		High Socio-orientation	Low Socio-orientation	High Socio-orientation	Low Socio-orientation
		"PROTECTIVE"	"LAISSEZ-FAIRE"	"CONSENSUAL"	"PLURALISTIC"
Mass media public affairs use	JrHi	−.35	−.27	+.24	+.29
	SrHi	+.01	−.15	+.24	+.27
Political knowledge	JrHi	−.52	−.39	−.26	+.01
	SrHi	+.14	+.33	+.43	+.56
Campaign activity	JrHi	+.02	−.07	+.36	+.33
	SrHi	−.06	−.26	−.17	+.13
System awareness	JrHi	−.51	−.24	−.33	−.12
	SrHi	+.02	+.26	+.40	+.57
Political affect	JrHi	−.13	−.03	+.18	+.15
	SrHi	−.24	−.01	−.01	+.13
Socioeconomic status	JrHi	−.37	+.16	−.07	+.59
	SrHi	−.34	−.09	−.13	+.30
IQ	JrHi	−.40	+.06	−.18	+.28
	SrHi	−.11	+.12	+.04	+.32

Note. Cell entries are standard scores, calculated as deviations from the overall mean for each variable (combining data from both grade levels), setting the standard deviation at unity. Data are from the Five Cities sample, with N = 641 for the junior high group and N = 651 for the senior high students (Jackson-Beeck & Chaffee, 1975).

classify as "highly socialized politically": protective, laissez-faire, consensual, pluralistic. Since not all interpreters would agree with this set of comparative value judgments on our part, let us review the findings of Table 8–6 in some detail.

It is clear from the standard scores in Table 8–6 that the "pluralistic" young-sters (high concept-, low socio-orientation) stand highest within their grade levels on nearly every index that is reported. The opposite family pattern, which we call "protective" in Figure 8–3—those with low concept- and high socio-oriented backgrounds—ranks lowest on almost every measure. Since socio-economic status and intelligence measures are also highest among the pluralistic families and lowest in the protective homes, the explanatory power of those structural variables was assessed; the pattern of relationships shown in Table 8–6 hold up even when both SES and IQ are statistically controlled (Jackson-Beeck & Chaffee, 1975). It is especially worth noting in Table 8–6 that the indices of campaign activity and political affect are already rather high even among the pluralistic children who are in junior high (7th, 8th grades). It also appears that the pluralistics (and the consensuals) have established habits of heavy use of the mass media for public affairs content even when they are in junior high school, a finding replicated with slightly younger children by Roberts et al. (1975). The measures of political knowledge and awareness of the political system show considerable growth from the junior to the senior high cohorts, however.

This set of findings suggests that family communication influences deter-mine, at least as early as the onset of adolescence, the general behavior patterns and feelings about the system in general that the child will follow during the secondary school years; i.e., one's media use, overt political activity, and politi-cal affect (trust and efficacy) are fixed rather early in the home setting; they do not change much in adolescence. Cognitive indicators of political socialization, on the other hand, continue to develop during adolescence although they too are heavily conditioned by the family communication environment; these are exemplified in Table 8–6 by the system awareness and political knowledge measures. Even though the degree of parent-child similarity in political orienta-tions is modest (Jennings & Niemi, 1968), parental behavior can be important because it determines the kind of communicatory environment in which the child learns to orient toward the political system and the news media.

In general, we can say that mass media use is not an isolated factor in the life of the developing citizen. It interacts in complex ways with one's network of primary group interpersonal communication contacts, and most fundamentally with the person's family communication background. Media inputs also have differential impacts depending on the extent to which the person is exposed to higher education. Both interpersonal communication and education are important socializing factors in their own right, but they are also necessary to an adequate comprehension of the role played by mass communication.

Multivariate Models of Political Socialization

The most commonly accepted model of the political socialization process in the research literature is that of Easton and Dennis, who consider political activity the ultimate outcome:

> We may conjecture that (the child) will be likely to acquire general orientations about support and begin to relate himself positively or negatively to the political community.... He becomes familiar with the notion of democracy and may begin to absorb some general impressions about theoretically fundamental regime norms.... Only later may he acquire a minimal knowledge of and begin to learn the skills associated with the roles through which these general regime norms may be fulfilled (1969, p. 90).

Similarly, Dawson and Prewitt (1969), conclude that an important, central pattern in political socialization research is a trend from basic to less basic orientations:

> Children acquire early the basic interpretive orientations through which political happenings and perceptions are filtered. Only later in life does the citizen fully appreciate the institutional complexities of political life. It is even later that the citizen comes to understand and appreciate his role as a participant in the political life of his nation (Dawson & Prewitt, 1969, p. 203).

This notion of a general model of political socialization seems to match empirical findings by many researchers. Data reported by Greenstein (1960, 1965), Hess and Easton (1960), Hess and Torney (1967), and Easton and Dennis (1969) all support the idea that children's political orientations and behaviors gradually become appropriate to the participatory form of democracy in the United States. However, the researchers draw attention to important limitations of their studies, and thus of an inductively derived general model; e.g., the samples consist of white middle-class children living in well established urban or suburban areas. Consequently, Dawson and Prewitt (1969) and Dennis (1968) caution that cultural variation is a poorly understood aspect of political socialization.

Research in Appalachia (Jaros, Hirsch, & Flero, 1968), and analysis of differences between blacks and whites (Bullock & Rodgers, 1972; Engstrom, 1970) suggest that the general model hypothesized by Easton and Dennis is limited to certain cultural conditions. Recent findings by Rodgers and Lewis (1975) and by Dennis and Webster (1975) indicate that children's generally favorable affect toward the President, traditionally thought to be the first and most basic political orientation an American child would develop, was massively eroded in the wake of the Watergate scandals.

Nevertheless, the general model persists in the literature and we must inquire into the most plausible position of mass communication in it. The conventional wisdom on the point seems to be that media use for public affairs information is an intermediate stage, which develops later in life than does basic affect and awareness of the system, but prior to the acquisition of patterns of overt political activity. This puts it in about the same position in the overall system of sequential events in political socialization as is the acquisition of political knowledge—which is the variable to which media use is most closely related in the data we have examined. Jackson-Beeck (1974) has devised a test of this model.

In Figure 8–4 we present the general model, as we interpret it from various sources, with mass media use incorporated at the stage where we would presume it to belong. The model is shown twice, so that we can test it with data from the Five Cities junior and senior high samples, separately. The data entries in Figure 8–4 are the results of a path analysis of the general model on these total samples; detailed tests of very different paths that we hypothesized for the four different family communication pattern types are presented in Jackson-Beeck and Chaffee (1975). Here we will limit ourselves to the general model derived from Easton and Dennis, as a vehicle for illustrating the path-analytic procedure in a highly simplified form.[6] In general, it survives both tests reasonably well, although this is no guarantee that it is the single best-fit model by which one might order these variables.

We have eliminated from Figure 8–4 any paths (standardized regression coefficients) that did not reach significance at the .01 level. This leaves us with a trimmed picture that is readily interpretable. Of the four antecedent variables at the left of the figure, intelligence is a major predictor, but it accounts only for variance in political knowledge, among the two intervening variables. System awareness and political affect both predict media public affairs use, even when all other variables are held constant in the multivariate analysis, but these relationships are fairly weak. Finally—and perhaps most important for our purposes here—the media use measure is a stronger predictor of campaigning activity than is political knowledge.

Phrasing our interpretation a slightly different way, we find that there is fairly consistent replication at the two grade levels of the following finding: media public affairs use is not as well explained by antecedent variables in the general model as is political knowledge, but it is a better explainer of campaigning activity. Since the latter is a variable that is often discussed as if it were a major stepping-stone in the general political socialization process, it would seem that media use explicitly (rather than simply as a source of knowledge) deserves at least equal attention in the elaboration of future models.

---

[6]Path analysis is an evolving methodology for testing complex causal hypotheses involving many variables, and is appropriate with data collected over time or at a single point in time. It is first necessary to specify one model (or a very few) in which some variables are hypothesized to precede others in a causal sequence; this model is then tested by assessing the extent to which it "fits" empirical data when partialing procedures such as multiple regression are applied. Variables that are more distant from the criterion variable in the model should, in general, be less strongly correlated with it than those that are closer to it in the hypothesized causal sequence. Acceptance of a model that has been tested in this fashion does not rule out the possibilities of other models that have not been similarly hypothesized and tested.

Figure 8-4. Simplified Path Model Testing Hypothesized Stages in Political Socialization

JUNIOR HIGH SAMPLE (N=641)

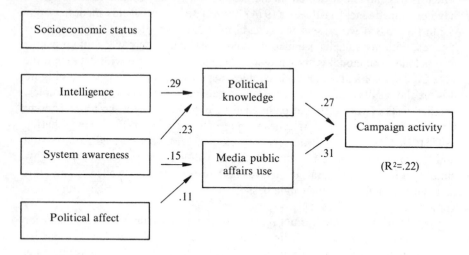

SENIOR HIGH SAMPLE (N=651)

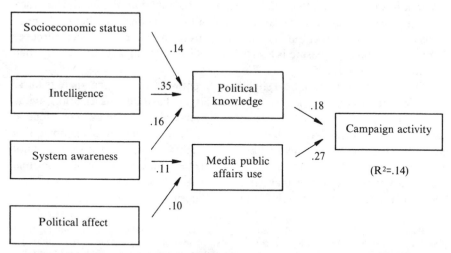

Entries are standardized regression coefficients between the indicated variables; only those that are significant at the .01 level are shown. Coefficients among the four exogenous variables (first column), and residuals for the two endogenous variables (middle column) are omitted here for simplicity. Complete path analysis appears in Jackson-Beeck and Chaffee (1975). Data are from the Five Cities sample.

Our procedure of testing the extant general model does not imply that we consider it the optimal image of the process on the basis of our review of empirical findings. We might be inclined to locate system awareness at a later stage in the model, and we would not necessarily consider campaign activity the ultimate outcome; a more complex dependent variable would come closer to our conception of what constitutes development into competent citizenship. But this section should suffice to demonstrate our most central point, that mass communication behavior has been a neglected variable in models of political socialization, relative to its empirical import when other factors are controlled.

Life Cycle Changes in Media Use

To this point we have virtually equated socialization with young people. That is the most common meaning of the term, but it is clear that political socialization can continue throughout the entire adult life cycle. We should be especially concerned with very *old* citizens, who might experience a phase of *desocialization* from political awareness and activity as they near the ends of their lives. This general point has not been studied empirically, but we can review some recent data (Chaffee & Wilson, 1975) that at least provide hints about the findings one should expect if media influences in political socialization were to be traced throughout the adult life cycle.

First, consider the number of hours a person spends in an average day watching TV.[7] This behavior is at about an average level—in terms of the overall norms for TV time for all persons—among young adults through the early thirties; in middle age, television viewing drops below the population norm; finally, in later life it climbs to above-average levels. Attention to public affairs programs on TV exhibits a slightly different life cycle, being lowest among young adults and highest after age 60.

Newspaper reading follows a curvilinear pattern across the years. It is low in young adulthood, grows through middle age, then drops off in very old age. A more drastic drop in the very late years is shown for the specific measure of most interest to us in this chapter—newspaper public affairs reading. This behavior reaches two peaks, which we might guess have different causes. The first occurs

[7]The age-cycle trends described here are based on two large-scale survey samples. One consists of 544 adult citizens of Wisconsin, interviewed in 1974 in a statewide survey conducted by the Wisconsin Survey Research Laboratory; results from that study have been reported in Chaffee and Wilson (1975). The second data source is the 1974 postelection national survey conducted by the Center for Political Studies at the University of Michigan. This sample of 1,552 persons was analyzed especially for this chapter, using the archive of the Inter-University Consortium for Political Research. There are some differences between the results from the two surveys; in this paragraph, only those statements which are supported by both data sources are included. A more detailed study of life cycle variation, including controls for education, employment, and other structural factors that exercise some control over media use, is in preparation.

in the person's forties, when it would seem that involvement in local public affairs news would be greatest; this is the "prime of life" stage of high participation and community visibility, when one's children are coming of age and one's years of local activity are coming to fruition in committee chairmanships, inside-dopesterism, and knowing-the-guy-who. The second peak in newspaper political consumption occurs around the age of retirement, as if the person had been "just waiting" for an opportunity to spend more time reading. With the onset of very old age, however, newspaper public affairs reading drops off to its lowest level throughout the life cycle. Whether this should be interpreted as a desocialization stage, or as signaling the end of socialization, is difficult to determine. We can assume that major inputs of new political knowledge become extremely unlikely once the aged person abandons the newspaper. Use of two other media, radio and magazines, also drops off sharply in very old age. Each reaches a single high point in use—around age 30 for radio, and about retirement age for magazines.

What is happening, overall, is that television supplants all other media in very old age. This might be because the content of certain media is ill suited to the interests of the aged, as in the case of radio. But a more general hypothesis would be that the audio-visual character of TV makes it an easier medium for consumption than do any of the media that are transmitted via a single sense modality—sight for the print media, sound for radio. Whatever the reason, it is clear that any theorizing about mass media as a source of political socialization in the late years of life should be limited to the single channel of television. Given the rather sorry record of that medium in terms of producing active, informed citizens at younger ages (see above), it is difficult to be particularly enthusiastic about this finding. The meaning of televised public affairs among the aged, and more generally the character of media political inputs at various points in the life cycle, are topics deserving much more extensive study than has been attempted to date.

We might consider in this connection whether life cycle patterns described above are due to aging of the person, or to the kind of media use that was normative within one's age cohort at the historical time of the person's socialization to public affairs media. As we noted earlier, the latter "socialization hypothesis" is at least partly supported by Jennings and Niemi's (1975) analysis of the CPS panel data. They found that the 1965 generation gap in news reading between the high school seniors and their parents—the parents reported much higher incidence of newspaper use—had persisted by 1973; there was little change over the eight-year period for either age cohort within these families. On the other hand, Danowski and Cutler (1975), comparing age cohorts from national sample surveys 1952–1972, concluded that from age 25 on there was solid evidence for the "aging hypothesis" in young adulthood; as the same cohort (as represented by different random samples) grew older, its level of newspaper news reading increased. The Jennings-Niemi and Danowski-Cutler findings are not necessarily contradictory, since they cover different periods in the life cycle. It could be that socialization-to-media effects hold the person's public affairs reading relatively constant in the first years of adulthood, but after about age 25 life cycle changes begin to take effect.

The least studied portion of the overall life cycle in the media-politics area is childhood. Atkin and Gantz (1975) have made a notable beginning in a survey of television news attention as a factor in political socialization of grade-school children beginning with kindergarten. Combining personal interview data from children and their mothers in a one-year longitudinal study, they were able to discern some causal patterns using time-lagged analysis based on the Rozelle-Campbell (1969) model. Their conclusion was that, over time, the extent to which parents discussed current events with their children predicted higher attention to TV news on the part of the child; this attention to TV news, in turn, predicted future gains in knowledge of public figures and current events. Hawkins, Pingree, and Roberts (1975) studied the reactions to media reports of the Watergate scandals in children as young as fourth grade. Many of their findings run counter to inferences about political affect and family communication patterns that other investigators had drawn from studies of adolescents and young adults.

Whatever future research determines about the little understood course of life cycle changes in the media-socialization relationship, it is obvious from these few findings to date that there will not be a single linear progression based on a monolithic developmental process throughout the range of ages. At different stages in life, media and political behavior indices may be increasing, decreasing, or remaining static, and the causal principles governing the relationship between these variables seem to differ radically at different ages.

A Media-Cultural Theory of Political Socialization

Having considered several alternative models of media effects, prior research findings, limitations on the kinds of research that are ordinarily done, and some new data bearing on these questions, we next consider a possible synthesis of what we have found. A number of thoughtful writers have suggested in various ways that postindustrial societies, in which the mass media are thoroughly diffused and virtually universally available, contain two latent subcultures. The first of these, and presumably the larger, consists of those persons who rely heavily on the electronic media (principally television but also radio, and sound and film recordings) for their contact with the greater world. Their political orientation is that of a passive consumer of all sorts of communication content, including whatever public affairs information happens to present itself via these easily attended sources. The second media culture supplements the ubiquitous electronic media with those of print—newspapers, magazines, books—which are far more laden with public information content and which can be much more selectively consulted by the person with a deep interest in a particular topic.

We assume that a child is not "born" a member of one of these two cultures, nor is it particularly a product of attributes of his home environment—such as the family's socioeconomic standing, or the parents' media habits. And yet, if these contrasting media cultures exist, presumably the developing child is gradually socialized to one or the other.[8] In speaking of a culture, we are implying that a complicated set of cognitive and behavioral characteristics gets adopted more or less as a unit, rather than piecemeal. These might include such traits as high levels of political knowledge, activity, discussion, and interest—which, as we have seen, are associated with the second, print-oriented, media culture. If this theory is valid, we should be able to trace a gradual divergence throughout the formative years between this print-centered subculture and the politically more passive, less knowledgeable electronic subculture.

From this point of view, it is not always appropriate to set specific hypotheses about causal relationships among these variables; they eventually come to have—at least at the point where the adolescent enters adulthood—a chicken-egg relationship to one another. It is clear that items of political information are learned from all kinds of mass media exposure in childhood and adolescence; more from television at an early age and probably in old age, more from newspapers in young adulthood and probably on into middle age. The import of this kind of theory for future research is to stress that the concept of "mass communication" is an overly broad one for organizing data collection and analysis. A single measure of media use is wholly inadequate for tapping the differential contributions made by each medium, and by exposure to particular types of content within each. Lumping into a single index measures of television and

---

[8]The concept of "two cultures" is recognizable as drawn from the writings of Snow (1964), who emphasized the divergence between the humanistic and scientific domains in intellectual life. A major difference should be pointed out, however. Snow was contrasting two methods of learning, and two bodies of knowledge, that are presumably equally valid and worthwhile although they involve separate groups of people and different kinds of knowledge. The two cultures that grow out of reliance on print and electronic media for one's information about the world are clearly not being characterized here as of equal validity; assuming relatively high expectations for political socialization, the print-based culture is interpreted here as generally superior to the electronic in terms of providing and storing knowledge. The opposite view, it should be noted, is taken by McLuhan (1964), who believes the electronic media provide the more realistic contact with the outside world. While intuitively interesting, McLuhan's propositions remain substantially undemonstrated. To some extent, either argument is overdrawn. There is a great deal of public affairs information provided via electronic media, most of it consisting simply of readings from a written script; at the same time, scandal sheets and ideologically constrained periodicals remind us that all that's printed is not news—although it can be quite entertaining. Media studies show that such informative electronic presentations as news specials and on-scene broadcasts of major political events attract listeners and viewers who customarily rely on the print media. These occasional uses of alternate news sources are essentially supplementary to one's basic diet, however. Each medium has historically developed a sphere of content specialization that allows it to attract a habitual audience that sustains it economically. The entertaining character of television, for example, has gradually influenced TV news presentations, leading to less journalistic and more jocular newscast formats.

newspaper exposure, or of public affairs and other types of content, is quite likely to lead to an inference that "nothing" can be attributed to "the mass media"—because the separate contributions of these sources to political socialization are in many respects opposite and will tend to neutralize one another. The immediate research need is for more particularistic research that specifies different contributions to political socialization from different forms of media experience. The urge to oversimplify by achieving a single broad statement for all kinds of people and all sorts of media content deserves stern resistance.

Current Directions in Mass Communication Theory and Research

There has been in recent years a flowering of new directions of growth in research on mass communication. Among these have been the study of political communication (Chaffee, 1975) and studies of the role of the media in child development (Comstock et al., in preparation; Roberts, 1973). Another important trend has been examination of units of analysis other than that of the individual. The work cited here on family communication structures is an example of the use of interpersonal or primary group units for defining empirical variables (see also Chaffee, 1972). A parallel trend has been the examination of larger social systems, such as communities, on a systematic, comparative basis (Tichenor et al., 1973). Cross-national comparative research has been hampered by the difficulty of measuring concepts in comparable fashion when media systems differ greatly; the psychological and sociological functions served by the mass media have been studied comparatively within that subset of nations that can be characterized as "media rich" (Blumler & Katz, 1974), and this has in some cases included settings that are not of the "post-industrial" class (e.g., Chaffee & Izcaray, 1975). Media effects research, which originated in the testing of "attitude change," has branched out to include cognitive and overtly behavioral outcomes, as well as those that are more narrowly attitudinal in nature; again, much of the research cited in this chapter exemplifies this trend. There is a decided tendency to pose hypotheses that are peculiar to certain classes of persons, or that are limited to a specific set of prior conditions not expected to obtain for all persons (Weaver et al., 1975; McLeod & Becker, 1974; Kline, Miller, & Morrison, 1974). This is part of a broader trend toward incorporating a greater number of variables into a single analysis. There is also a healthy inclination to resist taking popular assumptions at face value; an example is Edelstein's (1974) work demonstrating that the "credibility" people ascribe to mass media is only a minor factor in determining their reactions to the news they receive.

These lines of development are, taken together, rather encouraging from the standpoint of political socialization research. What is needed most is a fresh approach or two. We have suggested several in this chapter, but we certainly have not exhausted the possibilities that are implied by some of these new directions in the field: e.g., cross-national studies offer unique opportunities. Media availability tends to be rather similar from one place (and person) to another within a nation; in the United States, for instance, most citizens have access to a daily newspaper, three commercial television networks, a half-dozen radio stations, and a wide range of magazines, whether they live in the rural Midwest or in an urbanized coastal region. Many countries, by contrast, lack television entirely and have no strong print media or newsgathering system; nations also differ widely in the range and kinds of news the media are permitted to disseminate. It is possible to locate research projects where structural variation in media resources can be examined while many sociocultural factors are effectively controlled; this is particularly the case where different language groups have their separate media systems in the same community, or where a central city controls the media content for satellite cities within the same country (Chaffee & Izcaray, 1975). Communities located on international borders, especially where the two countries have different national languages and consequently separate media, seem to be "living laboratories" for the study of media variation in political socialization. Conversely, where international boundaries are crossed by same-language media, there is an opportunity to examine the socialization of youngsters in one country to the citizenship norms of the other; this phenomenon is currently a policy problem in Anglophone Canada, e.g., where a majority of the population is within the TV signal area of U.S. broadcasters.

The stage seems set, then, for a proliferation of research on mass communication in political socialization processes. While we have stressed the scarcity of research to date, there is every indication that we should not expect that situation to persist much longer. The next decade or so should see an opening up of many new lines of empirical inquiry.

Conclusions

We have ranged about the central question of mass communication in political socialization, exploring at least briefly several new directions of research. We have spent far more time examining original data, and new analyses of old data, than is usual in chapters whose purpose is to comprehend a broad area of knowledge. This has been necessary because we are dealing here with a set of phenomena that have not engaged the interest of empirical research very often or very deeply. The major conclusion that we would assert on the basis of this exploration is that the inattention to media use variables in political socialization research has been extremely shortsighted. There seem to be direct relationships among the major variables in this nexus, and many domains of subtle multivariate relationships that could prove highly fruitful in understanding how people come to exhibit the patterns of political behavior they do.

Let us review the six models of mass communication with which we began this chapter, and consider them critically in the light of the evidence we have examined. The first two models were those that presume that mass media variables constitute, respectively, appropriate dependent, or independent, variables vis-à-vis political behavior and affect measures. As our own data-handling decisions suggest, we would lean strongly toward the latter model, assuming that media behavior stands in an antecedent or causal relationship to political socialization. Media use habits appear to be well determined by family communication structures at least in early adolescence, to persist into adulthood, and to predict political behavior outcomes over time reasonably well. Since communication is almost by definition an intermediate event in some phenomenal chain, it would not seem appropriate to limit its role to that of one among many criterion measures of politicization.

The third model is that of limited effects of the mass media. As we indicated early on, this does not seem especially applicable to the study of socialization of youths to the political system. It is a model that assumes the existence of predispositions that control media use patterns, whereas socialization research inquires into the origins of those predispositions; media exposure begins at a very young age and seems to be a source of learning of political predispositions. To be sure, some people grow up as Democrats, others as conservatives, and still others remain apolitical; and these belief structures condition the interpretations they make of the mass media where partisan or tendentious content is presented. But in terms of the general global variables that are central to politicization irrespective of partisan direction—we are thinking of knowledge, affect, and activity—the media effects do not appear to be limited by individual predispositions. In some ways the mass media have little or no impact on political socialization, as we have seen; but in many respects they appear to play a major role even when other important factors such as education and primary group influences are taken into account.

The fourth model, in which media influence takes place only via an intervening process such as interpersonal communication, has not been explored sufficiently here to warrent acceptance or rejection. There is a close connection between interpersonal and mass communication, and one might indeed question whether the distinction between the two is as meaningful to the person as it might seem to the researcher. We have seen instances where interpersonal communication structures—in the family environment—made large differences in major indicators of socialization. We have also seen evidence of direct media-politicization effects that do not seem to be affected by interpersonal environmental factors. There is no essential need to choose between this indirect model and that of direct media influence, since either might hold under a given set of conditions.

The fifth model, that of contingent causation, seems to be well advised as a general procedure when dealing with media and political behaviors. We have noted instances where the direction of correlation between mass communication and politicization indices reversed itself for samples that were differentiated in their general orientations to politics. It seems reasonable to suspect that there are many more such situations—and that research to identify them will be important in building our understanding of this most imperfectly understood domain.

Finally, we consider the possibility that all of the statistical associations we have examined are spurious, artifacts of some set of unidentified variables that account for the observed correlations. While always conceivable, this conclusion seems most unlikely at this point. We have been looking, along the way in this chapter, at many other variables that one might expect to have major impact on the communication-socialization relationship: education, peer and family communication, age, and so forth. No all of the correlations we examined survived these tests, of course; our inferences have been qualified and limited in many ways. But the overall summation from the evidence reviewed above seems inescapably to be that mass communication plays an important, in some ways primary, role in the process of political socialization.

9

Perspectives on Adult Political Socialization—Areas of Research

Roberta S. Sigel and Marilyn Brookes Hoskin

Introduction

POLITICS GENERALLY IS CONSIDERED to be the domain of adults. Political scientists therefore have studied in great depth how adults are involved in it—whether or not they vote, how they vote, what political beliefs they hold, which beliefs are long-lasting and which transitory, etc. What they have not studied, or have studied very rarely, is how adults come to acquire such tendencies. Thus, what we have is a vast body of literature on the *manifestations* of adult political involvement and a dearth of literature on the *causes or antecedents* of involvement. We know the product but not the process. Hence we know more about adult political behavior than we do about adult political socialization.[1] This is all the more surprising inasmuch as political socialization is said to be the fastest growing subfield of the discipline. Research in the field, however, has for the most part limited itself to the study of young children, although in the last few years adolescents also have become the target for investigation (Flacks, 1970; Jennings & Niemi, 1974; Sigel & Hoskin, 1975).[2] The relative neglect of adults

---

[1]We shall not attempt here to define the term socialization. The handbook makes it abundantly clear that definitions differ but that there is agreement that it deals with a process—a process of learning and/or internalization. For another good summary, see Fred I. Greenstein, *International Encyclopedia of Social Sciences*, 1965.

[2]The same observation can be made for the socialization literature on childhood and adolescence, viz., that it tends to study the product rather than the process. For a more detailed discussion of this

makes it, of course, very difficult to write a review on the topic, but we shall try to close the gap as best we can.

Another difficulty we encounter in such a review is that the childhood socialization literature is not always very useful for a study of adults because it has tended to concentrate on a relatively narrow range of topics, such as children's attitudes toward political authority, especially the President, and on their love of country. Most literature on adult political involvement has stressed different areas, notably participation and policy preferences. This discrepancy makes it difficult to establish a bridge from childhood to adult socialization.[3] Another, and probably more serious, obstacle is the failure of childhood socialization research to look into the acquisition during childhood of values and behavior patterns which, although not political in themselves, are likely to have enduring or permanent political consequences. It is conceivable, e.g., that orientations toward such values as the work ethic, the norm of charity, or aggression, to name but a few, might be potentially more influential for the crystallization of adult political orientations than more explicitly political "lessons" learned in childhood (Sigel, 1965).

A third difficulty which confronts us is the dearth of materials on adults in non-American settings. In spite of the growing interest in new and developing nations and in comparative literature in general, we found little work done therein on adult socialization. The research that does deal with socialization to non-American settings tends to be on elite socialization and will be handled in another chapter of this volume. Our review, therefore, will suffer from a certain amount of national parochialism.

In most of our review we will deal with the socialization of those adults who since childhood have been part of and socialized into the prevailing American culture, i.e., people who have accepted the basic norms and values which the general culture has transmitted to them in order that they be "capable of adequate performance in ... [their] several roles throughout life, both as respects skills and attitudes" (Levy, 1952, p. 189). What we need to observe about these adults is the manner in which they learn to perform their uniquely adult roles or—more specifically—how the discontinuities occurring in adult life socialize individuals. The emphasis then will be on political and other discontinuities.

Within this focus we shall single out only those indigenous roles and/or subsystems which operate within the stream of the basic culture. We shall disregard adult socialization into the criminal subculture, the culture of the institutionalized, the culture of those living in religious orders, or the culture of

---

point, see Roberta S. Sigel, "Political Socialization—Some Reactions to Current Approaches and Conceptualization," paper read at annual meeting of American Political Science Association, New York City, 1966.

[3]The only general exception to the above statement is in the area of party identification where researchers have frequently commented on the persistence over the generations (Maccoby, 1954). This persistence, however, may be a testimony to the stability and relative rigidity of our stratification system rather than to the success of childhood socialization.

other atypical groups. Nor shall we discuss what Rosenblum calls "expedient socialization" by which is understood the learning of specific, narrow norms and behaviors (usually related to the work situation) by members "who have transferred participation from another society to the one in question but who maintain primary orientation to the former" (p. 174). Thus we shall exclude, e.g., American missionaries or technical experts working abroad for prolonged periods or, conversely, migrant foreign labor coming to the United States in search of employment but returning to their native land after having saved enough money.

Finally, we shall also pay little attention to a related question, viz.: What is the nature of adult socialization or, more accurately, desocialization followed by resocialization, of those adults who in their youth grew up in another culture and subsequently as adults enter the main culture? What happens if they want to function effectively in it? We are thinking particularly of members of subcultures who "want out," or dislocated victims of far-reaching political upheavals. We shall not ignore them, but the attention we shall pay to these groups and to this resocialization process will be—due to limitations in research—far scantier than the topic warrants.

All of these groups, the socialized and the resocialized, are confronted with the task of learning and adapting themselves to uniquely adult roles. This is not always an easy task, as Riley and associates (1969) have pointed out:

> Successful socialization beyond childhood involves a continual search for the delicate adjustment between the individual's internalized values and definitions and his specific judgments of the behaviors and attitudes appropriate to each new role situation. On the one hand, he implements his basic values in a specific situation; on the other, each new situation contributes to his basic value pattern as he generalizes the pattern (or modifies or reinforces it) to cover the new specific applications (p. 956).

The task which this review has set for itself is to attempt to answer the question: What political socialization do adults undergo for which childhood offered them but scant preparatory socialization or—put more cautiously—for which we have at the moment no empirical or otherwise visible evidence that childhood did offer them enough preparatory socialization? To answer the question we shall rely, wherever possible, on political science—specifically, political socialization— literature but we shall often have to go to other disciplines and documents and to make inferences from them about the political socialization which takes place in adulthood.

Theoretical Perspectives

There does not exist as yet a theory of adult political socialization, although three different approaches to the topic—three models—can be detected. The first and perhaps most prevalent one is derived from the assumption that attitudes learned early are the most enduring and hence are fair predictors of adult stances (Dawson & Prewitt, 1969; Easton & Dennis, 1969; Davies, 1965; Adorno et al., 1950; Stagner, 1954). Such an approach accords determinative influence to both obvious political preferences acquired in childhood and to the personality structure that is less visibly molded during that period but which underlies many permanent orientations to politics. In stressing the importance of early patterns, therefore, studies of the children's political world have advocated a theoretical pattern in which the persistence of early socialization is assumed. We shall call this the *persistence-beyond-childhood* model.[4]

At the other end of the theoretical spectrum is the approach which assumes that one's political orientations are malleable throughout the life cycle, given the appropriate stimuli to change. This model, which we could label the *constant change* model, while not excluding childhood socialization, argues that adulthood brings the organism into contact with new experiences (new settings, novel events, new responsibilities, changes in biological and social status) which have a powerful socializing impact on the individual. Some of this socialization may build on values and attitudes acquired in youth but in other instances it takes place *de novo* since there was no anticipatory socialization, and in yet others it may even require resocialization (as, e.g., in the adapting from a democratic and benign regime to an authoritarian and repressive one). The emphasis in this model is on the existence of environmental influences which will continuously create new political orientations or model them from their weak predecessors.

If the choice between cradle-to-grave orientations and constant change is too severe, an intermediate theoretical position posits the importance of *generations* as explanatory variables for adult attitudes. Such an approach accords events and changed settings a significant role in shaping attitudes by specifying that events and experiences will be interpreted differentially among age cohorts who share internal consistency in terms of educational trends, age at which political events took place, and subsequent peer influence in response to those events (Lane & Sears, 1964; Carlsson & Karlsson, 1970; Inglehart, 1971). The notion of generational change which culminates in overall aggregate changes thus specifies a level of event or systemic influence which is capable of inducing a change in orientation, without allowing any personal change of setting to enter as a universal factor in shaping adult views. In our review of the literature, we shall attempt to examine the research under discussion with an eye to its contribution to either of these three models. It might not be premature, however, to admit at the very outset that the findings tend to be sufficiently inconclusive to prevent us from reaching any definitive conclusion with respect to the superior explanatory power of any of the three models.

To study the course of adult socialization, we must look to novel or discon-

[4]David Sears makes a good case for four rather than three themes; see David O. Sears, "Political Socialization," in Fred I. Greenstein and Nelson W. Polsby (Eds.), *The Handbook of Political Science,* Vol. 2 (Reading, Mass.: Addison-Wesley, 1975).

tinuous conditions since we would not expect to observe any marked change in political behaviors or attitudes in situations which duplicate rather closely those experienced in childhood or adolescence. For that reason we shall all but ignore the impact of forces, roles, and affiliations, such as ethnic group and social class membership, which persist after childhood. Instead, we shall focus on potential discontinuities from childhood socialization. What are likely sources of discontinuities in the lives of most men? At its most general, we can say they would encompass all those situations and conditions with which the child has had no experience or for which he or she has not been socialized directly.[5] "Even though some of the expectations of the society are relatively stable through the life cycle, many others change.... We know that society demands that the individual meet these change expectations" (Brim, 1962, p. 310).

The expectations society makes are related to changes in the individual and to changes in society. We shall refer to the former as new social roles which the individual has to assume due to adulthood; we shall refer to the latter as changes in the sociopolitical environment. It is to these changes that we shall direct our review. With reference to the former we shall concentrate almost exclusively on two sets of new roles: those associated with sociobiological maturation and those related to occupation. With respect to changes in the environment, we shall focus on political events transpiring during adulthood, especially dramatic ones, and personal experiences of a sociopolitical nature.

With respect to the first, we shall ask ourselves: Does biological maturation from youth to old age and the statuses associated with it (husband, father, breadwinner, retiree, invalid, etc.) affect either a person's political beliefs or his practices or both, or do these essentially remain static from adolescence on? With respect to man's economic role, we shall focus especially on the socializing part played by occupation and its concomitant status. Third, with respect to the political environment, we shall observe what socializing impact changes in the environment (technological changes, new laws, wars, revolutions, etc.) have on the individual. In this discussion we shall make a distinction between changes over which the individual has no control (such as a revolution or depression) and those he may initiate himself (such as immigration) on the assumption that the socializing impact of voluntary versus involuntary experiences may well be differential. We shall proceed with our discussion in roughly the order outlined above. Whenever feasible, we shall assess the persuasiveness of the competing models of adult socialization in the light of the evidence we shall be able to muster.

---

[5]While it is no doubt true that the child is not oblivious of adult roles or important political events transpiring around him, it is highly unlikely that most children can experience them with the same immediacy as the adult. It is one thing to watch a father leave in the morning, briefcase or lunchpail in hand, and imagine the role of breadwinner; it is quite another to be one. It is one thing to watch the news of the war in Southeast Asia on the television screen; it is another to fight there. To discover the impact of such events and of such roles on the experiencing adult, we really cannot stop with childhood socialization but must observe whether or not they do indeed socialize the adult.

Sources of Adult Political Socialization

AGE AND THE ROLE OF THE ADULT

A good deal of ambiguity has surrounded research into the effect of age on political orientations, primarily because of a tendency to confound the questions of aging per se and generational differences (Dennis, 1968; Sears, 1969; Sears & McConahy, 1973; Abramson, 1974). Each implies a different working model of the influences on attitudes. The "change through the life cycle" model sees a regular and predictable progression of attitudinal development and involvement in politics which varies by age and age-related roles. While childhood political attitudes are mostly barren of real content and comprised mostly of affective evaluations (Greenstein, 1965; Hess & Torney, 1967; Sears & Whitney, 1973), adolescence ushers in a steady increase in the volume of political information which enriches the individual's involvement content and strengthens earlier dispositions (Jennings & Niemi, 1968; Milbrath, 1965; Hyman, 1959; Easton & Dennis, 1969; Sigel & Hoskin, 1975). At this point increased cognitive capacities open up a range of political orientations which were not possible to develop in the earlier years.

The developmental literature suggests that not until adolescence do individuals begin to develop the abstract reasoning skills and the capacity for reciprocal, sociocentric thought crucial for understanding politics and applying principles to concrete problem situations. At this point the mature political thought considered to be "adult" refines earlier notions of politics (Inhelder & Piaget, 1958; Merelman & McCabe, 1974; Sigel, 1975).

Political involvement is predicated not only on the cognitive capacity to process political stimuli; it also requires the interest or willingness to do so. The requisite interest involved in creating sustained political activity does not evolve as naturally as cognitive capacities. While theoretically the person of 18 or 19 should be as politically involved as his fellow citizen of 30 or 40, the reality is that the 18–25 age group expresses less interest and involvement in politics (Jennings & Niemi, 1974; Milbrath, 1965). Indeed, the age group which is in one sense most open to political influence because it has developed new political capacities and new reference groups, also is the group least concerned with politics: e.g., of the 12 million young people between the ages of 18 and 21 eligible to vote for U.S. President in 1972, at most 44% registered, and only about 20% voted, notwithstanding the tremendous appeal to the youth vote made by both parties. Youth's relative indifference to politics must be explained in terms of other, more pressing priorities: completing one's education, finding a job, finding a mate, establishing oneself as an independent individual separate from one's parents and home, etc. These take precedence over civic duties and concern with politics (Verba & Nie, 1972; Glenn & Grimes, 1968; Campbell et al., 1960; Butler & Stokes, 1967; Sears, 1969).

Nevertheless, distinct *views* emerge during this period and demonstrate at least the attainment of independent thinking during the late teens and early twenties (Jennings & Niemi, 1974; Merelman, 1969, 1971; Dennis et al., 1968). One postulate of the aging framework is that young people coming into contact with political and social ideas, but not yet confronted with the realities of political and economic participation, are more idealistic and reform-minded. A recurring attribute of youth is thought to be a faith in the future, combined with an impatience for the temporizing, compromising methods of their elders. Thus the young would be expected to form—and do form—the backbone of movements for civil rights, ecology, and world peace (Flacks, 1969; Gamson, 1968; Keniston, 1968; Feuer, 1969; Roszak, 1968). Far from constituting a sharp break with childhood socialization, these concerns of the "liberal" youths often are based on political values acquired during childhood. Flacks, e.g., pointed out that the young people studied by him came from predominantly liberal, even radical, homes and thought they were putting into practice the beliefs taught them by their parents. In fact, the only issue on which they judged themselves to be in disagreement with their parents was on the issue of how to translate belief into practice. "Whereas (students) overwhelmingly endorse civil disobedience, nearly half of their fathers do not" (Flacks, p. 190). The same holds for milder forms of political action, such as participation in protests and demonstrations. With this exception, Flacks concludes:

> Most students who are involved in the movement . . . are involved in neither "conversion" from nor "rebellion" against the political perspectives of their fathers. A more supportable view suggests that the great majority of these students are attempting to fulfill and renew the political traditions of their families (pp. 190–191).

While Flacks' findings lend support to the persistence model, a good case for the generational model can also be made by virtue of the fact that youth in general (and not just the liberal youth) are more liberal on a host of issues than the generation of their parents, particularly on issues relating to equality, social service, and the tolerance of dissent. A recent study of 17–20-year-olds showed them to be considerably more critical than their elders of the government's treatment of the poor, the aged, and the helpless. They are also more inclined to fault the United States for persistence of discrimination (Sigel & Hoskin, 1975). They show greater disposition to internationalism than does the over-50 generation. Some studies have found them to be economically more optimistic about both their own futures and that of the nation, and to believe more in working for optimal change (Bachman & van Duinen, 1971; Campbell et al., 1960). Others, however, have noticed a steady decline in trust (Hochreich & Rotter, 1970). Intergenerational differences also were demonstrated in eight European countries (Jennings et al. 1976). "With some noteworthy exceptions the filial generation emerges as considerably more 'liberal' and less conventional than its predecessor. . . . On the other hand, differences tended . . . to be slight to modest in the various responsibilities assigned to government." (p. 61) Apparently then even the alleged idealism and radicalism of youth has by no means been firmly established. Recent newspaper articles in fact suggest that on some issues, such as friendliness to labor unions, the youngest cohorts may actually be more conservative.

We do have one finding, however, which has often been cited as evidence of youth's greater propensity for radicalism and that is their participation in protests, demonstrations, and other unconventional behavior designed to exert pressure on government. Sigel (1976) in analyzing adolescents' advocacy of such measures found youth to view them not as radical tactics but as conventional ones, as "democracy between elections" not unlike voting and writing one's representative. One generation's radicalism may well be another's status quo—an observation which should alert us to the importance of contextual analysis in socialization studies.

In contrast to early adulthood, two changes appear between the ages of 25 and 30: involvement with more extreme or at least unorthodox movements and/or ideologies abates, but participation in more conventional politics increases. This phase tends to coincide not only with increase in chronological age but also with assumption of family responsibilities. Chronological maturation is said to have a deleterious effect on youthful idealism. Life experiences as well as new responsibilities incurred at about that age further complete the process (Verba & Nie, 1972; Milbrath, 1965; Glenn & Grimes, 1968). By the mid-twenties to early thirties most men and women are married, and many have begun to raise families. With this new status come the customary concerns over taxes, mortgage rates, schools. "It changes your outlook quite a bit when you have those mortgage payments, car payments, and kids to feed," the ex-radical president of Local 1112 of the United Automobile Workers is quoted as saying (New York Times, March 19, 1975, p. 28). Women begin to involve themselves in the problems of the schools, men in those of local taxation (March, 1953). The avid integrationist begins to worry about the "blackboard jungle" of inner-city schools for his children and moves to the suburb. The blue-collar worker, an economic liberal from way back, purchases a home, resents high labor costs in the building trade, and votes "No" on a referendum on higher pay for schoolteachers. Thus family responsibilities not only increase political participation but also affect the content and direction of political attitudes and behaviors, and the direction more frequently is toward conservatism rather than radicalism. Becoming a member of an adult family group also engenders a certain amount of political contagion among family members. Wives generally vote like their husbands,[6] and in a family where one person is interested in politics and votes regularly, the other adults—especially the spouse—will also vote even though he or she may be lacking in political interest (Glaser, 1959).

Sketchy though the literature is on political socialization during middle age,[7]

---

[6]Similarity of social status also explains this.

[7]The same holds for the general socialization literature on middle age. In a symposium on the topic, Daniel J. Levinson commented, "Research on mid-life development . . . seemed to be a

the existing evidence is fairly convincing that some political attitudes become more solidified in early middle age, and that adolescents and younger adults are more susceptible to attitude influence than their elders (Campbell & Valen, 1961; Agger et al., 1961; Milbrath, 1965). It is not so clear, however, how much of this progression is due to the stabilization of personality variables in the maturation process (Becker, 1964; Foner, 1974), and how much is due to generational forces which shape a particular age cohort in its political orientations. The lack of clarity is in part due to the unwarranted equation of life cycle with generation (Schaie, 1970; Abramson, 1974; Sears, 1969; Sears & McConahy, 1973). It is, we suggest, also partly due to an unwarranted extension of the interpretation of the general evidence that adolescents are more pliable than those older than they. That extension concludes that the young/idealistic/malleable syndrome contrasts with the old/realistic/inflexible syndrome and is due to age alone. Aging, there-fore, produces predictable political attitudes. In other words, "mature individu-als are widely thought to be unteachable" (Riley et al., 1968, p. 951). The evidence in the literature, we wish to suggest, is far from conclusive that older people are unteachable and less open to new ideas than young people. Some of the more recent studies, in fact, tend in the opposite direction and demonstrate considerable attitude change—at least on welfare issues—among those over 50 (Kirkpatrick, 1974; Pedersen, 1974). Nor is there solid evidence that aging brings with it a general increase in political conservatism. There is evidence to suggest that "each cohort tends to change as it ages in line with the general trend in society" (Riley, 1972, p. 133) although the aged probably change somewhat less. This has led Grimes (1974) to disagree with the "conventional wisdom" that aging leads to conservatism. It would be our conclusion that it does so in areas which constitute great departures from previous social customs (racial integration for example) and not so in areas where self-interest is involved (economic benefits).

Abramson is another researcher who has cast doubt on the notion of the aged's politics of inflexibility. In a cohort analysis (grouping people by date of birth and, consequently, by the era in which they grew to adulthood) he has presented persuasive evidence that change in attitude is more directly related to the life situation where politics has exerted a dramatic influence—especially the depression and, more recently, the turbulent 1960s (Abramson, 1971, 1974). At the same time that he confirmed that the younger people are more able to change, he also made the important distinction that attitudes developed when the indi-vidual is young (especially when that period corresponds to one of great sociopolitical change) have the power to persevere into middle age and old age. They are, therefore, more a function of the time period in which the individual came to adulthood and much less a function of pure age which predicts consistent change of attitude—from idealistic to realistic, from participatory to nonpar-

---

relatively lonely and uncharted territory. Very little research was being done on this topic and not much has been said about it anywhere." (Paper delivered to the symposium on "Social Character and Social Change" at the University of Delaware, October 23, 1974.)

ticipatory, from liberal to conservative (Mannheim, 1952; Cutler, 1974; Carlsson & Karlsson, 1970; Ingelhart, 1971; Sigel, 1970). Thus what seems to be greater and distinctly youthful liberalism may be more the acceptance of the prevailing status quo, which is more liberal than it was 20 years ago.

Two related situations confronting aging adults, especially those in urban settings, which could shed light on the controversy have unfortunately not been studied systematically. We have in mind retirement and urban violence. In a study of California pensioners, Pinner et al. (1959) found that for the majority retirement came unexpectedly and against their will, usually because of ill health, layoffs, etc. It often was accompanied by profound lack of self-respect, feelings of uselessness, and political uninvolvement. Even retirees who previously had belonged to organizations tended to reduce such contact. If to this we now add the fact that the majority of old people live in urban rather than small town or rural settings and therefore are exposed to more contact with violence than those living in nonurban or suburban settings, we might speculate that this might have political ramifications as yet not studied: e.g., it is well known that elderly adults, especially women, are particularly likely to be victims of muggings and assaults. Fear of such attacks in turn has caused many of them to be extremely hesitant to leave their homes and apartments, thus further increasing their social and political isolation. Political candidates, e.g., are said to find it impossible to organize meetings in older neighborhoods, especially in the late afternoon or evening. But political participation apart, is it not conceivable that the persistent and perhaps exaggerated fear of attack also leads to resocialization of attitudes on human relations? For example, the fact that in the minds of the public the perpetrators of such crimes are often thought to be members of certain minority groups, may lead to greater hostility and race prejudice than was customary when the retirees were young.[8] We know of no study as yet which has directed itself toward this particular problem. We do know, however, that advocacy of law and order, the death penalty, etc. is somewhat more pronounced among those over 50 years of age than among those younger.

Even less resolved is the question *why* political involvement diminishes after 50. One theory (Cumming, 1963) argues that *disengagement* is a normal and intrinsic part of the aging process: i.e., the decreased capacity for physical activity which often accompanies aging encourages a reduction of interaction with the environment, and that reduced activity eventually becomes necessary to maintaining the older person's morale. While this pattern has most frequently been observed in social and productive activity, it is logical to extend it to political activity as well (Horn, 1970; Agnello, 1973; Cutler, 1974). Thus, the

---

[8]The *New York Times* (March 20, 1974, p. 34) comments as follows concerning growing racial and ethnic tensions among the elderly: "One byproduct of economic adversity has been the growing animosity among the poorest groups. The retirees watching pennies in Miami Beach speak often with anger about refugees from Cuba, charging them with profiteering as landlords and with favoring fellow-Cubans at food stamp offices. This is despite the fact that a huge proportion of menial jobs in restaurants and hotels are held by Cubans."

decreased political interest and efficacy and greater resistance to change generally assumed to characterize the elderly is attributed to the natural process of aging and is assumed to be valid irrespective of the historical or social circumstances surrounding any one group of individuals (Foner, 1974; Argello, 1973).

Another explanation for the lessened involvement, especially in western industrialized nations, may be that the aged themselves consider it to be role-inappropriate to be overly assertive. They may believe that graciousness and dispensing of wisdom rather than wielding power is the proper role for Senior Citizens. This may be one reason why Neugarten (1963) found that people between the ages of 40 and 60 begin to shift from outer-world to inner-world orientations.[9] They are playing the role as they think it is expected of them. As this retreat occurs, they also begin to retreat from politics (Milbrath, 1965; Campbell et al., 1960; Kuroda, 1958; Berelson, et al., 1954; Cottrell, 1966; Crittenden, 1962) although voter turnout remains stable (Riley, 1968).

Riley et al. (1969) summarize the conclusion of this simple-aging or disengagement model: "The weight of evidence suggests that whether or not older people actively desire to withdraw, there may be a process of constriction, of diminished orientation toward achievement and involvement, that sets in with old age" (p. 957). It is a moot question, however, whether this gradual withdrawal or abdication from an active political role is inevitable or merely elderly people's response to society's refusal to assign to them socially and politically useful roles. Whereas the role of Elder Statesman may have become institutionalized in the United States—in fact, most political leaders in the United States are over 50—we have not attempted similarly to institutionalize the political role of Elder Citizen. Society in turn responds to the elderly's political withdrawal by showing them less concern and often neglecting some of their basic needs (such as health, housing, and safety). This neglect then contributes to the elderly's sense of powerlessness which rises dramatically in old age (Agnello, 1973). A vicious cycle then is set in motion; feeling powerless they give up trying to influence government and eventually lose interest in it. Glenn and Grimes (1968) question this interpretation and see no drop in political interest, quite the contrary. They attribute lower interest and involvement—where present—to the older group's lower educational status. They thus alert us to the pitfalls inherent in generational comparisons when two or more generations differ markedly in politically relevant characteristics.

The literature we have reviewed so far offers no definitive proof for either of the three models of adult socialization. The best and most conclusive evidence for one of them comes from the literature on party identification. This tends to offer support for the persistence-from-childhood model. Young voters, once they adopt a party identification, tend to stick with it and with increasing age become

---

[9]Neugarten's recent studies of the 55–75 age group suggest a reversal of this trend, with this group—in part because of high education levels—being politically active. (See her "Age Groups in American Society and the Rise of the Young-Old," *Annals of Political and Social Sciences,* September 1974, pp. 187–198.)

thoroughly entrenched in their original party identification (Campbell & Valen, 1961; Milbrath, 1956). People over 60 may vote less and participate less in other political affairs than they did when they were young but they are not likely to change parties. What constitutes the most conclusive proof for the persistence-beyond-childhood socialization model, however, is that this party identification in overwhelming proportions is the very identification learned in the parental home (Maccoby et al., 1954; Hyman, 1959; Jennings & Niemi, 1974). There is little to dissuade us from the conviction that early party identification, in spite of increases in ticket splitting and identification as "independents," is not among the most enduring political orientations studied so far.

Saying this is not to be equated with an assertion that party identification is among man's most important political orientations. The point has been made before but might be worth reiterating: viz., party identification may be, at least in the American context, a rather meaningless test of political socialization. Given the fact that party identification requires so little of most Americans—no dues, no activities, no attendance at meetings—and also given the fact that our parties are ideologically not very far apart—it is conceivable that identifying oneself as a Democrat or Republican has rather little meaning and that orientations on economic or racial matters have far more significance for individuals and more importance for the political system. Maybe we have studied party identification so much and attached so much importance to it simply because it was so easy to study.

Be that as it may, partisan attachments seem to persist into adulthood, and this is especially so if the early pattern was one where a positive *bias* for a specific party was steadily supported by consistent *positive* orientations from family and peers who were in *agreement* with the early position (Zajonc, 1968; Sears & Whitney, 1973; Blanchard & Price, 1971). Modifying this molded character of attitude development is the common adult acceptance and incorporation of the virtue of "independent" decision making. But a closer examination of adult claims to objective and independent partisan choices may reveal them to be a composite of early, reinforced, and socially acceptable decisions (Lane, 1962). Substantively, then, partisan orientations appear to be the most firmly entrenched of adult views. Party identification itself is the most widely documented persevering orientation (Converse, 1964; Sears, 1969; Jennings & Niemi, 1968; Hess & Torney, 1967). Although the claim that "a man is born into his political party just as he is born into probable membership in the church of his parents" (West, 1945) is certainly in need of some modification, it is true that strong partisan attachments—including those for the party's candidates—seem to persist through time.[10] Equally conclusive is the evidence which demonstrates that political

---

[10]David Sears, in a recent review (1969) of the literature, takes issue with this interpretation and writes:

On the basis of the evidence... late adolescents and young adults would seem to enter the electorate with relatively few family-based political predispositions. At that age, the number

participation and interest follow an age-related pattern. Participation is low in youth, reaches a peak in middle age, and drops thereafter. This is not to say that the question of when, if, and how much a person's participation and political interest falls off with the onset of old age has been resolved.

What, then, can we conclude about the socializing effect of biological maturation and concomitant change in social roles? Only two observations can be made with any amount of certainty: (1) Except in the area of partisan attachment, neither of the three models offers superior explanations for the political socialization occurring with maturation. (2) With respect to the socialization occurring after middle age, we can only conclude that research on the impact of aging on political orientations has not focused explicitly on the aged themselves. Somehow they seem far less interesting to the scholar than the preschooler or highschooler, and our knowledge about older adults' political socialization and resocialization therefore is quite incomplete. This is all the more regrettable inasmuch as those over 50—in fact, even those over 65—will soon become one of the largest single age groups in the United States.[11]

OCCUPATION

Despite talk of the cybernetic society, the work an individual does remains the largest single focus of his life and, partially in consequence of that fact, plays a large role in extending occupational habits to the political sphere (Kornhauser, 1965; Kohn, 1969; Garson, 1972; Rothschild, 1972).

Perhaps no other way so defines a person in our society as the type of work he does for a living. Work shapes his *outlook* (his beliefs and ideologies), his *habits and life style,* his *status* in society, and—sadly enough—often his appreciation of himself.

> In modernized societies, occupation represents a central place in life organization for a vast majority of adult males and a substantial minority of adult females. In temporal terms, occupation is challenged only by the family as the major determinant and locus of behavior.... In view of this overarching significance of occupation in the life of modern man... and woman, it is surprising that occupational socialization appears not to have excited scholarly interest proportional to its importance (Moore, 1969, p. 861).

Childhood and adolescence can offer anticipatory socialization for some aspects of the world of work but can offer no such preparation for others: e.g.,

---

who do not clearly share even a party preference with their parents is almost as great as the number who do, and on more esoteric matters the continuity is even slighter. This would suggest a relative openness of mind, though latent predispositions might exist which later would come to full strength (p. 387).

[11]Nineteen hundred seventy-five, according to U.S. Census figures, is the first year in our history that the average American family has dropped below 3 people, i.e., we are no longer at the point where we are replenishing our population, let alone increasing it. The proportion of people over 65 years of age has been variously estimated as between 10% and 12%.

Miller and Swanson (1958) found that the type of business setting in which a father worked (entrepreneurial versus bureaucratic) affected their child-rearing styles. These differences in turn conditioned offsprings to differential responses to authority relationships likely to be encountered in the work world. Similarly, the public schools' emphasis on punctuality, time consciousness, and scheduling, as well as the training in certain intellectual tasks, such as reading and arithmetic, all are preparations for employment in the modern economy.

Professional schools are another source of anticipatory socialization. Teachers' colleges are found to train for respect for political authority and established authority to a greater extent than do liberal arts colleges (Ziegler, 1966). Other professional schools, such as law and medicine, also indoctrinate their students. The young man or woman who enters law or medical school bent on helping the poor often graduates with views on health and law-related matters as conservative and establishment-oriented as those of his profession (Becker et al. 1961). In this limited sense then public schools and professional schools contribute to anticipatory political socialization.

Narrowly speaking, the way a man or woman makes a living is not a political act (unless they choose to make politics their profession) and might therefore seem to fall outside the topic of political socialization. In actuality, however, there is probably no other phase in a person's life of the same political impact— or potential impact—as his work situation. Because work defines status—at least in modern capitalist societies—it is closely related to political power and to the distribution of political goods and services. In addition, the conditions under which work is performed and the rewards received are major sources of political socialization: e.g., much of modern man's real or presumed political alienation has been atrributed to the alienation and dehumanization of industrial work (Bell, 1956; Marcuse, 1964; Lipset, 1970). Finally, certain occupations, for a variety of reasons, are associated with specific political or at least sociopolitical belief systems. All of these aspects of work, therefore, contribute to adult political socialization. For that reason we shall, in our discussion of occupation and political socialization, look at work from these three different perspectives: the socializing effect of the workplace itself; the extent to which certain occupations give rise to or are associated with specific political beliefs, and the socializing effect of occupational status.

THE WORKPLACE AS POLITICAL SOCIALIZER

THE FACTORY AS MODERNIZER

In perhaps the most basic political sense, the workplace can act as an initial and comprehensive introduction to modern politics. Alex Inkeles and David Smith, in examining the rapid modernization of some individuals in less developed regions, give major credit to the modern factory:

We conclude that the factory is unmistakably a school in modernity. In its own right, the organizational experience it provides serves consistently to change men in ways which qualify them as more modern in attitude, value, and behavior (Inkeles & Smith, 1974, p. 174).

Among the attitudes developed in the factory are respect for efficacy, readiness for innovation, "openness to systematic change," planning, and time consciousness. Each of these runs counter to some of the more traditional political environments, especially those in rural communities of underdeveloped countries. Lerner's earlier pioneering study (1958) of migration of hinterland peoples into the cities of the Middle East and into the changed occupational as well as social climates presented a similar picture of the process. Subsequent studies of peasant socialization in similar areas have borne out the particularly modernizing role which the urban workplace plays in bringing the individual into abrupt contact with elementary politics of the system (Frey, 1969). Socialization for modernity has powerful political implications because " . . . modern political and economic institutions alike make certain general demands on the people who work within them. They require . . . greater readiness to adapt to changes . . . indeed a propensity to be an innovator; more tolerance of impersonality, of impartiality, and of differences. . . . Neither type of institution has much tolerance for fatalism or passivity. . . ." (Inkeles and Smith, 1974, p. 4).

Whereas Inkeles and Smith see the factory mostly as a beneficial influence on formerly backward or nonmodern people, much of the current literature points to the factory as a prime source of political and psychological alientation. The noise of the assembly line, the monotony of the task, the insecurity of the job, and the impersonality of the organizational structure are related to political apathy or alienation and radicalism (Hampden-Turner, 1970; Rothschild, 1972; Seeman, 1966; Bell, 1968). This phenomenon seems to be especially pronounced among younger workers in heavy industry. Whereas older workers learned to ignore noise and monotony for the reward of having a relatively secure position with increasing wages, younger workers who are better educated and therefore socialized into higher aspirations have shown themselves to be less concerned with job security and more with personal gratification, especially in times of full employment (Howe, 1972; Widick, 1972). Their concerns have gone beyond simple employment to more enjoyable working conditions, fringe benefits, and, in some cases, involvement in company decision making (Rothschild, 1972; Kohn, 1969; Bell, 1969). As would be expected from this combination of lesser gratitude for work itself and unmet aspirations for real changes in the work situation, the rate of cynicism and general distrust and disaffection is higher among younger workers. Differing expectations brought to the contemporary workplace by younger or older workers, or by those from differing socioeconomic and educational backgrounds, thus may be critical in shaping work-related political dispositions (Wheeler, 1966; Sexton & Sexton, 1971). Lipsetz (1970) found supportive evidence for this pattern among automobile workers in the same plant but performing different tasks: those with more highly skilled tasks and individualized jobs were generally more satisfied with the work-place and less cynical about work, authority, trade unionism, and the system in general. Similarly, Kornhauser related the type of work to more generalized contentment with the authority system within which the individual sees himself operating—those doing the most routinized work being the most alienated (Kornhauser, 1965; Kohn, 1969; Dahl, 1970).

Unrealistic demands on the employed—whether worker or manager—which leave him tense and dissatisfied with himself are another potential source for political or economic alienation. Inkeles and others (1958), in a pioneering study of émigrés from Soviet Russia, discovered that the strain of the work situation for people in managerial positions frequently served as a primary impetus for emigration even though they otherwise were not alienated from the prevailing communist ideology. In a very different setting, Neal Gross (1958) found that some school superintendents experienced severe role strain when they realized that they had to wear "three hats" simultaneously; that of local politician, that of employee of the school board, and that of a true professional. A number of studies of local police forces similarly have documented that the political and social views of policemen experience considerable resocialization as a result of daily contacts with lower-class people, the underworld, corruption, etc., greatly increasing their cynicism and occasionally making them susceptible to corruption and other antisocial behaviors (Reiss, 1971; Wilson, 1968).

Just as work itself functions as a socializing agent, so can the lack of it. Studies of the unemployed (those unable but anxious to find steady employment) have shown them to undergo profound social and political changes. Jahoda and Lazarsfeld (1933), in a prewar study of unemployed males in an Austrian textile town, documented how men who had been active, alert members of the local community with much interest in politics and union affairs became apathetic and totally apolitical as a result of prolonged periods of unemployment. Far from becoming radicalized (although most of them had been Socialists before the layoffs), they simply withdrew from all public and political life. In sum, work in itself (or the absence thereof) and the kind of work performed, as well as the cultural setting in which it takes place, can function as an important agent of political socialization.

WORK AS A SOURCE OF POLITICAL BELIEFS

To this point we have stressed what might be called incidental factors of socialization—those attitudes and values acquired in adaptation (or reaction) to the workplace itself. There are, of course, more direct ways in which occupations become agents of political socialization. Those include primarily the notion of the occupation, or its practitioners, as the carrier of specific political credos. Some occupations are more directly connected to such credos than others, and some may become "political" only when the interest of the profession is conspicuously involved. In either case, the practitioner is more likely to share certain political orientations with his fellow practitioners.

In some instances, the holding of specific political leanings is essential to operating comfortably in the occupation itself. Social work as a profession, e.g., provides a type of work which virtually demands one sociopolitical outlook and precludes others: social workers are not apt to view poverty as an indicator of having fallen from divine grace, nor are they likely to look upon it as just retribution for laziness and/or lack of intelligence.[12] In contrast to people who do in fact hold such views, they are more likely to look upon the poor as victims of natural and/or social misfortunes who are entitled to help from the collectively more prosperous—the government. While there are variations within the profession itself, the occupation as a whole is unthinkable without the philosophical assumption of society's responsibility for its poor and disabled (Toren, 1972; Richan & Mendelsohn, 1973; Sprecht, 1972; Hancock & Willmot, 1965).

For somewhat similar reasons businessmen tend to share with each other certain political and quasi-political attitudes toward regulation, the system of taxation, work incentives, government welfare programs, and other areas of political concern (Ewing, 1964; Whyte, 1956; Lewis & Stewart, 1961). Their own self-interest, e.g., dictates opposition to government limits on profits. Not unexpectedly, however, there is somewhat more variation in the beliefs of businessmen than there is among social workers. Most social workers, after all, tend to work within social agencies of one kind or another,[13] whereas businessmen can be individual entrepreneurs or employees; they can work for small businesses or large corporations. Bernstein (1953) has shown that the political views of small businessmen vary considerably from those of corporation executives and can best be described as akin to nineteenth-century laissez faire views. The outlook of corporation heads, in contrast, is considerably less inclined toward laissez-faire and unrestricted competition. Also, foreign travel is credited with having socialized businessmen to a rather internationalist outlook in contrast to those businessmen who stayed home (De Sola Pool, 1956). In addition, big businessmen have learned to become somewhat more accommodating to public opinion than the small shopkeeper. In response to such opinion, Big Business in the United States had to undergo considerable resocialization, especially among top managements (Reagan, 1963). Whereas in the nineteenth century and during the pre-Second World War period, the philosophy of many top corporation executives could aptly be characterized by Andrew Carnegie's famous slogan of "The Public Be Damned," modern management gets inculcated with the importance of civic responsibility or—at the very minimum—with the importance of a good public image. Studies illustrating the general "mind set" that accompanies business careers indicate that this new role definition not infrequently gives rise to considerable role strain (Brown, 1960; Etzioni, 1961; Bendix, 1965; Ewing,

---

[12]Not that all social workers share identical views. Different schools of social work, different denominations, and different experiences of the practitioner with his/her clientele all affect the emphasis a social worker will place on the responsibility of the poor to help themselves.

[13]It would be interesting to study whether or not social workers who go into private practice, where they render services for a fee, begin to change their political views—views closer to those, say, of the medical profession.

1964). Witness the public relations efforts of major oil companies to portray themselves as guardians of the environment—responding, no doubt, to the public's concern over protection of vital natural resources. Hence, whatever narrow version of the essentially private nature of the business occupations might have been popular 50 years ago within the business community, the new corporate outlook demands projecting an image of concern for the public welfare. More than the occupation exerting a socializing influence on its practitioners, however, this example points to the previously mentioned influence of "generationally identifiable social climate changes."

The pattern of shared beliefs is well documented for the professions as well. Reviewing the extant literature on occupational groups and sociopolitical ethos lends support to the observation that those in distinct professions appear to share a great many political orientations (Blau & Duncan, 1967; Hall, 1969; Carr-Saunders & Wilson, 1933; Lynn, 1965). The medical profession's views on governmental policy are consistent with its members' class-associated biases as well as their definition of their profession (Roback, 1974; Garceau, 1941; Friedson, 1970; Stevens, 1971; Glaser, 1970). Similar works on lawyers (Eulau & Sprague, 1964; Carlin, 1966; Marks et al., 1972) and American civil servants and foreign bureaucrats have shed light on the process of politicization by expertise (Rourke, 1969; Glaser, 1968; Thompson, 1969; Eulau & Quinley, 1970; Suleiman, 1974; Wilensky, 1964; Corson, 1966). In the same vein, the research on the orientations of other neutral, "professionally nonpolitical" groups attests to their common political belief structures. Especially insightful is the work into the politics of military establishments (Janowitz, 1960, 1964; Huntington, 1967; Finer, 1962; Gutteridge, 1963). It documents that young officers are socialized into attaching great value to the concept "maintenance of a stable order," a concept which then facilitates political intervention by the armed forces. Similarly, recent programs to professionalize local police forces include socialization for enhanced self-respect and political assertiveness. This in turn has led police forces to increased assertiveness which has found expression in unionization, demands for competitive compensation, and, of late, even strikes against the public (Reiss, 1971; Wilson, 1968; Watson & Sterling, 1969; Halpern, 1974).

Also in point is the wealth of research on scientists. The stereotype of a scientist is that of a professional with a dedication to the pursuit of scientific truth that precludes attention to the politics of his work. The evidence indicates a contrasting pattern, with the politics of funding the status quo frequently obstructing the unfettered process of inquiry which the pursuit logically implies (Price, 1965; Nelson, 1968; Wood, 1964; Ladd & Lipset, 1972; Garceau, 1941; Glaser, 1960, 1964; Kornhauser, 1962; Hagstron, 1965; Hirsch, 1968). This conflict of intrinsic career behavior and values and the operative resources for that career more often leads to a shared group characteristic of at least implicit support of existing policy in return for the wherewithal to conduct costly and elaborate research—often with at least the footnoted privilege of offering "consultative" expert advice on the policy area in question.

Public school teachers are another allegedly neutral political group. With rare exceptions, they tend toward political conservatism or at least conformism. In part, this might be explained by the very fact that one of their occupational charges is to train the young for loyalty to the existing political system. In part, it might be explained by the fact that training, especially when it is received in teachers' colleges, leads the trainees if not to outright political conservatism at least to the eschewing of controversy and political conflict (Ziegler, 1966). It is a moot question whether this tendency was present in teachers prior to their entering training for the profession and was merely reinforced during it or whether training and practice led them to it. When we raise the question in this way we are, of course, raising the complex question of self-selection, or to what extent does a person choose a job compatible with his political value system and to what extent does the job socialize him to it? This is one of the many underresearched and hence unanswered questions in the adult socialization literature (Wheeler, 1966; Prewitt, Eulau, & Zisk, 1966–1967).

Labor unions may in some instances perform for industrial workers the same socializing function that the teacher's colleges do for would-be teachers. A great deal of attention has been paid both in the press and in the voting literature to union leadership's attempts to politicize the rank and file, especially as it concerns partisan electoral behavior (Berelson et al., 1954; Campbell et al., 1963). The prewar years also have seen the establishment of political education committees in most major industrial unions. In addition to direct involvement in politics, these organizations have, as the name suggests, attempted to *educate* workers to the meaning of political phenomena and to encourage them to participate. They have done this by means of house organs, workshops, summer camps, etc. The solid support given by labor to the Democratic party beginning in the 1930s, then, was often seen as proof of the effectiveness of these educational programs. It is debatable, however, just how influential and longlasting such programs really are. Kornhauser et al. (1956), e.g., showed that workers in a UAW plant who had Republican fathers did not support Adlai Stevenson nearly to the extent as did workers from nonpolitical or Democratic families. The support George Wallace got from some union members (Crespi, 1971) also casts some doubts on the effectiveness of the program. It is quite possible that the tendency to vote Democratic is much more the outgrowth of perceived economic self-interest than of socialization by unions. The unwillingness of the rank and file to follow its leadership on such issues as civil rights (especially as it affects job discrimination), elimination of immigration quotas, and free trade (Nimmo & Ungs, 1973; Sexton & Sexton, 1971) puts in question the extent to which an intermediary organization such as a labor union can socialize its members politically if the content of the socialization runs counter to previously acquired social and political values.

The study of another work-related attitude—viz., political radicalism among industrial workers—so far has raised more questions than it has answered. Although Karl Marx confidently predicted that the industrial proletariat would form the vanguard of political radicalism, this does not seem to have materialized, or at least industrialization has had very different consequences in different countries. "An almost classic preoccupation among analysts of American society has been the failure of that society to generate a radical working class in pursuit of socialist goals" (Rosenblum, 1973, p. 1). The lack of radicalism is often attributed to the steady influx of unskilled immigrants at the very time at which American industrialization picked up its greatest momentun (Handlin, 1951; Higham, 1963). These immigrants at the turn of the century offer an instructive case history of adult socialization and nonsocialization. Such immigrants, so the argument goes, were largely of rural origin and used to even harder work and lower wages than prevailed in U.S. mills. "The immigrant derived not only from a more or less alien culture but also from mean, impoverished circumstances. Entering the American economy on its lowest rungs, he commonly began by accepting wages and enduring conditions which Americanized employees scorned" (Higham, p. 45). Besides, few immigrants intended to settle here permanently but, rather, to return to their homeland, enjoying (they hoped) the improved status which their savings could promote. "This 'instrumentalism' of the immigrant was not likely to lead to protest against industrial capitalism" (Marshall, 1964, p. 168) or to any other form of political radicalism. The disinclination toward radicalism was strongly reinforced by the very conservative—nay, authoritarian—political and social outlook many immigrants imported into the United States from their native lands. Even those immigrants who eventually chose to remain permanently in the United States or Canada rarely abandoned their conservative stance on many social issues. Wilson and Banfield (1964) have shown how this conservatism has remained stable into our time and expresses itself in greater rejection of social welfare policies, less "public-regardingness," etc., and Greeley's surveys (1971, 1974) show ethnic groups from Eastern Europe to exceed other Americans in racial hostility. Politically, they participate less than other similarly located white workers.[14]

Current patterns in Australia rather parallel the earlier American ones. Italians who had migrated to the Commonwealth decreased their political interest and participation, especially during the first 10 to 14 years. This was most noticeably so for those occupying the lowest occupational rungs. "They became, in fact, less interested in passively participating in politics than they were back in Italy" (Wilson, 1973, p. 70). Rather than becoming radicalized, they became all concerned with making a livelihood and with its attendant problems. Wilson did not notice a similar pattern of detachment among British immigrants.

This differential orientation to a new work situation offers yet another clue why industrial work politicizes and radicalizes some but not others. In addition to the very real and immediate preoccupation with making a living, continuities and discontinuities in work patterns and social arrangements may well be a contribu-

[14]More recent research, however, refutes this but was received too late for inclusion—the authors.

tory factor to radicalization. Individuals will not resocialize easily in adulthood when the process requires great departures from engrained norms and habits. Work in a Buffalo steel plant may have seemed very strange for the Polish peasant used to tilling the soil. But docility, hard work, and acceptance of authority relationships were not. These he could get used to (Thomas & Znaniecki, 1958). Organizers for radical parties and/or unions consequently made little headway with these immigrants precisely because they were too insensitive to the extent to which docility had become internalized. Perhaps it is no coincidence that whatever radicalism existed in the U.S. working class was spawned either by those accustomed to a more egalitarian and individualized industrial workplace[15] or by immigrants from urban centers (mostly Jews and Germans) who migrated to the United States with fairly well articulated visions of a more just society. In short, radicalism sprang up where discrepancies between current industrial practices and previously espoused ideologies were most pronounced. It was not necessarily or exclusively a response to "bad" working conditions and/or low wages.

This has led some students of the international labor movement to point out that working conditions in and of themselves do not socialize for radicalism or conservatism but, rather, must be examined in the light of workers' past experiences and expectations for the future. The more conservative labor movement in Denmark is frequently contrasted with the radical nature of Norwegian labor (Galenson, 1952), even though both movements are, at least nominally, Marxist. Industrialization in Denmark was more gradualist and built on previous work habits; the new workers were craftsmen with a well established tradition of trade unionism. Consequently, the "workers looked upon political action as a means of supplementing union economic power in the daily struggle for better conditions of labor, and not for achieving any social millennium through radical change" (Galenson, p. 149).

We have dwelled at considerable length on this question of working-class radicalism because we wanted to bring home the point that all socializing situations, experiences, and roles are embedded in a larger societal context with its own past and present. Fully to understand adult socialization, we need to spell out more systematically than we have done so far what these societal contexts are and when and how they "socialize" adults and when they fail to do so.

We have dwelled on the pernicious and atomizing effects that the modern workplace has on the individual.[16] While this represents the most prevalent trend in the literature, it is not a unanimous verdict. There are others who see it either as an existing positive force within the democratic construct or as a potentially

---

[15]Commons (1908) and other early historians of the labor movement documented that the few militant labor organizations founded in the United States (such as the I.W.W. and the Western Federation of Miners) had far more appeal to native Americans than to immigrants.

[16]In this context it does not matter whether the workplace is an assembly line or a Madison Avenue public relations firm. The conclusion drawn is always the same: Modern work deprives man of identity, initiative, and dignity.

fruitful source of citizen training. Toward the former viewpoint, e.g., is William Kornhauser's proposition (1965) that the associational ties—such as labor unions and trade organizations—provided by modern industry are in themselves an important bond which helps to cement the political system and enhance its stability, and also serves as an outlet for citizen grievances as well as a psychological home for those who need to feel a sense of belonging. Etzioni (1968) noted that the sense of belonging often gives rise to a new group consciousness. Thus, "working-class individuals seem to join labor unions and labor parties not because they have working-class consciousness, but they seem to develop working-class consciousness because they have joined labor unions and parties" (p. 232). In other words, the performance of the intermediate association is still another important feature of the link between workplace and political socialization and an instance of potential political learning after childhood.

One relatively recent development along these lines need brief mention here, and that is the literature on worker participation in workplace decision making. During the postwar years the workplace as a laboratory for democratic citizenship has received renewed attention. The more it became evident that large segments of the population do not and perhaps cannot participate in the political process itself, the more some people, notably sociologists and political scientists, began to look for alternate loci for participation. The workplace has often been suggested as such an alternative (Dahl, 1970; Pateman, 1975; Cole, 1921; Thompson, 1970). The main outlines of the discussion trace the virtues of mass involvement in all quasi-political organizations which would extend their values to the political system, against the traditional pattern and systemic stability apparently fostered by limited participation in both political and parapolitical settings (Bachrach, 1967; Walker, 1966; Pateman, 1970; Dahl, 1963; Berelson, 1954; Eckstein, 1967). Here the argument runs as follows: There are many areas of worklife in which the worker could be consulted and ideally should participate in decision making. If this were to take place, it might enhance not only the worker's satisfaction and productivity but would also train him in essential political skills as well as lessen his sense of alienation. It should therefore operate as a more meaningful stabilizing political force than the prevailing apathy and thereby enhance the potential for democratic political life. At the moment of this writing (1974), the British Labor Government is proposing to Parliament just such a plan for codetermination in British plants and factories. Similarly, about a year ago an American labor union sent some of its assembly line workers to Sweden to work in a factory where workers were given a voice in work determinations. All of the above writings and experiments attest to the hope some have placed in the citizenship training aspects of occupational socialization.

In spite of the emerging trend of the sixties and seventies toward a "Participatory Economy" (Vanek, 1971), the more pragmatic assessment of the state of research into this phenomenon has been that its orientation suffers from a dual bias: one which slants the reporting to delve into the most obvious concerns of industry (production levels, relative absenteeism, overtime), and one which seeks to examine those aspects of the workers' attitudes which point to short-term, correctable problems in the areas of morale and job satisfaction (Blumberg, 1969). The gap is obvious: research into the larger questions of democratic attitudes, orientations toward the system and participation within it, and similar areas has gone largely unexplored. Thus, while we can extrapolate some information about the general political attitudes of the working class from the broader literature on public opinion, we are unable to draw on really significant research into the specifically political orientations of the worker as he relates to his occupational home. More particularly, we are unable to do more than suggest how the organizational setting and the individual's response to it might be utilized to frame an investigation of the possible influence of the workplace on enduring political orientations. Reflecting on the available evidence, we can only say that it is premature to draw conclusions about the socializing effect of the workplace per se. It would seem that it is not automatic that the workplace must have either a salutary and democratizing or an alienating effect on the individual. More logically, the type of work and type of expectation the worker brings to it will help to offset, reinforce, or challenge the obvious or inherent impact of the work situation.

So far we have focused mainly on the unitary thrust with which a given job or occupation socializes an individual; we have ignored ideological inconsistencies within occupations and strains across them. Let us turn to farmers as an instance of the former. As a rule, farmers tend to be economically and politically among the more conservative segments in the United States, staunchly defending the free enterprise system and rejecting government interference. This ideology does not prevent them, however, from asking for governmental subsidies when these are to their economic advantage (Lipset, 1950; Campbell et al., 1963). Similarly, newspaper publishers who tend to be economic conservatives are civil libertarians when questions of censorship and freedom of the press are involved. Self-interest, again, is at the basis of the political inconsistencies. Newspapers are businesses and hence share the business world's economic conservatism—but to conduct their business they require freedom of expression. What one must conclude is that group interests and occupational training patterns, rather than concern for ideological niceties, account for some of the inconsistencies of political outlook within occupations.

The persuasiveness of group interests rather than that of political ideology was made famous by Lipset (1960) in his essay on working-class authoritarianism (1960) where he demonstrated that the alleged liberalism of workers was based mainly on their shared economic group interests and did not extend to other facets of the liberal philosophy, such as respect for civil liberties, unorthodoxy, etc. In general, it can be said that the more coherent and similar the interests of members of the same occupation, the greater the likelihood that they will form an interest group whose goal is to secure maximum benefits from the government, i.e., they will organize themselves for the purpose of gaining political advantages. Organization in turn tends to politicize the group—or at least its leaders—thereby further socializing them politically. Organized members of a given occupation, consequently, tend to be more politically involved and aware than their unorganized counterparts (Berelson et al., 1954; Lipset, 1960).

In sum, it seems clear that occupations are one source for adult political socialization. What we do not know is just how continuous this socialization is with values and preferences acquired in childhood. Nor do we have data to answer the question how much self-selection into an occupation, and thereby into the political value structure congenial to it, is involved. Logic would suggest that there might be an interactive effect; occupations socialize and resocialize their members but people may also choose occupations whose value patterns do not subject them to too many discontinuities with patterns acquired during childhood socialization. Only systematic research into occupational choice versus occupational socialization will be able to answer the question.

STATUS AND OCCUPATION

While the way a man or woman earns a living is not ipso facto an indication of his or her status in society, the fit between the two generally is rather close. The literature on social status—and the related one on social class and ethnicity—is perhaps the most plentiful and best documented on the topic of socialization. Most of it is well known by now and beyond the scope of this essay which, as we stated at the outset, will conccentrate on discontinuities. Several observations, however, should be made generally: (1) the higher the prestige of a given occupation, the higher the social status enjoyed by its practitioners; (2) the higher the status of individuals, the more active they are likely to be politically (Verba & Nie, 1974); (3) the more active they are politically, the greater the variety of access points to political power brokers, and the more frequently these are used (Verba & Nie, 1974); (4) the higher the status, the greater the likelihood that the occupants' political views will tend toward the conservative—with the possible exception of views on civil liberties and civil rights (Stouffer, 1955). Conversely, people in low-prestige occupations, such as unskilled laborers, migrant workers, etc., enjoy low social status, are less active in politics, have less input into and access to political decision makers, and tend to be—economically, at least—more liberal (Lipset, 1960). As a consequence, the former come to be socialized to think of the political system as responsive and just and of themselves as efficacious while the latter think of the system as indifferent and of themselves as inefficacious.

Consciousness of status is closely allied to class consciousness. Although there is a tendency in the United States for more people to classify themselves as middle class than there is in most other countries, there is even in the United States considerable class consciousness. About half the working population and their children classify themselves as belonging to the working class (Center,

1949; Sigel, 1975). Such class consciousness is then translated into voting patterns. Although there does not exist in the United States a working-class or labor party of any consequence, Alfred and others have demonstrated that much voting is clearly class based (Alfred, 1963; Lipset, 1960).[17]

SOCIAL MOBILITY

What, however, happens to the pattern of early and reinforced socialization when the individual moves into a new—and, presumably, higher—status level where some attitudes are bound to be different from those with which he or she grew up? Unfortunately, the evidence available to attempt an answer to such a question allows for different conclusions. Some research has demonstrated empirically that at least overt political behavior is frequently affected by a change in social status. Thus Barber has related social mobility to a change in voting behavior (Barber, 1970) and Lenski, among others, has shown that status inconsistency often results in an alteration of voting behavior (Lenski, 1967; Geschwender, 1970). Prothro (1958) showed that upwardly mobile people who had lived outside of the South for a period of time were more likely to vote for Eisenhower than is customary for Southerners. Saenger (1946) found upwardly mobile urban Democrats also more inclined to vote for Eisenhower than stationary ones. Saenger and Prothro interpreted this as a strain toward status consistency. Downward mobiles, by contrast, tend to cling to their original party (usually the Republican) as if it were a last vestige of status and respectability. Bettelheim and Janowitz (1950) found that downward as well as upward mobility can create great strain and that such "mobiles" (they studied veterans of the Second World War) were considerably more prone toward racial prejudice and anti-Semitism and somewhat more inclined toward political authoritarianism than higher status ex-GIs or those less upwardly mobile.

Other studies refute the theory that behavior tends to be in the direction of the class of destination rather than that of origin. In some instances controlling for education and income levels reduces the amount of variance explained by the status inconsistency to a small amount (Treiman, 1970); and in others the attitude in question—race—was basically unchanged from the early socialization pattern (Knoke, 1972). Eulau and Schneider (1956) found that working-class people who thought of themselves as middle class in spite of this classification retain political behavior patterns characteristic of their class of origin. Some people have asserted that those in the process of status change resolve any conflict between class of origin and class of destination by adopting an inter-

---

[17]Status, of course, is affected not just—and perhaps not even mainly—by occupation but, rather, is dependent on family background, ethnicity, nationality, wealth, region, and even religion. Inasmuch as many of these are givens, dating back to childhood, they are more properly discussed under the heading of childhood socialization. We have alluded to them to alert the reader that there are group statuses in addition to occupation which act as agents of political socialization.

mediate attitude—between the expected early pattern and that characteristic of the new social status (Thompson, 1971a, 1971b; Abramson, 1972). In most cases the smaller transition is relatively easy, with few dramatic changes which could be readily attributed to the distinctive influence of a change in social status (Reiss, 1961).

Assimilation of subgroups is perhaps a special instance of status mobility. Most assimilation attempts tend to be in the direction of upward mobility. Here, again, success depends not only on perceived self-interest but on the strength of the motivational drive and on the congruence in socialization patterns between the two cultures. Silver (1974), in a study of Georgian, Ukrainian, and other non-Russian Soviet citizens, noticed that the willingness to shed ethnic identification (as expressed in identifying oneself for the census as a Russian-speaking, Russian national) was affected by one's striving for high-status jobs, urbanity, and the predominance of Russians in one's environment.

Warner and Srole (1945, cited in Rosenblum, 1973), dealing with the social systems of pre-First World War ethnic groups in the United States, similarly commented:

> The Jews, Armenians, and Russians, in the act of migration "burned their bridges behind them." Arriving with the design of establishing themselves in this country permanently, they were anxious from the first to strike roots to adapt themselves to the basic demands of the American society (p. 99).

Other groups, transient or permanent, have been far less willing to become "Americanized"—possibly because the socialization discrepancies were too dramatic. In America, e.g., the persistence of certain ethnic patterns has caused some analysts to be very dubious about the reality of the American "melting pot" (Glazer & Moynihan, 1963; Parenti, 1967; Wolfinger, 1965). Today's European scene offers another excellent illustration of the barriers an alien's early socialization erects against resocialization and/or assimilation. The "foreign workers" (mostly Yugoslavs, Turks, and Spaniards) in German and Swiss industries socialize well to the very novel job situations and at times even to the mores of big city life (intermediate socialization), but they are said to be indifferent to more basic socialization into the hostland's culture.[18] The conclusion we draw from these findings is that occupation and status changes, especially when deliberately sought by the individual, will tend to encourage resocialization but that the success of it will depend on (a) the strength of the individual's motivation to change; (b) the discontinuities between old and new statuses; and (c) the rewards flowing from change. Strong personal motivation, ample rewards, and small political discontinuities should predict to successful socialization to new and adult roles.

---

[18]Thus, officials in German towns complain about the difficulty they have in inducing foreign workers to send their children to school and to convince them to burden the young with fewer adult responsibilities.

Environmental Changes

In the preceding sections we have discussed individual changes due to maturation, occupation, etc. but have implicitly assumed that the sociopolitical environment would remain relatively unchanged. What transpires, however, when the political environment undergoes changes, especially very drastic changes, which are clearly discontinuous not only with childhood socialization but with the political norms and expectations for which a person has been socialized even during adulthood? This is the question to which we shall direct ourselves in the section which follows. To answer it, we shall make a distinction between environmental changes not initiated by the individual and those initiated by him or her. We think this is an important distinction because environmental changes not willed by the individual—especially if they are of the unwelcome kind—give the individual a sense of low efficacy over his environment whereas willed changes may have exactly the opposite effect. Consequently, each type of change may have a differential socializing impact.

EVENTS AND OTHER CHANGES NOT INITIATED BY THE INDIVIDUAL

Such occurrences may function as traumatic socializers, especially if they are unanticipated or coercive, such as revolutions followed by dictatorships and the like, but even less dramatic ones can create profound dislocations if they are very discontinuous from previous patterns. An illustration of the latter is Isaacs' study of India's ex-Untouchables (1965). The official change in the treatment of the Untouchables, although beneficial to them, was for some too novel and dramatic to permit them to alter their political values and behaviors. They continued to operate as though they were still Untouchables while others—usually the younger ones—modified their behaviors. An instance to the contrary is that of Southern whites who moved north for jobs or education. In spite of contrary preparatory socialization, they became significantly less racially prejudiced and learned to adjust to Northern mores with respect to race relations (Eddy, 1964). Similar observations were made in the South after the introduction of the civil rights legislation of the 1960s. In short, the environment in and of itself can act as a political resocializer for adults, but the success of the process will be related to the magnitude of rewards for resocialization and to the extent to which norms learned in a changed environment are continuous with norms learned in childhood. The greater the rewards and/or the congruence, the more likely it seems that adult socialization will "take."

Much social change, of course, occurs gradually rather than suddenly. The more gradual it is, i.e., the more continuous with previous socialization patterns, the more readily it can be accepted. The Woman's Liberation Movement is a case in point. Many of its stands have found favor with women for many decades (equal pay for equal work). Others (women being admitted to service academies) constitute more of a departure and hence are harder to accept for women socialized 50 years ago. Reynolds and Sigel (1977) in a comparison of college-educated mothers and daughters found mothers to be generally friendly to the Woman's Movement but less willing than their daughters to endorse its more radical departures from the traditional feminine role. This finding would lead one to conclude that resocialization is most likely to take place among those who are least threatened by it. Sharp discontinuities frequently fall into the threat category.

Dramatic and/or traumatic political events are another potentially socializing force for all those cognizant of it. It is interesting to note that this effect need not be dependent on the observer's direct contact with the event. Thus, e.g., the knowledge of the German extermination camps resocialized otherwise assimilated British and American citizens of Jewish faith into support of Zionism and later on the state of Israel and—in some rare cases—immigration to Israel. Among these were some who previously had rejected the notion of a Jewish homeland, considering themselves exclusively nationals of the state of their birth. Another event of this century with dramatic resocializing impact was the Great Depression of the 1930s. V. O. Key and others have documented that this event gave rise to a basic realignment in American party identification (Key, 1961; Campbell et al., 1960). The Great Depression is credited with having changed permanently the attitude of vast segments of the American public on the role of government in the economy and to have created in the "Depression Generation" a preoccupation with economic security previously unparalleled in our history (Centers, 1949; Elder, 1974).

The "Revolution of Rising Expectations" is given similar credit for the racial violence which erupted in our cities during the 1960s. The Kerner Commission on Civil Disorders (1968) noted a sharp break in socialization continuities between elderly and middle-aged blacks, on the one hand, and younger ones, on the other. The younger ones were far less convinced that working within the American political system would eventually yield social justice for the black man. They felt far more estranged from the system and considerably more willing to entertain the idea of the need for fundamental and systemic political change—if necessary, by violence. Instead of accommodation or manipulation (the favorite political tactics of the older generation), they favored confrontation. In other words, they intended to change the political environment to meet their needs rather than remaining socialized to the environment. Among the many explanations offered for this change have been all those factors which contributed to young blacks' expectations that the American polity would treat them better than it had treated their parents. This expectation, it is asserted, had been kindled in the public schools with their rhetoric of America as the land of equal opportunity and had been reinforced by expectations raised in the armed forces and the plentiful work in the defense plants of the North. When these expectations were dashed, frustration and resocialization set in. Sears and McConahy's analysis of the reactions to the Watts riots in Los Angeles suggests that the differential reaction of blacks to the violence of that period both resulted from, and will promote even further, a sense of a new generation—the new generation of urban blacks—having shared in the common experiences of the riot period (Sears & McConahy, 1973). Some people have speculated that for the new generation in general—and not just the blacks—the war in Vietnam (Pollock, 1974) and the postwar student movement might have had a resocializing effect (Keniston, 1968), although more recent evidence (Jennings & Niemi, 1974; Sigel, 1975) casts doubt on the persistence or pervasiveness of such resocialization.

Involuntarily shared negative group experiences also have possible resocializing effects—at least, this is the explanation often given for such phenomena as the "brainwashing" of American prisoners of war during the Korean War (Schein, 1956; Segal, 1957). Such collective behavior can well be categorized as a form of group-induced resocialization. It would then follow that select groups and whole generations, as a result of shared social experiences, undergo simultaneous political resocialization to beliefs and practices inconsistent with or different from those learned in childhood. While this fact is well documented, we do not know how lasting such resocialization is. One might conjecture that resocialization to relative proximate values and behaviors—such as advocacy of peace and nonintervention—will be more lasting than resocialization which is very dissonant from earlier learned norms—hence the impermanence of the effects of brainwashing.

Personal rather than national or cataclysmic experiences can have similarly resocializing effects. Malcolm X (1964), during incarceration, embraced and eventually expanded on the black liberation movement known as Black Muslimism. This encounter turned him away from a criminal career and into becoming a fighter for civil rights. Religious conversions have resocialized others. Mahatma Gandhi's nonviolence movement has been traced to such an experience. Martin Luther's break with the Roman Catholic Church—with all its ensuing political consequences—has been attributed to a similarly intense personal experience (Erikson, 1958, 1969).

ENVIRONMENTAL CHANGES INITIATED BY THE INDIVIDUAL

Probably no other type of behavior fits that category as well as does voluntary immigration to another country. Nationality is one of the more enduring attributes of modern men, and men do not give it up lightly. Yet, from time immemorial, men have left their native land for a variety of reasons, among them the desire to escape persecution and to find a better way to make a living and, since the days of national armies, in order to escape conscription. Depending on the motives for migration, the skills and attitudes of the migrant, as well as the reception received in the host country, some of these migration-resocialization ventures have proved to be successes and others to be failures. In general, it is safe to conclude that consonance with previous socialization patterns greatly increases the chances for successful adaptation to the new environment. A case in point is the fact that immigrants from Europe and the United States to Israel find the transition easier than those from Morocco, Tunisia, Iraq, and other nonwestern cultures (Tessler & Knuth, 1974; Matras, 1965). But even for immigrants from Europe and the United States the process involved some conscious training for Israeli citizenship (Eisenstadt, 1952; Shuval, 1963; Isaacs, 1967). Few of the immigrants from western countries managed to adjust without any resocialization pains. Isaacs showed how painful it proved for many U.S. citizens who had voluntarily gone to Israel in search of their Jewish identity—some never made it and eventually returned to the United States (1967). More to the point are the adjustment difficulties emigrating Soviet Jews are experiencing because the disparities between early socialization and resocialization are even greater. After having faced innumerable difficulties, if not outright dangers, before being able to obtain an exit visa from the Soviet Union, a fair number now find themselves unable to adjust to life in Israel. The reasons are clearly political. The Soviet Jews had grown up in an autocratic and all-pervasive political society where the state managed their lives. They were unaccustomed to having to search for employment, having to retool, etc. Russian émigrés' adjustment problems in the United States also point to the difficulties entailed in this type of resocialization. In an article in a Russian-language newspaper published in New York, the editor reflects on the problems faced by people who have spent their whole lives under communism. "They are used to having their jobs, their homes, their education provided by the state and even if they know intellectually that there is no such agency (in the United States) emotionally it is hard for them to adjust" (*New York Times,* March 9, 1975, p. 45).

CONTINUITIES IN SOCIALIZATION

So far we have concentrated mainly on those forces in a person's life for which childhood did not necessarily socialize him, i.e., we have stressed possible sources for discontinuities. In choosing this emphasis, we have omitted the many forces which make for continuities in the socialization process. In this latter context we are particularly thinking of such forces as race, religion, ethnicity, and—in the American setting—party identification, as well as such internal forces as personality. Forces such as these are covered in other chapters in this handbook. Moreover, they seem less appropriate for a discussion which focuses exclusively on *adult socialization* since that term by implication conveys *internalized change* occurring during *adulthood*. The reader should bear this focus in mind lest he get the erroneous impression that discontinuity of socialization is the rule rather than the exception. It is probably the other way around. Given relative stability in the objects of political attitudes—the institutions, leadership styles, international situations—the likelihood of attitude continuity is great. New socialization, then, has to come forth mainly in response to new and exclusively adult roles and in response to societal change. In either case the persistence-from-childhood model is probably the least applicable. The generational model might best explain gradual or limited change (as in our example of the Woman's Movement), but it is less adequate than the change model to account for sudden, far-reaching changes (as the party alignment following the Great Depression).

Concluding Thoughts

SUMMARY

From the evidence cited so far it would seem clear that there are important landmarks or way stations in an adult's life which socialize him (or resocialize him) to new political orientations and action. Such socialization takes place not because man necessarily wishes to reject values and behavior patterns learned in childhood, but because these are either inadequate for adulthood or irrelevant for the functions the adult has to carry out and the roles he has to play.

Adult socialization, then, takes place when man wants to (or is forced to) learn new, different, or additional ways of thinking, feeling, and behaving politically in order to cope with the new demands on him. Many of these demands arise in conjunction with new roles he has to perform; others arise in response to environmental changes with which he has to come to terms, and yet others may stem from the desire to meet personal, internal needs and tensions. Whatever the motive, it requires a new adjustment—a new socialization—if the dissonance between man and society is to be kept at a tolerable level. The legitimate needs of either—society and man—have to be met. Herein lies the importance of adult political socialization. If only the needs of the individual are met, deviant behavior—as that of the criminal—tends to ensue. If only the needs of society are met, the self-actualization of man tends to get crushed, which in the long run has disastrous consequences for society as well.

In our review of the literature, we singled out but a few of the important new roles and environmental changes which contribute to adult socialization. We have dwelled particularly on the role of occupation as a socializing agent because of its central position in modern industrialized society. We demonstrated that occupations tend to induce similarity of political outlook among their practitioners, which we explained by the pervasiveness of professional and/or occupational self-interest. We were unable to shed light on two related and very crucial questions; viz., is this similarity primarily a function of the occupation, or are occupations chosen by people who consciously or subconsciously have similar political tendencies? Second, what are the conditions which make some occupations more successful political socializers than others? In other words, what characteristics in occupations enhance the chances for similarity and solidarity and what are counterproductive forces? So far the research on adult political socialization has avoided that question.

Another role on which we have focused in our review is the sociobiological role of the adult individual in modern society (we emphasized particularly the role of the elderly in it). We have shown that political stances change during the maturation process—from aloofness to engagement to disengagement. We noted that the literature on this phase casts doubt both on the generational and the persistence-beyond-childhood models of socialization but neither does it offer definitive confirmation for the third model of socialization. Thus we were unable to offer any clear-cut answer to the question: Does aging per se bring about changes such as political disengagement, or is it our society which forces disengagement upon the aging?

A third source for adult socialization which we reviewed was the literature on the impact of historical events and political experiences. Here we found an even greater dearth of material. We consequently had to rely on voting studies, chronologies, and other histories as well as current accounts in order to draw inferences on the impact of such events on individuals. The conclusion we reached was that some such events do indeed socialize, desocialize, and resocialize individuals. Among the events we included in this category were immigration, exile, jointly shared experiences of great deprivations and/or extremes, and societal changes of wide-ranging character. There is very little in the literature, however, of a theoretical nature which suggests what type of event when experienced by what type of individuals under what type of conditions is likely to have a permanently socializing effect. To specify these parameters and then test them is a task which still lies ahead for the scholar of adult political socialization.

The general conclusion we reached was that at the stage of this writing there does not exist a systematic body of literature on adult political socialization, and that the literature which does exist lends no overwhelming support to either of the prevailing models of adult socialization but some support to each of them. In order to lay the groundwork for a systematic body of literature on adult socialization, we think three conditions have to be met: (1) The focus of childhood and adolescent socialization research needs to undergo some modification. (2) The concept of political socialization needs considerable conceptual clarification. (3) Contextual analysis needs to become an integral part of the research.

THE NEED FOR A CHANGED FOCUS OF CHILDHOOD SOCIALIZATION

We do know that in adulthood certain political values and norms are present among some people and form the basis for their opinions and behaviors. What we do not know is whether or not these norms and behaviors are recent acquisitions, close adaptations of general childhood values to specific situations, or far-reaching modification of values acquired earlier. We lack this knowledge because childhood socialization literature has focused on different political phenomena. Thus, while we know how children feel about the President, the flag, the policeman, etc., we know relatively little about their feelings toward international cooperation, racial equality, the government's role in economic issues, and other orientations which generally form the core of investigations undertaken with adults. More important than these omissions is the fact that the childhood literature has all but ignored the acquisition of those moral and social values which serve as a foundation for adult political beliefs and behaviors: e.g., children's attitudes toward the work ethic or toward the weak or helpless probably are potentially political attitudes, in that they are connected to attitudes such as liberalism and conservatism, ideas about social welfare, and the like. Chances are that they are more important for adult politics than children's views of the U.S. President. If we want to speak about adult socialization, we need to have as benchmark knowledge about these childhood values and norms, and the intensity with which they are held. Until such a time as we acquire this knowledge, we really do not know whether the political values exhibited by adults are new ones or modified ones, i.e., the result of adult socialization, or merely a continuation of norms learned in childhood. To illustrate this point: Blumenthal et al. (1971) found that the definition of violence differed with social class. Blue-collar males so categorized the behavior of demonstrating students whereas middle-class males were more inclined to so characterize the actions of the police. From the child psychology literature (Bronfenbrenner, 1958) we know that obedience is stressed more in working-class homes whereas independence is in middle-class ones. Could this be the explanation for the above differences among adults, or must it be sought in different life experiences during adulthood? We do not know and will not know until the study of childhood socialization begins to look at values and norms related to adult politics more than has been done up to now.[19]

THE CONCEPT OF POLITICAL SOCIALIZATION

The concept has been defined variously by different scholars in the field, and there is no point in dwelling on the differences. These differences notwithstanding, all definitions have two things in common: (1) They have described socialization as a *process*—a process by which values, cognitions, and norms are learned, internalized, and used as guides to action. But (2) socialization has been studied as a *product,* not a process. That is to say, scholars have neither observed how young people come to acquire the values they profess to, nor have they tried to ascertain observationally or experimentally whether these statements really constitute values for the respondents. All we generally know is that at a given moment (in an interview or on a questionnaire) a respondent will profess to holding to a given opinion or value. Whether or not this value has indeed become

---

[19]A step in this direction, albeit for different motives, is the work by Richard Merelman who has studied children's notion of poverty, and the work of Lawrence Kohlberg who has studied their notions of morality. (See, e.g., Lawrence Kohlberg, "Development of Moral Character and Moral Ideology" in M. L. Hoffman and L. W. Hoffman (Eds.), *Review of Child Development Research,* Vol. 1 (New York: Russell Sage Foundation, 1964), pp. 383–481, and Richard M. Merelman, "The Development of Policy Thinking in Adolescence," *American Political Science Review* 65 (1971), pp. 1033–1047.

internalized and whether or not it will subsequently form the basis for action is unknown to us. Under these circumstances, it seems legitimate to ask ourselves: How do we know that we are dealing with the products of socialization and not merely with verbal statements?

If we are dealing with verbal statements pure and simple, then what have we really learned about socialization? Let us cite an example. When we hear a person in an interview agree to the statement that "all men are created equal," the agreement could constitute a rather reflexive, "top-of-the-head" socially desirable response; or it could constitute the expression of part of a person's value system which guides his outlook on a host of related problems. In the latter case his agreement springs from values which he has internalized. But unless we can be sure that opinions do constitute such internalization, are we justified in speaking of the *process* of socialization? And if we are not so justified, are we really studying anything other than verbal responses which offer few clues how they came about and what they may lead to? The question, which may seem trivial, goes to the very core of this blossoming field we so confidently label as the study of political socialization.

CONTEXTUAL ANALYSIS

Finally, we think that adult socialization—more, perhaps, than the study of childhood socialization—needs to pay attention to the social context in which it takes place. To understand the significance of a given political act we must know the meaning attached to it by a given society at a given time. To cite but two examples: Staging a sit-in in a public building a hundred years ago would have been perceived as an act of near-insurrection. It has a far less ominous meaning in the year 1975, and participants are not likely to be viewed as insurrectionists. The simple act of asking for a passport in order to live abroad for a while has a very different meaning in the Soviet Union than it does in the United States. Adults who perform it in the Soviet Union are viewed as disaffected citizens who have resisted proper political socialization whereas no such conclusion can be drawn from the act of a U.S. citizen.

Not only do we need to understand the meaning of specific political acts but we also need to know what the role expectations are for the many different political roles modern men and women are called upon to play; roles such as citizen, community member, community servant, householder, taxpayer, etc. What are the socialization objectives for each and how compatible are they with each other? The questions just raised seem obvious but although they are obvious, they have not yet been answered satisfactorily as Matilda White Riley (1969) points out so lucidly in her discussion of socialization in middle and old age:

> Under ideal conditions, the roles he learns are integral parts of the social structure, embodying widely held values, and serving economic, political, and other societal ends. Thus, his learning depends only partly upon his own contributions.... It depends also upon social contributions....

As the outcome of socialization in such an ideal model, the individual learns new or changed roles and becomes committed to them, meanwhile relinquishing any conflicting prior definitions or commitments. Such an outcome is at once useful to the society and gratifying to the individual. For society personnel has been trained to man its key roles and perform necessary functions. For the individual, successful role performance has become a personal goal, rewarded both by social approval and by his own sense of self-approval.

How closely does the actual socialization of mature adults approximate such an ideal model? The answer immediately is apparent: not very. Yet what the specific disparities are and how they arise is less obvious. (Riley et al., 1969, p. 953)

Focus on these disparities and their origins is crucial for future research if the study of adult political socialization is ever going to answer any important questions with respect to the changes which occur after childhood. The absense of such a focus explains the current status of the field with all its inconclusiveness and lack of theoretical core. It also explains why in our review we have been unable to come forth with definitive answers and had to restrict ourselves mainly to the raising of unanswered questions.

10

Political Socialization Research
as Generational Analysis:
The Cohort Approach Versus the Lineage Approach

Neal E. Cutler

Introduction

THE PURPOSE OF THIS CHAPTER IS to explore the role of *generational analysis* in the study of political socialization. As will be noted, generational analysis includes two major modes of research, lineage analysis and cohort analysis. Although political socialization research is not typically characterized as being generational in nature, in fact much of the research in this field is of the lineage generational analysis genre.

Lineage analysis focuses upon intrafamily interactions, and in a socialization context the interest is typically upon the transmission of values and attitudes from the parental generation to the filial generation. In everyday usage the term *generation* often has this lineage connotation; e.g., we speak of a "three-generation" family or a "four-generation" family to describe the presence of grandparents or great-grandparents in the family unit. Generations qua lineage strata derive from anthropological inquiry and to some extent from sociological analysis (Eisenstadt, 1956; Troll, 1970).

The second mode of generational research, *cohort analysis,* focuses on the

The research project of which this chapter is a part has been supported by Administration on Aging Grant, 93-P-57621/9. Thanks to Paul Abramson for his insightful comments on a draft of this chapter.

unending succession of birth cohorts, each of which is born and socialized in a particular historical context. Consequently, each birth cohort represents the unique intersection of history, events, and individuals; and the aggregate biography of successive birth cohorts can be quite different, especially in terms of political socialization and political orientations. Generational analysis as cohort analysis substantially derives from a combination of classical European social philosophy (Mannheim, 1928; Heberle, 1951) and contemporary demography (Ryder, 1965).

Distinctions between lineage analysis and cohort analysis are rather critical for the study of political socialization. Many political scientists accept the main theoretical justification for the empirical study of political socialization as an attempt to understand continuity and change in political systems (Almond, 1960; Easton & Dennis, 1969). To the degree that this justification is accepted, then the concentration of efforts on lineage analysis and the analysis of children and adolescents, which have been typical of political socialization research, may be misguided. The problem arises because lineage analysis comparisons between parent and child are but a special case of the comparison between young and old. But, as will be demonstrated in this chapter, cross-sectional studies which exhibit differences between young and old—or between parent and child in the case of socialization studies—cannot legitimately draw inferences concerning the younger person's political development in the direction of the older person.

Observed *age differences* in a range of human attributes from personality traits to political attitudes can be descriptively portrayed by cross-sectional studies but cannot be "explained" by data derived from such studies. The old may differ from the young at any given point in time due to maturational factors, or because they are members of different birth cohorts and were raised in differing sets of social and political circumstances. Although chronological age is ambiguous with respect to the explanation of age differences, in most political socialization inquiries children are studied in the belief that observation of different age groups will provide evidence of the direction in which political maturation takes place.

By contrast, cohort analyses typically focus upon the attitudes or behavior of successive birth cohorts of adults. Rather than hypothetically projecting patterns of possible adult orientations from evidence of early life socialization, cohort analyses observe adults who have been socialized in different periods of time. Consequently, if early life socialization does have a lasting impact, such impact should be discernible from data describing adult cohorts. Studies of voting behavior, for example, reveal patterns which suggest the emergence of generational cohorts associated with the events of the Depression and the New Deal. Those individuals who can be identified as having voted for the first time in 1932 or 1936 exhibit patterns of attitudes and partisan predispositions different from both prior and subsequent cohorts (Campbell et al., 1960).

The purpose of this chapter, therefore, is the exploration of the lineage and cohort approaches to generational analysis as they provide frameworks for interpreting empirical research in political socialization. The organization of this discussion includes the following elements. Section One will briefly consider the implications of the fact that the study of political socialization is an interdisciplinary area of research. Since much of the research in this area is concerned with human development, Section One suggests that while students of political socialization have borrowed some of the concepts and analytic tools of human development research, they have not paid equal attention to the problems that occupy the attention of developmentalists.

Section Two explores the relationships between models of political socialization and the generational concepts of lineage and cohort. The section emphasizes the inherent ambiguity of chronological age as a variable in the study of socialization and human development.

Since much of the difficulty found in the lineage approach to political socialization research is rooted in the kinds of research designs employed, Section Three evaluates selected research designs in terms of the ambiguity of age as an analytic variable. Section Three also illustrates some of the problems inherently found in the attempt to deduce propositions about human development from data generated by cross-sectional research designs.

While both the lineage approach and the cohort approach can legitimately be referred to as generational analysis, the kinds of data and the kinds of inferences which each permits concerning the permanence of differences between generations (i.e., a "generation gap") are quite different. Consequently, problems can arise when a study is designed as a generational analysis of one kind, while the conclusions refer more appropriately to the other kind of generational analysis. Section Four presents an example of this kind of problem, based upon an internationally known lineage study of political socialization.

Although most studies of political socialization which address the question of generational analysis have employed the lineage approach, the cohort approach is beginning to be used in a range of studies. Section Five, therefore, briefly reviews some of the main examples of this emerging genre of research, while Section Six considers some of the methodological issues which have begun to emerge.

In concluding this introductory statement, two qualifying remarks should be made. First, although the cohort approach and the lineage approach are presented as alternative explanations, it is not being suggested that either cohort or lineage explains all of the variance in the dependent variables of political socialization research. Cohort processes and lineage processes operate simultaneously and interactively to effect patterns of political orientations.

Second, it should be kept in mind that any evaluation of the lineage and cohort approaches suggested here is made in the particular context of that body of political socialization theory which seeks to establish the linkages between early life socialization, and change and stability in political systems. Hence, there are other kinds of research in which lineage and cohort analysis are employed, and the evaluations and criticisms discussed here may not be germane to these other contexts.

One: The Interdisciplinary Problems of Political Socialization Research

The study of socialization within the discipline of political science represents a true instance of cross-disciplinary exchange. Historians of the sociology of knowledge will record that most of the theory, conceptualization, data collection strategies, and model-testing approaches have been borrowed from other social sciences. Most of this interdisciplinary borrowing is from sociology and psychology. From psychology comes the focus on child development, on learning, and on alternative models which explain how the young child acquires varying levels of cognitive knowledge, affective preferences, and social skills. From sociology comes much of the theory concerning the microstructural environment in which the child does his learning and developing: first and foremost the parents and family, but also peers, educational environments, communication systems, etc.

Two quite interrelated problems are associated with the kind of interdisciplinary borrowing which characterizes the study of socialization within political science. First, it is often the case that we borrow only the labels and part of the conceptualization from the cognate disciplines. Typically, we do not understand or fully appreciate the subtleties and problems with which the lender discipline is struggling. Consequently, we may be unaware that we have not really borrowed answers, but unsettled questions. Yet we tend to treat these as answers since we have our own unsettled questions to worry about. Second, since we either cannot or do not follow the controversies in the other disciplines, we may be unaware of new conceptual breakthroughs and suggested solutions to the problems which we have unwarily borrowed. Although there is symmetry in being ignorant of new answers to questions of which we are also ignorant, the ultimate result is the production of logically, conceptually, or methodologically uninformed research.

Such a situation has arisen with the study of political socialization. Whatever the macrotheoretical context of the study, or the microcontext of the actual research, political socialization represents research in human development. We look at human development in terms of particular traits, characteristics, modalities, and populations which are of interest to politics; and we look at the outcome of developmental processes in terms of concepts and theories which are part of the literature of political science. Nonetheless, we are engaged in research concerning social aspects of *human development over the course of the life cycle*— and thus we should be knowledgeable of controversies and developments which characterize the study of life cycle developmental processes.

It is in this context that the present discussion explores the generational bases of political socialization research: i.e., it is our contention that *the main issues which characterize "generational analysis" in the social sciences are of fundamental importance to students of political socialization,* and political scientists can be ignorant of these issues only at great intellectual risk. In particular, studies of human development increasingly recognize that the "age" of a respondent in a survey or subject in an experiment is an ambiguous variable, and that age differences which at first blush appear to suggest patterns in a life cycle developmental sense are really evidence of quite different phenomena, if they are evidence of anything at all.

In the context of multidisciplinary aspects of political socialization, it might appear somewhat farfetched to juxtapose political socialization—which has typically focused on children, adolescents, or young adults—with social gerontology, which has typically focused on the old or the very old. Yet there is in contemporary social gerontology research a number of issues which are applicable to the study of socialization and the political system (Schaie, 1965; Bengtson & Cutler, 1976).

Students of social gerontology focus not just on old people, but on the "processes of aging." Although the processes of aging at the beginning and at the end of the life cycle are not identical, it is nonetheless the case that certain models, concepts, and methodologies may be equally useful for the study of adolescent socialization and the analysis of old-age disengagement. If chronological age is an ambiguous social indicator in the analysis of human development across the life cycle, then gerontologists and socialization researchers alike must be aware of the analytic issues through which the ambiguity is expressed.

Thus, the study of political socialization is but a specialized component of the more general study of human development. At the same time, however, there are serious controversial issues (both questions and proposed answers) in the study of human development which are seldom raised in studies of political socialization. The generational approach to questions of human development provides a vocabulary and an organizing conceptual framework in which these issues can be raised, discussed, and researched.

Two: Generational Concepts and Socialization Models

THE AMBIGUITY OF CHRONOLOGICAL AGE

An individual's chronological age describes two sets of facts about him—facts which may be labeled as "maturational facts" and "generational facts." First, the notion of maturational facts derives from a general understanding of life cycle development which implies that biophysiological development, defined in *social* terms, is important to the social scientist: i.e., if we know a person's age, we presume to know, *in general,* that the person is likely to have undergone certain life cycle experiences and not undergone others, although it is not the case that biophysiological variables are always predictive of psychological and social variables (Woodruff, 1973, 1975). Thus, a person who is 22 years of age can be generally assumed to have undergone puberty, some dating, completion of high school, perhaps some college; the same person, however, is unlikely to have undergone retirement, widowhood, grandparenthood, etc.

It is obvious to citizens and social analysts alike that sequences of developmental events are not always ordered the same way for all individuals: some graduate from high school at age 16, and thus begin their career (or their college education and later their career) earlier than most. Some individuals marry and have children at very early ages, and thus may become grandparents at age 42, an age when many of their age peers have their oldest child in junior high school. And we know that some occupations, companies, or labor unions facilitate retirement at age 55 while other individuals are working into their seventies. Despite these exceptions to the general model of life cycle development as a sequence of ordered events, chronological age does typically index stages of social maturation (Bengtson, 1973).

Second, chronological age indexes the year in which the person was born and, consequently, the general historical milieu in which he or she was raised, educated, and *socialized.* Demographers, recently followed by other social analysts, refer to individuals who are born in a particular time interval as members of the same *birth cohort.* While the details of any particular research design would dictate whether that time interval was a year, a five-year period, or a decade, the basic concept of the birth cohort remains the same (Evan, 1959; Ryder, 1965; Cutler, 1968; Hyman, 1972).

There are a number of conceptualizations from the writings of social theorists, demographers, and sociologists which note the importance of the historical milieu as a critical agency of socialization and learning (Bengtson & Cutler, 1976). The basic point of these analyses is that individuals raised in different historical contexts will have been exposed to quite different sets of cultural, social, and political events. Hence the nature of their attitudes and even the essence of the processes of their socialization can be different (Bengtson, Furlong, & Laufer, 1974; Cutler, 1975a).

Observed patterns of political attitudes, at a particular age in the life cycle, may be indicative of processes of human development or evidence of the generational impact of particular sets of events and experiences. Since chronological age is simultaneously an indicator of both the maturational facts and the generational facts, age cannot be used as an unambiguous indicator of either phenomenon (Cutler, 1974a).

But how does this problem influence the study of political socialization?

Conceptually, the distinction between generational and maturational interpretations of age differences concerns the linkage between childhood socialization and adult political orientations—a linkage which is implicitly, if not explicitly, assumed in most studies of political socialization. Both individual-level and system-level studies of political socialization typically observe children and adolescents in terms of what can be learned about adult political orientations; i.e., it is typically assumed that there is a *linkage* between the political attitudes of children and the attitudes which those same individuals are likely to hold when they become adults.

As Schonfeld (1971) notes, however, this linkage—on which much of the justification of child-based research rests—is in reality a *missing linkage*. Few studies have attempted to test the connection between childhood political responses and later life political attitudes (let alone behavior). Yet if we carefully observe individuals of particular ages in order to "guess" what they may evolve into via the processes of life cycle development, it should be recognized that the age datum that is employed to index maturational life stage simultaneously indexes the individual's location in the historical-generational flow of time and events.

This problem is exacerbated as studies of political socialization begin to accumulate and report maturational *regularities* in the manner and mode of political learning. Since studies of political responses among children and adolescents have typically not been longitudinal in nature, why should it be assumed that the differences between 10- and 15-year-olds in 1960 will be descriptive of differences between youngsters who will be 10 and 15 years of age in 1980?

The long-term generality of age-based maturational sequences of political orientations, thus, is called into question as it is recognized that chronological age is an inherently ambiguous indicator, indexing both maturational facts and generational facts. For political socialization research this is a particularly difficult problem since both generation and maturation represent plausible explanations of the genesis of political orientations. Individuals are influenced by the social and political context in which they are born and raised; and individuals undergo processes of maturation and development which can affect the way they see the world and the way they view the political system.

Yet this ambiguity of maturation and generation has even more disarming impact. Before we can worry about whether or not patterns of adolescent political aging can be generalized to future generations, we must be concerned that the evidence of adolescent development is itself accurate—even in a single historical context. Just as the differences between 20-year-old and 50-year-old adults can be due to either maturational differences or generational differences, so it might be that the differences between the 10-year-olds and the 15-year-olds observed in the same attitude survey may just as well be due to generational differences— either in the larger political environment or the more local educational environment—as due to developmental processes (Nesselroade & Baltes, 1974).

ALTERNATIVE MEANINGS OF THE GENERATION GAP

The issue of generational versus maturational interpretation can also be placed in the theoretical context concerning the assumed relationship between political socialization and sociopolitical change. While a generation gap could exist between all young people and all adults at a particular moment in history, in the 1960s the gap was often described as being between parents and their children (Bengtson, 1970). Since many studies of political socialization have focused on the attitudinal similarities and differences between parents and their children, we can profitably examine parent-child differences in terms of two conceptualizations of the generation gap.

When a journalist or a scholar refers to a generation gap, he should be quite specific as to what kind of gap is really being described. On the one hand, gaps may be identified between children and parents which, although real and large, can be described as being rooted in the inherent developmental differences between the children and the parents. Each participant in the socialization relationship has a different "developmental stake" in that relationship: while the parents want consolidation of values and perpetuation of their values through their children, the children want to express themselves, to be independent, and to experiment with new values and life styles (Bengtson & Kuypers, 1971). (For an alternative view, see the Weissberg and Joslyn chapter in this volume.) Such a family-based gap may be referred to as a *lineage gap*. While the gaps may be real and wide, if they are rooted in maturational differences they may be expected to diminish as the child matures and eventually becomes a parent himself.

While the generation gap as lineage gap is relatively transitory, the alternative meaning of generation gap signals more permanent difference. Aside from the special nature of the parent-child relationship, it should be recognized that parents and children are each members of different generational birth cohorts. Each cohort has been born in a different political context and has been raised at times when different issues, events, and ideologies were dominant. To the degree that each birth cohort is indeed different in terms of its political socialization experiences, we might see the beginnings of more permanent differences between young and old, between parent and child (Cutler, 1975a).

Defined in this way, the generation gap is a *cohort gap*. The differences between adults and youngsters, between parents and their children, are reflections of the different political themes which dominated the formative years of their political learning. The cohort gap is not necessarily a large gap; successive cohorts need not have been exposed to drastically different sets of experiences and events. Nonetheless, each cohort represents a unique intersection between man and civilization; indeed, Mannheim found the dynamics of systemic social change in the "fresh contact" between youth and society which is unique for each cohort of individuals (Mannheim, 1928). The main point is that the cohort gap, wide or small, is not rooted in the transitory developmental phases through which most individuals mature and change. Consequently, any basic differences which characterize the young and the old are, given the cohort gap model, likely to endure.

In summary, this discussion suggests that two key concepts in the study of political socialization—age and generation—are ambiguous. They are ambiguous since empirical differences in age distributions of political orientations could represent either differences in developmental life stage or differences rooted in the historical milieu of cohort membership. Similarly, the term generation gap may represent a lineage gap—maturational differences magnified by role differences in the family system—or a cohort gap—relatively permanent differences rooted in the unique interaction between a birth cohort and the historical context of its socialization.

What is important about the ambiguity of age and of generation is that it is the same ambiguity: i.e., the lineage approach and the cohort approach to generational analysis are simply special cases of the more general issues inherent in the analysis of chronological age. Consequently, researchers should recognize that since parent-child differences are also young-old differences, analysis of chronological age can not distinguish permanent schisms from temporary developmental differences. The child's orientations may reflect his status as offspring subject to maturational change, or they may reflect the enduring influence of cohort membership.

This dilemma has its counterpart at the level of the social and political system since, as ideal types, the lineage and cohort models suggest different models of social change. The maturational or lineage orientation, in suggesting that young-old differences are temporary and rooted in the processes of individual development, implies a somewhat cyclical view of society. Children may have differences with their elders and parents, but such differences can be expected to diminish as the child matures, becomes like his or her elders, and eventually assumes the role of elder, a process that may be expected to recycle through each successive biological generation.

The cohort approach suggests a more dynamic model of social and political change. Since each new birth cohort has "fresh contact" with the social system, and since the intersection between birth cohort, history, and social system is by definition unique for each cohort, the potential for substantial social change is always present. To the degree that cohort differences persist throughout the life cycle of the cohort members, the cohort model has within it the potential for substantial system change. Periodically, and perhaps unpredictably, the intersection of cohorts and events will produce a population so structured in terms of numbers and social composition as to alter the course of history.

Three: Research Designs in Political Socialization

The concepts described in the previous section are difficult to disentangle empirically due to the nature of the research designs typically employed by students of political socialization. Basically, such research employs two different designs which are germane to the issues of lineage, cohort, and developmental differences described here.

THE CROSS-SECTIONAL "DEVELOPMENTAL" DESIGN

The simplest, and perhaps most prevalent, "political socialization study" is the analysis of the political attitudes of a sample of young persons—where "young" may be from earliest elementary school through college students. The immense growth of political socialization as a field of research within political science was legitimized by the study of the political attitudes of young persons. Consequently, most if not all of the attitude scales and measurement strategies which had been developed to assess the political orientations of adults could be employed, often with little or no adaptation, to the study of youthful samples—and the result was labeled as "political socialization research." If, theoretically, a developmental linkage was assumed between the attitudes of adolescents and those of adult members of the political system, then it became imperative to identify and map the attitudes of adolescents.

While many of these studies are important descriptions of the political orientations of youth, they are not particularly useful for assessing the degree to which children learn from various agencies of socialization, or the degree to which the orientations of adults are developed during the youthful years of the life cycle. Furthermore, in many of these descriptive studies children are not specifically studied in terms of developmental patterns. Thus, such studies do not directly enter into the dialogue concerning the developmental and the cohort interpretations of observed chronological age differences.

The groundbreaking political socialization studies of the early 1960s (Hess & Easton, 1960; Easton & Hess, 1962; Greenstein, 1965), although cross-sectional in nature, were specifically designed to examine respondents of different maturational levels. Easton and Hess studied elementary school children in grades 2 through 8, while Greenstein focused in grades 4 through 8. In each case samples were drawn from the successive age or school grade intervals in the belief that these ages represented maturational or developmental gradients typical of any individual: i.e., while no single individual was actually observed from grades 4 through 8, the logic of the research design suggested that differences observed cross-sectionally would be developmentally generalizable to the individual-level process of development.

In the context of the argument presented in the previous section, however, one of the basic problems with the cross-sectional design is that developmental inferences cannot be legitimately drawn from data collected at one point in time. Just as the difference in the Republicanism of people age 30 and people age 50 may be due to cohort factors rather than maturational factors (Crittenden, 1962; Cutler, 1970a; Glenn & Hefner, 1972), so socialization researchers should recognize that differences between samples of fourth graders and eighth graders measured at a single point in time may be due to other than maturational processes.

Some might argue that although the cohort approach represents a plausible explanation of differences across the adult age span, it is not a useful explanation of childhood development. Yet while we may believe that differences between fourth graders and eighth graders are symptomatic of individual differences occurring over a four-year period of life cycle development, such belief does not substitute for appropriate research design and data analysis. In fact, one recent psychological study of personality development over a three-year period, examining changes in junior and senior high school, found that cohort differences were greater than developmental differences over the study period (Nesselroade & Baltes, 1974). Yet the authors specifically note that had the data been analyzed as if generated by a typical cross-sectional research design, the analysis would have revealed substantial individual developmental change—the opposite of the phenomenon which was in fact documented.

THE CROSS-SECTIONAL PARENT-CHILD DESIGN

While early studies of political socialization concentrated on the discovery of the child's developing imagery of politics, thereby reflecting intellectual influence of developmental psychologists (e.g., Hess & Torney, 1967), the second major thrust in political socialization research has been the assessment of the contribution of different agencies of socialization. In this context, the family has loomed as overwhelmingly important. Indeed, in the first major synthesis of political socialization findings, Hyman (1959) concluded that the family is *the* most important agency of political socialization.

There are two kinds of parent-child research designs, which might be characterized as the expensive model and the economy model. In the economy model only the adolescent is interviewed, and the attitudes of the parent are assessed by the child's report of the parent's likely response. While this approach is certainly less expensive than the direct assessment of the parental response, there are clearly problems of child ignorance or misperception of the parental political belief. Indeed, Connell (1972) comments that the reason Hyman was evidently so impressed with the prominence of the family in matters of political socialization is that most of the studies then available were based on the economy model design, with the result that the parent-child correlations were consistently high.

The more expensive, and consequently more contributory, parent-child research design is one in which the parents and the children are each surveyed, providing independent estimates of the parent's response and the child's response (Dodge & Uyeki, 1962; Jennings & Niemi, 1968, 1974; Dennis, 1964; Bengtson & Black, 1973; Renshon, 1974; Tedin, 1974). Studies of the "transmission" of values and attitudes from parents to their children, a major theme in the investigation of agencies of political socialization, virtually require independently collected parent-child information in order to determine if children really do possess the same (or similar) attitudes as their parents.

While the true parent-child study facilitates the direct comparison of the child's responses with the parent's responses, there are inferential problems in attempting to interpret the results. These interpretive problems, in turn, are embedded in the previously discussed distinctions between *lineage* and *cohort*. Since this research design is cross-sectional, there is no way to determine empirically if the observed differences between parents and their children diminish or disappear as the children grow older and assume adult roles (a "lineage gap") or if those differences remain throughout the lives of the parent and the child (a "cohort gap").

In other words, how does the analyst interpret parent-child differences and parent-child similarities? One of the serious problems is that a mixed pattern of parent-child similarities may lead to mixed criteria for interpreting the data in lineage versus cohort terms. A pair of examples of this problem may be taken from the Michigan national political socialization study. In the monograph reporting the study (Jennings & Niemi, 1974) generational (i.e., cohort) discontinuities—as contrasted with lineage or maturational differences—are deduced in one instance from parent-child *differences*, while some 20 pages later cohort discontinuities are deduced from parent-child *similarities*.

In the analysis of a Cosmopolitanism Index, the authors found that the parents were less cosmopolitan than their children, and concluded: "Unlike some of our previous measures, this one may be more vulnerable to a true generational discontinuity" (p. 268). Thus, cross-sectional parent-child differences are interpreted as a cohort gap. Twenty pages later, when parent-child differences among black families are analyzed, the authors find evidence of a cohort gap in parent-child similarities: "Greater [generational] change among blacks might mean that currently, as students, they are very similar to parents" (p. 289). Thus, in the first example cohort differences are indexed by parent-child dissimilarities, while in the second example cohort differences are indexed by the opposite kind of data, parent-child similarities. This is not to say that Jennings and Niemi do not convincingly argue their positions. The point is that cross-sectional data comparing young and old (of which parent-child comparisons are a subset) are inherently ambiguous as to the explanation of observed age differences. As our review of the Jennings and Niemi monograph observes, "While age *differences* can be identified, age *changes* cannot be thereby verified or predicted" (Cutler, 1975b).

THE INHERENT AMBIGUITY OF CROSS-SECTIONAL DESIGNS: TWO HYPOTHETICAL EXAMPLES

To clarify and emphasize the problems of employing cross-sectional research designs in political socialization research, two examples which use hypothetical data will be presented. The examples serve to emphasize the fact that chronological age simultaneously represents both maturational facts and generational facts. In many research contexts, both a maturational and a generational interpretation may be consistent with the data; consequently, the cross-sectional research design itself can do little to provide an explanatory solution.

In the first example, the hypothetical age distributions in Table 10–1 are assumed to be based on data collected in 1970. These hypothetical data represent the way in which age patterns in political orientations are typically presented, and the usual description would be: as age increases, the characteristic decreases. Description, however, is not the same as interpretation, and often the interpretation is the more important contribution of the analysis. Thus, if in Table 10–1 the characteristic was agreement with the policy of legalizing marijuana use, then the typical interpretation of the data might be: the older a person gets, the less he is likely to support the legalization of marijuana.

The problem suggested by this example is that while the description is accurate (the characteristic indeed does decrease as age increases), the interpretation implies maturational change as the cause of attitude changes. There are at least two possible fallacies in this interpretation (Riley, 1973). First, since the hypothetical data are from a single year (a poll taken in 1970), there can be no evidence of maturational change over the life cycle. Second, the groups defined in terms of their chronological age represent different birth cohorts, each of which was born and socialized in a different set of historical and political circumstances. Thus, Group A was born in 1945–1952, Group B in 1925–1944, Group C in 1905–1924, and Group D before 1905. Certainly we might expect that people socialized in the first decade of this century will have different attitudes toward the legalization of marijuana than those born after the Second World War. The issue illustrated here is that for many political variables both cohort and maturational explanations are plausible, yet the cross-sectional research design cannot distinguish between the alternative explanations.

Table 10.1. Hypothetical Age Distribution in 1970

Group	Chronological Age	Year Born	Characteristic
A	18–25	1945–1952	80%
B	26–45	1925–1944	60%
C	46–65	1905–1924	45%
D	66+	before 1905	30%

This argument can be further clarified by returning to the hypothetical data, but considering the characteristic to be the educational attainment of the individual, with the percentages describing the proportion of each age group that has "high education"—at least a completed high school education. (In fact, the hypothetical percentages given in Table 10–1 are the real approximate percentages of each age group, in 1970, that have completed at least 12 years of schooling.) In this view of the percentages, the summary description remains the same as in the marijuana example: as age increases, the characteristic decreases.

While the description is the same, the interpretation must be quite different. It would be quite difficult to argue, using the maturational interpretation, that as the person gets older his level of education decreases! For any individual, level of attained formal education cannot decrease (although, for a small number, educational attainment increases during the adult years). Clearly a cohort interpretation, suggesting differences in the historical context of early life socialization, is more valid: those cohorts born before 1905 did not have the same opportunity for educational attainment as those born after the Second World War.

The hypothetical percentage table, therefore, demonstrates that an age distribution of a characteristic does not always imply age changes produced by ontogenetic processes. While the maturational hypothesis may be appropriate for certain biological or physiological characteristics, for a variety of psychological and sociological characteristics the generational or cohort hypothesis may provide the more plausible explanation. This may be particularly true for political orientations, since attitudes toward elements of the political system typically represent the joint contribution of the individual's psychological predispositions and the "objective" nature of political affairs (Greenstein, 1969; Renshon, 1974).

The second example, illustrated by Table 10–2, contains three hypothetical cases presented by Nesselroade and Baltes (1974). In each example it is assumed that the true cohort-specific developmental changes for each of the birth cohorts are represented by the broken lines. The age gradients which would be produced by a cross-sectional analysis undertaken in 1960 are represented by the solid lines. The distortion introduced by the cross-sectional method is illustrated in general by all three examples; i.e., in each case the line demonstrating a cross-sectional portrait of the age changes fails to accurately portray the actual age gradient of any of the separate age cohorts.

In Example A let us assume that the dependent variable is a liberalism scale, and that the higher values indicate greater liberalism. The (broken) lines representing each birth cohort, each of which is measured from age 10 through 50, describe three generalizations: (1) each successive cohort (born in 1910 through 1950) is more liberal on this scale than the preceding cohort; (2) each cohort becomes more liberal as it ages; and (3) the historically more recent cohorts exhibit greater acceleration in their increased liberalism. Measured cross-sectionally in 1960, however, an entirely false curvilinear pattern is given. The cross-sectional design happens to sample the 1950 cohort at age 10, the 1940

Table 10-2. Three Hypothetical Age Gradients

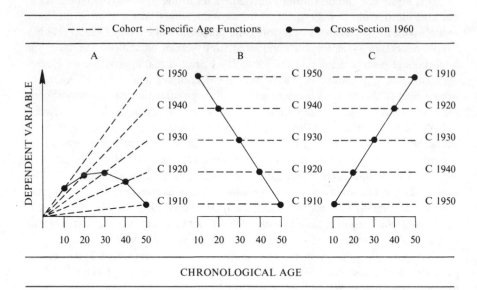

CHRONOLOGICAL AGE

Source: Nesselroade and Baltes (1974), p. 4.

cohort at age 20, the 1930 cohort at age 30, etc. Indeed, those respondents in the cross-sectional design who happen to be the 40-year-olds and the 50-year-olds are representatives of the more conservative cohorts.

Examples B and C are even more extreme illustrations of the problems of cross-sectional designs. Example B presents the unlikely situation in which each cohort exhibits absolutely no attitudinal change over the course of the life cycle, but with each of the cohorts being more liberal than the prior cohorts (with the opposite situation portrayed in Example C). Yet the cross-sectional sampling of age groups in 1960 falsely indicates a pattern in which there is progressive and linear decline in liberal attitudes across the life cycle. This distortion is clearly created by the fact that the sample of 10-year-olds is part of the most liberal cohort (1950), while the sample of 50-year-olds is part of the most conservative cohort. Hence, the cross-sectional pattern suggests a relationship between maturation and political beliefs which is not characteristic of any of the cohorts whose political beliefs have been sampled. As in the example of Table 10–1, these age gradients demonstrate the virtual impossibility of distinguishing cohort and maturational explanations through the use of cross-sectional data.

Four: The Noncorrespondence of Lineage and Cohort Groups

An additional set of research problems is suggested by the following pair of observations: (1) the concept of generation in the several social sciences can refer both to lineage and to cohort; (2) research designs which attempt to elucidate variations correlated with either one of these two concepts do not at the same time necessarily provide information relevant to the other. The problem arises when a lineage-based research design uncovers evidence of a generation gap, but the research findings are communicated in a way which implies a cohort gap. In a sample of two-generation families, for example, all of the parents constitute "a generation" and all of the children represent the "other generation"—*in lineage terms*. Yet it is not necessarily the case that the sample of parents, which is homogeneous with respect to the lineage-generation attribute, is also homogeneous with respect to the cohort-generation attribute. Indeed, a visit to the fathers' waiting room in a maternity hospital or to a fifth-grade PTA meeting—which suggests that the children in each case constitute a homogeneous birth cohort—would demonstrate that the parental (lineage) generation is not composed of a single generational cohort.

In this section we will attempt to illustrate empirically this noncorrespondence of lineage and cohort generational groups through a brief analysis of the parent sample of the Michigan socialization study. This study is an outstanding example of true generational analysis in that it is concerned with both lineage and cohort variations. Consistent with much political socialization research, Jennings and Niemi originally focused upon a lineage analysis of the transmission of political orientations from parent to child, based upon independent interviews of parents and their children collected in 1965 (Jennings & Niemi, 1974). The study was extended to a modified cohort design in that the same parents and children were reinterviewed in 1973 (Jennings & Niemi, 1975). What is important to keep in mind, however, is that through the second wave of interviews two different kinds of generational analysis—lineage and cohort—become possible. Furthermore, while the parent and child generation groups retain their homogeneity with respect to the lineage generation attribute, and while the sample of 1965 high school seniors remains homogeneous with respect to its birth cohort attribute, it is not necessarily the case that the parental lineage generation is homogeneous with respect to cohort. In short, we have a situation in which two groups are clearly identifiable with respect to one generational attribute but not so clearly identifiable with respect to the second generational attribute. To illustrate this proposition, our analysis considers the age distribution of the 1965 sample of parents.

In the national sample of 1,909 parents for whom age data were available, the average parent was born about 1917 (median = 1919, mean = 1917). The standard deviation of this age distribution is 6.8 years, so that theoretically a calendar range of approximately 14 years is required to encompass the 68.3% of parents who represent the range of one standard deviation above and one standard deviation below the mean year of birth. As an illustration of the relative lack of cohort homogeneity among those who are of the same lineage generation in this sample, we may consider the likely generational, historical, and consequent life experiences of parents found at the edges of this plus/minus one standard deviation group. Empirically, 67.3% of the sample was identified between the birth years 1912 and 1924. Of course, our interest is not in the attitudinal or behavioral characteristics of parents specifically born in these years; rather, our intent is to illustrate the range of cohort differences represented by the middle 68% of the parent sample.

Table 10–3 indicates the year in which each of these two parental cohorts arrived at a particular age in their life cycle. The ages chosen are arbitrary, but they illustrate important stages in the development—especially the political socialization—of these parents as adolescents and young adults. For each group, three ages or life stages are portrayed: age 10—an age when, according to some analysts, much of basic political socialization has taken place; age 18—the end of the formal school process for many people, and the age at which their children were interviewed in 1965; and age 25—an age which generally represents the early stages of adulthood, involvement in the formal political system, as well as the beginnings of family and occupation.

These two illustrative birth cohorts were raised in and have directly experienced quite different sets of events. The older cohort, born in 1912, was raised just after the First World War. The country came to celebrate the Roaring Twenties, and these children were exposed to what have been looked back upon as the relatively happy times between two world wars. The 1924 cohort, by contrast, wound up their first decade of life in the midst of the Great Depression. Through the eyes and experiences of their family, they may have experienced rather traumatic changes in day-to-day resources and general life style. In foreign policy, the Peace of Versailles was unraveling, and the United States was watching the political development of National Socialism in Germany.

The 1912 cohort arrived at age 18 at the beginning of the Depression. Immediate plans for college, for marriage, for particular occupations may have become precipitously frustrated. What may have been a lifetime of planning by the family and the adolescent was dramatically changed, and the future for these individuals was probably quite uncertain. By contrast, the 1924 cohort arrived at

Table 10.3.   Life-Stage Calendars for Selected Parent Respondents[a]

YEAR BORN	AGE 10	AGE 18	AGE 25
1912	1922	1930	1937
1924	1934	1942	1949

Source.   The data were made available by the Inter-university Consortium for Political and Social Research through the USC Political and Social Data Laboratory. The data were originally collected by the Center for Political Studies, Institute for Social Research, University of Michigan.
[a]Parents born between 1912–1924 inclusive represent 67.3% of the 1,909 respondents in the 1965 national sample of the Michigan Socialization Study.

age 18 with a substantially different set of political, social, and economic experiences. While their early years found them confronting the Depression, by age 18, in 1942, the country had seen a new war in Europe and in Asia into which, after a somewhat divisive domestic debate, the United States was drawn by the event of Pearl Harbor. Military service and economic rationing began to be common experiences.

Finally, looking at the important developmental period between age 18 and age 25 for these two groups, we again see quite different sets of politically salient events. The 1912 cohort spent this period totally in the Depression years. Economic hardship was exacerbated by the frustrations in the starting of occupational and family careers. Additionally, the Depression ended as war preparedness began. By contrast, the 1924 cohort ended the 18–25 age period in the early years of the postwar economic boom. Victories were seen in both the European and Asian theatres of war, although the latter victory marked the beginning of the nuclear age. With demobilization families were reunited although, for many, families were not as whole as they had been.

It is clear, consequently, that this sample of parents does not represent a single generational cohort; even these "modal" parents have undergone substantially different social, economic, and political experiences. Considering the parents whose year of birth is beyond plus/minus one standard deviation in the distribution, we find individuals whose adolescent and early adult life experiences are even more dissimilar.

It may be concluded, then, that the two "meanings" implied by the concept of generations do not operationally define the same populations. All of the almost 2,000 parents in the Michigan socialization study are parents of high school seniors in 1965 and are thus homogeneous with respect to the lineage conception of generations. When these parents are analyzed in terms of cohort, however, they are not found to represent a homogeneous group. While 68% of the parents were born between the years 1912 and 1924, some were born as early as 1898 while the youngest natural parent of a 1965 high school senior may have been born as recently as 1930.

Five: A Brief Overview of Generational Studies

The salience of the generation cohort concept in political analysis may be illustrated through a review of the small but growing number of relevant studies which have been reported in the literature. As mentioned previously, the lineage approach to generations is well represented in contemporary research by parent-child socialization studies. A less expansive research tradition characterizes the cohort approach to generational analysis. As this overview illustrates, however, varieties of cohort analysis are becoming applied to an expanding set of research questions, incorporating increasingly sophisticated methodological advances.

The main components of our review will focus upon several recurring issues in political research that have been investigated through cohort analysis. These areas include patterns of political party identification, changes in the independence and partisanship of the American public, political alienation, political tolerance, and attitudes toward domestic policy. Section Six will then briefly review some of the emerging methodological issues discussed by the increasing number of cohort analysts. In concluding this chapter, we will note the way in which a variant of generational analysis has been applied to cohorts of teenagers by a team of developmental psychologists. Their studies demonstrate that cohort rather than maturational differences can be identified in samples of respondents which are as close in age as six months.

POLITICAL PARTY IDENTIFICATION

Campbell and his colleagues in *The American Voter* (1960) argued that the Depression and New Deal period had a dramatic impact on those citizens who were new voters in the 1930s such that those events crystallized what could be called a "generational effect." Using survey data collected in 1952 and 1956, they noted that those respondents who had initially voted in 1932 and 1936 were more Democratic in their party identification two decades later than would be predicted on the basis of such factors as their social class and 20 years of aging. The issue of aging is an important one since, on the basis of some gerontological and psychological studies (Cutler, 1977), it has been assumed that individuals become more conservative as they age. In this context Campbell and his colleagues noted that even among those young first-time voters who were swept up in the Democratic tides of 1932 and 1936, a substantial proportion should "normally" move to Republican party identifications as they aged. That they did not so change, these authors argued, was evidence of a generational effect.

A study employing Gallup survey data over the period 1946–1958 tested the aging-conservatism hypothesis, and operationalized conservatism as identification with the Republican party (Crittenden, 1962). In each of four cross-sectional surveys, it was found that the older respondents were more Republican in party identification than were the younger respondents. Since the pattern was similarly found in each of the surveys, it was concluded that the processes of aging impelled individuals to change, and to change in the direction of Republican party identification.

Seven years later a reanalysis of the published Crittenden data using a formal cohort analysis model concluded that the data provided no evidence of a conversion to Republican party identification as a concomitant of the aging process (Cutler, 1970a). Furthermore, the later study found that none of the birth cohorts which could be traced over the 1946–1958 period were characterized by the monotonic increase in Republicanism hypothesized by the earlier study.[1]

[1]Various perspectives on the Crittenden-Cutler cohort controversy are included in Hyman (1972), Riley et al. (1972), and Spitzer (1973). The two original articles, including rejoinders and comments in which neither author changed his mind, are reprinted in Kirkpatrick (1976).

Fortunately, three years later a new study was published which confronted the very same question. Where Cutler had only reanalyzed the published Crittenden data, Glenn and Hefner (1972) brought to the issue a more expansive data base and a more finely calibrated application of cohort analysis than was the case in the earlier studies. Like Crittenden, Glenn and Hefner descriptively noted that the older age groups were more heavily populated by Republican identifiers than were the younger age groups. Their analysis, however, focused upon a cohort analysis of the data in order to see if old-age Republicanism was to be explained by generational factors or by a process of old-age partisan conversion. Glenn and Hefner concluded the former:

> This study should rather conclusively lay to rest the once prevalent belief that the aging process has been an important influence for Republicanism in the United States. Aging cohorts *have* become more Republican in a relative sense as a result of a secular trend away from Republicanism in the total population. However, this trend has grown to a large extent out of the dying off of the older, more Republican cohorts . . . and therefore the failure of aging cohorts to conform to it in no sense implies that aging exerts influence toward Republicanism (p. 47).

PARTISANSHIP VERSUS INDEPENDENCE

In recent years political scientists and professional politicians alike have noted the growing disenchantment on the part of the American electorate with the two major political parties. One of the most notable indexes of this apparent trend is the marked number of respondents in various polls, surveys, and studies who declare themselves to be "Independent" rather than either Democratic or Republican. When explanations of trends in increasing independence are considered, the generational concept is particularly important.

As most analysts recognize, behavioral trends may be the consequence of one or more of several interrelated factors: e.g., the whole society may be responding to particular events or crises—i.e., a "period" effect. Or, the weak partisanship which may be "typical" of new voters may have temporarily affected the electorate as the numerically large postwar baby boom generation came of age politically. Or, a process of demographic change may be taking place in response to recent political events; hence, each incoming cohort may be more independent than the last while at the same time the older and more partisan generations are dying out of the political system.

Two studies have specifically focused upon a generational analysis of trends in independence in the United States. Applying cohort techniques to a large data base, Glenn (1972) successively eliminated each of a number of plausible explanations for the increasing independence of the 1960s: e.g., he demonstrated that the societal increase in independence was not the statistical result of the entrance into the political system of large numbers of independent-leaning young voters of the postwar baby boom cohort.

Examination of the cohort trends in total partisanship patterns (Republicans,

Democrats, and Independents) allowed Glenn to examine the hypothesis that the Democratic majorities begun in the New Deal era are unraveling and regrouping into a Republican majority. The cohort analysis demonstrated that the growth of the Independents is at the expense of both major political parties, and is not simply a transition phase from Democratic to Republican majorities. Similarly, separate analyses of Southern and non-Southern respondents demonstrated that the national trend in independence is not simply a result of Southern defections from the Democratic party.

Finally, by juxtaposing the cohort analysis of independence patterns with analyses of attitudes reflecting political apathy and political radicalism, Glenn eliminated two additional hypotheses: (1) that independence typically reflects an apathetic attitude toward politics and that growing independence is consequently a reflection of growing societal political apathy; and (2) that independence is a reflection of the disaffection with both parties by the growing political left which was particularly radicalized by the 1968 presidential conventions. Glenn's analysis showed that the Independents in recent years are no more apathetic than are partisans, nor are Independents more or less "leftist" (by self-identification measures) than are partisans.

Having eliminated several hypotheses, the one explanation which Glenn's data did support was a generational one. From 1945 through 1957, the youngest 10-year age group at each sampling point exhibited a relatively constant proportion of independents (about 25%). The 1957–1971 period, however, witnessed an abrupt acceleration in the independence of each new cohort entering the electorate. Furthermore, statistical tests demonstrated that the most dominant factor in the increasing societal independence was the addition of young adults to the electorate whose *level* of independence was higher than historically prior cohorts.

At this point, however, Glenn's analysis stopped since the data could not provide a basis as to *why* the incoming generational cohorts were substantially more independent than their predecessors. Glenn's proposed explanation rests on what might be called the growing ideological impurity of the two major parties: the Depression–New Deal period brought to each party a section of the electorate generally defined in terms of wealth and status, and politically tied to its party mainly in terms of socioeconomic issues. The politics of the 1960s, Glenn suggests, produced a set of political issues in which the parties' programs conflicted with the general feelings of its own socioeconomically defined constituency. Hence, Glenn suggests that "careful empirical investigation of the interrelations, and trends in the interrelations, among class, the various dimensions of liberalism-conservatism, and party support could probably throw much light on the changing character of American politics" (p. 512).

It is precisely such a thesis which is carefully investigated in a series of generational cohort analyses recently published by Abramson (1974, 1975, 1976). Underlying much of Abramson's research is the hypothesis that the locus of generational change in patterns of American partisanship is a basic change in the relationship between partisanship and social class. The argument is cast in terms of differing patterns of generational political socialization:

The young may have had formative experiences different from those of their elders. Whereas their elders may have had formative experiences that contributed to a high relationship between social class and partisan choice, young voters may have had experiences that contributed to a low relationship (Abramson, 1974, p. 99).

Using the cohort analysis framework, Abramson examines cohort patterns in the correlation of partisan presidential voting with standardized occupation-based measures of social class. Contrary to hypotheses which argue that the connections between social class and partisanship are weak for young adults but "naturally" become stronger as the adult increasingly participates in society and politics, the analysis demonstrates that among the postwar cohorts the class-politics correlations are low even as the cohorts age beyond their young adult years (Abramson, 1974, pp. 95–96).

The dramatic postwar reduction of the class-politics correlation—signifying that many working-class persons do not prefer the Democratic party and that many middle-class persons do not prefer the Republican party—is thus related to the national trends in increased independence. The weakening of the class-politics relationship does not necessarily result in "conversions" to the opposite party; the response is also a withdrawal of regularized identification from either party. Thus, Abramson finds that the overall levels of partisanship among the more recent historical cohorts is substantially less than historically prior cohorts: "This analysis strongly suggests that the relatively weak party identification among the young results from the fundamental differences between their socialization and that of their elders. It provides virtually no evidence that this low level of identification is only temporary" (Abramson, 1976, p. 474).[2]

POLITICAL ALIENATION

Recent studies of political alienation have variously attributed trends in alienation to such factors as location in the life cycle (e.g., youthful alienation or the

---

[2]That increases in independence are indeed generational rather than maturational in origin is supported by the Michigan socialization panel study mentioned earlier. While the maturational hypothesis would predict increased partisanship in the "children" sample, from age 18 to age 26, such increase was not found. On the contrary,

the change in the partisan distribution of the filial generation between 1965 and 1973 is startling. The proportion of Independents, already very high in 1965, rose another 12% to include almost half of the sample. At the same time, the proportion of strong identifiers was cut nearly in half. Such an increase in the proportion of Independents at a time in the life cycle when we would ordinarily have expected the beginning of a long term decline provides a compelling argument for a generation effects interpretation (Jennings & Niemi, 1975, p. 1325).

A study using a multiple regression approach to cohort analysis also supports the general conclusion that there are strong generational net effects in recent patterns of increasing societal Independence (Knoke & Hout, 1974).

consequences of old age), generational units whose socialization reflects an enduring alienation toward societal and political institutions, and general social trends not isolated in any segment of society.[3] Consequently, cohort analysis can make a contribution to this area of inquiry in that a single set of data can be examined for evidence of each of these three competing explanations. Interestingly, the two studies which can be noted in this context employed the same basic data: the set of three political alienation items included in the presidential election surveys conducted by the Center for Political Studies at the University of Michigan.[4]

A cohort analysis of the three political alienation items, at eight-year intervals over the 1952–1968 period, was reported by Cutler and Bengtson (1974). This analysis concluded that neither aging factors nor generational factors appeared to account for the trends in political alienation. Indeed, for all age groups and cohorts, and for each of the three indicators, the pattern was virtually identical: (1) alienation substantially decreased between 1952 and 1960, (2) it increased between 1960 and 1968, and (3) in virtually every cohort and age group the level of alienation in 1968 was higher than it was in 1952. Separate cohort analyses for high and low education groups revealed the same patterns as was found for the whole samples. Thus, it was concluded that a period effect explanation best accounted for the observed trends.

A second study of political alienation employed the same three questionnaire items, using all of the quadrennial presidential election year surveys from 1952 through 1968. Unlike the Cutler-Bengtson study, House and Mason (1975) did not employ a formal cohort analysis by which the political alienation of different cohorts and age groups could be traced over the study period. Rather, the researchers employed a form of multiple regression analysis, the task of which is the estimation of the net variance explained by each of several variables when the others are held constant.

House and Mason concluded that the trends in political alienation over the 1952 to 1968 period reflected aggregate "period effect" fluctuations in the population as a whole. The multivariate analyses demonstrated that the trends were neither the simple reflection nor the aggregation of changes in any identifiable age, cohort, region, sex, education, or income group within the population. Thus, although this analysis used an expanded data set and different analytical tools than the cohort analysis employed by Cutler and Bengtson, the two studies yielded virtually identical conclusions.

These applications of generational analysis to trends in political alienation

---

[3]Age-oriented alienation explanations are suggested by Cumming and Henry (1961), Freidenberg (1969), Whittaker and Watts (1969), Agnello (1973), and Bengtson (1973). Generational explanations are suggested by Flacks (1967) and Bengtson (1970). Period effects explanations of political alienation are suggested by Scammon and Wattenberg (1970) and House and Mason (1975).

[4]"I don't think public officials care much what people like me think." "People like me don't have any say about what the government does." "Sometimes politics and government seem so complicated that a person like me can't really understand what's going on."

serve to illustrate two important points. The first concerns the critical difference between cross-sectional and longitudinal analyses. Although previous cross-sectional studies of alienation have established statistical relationships between different age categories and the indicators of alienation, such relationships must be considered only as hypotheses to be tested in the more appropriate context of longitudinal data and related analytic strategies. Second, the fact that both Cutler and Bengtson and House and Mason concluded that recent American trends in political alienation were best explained as historical period effects demonstrates that variants of cohort analysis are a useful approach even when a generational explanation is not the correct (or anticipated) explanation.

An attribute related to alienation is tolerance, the subject of the classic Stouffer study of "communism, conformity, and civil liberties." Although Stouffer found the younger respondents in the mid-1950s to be more tolerant than the older, he recognized that cross-sectional data could not be used to distinguish between the generational and maturational interpretations (Stouffer, 1955, p. 89). The inclusion of the Stouffer tolerance scale items in a 1972 attitude survey provided the basis for a formal cohort analysis in which the two competing explanations could be examined. The analysis found that all cohorts exhibited increased tolerance, but that cohorts in the younger years of their life cycle increased at a faster rate than did cohorts observed in their older years (S. Cutler & R. Kaufman, 1975). Hence, while both generational and maturational effects were present, the slower rate of change within the older cohorts, in the context of societal increases in tolerance, tended to inflate the appearance of generational distinctions.

DOMESTIC POLITICAL ATTITUDES

Although political scientists have long been concerned with sources of and variations in domestic political attitudes, there are few cohort studies in this area. Unfortunately, the three which can be noted here do not cumulatively address the same set of issues, although they are illustrative of interesting generational patterns.

As part of a larger analysis, Klecka (1971) examined aging and generational patterns of American attitudes toward the issue of federal aid for local public education over the years 1956–1968. During this period a substantial trend affected all age and generation groups; in 1956, 82.3% of the total electorate favored federal aid to education while 12 years later, in 1968, this majority support had declined to only 36.8%.

Klecka found that the biggest shift in the electorate was between 1962 and 1964, a period which also marked the end of relative similarity among age and cohort groups. As of 1964, the older cohorts tended to exhibit substantially less support for federal aid to education than would be predicted on the basis of the overall trend; similarly, the young cohorts which had recently entered the electorate showed a more positive attitude than the general trend.[5] Consequently, Klecka concluded that the generation effect was somewhat stronger than the aging effect, and that for this particular attitude the national unanimity of the late 1950s had been replaced by the "generational polarization" of the late 1960s (Klecka, 1971, p. 368).

Cutler and Schmidhauser (1975) report a cohort analysis of attitudes toward federal involvement in the financing of medical care programs. Although it is often thought that the aging process is responsible for conservative political beliefs, studies of attitudes toward federal involvement in various welfare and social service programs have suggested that a "group benefits orientation" toward specific policies might override more general "ideological" conservatism toward such policies (Campbell et al., 1960; Campbell, 1971). A specific test of this possibility was carried out with respect to the aging population and federal involvement in medical care programs. While some studies have suggested that both objective chronological age differences (Schreiber & Marsden, 1972) and subjective feelings of old age (Cutler, 1974b, 1975c) are strongly associated with support of federal medical programs, such studies have been cross-sectional in nature, and have not established whether the age patterns represent the effects of aging or of generational differences.

The analysis reported by Cutler and Schmidhauser focused upon within-cohort changes in attitudes toward federal involvement in medical aid programs over the 1956-1972 period. Four separate cohorts, each maturing from age 61-64 to age 65-68, were observed. These data were compared both to the overall trend for the electorate and to four additional cohorts which were observed maturing from 21-24 to 25-28 years of age. The results showed that, within the ebbs and flows of the national trend, the aging of the older cohorts was always accompanied by higher levels of support and more positive changes in that support than was the case either for the total electorate or for the younger cohorts.

Attitudes toward federal aid to education and toward federal involvement in medical care financing may be considered as components of a more general liberal-conservative ideology. While one research question concerns whether aging and generational factors influence the formation of specific attitudes, another concerns the influences of these factors upon the ideology itself. This latter question was the focus of a cohort analysis of age and generational correlates of change in the social welfare ideology of the American electorate over the period 1956-1968.

Kirkpatrick (1976) found both aging and generational patterns underlying a

---

[5]Klecka designed an innovative approach for estimating the strength of any generational or aging effects which may have developed apart from a general trend. The method is based upon estimating the attitudes an age or cohort group might be expected to have if that group changed at the identical rate as the national trend. If the group's actual change between two time points was larger or smaller than the estimated change, then the deviations could be considered as evidence of the age or generational effect.

1956–1968 sequence of ideological constraint correlations.[6] For both the earliest and more recent cohorts in the study, aging over the 1956–1968 period appeared to be accompanied by increases in the correlations; i.e., for these cohorts attitudes on the three items identifying the social welfare ideology came closer together. A number of statistical tests concerning whether generational or aging effects were dominant in the data resulted in the mixed conclusion that both aging and generational effects were present. What Kirkpatrick concludes, therefore, is that while aging seems to bring about a more tightly clustered set of social welfare attitudes within all the observed cohorts, the effects of maturation are clearly greater for some cohorts than for others.[7]

Six: Analytic Issues in Generational Cohort Analysis

The final section of this chapter reviews some of the conceptual and methodological issues concerning cohort analysis in socialization and generational research. Although the cohort analysis of attitudinal data within the social sciences is less than 20 years old, the recent expansion of cohort analysis techniques has brought forth a small but increasing number of articles concerning alternative methods and analytic problems. This discussion cannot provide a methodological primer; rather, it will introduce some of the major issues, and hopefully provide sufficient bibliographical references for focused "further reading."

Contemporary generational analysis is typically traced to Mannheim's classic essay on the "Sociological Problem of Generations" (Mannheim, 1928). The significance of the generation concept, in Mannheimian terms, is that each new birth cohort has "fresh contact" with society and, consequently, with society's ever current reinterpretation of past history. Thus each new generational group—the term cohort was added to this line of inquiry later—has within it the seeds of sociopolitical change (Bengtson & Cutler, 1976).

Yet, for purposes of empirical social analysis, the concept of *generation* was a difficult one to operationalize since over the centuries it had taken on a variety

[6]Kirkpatrick defined the strength of an attitudinal ideology as the magnitude of the correlations among the separate attitude questions: the greater the average interitem correlation for the set of items, the greater the attitudinal constraint reflective of the underlying ideology. To measure ideology, Kirkpatrick used attitudes toward the issues of federal aid to education, federal involvement in medical care, and federal involvement in employment guarantees.

[7]Additional areas which have been the subject of generational analysis include foreign policy attitudes in the United States (Bobrow & Cutler, 1967); Cutler, (1970b); foreign policy attitudes in Western Europe (Inglehart, 1967, 1971); the relationship between age factors, mass media behavior, and political socialization (Cutler & Danowski, 1975; Danowski & Cutler, 1975); and the political choices of successive generations of college graduates (Lipset & Ladd, 1971). As generational cohort analysis has become more widely known through research applications as well as methodological summaries and reviews (some of which are cited in Section Six), more and more examples of the approach are becoming available. Thus, while the brief review in this chapter has attempted to be comprehensive, it is by no means exhaustive.

of meanings. Mannheim had found various estimates of the length of a generation, ranging from 15 to 30 years, although he personally preferred the 30 year
interval (1928, p. 278). Traditionally, a generation became defined as "the
average period from a male's birth until the birth of his first male child. Nowa-
days a generation so defined is much closer to twenty years in duration" (Foote,
1960, p. 6). In his essay "How Long is a Generation?" Berger (1960) argued
that, since the pace of technological and social change has speeded up in the last
70 years, the time separating generations appears to be shrinking. Consequently,
it may be inappropriate to define or delimit generations in terms of biological or
lineage concepts.

Since a birth cohort may be operationally defined in terms of any interval of
years, since the choice of the interval may be either theoretically chosen or
imposed by the availability of data, and since the notion of a birth cohort specifically distinguishes a generational cohort from the lineage connotation of the
generation concept, the concept of *generational cohort analysis* has gained relatively widespread acceptance in the several social sciences. Given the precise
statistical identity with which *cohort* is typically imbued, it may never find
acceptance by literary and historical analysts whose interest is in long-range
social and cultural movements (Mariás, 1968; Rintala, 1968). Alternatively,
however, contemporary historians whose interests include generational change
have found the more precise concept of cohort to be quite complementary to
more traditional embodiments of the generation concept. Writing in the *American Historical Review,* for example, Spitzer (1973) noted the similarity of themes
found in both classical historical analysis and contemporary sociopolitical analysis
of generational issues.

The beginning of contemporary cohort analysis employing old public opinion
polls is found in Evan's exploratory essay (1959). Subsequently, cohort analysis
has become virtually synonymous with the secondary analysis of archival attitude
survey data since the cohort researcher must locate at least two polls or surveys
which contain comparable attitude items. Indeed, one of the most comprehensive
reviews of cohort analysis is located in Hyman's (1972) monographic discussion
of alternative approaches to the secondary analysis of archival public opinion
data.

Because cohort analysis is a form of trend analysis, the researcher must
recognize that sampling techniques of the 1940s and 1950s were not as efficient
as the sampling techniques of more recent years. In particular, in the earlier
years commercial pollsters typically underrepresented the lower socioeconomic
strata of society. Consequently, Glenn and Zody have analyzed a number of the
problems which the cohort analyst faces when using and comparing old data and
more recent data (Glenn, 1970; Glenn & Zody, 1970; Zody, 1969). As an
example of the problems precipitated by improvements in survey research
technology, Glenn (1970) demonstrated that since the more recent surveys have
"discovered" additional lower SES respondents, a cohort analysis spanning
several decades can present the erroneous statistical portrait of a cohort which in

the later years becomes less educated than it was in the earlier years. More importantly, Glenn notes, any social or political attitude which is likely to be correlated with education will be inaccurately portrayed in trend analyses unless appropriate statistical controls are employed.

Beyond initial questions of the comparability of data sets, questions concerning alternative modes of cohort analysis arise. Consideration of the three key variables which underlie cohort trends—cohort, age, and period—reveals that each of the variables is a statistical function of the other two. Thus, any observation of a cohort is the observation of a particular age group at a particular point in time. Or, any observation of an age group is the observation of a particular generational cohort at a particular point in time. The most complete statement of this "cohort analysis problem" may be found in the introductory chapters of *Aging and Society: A Sociology of Age Stratification* (Riley, Johnson, & Foner, 1972). In this landmark volume, Riley and her colleagues note that society may be characterized as a population system in which new generational cohorts are continuously being added, while older cohorts are continuously dying off. At the same time, each of the cohorts is aging. Furthermore, the processes of aging and of generational replacement take place in the context of events and trends in society which may or may not differentially affect all age and generational groups. Hence, the task of the social analyst is to disentangle all of these interrelated dimensions of the problem (see also the discussions by Carlsson & Karlsson, 1970; Cohn, 1972; Riley, 1973; Maddox & Wiley, 1976).

Beyond theoretical discussions of cohort analysis, the major dialogues have concerned alternative approaches to the analysis of cohort data. Three general approaches may be identified, the first two occupying the attention of sociologists and political scientists, and the third being the focus of much psychological research. One predominant method, introduced by Evan (1959) is the construction of an age-by-time cohort matrix. As illustrated in Table 10–4, this formal cohort matrix allows the investigator to observe the aging process within cohorts, to observe summative or patterned differences between cohorts, and to note trend patterns for the total society.

While the cohort matrix approach is relatively straightforward, a number of issues have arisen: for example, the controversy between Crittenden (1962) and Cutler (1970a) (see footnote 1) concerned how cohorts should be analyzed in the context of general societal trends. This issue, in turn, raises a broader question as to the form of data to insert into the cohort matrix. Most cohort research employs percentages or frequencies; a small number of studies, however, has employed bivariate correlations (Abramson, 1974; Kirkpatrick, 1976), partial correlations (Cutler & Danowski, 1975), and expected versus observed "deviation proportions" (Klecka, 1971).

An alternative to the cohort matrix approach is the multiple regression "net effects" model proposed by Mason et al. (1973). The goal of this approach

Table 10-4. Cohort Analysis Matrix: Five-year Intervals

1956[a]	1961	1966	1971	1976
21-25[b]	21-25	21-25	21-25	21-25
26-30	26-30	26-30	26-30	26-30
31-35	31-35	31-35	31-35	31-35
36-40	36-40	36-40	36-40	36-40
41-45	41-45	41-45	41-45	41-45
46-50	46-50	46-50	46-50	46-50
51-55	51-55	51-55	51-55	51-55
56-60	56-60	56-60	56-60	56-60
61-65	61-65	61-65	61-65	61-65
66-70	66-70	66-70	66-70	66-70
71-75	71-75	71-75	71-75	71-75

[a]Each column is represented by a sample survey taken in the given year.

[b]The cohort represented by the uppermost pair of diagonal lines was born in 1931-1935. Thus the entries in this diagonal "row" may be read as follows: "The cohort born in 1931-1935 was 21-25 years old in 1956; it was 26-30 years old in 1961, 31-35 years old in 1966, etc."

differs from the cohort matrix approach in that the task of the regression model is to estimate statistically the explanatory power of age, cohort, and period in the presence of additional explanatory or control variables. In estimating the amount of variance explained by age, cohort, and period in the presence of the other variables, the net effects of the primary variables suggest their independent explanatory power.

Mason and her colleagues provide a detailed mathematical account of the underlying assumptions of the model. In the context of the present discussion, what is more important than the mechanics of this alternative is how the cohort matrix and the cohort regression models differ in their goals and procedures. As noted, the main goal of the regression model is the statistical estimation of effects, using a proportion of variance explained criterion. The cohort matrix approach, by contrast, is typically concerned with the tracing of longitudinal patterns of between-cohort succession or within-cohort maturational change. As part of this distinction, the nature of the data analysis is quite different. The cohort matrix approach (illustrated in Table 10-4) presents the measurements on the dependent variable serially for each of the time points. The regression approach—in which age, cohort, and period are treated as three variables in a larger cluster of predictor variables—combines all of the respondents from the collection of cross-time surveys into a single data file. The regression analysis of this "macro-file" thus produces summary statistics and regression weights for the aggregated data set, enabling the researcher to determine the relative predictive power of age, cohort, and period variables.

Although the Mason approach has not yet been widely used, it can potentially make a substantial impact upon the field of generational analysis. The regression method makes its biggest contribution precisely in that area where the cohort matrix approach is often lacking: a precise statistical statement of the relative weight of age, cohort, and period factors in explaining a dependent variable.

On the other hand, at least two problems with the regression approach should be noted which may limit the potential value of the regression approach. The first concerns the relatively narrow range of substantively interesting questions to which the regression approach is limited by its own statistical complexity. As discussed by Glenn (1976), in the refinements of the statistical model Mason and colleagues note several limiting assumptions with which the model must work. Glenn suggests that these limitations are so substantial that many of the areas of interest to cohort analysts cannot be legitimately investigated using the approach. In one application of the model, Hout and Knoke (1975) note the requirement of choosing any pair of cohorts, age groups, or time periods, and artificially reducing the variance in the pair so that the regression technique would work. Since the data included 16 age groups and 21 cohorts, there were 25,200 possible pairs. On the basis of intuitive judgment, they chose 10 pairs in which to replicate the regression analysis. One wonders, however, what the regression results might have been using any of the other 25,190 available combinations.

A second problem is that the regression analysis approach combines age, cohort, and period with other variables in such a way that the pattern of intracohort change or intercohort differences is lost. This contrasts with the cohort matrix approach in which patterns of intracohort variations in political, educational, or social class differences are precisely the focus of the analysis (e.g., Abramson, 1976).

To the degree that such problems can be overcome, the regression approach is likely to provide an important complement to the cohort matrix approach. Examples of its use include studies of political alienation (House & Mason, 1975), the salience of alternative political issues (Douglas, Cleveland, & Maddox, 1974), partisanship (Knoke & Hout, 1974), and changes in voting turnout (Hout & Knoke, 1975).

CROSS-SEQUENTIAL RESEARCH DESIGNS

While the cohort matrix and the cohort regression models have dominated studies of age, cohort, and period effects in political science and sociology, developmental psychologists interested in the identical set of analytic issues have developed cross-sequential analysis, a set of techniques methodologically linked to analysis of variance procedures. It is particularly appropriate to end this discussion with a brief introduction of cross-sequential analysis strategies. As stated at the beginning of this chapter, the study of political socialization is an example of interdisciplinary borrowing; since much of the explicit or implicit borrowing is from psychology, it is important to note the substantial attention which developmental psychologists have paid to the cohort analysis problem.

Like political scientists and sociologists, psychologists recognize that cross-sectional and longitudinal measures of the same variables can yield quite different results. More precisely, researchers recognize that single cross-sectional studies of age-graded phenomena cannot provide valid information about age-developmental processes—clearly a prime concern to developmental psychologists. Schaie (1965) presented a "General Developmental Model" which described the three intertwined variables of age, cohort, and "time of measurement," each of which is a statistical function of the other two. To disentangle these variables, he proposed that each pair of the three be studied separately in analysis of variance designs in which main effects and interaction effects could be detected. In order to make decisions about which effect provided the best explanation for the data, Schaie prescribed a number of rules or propositions concerning the comparison of main effects and interaction effects across the three sets of analysis of variance (Schaie, 1973, 1977). Most of the applications of the Schaie model have been in the area of intelligence (e.g., Schaie, 1972; Schaie & Strother, 1968; Nesselroade, Schaie & Baltes, 1972; Woodruff & Birren, 1972). One review concludes that all of these studies "have shown substantial and complex differences between the ontogenetic patterns of different generations or cohorts" (Nesselroade & Baltes, 1974, p. 5).

Alterations and discussions of the model continue to evolve (Baltes, 1968; Schaie, 1970; Baltes & Nesselroade, 1970; Schaie, 1973). The important point for the present discussion, however, is that data which are structurally similar to that which political scientists typically have at their disposal (i.e., independently collected samples which, when stratified by age, yield quasi-longitudinal samples of the same cohorts) can be systematically analyzed for the presence of the effects of maturation, generation, and historical period.

While it is not surprising to find cohort differences in samples of adults, it is particularly relevant to students of political socialization that some applications of the Schaie model have revealed age differences among adolescents which are cohort rather than developmental differences (Baltes & Reinert, 1969; Baltes, Baltes, & Reinert, 1970; Baltes & Nesselroade, 1972; Nesselroade & Baltes, 1974). The most recent of these studies provides a good example of cohort research applied to adolescents. Using a variety of personality and ability development tests, Nesselroade and Baltes (1974) tested four one-year birth cohorts—at ages 13, 14, 15, and 16. A year later the cohorts (using the same panel of respondents) were tested again, and a third test was taken in the following year.

The results indicated that, although there were both cross-sectional age differences as well as longitudinal age differences in several of the dependent variables, age was not a particularly relevant variable. Variation in the dependent variables seemed to be more influenced by time of measurement than by age. The authors conclude that "the outcome was clear-cut and offered persuasive evidence for the importance of historical time effects and the need to employ both sequential strategies and appropriate controls in developmental research" (Nesselroade & Baltes, 1974).

Conclusion

The earliest study in the sequence of psychological studies of adolescent development mentioned above provides an appropriate basis for concluding this chapter. In that study, Baltes and Reinert (1969) examined three different cohorts of 8-year-olds, and three additional cohorts of 9-year-olds. Each of the *cohorts* (not individuals) was tested twice, separated by 5 months. Each of the three cohorts in the first group were measured as they "aged" from 8 years and 4 months to 8 years and 8 months; the aging of the 9-year-olds was similarly tested. Studies of political socialization, by contrast to Baltes and Reinert's study of adolescent cognitive development, typically neither identify nor analyze age groups in time units of less than 1 year. Even more telling is the fact that cross-sectional sequences of age differences in political socialization research are virtually always treated as evidence of ontogenetic change.

The orientation of this chapter has been that the importance of political socialization derives not so much from knowledge of children's attitudes, but from knowledge of how adolescent or young adult experiences affect adult attitudes and behaviors and, consequently, the functioning of the political system. It has thus been argued that political socialization research be undertaken in terms of generational analysis. Furthermore, we have endeavored to distinguish between the lineage and the cohort conceptualizations of generation. The lineage approach has stimulated a number of parent-child studies in political science. As with other cross-sectional studies of differences between young and old, these parent-child studies cannot distinguish relatively temporary differences which are attributable to differences in physiological and social maturity, from potentially permanent differences which are rooted in the intersection of history and socialization, and which are unique for each new birth cohort.

For these reasons, the consequences of political socialization are best observed and analyzed through the investigation of birth cohorts which may be identified in terms of when they were born and socialized. Research designs in political socialization should reflect the strengths and weaknesses which are offered by, and are inherent in, the lineage and cohort approaches to generational analysis. A growing literature employing generational cohort analysis has demonstrated that variations in political attitudes and behavior can often be traced to the historical context of the cohort's socialization. Yet our overview of this emerging genre of research has suggested that the methods of generational analysis are not limited to those research questions where the investigator antici-pates a generational explanation. By its very nature, cohort analysis helps to differentiate between cohort, aging, and period effect explanations. Although much remains to be done in the application of generational cohort analysis to questions of theoretical interest to political scientists, the extant studies have demonstrated that differences which appear in cross-sectional studies to be mat-urational in nature are often better explained in generational cohort terms.

This, then, leads back to the adolescent developmental study undertaken by Baltes and Reinert (1969). The two test sequences for each of the cohorts were separated by only 5 months—just as the cohorts themselves were separated by only 5 months of age. *Analogous to most political research of this kind, all of the data were from independent cross-sectional samples.* The authors note that if the analysis had been undertaken using traditional cross-sectional methods, then the aging or developmental processes would have looked much stronger than was in fact the case:

> The present results argue for the consideration of cohort effects in cognitive develop-ments of children in dealing with cohort populations separated by intervals as small as a few months (p. 176).

While we would not argue that political scientists should look for generational differences in cohorts of children which are separated by only a few months, it is clear that students of political socialization would do well to conceptualize their studies in terms of the concepts and techniques of generational analysis.

PART THREE

OUTCOMES OF
THE POLITICAL
SOCIALIZATION PROCESS

11

Political Socialization and Models
of Moral Development

Daniel A. Friedman

GIVEN THE DESIRE TO TRANSLATE competing social theories into public policy under conditions of limited material resources, theories serve ideological functions. The implementation of "theory" determines not only the allocation of scarce resources—i.e., wealth, esteem, and enlightenment to future researchers and citizens—but determines the "world view" of future generations.

Our choice of pedagogical theory has political outcomes. Children may learn as active participants by discovering or they may be passively taught. Obedience may be instilled by aversive and symbolic rewards or it may be produced through empathy and reason. Different kinds of obedience may result in the two treatment groups—the one based on fear of authority or response to what may be a punitive reward system, and the other based on participatory conceptualizations of social justice: e.g., Lepper, Green, and Nisbett (1973) found that extrinsic rewards (gold stars) decreased the subsequent intrinsic interest in the target activity for young children. Children are socialized to accept different sources of authority as legitimate. They may be socialized to accept unfulfilling symbolic representations of reality (i.e., gold stars). Or they may develop loyalties and respect on the basis of understanding.

Is it improper to refer to social theory as theory if it can be demonstrated that a social theory has an ideological component? I think not. By separating out the varied aspect of a social theory one can refer to empirical, testable propositions and to their ideological implications.

This chapter represents a portion of a doctoral dissertation submitted to the graduate division of the University of Hawaii.

Moral issues—i.e., how we ought to act or how we ought to be motivated—are not usually perceived and discussed as part of a particular theoretical orientation. The efficiency of a socialization technique (e.g., behavior modification) or the explanatory power of a theory are issues which are aired "publicly" (if not in university classrooms then in academic journals). What receives less attention are the ideological issues of ethics and politics. Psychological theories of moral development are vulnerable to this sort of critique. These are theories upon which school curriculums are built and social policy is made. Ostensibly these theories are concerned with hypotheses, empirical statements, and tests concerning the moral development of children and adults. Yet these theories contain ethical statements—i.e., value statements about man's basic nature—"evidence from history suggest that to expect people to be compassionate, charitable and tolerant is patently unrealistic" (Hogan, 1973, p. 231)—and develop metaethical positions, i.e., virtue is the product of affect or cognition or natural selection.

The subject matter of psychological theories of ethics (i.e., what is deemed by the theorist or theory as moral behavior) and the conceptual framework used to interpret moral development (i.e., the selection of concepts for inclusion or exclusion in analysis) are matters of political interest as are the more overtly expressed biases of the theorist.

Self-Control as an Example of Political and Moral Behavior

Let us examine a single case to illustrate this point. If we accept that self-control[1] (often referred to as a moral virtue) is a moral characteristic to be instilled in our citizens, we have made a political choice. Community resources are allocated (classroom time is spent instilling this virtue); the community or agents of the community have identified a social virtue and ranked its worth against other possible social virtues (more time may be spent developing undesirable qualities such as nonconformity). These decisions reflect the community's social structure and preferred values and channel the lives of future members in one particular direction rather than in another.

But the decision is considerably more complicated than the opting for a specific moral virtue. Self-control implies the internalization of rules. Rules can be internalized in a variety of ways, i.e., different techniques may be used to effect internalization. But the political-social implications of the internalization techniques and the resulting effects differ.

---

[1]In the past much of the study of moral behavior has been limited to the study of resistance to temptation. Graham, e.g., states: "The term 'moral' may be used in three main senses. 1) It may be used to refer to 'resistance to temptation.'. . . 2) It may refer to the control of behavior by reference to 'internalized' standards rather than by reference to the possible consequences of the behavior for the actor. . . . 3) It may indicate behavior which is carried out by reference to rules or principles which are rationally accepted in the sense that reasons for accepting them are understood and felt to be legitimate" (1972, p. 10).

Hoffman lists three different types of internalization. "The first and most primitive one is based on conditioned fear or anxiety. . . . The second is based on the actor's positive orientation toward an absent reference group or person in the manner discussed previously; that is, the actor believed in the standards and employs the moralistic evaluations which have been transmitted by the significant others whom he respects and with whom he identifies. In the third and most advanced type, the individual experiences the standards as an obligation to himself rather than to some reference figure" (Hoffman, 1974, p. 264). The political implications are quite clear. Is self-control to be construed as externalized control whose sanctions depend on fear, anxiety of disapproval and punitive measures? Kohlberg responds: "Insofar as inhibition of action is determined rigidly by the paradigms of classical conditioning, it indicates the absence of self-control in the usual sense" (Kohlberg, 1969, p. 410). What kind of self-control should a polity opt for? Should the decision (with regard to self-control) be based on explicit ideological criteria or unstated (but ideological) spinoffs of a psychological theory?

A recent study by Judith Long-Stevens (1973) is illustrative of this problem. She conducted an experiment in which an actor posing as a child (in a manner believable to the adult subjects) performed the same play sequence (on videotape) with three different emphases. Although the transgressions are the same in each sequence (and all end with the child hitting an adult) in one run-through the child is portrayed as underactive, in one as normal, and in a third instance as hyperactive. Despite the fact that in all three cases the child performed identical transgressions, the passive and hyperactive child elicited much stronger punishment responses than the child whose mannerisms were normal.

This suggests that there is an unstated and perhaps unconscious model of "proper" behavior that is used by American families to socialize their children. In this model mannerisms are judged as well as consequence (we could now add style to consequence and intent in moral dilemmas) in determining punishment for a transgression. American children are being taught to regulate their lives at a uniform and moderate speed. People who respond too quickly or too slowly are punished. Uniformity and moderation may be as political a lesson as saying the pledge of allegiance every morning.

Socialization of qualities such as uniformity and moderation in children is reflected later in the type and quality of political interaction among adults (i.e., tolerance of dissent, restriction on the kinds of people entering the political arena and the kinds of political statements permissible).

The Learning Theory Approach to Moral Development

For those educators who place a premium on the importance of autonomy and spontaneity in the child (as well as adult), both learning theory and modeling approaches to moral development are deficient in certain respects as modes of political socialization. Both of these approaches stress the importance of fitting the individual into an existing pattern of social relationships. They have represented the political interests of the status quo. Power and authority flow downward and the child is manipulated into the desired shape. Studies of resistance to temptation have been of special interest to learning theorists because it has ranked high on the list of traits considered desirable by the general community and because it represents a moral virtue which is consistent with social conformity and therefore not controversial.

Resistance to temptation is used as a measure of whether social prohibitions (resistance) have greater force in determining behavior than personal desires (temptation). Acting out existing social prohibitions is good. Acting out egoistic desires is bad. Temptations, however, *could* be altruistic or "self-sacrificing," i.e., I have been tempted to give up a materialistic life style and decrease the small but disproportionate strain I place on the world economy. Resistance to temptation denotes the acceptance of extant social norms.

The learning theory approach to moral development has usually been based on operant conditioning. Moral values in this approach to learning are not seen as "fundamentally different from such behavioristic constructs as Hull's (1943) habit strength or Tolman's (1949) equivalence beliefs" (Hill, 1972, p. 263). Learning theory defines morality in terms of specific acts and avoidances which are learned on the basis of rewards and punishments (Hoffman, 1970, p. 262). The model, then, is seen as value free inasmuch as it can be put to use by any number of political ideologies. In fact, however, operant conditioning is used to maintain the system of political values which are supported by those who control the rewards which may be distributed (praise, affection, gold stars). To state that the theory itself is value free is to ignore the political use to which the theory is being put. It is also to ignore the semantic rules (which are value laden) used to link concepts in the theory with observations, as described by Shapiro (1974).

Hill, e.g., views resistance to temptation as a matter of avoidance learning.

> This relating of conscience to avoidance learning suggests that independent variables known to be effective in animal avoidance learning would be among the most appropriate ones for study in connection with the development of conscience in children (Hill, 1972, p. 268).

The problem, seen from this perspective, is a technical one: e.g., how can we inflict punishment in such a way that we will best achieve some set of stated goals? Aside from the ideological considerations of such an approach to education, there are empirical questions which arise from the implementation of such practices.

The Hartshorne and May studies (1928–1930) point to the situation specificity and longitudinal instability of moral character traits (Kohlberg, 1969, p. 367). Further studies have borne out this finding:

> The ordering of individuals on motivated traits like dependency, aggression, affiliation, anxiety, need achievement, and conscience-strength either predicts very little or

not at all to later ordering on these same traits, if the two orderings are separated by many years... (Kohlberg, 1969, p. 369).

We can effectively constrain our children to obey all the rules we set down for them. The behaviors children are learning may be so specific that they are useless in predicting their behavior in the adult community. "Reinforcement learning theories are not theories of structural change; i.e. they do not assert that child-hood learnings are irreversible or that they should determine later behavior in different situations" (Kohlberg, 1969, p. 364). Through conditioning, the child is learning a hedonistic model of the world (good behavior is characterized by the avoidance of pain and the gain of pleasure as ministered by authority figures).

LOVE WITHDRAWAL

Aversive reinforcement scheduling does not rely solely on physical punish-ment, but also on psychological deprivations such as love withdrawal. Hill describes the entire gamut of possible conditioning agents, i.e., scolding, ridicule, and the withholding of positive reinforcers (1972, p. 268). Love with-drawal is possibly the most effective of aversive conditioning agents. "However, the desire to continue receiving love from the parents may persist after the child has outgrown the need for other parental rewards, such as gifts and privileges. Discipline by withdrawal of love, in an atmosphere of warmth, might therefore be even more effective than other forms of discipline by denial of reward in producing persistent avoidances" (Hill, 1972, p. 285).

As in the previous examples of the use of conditioning to promote moral development, empirical research does not support the contention that reward-punishment schemes lead to moral development. Hoffman suggests that power assertion is negatively related to an extensive list of moral development studies and indices (1970, p. 291, Table 3, Table 4,). Power assertion techniques by parents have also been shown to lead to aggressive behavior by the child toward his peers. The rationale for the failure of power assertion to influence moral development is that (1) it elicits hostility in the child; (2) provides him with a model who expresses hostility; (3) the absence of affection "fosters the image of the parent as an arbitrary, punitive, and unrewarding person—someone to be avoided rather than approached and emulated" (Hoffman, 1970, p. 331).

Love withdrawal is possibly a more subtle socializing technique, though equally manipulative and punitive. It depends, however, on the prior establish-ment of positive affect between parent and child if it is to be successful.

The effect of this technique is to instill anxiety in the child when he commits an undesired act. Judiciously and effectively practiced by the adult, the use of love withdrawal will socialize the child in level two of the three levels of rule internalization discussed earlier. Socialized by this technique, children turn to authority figures for the proper definition of what is right and wrong (and thereby obtain gratification). The relationship between love withdrawal and moral development is at best inconsistent and probably nonexistent (Hoffman, 1970, pp. 291, 300–301). Hoffman notes that "there is some evidence that love withdrawal may contribute to the inhibition of anger" (1970, p. 301). What the child learns when his parents practice love withdrawal is that in order to avoid losing love he must control his impulses.

BEHAVIOR MODIFICATION IN THE CLASSROOM

A natural outgrowth of the principles of learning theory[2] has been the use of behavior modification in the classroom. Behavior modification is viewed by some educators as the streamlining of traditional educational practices. In the past rewards and punishments were often ambiguous and meted out inconsistently. The newer approach stresses efficiency and consistency.

Behavior modification seeks to correct the moral growth of the child: i.e., behavior modification is used to alter specific behaviors of the child that are viewed by the authority figure as "disruptive," "undesirable," or "inappropriate." Behavior modification is used when the child does not behave as he ought to behave.

Arguments in favor of the use of behavior modification are based upon traditionalism and efficiency. Behavior modification supposedly harnesses techniques we have always used and makes them more efficient. It is thought necessary in many instances if a teacher is to be "successful" in imparting information and norms to his or her charges.

While all the above may be true, it is also true that behavior modification of children by teachers is systematically manipulative.

> For example, if a child announces on entering the classroom that he is going to work with the paints, the teacher is in a position to use this activity as a contingent upon which the child will first work at the class assignment set by the teacher and then will be rewarded with freedom to paint for a few minutes (Fein, 1974, p. 207).

Behavior modification tends to sweep under the rug the prior political questions of what "appropriate" behavior entails and who determines when behavior is appropriate or inappropriate. These decisions are left to the teacher while the child is seduced or cajoled from his or her original goals. The child is not

---

[2]Space does not permit a fuller exegesis of the learning theory approach to moral development. The reader is advised to review the works of Aronfreed (1968, 1970, 1971), of Rosenhan (1972), and of Hogan (1973, 1974).

Perhaps more interesting is the research in modeling reported (Bryan & London, 1970; Bryan & Walbek, 1970). The implications of their findings are (1) that children's behavior is affected by behavior modeling and not by exhortations and; (2) that children are able to tolerate a very high degree of inconsistency between ideology as verbalized (self-conscious word systems) and ideology as expressed in attitudes and behavior. Bluhm (1974) has an excellent discussion of the two ways in which the term ideology is used. The child may be learning two separate models in school. The first (which greatly affects his own activities) are patterns of behavior. The other is a model of verbal platitudes which hardly registers on the child's cognitive framework.

regarded in this system as a thinking, motivated organism who is "voting" via his actions. No attempt is made to find the source of his rebellion. No attempt is made to alter the child's environment.

An Overview of Piaget's Psychological System

Piaget holds that cognitive processes are ordered by structures. Structures have three characteristics, i.e., wholeness, transformation, and self-regulation (Piaget, 1970b, pp. 22–23). Wholeness refers to the fact that a set of laws govern all the elements of the system as an entity. Transformation implies that the laws which govern the system are dynamic in that they allow the elements of the system to form and combine in new ways, i.e., the law of addition allows us to transform a number by adding to it (Piaget, 1971, p. 23). Self-regulation implies that "in order to carry out these laws of transformation, we need not go outside the system to find some external element" (Piaget, 1971, p. 23). The developmental process carries with it the necessity for reformulating new structures as the old ones are inadequate to perform increasingly difficult cognitive tasks. The genetic maturation of the individual and the increasingly complex social interactions of the child-adult provide the composite elements with which the organism interacts to create new structures.

Cognitive structures are composed of schema (sensorimotor concepts) and operations. Operations have certain characteristics; they are internal, reversible, and connected to other operations. Operations define the laws by which elements in the system relate to one another. These laws consist of hierarchical categories called lattices and a series of mathematical relationships called groups. The number of groups increases as the cognitive-structural complexity of the individual increases: e.g., there are laws of (1) composition—$A \times B = C$ where C is part of the system; (2) associativity—$A \times (B \times C) = (A \times B) \times C$; (3) identity—$A \times I = I \times A = A$; (4) reversibility—$A \times A' = I$ where A' is the inverse of I. And there are groups for special identity, negation, reciprocity, and correlations (Phillips, 1969, pp. 69–71; Flavell, 1963, pp. 135–142).

Leaving aside the problem of the organism's inherent capabilities, it becomes clear that Piaget believes that social life has a great deal to do with the fact that cognitive structures are defined in mathematical relationships in which we are constantly finding equivalencies and making transformations: e.g., in order for social interaction to exist, individuals must be aware of a consistent outcome of similar actions (or identity $A \times I = A$). Life is seen as a great chess game of mathematical transformations.

> Intellectual interaction between individuals is thus comparable to a vast game of chess, which is carried on unremittingly and in such a way that each action carried out with respect to a particular item involves a series of equivalent or complementary actions on the part of the opponent; laws of grouping are nothing more or less than the

various rules ensuring the reciprocity of the players and consistency of their play (Piaget, 1950, p. 165).

Piaget discusses the composition, etiology, and consequences of these structures in depth. Kohlberg's phenotype description of moral structure is much more complex than Piaget's. Kohlberg's understanding of the importance of structure is not questioned. But his treatment of the composition and etiology of cognitive structure is not completely adequate. Eliot Turiel has recognized these deficiencies and has begun research on the mechanisms of transition from stage to stage of moral development (1974).

PIAGET'S STAGES OF MORAL DEVELOPMENT

Piaget observed children at play and presented them with moral dilemmas. His subjects were mostly between the ages of 5 to 13. The results of his studies indicated the existence of two moral stages: the heteronomous stage in which the child was absolutistic, morally "objective," egocentric, and dependent on authority for his decision making; and the autonomous stage in which the child was morally "subjective" and thought out the meaning of moral acts. Kohlberg notes that there are 11 aspects of Piagetian moral stages though he reservedly accepts only 6 of these dimensions and states that the nonvalid remaining 5 dimensions stem from a social emotive background rather than one of cognitive development.[3] Piaget views the natural condition of the child as one of powerlessness. It is partly the absence of this power which forces the child into a position where he

---

[3]"1. *Intentionality in judgment*—Young children tend to judge an act as bad mainly in terms of its actual physical consequences, whereas older children judge an act as bad in terms of the intent to do harm. 2. *Relativism in judgment*—The young child views an act as either totally right or totally wrong, and thinks everyone views it the same way.... 3. *Independence of sanctions*—The young child says an act is bad because it will elicit punishment; the older child says an act is bad because it violates a rule, does harm to others and so forth.... 4. *Use of Reciprocity*—Four year old children do not use reciprocity as a reason for consideration of others, whereas children of seven and older frequently do.... 5. *Use of punishment as restitution and reform*—Young children advocate severe painful punishment after stories of misdeeds; older children increasingly favor milder punishments leading to restitution to the victim and to the reform of the culprit. 6. *Naturalist views of misfortune*—Six to seven year old children have some tendency to view physical accidents and misfortunes occurring after misdeeds as punishments willed by God or by natural objects... (Kohlberg, 1964, p. 399).

In contrast to the six aspects listed, five others suggested by Piaget's stage theory do not hold up a general dimension of moral development. The five questionable dimensions are those derived from the social emotional rather than the cognitive components of Piaget's stages, for example, his concept of a shift from unilateral respect for adults to a mutual respect for peers.

These five dimensions are: modification of obedience to rules or authority because of situational demands or human needs; maintaining peer loyalty demands as opposed to obedience to authority; favoring direct retaliation by the victim rather than punishment by authority; favoring equality of treatment rather than differential reward for virtue for conformity to authority; punishment based only on active individual responsibility rather than collective responsibility.

The research results introduce a third qualification into Piaget's interpretation of his dimensions of development. Piaget's dimensions do not represent definite unitary stages which cut across the

must accept the rules of adults as unquestionable laws. This follows not only from the child's dependence on the adult, but from his fear and admiration of the adult (Piaget, 1965, p. 332). At this stage (heteronomy) the child's thought processes are constrained by the necessity of pleasing the adult. This constraint in turn hinders the child's ability to possibly contest the adult by reasoning out problems for himself. The social development process which accompanies the child's cognitive development goes from the unilateral of child for adult to the mutual respect of equals. Obviously, since most of us do overcome to greater or lesser degrees the initial cognitive constraints experienced by children, we might question how this was accomplished. Piagetian theory explains social development via mechanisms of cooperation, equilibration, role taking, and the desire for competence. In the case of extreme authoritarian parents, the constraint of the child may not be broken and may in fact be passed on:

Even when grown up, he will be unable, except in very rare cases, to break loose from the affective schemas acquired in this way, and will be as stupid with his own children as his parents were with him (Piaget, 1965, p. 192; emphasis added).

Kohlberg's Stages of Moral Development

Lawrence Kohlberg has devised a six-stage theory of moral development based on 28 aspects of moral judgment. These stages have been defined in various (but consistent) ways. Twenty-five of these aspects are listed in Kohlberg (1969, pp. 378–379). The stages are:

1. *Punishment and obedience orientation*—The physical consequences of an action determine its goodness or badness regardless of the human meaning or value of these consequences.
2. *Instrumental relativist orientation*—Right action consists of that which instrumentally satisfies one's own needs and occasionally the needs of others.

---

separate aspects of moral judgment. Within age and IQ groups, a child who is at the autonomous stage on one aspect of morality (for example, intentionality) is not especially likely to be autonomous on another aspect of morality, for example, naturalistic justice or reciprocity'' [Mac Rae, 1954; Johnson, 1962] (Kohlberg, 1964, p. 399).

Martin Hoffman, however, notes that "consistency across content areas within a given attribute" (i.e., is objective responsibility with regard to lying associated with objective responsibility with regard to stealing?) is also of importance. The evidence tends to be positive but inconclusively so, for the first type of consistency. Thus high consistency was found within the following attributes by Johnson (1962): imminent justice, objective responsibility, retributive justice and expiatory punishment; and within imminent justice, objective responsibility, and absolute moral perspective by Mac Rae (1954). Boehm and Nass (1962), however, found considerable specificity as regards objective responsibility. The evidence for consistency across attributes, which comes from Johnson and Mac Rae studies, is less clear cut. Thus, while Johnson reports positive relations among his moral attributes, Mac Rae found his attributes to be independent of one another.

3. *Interpersonal concordance or "god boy–nice girl" orientation*—Good behavior is that which pleases or helps others and is approved by them.
4. *"Law and order" orientation*—There is orientation toward authority, fixed rules and the maintenance of the social order.
5. *Social-contract legalistic orientation*—Generally, this stage has utilitarian overtones. Right action tends to be defined in terms of standards that have been critically examined and agreed upon by the whole society.
6. *Universal ethical-principle orientation*—Right is defined by the decision of conscience in accord with self-chosen *ethical principles* appealing to logical comprehensiveness, universality, and consistency. These principles are abstract and ethical (the Golden Rule, the categorical imperative); they are not concrete moral rules like the Ten Commandments (Kohlberg, 1971a, p. 87).

The method by which Kohlberg assesses moral development is to relate moral dilemmas to children and adults in which there is no correct answer (stories in which cultural values conflict) and then code the response on the basis of thought process rather than end choice. One complex Kohlbergian story could be simplified to the following: Would you steal a drug in order to save your wife's life? At Stage 1 the arguments might be: "Pro—If you let your wife die, you will get in trouble. You'll be blamed for not spending the money to save her and there'll be an investigation of you and the druggist for your wife's death. Con—You shouldn't steal the drug because you'll be caught and sent to jail if you do" (Kohlberg, 1971a, p.91).

Political Values in Cognitive Developmental Theory

In contrast to the socialization practices growing out of learning theory in which socialization is a consequence of unequal relationships is the democratic bias in Piagetian and certain neo-Piagetian psychological theories. To the extent that socialization is transmitted from adult to child with the adult controlling the socialization process it is an unequal experience. Learning theory proceeds from an assumption that adults should control the socialization experience. Cognitive development theory holds that the child can learn by self-discovery in the course of testing and experimenting in the social and physical realities he perceives. In the cognitive development model the adult is controlling access to the environment from which the child is able to construct his own reality. In the learning theory model the entire process is ideally controlled by the authority figure.

A number of premises about man's social-psychological nature exist within Piaget's and Kohlberg's theories of moral development. These premises express the developmentalists' own sense of moral right (i.e., both Piaget and Kohlberg believe that higher stages of cognitive development are "better" than lower stages). They are also propositions concerning the natural and preferred state of man.

These premises or propositions about man's nature are supportive of a democratic social system. The propositions underlying these cognitive developmental theories are democratic in their stress on equalitarianism and the self-worth of man.

The democratic propositions expressed in these theories are: (1) children ought to be autonomous (i.e., not controlled by fear or intimidation but enjoying independent participation); (2) men ought to treat each other with respect and dignity; (3) men are capable of rationality; (4) justice should be based on the equality of reciprocity between individuals; and (5) human beings can learn generalizable principles as well as specific behaviors.

Piagetian and Kohlbergian theory suggests that the above mentioned states of existence are promoted through the use of certain socialization mechanisms. These mechanisms are: (1) the use of language; (2) cooperation between individuals; (3) the use of role taking; (4) mastery and competence as motivating forces in the individual; and (5) the use of situations of "disequilibria" (a Piagetian equivalent of cognitive dissonance). The structure of the socialization experience is meant to be democratic.

If one wished to promote intellectual growth, the cognitive psychologist (of Piagetian persuasion) would argue that one should employ the mechanisms of role taking, cooperation, etc. These mechanisms, if employed effectively, result not only in the enhancement of cognitive growth but lead to democratic value outcomes. The child learns to respect and treat others as equals.

Developmentalists such as Piaget and Kohlberg believe that both man's capabilities for rationality and his ability to utilize generalizable principles stem from the interaction and maturation of cognitive structure and environment. The most productive environment for cognitive development as expressed through moral judgments should be democratic.

The use of and meaning of these mechanisms are particularly important in understanding the difference between Piaget and such neo-Piagetian theorists as Kohlberg and Ausubel. The democratic bias enumerated above holds true in both Piaget's and Kohlberg's theories despite a differing emphasis on the mechanisms of cognitive development. David Ausubel, another cognitive theorist, selected only certain of the aforementioned socialization mechanisms as salient to his theory and this has resulted in different value outcomes discussed below.

MORAL JUDGMENT—COGNITION VERSUS AFFECT

Piaget did his groundbreaking work on moral judgment in the 1930s and has not revised his initial effort. Kohlberg greatly enlarged upon and altered some of the Piagetian framework.[4] Moral judgment, in these theories, is seen as the most important factor in moral action.

---

[4]Piaget discusses two stages of moral development (heteronomous and autonomous). Moral maturity within this typology is usually achieved by age 12. Kohlberg used six stages in his typology

As learning theory becomes vague in its treatment of cognition, cognitive development theory is equally vague in its treatment of affect. Although their moral judgment systems do not claim to be based on emotional response, it is possible that many of the cognitive development mechanisms engender emotional as well as cognitive change. Kohlberg and his students have reported a number of behavioral findings linked to the moral judgment response category. These include the cheating behavior of grade school and college students (Kohlberg, 1971, pp. 78–79) and a number of more political behaviors (participation) discussed further on.

Piaget views moral judgment as an extension of the logical thinking process. Kohlberg's later essays hedge on this view of moral judgment. Both theories assume that the core of moral development resides in cognitive development. Both theories postulate hierarchical invariant stages through which the child progresses (develops). In the Piagetian framework, the ideal model for human reasoning (and in this case moral judgment) is based on a system of Aristotelian logic. Kohlberg is ambiguous about this point.

Kohlberg believes that each increasing stage on his hierarchy represents a greater differentiated structure, more stable and consistent, capable of handling more moral problems and conflicts. There is an inner consistency and logic in each stage's structure based on its relationship to the previous stage. Abilities, however, to complete Piagetian tasks do not completely coincide with the expected moral judgment level of the subject, i.e., there is a different logical system in one than in the other. Kohlberg states that cognitive development on Piagetian tasks (i.e., adjusting a pendulum to increase its frequency) is a necessary but not sufficient condition for moral judgment. It is necessary for subjects to be able to solve certain Piagetian tasks before they can reach certain moral levels. The achievement of a certain level of moral development entails the ability to solve a certain level of Piagetian tasks (i.e., the pendulum problem, balancing weights on a scale, or determining the relative flexibility of rods of different lengths, diameters, and material). The ability to reach a particular Piagetian level does not indicate automatic success on the moral judgment level of corresponding difficulty (Kohlberg, 1971b, p. 187).

> The correlations between general cognitive maturity and maturity of moral judgment are not one-to-one but of the order that a certain level of cognitive maturity is a necessary but not sufficient condition for a given level of moral judgment (Kohlberg, 1971, p. 45).

Keasey and Keasey (1974) report similar findings, i.e., that logical operations are a necessary but not sufficient condition for principled moral reasoning. If the later statement is true and Aristotelian logic is a necessary but not sufficient condition for moral development, what creates a situation that is necessary and

---

(outlined above). Moral growth is ongoing (through adulthood) in the Kohlberg system with few people reaching Stage 6 and a majority of Americans at Stage 4 (Kohlberg, 1974).

sufficient? Followers of Kohlberg suggest (Keasey & Keasey, 1974) that this is an example of *décalage* (lag between different areas of logical development). But individuals may achieve very high levels of cognitive development and display much lower levels of moral judgment à la Kohlberg (e.g., Albert Speer). *Décalage* is an unconvincing explanation. It seems more likely that, aside from the increasing cognitive complexity of Kohlberg's stages, the different moral levels are also tapping affectual responses which Kohlberg's theory does not adequately incorporate or explain.

Social Mechanisms of Cognitive Growth

Piaget writes that cooperation is the basis of the permanence of meaning and the social background for the development of concrete operational thought from intuitive thought. *It is also the basis for valuing the concept of reciprocity between individuals.*

> In particular, it is very difficult to see how concepts could conserve their permanent meanings and their definitions were it not for cooperation....
>
> To say that an individual arrives at logic only through cooperation thus simply amounts to asserting that the equilibrium of his operations is dependent on the infinite capacity for interaction with other people and therefore on a complex reciprocity. But this statement contains nothing that is not obvious, since the grouping within him is already nothing more or less than a system of reciprocities (1950, p. 164).

He continues: "Grouping is a co-ordination of operations, i.e. of actions accessible to the individual. Co-operation is a co-ordination of viewpoints or of actions emanating from different individuals" (1950, p. 163).

The question of which comes first—or which causes which (does grouping cause cooperation or vice versa since groupings exist in intuitive thought?)—is a problem more or less unresolved by Piaget except for his statement that both feed into and strengthen each other (1950, pp. 162–163). At one stage of development, the child possesses the cognitive apparatus for grouping but not for social cooperation. Descriptively, this is accounted for by the child's inability at this stage to clearly distinguish his own point of view from others (egocentrism) and his tendency to focus on only one aspect of a dilemma (centration) (1950, p. 160).

Without social cooperation, complex logical operations cannot be formed because the child is dependent on authority figures and is egocentric rather than independently attempting to solve problems. The points to be stressed here are the importance of cooperation for the development of logical thinking and the importance of both logical thinking (rationality) and cooperation for the maintenance of a democratic social structure.

Educators such as Johnson and Johnson concur: "Without cooperation among individuals, no group, no family, no organization, and no school would be able to exist'' (1974, p. 218).

Despite the importance of cooperation in social development, Johnson and Johnson state that of three possible goal structures which schools may use (i.e., cooperative, competitive, and individualistic goal structures) it is the cooperative structure which ''is the most underutilized in current educational practice'' (1974, p. 213). They cite experimental evidence demonstrating that American children are more competitive than children from other countries and that competitive tendencies in children often interfere with cooperative problem solving (1974, pp. 217–218).

Lasswell cites the multiplication of particular and special interests at the expense of common norms and interests as one of ''the most obvious challenges to the internal public order of advanced bodies politic'' (Lasswell, 1969, p. 34). The cognitive developmental model of moral development stresses the importance of social cooperation in the development of cognitive structures.

THE IMPORTANCE OF ROLE TAKING IN MORAL DEVELOPMENT

Moral maturity in Kohlberg's system is partly dependent on the individual's ability to understand the perspective of others. Kohlberg believes that understanding the viewpoint of other members of one's social group facilitates the values of reciprocity and equality (which he sees as the end states of moral development). If his assumptions are valid, institutions which support role taking create an environment where equality and reciprocity are valued. Hence ''democratic leadership,'' which requires more role taking than ''autocratic leadership,'' would have greater probability in producing these preferred value outcomes. Kohlberg stresses the importance of shared knowledge for individual development.

> All social knowledge implies an act of sharing, of taking the view point of another self or group of selves....The motivational problem usually proposed to socialization theory is the question of why the ''selfish'' or impulsive infant develops into a social being.... The answer of developmental theory is that the self is itself born out of the social or sharing process, and therefore, motives for self-realization or self-enhancement are not basically ''selfish'' in the pejorative sense, but require sharing ... developmental theories assume a primary motivation for competence and self-actualization which is organized through an ego or self whose structure is social or shared (1969, p. 416).

Kohlberg links role taking to empathy. ''Perceived harm to others is as immediately, if not intensely, apprehended as harm to the self. Empathy does not have to be taught to the child or conditioned; it is a primary phenomena'' (1969, p. 436). Empathy is a precondition for ''experiencing a moral conflict'' (1971a, p. 64). But the important question for Kohlberg is not how one *feels* but how empathy acts to structure a moral dilemma. "The moral question is 'whose role do I take?' or 'whose claim do I favor?' The working core of the utilitarian principle is the principle of justice, 'consider each person's welfare equally, not the maximization principle' " (1971a, p. 64).

COMPETENCE AND AUTONOMY IN KOHLBERG'S SYSTEM

A crucial factor in the child's cognitive development is his or her inborn desire for social competence which implies a "need to understand" at least the social environment. This, if true, presents some interesting political implications. We would wish to structure the social system in schools such that the child could continually test and demonstrate his competence. Children would not be placed in situations wherein they feel incompetent since this would hinder cognitive growth (Hoffman, 1970, p. 268).

From a Piagetian perspective, parents can contribute to their child's cognitive growth—"movement towards autonomy" (1971a, p. 268)—by establishing relationships of mutual respect and equality. "One must place oneself on the child's own level, and give him a feeling of equality by laying stress on one's own obligations and one's own deficiencies" (1971a, p. 268). The child should not be given unsolvable tasks: "The parent can contribute to the young child's movement toward autonomy by burdening him with fewer demands whose reasons he cannot grasp and which he is therefore apt to place on the same plane as actual physical phenomena" (1971a, p. 268).

Kohlberg believes that there is an innate striving for competence via being able to control the environment. Infants attempt to control their environment in simple physical ways. Young children of 6 or 7 become increasingly sensitive to social definers of competence.

> The child's initial desires to perform competently, to succeed, rest on intrinsic competence motivation. The infant struggles to master a task without the least concern for adult reward for performing the task, and without the least concern for the adult's judgment as to whether or not he is doing right (Kohlberg, 1969, p. 420).

In defense of this position, he argues that (1) babies frequently imitate the behaviors of adults who are unimportant to the babies emotionally; (2) the imitated behaviors are "often not those immediately associated with affectively significant events" (Kohlberg, 1969, p. 436).

Brofenbrenner's summary of the results of modeling studies supports Kohlberg's claim that self-mastery or competence is a motivating factor in the child's social development.

1. The potency of the model increases with the extent to which the model is perceived as possessing a high degree of competence, status, and control over resources.... *The status of the model emerged as a more powerful*

factor than the degree of reinforcement received by the child (emphasis added).

2. The inductive power of the model increases with the degree of prior nurturance or reward exhibited by the model....

3. The most "contiguous" models for the child are likely to be those who are the major sources of support and control in his environment; namely, his parents, playmates, and older children who play a prominent role in his everyday life....

4. The inductive power of the model increases with the degree to which the person perceives the model as similar to himself.

5. Several models, exhibiting similar behavior are more powerful inducers of change than a single model....

6. The potency of the model is enhanced when the behavior exhibited is a salient feature in the actions of a group of which the child already aspires to be a member....

7. The power of the model to induce actual performance (as distinguished from acquisition) is strongly influenced by the observed consequences for the model of the exhibited behavior (Bronfenbrenner, 1970, pp. 132–134).

Kohlberg notes (1969, p. 441) that the results of modeling studies by MacDonald and Ross (1963) show that the child is more concerned with social approval than concrete rewards (Kohlberg, 1969, p. 453). These observations can be interpreted as showing that reinforcement via rewards may be successful for short-range behaviors but that "cognitive stability" in large measure depends on the child's definition of "good" and "right."

> The child understands that whether or not he gets candy for a performance is highly specific to the situation and the adult, and that the more generalized component of his learning is that of whether the act is good or bad (Kohlberg, 1969, p. 442).

Whereas learning theorists focus on needs as physiological states and learning as dependent on rewards which initially emanate from outside the organism, Piaget suggests what is learned is determined by (1) what the organism can understand from the learning experience, and (2) his cognitive need for successful solution (Mischel, 1971, p. 332). Need is seen as the discrepancy "between one's schemas and the situations one encounters—this is what motivates the child to deploy and develop his schemas, he needs to accommodate those schemas in order to assimilate the situation he has encountered" (Mischel, 1971, p. 329). This state of disequilibria (referred to as the equilibration process or the mechanism of cognitive match) has been successfully employed in raising the moral judgment level of elementary and high school students (Kohlberg, 1969, p. 403). The idea of cognitive match as a mechanism for inducing cognitive restructuring would appear to be easy to implement within the elementary schoolroom.

Contrasting Ausubel with Piaget and Kohlberg

Not all cognitive developmental theorists believe in the democratic values their model advocates. Whether this indicates a confusion on their part with the value outcomes of the Piagetian-neo-Piagetian theory or an appreciation of the theory but a discomfiture with its value outcomes is difficult to assess. David Ausubel is an example of such a theorist. In his treatment of the determinants of change in Piagetian stages (Ausubel, 1970), he emphasizes language acquisition and use. However, in his treatment of moral development Ausubel sounds remarkably like Piaget and Kohlberg (Ausubel, 1971, p. 203).

Two differences in approach between Ausubel and Piaget-Kohlberg are: (1) Ausubel believes that cognitive drive arises not from the structure of thinking but from the experience of satisfaction with correct solutions; (2) Ausubel stresses the importance of the child's understanding of obligation. These differences notwithstanding, it is difficult to reconcile Ausubel's position on adult socialization with the values implicit in the cognitive development model of socialization.

> Particularly in our utilitarian, competitive and status-oriented culture, such extrinsic considerations as ego-enhancement, anxiety reduction, and career advancement become with increasing age, progressively more significant sources of motivation for school learning. Although educators theoretically decry the use of aversive motivation, they implicitly rely on it, as well as on other extensive motivations, to keep their students studying regularly for their credits, degrees and diplomas. They do this because they recognize, at least implicitly, that cognitive drive and anticipated rewards for hard work are not sufficient to overcome both inertia and the typical human proclivity toward procrastination and aversion to sustained regular and disciplined intellectual work (Ausubel, 1971, p. 360).

The model stresses egalitarianism, reciprocity, autonomy, and cooperation but the theorist (at least in this case) does not believe it will work. And, while he does not seem to favor the values he sees as currently holding sway in our society, he would not attempt to alter the status quo.

Structured versus Nonstructured Thought

The debate over structured versus nonstructured thinking is reflected in the differing approaches of learning theorists and cognitive developmentalists. The cognitive developmentalist argues in favor of the learning of generalizable principles rather than specific behaviors. In criticism of the Bereiter-Englemann training program which attempted to teach young children basic learning skills, Kohlberg noted that "some children had been successfully taught competence in adding and subtracting written numbers ... but failed to conserve numbers or even to say correctly that seven (raisins) were more than six (raisins)" (1970, p.

46). Teaching principles which are generalizable not only endow the child with greater flexibility (and therefore more choice options), but the teaching of such principles involves the child as an active and the central participant in the learning experience. It is the child who must recognize deficiencies in his own thought processes (through the process of disequilibria or equilibration). It is the child who must actively restructure his own thought processes when they do not adequately explain the environment.

Modeling and Cognitive Developmental Theory

Learning theorists using modeling techniques have tried to train children to use cognitively sophisticated responses (as defined in Piaget's model). Their success might (1) indicate a method of hastening the moral development of children, or (2) undercut the explanatory value of the cognitive developmental theory of moral judgment by demonstrating an effective alternative to role taking, equilibration, and other socialization mechanisms employed in developmental theory.

According to the developmentalists, moral thought is organized and restructured in a series of invariant stages. If modeling techniques were to enable children to quickly reach a preferred stage of moral judgment without passing through the previous stages, there would be cause to greatly alter if not discredit the developmental approach.

Bandura and McDonald (1963) found that children could be trained to respond to moral judgments which were contrary to their initial orientation regardless of whether the initial responses were "objective" or "subjective." In the Piagetian framework which was used, objective or immature responses occur when blame is assigned (by the child) in relation to the consequences of an act. Subjective or mature responses occur when blame is assigned in relationship to the intentions of the actor.[5]

Cowan, Langer, Heavenrich, and Nathanson (1969) successfully replicated the Bandura and McDonald study but questioned the learning theory interpretation of the results. They were not satisfied that learning theory adequately explained the rapidity with which responses were learned, or the generalizability of the responses or the instability of certain learned responses or the difference in modeling effects on groups being trained in an upward (toward mature judgments) versus a downward direction.

Bandura (1969) responded by critiquing Cowan et al.'s statistical methodol-

---

[5]The oversimplification of the Piagetian model in regard to consequences and intentions has been questioned by a number of researchers. The work of Gutkin (1972), Armsby (1971), and Walster (1966) indicates that intentions play a more important role in children's judgments than Piaget originally assumed and that consequences play a more important role in adult judgments than originally assumed.

ogy and interpretation as well as by reiterating his acceptance of a mediating process which would allow subjects to "abstract common attributes from diverse modeled responses and formulate a principle for generating similar patterns of behavior" (Bandura, 1969, p. 278). Schleifer and Douglas (1973) also replicated Bandura and McDonald's findings but altered the experimental setup to reduce possible response bias. But, like Cowan et al., they questioned whether the experimental results repudiated Piagetian theory. They note a difference between trained and untrained responses.

> However it was clear that many of the trained children could not adequately generalize the concept of intentionality to very complicated moral situations which were designed to control for response sets. Compared with a nontrained high level group of the same age, many did not do as well in coping with some of the pairs of stories. This suggests that training cannot completely duplicate the normal developmental process (Schleifer & Douglas, 1973, p. 67).

Schleifer and Douglas also adopt Turiel's view that modeling may in fact provide the child with an alternative point of view and stimulate reflection much in the manner that role playing or disequilibration might instigate the child to further reflection.

Criticisms of the Cognitive Development Model of Moral Development

A number of critiques of Piaget's and Kohlberg's research methodologies have been made by a diverse set of critics. Although all of this criticism tends to show up the shortcomings of developmental theory, some of the most interesting criticism has been directed by developmentalists aiming to increase the accuracy of the model rather than to disprove the theory. Some criticism, such as Brainerd's (1973), was focused not on moral judgment but on other Piagetian tasks (transitivity and ordinality). But Brainerd's analysis seems equally applicable to the moral judgment stories and interpretation.

Brainerd notes that two types of criticisms have been made of Piaget's clinical method of investigation—"stimulus" criticisms and "response" criticisms.

> The stimulus criticisms...concern methods of task *presentation* and they include the usual sources of Type II error in studies of children's reasoning: inattentiveness, forgetting, misunderstanding instructions etc. ... the response side has been whether children's *judgments* or *explanations* of these judgments are the minimum necessary evidence that the structure presumed to underlie the solution of some given task is in fact present (Brainerd, 1973, p. 172).

Brainerd is concerned with the response criticisms made of Piaget. Understanding these criticisms are, I believe, central to understanding and accepting the accuracy of Piaget's or Kohlberg's stage theory of moral development.

Brainerd does not discuss Piaget's work on moral judgment (in which judgments and explanations were used to measure moral development). He reviews the work in Piagetian transitivity and ordinality experiments in which different experimenters reached different conclusions as to the ages when these conceptions were acquired. The discrepancies in research findings could be accounted for by the difference in response criteria (judgments versus explanations) used by the experimenters.

> Gruen proceeded to reanalyze the data of his doctoral dissertation...which was concerned with number conservation, and he found, in line with his hypothesis, that more subjects were inferred to possess conservation when the judgment criterion was applied than when the explanation criterion was applied. On the basis of this finding, Gruen concluded that the judgment criterion is more consonant with non-Piagetian theory. Subsequent research has either directly . . . or indirectly . . . supported the proposition that the judgment criterion is the less stringent of the two (Brainerd, 1973, p. 1974).

Is verbal performance a precise measure of competence? Brainerd is doubtful since developmentalists consider language as a subset of thought.

> *It should be recalled in this regard that, according to Piaget, language bears a very special relation to cognitive structure. In particular, language is a dependent variable vis-a-vis cognitive structure. Logically, this implies that all identifiable structural properties of language are, in some sense, inherent properties of the cognitive structures. This, in turn, implies that one can discover some though certainly not all, of the properties of cognitive structures via the study of language* (1973, p. 178; emphasis added).

Simpson raises a similar point (1974) when she decries the cultural biases of Kohlberg's test since it is dependent on verbal responses.

McCann and Prentice (1973) found that delinquents possessed a higher level of competence on a Piagetian moral judgment test than their "normal" performance on such a test would indicate. Delinquent adolescents were capable of increasing their intentional choices (judgmental responses to Piagetian stories indicative of a "higher" level of moral development than stories stressing "consequences") by 20% under experimental conditions. These particular experimental conditions were unusual in that subjects were motivated to produce "correct" responses via set (the delinquent was told to match the imagined response of a teacher) and a monetary reward for correct responses. Financial payment was made at the conclusion of the experiment. Subjects were *not* informed after each choice whether they were right or wrong. The results suggest that delinquents are capable at times of making more sophisticated verbal responses than they would ordinarily care to make.

Kohlberg's research has been criticized for a number of methodological reasons. Kurtines and Greif list the following faults in research findings stemming from Kohlberg's model: (1) different studies using the Kohlberg model have not necessarily used identical moral dilemmas in assessing subjects' moral stage. Researchers choose from nine basic stories but do not specify which stories they used; (2) at least two systems of scoring Kohlberg's stories have been used: a global system and a detailed system (1974, p. 455); (3) Kohlberg has not always specified his sample size and statistical analysis of some of the earlier moral judgment studies was faulty (1974, pp. 461, 464); and (4) the test appears biased against females, i.e., women do worse on Kohlberg's test than do males although Kohlberg ascribes this difference to the different role men and women occupy in our society (1974, pp. 456, 467).

In addition, the research of one of Kohlberg's closest collaborators, Elliot Turiel (1974, forthcoming), indicates that Kohlberg's original coding scheme was inaccurate. Subjects in transition from Stage 4 to Stage 5 gave a response set which was similar enough to Stage 2 that Kohlberg assumed it was Stage 2 and was unaware of the transitional nature of this "stage." Kohlberg now codes this response as Stage 4 ½ but this is not likely to satisfy Turiel. At the least, it would require the recoding of earlier studies of moral development such as the Haan, Smith, and Block study (1968) which adopted Kohlberg's framework and categorized a large number of arrestees from the Berkeley Free Speech Movement. Many of these students were ranked as Stage 2 and Stage 5 whereas they probably would be recoded Stage 4 ½ and Stage 5.

A study of "hippies" by Haan, Stroud, and Holstein (1973) comparing the moral judgment stages of Kohlberg with the ego stages of Loevinger found evidence in support of Turiel's claim. Many of the subjects in this later study appeared to be in a transitional stage. The following bits of evidence suggest that they are in flux:

a) they are most frequently designated as transitional in terms of ego development;
b) the Moral Stage 2's who were also Ego Stage ¾'s did not appear fixedly regressed to an immature stage, but rather seemed uncertain and uneven;
c) those subjects who were most likely to be transitional in development, again the Moral Stage 2's, were also seen to be functionally the least coping (p. 609).

To be uncommitted in one's relations to others and to be unclear about one's self is probably manifested functionally as being less coping" (Haan et al., 1973, p. 609).

Turiel claims that "moral judgment constitutes only one aspect of social conceptions and that there exist other dimensions of social development that should be analyzed separately" (forthcoming, p. 3). This represents a broader and more inclusive perspective than Kohlberg's. It is an attempt to extend and integrate the structural stages of cognitive development to other realms of social thought. Turiel is now testing a developmental theory of social conventions (which he believes is a separate social dimension from moral judgment but which he also believes influences specific moral judgments, i.e., judgments concerning sexual conduct [forthcoming]). If Turiel is successful, his model may bolster the claims made by adherents to Kohlberg's moral judgment theory by providing further explanation of anomalous cases: e.g., Turiel cites an unpublished study by Gilligan in which "sexual stories were a) more variable and b) scored at lower stages of responses on the standard stories" (Turiel, forthcoming, p. 14).

It seems equally reasonable to me that cognitive theories of moral development could be strengthened (better explain judgment responses) if they would further investigate and integrate the role of affect in judgmental responses. Cognitive developmentalists stress the importance of cognition over affect in making judgmental responses. But the precise role of affect in this process is not always clear, is usually an underdeveloped portion of developmental theory, and seems to differ slightly from theorist to theorist.

Ausubel, e.g., states that as the child grows cognition becomes increasingly more important than affect in making moral decisions. "This trend is manifested in at least three different ways: 1) in the bases on which moral values are selectively-internalized; 2) in the basis on which feelings of obligation to abide by these values are interiorized; and 3) in the actual processes of reaching an action decision in behavior involving moral issues" (Ausubel, 1971, p. 201). If moral belief and action differ, it is probably due to insincerity or a confusion of moral beliefs.

Mischel cites Piaget's discussion of affect (unfortunately, Piaget's book on this topic has not been translated): "Affect and intelligence are complementary facts of mental development... all conduct has both 'structure' and 'energy': affects provide the latter, while structures of intelligence constitute the former" (Mischel, 1968a). How this works out and what it means is still unclear—especially in the work of Kohlberg.[6]

It is unclear why developmentalists argue that cognition will influence the accompanying affect one might feel in reaching a moral judgment; i.e., do we

---

[6]The following citations from Kohlberg demonstrate both ambiguity toward the role of affect in moral judgments and belittle the importance of affect in moral decision making. Kohlberg believes that the affect which accompanies a moral judgment is similar to the affect which an astronomer might feel upon discovering that a comet would hit the earth (1971b, p. 189). In a more theoretical argument he states:

1) "Affective" and "cognitive" development are *parallel;* they represent different perspectives and contexts in defining structural change (1969, p. 349).
2) The *development* of cognition and the development of affect have a common structural base (1969, p. 389).
3) What is being asserted, then, is not that moral judgment stages are cognitive but that the existence of moral stages implies that moral development has a basic structural component. While motives and affects are involved in moral development, the development of these motives and affects is largely mediated by changes in thought patterns (1969, p. 389).
4) Moral judgment stages or sequences are to be described in cognitive-structural terms even in regard to "affective" aspects of moral judgment, like guilt, empathy, etc. (1969, p. 390).

Why make the distinction between affect and cognition if affect is always defined in terms of cognition?

[7]In a cross-national study of three universities (England and France), O'Connor (1974) also concluded that "Kohlberg's moral reasoning variable was the single best predictor of activism from among the... variables employed in this study" (p. 77).

feel differently when we learn the circumstances of a malfeasance, and yet disregard the possibility that our feeling states might influence our cognitive perceptions?

Political Research Utilizing the Cognitive Development Model

Despite the above mentioned criticisms of the Piaget-Kohlberg model of moral development, this model is widely used by researchers studying ethical beliefs, political behavior, and ideology and it has yielded fairly consistent and interesting results. Haan, Smith, and Block (as reported in Haan et al. [1968], or Smith [1969], or Block et al. [1968]) gave 957 college students and Peace Corps volunteers Kohlberg's moral judgment scale along with several other psychological and social measures—i.e., adjective Q sorts in which subjects described themselves and a measure of perceived parental child-rearing practices. Most interesting of their findings was the attempt to relate political activism and moral judgment. Haan et al. found that students at Level III (stages 5 and 6) were disproportionately active in political demonstrations (Haan et al., 1968, p. 188, Table 7; Smith, 1969, p. 336) but that there were also a substantial minority of Instrumental Hedonists at Level I among the FSM male arrestees. Smith wondered:

> Are these really "moral primitives" corresponding to the public image, or are they rather a special worrisome breed of "postmoral" young people who are unprincipled "on principle?" It is hard to say, but I would venture that these students are quite unlike people in the general population who would be so classified (Smith, 1969, p. 336).

Turiel's analysis of transitional stages (1974) indicates that many of those previously categorized as Stage 2 are actually in a state of transition from Stage 4 to Stage 5. This sample would have to be recoded in order to separate out the Stage 4 ½ (transitionals) from Stage 2. The effect of the recoding probably would further weight the evidence that the majority of FSM protesters questioned were of high moral ideals (predominantly stages 4 ½, 5, and 6) and not participating out of hedonistic (Stage 2) needs.

Smith, Haan, and Block divided the student sample into four political categories. These were identified as follows:

> *Conventionalists,* who belonged to fraternities or sororities but were below the median of the total sample in both social service activities (volunteer work) and protest activities (such as picketing, demonstrations, and sit-ins). Differential participation in social service and protest activities was the basis for defining three additional types. Those who were high on social service but low on protest activities were called *Constructivists;* those who were high on both, *Broad Spectrum Activists;* those who were high only on protest activities (and indeed check *no* social service activities) *Dissenters* (Smith, 1969, p. 333).

Regarding the moral judgments of these different groups Smith concluded:

> The Inactives, the Conventionalists, and the Constructivists all fall mainly at Level II—Morality of Conventional Role-Conformity. It is the two types who had engaged in substantial protest activity, the Broad Spectrum Activists and the Dissenters, in which principled morality is especially frequent (Smith, 1969, p. 337).

Fishkin, Keniston, and MacKinnon (1973) conducted a similar study in 1970 using 75 undergraduates from eight major campuses as subjects. They concluded:

> Subjects who reasoned at the conventional moral level were politically conservative, while the preconventional subjects favored violent radicalism. Further analysis showed extremely high correlations between stage 4 (law and order) reasoning and conservatism. Postconventional moral reasoning was associated with the rejection of conservative views but not with the acceptance of radical ideology (Fishkin et al., 1973, p. 109).

As in the Haan, Smith, and Block study Fishkin, Kenniston, and MacKinnon found that preconventional reasoners (Stage 2) were more like postconventional reasoners (stages 5, 6) than either of these groups were like conventional subjects (Fishkin et al., 1973, p. 114). The researchers, however, distinguished between the "acute moral 'regression'" of the Stage 2 reasoners (which was associated with the acceptance of slogans of violent radicalism) and the higher stages (5, 6) in which reasoners disagreed with conservative slogans, but were not in agreement with radical slogans "whether violent or peaceful" (1973, pp. 114, 117).

Like the Haan study, the Fiskin research should be recoded so that Stage 2 and the transitional Stage 4½ are distinguished. Unlike Haan, Smith, and Block, who used a behavioral measure of political activity,[7] Fishkin, Kenniston, and MacKinnon used a list of political slogans which subjects indicated their liking for (or dislike of) on a five-point scale. This is at best a weak measure of ideology.

In a slightly different vein is the work of Fontana and Noel (1973) who attempt to piece together the relationship between social role and moral judgment. Fontana and Noel examined the moral judgments of administrators and faculty of a university and compared both social role and political ideology with the level of moral judgment of their subjects. Some critics (Simpson, 1974) believe that Kohlberg's scale is culturally biased. The findings of Fontana and Noel do not dispute this contention. But their results do begin to shed light on the kind of social structure (or at least the kind of social roles) that produce a particular kind of ethical being (i.e., Stage 3 or Stage 4 or Stage 5). Among their findings were these:

1. Administrators were higher than other groups in their use of stage 4 reasoning. . . .
2. Individuals on the right were highest and those on the left were lowest in stage 4 reasoning. . . .
3. Leftists are higher than rightists in their use of stage 2 reasoning. . . .

4. Only minimal differences were found in moral reasoning between activist and inactivist students. . . .
5. Activist faculty reasoned more at stages 5 and 6 than inactivist faculty did; and inactivist faculty reasoned more at stage 2 than did their activist counterparts. . . .
6. Two findings emerged across role groups for field of specialization, namely, that natural scientists reasoned more at stage 4 and less at stage 5 than did social scientists and individuals in the humanities (Fontana & Noel, 1973, pp. 426–428).

As in the above mentioned research, the coding procedures regarding Stages 2 and 4 are suspect.

Support for the cognitive developmental approach is evidenced in the work of June Tapp (Tapp & Levine, 1970; Tapp & Kohlberg, 1971) and Joseph Adelson (Adelson & O'Neil, 1966; Adelson, Green, & O'Neil, 1969; Gallatin & Adelson, 1971).

June Tapp is concerned with the development of legal rule systems. In a cross-cultural study of 406 children, she has noted their changing perceptions of authority figures, rules, justice, and punishment (Tapp & Levine, 1970). Later she attempted to match her findings from two studies (one using a sample of United States youths from kindergarten to college and the other a six-country study of middle school preadolescents) with the results of Kohlberg's studies.

Tapp found a developmental trend to children's perceptions of rules. The changes Tapp perceived corresponded well with the stage model of moral development discussed by Kohlberg. As children grow from primary schoolers to become adolescents, their views of rules change in a number of ways. Young children perceive obedience to rules as a consequence of the negative sanctions of rules (Level II of Kohlberg's scheme). As children grow older they (in this case a proportion of the sample) give rational-utilitarian reasons for obeying rules (Kohlberg's Level III). Similar correspondences were found in children's perceptions of the mutability of rules—i.e., rules cannot be changed (Level I) to rules can be changed depending on social utility or mutual agreement (Levels II, III). Children's perceptions of the conditions under which a rule may be broken also changed—i.e., rules can be broken but *should* not be broken (Level I), rules can be broken depending on the morality of the circumstance (Level II), rules can be broken depending on the morality of the rule (Level III).

While the work of Joseph Adelson et al. (as cited above) does not attempt to relate Kohlberg's theory of moral judgment to their findings on children's political conceptualizations, the findings of Adelson et al. do mesh well with Kohlberg's theory and are in many instances similar to Tapp's results.

The research of Adelson and his colleagues outlines the change in children's political thinking from concrete, absolutist, restrictive, and authoritarian to complex, philosophic, and social, e.g.:

Younger children particularly those below 15 ... conceptualize government in terms of specific and tangible services... younger adolescents are usually insensitive to individual liberties, and opt for authoritarian solutions to political problems—at the

> same time, they are unable to achieve a differentiated view of the social order, and thus cannot grasp the legitimate claims of the community upon the citizen (Adelson & O'Neil, 1966, p. 295).

Or:

> Significant changes in the view of law take place between 13 and 15. Level of discourse shifts from concrete to abstract; a restrictive emphasis is replaced by a stress on the positive aims of law; a conception of amendment is increasingly present in later years, as in an emphasis on the intrapsychic effects of law (Adelson, Green, & O'Neil, 1969, p. 327).

In addition, these theorists are sympathetic to a cognitive developmental interpretation of their results. Changes in political thought are at least partly attributed to changes in cognitive development *as postulated in Piaget's theory* (Adelson & O'Neil, 1966, p. 305).

Cognitive Development and Political Thinking

In Piaget's model of development children progress from a state of irrationality to, presumably, the rationality of adulthood. Using Gibson's description of rationality, we can illustrate the irrationality which characterizes much of children's thought.

> In most anything we do there are in fact disadvantages as well as advantages, to be rational we must count the cost, or—to put it another way—consider whether our ends on balance justify the means. Much of the rationality of any action consists in considering means for reconciling different ends, and where they cannot all be achieved at a given time, in considering which is likely to be most satisfying in the long run, which can be postponed till later and so on (1960, p. 158).

Merelman (1969) describes four types of child-like thinking outlined by Pinard and Laurendeau: realism, artificialism, dynamism, and animism. They are categories used to refer to interpretations of reality which do not conform to the "adult" construction of reality.

Artificialism refers to the child's belief that social and natural phenomena are attributable to supernatural forces (i.e., clouds are pushed by God—Merelman, 1969, p. 754). Realism refers to the child's acceptance of subjective phenomena as objective phenomena, i.e., dreams "have an origin external to the dreamer." Dynamism refers to the belief that causation is either supernatural or wholly personal. Animism is the label attached to the child's anthropomorphic views.

Merelman is interested in these processes because his conceptualization of ideology embodies a high degree of rationality—i.e., "if a person, because of some views of individual morality, favors a balanced budget, he cannot at the same time, believe in extra-budgeting social welfare payments to his own group" (1969, p. 751). Realism, artificialism, dynamism, and animism are examples of children's thinking processes which result in irrational conclusions by the standards of adult observers. How can means and ends be properly considered if the future is at the whim of supernatural forces?

Merelman is interested in the growth of rational thought in children so that he can understand the development of political ideology.

> To sum up, the individual must be able to reason from cause to effect. The causes of effects in the political world must seem partially and/or potentially under human control, and the principles by which causes and effects are linked must be transmissible (1969, p. 753).

We often perceive adults make what appear to be irrational decisions—decisions which, given the actors' goals, are lacking in forethought or foresight. The lack of adult rationality may be viewed by stage theorists as the consequence of a gap or lack of cognitive development in childhood (since thinking in a higher stage of development is dependent on the existence of the previous stage of cognitive development).

Ronald Johnson has proposed an alternative interpretation which is that the success of adults in solving Piagetian-type tasks is a matter of relativity. He surmises that if adults were given tasks of comparable difficulty, as the Piagetian tasks are to children, the incidence of what psychologists term precausal thought would be equally high: e.g., "Dennis found that many college students in his sample believed that the sea is a living organism because it moves" (1969, p. 754).

Or note the persistence in adulthood of the "just world" hypothesis. Studies by Lerner and Simmons (1966), Lerner (1971), Stein (1974), and Chaikin and Darley (1973) indicate that people have a need to believe

> that a relationship exists between one's actions and one's outcomes such that rewards are obtained for appropriate effort and skill, and punishment or lack of reward accrues only when those have been justified by one's behavior.... It is preferable, according to Lerner, to imagine that the person's actions brought misfortune upon him, that is, his behavior was responsible for his suffering. If such is clearly not the case, however, it will accomplish the same purpose to devalue the luckless one's inherent personal worth (Stein, 1974, p. 805).

Piagetian problems appear relatively simple to adults since adults have accumulated many years of experience in manipulating the variables presented in the problems. The questions Piaget poses are familiar problems to an adult but are new to the child. Political problems are not as familiar to many adults. Perhaps by using some Piagetian categories of preoperational thought we can discern types of laws which adults make in their political cognitions.

The descriptive categories Piaget uses to characterize preoperational thought are not restricted to those referred to by Merelman. These categories often represent different degrees of generality and sometimes overlap one another, i.e., animism and egocentrism overlap. Two descriptive categories not discussed by Merelman are "centered thinking" and transductive thinking.

Centered thinking occurs when the child pays attention to only one aspect of a problem. Two jars hold the same amounts of water but the child believes one contains a greater volume because it is taller. Children sometimes give objective moral judgment responses because they attend to one aspect of the story (the consequences of the act) to the exclusion of the relevant portion of the story (the intentions of the actor) (Crowley, 1968). Likewise, adults sometimes focus on one aspect of a "problem" to the exclusion of other facets of the dilemma (Slater, 1970, p. 61).

> "But mother, I'm going to jail—I'm a political prisoner."
> "Well at least they'll give you a decent haircut."

Transductive reasoning exists when the child reasons from the particular to the particular. "A causes B, therefore B causes A....Daddy's getting hot water, so he's going to shave" (Phillips, 1969, p. 65). It also characterizes a child's limited ability to order categories. The example offered in a Piagetian story is that Jacqueline, at 25 months, was unable to distinguish illnesses with reversible and irreversible effects (e.g., influenza versus humpback). "A is like B in some way; therefore, A is like B in every way" (Phillips, 1969, p. 67). Phillips' footnote at this point is: "Again this is a fairly accurate picture of the rigidity that can be found in the thinking of many adults in certain situations (e.g., A and B both have dark skins; B is shiftless and irresponsible; therefore, so is A).

Watergate and Moral Development

The great salient moral issue of recent domestic politics is the crisis of Watergate. It is difficult to determine how much of the Watergate phenomenon (i.e., illegality, trickery, and hypocrisy on the part of legitimate sources of authority) has been symptomatic of the public and private sectors of American life. The comparative import of Watergate, the Vietnam war, and the economic difficulties of the mid-seventies in eroding public confidence in "legitimate" institutions may be an unanswerable question. Certainly we may expect greater concern in reestablishing the recognized moral character of our political leaders as well as renewed interest in effectively socializing shared moral values. The lack of moral criteria among the population and moral rectitude in the community's leadership has disastrous implications for the nation's social solidarity and acceptance of authority as legitimate.

The pervasiveness of the Watergate phenomenon in American life is implicitly acknowledged by Kohlberg in a speech he gave at the 1974 APA convention.

> Hopefully, if the American public has rediscovered the constitution the American psychologist will rediscover Dewey. Psychology perhaps in the next few years may take up where Dewey and James left off. No more gimmicks, no more bugging, no more beyond freedom and dignity, no more cost accounting, no more encounter group

expression of feeling at the loss of dignity of others, no more psychiatric profiles used to dump on people you don't like. Just straightforward science openly interviewing people and in participant observation of their actions. Just straightforward justice and democracy (Kohlberg, 1974, p. 10).

Kohlberg's general analysis of Watergate is that President Nixon was morally blind. His published statements were never above Stage 4 of Kohlberg's system nor do they indicate an understanding of Stage 5. The moral level of general public opinion in the United States also is at Stage 4. The Constitution, however, is a Stage 5 document and many of the eventual opponents of Nixon during the Watergate struggle (Ervin, Baker, Cox, and Richardson) were at Stage 5 in their moral cognitions.

The former President was unable to understand the responses of his opposition. "Nixon's last comments before deciding to resign were comments of bewilderment. After all the stage 2 exchanges of favors Nixon had done in getting Republican Congressmen elected, how could they vote to impeach him? Nixon then was destroyed by his own cynicism, by his inability to believe there was any power to moral principles or to a constitution which embodied them" (1974, p. 5).

Kohlberg cites Watergate as the third great morality tale of the post-Hitler era, the other two being the civil rights struggle and the Vietnam war. He significantly overlooks the McCarthy hearings. Through Watergate (or so Kohlberg believes) "the public came to understand that Nixon's Watergate violations of law were not only violations of isolated individuals challenging the system on moral grounds but were violations of the civil rights of every American—of the heart of the constitutional system.... Thus, the American public's mood passed from apathy to indignation to a greater faith in our own stage 5 system" (1974, p. 9).

Dan Candee, a Kohlberg research associate, interviewed 400 college and graduate students in an empirical study of the response to Watergate made by people of different stages of moral judgment. Candee began with the hypothesis that regardless of their political affiliation persons categorized as stages 5 and 6 share certain beliefs which are congruent with the values necessary for a democratic tradition, i.e., "the area that is absolute is the protection of human rights, above all the rights to life and liberty" (Candee, 1974, p. 26).

Candee found that subjects in stages 5 and 6 were more supportive of democratic principles than those in lower stages.

On every question, stage 5 subjects of both political parties, endorsed the content choice which was consistent with democratic principles more often than did stage 3 or 4 subjects. However, in terms of absolute consensus the results were more complex. Sometimes, there was as much agreement among stage 3 subjects, across party lines, for their alternatives as there was among stage 5 subjects (1974, p. 19a).

These studies are small steps toward understanding the impact of Watergate. Arterton (1974), using third-, fourth-, and fifth-grade students in a Boston elementary school, attempted to replicate the Easton and Dennis findings of 1962 (i.e., on children's perceptions of the President). He hoped to discern via Watergate whether children's perceptions of the President as benevolent and infallible were part of their developmental process or whether they were subject to change as a consequence of the politics surrounding them.

Arterton found that the "effect of Watergate has been to transform the President into the malevolent leader" (1974, p. 285). Arterton concludes that if Easton and Dennis are correct in their supposition that the child's perception of the President is central for building diffuse support of a political system then a generation of children will have been socialized with strong feelings of suspicion and cynicism toward the government. However, it is also possible that the replacement of Nixon as President may result in the redistribution of response set back to the 1962 distribution.[8] The deterioration of attitudes "toward other parts of the political system poses a more serious question for the future stability of our political institutions than does the rapid and complete shift in attitudes toward the President" (1974, p. 287).

A review of some of the data suggests an alternative interpretation. The study was conducted in Boston, Massachusetts, in a high-SES suburb. Arterton notes that Easton and Dennis grouped their indicators into five dimensions which vary from those high in affective content (e.g., attachment) to those high in cognitive content (e.g., leadership).[9] A comparison of the responses between 1962 and 1973 indicate that children still rank the performance capabilities of the President very high. Ratings on the affective dimensions of the Easton-Dennis measure dropped from positive to negative: "Differences are less pronounced, however, for scales of perceived power and leadership; in these indicators the president still receives positive ratings, though less positive than in 1962" (1974, p. 274).

Surprisingly, Arterton found a low percentage of children able to correctly identify Watergate figures. This finding is corroborated by the studies of Friedman (forthcoming) and Lupfer and Kenny (1974) who discovered low levels of factual comprehension of Watergate among primary school students.

These findings should not have been as surprising as they first appeared. The studies by Adelson, Green, O'Neill, Tapp, and Levine discussed above suggest that the child's conception of the government is removed (from his daily experience) and oversimplified. The events of Watergate, on the other hand, are fairly complex and have unraveled piecemeal over a protracted period of time. It may be that the cognitive aspects of the judgments made by young children on Watergate were not salient, i.e., there was not much information being processed about the case itself and the actors and institutions represented were not clearly

---

[8]Arterton relies here on his interpretation of Kohlberg that children at stages 1 and 2 are moral absolutists and swing from one evaluative extreme to another. Given the context—i.e., children evaluating a person acting out the unique role of President—I think this is an oversimplification of Kohlberg's views and an oversimplification of the socialization-evaluative process.

[9]Arterton acknowledges that the questionnaires "are measuring surface level cognitions rather than basic orientations" (*Ibid.*, p. 287).

defined or understood by the children.[10] The affective dimension, however, was quite salient. And for this reason I believe that the children were reflecting the concern and attitudes they perceived in their parents and other significant adult models. (Parental responses to Watergate were not studied.) This does not mean, as Arterton states, that transference of perceptions from the father to the national collectivity ought to be mirrored by a parallel transference of feelings from the President to the father. The data did not support Arterton's statement since father ratings between 1962 and 1973 did not change significantly while ratings of the President did.[11]

Lupfer and Kenny (1974), however, found that after Watergate a majority of youths in their sample continued to evaluate the President positively although an increasing number of youths voiced negative or ambivalent feelings about the President. The authors believed that negative affective responses were directed at Nixon and not at the office he held. Lupfer and Kenny drew their sample from third-, fifth-, seventh-, ninth-, and eleventh-grade students of varying SES backgrounds from public and Catholic schools in Memphis, Tennessee. They note that the difference in affect demonstrated by the Boston children in Arterton's study can "probably be attributed to the attitudinal environment in which the two groups live: the Boston children residing in a 'liberal Democratic' probably highly politicized environment: the Memphis youths ... residing in a conservative environment which is not politicized" (Lupfer & Kenny, 1974, p. 15).

Can we project the future political behaviors of these students from the results of these studies? Will the effects of Watergate be long lasting? The cognitive and affective perceptions of children vis-à-vis the government are subject to change. Despite the positive affect displayed by many school children in 1962 toward the President, many of these children later became rebellious in their political actions.

Probably as long as the cognitions about government remain undeveloped and malleable, the affective responses of children to the government will also remain in flux. As the cognitions of children mature and the saliency of the government (to them) increases, I would expect the affect they feel toward institutions of legitimate authority to become more fixed. At that point, one might make

[10]Lupfer and Kenny (1974) found that cognitions about the presidency did change among students in their sample of third, fifth, seventh, ninth, and eleventh graders in Memphis, Tenn. Children were able to cite more performance roles of the President and were more specific in their illustrations. The evidence is not depicted by grade although the authors state that only older children shifted towards more *accurate* descriptions of the President's roles. These findings may indicate an increasing saliency of the office of the President as a consequence of Watergate, but switching from general to specific descriptions does not necessarily indicate an increasing sophistication in comprehending the politics and meaning of the presidency.

[11]To briefly outline the difference in relationship between child and parent versus child and President, I would list: (1) the authority of parents is derived from the child's dependency on them; (2) the parent is a primary figure in the child's life and while many of his attributes may be magnified and mythologized he is in comparison to the President a real and understandable figure; (3) the authority of the President as a father figure is derived from the child's perceptions of the esteem with which the President is treated by adults.

somewhat reliable observations and predictions about the future political be-havior of the sample.

Political studies of primary school children and Watergate which do not take a cognitive developmental approach are significant primarily as social indicators of parental responses to Watergate. An affective study of high school students is probably a more reliable measure of the effects of Watergate on inputs to the political arena than is a study of primary school children. The affect which high school students feel toward the Watergate crisis can then become part of a more stable cognitive structure, e.g., we would therefore expect the affective response to be more enduring. Regardless of the cognitive sophistication of their views of government, high school students will shortly be acting (or not acting) in the formal political arena. Even if their affective orientation toward the govern-ment is short lived or potentially malleable, it may still direct or indicate the direction of political activity among these students.

Public Policy and Moral Development

Little has been published concerning moral development and public policy although moral development will increasingly become a concern of public policy makers. Two programs in particular are receiving attention from elementary school educators.

Simon, Raths, and Harmin have advocated an eclectic pedagogical device called value clarification. The roots of value clarification are not within a particu-lar psychological theory. Schools seem to be increasingly adopting this approach to character education. Seven precepts are spelled out for the adult who wishes to help children develop values (Raths et al., 1966, pp. 38–39):

1. Encourage children to make choices, and to make them freely.
2. Help them discover and examine available alternatives when faced with choices.
3. Help children weigh alternatives thoughtfully, reflecting on the consequences of each.
4. Encourage children to consider what it is they prize and cherish.
5. Give them opportunities to make public affirmations of their choices.
6. Encourage them to act, behave, live in accordance with their choices.
7. Help them to examine repeated behaviors or patterns in their life.

Although value clarification appears to me as a step in the right direction, toward democratic socialization, it also appears to have limitations. Value clarification deemphasizes the structural forces in the school and at home which impinge on the child's possible choices (i.e., the choices which he recognizes as existing and the choices he recognizes as viable). The child is assumed (so it appears to me) to be living in a democratic environment out of school. In school he learns value clarification which is intended to be supportive of democratic pluralism. This, of course, might be just the price one must be willing to pay to bring any form of democracy into the elementary school system.

Kohlberg's initial response to moral education was to advocate (as he still does) classroom discussions of moral dilemmas. Previous studies (Rest, 1973; Turiel, 1972) indicate that people prefer moral arguments which are more preferable to the participants (i.e., more developed) than the viewpoints initially expounded.

Scharf (Scharf et al., 1973, as reported verbally and as discussed in Rest, 1974) found that discussion groups were only partially successful when conducted in a prison setting. He found that "prisoners conceptualize prison life at a lower stage than their moral judgments of hypothetical dilemmas. Hence prison life gives the inmate little impetus for developing a higher stage of understanding of the moral basis for law, society and cooperation" (Rest, 1974, p. 249).

The response from the Kohlberg-Scharf group has been an attempt to restructure both prisons and schools in pilot projects called the just school and the just prison. Evidence and description of these ongoing projects is at present mostly anecdotal.

Conclusions

Increasing fears about the lack of social solidarity and legitimacy of institutions in America probably will lead to increased interest in sponsoring programs which promise "moral" development. Different models of moral development, however, embody different values of what is correct, desirable, and moral behavior. These psychological models are competing for our present and future resources. Ironically, the model we choose today will also exert its influence over the model we may consider possible tomorrow. Our sense of reality is constructed out of the psychological, social, and political models we are socialized with and employ.

It is suggested above that a purely learning theory model of moral development is not democratic as a process and often coexists with a constraining view of man and human nature.

While a developmental approach (as exemplified by Kohlberg) has a number of methodological problems and has yet to incorporate the findings of learning-modeling theory, a number of studies (some of which are reported here) verify meaningful and consistent results. The Kohlberg model of man—i.e., the last stages towards which his system is directed—is a model which is democratic in process and goal.

Kohlberg's model is one of several models of moral development which might be successfully implemented, i.e., adopted by schools and/or other socializing agencies. The ideological import of these models differs and our choice of programs will eventually reflect these differences.

12

Preference and Politics:
Values in Political Psychology and Political Learning

Elizabeth Léonie Simpson

Introduction

THE STUDY OF POLITICAL, LIKE OTHER HUMAN, VALUES has been approached, both philosophically and scientifically, from many different directions and by many means of transportation. Description abounds but, in the main, little approaching clarity as to the specific contents of the general idea of political values and even less suggesting consensus about their acquisition through socialization.[1] While a precise and elegant statement of the nature of values utilized in theory and research would carve away much of the hydra-headed exploration and exclude heuristically valuable, if idiosyncratic, work, some assumptions may be put down here.

Usually the term *values* implies choice (which need not be conscious) and a range from which choices of varying saliency are made from time to time. A *value system* is an inner organization of these values, roughly hierarchically arranged according to a system of priorities which varies situationally. Values may be expressed in words or in other behavior; the one cannot be assumed from the other. Values truly held are a component of personality. They affect each other and, in fact, a value which represents an end goal may become a means for

I wish to thank Fred Greenstein and Milton Rokeach for helpful comments on an earlier version of this chapter.
[1]A general introduction to the field of value theory and application and an extensive bibliography may be found in Rescher (1968).

the attainment of other values. Above all, a full understanding of the meaning of any value for the psychic economy of the individual cannot be derived from knowledge of that value alone. The person becomes comprehensible only in the light of the interplay among his values within a given social environment.

C. Kluckhohn (1951, p. 395) has suggested that a value is "a conception, explicit or implicit, distinctive of an individual or characteristic of a group of the desirable which influences the selection from available modes, means, and ends of action." Smith (1969, p. 102) drew the core of the above statement as "conceptions of the desirable that are relevant to selective behavior." Either of these definitions serves the general purpose here for, whatever else they may be, values as related to the political system are always learned preferences which, from their pale and evanescent forms as opinions, interests, and attitudes to the stronger, more lasting forms of motivation, represent the belief that some thing, state, or way is better or more desirable than some other. Political socialization, then, is the arousal and maintenance of particular, effectively shared values.

While not all explorations into value learning are of direct relevance to political socialization, the number of values which interact with and shape political systems is large. Those who would enter this broad and hazardous territory of conceptual jungle may choose to attack those of order, justice, equality, freedom, law, conservation, acceptance or tolerance, dominance or superiority, authority, individualism, etc. The list is long and bounded only by the limitation of interest in an expanding field. Fundamental work in the field has not always been investigation into the obvious, direct expression of political preference. From a collection of value measures assembled for political researchers by Robinson and Shaver (1969), three studies serve as examples: Morris' (1956) *Paths of Life*, F. Kluckhohn and Strodtbeck's (1961) *Variations in Value Orientation*, and the Allport, Vernon, and Lindzey (1960) *Study of Values*.

The first of these is an attempt to measure conceptions of the good life by asking subjects to rank paragraphs describing life styles according to their level of preference. Like the study of values, this work has been used cross-culturally and has produced at least theoretically comparable value profiles from nation to nation. The statistical analyses, however, have run away with the data which is analyzed and presented in a wide variety of forms and complexity, given the simple nature of the instrument. Even more unfortunate is the lack of clarity in the paragraphs comprising the instrument itself. The language is difficult and ambiguous. (Just what does it mean to say that life tends "to become sickled o'er with the pale cast of thought"? To die "with cosmic good manners"?) With all that connotative sweep, the wording is so vague and abstract that cross-cultural, cross-language validity seems extremely suspect. Nevertheless, with all the limitations of instrumentation and analysis, in a preliminary way such ranking does provide a means of assessing life style preferences related to political choices and the demands made on the political system to provide for the general welfare by facilitating those choices.

Kluckhohn and Strodtbeck attempt to assess value orientations as complex, patterned principles which give order and direction to acts and thoughts related to the solution of five universally human problems: the definition of *human nature,* the relationship of *man to nature,* stances toward *time* and toward *activity,* and the relationship of *man to his fellows.* (Due to lack of funds, *human nature* was not actually measured.) Possible responses were postulated in a three-step range, e.g., orientation toward *man-nature* relationships could be with man subjugated to nature, in harmony with nature, or as the master and controller of nature. However, the findings are of heuristic value only, due to a number of factors, the most notable of which is the small size of the sample—a total of 106 from all five groups (Levitin, 1970). To the distress of bias-conscious ethnic leaders, in the absence of methodologically superior studies, this research has been widely quoted without reference to the sample size or lack of conventional tests of reliability.

Since its inception, Allport, Vernon, and Lindzey's *Study of Values* has spawned ramifying generations of offspring. There are a total of 687 items in the bibliography of the measure. It continues to be revised (through 1970), to influence the development of similar tests (e.g., Thomas, 1970), and to be used productively in research such as that conducted in 1968 with a national sample of high school students from the tenth to the twelfth grades. (For a comprehensive review of the literature, see Hogan, 1972.) Despite its name, this instrument is by no means designed to measure personal or social preferences as such but, rather, their conative function. It yields a broad profile of the dominant interests or motives of the subjects among those of the six types of man described by Spranger (1928): the theoretical, the economic, the aesthetic, the social, the political, and the religious. Values are "interests" or "interest systems." As Tisdale (1964) suggests, Allport's definition of value appears to be "an individual, generalized disposition which is easily aroused and acts not only to direct behavior, but to drive it as well."

Allport's conceptualization implies that values are components of personality and, indeed, many researchers and scholars have described politically relevant dimensions of personality which may function as personal or social values. Although the studies are concerned with preferences which may or may not be consciously chosen, they rarely appear under a title which makes immediately clear their value emphasis. Perhaps best known among these is that research which has to do with authoritarianism (Adorno et al., 1950), tolerance (Martin & Westie, 1959), dogmatism (Rokeach, 1956), and related aspects of personality such as status concern (Kaufman, 1957), rigidity as constriction and inhibition, conservatism, intolerance of disorder and ambiguity, observational and perseverative tendencies, social inversion, and anxiety and guilt (Rehfisch, 1958), rigidity as opposition to change as such and intolerance of ambiguity (Meresko et al., 1954), and intolerance of ambiguity as threatening rather than desirable (Budner, 1962), and as conceptualized in the original work on the authoritarianism syndrome (Frenkel-Brunswick, 1951). Other work on dimensions of personality which may be perceived as indirect values includes that on politicoeconomic radicalism-conservatism (Comrey & Newmeyer, 1965; Nettler & Huffman, 1957; Hetzler, 1954), liberalism-conservatism (Kerr, 1952), and generalized conservatism (McClosky, 1958).

Values such as belief in people, trust, generalized justice, and equality have been studied in the attempt to determine the relation between individual and aggregate models of humanity and their assumed effects upon political systems: e.g., Christie and Merton's (1958) *Machiavellianism* and Wrightman's (1964) *Philosophy of Human Nature* measures have both been applied in a wide variety of research settings in a comprehensive study of racial attitudes, and have been found to be almost the only scales which predicted favorable changes in attitudes toward Negroes (Wrightsman & Cook, 1965).

There is a conceptual tidiness about dealing with single or sets of values, rather than values imbedded in a field as components of personality, even when those values are seen as clusters, equal in valence and salience, or upwardly or downwardly mobile in rank as competing entities in varying environments. It is possible to isolate and contain the phenomena being described, rendering them both more readily identifiable as conceptual categories and more abstract and inaccessible in that the attributes of those categories may vary widely from user to user, as well as from group to group and from culture to culture. But the question of the proper way to approach the study of political values is not so easily settled.

An example will serve to illustrate the dilemma: Are *violence* and *aggression* aspects of personality or preferences which are much more narrow, whether consciously or unconsciously held?[2] In manifest aggression, the predispositions of the individual are shaped by cultural factors which are interpreted and acted upon by the ego. These are triggered by situations which activate specific values or systems of values, rearranging their hierarchical order or redistributing them laterally as they become motivating forces. A sharp distinction, however, needs to be made between the appearance of aggressive drive and the instrumental aggression which functions as a means value for the attainment of other specific goals. Someone may be generally violent without holding violence as a personal value; in the reverse way, a person may value violence as a preferred means for specific purposes and yet not be a violent person. Civilized humans who adaptively learn to value violence have been described over and over again. Brutus was one. The possibility that, as a central value of small cohesive groups, violence directed at the transformation of society may at the same time redeem the self-respect of the oppressed, is described in Sorel (1908). It appears in the image of humans recreating themselves, presented by Sartre in the preface to Fanon's *Wretched of the Earth* (1963).

An aggressive or violent personality, then, may or may not be one which

[2]This example of violence and aggression as values was taken from S. Feshbach, "The Dynamics and Morality of Violence and Aggression: Some Psychological Considerations," an unpublished paper based on an address given at the 1970 Western Psychological Association meetings.

values aggressiveness or violence. If the violent or aggressive human does not *prefer* violence or aggression, and is competent and healthy, his behavior based on choice will reflect those values he does hold. His violence and aggression will be controlled. The view of values as components of personality implies a stability which is largely supported by sources beyond the will. Humans must have within them the capability and the freedom to choose among available values for the fact that they do select some over others to have any meaning. Like it or not, students of political socialization are inescapably drawn into consideration of free will and the responsibility of the individual to choose for himself. Must the individual (or the culture) inevitably have developed the value system which he or she did indeed select? Do values with their threefold cognitive, affective, and conative aspects imply *conscious* choice or the unfolding of preprogrammed preferences which are the outcome—at least to a very large degree—of genetic and social pressures beyond the individual's control? And if an individual is not aware of his values, is he then still responsible for them? These are philosophical questions both wide and deep which form the infrastructure for serious theoretical and empirical investigation into the development of political value systems.

Origins of Values

Social scientists have long recognized that the development and application of political value systems of any kind depends upon more than a narrow, stereotypically defined socialization process alone. Like other aspects of personality, the surgence and utilization of values depends upon specific social processes and structures with which the individual interacts, the surrounding cultural environment in which such learning takes place, his or her predisposition to mediate as well as internalize culturally available values (based on previous personal history), and the situations in which he or she may be asked to act.

Hyman (1959, p. 18), the conceptual father of political socialization, defined socialization of the individual as the "learning of social patterns corresponding to his societal positions as mediated through various agencies of societies." In his delineation of the field, this sociological, structural rather than dynamic, approach emphasized the effects of social institutions as the inculcators of culturally shared political values whose transmission acted as a conserving force for the political system. Measurements of preferences were intended to uncover the extent to which the child had learned the values taught, without regard for the effects of the biosocial characteristics which the learner brought to the task of acquisition. This view of socialization is consonant with that of the social learning theorists to whom the acquisition of values is highly dependent upon reinforcement contingencies and excludes motivational and affective factors.

Some researchers, however, have interfaced Freudian theory (in which social environment pressures, in acting upon the innate nature of the individual, pro-

duced early, unconscious, and deep-seated political orientations) with the structural approach (George & George, 1956; Lane, 1962; Lasswell, 1930, 1948).
Connections between the child's orientation and the adult stance which directly
influences the political system were posited by Greenstein (1965); in the same
year, David Easton's (1965) systems theory appeared, encouraging the use of
survey research methods for the exploration of positive citizen affect, irrational
and latent, which provides diffuse support for the extant political system. In
Easton's view, this nonanalytic support represents superordinate values which
shape the generalized attitudes toward power and authority which function toward the maintenance and transformations of the political systems.

With the crucial role it plays in the balance maintaining the stability of the
political system, political socialization has been concerned with values origi-
nating with various sources of influence (see, e.g., Niemi, 1973). The most obvious of these sources, and commonly remarked upon, are the family and the school,
although religious training, media exposure of political events and public behavior of officials (such as powerfully displayed throughout the Watergate scandals), peer interaction, and the social environment provide important learning
experiences. (See also a panel study by Brookes & Sigel, 1974, suggesting that
government performance strongly influences young children's attitudes.)

Niemi (p. 128) provides recent evidence suggesting that family contacts have
much less impact in comparison with the general environment than has been
previously believed (see also Jaros & Kolson, 1974) and that the balance of
influence between the two parents is "remarkably even and, if anything, is
tipped in the mother's favor." He also sums up school effects as "highly variable" and the result of extracurricular activities—contrary to widespread
belief—to be virtually nil. Some of the vivid accounts of environmental sources
of political value development have come from descriptions of collectivization of
child rearing in Israel and in the Soviet Union (Bettelheim, 1969; Bronfenbrenner, 1970; Azreal, 1965). Niemi (1974, p. 5) advocates a "less simplistic view
of a direct relationship between child-adult attitudes and behavior, recognizing
instead the unique contribution of each child in his or her own socialization and
the role of the surrounding environment apart from particular agents such as
family, school, and friends."

Other models of value learning have focused less specifically on early childhood, adolescence, and early maturity and both the scope and sequence of the
cognitive, conative, and affective content learned. These studies have shown
interest less in narrowly defined values than in those applicable across systems,
e.g., the nature of law (such as belief in the fairness of law which erodes as the
child matures), authority, rights, etc., which appear in a predictable sequence
and form dependent upon environmental constraints or facilitations.

Fundamental orientations toward power, legitimacy, obedience, justice,
equality, and social responsibility have been investigated both cross-sectionally
and longitudinally in the process of development: e.g., Piaget's (1932) cognitive
developmental approach to the study of these concepts involves the analysis of

thought structures at various ages. According to his theory, these stages are characterized by, first, the fact that they are integrated wholes which differ qualitatively, not just quantitatively; second, each new stage is an integration, and replacement, of the prior one; third, it is the product, not of passive cultural transmission, but of active cognitive synthesis on the individual's part; and, fourth, the stages occur in a sequence which is the same for all individuals, no matter their cultural background—the characteristic which remains only debatably grounded in empirical evidence.

From his clinical studies of children, Piaget found a two-stage developmental shift from respect and submission to authority to self-government and control. The first stage—of heteronomous morality—is one of moral realism and external constraint. The individual is a moral absolutist. He thinks in terms of total right or wrong which is defined by whether actions conform to established rules or elicit punishment, or the magnitude of their consequences. He believes in "immanent justice"—that any violation of social norms will be swiftly followed by misfortunes caused by supernatural forces. Development to the second stage includes the view that, since rules are established and maintained through reciprocal social agreements, they may be modified in response to human needs. The intentions of the individual matter and punishment is no longer seen as impersonally ordained but, rather, as appropriate to the wrong done. Blind obedience to authority gives way to conforming to peer expectations, gratitude for favors, and the development of empathy.

Piaget concluded that the essence of morality was respect for rules of social order and a sense of justice—i.e., concern for reciprocity and equality among individuals. The child-adult relationship was intrinsically heteronomous; autonomous moral maturity, guided by higher cognitive processes, was the product of egalitarian interactions among peers. Although Piaget does not directly concern himself with the political implications of his findings, at least theoretically, the stage development of the majority of their members may be expected to exert a powerful effect upon the political forms of groups and societies.

In his studies of Australian children, Connell (1971), like Piaget, has used a developmental model to explain the acquisition of political attitudes, beliefs, and values. For the young child, contact with politics is entirely through adults, indirect, and "as outside of his control as the weather." Up to the age of 9, he does not see politics as a sphere of life in which choices must be made between alternatives. The few consistent attitudes developed remain so only under systematic instruction from adults. As he matures, when he begins to recognize political alternatives, he develops consistent preferences which gradually may form an ideology. Only later, usually in late adolescence, this ideology may extend into recognition of himself as a political actor. Connell believes that this later development is basically due to the creative activity of the child and not to adult intervention. The child builds individual structures through selective appropriation of materials provided by a diverse environment. (Here Connell is in agreement with both Piaget and Kohlberg who see structural integration of experience provided by the social environment as the cognitive work of the individual.) The construction of political values, then, is not a mechanical function or the results of inputs of a single system, but a contingent, historical process in which the children are subject to all the many influences of different overlapping groups.

The work of Adelson and his colleagues (Adelson & O'Neil, 1966; Adelson, Green, & O'Neil, 1969; Gallatin & Adelson, 1970) is instructive, both because it parallels the sequence found by developmentalists such as Piaget and Kohlberg (whose work is considered in more detail in Friedman's chapter in this volume), and because this sequence moves from the values rooted in self-interest found in preadolescent children to later ones sharing that interest with a commitment to community welfare—values which in some may be expressed and actualized even in the absence of direct personal benefits. In much the same way that Piaget's very young subjects conceptualized authority and Kohlberg's defended their choices in resolving moral dilemmas, these children saw law as a powerful and abstract, almost mystical, force to which their individual rights were subject. During adolescence, personal responsibility becomes clearer as does the human origin of rights—i.e., that they are granted by the social group. For some, authority may be redefined at that time as centered in the autonomy of the individual and political authority in particular viewed with skepticism (Hess & Torney, 1967).

These developmental trends and others appear to mediate the favorable attitudes and diffuse support for the political system which Easton (1965) and others found in American children, for by no means do all American adolescents *accept* democratic norms and values (Remmers, 1963). As Merelman (1971) has pointed out, civics courses and extracurricular participation do not appear to affect political orientations and the high school, as a social institution alone, has not increased understanding or support for democratic values. Massialas (1972) comments that activism is conspicuously absent from civic education programs in schools at all levels (as indeed is realism), and that schools inculcate passivity and compliance through authoritarian direction, rather than the opportunity to participate actively in the process of learning. Political values, he insists, are learned by practice in the classroom (e.g., through the use of inquiry methods); open discussions of value positions must be clear and explicit, as well as multidisciplinary, cross-cultural, and focused on social issues.

Times are changing, however. There are signs that in some American high schools the distribution of power and authority is becoming less hierarchical and more broadly shared. Students are seeking to actualize such traditionally symbolic bodies as the Student Council. Teachers actively participating in the political process for their interests are acting as role models for students learning the expressed values. Perhaps most important, alternative schools committed to democratic values of equality, freedom, participation, and sharing of power are beginning to emerge.

Most educational institutions now entrusted with the task of transmitting democratic values may not be teaching what we believe they are—either through the curriculum or through the social processes which express actualized values. Alternately, apart from developmental trends, there may be persons who are unable to support those values, even under conditions of continuing exposure to them. *There is no one-to-one correspondence between childhood socialization and adult attitudes.* The present findings raise serious questions as to *which* adolescents do not now support these values, their social and psychological characteristics, and the etiology of this failure. Wallas (1921), Lasswell (1965), Davies (1965), Inkeles (1961), Almond and Verba (1963), Knutson (1972), and Simpson (1976) have linked socially determined psychological deprivation to the nonacceptance of democratic values and consequent behavior in adults.

Drawing on Maslow's (1954) theory of needs in a study of three socioeconomically diverse adolescent groups, Simpson (1971) explored relationships between the lack of psychological gratification and the development of democratic values. The latter included tolerance, belief in the validity of the experiences of others, belief in the rights of others and in the capacity of the individual to choose rationally for himself, belief in the ability of the individual to influence his environment, his life, and his future, and belief that human nature is fundamentally good and trustworthy. To varying degrees, dependent upon a combination of innate and social environmental factors (including the effects of formal social structures and processes), psychological deprivation was found to be related to the internalization of these democratic principles.

Values Expressed in Behavior

Values may be expressed in verbal behavior and/or enacted in other ways which may or may not be congruent with what is expressed verbally. This relationship between what is said and what is done has long troubled researchers, for there is often an almost bizarre incongruence between the values and beliefs which have been learned in the form of verbalized ideologies and the values and beliefs which have been learned as a consequence of observation, experience, and imitation of behavior. At home, as well as within the schools, learners are affectively conditioned to express democratic values, e.g., while at the same time they are often positively reinforced for acting out a most undemocratic ideology. Ideals are taught directly which conflict with what is experienced; intellectual independence and critical thinking are penalized so that the student's training often consists largely of attempts to instill conformity and unquestioning patriotism.

As a means of shaping behavior, exhortation and direction appear to be far less effective than behavioral models presented for imitation and techniques which assist the cognitive development of the learner. Research by Bryan and Walbek (Bryan & London, 1970) not only supports the previous statement, but also suggests that a high degree of inconsistency is tolerable between expressed and enacted values—either because verbal ideology is learned only so superficially that the cognitive dissonance aroused by the conflict is minimal, or because compartmentalization is more effective than the proponents of cognitive dissonance (Festinger, 1957) or balance theory (Heider, 1958) would have us believe.

The gap between opinion and behavior is an old story (Hennessey, 1970). Conflicting messages abound and researchers have generally found it difficult to match verbal and enacted expressions of values, partly perhaps because of deeply-lying contradictions within personality, but also no doubt because of contradictory elements within the social environment. According to social learning theory, correspondence between the two is not likely to occur unless both have been subject to the same treatment by socializing agencies; according to developmental theory, biosocial change, including role-taking opportunities and appropriately timed conflicts, may bring the learner to congruence at the principled level. In his clinical studies, Piaget (1965) found a developmental lag in the young child which allowed behavior to be manifest before corresponding reasoning had appeared. Grinder (1964) attempted to test whether moral values and behavior were related and concluded that they were not and that the behavioral and cognitive dimensions of conscience developed independently. Kohlberg (1964) and Pittel and Mendelsohn (1966) reviewed similar studies and reached similar conclusions.

From their massive study of children's values, Hartshorne and May and their collaborators (1929–1930) concluded that they had settled another perplexing question about behavior based on social values: Are the islands of segmented behavior which are perceived separately joined below the surface? Do values generalize from situation to situation or are they situation-specific? While Hartshorne and May found that the latter was true, Burton (1963) reanalyzed their data and found that a generalizable factor did exist but that, as situations became less similar, moral consistency grew weaker. Johnson (1962), attempting to assess generality by determining the amount of association between responses to moral judgment questions (modeled on Piaget's work), concluded that responses were related both logically and empirically and, contrary to expectations, moral judgment was consistent.

Kohlberg reports that, among those who reason at the principled levels, many fewer students cheat. Although the data have been questioned (O'Connor, 1974) in an experiment conducted by Milgram at Yale, Kohlberg (1971) also found that those subjects who reasoned at the highest stage, applying autonomous, universal principles of justice and equality, tended to refuse to give electric shocks to the persons whom they were ordered to shock in the course of the study. More of those reasoning at lower levels did not refuse. In their study of Berkeley activists, Haan, Smith, and Block (1968) also found convincing evidence that moral reasoning and values are related to principled action: a significant proportion of those politically involved in social change were drawn from among those who demonstrated reasoning at the principled level. From among the 50 variables used in O'Connor's study, he found principled reasoning to be the single best predictor of activism among students studied in Great Britain and France.

In an apparent paradox, Gough's (1949; Gough & Petterson, 1960) Socialization Scale, which does not directly seek to assess any of the areas historically considered integral to the definition of morality (such as rectitude of verbal values, moral knowledge, amount of guilt, strength of conscience, resistance to temptation, or attitudes toward conventional, externally defined norms), is the clearest predictor of ethical behavior available today. Scores on this psychological measure form an isomorphic continuum with sociologically defined deviance. Delinquency and crime, as well, can be predicted. In fact, the discriminatory power of the instrument is sufficient to differentiate among various subgroups according to the severity of their offenses and the amount of recidivism they show. Gough's measure is one of personality and presents impressive evidence that prediction of behavior demonstrating values in a particular situational context may depend more upon the person's generalized view of what he *is* and less upon what he *attests* about his principles or how he arrived at them.

While widespread incongruence between what is said and what is done is unsettling, the political importance of values may lie largely in the latter—in habitual patterns of behavior rather than in conscious agreement on any set of expressed democratic principles. The question is whether values act as constraints on individual political choices. The answer does not seem to be invariably "Yes"; it is more complicated than that. Reporting results of a 10-nation study of civic education, Judith Torney (1975), e.g., presented evidence that students who support democratic values are less likely to support their national government, and vice versa. Lane (1972), too, argues that values constrain choice, but that general principles do not decide political preferences nor does any one value except in cases of "unfree" obsession. Perhaps it is just as well that general agreement on values is not necessary for system functioning since considerable evidence exists that consensus is rare, especially when principles of freedom, equality, and tolerance are encountered in their applied, specific forms (Prothro & Grigg, 1960; McClosky, 1969; Zellman & Sears, 1971).[3]

In 1971 the International Study of Values in Politics published a report, *Values and the Active Society* (Jacob, 1971), of their pioneering attempt to explore the effects of individual values on change at the social level. This consisted of a four-nation (United States, Poland, Yugoslavia, and India) study of the relationship between the active social involvement, both governmental and voluntary, of communities and the values of their national leaders. Building on the assumption that human values are utilized in the decision-making process and

---

[3]Zellman and D. O. Sears offer an example of the discrepancy between acceptance of abstract principles and their concrete application in the study of nearly 1,500 schoolchildren in grades 5 through 9. Most of these children acquired support for *free speech* in slogan form, without learning its concrete implication. Tolerance for free expression in concrete instances was largely dictated not by the general principle, but by the child's attitude toward the specific dissenting group in question.

that social development within communities is at least in part a function of political leadership, the cross-national research team interviewed almost 4,000 political and governmental officeholders to determine their commitment to nine values: *innovative social and economic change; propensity to act* (as against caution and avoidance of risk); *economic development and improvement of standards of living; economic equality or lessening inequalities; widespread public participation in decision making; avoidance of conflict in the community; national interests and goals; selflessness in behalf of public duty; and truthfulness in public conduct*. Validity of the value self-report was determined on the basis of consistency. Information gathered from at least 30 local units in each country provided an index of "social mobilization."

Of these nine values, data from three (*truthfulness, selflessness,* and possibly *sense of national commitment*) suggest a transnational basis; major international differences appear on the remaining six. Of these, three (*economic development, economic equality,* and *conflict avoidance*) paralleled the economic levels of the countries: most strongly held in India, followed by Yugoslavia, Poland, and the United States, whose leaders vigorously rejected the value of *economic equality*. Two values emerge as universal within the sample: *truthfulness in public conduct* and the *subordination of self to public interest by public officials*.

Leaders who were change oriented varied in their concern for *economic equality, political participation,* and *strengthening the nation*. Some were committed to all three goals. Characteristic national profiles differed widely: Americans rejected *economic equality;* Indians tended not to value *widespread participation*, although Yugoslavia and the United States espoused it. Poles linked change to nationalist values. One demographic factor cut across all four nations: *education*. Interestingly, the greater amount of formal education any leader had, the *less* he favored economic equality.[4]

Jacob (1971, p. 33) suggests that human factors in political decision making may be overwhelmed by other factors such as the availability of resources or entrenched political authority and, in fact, that in many countries the capacity to master their destinies may be lost to human beings. " 'Development' will, or not come, by secular tides, and not by human initiatives." To a certain extent, the major findings of the study support this pessimistic view: the "active community, vibrantly responsive to varied pressures for social change, can be the work of human leadership motivated by a particular set of values" (p. 313). However, the effects of these values may be deeply conditioned by others, such as material conditions, the social system, or entrenched political organization. Certainly the

---

[4]Niebuhr (1932, p. 117) writes, "The moral attitudes of dominant and privileged groups are characterized by universal self-deception and hypocrisy.... The reason why privileged classes are more hypocritical than underprivileged ones is that special privilege can be defended in terms of the rational ideal of equal justice only, by proving that it contributes something to the good of the whole....The most common form of hypocrisy among the privileged classes is to assume that their prizes are the just payment with which society rewards specially useful or meritorious functions."

dynamics of developmental change are not universally and systematically predictable from leadership values.

Striking differences between countries suggest that the role of values in the
determination of social change is not uniform; the influence of values must be
analyzed in conjunction with basic environmental conditions. "Only in India is
there a clear association of leaders' values with social mobilization in communities, an association apparently unaffected by economic resources, social
structure, political differences or other factors" (p. 14). In Poland, local leadership values are rendered negligible by the fact that social and economic policies
are centrally determined, i.e., by higher elite values. In Yugoslavia and the
United States, community affluence overwhelms leaders' values and all other
factors in accounting for community activeness. Even more interesting was the
finding that *within*-nation diversity exceeded that of *between*-nation differences.

Value Change

At the personal level, the explanation that reaction takes place when dissonance or imbalance occurs between two cognitions held by an individual, such as
that described by Heider (1958) or Festinger (1957), where conflict forces an
inner shift, or between an individual's generalized perception of his actual self
and his ideal self, does not seem to account for many classes of value change.
Rokeach (1971) experimentally established another type of imbalance—that between the individual's image of his self and his perception of his performance or
behavior in any specific situation: e.g., awareness of value inconsistency (between two expressed values—e.g., *freedom* and *equality*—or between an expressed value and an enacted value—*equality* and *failure to participate in a civil
rights demonstration*) led to highly significant changes in values and attitudes that
were evident 3 to 5 months after the experimental treatment. Long-range behavioral effects of the experimental treatment were found through unobtrusive
measures and observation of natural events.

Rescher (1969, p. 72), impressed with the importance of examining value
processes as social and political indicators, posits seven ways in which values
change, either diminishing or increasing.[5] How are new values selected? The
intrusion of outside forces and breakdown in the adequacy of existing institutions
are two common explanations. Rescher suggests that the social environment is
the major contributor and that values change because of external changes in

[5]Values increase through (1) acquisition of new ones, (2) increase in distribution (i.e., area of
use), (3) rescaling upward toward higher values, (4) widening deployment, i.e., usage, (5) increased
emphasis, (6) restandardization by a raising of standards, and (7) retargeting by adding implementation targets or giving a higher priority to existing ones. The opposite, value diminishing, is easy to
infer.

degree and kind of information and social and political ideology. Values may become irrelevant or erode through boredom, disillusionment, and reaction or be affected by economic-technological change or change in demographic factors. Further, he suggests that the character of the change can be predicted on the basis of comparing cost to benefit—using the cost-effectiveness approach of economic analysis.

Rescher's interesting prediction of value change depends more upon the mechanism of broad social processes and less upon clearly definable individual psychodynamics. In two studies of value change in Yale students done a decade apart, Lane (1969) and Keniston (1968) also describe the pressures which the social environment exerted toward conforming values. During the 1950s and early 1960s pressure was toward a conservative norm; 10 years later the radical activity of students expressed, not rebellion, but the faithful implementation of values inculcated at home.

Inglehart (1971), in a report of a six-European-nation study, describes the transformation of basic value priorities as a result of changing conditions influencing socialization. He sees value as ranked in a hierarchical order at the top of which are those representing the most important needs which remain unsatisfied at a given time (cf. Simpson, 1971; Aronoff, 1967). Economic issues and *instrumental* or *acquisitive* values have given way to life style issues and *expressive* or *postbourgeois* values. Inglehart rejects the developmental life cycle explanation of value change held by Erikson (1968)—that values are selectively utilized at particular times of life—in favor of what he believes to be a more parsimonious, generational one based on his findings of an intergenerational difference with considerable intracohort stability. According to him, a given value hierarchy is attained during the formative years and retained throughout life. Inglehart not only found younger cohorts more likely to have postbourgeois values; he found those values to be predictive of approval of student demonstrations and of supranational European integration.

It seems likely that some combination of cognitive shift, life developmental, and social-psychological theories (in which modification in the cultural environment and structural supports are also taken into account) is needed for the understanding of the development and maintenance of individual and group values manifest in field behavior. Future values of noninvolvement or greatly increased involvement and group, rather than personal, responsibility will have tremendous implications for political systems. Mankind-oriented values may be the forerunners of a supranational political system; technologically developing countries may demand economic, as well as political, rights. A society in which the pleasure, rather than the work, ethic predominates (especially one using drugs widely) and in which education is denigrated to serve only personal ends, is likely to find itself a slave society in which information is the monopoly of the elite. Those who reject participation and the struggle for shared power may find that the decision is one which is extremely difficult to reverse. If this is the choice made, in this respect the leisure society may be even more of a threat to democracy than unpopular foreign wars.[6] The relationship of economic and social security to democratic government may be curvilinear with despotism, the natural outcome when the needs of individuals and groups are met without demands and pressures. Who will write the programs of the programmers when power is reserved only for those who have access to specialized knowledge?

The forerunner of group, rather than personal, responsibility in the economic realm is found in no-fault automobile insurance, in which reparation for damages is made without blame being assigned, in "dissolution" rather than "divorce," and in the proposition that everyone is entitled to a minimum financial base regardless of whether they have earned the money or led conventionally upright lives. Socially and ethically, the trend toward group responsibility as a preference is seen in the massive negative response to the Calley trial and the minimal assignment of individual responsibility—even at the symbolic level—to his acts at My Lai (Kelman & Lawrence, 1972). Many people in the nation perceived those acts as social system breakdown, rather than personal failure. They believe that the man was so thoroughly emmeshed in the nexus of the military system that responsibility was not assignable because freedom to choose did not exist. If the citizen is not responsible for his moral choices, can he be held responsible for his political ones? Or will governance be left to the "group," to the "state"?

Contemporary Research: Two Approaches

Any analysis of the development of individual preferences and their effects upon political systems must concern itself with two major contemporary thrusts in research theory and methodology: the one (an outgrowth of Piaget's work), the sequential cognitive developmental emergence of ethical values and modes of reasoning which are directly related to their political counterparts (Kohlberg, 1964, 1969, 1970, 1971a, 1971b), and the other, an examination of instrumental and terminal value systems, which include political values empirically derived (Rokeach, 1950, 1968, 1971, 1973).[7]

---

[6]Leisure may not mean that these values are chosen: witness recent increases in social and political involvement, particularly on the community level. Fears for the hedonistic society may also be premature: in a national sample, distributions for values of *pleasure* and *an exciting life* were heavily skewed at the low end of Rokeach's (1973) *Value Measure*.

[7]Kohlberg's theory and experimental work are discussed more fully by Dan Friedman in his essay on moral development within this handbook. John Stewart, in his work at Michigan State University, suggests a transactional developmental approach which draws on Kohlberg in describing democratic political relationships and structure from the small group to the state. See, e.g., *The School as a Just Community: A Transactional-Developmental Approach to Moral Education,* Values Development Education Program, 213 Erickson Hall, Michigan State University, East Lansing, Mich. 48824.

PREFERRED MORAL CONCEPTS AND REASONING: KOHLBERG

Moral values generally carry more than a sense of desirability; they also carry a sense of obligation—something or some way is preferred because it is felt that it *should* be. During the last century morality has been studied scientifically from four principal points of view: (1) the sociological restructuring of traditional moral theory, as in the work of Durkheim (1961) and Piaget (1932); (2) the psychoanalytic study of morality, e.g., Freud (1933) through Hartmann (1960); (3) an anthropological approach encompassing both institutional and personality studies, e.g., Kluckhohn (1951); and (4) the sociohistorical treatment which relates morality to other aspects of society, e.g., Weber's (1930) explication of the relationship between capitalism and the Protestant ethic and Marx's postulation of morality as a superordinate structure of the economic system.

From these points of view has evolved an application of science to moral judgment, as defined by philosophers, which involves (1) the structure of the moral situation (what the problem is and what principles are relevant), (2) the interpretation of those principles, and (3) the ordering of the values or principles that constitute choice (Edel, 1968). To the latter area has been added the concept of development and of increasing moral maturity, with the various phases of moral understanding and processes ranked in an evolving pattern of growth. That the *structure* of morality, rather than the content, may provide a more adequate means of describing ethical growth is suggested by Kohlberg's typology of stages of moral development.[8]

Kohlberg's work has important implications for the understanding of the effect of individual political socialization upon the political system. Most citizens—those who ground their ethical and political values in the already established institutions of the nation—reason at the conventional level (Kohlberg's stages 3 and 4). Postconventional reasoning at Stage 6 has been associated with leftist political activity (Haan, Smith, and Block, 1968). These findings seem quite consistent with the international ones Torney (1975) has reported of association between democratic values and rejection of the national government. If principled values are successfully taught in sufficient number, systemic alteration—including the loosening of group cohesion, the breakdown of traditional hierarchical institutions, and increased equality in the sharing of power and wealth—may be the outcome.

The choice to attempt such education would in itself be a political one.[9] Its

---

[8]Kohlberg is actually concerned with *structure* (stages representing abstractions of the form in which reasoning appears), *process* (reasoning), and *content* (concepts of justice, law, equality, etc.). Cf. John Dewey's *Theory of Valuation* in which he points out that, unfortunately, the use of the term *value* as a noun rather than as a verb implies a static entity, rather than a process of valuation.

[9]Whether such training would be widely acceptable, given the cultural values of Americans, remains to be seen. In his national survey, Rokeach (1970) found *intellectual, logical, and imaginative* ranked fifteenth, sixteenth, and eighteenth. When *knowledge, reason,* and *imagination* are not

success would depend on the availability of principled teachers (since children seem to have difficulty in learning higher level values from ones who function at a lower level) and the continuing, comprehensive structural supports needed for pattern achievement and persistence. Preparation for the change in values would have to come from the latter and, in order to achieve it, the change in values would already have to exist—the not unusual problem of producing the chicken to lay the egg. The implied connection between preferred ethical concepts (and the effective and cognitive processes utilized in their application to moral dilemmas) and type of political regime invites further study in this important area at the same time that the complexity and inconsistency of the methodology presently utilized discourages it. (For a critique of theory and research with emphasis on the claims made for cross-cultural universality, see Simpson, 1974.)

VALUES AND POLITICAL BELIEFS: ROKEACH

According to Rokeach, values and value systems function within the individual in a variety of ways—as multifaceted standards, as organizers of principles and rules for decision making and conflict resolution, motivational forces, adjustive or utilitarian content, ego-defensive mechanisms, and, in the knowledge function, as organizers of perceptions and beliefs and self-actualization goals. They are enduring although not completely stable so that change, both individual and societal, can occur and they are relative—i.e., the notion of a value system implies a rank ordering of all values on a single continuum. Decision making requires the balancing of one against the other and through experience and maturation we learn to order each in priority and importance relative to the others. Rokeach uses the analogy of the parent who loves all his children in an absolute, unqualified manner but who, from time to time, is forced to show preference for one over the others because of situational factors.

The problem with this analogy is the difficulty encountered in describing this decision-making process as one in which all other values are clearly subordinated to one. Only when one of the values in competition is overwhelmingly a central issue is the outcome likely to be quite so tidy. Perhaps this may also occur when the ranked values are selected at the verbal level and the process remains devoid of obvious behavioral consequences. In many decisions, however, value conflicts are reconciled in such a way that no one value is either complete winner or complete loser and most competitors get a share of the prize money. *Equality*, e.g., is not absolutely sacrificed to *status* or *power*. In most situations, a multidimensional, dynamic model, ramifying laterally and with complex linkages among its parts, may be as realistic as a neat, static, hierarchically organized one.

---

valued generally within a group, it seems unreasonable to expect to find them utilized specifically in the political domain. Political education had traditionally been aimed at the uncritical inculcation of a constellation of patriotic traits.

Values, for Rokeach, have cognitive, affective, and behavioral components. Those which are *instrumental* or means oriented may be concerned with either *morality* (interpersonal behavior, conscience, guilt) or *competence* (personal behavior, especially the sense of adequacy); those which are *terminal* or goal oriented are either *personal* (self-centered) or *social* (society-centered). Instrumental and terminal values are related to each other, yet separately organized into relatively enduring hierarchical organizations along a continuum of importance. Value change is seen as a reordering of priorities in a system developed by socialization within a given culture—a view congruent with the one held by Kluckhohn and Strodtbeck (1961) that all orientations exist within every culture but are differentially preferred.[10]

The instruments developed by Rokeach consist of two lists of values—one *terminal* and the other *instrumental*—with very brief explanations beneath each. Terminal values for Form E are *a comfortable life, an exciting life, a sense of accomplishment, a world at peace, a world of beauty, equality, family security, freedom, happiness, inner harmony, mature love, national security, pleasure, salvation, self-respect, social recognition, true friendship, and wisdom.* Instrumental values are *ambitious, broadminded, capable, cheerful, clean, courageous, forgiving, helpful, honest, imaginative, independent, intellectual, logical, loving, obedient, polite, responsible, and self-controlled.* These values were chosen as "reasonably comprehensive" and socially desirable, but not implausibly positive, and the subject is asked to rank them in order of their importance to him.

Rokeach has addressed himself to the major question as to whether value meanings are similar to all subjects by suggesting that (1) predictability to behavior is what concerns the investigator, and not meaning, (2) correlations between ranking on the evaluative factor of Osgood's (Osgood, Suci, & Tannenbaum, 1957) semantic differential and the simple ranking are high and yield essentially the same information, and (3) the reliability and validity with or without definitions are essentially the same. It is the psychological, and not the semantic, meaning of the values that matters and that is determined by observation of relationships between them.

Some interesting and politically relevant relationships between values, attitudes, and certain personality variables have been found (Rokeach, 1971, chap. 4). E.g., university students studied by Rim (1970) who were high in dogmatism care less for *equality, freedom,* and *broadmindedness* than those who were low in dogmatism; high dogmatics cared more for *salvation, social recognition,* and being *obedient.* Feather (1969) found a similar pattern among students in southern Australia, while Rim in Israel found that highly dogmatic males, although

---

[10]It is difficult to see how new values could arise solely through a reordering of priorities. Rokeach (personal correspondence, 1972) argues that none do, that it is not possible. How, then, are cultural evolution and such values as widespread political participation, universal education, and equality of economic opportunity—which did not exist even a few hundred years ago—to be explained?

valuing *broadmindedness* and *independence* less, ranked *equality* high—an interesting confirmation of the power of cultural environment and prevailing institutional norms regarding egalitarianism. Rim also found that high F-scorers among the students—authoritarians—ranked *family security, polite,* and *clean* significantly higher than did low F-scale scorers. Stressed values of *national security,* a *comfortable life, social recognition,* being *ambitious, polite,* and *obedient,* and significantly less important values of *happiness, inner harmony,* and being *broadminded* and *cheerful* were related to intolerance of ambiguity. *Equality,* being *ambitious,* and *independent* are significantly more important to high Machiavellians—those who believe that others can be manipulated (Christie & Merton, 1958)—than are *freedom,* being *courageous, imaginative,* or *loving.* Conceptualizing ambiguity as a diffuse value or goal, Budner (1962) found intolerance of it associated with authoritarianism, conventional attitudes, and (male) Machiavellianism. To a large degree, these findings support what is already known about the correlates of dogmatism and intolerance of ambiguity.

Rokeach hypothesized that whatever attitudes exist must be in the service of, and therefore significantly related to, some subset of values, but that they will be differentially related to particular values. From data gathered in 1968 from a national sample, e.g., he found values differentiating between those prejudiced against the poor and those prejudiced against blacks. The average adult American racist held value patterns similar to those of the poor and uneducated in many ways. A marked exception to this rule was *equality,* which was more related than any other value to attitudes of racial tolerance. *Equality* did not discriminate between rich and poor of either black or white. It did between uneducated and educated of both races, although the *equality* difference between racists and nonracists was far greater.

Rokeach's approach to values is descriptive. However, as he wrote, even though there were no theory readily available which would account for his findings, major value differences could have been predicted on intuitive grounds. "Thus of all 36 values *equality* is the one that best predicts reactions to the assassination of Dr. Martin Luther King, attitude toward blacks, the poor, Vietnam, student protest, and church activism. *Salvation* is the value that is most related to perceived importance of religion, to differences in religious orientations, and to an anticommunist attitude. In the United States, at least, *salvation* and *obedient* are the two values that are most associated with high scores on the Dogmatism Scale" (1971, chap. 4, p. 24). Some results have run contrary to expectations: "hawks" value *a world at peace* just as highly as "doves"; *national security* is ranked just as low by those opposed to communism as by those sympathetic to it; *broadmindedness* is valued just as highly by those pleased or afraid after King's assassination as those ashamed, saddened, or angered. Interpretation of these findings requires consideration of the relationship of one value to another—its instrumentality or relative status—and also the ways in which the same value may perform very different functions within the psychic economy of different persons. For hawks, e.g., the value *a world at peace* may be firmly linked with the value of American global dominance, and so have a very different meaning from the same value with equal status held by doves.

Value differences discriminated among the social groups studied, and not always along generally accepted lines: e.g., while male-female differences generally seem to reflect the ways western men and women are socialized into their cultural roles, some stereotypes are threatened: women are no more romantic than men, no more affiliative or egalitarian, and no more concerned with national security or aesthetics than are men, while men are as concerned as women with family security and responsibility. Conventional wisdom about economic groups is questioned, as well. The values *clean* and *comfortable life* best distinguish poor from rich since, being taken for granted, they have lost their saliency for the latter. The data lend credence to Lewis' (1966) concept of the culture of poverty as opposed to the culture of affluence, with value differences more pronounced at the extremes. Interestingly enough, Rokeach's findings do not support current opinion that the poor are hedonistic and present oriented, for differences in rankings between income groups for values of *self-control,* an *exciting life,* and *pleasure* are not significant. The only value that continues to show large differences between black and white Americans when income and education are controlled is *equality* which also differentiates between militant blacks (who rank it low) and nonmilitants—a pattern consistent with the separatist stance of the activists.

Rokeach also presents evidence for generational differences in value rankings and, *perhaps even more important for the understanding of political socialization, for the view of value change as an ongoing integrative process which by no means ends with the close of the psychosocial development of the adolescent.* This notion is closer to Erikson's conceptualization of the stages of life than to Freud's developmental theories and in contradiction to prevailing theories of early political socialization and value stability in maturity.

In exploring an approach to political orientation which does not depend upon ordering along a single continuum of left-right or liberalism-conservatism, Rokeach attempted to use the value framework to make comparisons "across historical time and cultural space" (1972, chap. 6, p. 5) among the positions which varying political systems take in regard to two values: *equality* and *freedom.* All major systems must be concerned with the consequences of unequal distribution of power and scarce resources and hence must take a stand to advance their own self-interests ideologically and to oppose competing interests. Usually those possessing greater power and resources (and those who are potential possessors) will attempt to maintain their freedom, even at the cost of maximizing social inequality; those who identify themselves as less powerful and wealthy may stress social equality in order to increase their freedom. When *equality* and *freedom* are conceived as variables ranging from high to low, four types of value orientations appear which seem conceptually coordinated with the four major types of contemporary political orientations. *Socialism* places a high value on both *freedom* and *equality; fascism* places a low value on both of these.

Communism places a high value on *equality* and a low value on *freedom* while *capitalism* reverses the ranking of these values. As stated above, it is the relationship between the ranks of these two values which is psychologically important to the individual. The meaning and affective loading of one concept have to be considered in the light of the meaning and affective loading of the other. It can hardly be said, therefore, that the concept of equality has the same meaning in any of these societies.

To determine the empirical validity of this two-value model, writings from these ideological orientations were analyzed, counting negative and positive references to these specific terminal and instrumental values as well as synonymous ones. The results for terminal values were in nearly perfect agreement with the model, and disclosed other related value differences as well: Hitler expresses his antipathy for *equality;* Goldwater ignores it. Not surprisingly, *racial purity* is important to Hitler; *wisdom* is not. Goldwater and Hitler both value *national superiority; national defense* is important to all but the Socialists. Most interestingly, the correlations expected among the ideologies adjacent to each other on the left-right continuum—communism to socialism to capitalism to fascism—do not occur. Socialism, rather than capitalism, turns out to have the ideology most differing from fascism; capitalism is most different from communism. Similarities among the four political orientations are in instrumental rather than terminal values, but even these are not strong. The only consistent finding is that fascist value systems are more unlike socialist than communist or capitalist systems.

Although the total continuum of political variations does not exist in the United States to the degree present in some other countries, data from a 1968 American national survey lent support to the results of the content analysis. Supporters of McCarthy ranked *equality* and *freedom* in first and second place; Wallace supporters ranked them eighteenth and first, respectively. Rokeach suggests that the liberalism-conservatism dimension in American politics is really an *equality* dimension, with *equality* highly valued by liberals and hardly valued by conservatives, but that in other countries, such as Russia, *freedom* is the more differentiating value. The two terminal values together describe the four political orientations parsimoniously. Since the writings analyzed came from different cultural areas, were written at different times (within the twentieth century), and were originally written in different languages, Rokeach concludes that content analysis to determine values can indeed be applied across history and culture.

While there are methodological questions unresolved in his discussion, e.g., those concerning the selection of the exact sample chosen for analysis, a larger issue involves the meaning of the results. The *Value Survey* and the values culled from speeches and writings represent the presentation of preferences both to others and to the self which are expressed verbally. As such, they seem to differentiate some known groups clearly. But how important this differentiation and these preferences are without behavioral referents may be another matter.

Could these techniques be used in conjunction with other, observational indices of value measurement? Could political behavior, situationally expressed, be predicted by knowledge of these values? These are hardly new questions. Rokeach's approach seems to offer new bottles for this old wine and, indeed, an interesting method of producing it. Whether it, in conjunction with other modes of measurement or alone, can produce more than *ex post facto* inferences about political behavior and how it is learned remains to be seen. It appears that the crucial question lying across the gap from verbal values to action is one of motivation: how, and why, do these values, once identified, become actualized in behavior?

Needed Research

The concern of political psychologists is with those learned values which, directly or indirectly, find their expression in political behavior. As may be seen from this brief attempt at review, findings to date are not only sporadic and lacking in generalizability, they are often conflicting. Predictive answers to these fundamental questions have certainly not been found: What is the relationship between the values of adults which are verbally expressed and those which find their expression in political behavior on both micro- and macrolevels? What is the relationship (if any) between the verbal and other behavioral values of the young child and those he or she holds at various later stages of adult life? While Beck (1974), among others, has found no one-to-one correspondence between childhood socialization and adult attitudes, we still do not have enough information for a reliable, widely applicable answer to that question. What are the effects of group membership and other social environmental factors upon value persistence and change?

In regard to the first of these questions, studies such as those by Rokeach (1971), Flacks (1967), Haan, Smith, and Block (1968), and O'Connor (1974) which have been cited above serve largely to point to the empty well of our ignorance. For that matter, what *systematic* knowledge do we have of the origins of the value systems of members of known groups and individuals whose political behavior is manifest—groups such as the Southern Christian Leadership Conference and the Black Panthers? What do we know of the Berrigans, Martin Luther King, Eldridge Cleaver, or Rockwell—the now-dead American Nazi party leader—or the road which they traveled to leadership? We need not only idiographic studies, but those intensive (and expensive) ones based on interview and observation-participation which provide an understanding of the political person—at all ages—at work acquiring, modifying, and applying his value systems.

We need, also, to understand more about the nature of altruism and of the learned values underlying "helping behavior" (Macaulay & Berkowitz, 1970) and prosocial behavior in many variants which does not provide direct benefits to the actor. Perhaps most important, we need to explore the process of movement from tribal to universal altruism—the enlargement of the inner circle for the sake of whose membership one is willing to sacrifice something of the self—and to examine the effects of diverse techniques of altruistic transformation on both persons and groups (Sorokin, 1954) under field conditions as correspondent to reality as objective observation will allow. Under what specifiable conditions might altruism, like passive resistance or personal courage, be maladaptive? Is it possible that personal and group altruism and political democracy are associated in a curvilinear way? Can a measure parallel to Gough's Socialization Scale be devised to predict prosocial, instead of antisocial, behavior?

More should be known, too, about the value systems of leaders and policy makers. What effects do their roles have upon already formed values, e.g., how are their values impeded or implemented systemically? To what extent can constitutional democracy survive if leaders value secrecy and the restriction of information when the maintenance of access to information would strengthen the political and economic positions of others? In short, when is hypocrisy among leaders *valued* as a life style (Niebuhr, 1932, p. 117)? What are their preferred images of private and public welfare, their valued ends and means?

Past findings on male-female differences need to be reexamined and the effects which sex-linked perception of values have on behavior. To what extent have changes in past child-rearing practices and institutional socialization affected sex differences in political behavior? Jane Jacquette (1974) and her co-authors have attempted a preliminary description of the effects of cultural values on female, as opposed to male, political socialization, e.g., female "moralism" and awareness of the discrepancy between the norms and reality of democratic practice. According to Bronfenbrenner (1962), girls have been more exposed to affection and less to punishment; their discipline is "love-oriented" and they become more obedient and cooperative than boys at comparable age levels, but also more anxious, timid, and dependent. Extending love techniques of socialization to males may be producing conformance, less enterprise, and less self-sufficiency—more, he writes, "of the virtues and liabilities commonly associated with female character structure" (p. 78).

Since politics is conceptualized in terms of power, aggression, and conflict, does Bronfenbrenner's assertion mean that fewer men will be active participants in the future? Women have been socialized to value submission, dependence, passivity, and conformity; culturally taught, role-specific values may be an important determinant of low politicization and weak interest on their part. There are marked sex differences in views of political, as well as social and economic, roles and studies which show women to be apolitical in comparison to men imply that differential values explain the finding: women simply prefer domestic pursuits and the narrow sphere of home and family. If this is the case, then as feminine values change, degree of involvement should also change. If politics is not to continue to be seen as the almost exclusive province of men, educational concern should lie with the microlevel of the political system (e.g., at school and at home), where the child learns basic views of power and authority, and should deemphasize the distant macroformal system of institutions and roles where power—at least today—is still defined largely by masculinity.

Studies are needed of preferences for cooperation and of the "too uncritical glorification of co-operation and mutuality [which] results in the acceptance of traditional injustices and the preference of the subtler types of coercion to the more overt types" (Niebuhr, 1932, p. 233). At the same time, more work is needed to understand the dynamics of competition as a value and the stress caused by the need for achievement in which self-esteem and the sense of worthiness are dependent upon personal, competitive accomplishment. (See Deutsch, 1969, for a useful discussion of conflict, cooperation, and power.) We need to understand how instrumental values become rigidified into goals, to examine under what conditions peace rather than war is preferred as a dynamic social process, or civil disobedience, nonviolence, and pacifism conceived as coercive means in the struggle against power (Putney, 1962). When is mainte- nance of the status quo, stability, and law and order opposed to change and personal freedom? Or diversity opposed to uniformity? We need to know more about the many faces of equality as a value—from distributive justice to social fraternity—and the preference pattern for tolerant behavior which may in some cases support diversity and in others, as Marcuse (1969, p. 123) wrote, "in reality, favors and fortifies the conservation of the status quo of inequality and discrimination."[11]

We need to examine more evidentially the determinants and correlates of the preference for power, not in the polarized terms of the past ("Power-seekers are sick people; power-seekers are healthy self-actualizers" or as opposed to love [Sampson, 1968]). Rather, we need to understand power as a multidimensional instrumental or end goal serving either prosocial or antisocial purposes, prodem- ocratic or antidemocratic ones. See McClelland (1975) for a comprehensive defi- nition of power orientations as inner experience and its application to empirical studies in the United States, India, and Mexico.

It is hard to imagine political democracy surviving where the imitation of those with social power which Bandura, Ross, and Ross (1963) found in their young subjects is translated wholesale into a preference for following or obeying rigidly those who have control of the allocation of resources through possession of political power. This would be particularly true if such power were not distributed pluralistically but, rather, isolated in the hands of a small group of elites described by C. Wright Mills or as Marx's capitalist class. (On the other hand, widespread acceptance of power as a cultural value may help to maintain a

---

[11]Marcuse continues: "The tolerance which is the life element, the token of a free society, will never be the gift of the powers that be; it can, under the prevailing conditions of tyranny by the majority, only be won in the sustained efforts of radical minorities, willing to break this tyranny and to work for the emergence of a free and sovereign majority—minorities intolerant, militantly intol- erant and disobedient to the rules and behavior which tolerate destruction and suppression."

pluralistic balance through competition.) Certainly not enough is known about who values power, under what conditions this value is actualized into behavior, or whether the experimental findings with children earlier cited also hold for adults at various ages and are supported by field work and other observations. Much remains also to be known of administrative power—in organizations dealing with problems of the production of goods and services and in those involved in the administration of the law and norms of justice. (For an argument on the inevitability of democratic values in industrial administration under conditions of chronic change, see Bennis, 1966.)

Studies are needed of the effects of controlling drugs on value systems, their development and modification: what do anxiety-relieving or other drugs do, if anything, over time (Somit, 1968)? London (1969) suggests that the technology for drugs producing, e.g., courage or suggestibility already exists. While it is difficult for humanists, both scientific and lay, to accept the machine model of man he describes, we need to know more about the circumstances under which the value systems of followers, as well as leaders, can be radically and permanently altered (Koestler, 1941; Lifton, 1961; Paul, First Century A.D.). (See Jaros, 1970, for an initial study on biochemical desocialization.) This problem is part of a larger one which has to do with the nature of value change, both over time and over group membership and especially as it is manifest in behavior.

Unknown possibilities may exist for variation within and between value systems. How do preferences differ between groups? How do they develop within them? On what basis are they selectively borrowed from other groups? The study of utopias needs to be included here, both their conception—for many do not live to birth—and the behavior which characterizes their maturation and death. Although, like the utopian socialism of the eighteenth-century Enlightenment, some communes today are based on a vision of the past, most utopias are part of the imaginative trait pool of social invention from which tradition-maintaining groups draw for cultural change. The vision of the ideal provides a new species and broadens the range of the available from which choices may be made (Mannheim, 1936, pp. 257–263).[12]

Adelson (1971, p. 1038) suggests that utopianism is "a matter of class and social position, not fundamentally a youth phenomenon," as has sometimes been assumed, with those most inclined to such innovation today drawn from inner-city adolescents who feel despised and rejected and young suburban intellectuals who are morally troubled and see themselves as innovators and leaders. Neither

---

[12]Mannheim felt strongly about the function of utopian thought for man:

But have we reached the stage where we can dispense with strivings? Would not this elimination of a tension [that created by utopianism] mean the elimination of political activity, scientific zeal—in fact of the very content of life itself? (p. 257)

The disappearance of utopia brings about a static state of affairs in which man himself becomes no more than a thing. We would be faced then with the greatest paradox imaginable, namely that man, who has achieved the highest degree of rational mastery of existence, left without any ideals, becomes a mere creature of impulse (pp. 262–263).

biosocial development nor identification with parental values (Flacks, 1967) alone seems adequate to explain this phenomenon and it seems likely that the creation of new patterns of organized values is a complex matter in which personality and social situation are intricately interactive. Mannheim (1936, p. 261) expressed his awareness of this and of the emotional aspects of the development of new ideas and values when he wrote that the individual who is bound into a system of relationships, which hamper his will and rest upon his uncontrolled decisions, is free to choose only when he is made aware of the motives hidden behind his decisions. (For an excellent historical reprise of the "utopian mentality" in modern times, see Mannheim, 1936.)

Utopias are the product of imagination, among other things, and only one of the ways in which imagery functions in the renovation of political and social systems. Visions, including dreams of power and authority, may be of many kinds, but the process itself may be of political significance. Although the association has hardly been explored empirically, a theoretical relationship between the capacity to fantasize and imagine and the development of certain kinds of motives and value systems has appeared in the literature (Simpson, 1976; Merelman, 1969; Klinger, 1971; Atkinson, 1958; Cox, 1969). Clinicians have been aware for many years that the unfolding creative process, manifest in a wide variety of art forms, has inherent integrative qualities. Can the relationship between this developmental process and value change be demonstrated under controlled conditions?

For what behavior will future humans be held responsible by the values of their groups and their leaders? Will their values be seen as something which they select and from which they select? Will guilt disappear and shame replace it when the culture disapproves but, as a group, still accepts the responsibility for coping with the results of individual behavior? Where impersonal or group responsibility has appeared in the past, it has been in socialistic or communistic societies. Can there be political democracy as we know it without individual responsibility among leaders and among followers? Niebuhr (1948, p. 248) discriminated "between the evils of the social system and the individuals who are involved in it. Individuals are never as immoral as the social situations in which they are involved or which they symbolize." Evil as system failure removes that distinction. The person becomes a poorly functioning part; a model of humanity appears which is less the individual and more the individual's membership, less human and more a machine within a machine—a person who can get out of order but never be wrong or bad as long as conforming to group expectations.

Perhaps even more than in other areas of study, in examining the learning of political values the researcher must enter the world he wishes to study if his images are to be real. At the same time, he must beware of areas where the subjects are influenced by the observer's presence, use a variety of methods from his armamentarium, and include in his work the study of dynamic interaction processes. He must attempt to find out what individuals know of their own values (and are willing to disclose); if he can, he must tap those deep sources which are unknown to those who draw upon them. He must observe political values imbedded in political behavior and the effects they militate and seek the causes, wherever possible, which will shape the world for which he, his subjects, and all human beings will be responsible in the future. No small task for any kind of political socialization!

13

Childhood Learning About War and Peace: Coming of Age in the Nuclear Era

Howard Tolley, Jr.

THE INCREASED POTENTIAL FOR NUCLEAR ARMAGEDDON and repeated forecasts of a war pitting the have-nots against the advantaged lend added significance to contemporary socialization research. For if, as many have long assumed, wars do indeed begin in the minds of men, then a program of socialization for peace might save future generations from assured self-destruction. Boulding, Reischauer, Heilbroner, and other commentators have evaluated the threats to human survival and reached different conclusions about man's ability to adapt in time. Emerging values about war and peace therefore generate interest far beyond the classroom, and world conditions require answers to major questions, both old and new. Is the will to fight instinctive in human nature? How does wartime experience affect the child? Which agents of socialization most influence war-related knowledge and attitudes? Can formal peace education significantly affect behavior and values?

American children have lived with the reality of cold war, the Vietnam conflict, and nuclear proliferation through the most important years of early political learning. Exposure to media reports of actual military combat and the bitter divisions generated by the antiwar movement taught basic, fundamental lessons. This chapter examines the process of learning about war and peace first by summarizing the ethologists' account of the origins of human aggression. Following assessment of research into socialization during a particular war, the analysis turns to evaluate childhood learning about war and peace in general. Finally, the chapter examines research attempts to weigh the relative significance

of various socializing agents, noting in particular recent efforts at peace education in the elementary and secondary school curricula. The conclusion offers
suggestions for future research needed to address unanswered questions in the
field.

Origins of Human Aggression

To what extent can individual aggressiveness and international war be traced
to child-rearing practices? The question remains unanswered. Society is alternately portrayed as the corrupting agent of innocent youth or as an essential
restraint on the antisocial impulses of man's natural disposition. At a young age,
many children develop aggressive tendencies, personality traits frequently cited
as an underlying cause of war. Hostility, violence, and aggression may stem, on
the one hand, from a single biological root or, on the other, from a complex of
social causes. Do children fight because it is their nature to do so? Or does
society itself teach the young to be aggressive?

One theory attributes aggression in the child to instinct and regards its
emergence as a natural development. New parents observing the ferocity of an
infant's tantrum may indeed wonder whether Baby has carried some asocial
behavior into the world with him. The Swiss psychologist Jean Piaget regards
both compassion and vengeance as instinctive in the child, concluding:

> It is very difficult to say ... whether the fit of rage of a baby of a few months old
> merely expresses the need to resist unwelcome treatment, or whether it already con-
> tains an element of revenge. At any rate, as soon as blows appear (and they do so at an
> extraordinarily early date, independently of any adult interference) it would be hard to
> say where fighting ended and revenge began (1965, p. 229).

In the same manner, Freud offers a Greek term, *thanatos,* and the Latin phrase,
Homo homini Lupus, to describe the innate death wish and wolf-like aggressiveness which characterize men from birth. "The tendency to aggression is an
innate, independent, instinctual disposition in man" (Freud, 1961a, p. 29).

Lorenz, Hess, and other ethologists also contend that biology, rather than
childhood socialization, determines human aggression. Ardrey (1966) interprets
man's lust for battle as an urge to preserve territorial control, and in *African
Genesis* (1961) suggests that the first human tools also served as weapons for
killing. The literature of ethology describes at length instances of violence among
animals which closely resemble conflict among men. Lorenz (1966) asserts that a
child's aggressive behavior has been dictated by evolution and hereditary processes beyond individual or social control.

> Unreasonable and unreasoning human nature causes two nations to compete, though
> no economic necessity compels them to do so; it induces two political parties or
> religions with amazingly similar programs of salvation to fight each other bitterly and

impels an Alexander or Napoleon to sacrifice millions of lives in his attempts to unite the world under his scepter.

Storr (1968) compares aggressive drives to sexual instincts, noting the general belief in an innate physical urge to mate. Why, then, cannot the similar forms of physical arousal associated with violent anger be attributed to inherent traits? Golding's popular novel (and a subsequent film version) *Lord of the Flies* portrays a group of schoolboys stranded on a small island who coalesce, seemingly by instinct, into rival groups prepared to fight to the death. Finally, Desmond Morris' view of man as a "naked ape" supports the ethologist position in the nature versus nurture debate.

In rejoinder, behavioral scientists condemn ethology as a combination of false analogy, inaccurate evidence, and misconstrued theory (Montagu, 1973). Rather, they maintain that children learn aggression; society is the teacher. Montagu unequivocally declares: "In spite of periodic attempts to revive the idea of the existence of instincts in man, the notion has no scientific validity whatever" (1973, p. xiv). In support of that claim, Montagu cites psychological studies dating back to 1918 and presents essays by 20 contemporary behavioral scientists. Regrettably, part of the debate degenerates into an attack *ad hominem*—on Ardrey as a dramatist and Lorenz as an apologist for Nazi racism. The critique of the ethologists' methodology carries greater weight, since Lorenz' primary research with geese and selective reference to fighting baboons will not support an evolutionary theory of aggression. Some of the primates most closely linked with man, such as chimpanzees, reveal no inclination to fight.

Therefore social customs and different methods of child rearing explain childhood aggression, a variable largely dependent on individual circumstances as well as personality traits. The relative incidence of violence and teenage gangs in urban ghetto and middle-class suburb testify to the importance of social environment. Overly strict parents who brutalize the young or merely ignore their needs for affection create and nurture enduring hostility. Malinowski traces interpersonal conflict to appetitive frustration in childhood and the denial of basic physical or emotional needs.

> The simplest analysis of human behavior shows that aggression is a derived impulse. It arises from the thwarting of one or the other of the basic psychological drives ... or culturally determined interests, appetites or desires. When sex, hunger, ambition or wealth are threatened, aggression occurs (1966, p. 22).

Parents, either through harsh punishment or neglect, may promote violent behavior by creating a need for affection.

On the other hand, Parsons contends that even concerned, attentive mothers contribute to anxiety and aggression by offering their love as a reward for achievement. Children learn that to succeed or perform above expectations earns praise and affection; failure brings a reprimand or worse. Parsons contends that such child-rearing practices nurture the violence and hostility which ultimately cause international war (1954, p. 304).

> The typical Western individual ... has been through an experience in the process of growing to adulthood which involved strains of such severity as to produce an adult personality with a large reservoir of aggressive disposition; the bulk of aggression so generated must remain repressed and becomes free floating to be mobilized against external scapegoats.

Social relations beyond the home may also stimulate individual hostility. Robert LeVine maintains that ethnocentrism characterizes most communities, and that fighting between societies serves as a "safety valve" releasing aggression that might otherwise turn members of the in-group against each other. Similarly, children's exclusive peer groups often express virulent hostility to newcomers or outsiders, behavior that may satisfy basic psychological needs to belong or to project personal inadequacies. Affection for some becomes inextricably involved with hate for someone else.

The Robbers Cave experiment involving two youth groups at a scout camp in Oklahoma illustrates the principle. Camped in close proximity, the members of each group regarded the other as the enemy at their first encounter. Soon the "Eagles" and "Rattlesnakes" established strong in-group identity, and fighting erupted between the groups despite the boys' individual similarities (as in *Lord of the Flies*). Only by careful engineering could the adult supervisors bring the boys to a stage of cooperation which ultimately resolved the conflict (Nesbitt, 1973). If internal order does depend on external hostility, as LeVine suggests and the Robbers Cave exercise indicates, then there is no escape from violent conflict. Apparently, men will associate and fight others similarly organized no matter how large or small the groups might be. LeVine thus concludes: "There appears to be a correlation of internal solidarity, trust and sociability with external hostility" (1965).

At the same time, however, certain families committed to nonviolence have successfully raised children in the pacifist tradition despite the pressure of social forces. Their individual success raises hope that perhaps an entire society could free itself of violence with a foresighted approach to raising children. Anthropologist Geoffrey Gorer reports on three such societies where war and murder are unknown. Small tribes had retreated into remote areas of New Guinea, the Himalayas, and the Congo rain forests rather than resist invasion. Subsisting as hunters and gatherers, the peaceful groups were less successful than their more aggressive (in New Guinea, cannibalistic) neighbors. In lieu of violent conflict, Gorer noted "enormous gusto for physical pleasures—eating, drinking, sex and laughter." Such customs demonstrate that social rather than biological stimuli cause aggression, that man has no killer instinct. Gorer found that, when raising children, all three societies made

> very little distinction between the ideal characters of men and women ... particularly have no ideal of brave, aggressive masculinity .... No child, however, grows up with the injunction "All real men do ..." or "No proper woman does ..." They do not have heroes or martyrs (1968, p. 34).

For one school of behavioral theorists, then, "aggression is a cultural acquisition, not an original trait of human nature" (Durbin & Bowlby, 1950, p. 26).

Underlying political or ideological, rather than purely scientific, concerns may explain the intensity of the nature versus nurture dispute. For those who assert the importance of instinctive drives share a pessimistic view of man's ability to reduce violent conflict by rational means. Liberal behavioral scientists, on the other hand, deride "simplistic" explanations which trace all human aggression to a single cause beyond human control. Eisenberg regards the ethologists' despairing view of inborn drives as a self-fulfilling prophecy. "Men and women must realize that mankind can become fully human in order for our species to attain its humanity. Restated, a soberly optimistic view of man's potential ... is a precondition for social action to make actual that which is possible" (1973, p. 56).

The origins of human aggression remain subject to dispute, although few would insist that instinct alone dictates human behavior. Obviously society can and does modify political conduct, and socializing agents significantly influence the extent to which children accept or reject international war. A growing body of literature offers persuasive evidence that children acquire basic political values, including pacifist or militaristic sentiments, early in childhood.

Understanding the Reality of War

Psychologists wrote the first major works on children and war following the Second World War bombing raids on London which separated families and confronted many children with the reality of military destruction. Anna Freud concluded that exposure to such violence worked less harm on children's mental health than the separation from parents during evacuation. The model of adult society in wartime did encourage aggressiveness and juvenile delinquency, and disorders such as enuresis were frequently noted. Nevertheless, Freud and Burlingham declare that violent conflict does not unduly shock young children (1944, p. 29).

> In the very young no restraints yet exist on violent impulses.... It is a common misunderstanding of the child's nature which leads people to suppose that children will be saddened by the sight of destruction and aggression.

A questionnaire survey conducted by Preston in New York in 1940 supports that conclusion since, in general, older children condemned war more than the youngest. In addition, the American study confirmed that children formed opinions of the Second World War with little factual knowledge. Dramatic events and prominent personalities aroused the greatest interest, while more abstract issues did not register. Preston (1942, p. 85) found that despite the children's ignorance there was "little hesitation shown in expressing attitudes or taking sides. While the degree of partisanship varied, there was far short of general acceptance or the blind partisanship which ignores the faults of the objects of one's sympathies.''

Lippit and Zander's comparison of boy scouts and nonmembers during the Second World War revealed the former more involved in civil defense and military support activities. The scout units provided a suitable means of organization, and the official creed has traditionally encouraged patriotic loyalty. In a 1944 study of children aged 6 and 7, Geddie and Hildreth found unexpected knowledge of wartime events. Boys seemed far more interested than girls in the conflict, and parents appeared to contribute most to the children's outlook on war. Rautman and Brower (1945, 1951) compared children's stories during the Second World War with essays composed in peacetime five years later. They noted a decrease in references to war themes, and the children in peacetime concluded their stories with more happy endings. By contrast, Japanese children who survived the Hiroshima blast have recounted in graphic detail the horror and terror of their war experience, a traumatic shock that left unhealed scars (Osada, 1963).

Since the end of the Second World War children in the Middle East, Northern Ireland, Southeast Asia, and eastern Nigeria have all been exposed to the horror of prolonged, bloody conflict. Journalists' accounts confirm the obvious brutalizing effects of their experience. Increased school truancy, juvenile delinquency, psychological disorder, and enuresis observed among children in Northern Ireland parallel the earlier findings by Freud and Burlingham. Cook and Jackson (1973) found Belfast children made relatively fewer negative judgments about war than American respondents. Similarly, the 10-nation Civic Education Survey reports that "Israeli students reject war somewhat less than those in other nations" (Torney, 1974, p. 14). Israel's military victories and the 1949 war which established the Jewish state explain the result. Naturally, the primary concern in time of war must be to guarantee the physical safety of children, and the few accounts which have appeared necessarily concern innocent suffering rather than childhood socialization.

VIETNAM

U.S. involvement in Southeast Asia provides a more recent and suitable test of American children's response to actual military conflict. Preadolescents' 1971 opinions about American intervention closely resemble views of the adult public at that time (Tolley, 1973). Despite majority support for American involvement among third graders, after age 10 more children displayed reservations about U.S. policy.

> Most believed their country made a mistake in Vietnam, and half favored a withdrawal of American forces "even if they lose."... At the same time, however, a large majority hoped for a United States victory. Thus, although the war may have raised

serious doubts in the minds of many children, most still retained an underlying commitment to the nation's success and did not wish to see a United States defeat (p. 26).

Parents and school had the greatest impact on attitudes toward American policy, while multivariate analysis revealed that the media, religion, and military parentage seemed far less important. Black children displayed much greater opposition than whites to American involvement, resulting both from disproportionate loss of conscripted relatives and from a sense of discrimination.

By contrast, children's knowledge of the Vietnam war depended less on parents and school than on personal variables such as age and sex. Despite the absence of sex-related opinion differences, boys knew considerably more about Vietnam than girls. Age correlated significantly with information levels. In addition, higher income consistently accompanied improved knowledge of the war, while students from lower status homes who read less clearly knew less about Vietnam. After five years of active American participation in Vietnam, however, children did not comprehend widely known facts about the war. Less than half surveyed knew the United States was assisting South Vietnam rather than North or ''East'' Vietnam. The weak association between knowledge and attitudes raises doubt about the children's capacity to offer factual support for their emerging beliefs about the war.

The Vietnam war experience influenced not only the children's outlook on international conflict, but apparently contributed to rising cynicism about the President as well. Throughout the 1960s socialization literature referred to a positive idealization of the President. Greenstein (1961) felt children regarded the President as a ''benevolent leader,'' and in 1968 Greenberg reported that even black children regarded him as a kind, grandfatherly figure. By the close of the Vietnam war, yet prior to the Watergate revelations, the President's credibility and infallibility were already suspect. Less than a third of the children surveyed in 1971 approved President Nixon's Vietnam policy, and only 22% believed he told the truth about the war. Less than a fourth indicated they would support the President in wartime if they felt he was wrong (Tolley, 1973). Greenberg concludes the war may be ''one of the most significant socializing events of our time, playing as powerful a role as did the depression for the parents of the past generation'' (1970, p. 12). Clearly, the young adults conscripted to fight in Vietnam found the experience a major catalyst for political reeducation. Lifton (1973) observes that Vietnam Veterans against the War turned against the ''John Wayne'' ethic of loyal, courageous service, adopting instead the compassionate, antiwar values of the counterculture as represented by Country Joe and the Fish. Jennings and Marcus (1977), on the other hand, found that although military service severely affected particular individuals, generally Vietnam combat experience had a modest impact on political attitudes.

Exposure to televised scenes of military conflict, the patriotic displays in support of a popular war, and violent protest against America's Vietnam involvement have socialized the young both to modern war and to the national leaders who wage such battles. Although the reality may seem more remote in peacetime, socialization to international conflict remains of critical importance.

Conceptualizing War in the Abstract

In the absence of war's immediate horror, children nevertheless learn about the history of international conflict, develop some degree of acceptance, and form expectations for the future. Pierce (1930), e.g., found that American civics texts glorify national heroes and portray only the successful, romantic aspects of United States military efforts. Idealists determined to save succeeding genera-tions from the scourge of war, as well as patriots committed to maintaining psychological defenses against foreign enemies, have both attempted to under-stand and mold the socialization process. Past research has explored when the child first understands the concept of war and how that appreciation changes with age. The impact of other variables such as sex, race, and economic status have also generated frequent inquiry, as has the still unanswered question whether individual attitudes contribute to the incidence of international war. More recent studies focus on differing perceptions of nuclear and conventional war; cross-generational comparisons facilitate attempts to evaluate the effects of the threat of nuclear holocaust and the antiwar movement on children's commitment to peace or expectation of war.

The first major investigations of war-related attitudes began in the 1930s as Americans reexamined their involvement in the First World War. The public debate over the causes of war, international involvement, and U.S. isolationism presaged a similar reappraisal of the Vietnam experience 40 years later. In a 1933 study by Paul Limbert more than half the children responded that a man had a duty to support the country in every way possible during war, while one third approved participation only if the war was considered just and necessary; the remaining 10% expressed a pacifist position. On agree-disagree items measuring appreciation for military values and symbols, slightly less than half felt American soldiers and sailors were always well behaved, and 46% thought every boy ought to be trained to be a soldier in war. Limbert concluded that upper status children are better informed about war and less inclined to support military action (1933, pp. 67–71).

More recent research in England and Norway has examined how children begin to understand the concepts of war and peace. Peter Cooper concluded that English children had fairly well defined ideas about war and peace by age 8 (1965, p. 3). In the following years

> a child loses his pre-occupation with the physical facts of war and particular events and people, and concentrates more and more on fighting, killing and dying; these he evaluates as disagreeable. Thus with the approach of maturity, the image of war

appears to lead to a negative view of aggression, but with little reference to the international scene or particulars.

In contrast to Preston's conclusion, Cooper observed a greater acceptance of war among older children. "The justifications for war are multiplied" with age, although older children may not like or glorify war any more than others (p. 6). Age does not, however, modify a child's image of peace, a far less tangible concept "usually interpreted . . . to mean inner peace and the absence of conflict" (p. 6). In comparison with the 300 English children surveyed, Cooper found 100 Japanese respondents somewhat more opposed to war but less able to display formal operational skills in reasoning about war.

Alvik replicated Cooper's method in an attempt to apply Piaget's stages of intellectual development to children's emerging concepts of war. Norwegian children aged 8 to 12 demonstrated the concrete operational mode when discussing war. Apparently, adolescents cannot fully conceptualize war in the formal operational manner until after age 14, and during the earlier concrete operational stage television imparts significant information. Alvik also found that children compare peace to silence or quiet, an inactive concept rather than a "state which must be actively maintained" (1968, p. 189).

In contrast to Alvik's Norwegian respondents, Haavelsrud (1970) found that German adolescents surveyed in Berlin had a more highly developed understanding of the concept of war. Perhaps the results, comparable to Cooper's findings with English and Japanese children, can be attributed to the legacy of the Second World War. A large majority of the Berlin students replied that Germany's former enemies had been "right" in the Second World War, and Haavelsrud found little evidence of dissonance among 17-year-olds with such unpatriotic sentiments. Students at all ages gave a much more detailed and vivid description of war than of peace; similarly, Haavelsrud found responses describing the causes of war and prevention of war revealed a more highly developed appreciation of the former. A preoccupation with military equipment and the concrete aspects of war rather than with individual suffering distinguished the younger children from older respondents. Finally, the absence of consistent sex differences in Haavelsrud's research appears of particular significance in light of earlier studies in both Europe and the United States.

SEX DIFFERENCES

Traditionally, girls and boys have been conditioned from birth by both indirect and more formal training to demonstrate "ladylike" or "manly" behavior. "A low threshold for anger, direct aggressive retaliation and frequent sexual behavior . . . are disproportionately punished in females, whereas males are given greater license in these areas" (Kagan & Moss, 1962, p. 28). Boys develop weaker inhibitions against aggression, becoming less passive and restrained. A docile mother or active father provide models for the growing child, who soon learns whether doll or miniature soldier is the right toy. In father-absent or mother-dominant families, Langton (1969) found that boys became more authoritarian as a result of overprotection or the absence of an appropriate model. Maccoby and Jacklin (1974, p. 274), following an extensive review of the most recent research on power relationships, conclude that "the evidence for greater male aggressiveness is unequivocal." Since the sex differences observed appear prior to any differential socialization experiences, Maccoby and Jacklin attribute male aggression—at least in part—to higher hormone (androgen) levels in boys.

Despite their generally inferior performance in school, "boys usually demonstrate a clear superiority in factual knowledge of public affairs" (Burton, 1936, p. 264). At the same time, Piaget discovered that boys have a far better "legal sense" than girls. "We did not succeed in finding a single collective game played by girls in which there were as many rules, and above all, as fine and consistent an organization and codification of these rules" (1965, p. 77). In summary, Hyman notes, "Boys are apt to be better informed politically, more interested in public affairs and more attuned to the politically relevant aspect of the news media and other communications" (1959).

Sex differences have consistently appeared with great clarity on measures of war-related attitudes and knowledge. It is no surprise that males are better able to answer factual questions about war, and their greater interest in war play in childhood might also be expected. In 1942 when Geddie and Hildreth asked 21 nursery school children to choose between a number of pictures, 9 boys and none of the girls preferred photographs with a war theme. Cooper (1965) observed that girls made less reference to concrete aspects of war and condemned war to a greater extent than boys who found it justifiable and necessary. Girls not only display less interest in the strategy and methods of conflict, but also hold different attitudes as a result of their "moralistic orientation." Greenstein comments that women are "less willing to support policies they perceive as warlike or aggressive" (1965, p. 107). College students express similar differences according to sex, as revealed by Putney and Middleton in a study of attitudes toward nuclear war. Men, they report,

> are more certain nuclear weapons should be used. On the other hand, they expect lighter casualties, and are more likely to believe that the United States could achieve a meaningful victory in a nuclear war. They are more confident that they personally would survive the war and they would want to survive it; the males are also more likely to have a knowledge of nuclear weapons (1962, p. 306).

Rosenberg et al. came to the conclusion as recently as 1970 that (p. 76) "males are more willing to temporize with human life as an ultimate value than are women."

Nevertheless, the 1971 survey by Tolley revealed no significant sex-related opinion differences in children's orientation either toward the Vietnam conflict or war in general. Girls expressed no greater opposition to American intervention in Southeast Asia, nor did boys demonstrate greater acceptance or tolerance for war in the abstract. Only on a measure of knowledge, a Vietnam fact test, did boys demonstrate higher information levels than girls. Haavelsrud, too, found inconsistent and ultimately insignificant sex differences among the German students. Perhaps in future, the developing movement for women's rights may increasingly contribute to a socialization process that minimizes sexual differentiation in political values as well as in other beliefs.

The uncertain nuclear balance of terror has provided an equally contemporary focus of socialization research in the United States since the early 1960s. Wrightsman (1964) found a direct correlation between children's fears of nuclear war and their parents' expectation. Of 311 children questioned by Escalona in 1962, 70% mentioned the possibility of war, reflecting a profound uncertainty and disturbing fatalism. Escalona concludes that children come to distrust authority figures unable to cope with danger, thereby complicating their own ego development and identity problems. Ninety-five percent of Button's survey respondents had heard of nuclear weapons: "Belief in the basic inevitability of world war did tend to increase significantly with grade level, and a majority of students at the ninth and tenth grades agreed 'there is a good chance we will all die in the next world war'" (1971, p. 349). Thus Button confirms the fatalism noted by Escalona, reporting that a majority felt there was nothing they could personally do to facilitate peace.

While the balance of terror remained stable through several cold war crises of the 1960s, the repeated incidence of controlled violence and conventional military conflict rekindled interest in aspects of international socialization bearing on war-related attitudes. Targ (1970) compares the increased acceptance of war in early adolescence to Morgenthau's realism or *Realpolitik*. Wars are seen as bad but legal; children regard military alliances and treaties as necessary and nonaggressive. According to Button, "Established norms of international law and morality are deprecated" (1973, p. 350). In the same manner, Targ finds both an increasing justification of destructive war and increased acceptance of a "just war," an adolescent belief system that comes to approximate closely that of the adult public.

Essays by several children quoted by Tolley (1973) illustrate the results so often confirmed. One sixth-grade girl wrote: "War is horrible, but we have to learn to live with it." A similar ambivalence appears in the essay of another 11-year-old: "I don't think war is good, and I don't think we should have it. I guess it's o.k. if it's over a good cause and doesn't last very long." What do children feel is a "good cause" for war? One third in Tolley's survey believe that war is good "if the U.S. beats the communists." Far more, however, regard defense of the nation's freedom as the primary objective. One boy explained that conviction as follows: "We have to go to war for a purpose, to have a free country. . . . Every country has got to go to war sometime or another to defend themselves."

These quotations illustrate that attitudes toward war have several dimensions and often encompass inconsistent beliefs. On the moral plane, children condemn war as wrong although on a different level feelings of patriotic loyalty may result in support for military action against the enemy: e.g., men who unconditionally renounced violence in principle nevertheless rallied in the nation's behalf during the First and Second World Wars. In a third area, children predict the likelihood of future wars without reference to moral judgments or patriotic commitments (Tolley, 1973, p. 32).

Although children almost unanimously condemn war on principle, that repudiation clearly has important limits; children condone international conflict as an alternative to what they deem even greater evils. There may be no undue glorification of military conflict, but the young do justify war conducted for national defense or against a hostile enemy. Only 10% in Tolley's survey indicated they would not fight in any circumstances. That percentage for declared pacifists closely resembles figures reported by Limbert and Preston following their work in 1933 and 1940, respectively. (As Preston suggests, it is unlikely that all who profess nonviolence would practice it during a national emergency.) Despite Vietnam antiwar protests, the 1971 study shows about the same proportion of avowed pacifists as do studies conducted before the Second World War.

In assessing the likelihood of future wars, preadolescents believe it is extremely hard to prevent international conflict, and they do not expect to inherit a peaceful world. Early in life, then, Americans learn to regard war as a regular feature of international relations.

Primary Socializing Agents

Behavioral scientists have explored in depth the important questions so well phrased in Torney's query "Who did it?" (1974). The influence of family, school, media, church, peers, and others have all generated considerable study, although the common dependent variable in such research has rarely been attitudes toward war. The existing literature thus offers little of substance on agents of socialization to war and peace, despite numerous research hypotheses. Evidence that violence in the media fosters aggressive behavior, e.g., indicates a need to examine how television affects international orientations, if at all. Similarly, authoritarian parents have a predictable impact on a child's psychological development, although the effect of harsh treatment on militarism remains unclear. Beyond a few unsupported generalizations about antiwar sentiment among the affluent, insufficient data exists to explain the relationship between socioeconomic status and pacifist views. Finally, contradictory findings about sex-related and religious differences indicate that the primary socializing agents for war-related attitudes remain at best vaguely understood. A brief overview of the three most important sources—family, media, and school—illustrates what has been accomplished and what remains to be done.

THE FAMILY

The popular notion of a "generation gap" has led many to conclude that on reaching adolescence a child will intentionally reject a parent's opinion and may deliberately cultivate a distinctive viewpoint. After an extensive national survey of 12,000 children, Hess and Torney document that subjective impression: "The effectiveness of the family in transmitting attitudes has been overestimated" (1967). Helfant also found less agreement within families than earlier studies might suggest (1952). Nevertheless, research by Hyman (1959) and Jennings and Niemi (1968) as well as the 1952 Erie County study have consistently found strong family influence on voting behavior and party affiliation. Yet none of these studies dealt with questions of war and peace, issues which might produce quite different results.

Lawrence Wrightsman reports that children's fears about nuclear war bear a direct relation to parents' concerns (1972), and a subsequent study of attitudes toward the Vietnam war indicates significant family influence.

> Even young people who said they learned little or nothing from their parents expressed opinions similar to those they reported their parents holding. Children may only grudgingly acknowledge the influence, but parents clearly determine much of what they believe about Vietnam (Tolley, 1973, p. 114).

Nevertheless, Tolley found no significant opinion differences between children of civilians and those of career military personnel. Nor did parents convey as much factual information about Vietnam as the media or teachers. Perhaps most important, school had a significantly greater impact than family on children's general orientation to war (Tolley, 1973, pp. 46–48).

Jennings and Niemi offer a possible explanation for what may seem contradictory assessments of parental influence (1968). At a time when parents articulate firm opinions on prominent issues, children mirror their views; when parents deal with abstractions or are undecided, no correlation appears. Thus the controversy over Vietnam resulted in greater parental influence for the preadolescents surveyed. Hess and Torney based their conclusions on data collected in 1960, prior to the intense polarization of later years, and their research considered more abstract values; consequently, parents' attitudes seemed less significant. Moreover, Hess emphasized that the school was "particularly important in low socio-economic areas" but he paid little attention to the relative importance of family and school in higher socioeconomic groups. Tolley's research suggests that in many cases upper-status parents make a major contribution to socialization to war, and his findings add to "the considerable evidence against the theory that attitudes are formed generally in terms of opposition to parents" (Hyman, 1959, p. 72).

A family's socioeconomic status may also affect children's orientations to international conflict. Rosenberg found that adult respondents from the lowest and highest income groups consistently opposed the Vietnam war more than those at intermediate levels (1970). Similarly, children in upper-income homes demonstrated stronger opposition to American intervention in Vietnam and also had higher information levels (Tolley, 1973). The Vietnam study found no correlation between factual knowledge and attitudes, however, so that both the well informed and misinformed shared similar attitudes toward U.S. policy. Cognitive dissonance appears at an early age, and value judgments about war and peace precede factual understanding for both children and adults. The rapid growth of the mass media in the United States has now introduced potent new socializing agents into the American home with the capacity to convey both facts and values to an audience of unprecedented size and economic diversity.

THE MEDIA

Television has become an increasingly important agent of socialization, particularly for children, who spend more hours before the set than they do in school. In assessing the consequences of such overexposure, the media's most ardent critics have accumulated impressive statistics:

> Between the ages of 5 and 14 the average American child witnesses the violent destruction of 13,000 human beings on television. . . . One television station showed in one week, mostly in children's viewing time, 334 completed or attempted killings (Guitar, 1968, pp. 37, 41).

Violent incidents involving use of force against others "were depicted on the three networks at the rate of eight times an hour" in 1968–1969 (Milgram, 1973, p. 1). Violence may become associated in children's minds with the just and good when the "hero" typically requires, and justifiably employs, extreme force to resolve conflicts. Moreover, children who regularly observe hostility and violence in a fictional context become coarse, indifferent, and insensitive to its use in society. Thick skinned, passively jaded, "child viewers cannot afford to get involved, for if they did their emotions would be shredded. So they 'keep cool' distantly unaffected" (Guitar, p. 45). In the same manner, television conditions children to accept the violence of war as routine and commonplace, and there are no countervailing peace commercials.

In response to critics, the industry has refuted the more sensational allegation that television violence causes juvenile delinquency or increases personal aggression. Their contention, that televised violence is not a significant determinant of aggressive behavior, has wide support. Milgram (1973) set out to measure the effect of television programming on anti-social behavior with an elaborate test involving a specially prepared segment of "Medical Story." Despite repeated showings, both to the general public and select audiences in New York, Detroit, and St. Louis, several variations of the experimental design failed to differentiate between the control group and viewers who watched the antisocial broadcast. For most viewers "the predisposition to committing acts of delinquency must be there for television to lead to anti-social acts" (Himmelweit, 1962, p. 209). Although television may not be a causal factor in criminal conduct, there is little evidence to support the industry's claim that action programs are a "safety valve" stimulating a cathartic response which reduces viewers' aggressive drives. On the contrary, the media reinforce deviant behavior of the emotionally disturbed (Schramm & Parker, 1961).

Himmelweit (1958) found that English children, even adolescents, were disturbed and often frightened by the high incidence of personal assault and especially by verbal acts of aggression. Fictitious conflict created much greater anxiety for children than film documentaries of actual violence. Rioting, shooting, and warfare in newsreels had no greater impact than a western shootout, indicating that television may indeed desensitize the viewer. Himmelweit explains that since children have no direct experience with war they feel little compassion for its victims, but when the media depicts an identifiable situation, whether fictional or real, they demonstrate concern.

Television coverage of war scenes may not, therefore, unduly shock child viewers, although those young people should prove better informed as a result of broadcast news. Based on surveys in Seattle and Vancouver, Haavelsrud concludes unequivocally that "mass media is the major source for developing concepts related to war and peace among high school students" (1971b). Peers, teachers, family, and religion trail in importance in that order, as confirmed by Hollander (1971). In particular, Haavelsrud found television had the greatest utility in developing children's concept of war, but was less frequently cited as a source relating to peace or war prevention. Especially among the American children surveyed, Haavelsrud found

> more sources of orientation … geared to the notions about war and causes of war than the development of peace and prevention of war. On the other hand, Canadian subjects seem to regard parts of the communication structure more conducive to the development of orientations about peace and prevention of war (1971c, p. 11).

Although Tolley polled a younger sample than Haavelsrud (aged 8 to 14), the methodologies are similar to the extent that each survey asked the children themselves to rate the importance of media influence. As with the Seattle and Vancouver high school students, the younger children polled in the New York metropolitan area (at about the same time) indicated that television was their most important source. Further analysis of the New York sample, however, revealed no significant attitude differences between viewers and nonviewers, either on general orientations toward war or opinions of U.S. Vietnam policy. Tolley did find that regular viewers had significantly more factual information about Vietnam than nonviewers, and in that sense children correctly identified the source of their knowledge. Television viewing did not, however, appear to modify attitudes about the Vietnam war or acceptance of war in the abstract.

Perhaps the media's ultimate impact on children's beliefs involves a more elaborate chain of communication through parents, teachers, or others, similar to the two-step process described by Katz (1957). Tolley reports a rather complex pattern of influence: parents exercise the dominant influence on Vietnam-related attitudes, schools on general orientation to war, while the media affect information levels the most. Haavelsrud makes no such distinction, but does differentiate between the importance of the mother and father in developing moral concepts. The ambiguous findings from the two studies make it uncertain whether children not only learn the concept of war, but also form value judgments about war and peace as a result of media exposure.

Haavelsrud and Tolley do concur on the decreasing importance of television for older children. At the high school level, newspapers and magazines apparently replace the visual media as primary source material, particularly among upper-income groups. Clearly the mass media now offer unprecedented opportunities to observe military activities firsthand, and one survey revealed that 80% of the children polled had seen Vietnam combat on their home television (Tolley, 1973). Undoubtedly children today know far more about war than earlier generations as a result of media coverage. It seems unlikely that television has also contributed to a better understanding of peace, and the long-term effect of media programming remains uncertain.

THE SCHOOL

Educators frequently debate whether family, the media, or school play a larger role in political socialization. The question remains moot. Hess and Torney, on the one hand, believe the importance of the home has been seriously exaggerated. Public education is the most "central, salient, dominant force" in political socialization (1967, p. 106). Their research showed that schools cultivate reverence and awe for the government through ritual indoctrination and patriotic ceremonies—the pledge and salute to the flag, the national anthem. Those routines foster an

> attitude of submission, respect and dependence manifested in the gestures and words surrounding these acts and the group nature of the behavior. These rituals establish an emotional orientation toward country and flag even though an understanding of the meaning of the words has not been developed (1967, p. 106).

In addition, school textbooks typically glorify national heroes and portray the homeland in its most favorable light. "From schoolbook descriptions one would draw the conclusions that war is a natural and normal relationship between nations; it is dreadful but inevitable, and its horror is full of interest" (Stephens, 1967, p. 257). During wartime, public education has promoted student morale to assist the national cause with activities like the school garden armies and cadet units of 1918. The absence of such activities during the Korean and Vietnam wars reflects in part the more limited nature of the conflict, as well as reduced levels of public support.

At no time, however, have American schools offered systematic indoctrination comparable to the extensive influence exercised by totalitarian regimes. In fact, during the Vietnam war, public school teachers largely abdicated responsibility for dealing with the bitter controversy. Tolley attempted to poll teachers along with each class surveyed and met considerable resistance. Some teachers protested that young children should not discuss such controversial material, confirming the children's report that they rarely studied the Vietnam war in school. Similarly, Burton concluded that sources outside school had more utility in acquiring civic information (1936).

Although less important than family and media in affecting opinion or knowledge of the Vietnam conflict, schools did appear to have the greatest impact on general orientations to war. As might be expected, children in Friends schools differ considerably in outlook from military academy cadets, but similar attitude differences also appear in public and private school students of the same socioeconomic background. Public institutions may not inculcate a blind patriotism, but they do appear to contribute to a greater national loyalty and acceptance of war than private schools (Tolley, 1973). Differences in staff and curriculum, as well as the required patriotic observances in state-run schools, explain the result. In peacetime, Hess and Torney's assessment of the school's primary importance undoubtedly applies. When the community becomes deeply polarized on a war issue, however, it appears likely that the public school teaching staff will avoid what might be considered partisan remarks, while private school instructors may support one particular viewpoint. Similarly, Zeigler found that on 8 of 10 domestic and international concerns "a majority of teachers preferred noninvolvement" (1967, p. 98).

Targ offers one possible solution to the difficulties inherent in discussion of contemporary problems—a simulation exercise. Children aged 9 to 12 who participated in an Inter-Nation Game recorded no significant change in evaluations of war or in action preferences, but did alter some international beliefs. Perhaps most significant, the simulation exercise markedly improved the children's understanding of participant roles, the foreign secretary, organizations like the United Nations, and concepts such as economic development.

The need for effective socialization methods in the elementary school appears more pressing in light of the apparent failure of the high school civics curriculum to influence political orientations. Langton and Jennings declare there is no significant change in students' attitudes, although the course does improve their factual knowledge (1968). Children learn what to believe in the elementary years before they know the facts; high school students may indeed learn *why,* but their assumptions remain stable, relatively uninfluenced by new learning.

Numerous attitude surveys of college-level students attest to the interest of university faculty in self-evaluation and their concern for measuring the impact of favorite course offerings on "impressionable" freshmen. To their regret, pre- and post-tests generally reveal insignificant attitude change, although undergraduates may demonstrate a spontaneous shift of opinion. In a four-year longitudinal study of 282 students at the University of Kansas, Smith found increasing opposition to military conflict during college, although the faculty made no effort to encourage pacifism (1937). Despite its limitations as a guide for modifying the attitudes of postsecondary students, the literature does contain several valuable reports on the relevant beliefs of undergraduates. Putney and Middleton (1962) surveyed 1,100 students in 16 colleges to explore important factors associated with acceptance or rejection of nuclear war and pacifism. Day and Quackenbush (1942) differentiate between defensive, cooperative, and aggressive war in an effort to clarify the meaning of war acceptance.

Antiwar protest initiated by campus activists during the 1960s generated renewed interest in research with undergraduates. Keniston (1968) interviewed a select sample of new left activists during "Vietnam Summer" and reports that the student leaders opposed the ends of U.S. policy in Southeast Asia, rather than the use of military force to realize national objectives. Further, some radicals wanted not only to end the war, but also to politicize a larger constituency in the United States, if necessary through disruption and more violent tactics. Keniston concludes that childhood learning experiences pointed toward, but did not finally determine, a radical-activist adult life and that the political, social, and historical forces of the 1960s had a decisive impact. In early childhood the activists

> were more attuned to the historical currents in their lives than are most children. Also from an early age they began to think of themselves as special and different people; they became sensitive to and inoculated against the issue of violence, struggle and conflict; and they developed an important ambivalence toward their fathers as being on the one hand highly principled, but on the other hand often ineffectual (Keniston, 1968, pp. 75–76).

The World Law Fund capitalized on the emergence of new student interest and supported the creation of a Consortium on Peace Research, Education, and Development in 1970. University research and training centers, and as many as 150 peace education programs nationwide, offer interdisciplinary courses which consider the ethical, social, economic, and political aspects of international war. Avowedly pacifist by design and intent, the World Law Fund, the Center for War/Peace Studies, and related organizations distribute appropriate literature and publish the *International Peace Studies Newsletter* in an effort to build a framework for a peaceful world order (Sievert & Langer, 1973). Linked to that academic program in American universities is an even more fundamental effort to revise the elementary and high school curriculum in order to socialize the next generation to a world at peace.

Peace Studies Curricula

The obvious, terrible risks involved in a third world war, combined with an abiding liberal faith in man's ability to master his destiny, motivate those curriculum developers committed to a program of peace studies. "The institution of war presents a problem that can be studied and is amenable to human intervention and resolution" (Nesbitt, 1973, p. vii). Further assuming the critical importance of early childhood learning leads to the inescapable conclusion that "elementary and secondary schools of this country have a responsibility to prepare their students to deal with and eventually control war and violence" (Education on War, Peace, Conflict and Change, 1970, p. 20). The National Defense Education Act, launched after the successful orbit of Sputnik I, illustrates that the government concurs at least in part on the importance of childhood learning for realizing national goals. Unfortunately, from the standpoint of those advocating a peace studies curriculum, that early initiative sought to train scientists for war, and the nondefense goals of the 1966 International Education Act have never been implemented with the required appropriations. Concerned that less than 10% of American undergraduates studied international affairs, Congress originally anticipated expenditures of $90 million for university activities in 1969, but ultimately approved only $19.1 million in that year for language and area programs.

In a comparison with "spaceship Earth," Boulding has written eloquently of the need for curricular reform at a time of growing population and limited food supplies. "The kind of organization, ethic and conduct which may be quite appropriate to a great planet are quite inappropriate for the crowded and precarious conditions of a spaceship" (1968, p. 648). Taylor decries the ethnocentrism apparent in data revealing that less than 10% of U.S. teachers had any courses containing nonwestern historical material, and less than 2% of the time in high school is now spent on nonwestern material (Education on War, Peace, Conflict and Change, 1970, p. 42). The answer, according to Torney and Morris, is not only to broaden course content, but to profit from the findings of earlier socialization research. Although war cannot be studied by the very young, conflict can. Torney and Morris thus recommend helping children analyze a conflict situation, exploring ways in which it might have been resolved or could have been prevented. In addition, exercises can be designed which "deliberately train functions . . . to inform children that peace is a pattern of active cooperation" (Alvik, 1968, p. 189).

Peace studies curricula rely on a variety of teaching methods. For high school students, the Thorpe syllabus sets out a 12-week program of readings on international law and organization accompanied by appropriate films and class discussion. Simulation exercises and fictional scenarios depart from the standard teaching format, and the popular case study method draws on historical material, such as documents from the Cuban missile crisis. In all forms of conflict resolution study, the students can explore alternate outcomes, both for interpersonal differences and at the level of world order. Enthusiastic accounts of peace studies lessons in Diablo Valley, California, and Dade County, Florida, have appeared periodically since the mid-1960s, but there have been no reports of subsequent studies examining the long-term effect of such instruction on students' values.

It may nevertheless be concluded that the programs represent a well intentioned effort to take advantage of whatever opportunity exists for giving human nature a peaceful bent. Moreover, even if the curriculum developers fall short of their professed goal of curbing international war, they may nonetheless mitigate the virulence of interpersonal conflict at a lower level. For all the disdain expressed by "hard headed realists," the idealism of a peace studies curriculum offers a preferable alternative to the too-often-self-fulfilling prophecy of *Realpolitik*.

Some fundamental doubts and reservations, however, remain. First, the age group exposed to the peace studies offerings appears too old for maximum impact. So many studies have now documented the importance of early political learning that a syllabus which requires a high school reading level has limited value. Granted that a suitable high school curriculum might reinforce pacifist sentiments, it would still not accomplish the primary objective of creating those values, attitudes which form before the development of advanced reading skills. Boulding (1968) notes a second inherent problem. Since "any attempt to diminish glorification of the nation state would be viewed with suspicion," over-zealous pacifists "could create anti-international results with conservative teachers" (p. 648).

Third, the basic premise of world studies could prove fallacious. Perhaps increased familiarity with foreign ways will not promote understanding, as expected, but, rather, contribute to a heightened appreciation of irreconcilable differences. Does full exposure necessarily entail empathy and mutual trust? Finally, the arguments raised by hard-line opponents of unilateral disarmament merit consideration. Of course, one state must begin the difficult process of socializing youth to a world of peace, but there would be obvious dangers to any nation which has disarmed its citizenry without prior guarantees of security from rivals who have pursued more traditional forms of competitive, aggressive child rearing. Efforts to develop a peace studies curriculum are neither futile nor misguided, but the first tentative efforts at curricular reform require additional improvement. Existing doubts might in part be resolved by further research into several important, recurring questions left unanswered by prior socialization research.

Directions for Future Research

Perhaps the most glaring deficiency in studies of child socialization, an oversight equally characteristic of the curriculum reform movement, is the failure to connect the child's emerging value system with observed behavior. For the ultimate test of high ideals comes when difficult events require unpopular conduct. Too frequently, researchers note "significant opposition to war" without considering whether such a commitment would hold firm during an attack on the United States. Day and Quackenbush (1942) attempted to differentiate between student support for offensive and defensive war but here, too, the authors are unable to demonstrate whether actual behavior conformed to professed values in a conflict situation. Although few opportunities would permit testing the consistency of beliefs and conduct in wartime, respondents might be involved in a more immediate conflict situation as a possible measure. As long as the values taught by family, school, and church can be overcome by a month in marine boot camp or battlefield experience, socialization research must attempt to bridge the gap between belief and conduct.

Even with conventional approaches, improved methodology would produce more reliable results. On the one hand, "the scope of socialization research must be enlarged to include parents and teachers as well as children. For only by obtaining an independent assessment of the attitudes of parent and teacher can their impact on children's beliefs be accurately determined" (Tolley, 1973, p. 134). On the other hand, research is needed to trace the development of war-related attitudes over time in a genuinely longitudinal study design. Future studies of children and war should be carried through the high school years at least, since the child's early outlook on complex world affairs may continue to evolve in late adolescence. Perhaps some of the existing uncertainty about how children's orientations to war and peace change with age could be resolved with an improved study design. The continuing doubts about the use of a written questionnaire format with young children (Vaillancourt, 1973) reveals a need for a variety of approaches—interviews, essays, drawings, and other informal techniques.

> One immediate research need is for a comparative study of alternative methodologies. One group of children might, for example, write essays and draw pictures on a given political subject before being interviewed on the same topic. Conclusions drawn from these two approaches might then be compared with findings based on a written questionnaire survey of the same children. Future studies of political learning would profit immeasurably from comparative testing which determined, for example, at what age children first give reliable answers on a written questionnaire (Tolley, 1973, p. 133).

Finally, for all their "world-mindedness," behavioral scientists examining socialization to war and peace have focused primarily on American children. Torney has appealed to political scientists to correct the imbalance and attend to the important research under way in Europe. Numerous opportunities for cross-national comparison exist in both Third World "neutral" states and in those rent by frequent civil or international war.

Granted the funds, opportunity, and methodology required for improved research, what subjects merit further study? One variable too long ignored, perhaps because of preoccupation with American children, has been religion. Eight times during a quarter century, in Ireland, the Middle East, and South Asia, religious differences have contributed to prolonged, unresolved warfare. Even in the United States, the consistent research finding that formal civics courses fail to affect a child's political orientation illustrates that political beliefs frequently have no factual or rational support. Further, evidence of cognitive dissonance in adolescence ought to concern liberal curriculum developers bent on educating high school students to the futility of war. Apter's concept of "Political Religion" suggests that in developing nations charismatic leaders may acquire a mystical authority as prophet or missionary with greater impact on citizen values than church religion (1965, p. 303). Nonrational, inspirational modes of acquiring political beliefs might also merit study in the industrialized democracies.

Socialization to the balance of terror certainly deserves additional consideration, since it is impossible to determine whether children today willingly accept the likelihood of total nuclear war. The younger children polled by Tolley

> seem more willing to use atomic bombs in Vietnam than did the older. It must be wondered how and when young people first learn the possibility of nuclear holocaust and whether they understand the ideas behind deterrence. Statesmen and some scholars often insist that nuclear war is no longer a feasible mode of international conflict, but additional study is needed to determine whether children accept that idea (1973, p. 134).

Doomsday may not come in the form of a nuclear holocaust, however, according to the Club of Rome's alarming forecast; consequently, research is needed on how American children in particular develop views on energy consumption, overpopulation, famine, and the sharing of scarce resources at great personal cost. Americans, 6% of the world's population, now consume nearly one third of the fuel reserves and an even more disproportionate share of other resources. Toynbee's vision of a "stockade society" and Hardin's concept of the "lifeboat ethic" both suggest that the next major world struggle will involve the "haves" versus the "have nots." Future research ought to be guided at least in part by expectations of what the future will bring. The weakness of antiwar attitudes among U.S. children noted by Torney (1974) combined with the grave challenges facing America pose significant problems.

If even the most moderate predictions of impending hardship prove true, individualism, materialism, and related cultural values acquired in youth could ultimately determine the future of world order. Has socialization research, then, shown disproportionate concern for theory and abstract issues, when the times demand more immediate answers to immense difficulties? Sex-related differences and age-specific viewpoints have been explored in sufficient depth. New studies might better ask whether the political values presently acquired by youth are suitable for life in the twenty-first century. The doomsayers no doubt overstate their case, yet the statistical logic of their most soundly based projections offers a timely reminder that socialization studies too must look ahead. Although prior studies of socialization to war present at best a fragmentary picture, better use can be found for the most frequently replicated findings. Socialization theory developed in past research should prove of utility in meeting the challenge of the future, and the times require a more practical application now.

14

Socialization and the Characterological
Basis of Political Activism

Kenneth J. Gergen and Matthew Ullman

POLITICAL MOVEMENTS IN THIS NATION have seldom involved large segments of the populace. Although highly visible, those groups most strongly invested in altering the status quo have generally enlisted only a minority of the population. Presidential elections do motivate large numbers of people to engage in a political act, but even this quadrennial appeal seldom influences more than 60% of the eligible voters. This is not to disparage the importance of political activism in the culture. Many successful revolutions have been achieved by small numbers. Largely because of the potential power of such movements in producing change, a strong demand for systematic understanding has developed. Many behavioral scientists have attempted to construct general theories of political activism (cf. Toch, 1965; Schwartz, 1970; Feuer, 1969; Le Bon, 1913; Edwards, 1927; Adams, 1913; Blumer, 1951). Research has documented a number of important precipitating conditions (cf. Davies, 1962; Zawadzki & Lazarsfeld, 1935; Killian, 1964), and arguments for and against the use of political disorder have been elaborated (cf. Sennet, 1969). However, most important for present purposes, intensive inquiry has been made into the character of those who are moved to action versus those who remain uninvolved. It is this issue which is most closely tied to the sphere of political socialization. Thus, the present chapter is addressed to the character of the political activist as it is articulated with his or her relevant socialization experiences.

Our discussion will be divided into five related segments. At the outset, we shall briefly discuss a number of central assumptions that undergird the inquiry into the character of the activist. Then we shall undertake a broad-scale review of the major empirical contributions. We shall be most concerned with attempts to determine the specific dispositions that successfully predict engagement in political movements. Once we have reviewed this literature, we shall be in a position to step back and ask about the adequacy of the major research paradigms. We shall be particularly concerned with feasible means of improving on the methods traditionally employed in such research. We shall then return to the basic assumptions that we initially described. Both the appraisal of the present literature and recent developments in related fields suggest that many of the basic assumptions are misconceived. In this section, we shall argue for an abandonment of many of the initial assumptions. The final section will allow us to complete the discussion on a more optimistic note. Specifically, we shall elaborate on what we feel to be the potential of future investigation in this domain.

The Assumptive Basis of a Science of Political Activism

Research on personal dispositions underlying political activism has been undertaken for a variety of different purposes, and not all investigators share similar viewpoints concerning their endeavors. Within this broad array, however, two distinct orientations may be isolated. On the one hand, there are the behavioral scientists who strive to accumulate knowledge in the traditional sense. Their attempt is to build viable theories of political activity, and their work is essentially carried out in the hypothetico-deductive mold. This orientation tends to dominate the research spectrum and may be considered "normal science" in Kuhn's (1962) sense. In contrast, other investigators are concerned primarily with documenting the character of a single movement at a particular point in history. While the former group is striving for transhistorical principles, the latter is more concerned with description of history in the making. We shall return to the distinction at the close of this chapter. However, for now it is important to spell out some major assumptions underlying much research within the former and more dominant orientation in the behavioral sciences. Four major assumptions deserve attention.

1. PERSONALITY AS A DETERMINANT OF POLITICAL ACTIVISM

Central to the behavioral science orientation is the deterministic assumption that all behavior can be understood in terms of its causal antecedents. Although most behavioral scientists agree that political behavior is the result of multiple determinants, the research with which we shall be concerned in this chapter has argued that personal dispositions must be taken into account in understanding political activism. Such an argument has much to recommend it. After all, thousands of people may be faced with very similar life circumstances, and yet only a minority of them seem to respond to these circumstances with political commitment. It seems impossible to account for these differences on the basis of contemporary circumstances alone. One must attend to the underlying personal dispositions of the committed versus the passive. It is assumed that individuals develop over time stable and enduring styles of behavior, and that these individualistic styles pervade their activities across diverse situations. Political activities should be no less influenced than any others. This line of thinking follows an estimable tradition, possibly beginning in 1897 when Frederick Jackson Turner called for research to determine "what kinds of people tend to be Whigs, what Democrats, or Abolitionists, or Prohibitionists, etc." The classic explorations of Smith, Bruner, and White (1956) on the dynamic underpinnings of political opinion, the work of Lasswell (1948) on the power needs of those in political office, and Lane's (1959) detailed studies of the relationship of political behavior to the personal problems faced by the individual all lend support to the endeavor.

2. SOCIALIZATION AS THE CORNERSTONE OF PERSONALITY DIFFERENCES

Because people seem to differ in stable and enduring ways, the major question arises as to the source of such differences. In this case, the assumption underlying most research in this area has deep roots in the psychoanalytic perspective. As Freud persuasively argued, the first six years of life are of inestimable importance in establishing the basis for adult personality. While later theorists disagreed on the precise mechanism at stake or viewed the formative years as continuing into adolescence, the initial orientation continues to dominate the field. Essentially, it is assumed that those major personality differences influencing political activism are the result of critical socialization experiences. Socialization practices implant in the individual the particular styles or dispositions that form his or her individual character and that influence, among other things, his or her level of political participation. This line of thinking has played a critical role in the entire development of the field of political socialization. The influential works of Greenstein (1964), Easton and Dennis (1969), and Hess and Torney (1967) have all shared similarly in the emphasis placed on the preadult years, as have the scores of more recent investigations in this area.

3. THE ACCUMULATION OF KNOWLEDGE

The third major supposition underlying behavioral science research on political activism rests on the positivistic tradition of the field. The positivist model (cf. Kaplan, 1964) essentially envisions the scientist as one who observes the state of nature, formulates principles or hypotheses on the basis of inductive logic, and through deduction constructs empirical tests of these principles. Over time, the empirical evaluation of the theoretical principles allows one to dispense with those having poor predictive validity and to elaborate with increasing precision those principles of robust predictive value. As an increasing number of facts become available to us, our general knowledge of political activism should be improved; e.g., if one views political movements as primarily invested in altering the normative structures of a society, then it is reasonable to suspect that particular types of personality variables should predict political activism. People with strong needs for stimulation, who prefer high levels of risk, who are without strong emotional dependencies, who are "open-" as opposed to "closed-minded," and so on should all be more inclined to engage in activistic movements. Hypotheses derived from this line of thinking can be tested in virtually any era, and over time it should be possible to verify or to invalidate this particular conception of political movements. Of course, there are competing conceptions that could also be put to empirical test, and there are also many researchers whose primary interests lie in a particular personality constellation as opposed to political activism per se. The important point is that in all cases the assumption is made that through empirical testing our knowledge of political activism and its characterological basis may be improved over time. It may even be ventured that one major reason for publishing a handbook such as this is to provide future researchers with the fund of knowledge thus far established.

4. THE DEVELOPMENT OF INTEGRATED THEORY

The fourth major assumption underlying much contemporary research on personality and political activism may be derived from the preceding. If we can accumulate factual knowledge concerning the roots of activism and if we can improve on the predictive ability of our hypotheses over time, then it should ultimately be possible to build an integrated theory of political activism. From the plethora of facts, we may construct a more general understanding of the personal antecedents of activism. Ideally, this more general theory would treat both personality and political activism within a broader social context. This "constructivist" assumption is closely wedded to the mechanistic orientation underlying major sectors of the behavioral sciences. From this standpoint, an understanding of the whole can be constructed from our knowledge of the constituent parts. Thus, the continued isolation of relations among particular personality, political, and institutional variables should ultimately yield an understanding of the general patterns of behavior.

Personal Correlates of Political Activism

Having glimpsed several of the major assumptions underlying research in this domain, we may fruitfully examine major research contributions. We shall first discuss a range of studies in which personality variables have been linked to various forms of political activism or participation. In the case of political participation, we shall primarily be concerned with social movements with vested interests either in changing or maintaining some aspect of society. Thus, we shall be particularly interested in revolutionary groups, the civil rights movement, women's rights activists, the antiwar movement, and so on. Although we shall not be specifically concerned with general levels of party participation, we shall include relevant data where they suggest a broader or more integrated interpretation.

After reviewing major work relating personality factors to political activity, we shall turn to individual difference variables not strictly related to personality: e.g., keen interest has been shown in the economic-class basis of political activity. Religion, family background, and intelligence will also receive attention.

In the case of personal dispositions, the following lines of research have been singled out for attention.

AGGRESSION

In our society, it is commonly believed that political participation represents a socialized form of aggression. The wellsprings of such aggression are generally traced to early socialization. Bandura and Walters (1963), Kagan and Moss (1962), and Bettleheim (1952) have all provided empirical demonstrations of the manner in which aggressive traits may be developed during the early years. The extensive literature in this area has been reviewed by Becker (1964). With respect to the political sphere, the large amount of terminology that is used to describe political activity suggests the link between aggression and political behavior: e.g., we commonly speak of "political battles," "campaign tactics," "victory celebrations," and the "political arena" with its overtones of violent gladiators fighting for victory before bloodthirsty crowds. Milbrath (1965) has made intensive use of this simile in his analysis of political behavior. Psychoanalytic theory provides a particularly rich base from which to generate hypotheses on the relationship between aggression and political activism. According to Freudian theory, the taming of aggressive impulses is one of the primary tasks of childhood socialization. Depending upon the manner in which this is accomplished, conflict over the repression of hostility frequently results within the individual. Although this intrapsychic conflict may be repressed from consciousness, it remains within the person and creates an uncomfortable state of anxiety which causes a venting of the frustrated impulse through one or more of the defense mechanisms. In the case of aggression, it has been speculated that the political process is an appropriate sphere in which this can occur (cf. Lane, 1959).

With the pervasive controversy over protest demonstrations, electoral contests, intra- and international rivalries, etc., it seems clear that hostile and aggressive drives can be easily channeled into varied types of political activity (cf.

Lasswell, 1930, 1954; Schiff, 1964; Wolfenstein, 1967; Rohter, 1969). Further, the existence of competing candidates, groups, political parties, and governments provide ample opportunity for the projection of one's forbidden aggressive impulses onto others, and the democratic value of participation in politics enables one to easily rationalize political involvement. Thus, many investigators have hypothesized that the trait of aggressiveness or hostility will be linked with political activism. Some have even postulated that political participation will be facilitated by a capacity for externally expressed aggression and extrapunitiveness.

Most of the empirical work on aggressive or hostile impulses suggests that such impulses are positively related to various forms of political activism. Investigating the radical right, Bell (1964), Hofstadter (1964), Schiff (1964), Faia (1967), Chesler and Schmuck (1963), Broyles (1963), Grupp (1969), Rohter (1969), Elms (1969), and Eysenck (1954) have all found a high degree of hostility in members of such groups as the John Birch Society, the Christian Anti-Communist Crusade, the Minutemen, etc. Closely related, Lasswell (1947) has noted the same relationship in a study of Hitlerism. While such research has often been conducted by liberals, and its ideological biases are thus rendered questionable, many investigators have also located high levels of aggressiveness within leftist circles. Fishman and Solomon (1963) and Coles (1964) have described young civil rights demonstrators in such terms. Allport (1929) and Wolfe (1921) have both reported a high degree of hostility associated with left-wing activism, as did Whittaker and Watts (1971) in their inspection of leftist student activism and Goldschmidt, Gergen, Quigley, and Gergen (1974) in their probe of the Women's Liberation movement. These findings are also upheld in two somewhat unconventional studies: Wolfenstein's biographical investigation of three "revolutionary personalities"—Lenin, Trotsky, and Gandhi (1967), and Hendin's study of 15 college activists by means of psychoanalytic interviews (1971). Broad studies not distinguishing among ideological leanings have lent further support to the positive relationship between aggression and activism. Helfant's investigation of political attitudes (1952), Lasswell's examination of general activism (1930) and political participation (1954), Lane's work on political participation (1959), Baird's research on general student activism (1970), and Blumer's study of social movements (1969) have all provided supporting evidence.

Unfortunately for our sense of order, there are exceptions to this general pattern. Keniston (1968), examining in depth 14 Vietnam war protestors, found a low degree of hostility, a result sustained by Fishman and Solomon (1946b) in their more generalized study of student peace demonstrators. McCloskey (1958), inquiring into political ideology, reported a high degree of hostility in conservatives but low levels in liberals, whereas Shils (1954) found that both "right" and "left" authoritarians manifested higher levels of hostility than nonauthoritarians. Clearly, then, the vast majority of the studies in this area indicate a positive correlation between aggression or hostility and various forms of political activism. However, exceptions do cast doubt on the generality of the pattern.

OPTIMISM-PESSIMISM

An essential faith in the rationality and goodness of one's fellow citizens and in the possibility for beneficial change should play an important part in the individual's motivational system. The pioneering work of Erik Erikson (1950, 1959) on the development of trust in the young child and the relationship of trust to optimism is strongly compelling on this point. The possibility that such differences in basic trust in a beneficial future should be articulated with political activism has been spelled out by both Lane (1959) and Keniston (1967). In particular, it has been reasoned that the political participant must feel that his or her work is not in vain and that improvements are possible. If one believes that all one's actions may be in vain, that one cannot trust the results of political participation, then little participation should take place. For these and other reasons, many investigators have hypothesized that personal optimism should correlate highly with political activism.

Unfortunately, investigations exploring the personality dimension of optimism-pessimism disclose a confused picture with no clear trends. Several general studies link optimism to political activism. Bronfenbrenner's work on community participation (1960) and Blumer's inspection of social movements (1969) are classic in this respect. Examinations of left-wing student activism (Fishman & Solomon, 1964b), the antiwar movement, (Keniston, 1967), and the Berkeley Revolt and related Free Speech Movement (May, 1965; Somers, 1965; Smith et al., 1967) point to the same relationship. Further support for this linkage is derived from research on the radical right, including findings by Westin (1964) in his investigation of the John Birch Society and Wolfinger et al. (1969) in their inquiry into the Christian Anti-Communist Crusade. Rosenberg's study of political apathy (1954) also suggests that optimism is related to activism, for his findings tie pessimism to political apathy. Yet McClosky (1958), in his study of political ideology, found that his subgroup of leftists ranked as optimistic but that the rightists were pessimists. Confusing the picture still further, Milbrath's review of general political participation (1965) found pessimism positively related to political activism. This finding is echoed in a number of studies of leftist activism. In their examination of student activism of the left, Jacobs and Landau (1966) linked pessimism to activism in research covering many of the same activities that were probed by investigators mentioned above, such as antiwar, FSM, SDS, and SNCC participation. In his investigation of civil rights activism, Coles (1964) uncovered the same relationship as Jacob and Landau, as did Hoffer (1951) in his scrutiny of general leftist activism, Lasch (1965) in his historical summary of radicalism, and Wolfenstein (1967) in his examination of the "revolutionary personality."

From our perspective, research into the optimism dimension seems overly influenced by the search for *general* personality styles. It seems quite possible that activists may often be both optimistic *and* pessimistic, depending on the domain of concern. They may be pessimistic, e.g., concerning the status quo, and optimistic with respect to their own political movement. They may be pessimistic with respect to "people in general" and optimistic with respect to their own contribution. Differentiation of the domain of optimism versus pessimism is highly recommended for future research in this area.

AUTHORITARIANISM

In their seminal work on anti-Semitism and ethnocentrism, Adorno, Frenkel-Brunswick, Levinson, and Sanford (1950) developed the concept of the authoritarian personality. At that time the authoritarian individual was viewed as a character type, and the pure type was characterized by such traits as rigidity, prejudice, submissiveness to authority, harsh dominance toward subservients, dogmatism, alienation, intolerance of deviations from norms, aversion to ambiguity, and exaggerated concern with sex. Although one or another of these traits is occasionally maintained in the present-day literature, for the most part contemporary research has emphasized two major characteristics: (1) a preference for viewing personal relationships along dominance-submissiveness dimensions, in which one accepts orders from an unquestioned authority above and in turn demands extreme deference from those below, and (2) a relative intolerance of ambiguity (cf. Brown, 1965; Sanford, 1973). The scale most commonly employed is the 26-item *F-scale,* developed by the initial group and used in more than 300 studies. Although this scale was developed in the study of fascism, it is often viewed as a measure of general authoritarianism, a personality syndrome divorced from ideology. The initial view of an ideology-free measure has had a troubled history. In a study of ward committee chairmen, Harned (1961) found authoritarians were low in their commitment to any ideology. However, Barker (1963) found that the F-scale identifies only authoritarians on the right; left-wing authoritarianism does not seem to be tapped by the scale. Similarly, Janowitz and Marvick (1953) did find strong ideological leanings (to the right) among authoritarians. In an attempt to develop a scale measuring general authoritarianism, Rokeach (1960) has developed a dogmatism scale that has been used with some success in more recent research.

Early childhood antecedents of adult authoritarianism have been explored by a number of investigators. Adorno et al. gave initial impetus to such inquiry by exploring early childhood dynamics of authoritarian and nonauthoritarian subjects. Since that time more precisely controlled research has shown that the authoritarian individual generally seems to come from a home in which the parents themselves were highly authoritarian. So common have such findings been that developmental psychologists have made a primary distinction between authoritarian child-rearing methods and others (such as democratic or permissive). The influence of those differential child-rearing atmospheres has been amply documented.

For our purposes, studies of the relationship between authoritarianism and political activism may be divided into two classes: studies of the degree to which authoritarians are likely to involve themselves in any political activity at all, and studies concerning the distribution of authoritarians among the various ideologies.

Research examining the relationship between authoritarianism and degree of political participation has yielded mixed findings. Lasswell (1930), probing general political activity, revealed that political activity and authoritarianism are related in a positive manner, as did Froman's (1961) investigation of political behavior, from voting to holding office, and DiRenzo's (1967) study in which he drew his subjects from the Italian Chamber of Deputies and utilized Rokeach's dogmatism scale. Westin (1964), Rohter (1969), and Elms (1969), in their studies of the radical right, and McClosky (1958), in his inquiry into political conservatism, all point to a high degree of authoritarianism in right-wing activists. DiRenzo (1968) further found that Democrats rank low in authoritarianism, but that Republicans cannot be characterized as high on this dimension. Bay's research on student political participation (1967) reveals that their rightist subgroups manifest high levels of authoritarianism and that their leftist subgroups rate low on the same dimension. Further support for these latter findings is provided by Keniston's discussion of the literature on student dissent (1967). In sum, a substantial number of studies indicate that authoritarians are more involved in politics in general, and that their involvement is typically in right-wing activities.

Yet this picture is far too simple, and does not do justice to the literature. Both Sanford (1950) and Milbrath and Klein (1962) have found that authoritarianism is associated with a disinclination to participate in political affairs. Janowitz and Marvick (1953) linked authoritarianism to feelings of political ineffectiveness and found that authoritarians tended not to vote in elections. Consistent with this view, Lane (1955) reported that authoritarians are less likely to campaign and have a lower level of political interest. Finally, studies by Barker (1963) and Christie et al. (1958) found no relationship between authoritarianism and general political participation. In terms of ideological commitment, Levinson (1950) and Shils (1954) found in their research that political activists of both extreme ideological persuasions rated higher on authoritarianism. Flacks (1967) also demonstrated that anti-SDS activists were characterized by a low degree of authoritarianism, and Elms' (1969) examination of right-wing extremisms showed no difference between activists and controls on a measure of authoritarianism. In sum, it is virtually impossible to reach any generalized conclusions about the relationship between authoritarianism and political activism. We shall return to this issue later in the chapter.

GROUP AFFILIATION

Participation in the democratic political process usually involves a high degree of social interaction. Through his association with others of similar feelings and political views, the politically active individual may be provided with a strong network of supportive social relationships. In this sense, political activism can serve an "adjustive" function for the individual (Rohter, 1969). In particular, it has been hypothesized that those who need frequent and active contact with others (i.e., those ranking high on group affiliation) will tend to engage in political activism more frequently than those who are low in affiliative needs. The development of such needs during the early childhood years has been traced in detail.

Examinations of the trait of group affiliation as it relates to political activism show striking unity in their findings. Broad studies not distinguishing as to ideological direction, such as Rose's research on group leadership (1962), Fishman and Solomon's work on general political activism (1964a), Gelineaux and Kantor's investigation of social service involvement (1964), and Blumer's inspection of social movements (1969), suggest that activists are generally high in measures of group affiliation. Probing the radical right, as manifested in the Christian Anti-Communist Crusade, both Chesler and Schmuck (1963a) and Wolfinger et al. (1969) report this same relationship. Examinations of leftist activism also support these findings. Hoffer (1951) in his examination of general activism of the left, Shils (1954) in his work on authoritarianism, Keniston (1968) in his investigation of antiwar activism, and Bittner (1969) in his study of radicalism all link activism to high needs for group affiliation. Inspecting student participation in mass demonstrations, Bakke (1966) found a positive relationship between activism and need for group affiliation, as did Flacks (1967) in his probe of students involved in SDS activities and Keniston (1967) in his review of work on student leftist dissent. Whittaker and Watts (1971), however, reported no difference between activists and controls on this trait. In sum, the research relating group affiliation to political activism strongly suggests a positive link between the two.

ALIENATION

The term "alienation" has been variously used to refer to the feelings of powerlessness, meaninglessness, normlessness, isolation, self-estrangement, inefficacy, cynicism, and lack of social-rootedness (Seeman, 1959; Levinson, 1968; Knutson, 1972; Yinger, 1973). Despite the difficulties of dealing with such a multidimensional concept, some coherence is provided by Yinger's definition of alienation as "the experienced loss of a relationship and of a sense of participation and control, with reference to prevailing social structures" (1973). Unlike many of the traditional dispositions relevant to political activism, alienation is most often viewed as a reaction syndrome triggered by the prevailing social circumstances. The social or economic structure of the society may generate alienation at virtually any point in the individual's life. To be sure, certain individuals may be rendered more sensitive to such circumstances as a result of earlier socialization; but, presumably, contemporary structural characteristics carry the most important causal weight. Many have reasoned that the alienated person should be less inclined toward political activism. Having little sense of participation or control, the alienated person should be politically apathetic. Others have theorized that alienation will first lead to quietude and apathy, but that as the individual's desperation increases he will seek expression in some form of political extremism (cf. Kornhauser, 1959; Wolfinger et al., 1969). And, too, it may be argued that the alienated person should be more inclined to join in movements which invite participation and renew the individual's sense of control.

Given such conflicting views, it is not surprising to find highly variable research results. Lasch (1965), in his historical summary of radicalism, linked it with high alienation, as did Wolfenstein (1967) in his exploration of the "revolutionary personality." Some studies of student activism of the left reinforce these findings. May (1965), investigating the Berkeley Revolt and Free Speech Movement, and Watts, Lynch, and Whittaker (1969), examining student leftist dissent at Berkeley, found that their activist subjects were marked by a high degree of alienation. In the realm of the radical right, inquiries by Chesler and Schmuck (1963a) and Rohter (1969) yielded the same relationship between activism and high alienation. Lofland and Stark's work on religious extremism (1969) revealed that "activists" in this area are also characterized by a high level of alienation. Yet other systematic inquiries yield opposing findings or no relationship at all. In his probe of general student activism, Baird (1970) showed that activists ranked low on alienation, as did Wolfinger et al. (1969) in their study of the radical right. Examining general political participation, Erbe (1964) tied participation to low alienation. Finally, in Cowdry, Keniston, and Cabin's investigation of antiwar activism, as manifested in actions taken against the draft (1970), no correlation was found between activism and alienation. Clearly, no general conclusions may be reached in this case. We shall discuss a number of reasons for such inconsistencies later in the chapter.

AUTONOMY

It has been noted that the political activities of the "youth movement" are often characterized by strivings for autonomy and independence from adults and adult values (cf. Fishman & Solomon, 1964a). Needs for autonomy may be particularly salient to the adolescent (cf. Erikson, 1968). However, as research by Kagan and Moss (1962), Bandura and Walters (1963), and Rheingold and Bayley (1959) suggests, persistent needs for autonomy may be developed in the preadolescent period. The conditions fostering such tendencies have been discussed in detail by Maccoby and Masters (1970). For the autonomy-prone individual, the political movement is said to offer an opportunity to be integrated with an organized group while at the same time facilitating a break in parent-child bonds. Although some theorists have maintained that political involvement may simply be the displacement of dependency attachments from one group to another, it appears that the essential element is the belief on the part of the youth involved that such participation really does facilitate autonomy. Such a function may be served by the wide range of action opportunities in novel settings afforded the activist. Therefore, we might hypothesize that autonomy will be positively associated with political activism.

Studies generally reveal a direct connection between autonomy and political activism, particularly in the area of the ideological left. Examining general political activism, Fishman and Solomon (1946a) noted a significant correlation with autonomy, a finding that is paralleled in Kerpelman's work on broadly based student activism (1972). More specific studies of student activism of the left uniformly support these findings. In the case of left-wing student dissent (Whittaker & Watts, 1971; Hendin, 1971), civil rights and peace activism (Fishman & Solomon, 1963, 1964b; Keniston, 1968), and the Berkeley Free Speech Movement (Trent & Craise, 1967; Smith et al., 1967; Heist, 1965, 1966), a strong positive association between autonomy and activism is reported. In a study of student political participation, Bay (1967) upheld these results with regard to his leftist subgroup but found that his rightists ranked low on autonomy. Lane's work on general political participation in adult populations (1959) also revealed this inverse relationship between autonomy and activism. In sum, substantial evidence links a high degree of autonomy with student activism of the left, but findings do not suggest that such is true for right-wing groups or for adults in general.

CONFORMITY

Like autonomy, the issue of conformity is typically raised with regard to youth and political activism (cf. Fishman & Solomon, 1964a). Tendencies toward conformity have again been traced to early socialization practices (cf. Kagan & Moss, 1963; Hurlock, 1974). As the common stereotype has it, the nonconformist or anticonformist youth is generally more prone toward political activism. To some degree this view has validity, for commitment to many youth movements frequently involves renunciation of the values, patterns, and ties of the established adult culture. From this basis we might speculate that tendencies toward conformity, at least among the young, would be inversely related to political activism. Yet a strong alternative argument exists. Involvement in a youth-oriented political group may simply involve a shifting of one's conformity needs from the framework of the common culture to that of the splinter group, possibly with greater pressure and sanctions enforcing adherence to the group's values. In this light, we might expect there to be a positive association between conformity and political activism.

Although few in number, investigations relating conformity to political activism point to an ideological difference on this dimension. Studying general activism, Reed (1925) and Tomkins (1963) noted that only right-wing activists were characterized by high needs for conformity, a result also obtained by both Hofstadter (1964) and Schiff (1964) in their work on the radical right. Levinson's inquiry into political ideology and group membership (1950) sustained this relationship with regard to its rightist sample, but showed the leftist subgroup to be marked by a low level of conformity. Additionally, in their probes of student activism, Smith (1969) and Flacks (1970) found leftist activism related to low conformity. On the other hand, Kerpelman's study of student activism of the right, left, and center (1972) revealed no differences among the different ideological subgroups on ratings of conformity. Thus, the limited research in this area suggests that conformity is directly linked to rightist activism and inversely related to activism of the left. However, given the possibility for ideological bias in this case, further inquiry is merited. In particular, the reference group related to the conforming tendencies is in need of specification. Rightists may simply be more sensitive to the views of different reference groups than are leftists. The demand for conformity is not necessarily less in leftist political groups.

POWER AND DOMINANCE

Since the time of Hobbes and Nietzsche, the need for power or dominance has often been posed as the primary motivator of political activity. Lasswell (1948, 1954) has argued that many individuals learn early in childhood (particularly during the resolution of the Oedipal conflict) to rely on power or dominance as an effective manner of coping with the world. More recently, McClelland (1975) has extended these views by discriminating between the mature and immature orientations to the use of power. However, according to Lasswell, these motives may later facilitate political participation through displacement and rationalization of the public interest. The training of dominance patterns through early periods of socialization has been undertaken by Kagan and Moss (1963), and the family backgrounds of those differing in power orientation studied by Winter (1973). Several theorists (cf. Lane, 1959; Milbrath, 1965) have also proposed that persons ranking high on dominance tendencies will devote their energies in areas other than politics. Political success is usually predicated upon harmonious personal interaction. It is highly probable that an individual with a strong power orientation would constantly alienate his supporters and therefore frustrate his own goals. Additionally, it has been noted that the democratic political system is not the most fruitful context in which to demonstrate tendencies toward domination; many other environments (e.g., home, industry, finance, military) allow more direct expression of personal power needs. From this viewpoint, political activism should not be correlated with high power or dominance tendencies.

Research on the relation of dominance or power needs to political activism reveals no clear trends. Browning and Jacob (1964) found that candidates for powerful political offices were higher in need for power than candidates for lesser offices, and Donley and Winter (1970) have shown how power needs of union presidents may have dictated their political policies. Kerpelman (1972), examining ideologically varied student activists, reported a high degree of dominance across the spectrum. In their investigation of student activism of the left (civil rights, sit-ins), Fishman and Solomon (1963) also found high dominance expressions. Inspecting general political participation, Milbrath (1960), Jenson (1960), and Milbrath and Klein (1962) discovered very slight trends linking dominance to activism (only one was statistically significant). Related to this, McConaughly (1950) showed that a sample of South Carolina legislators rated only slightly higher on dominance than is the norm for adult males in the state. McClosky's probe into political ideology (1958) sustains these results with regard to his leftist subgroup, but discloses that his rightist subgroup is characterized by low levels of dominance. Studying radical rightism, Hofstadter (1964) also revealed an inverse relationship between dominance and activism. Yet Lane (1965) failed to find an association between dominance and political activism in his investigation of general student political participation, and Whittaker and Watts (1971) reported no difference between activists and nonactivists on this dimension in their study of student left activism. Thus, no clear pattern emerges from the work on dominance and power.

DISTRUST

As Lane (1959) has argued, it seems doubtful that individuals who characteristically distrust the intentions of others and the responsiveness of the political structure are psychologically equipped to be politically active. To join a movement or to participate in the political system strongly suggests that one trusts the cooperative and mutually supportive character of the movement or certain groups within the system. Much the same reasoning prevailed in our earlier and closely related discussion of optimism and pessimism. Yet it also seems possible that a general distrust in the established order or in human nature in general, might also motivate political activity, either to overcome the established order or to ensure that "human nature" will be kept in check.

Limited inquiry into the relationship between distrust and political activism lends partial support to both viewpoints. In his work on political ideology, McClosky (1958) revealed that rightists are marked by a high degree of distrust. This relationship was also found in studies of the radical right, such as Morris' scrutiny of the Christian Anti-Communist Crusade (1961), Westin's probe of the John Birch Society (1964), and Rohter's work on right-wing activism (1969). Coles (1964), investigating civil rights activists, and Wolfenstein (1967), examining three "revolutionary personalities," both linked activism to high distrust. In addition, Shils' research on both right and left authoritarianism (1954) yielded the same results. Yet Bronfenbrenner (1960), in his inspection of community participation, reported that activists are characterized by low distrust, as did Rosenberg (1956) and Lane (1959) in their work on political participation. Future work must not only discriminate between political ideology but differentiate more carefully the targets of distrust.

SELF-ESTEEM

As noted above, harmonious interaction with others is an essential component of much political activity. One personality dimension often singled out for its unique contribution to social well-being is self-esteem—the degree to which the individual values himself or believes himself worthy of others' regard. The early roots of esteem development have been traced by a variety of investigators. One of the first was the neo-Freudian Harry Stack Sullivan, whose case analyses convinced him that esteem development commenced during early infancy when the child was fondled and fed (cf. Sullivan, 1953). Erik Erikson (1950) and Carl Rogers (1961), again using the case study method, also traced the rudiments of self-esteem to the early years. On a more systematic basis, Coopersmith (1967) has carried out careful objective assessment of developing children and has observed a number of child-rearing patterns which correlate substantially with self-esteem. Rosenberg (1965) has carried the focus into the adolescent years, and with a large-scale questionnaire study shows how a variety of parental, peer, and structural variables may influence esteem level.

Turning to the question of political activism, several investigators (cf. Riesman, 1952; Milbrath, 1965) have speculated that without a reasonably high level of self-esteem an individual will have great difficulty interacting effectively with other people. According to this position, liking oneself and feeling personally competent (i.e., high feelings of self-esteem) will promote social participation in general and political participation in particular. Thus, in this case, a positive correlation between self-esteem and political activism would be expected. On the other hand, a number of theorists (Rosenberg, 1951; Lane, 1959) maintain political activity will serve to enhance the individual's self-esteem, and therefore will be adopted by those who are marked by a low ranking on this dimension: e.g., according to Rohter (1969), political activism may serve "ego-defensive needs" (by derogatory labeling of individuals and groups who threaten one's sense of self-esteem); they may also serve a "value-expressive function" (by allowing the activist to express his or her central values in a manner which increases feelings of status and gains social acceptance from others who share these values); and, finally, activism may play an "adjustive" role (by placing the individual into supportive social relationships). Clearly, this perspective leads to the hypothesis that there will be an inverse relationship between self-esteem and political activism.

Studies relating self-esteem to political activism disclose a complicated picture. Several broad inquiries, such as Lasswell's investigations of general political activism (1936, 1954), have linked low self-esteem to activism. Probing the radical right, both Proshansky and Evans (1963) and Rohter (1969) noted that right-wing activists were characterized by low self-esteem, as did Lane (1959) in his examination of political participation. McClosky (1958), scrutinizing political ideology, supported these results with regard to his conservative subgroup but revealed that liberals showed a high degree of self-esteem. Yet Hendin (1971) found an inverse relationship between activism and self-esteem in his inquiry into student leftist activism. Confusing the issue even further, however, studies of general political participation reported by Allport (1945) and Milbrath and Klein (1962) associated activism with high levels of self-esteem. In sum, investigations of the relationship between self-esteem and political activism have unearthed a range of disparate results. We shall return to this issue later in the chapter.

ALTRUISM

Most political movements hold forth the promise of achievement for the social good. Regardless of the validity of this claim, a great many political participants may be attracted by such possibilities. In particular, it has been noted that this orientation toward bettering the world is common to all of the political activities comprising the "youth movement" (Fishman & Solomon, 1964a). The roots of such orientations in early socialization have been carefully discussed by Hoffman (1970). As a result of this line of thinking, we might predict that altruistic tendencies on the part of the individual will be positively associated with political activism.

Limited work on the relationship between altruism and political activism is mildly suggestive of a positive link, although some evidence opposes this trend. Examining general student political activism, Fishman and Solomon (1946a) noted a positive relationship between activism and altruism, as did Gelineaux and Kantor (1964) in their investigation of individuals involved in social service work. In their focus on the radical right, Chesler and Schmuck (1963a) found that members of the Christian Anti-Communist Crusade were characterized by a high degree of altruism. Similar results have also been obtained on the other side of the ideological fence. Studies of leftist student activism by Fishman and Solomon (1963), Keniston (1967), and Peterson (1968) all suggest a positive association between activism and altruism. Levinson's probe of political ideology and group membership (1950) sustained this relationship with regard to his extreme leftist subgroup but found that the highly rightist subgroup ranked low on altruism. In addition, results from several general investigations ran counter to the findings on leftist student activism. Baird (1970) showed that student activists were marked by a low degree of altruism, while in his work on student activism of the right, left, and center, Kerpelman (1972) found no correlation between altruism and activism. Thus, moderate but disputed indications of a generalized correlation between altruism and political activism emerge from the data.

OTHER PERSONAL FACTORS

Limited empirical scrutiny of the association between political activism and several other personal factors has also been undertaken. One such dimension is birth order. Several investigators have linked first-born sibling status to activism. In their work on student peace demonstrations, Fishman and Solomon (1946b) noted that 45% of their activist group were first-borns; studying the Berkeley Free Speech Movement, Watts and Whittaker (1966) disclosed that 60% of their activist sample were eldest children. Schiff's probe of conservative activism (1964) revealed that all but one of their right-wing subjects (N = 47) were eldest or only sons in their families. However, without accurate indications of the proportion of first-borns in the sample from which the activists emerged, it is difficult to determine the significance of these findings.

Scanty research has also been carried out in the relationship of personal consistency to political activism. Reed (1925) found that left-wing activists exhibited a high degree of consistency while activists of the right rated low, a result that was supported as well by Harper's work on political attitudes (1930) and Soares' investigation of student activism in developing countries (1966). Allport (1929), in his examination of political opinions, disclosed just the opposite; his findings ranked the rightist subgroup high on consistency and the leftists low on the same dimension. Yet Westby and Braungart (1966), probing student activism of the left and right, revealed that activists of both ideological persuasions were characterized by a high level of personal consistency. Finally, Helfant's inspection of general political attitudes (1952) also linked activism and consistency in a positive manner. Thus, no general conclusion seems merited.

A few researchers have examined the relationship between activism and locus of control. Gore and Rotter (1963), inspecting black civil rights activists, obtained a positive correlation between internality of control and willingness to participate in social action. Geller and Howard (1972), however, found no relationship between activism and locus of control in their inquiry into student antiwar activism. The latter finding was replicated by Thomas (1970) who found Rotter's 1-E scale insignificantly related to six separate measures of political activism. Finally, Renshon (1974) found that persons experiencing low personal control were more likely to participate in political affairs.

INTELLECTUAL ABILITY

The intellectual background of activists has been of great interest to investigators in the area. Although intelligence is not viewed as a personality trait, as an ability it is highly valued in the society. Often, it appears that investigators evaluate the validity of a movement on the basis of the intellectual competence of its membership. Given the liberal background of most investigators in the area, it is not overly surprising to find high intellectual ability linked with activism in general and left-wing activity in particular. Probing general community participation, Bronfenbrenner (1960) found a positive relationship between the degree of intelligence and the level of activism. This result is uniformly supported by studies of the political left. Broad investigations by Allport and Hartman (1935), Krout and Stagner (1939), Mussen and Wyszynski (1952), and Keniston (1968) suggest a positive relationship between measures of intellectual ability and leftist activism, a trend which is further confirmed by data from a variety of more specific studies. Harper (1930), inquiring into the political attitudes of American educators, and Keniston (1968), examining participants in a Vietnam summer war protest, found activism associated with higher levels of intelligence. Investigators studying student dissent of the left, such as Crotty (1967), Trent and Craise (1967), Flacks (1967), Gergen and Gergen (1970), Peterson (1968), Block, Haan, and Smith (1968), Hendin (1971), and those who focused on the Berkeley student revolts and the related Free Speech Movement (May, 1968; Heist, 1966) have reported similar findings. Consistent with this ideological picture, McClosky (1958) revealed that conservatism was linked to lower levels of intellectual ability. These findings receive further support in research which examined and distinguished between activism of the left and that of the right. Allport's study of political opinions (1929), Somers' examination of the Berkeley revolt and Free Speech Movement (1965), and Bay's investigation of student activism (1967) all found that activists of the left were marked by a high degree of intelligence, while those of the right exhibited low levels of intellectual ability.

Exceptions to this pattern do exist, however, and inhibit self-congratulatory conclusions. Kerpelman (1969), investigating student activism of the right, left, and center, revealed no differences in degree of intelligence among the three activist subgroups or between them and their matched control groups. These results were fully replicated by Abramowitz (1972). Furthermore, Schiff's investigation of radical rightism (1964) supports these findings as do Watts and Whittaker's work on the Free Speech Movement at Berkeley (1966) and Cowdry, Keniston, and Cabin's examination of Vietnam war draft registers (1970). In a related vein, Gelineaux and Kantor's study of students involved in social work (1964) demonstrated similar null findings. More distressing for our sense of order, Watts and Whittaker (1966) found that, in the case of the Berkeley student revolt and Free Speech Movement, a negative relationship existed between intelligence indicators and engagement in the movement. In sum, the research connecting intellectual ability with political activism does not show a clear-cut relationship.

RELIGIOUS BACKGROUND

Although less theoretically based, religious background has also been of lively interest to investigators of political activism. Such research usually discloses a difference along ideological lines: right-wing activism is typically associated with some form of Protestant religious background, while leftist activism is often found to be related to Jewish upbringing or the lack of any strong religious tradition. Studying general political activism and ideology, Allport and Hartman (1925) noted that liberals had little interest in matters of religion, while Allport (1929) showed that rightists tended to be Protestant. In his examination of student activism, Peterson (1968) revealed that rightist activists were predominantly Protestant and leftist activists were characterized by very little religious background. Gelineaux and Kantor (1964), inspecting student involvement in social service work, reported that students active in this area were predominantly Jewish. Probing student participation in peace demonstrations, Fishman and Solomon (1964) found that very few Catholics were involved and that 51% of the subjects reported a nonreligious upbringing. Research on student leftist activism by Flacks (1967), Keniston (1967), Mankoff and Flacks (1971), Gergen and Gergen (1970), Geller and Howard (1972), Lipset (1965), Selvin (1965), Somers (1965), Watts and Whittaker (1966), and Smith et al. (1967) reveals the existence of a disproportionately high number of Jews and low number of Protestants in the activist membership.

Investigations of the radical right have also focused on religious background. As indicated, they point to just the opposite relationship of that generally found in the student left. Inquiries by Lipset (1960), Morris (1961), Proshansky and Evans (1963), Chesler and Schmuck (1963a), Wolfinger et al. (1969), Rohter (1969), Grupp (1969), and Elms (1969) all highlight the unrepresentatively high proportion of Fundamentalists and Protestants active in various organizations of the extreme right wing. A dispute exists in the literature over the representation of Catholics in the radical right. Lipset (1960) reported that there were very few Catholics in his examination of the John Birch Society, yet Westin (1964) pointed to the existence of a high proportion of Catholics in his probe of the same group, a finding which Lipset (1964) sustained in his discussion of the sources of the radical right. However, complicating the picture established so far, Goldschmidt et al. (1974) found that daughters of nonreligious parents were most likely to be involved in Women's Liberation activities, with Protestant offspring less likely to be active in the movement and Catholic and Jewish women *least* likely to be involved. In sum, much of the empirical work upholds the general relationship of an association between Jewish or nonreligious upbringing and leftist activism and Protestant or Catholic religious background and activism of the right. However, firm conclusions are not merited.

ECONOMIC BACKGROUND

In light of Marxist speculations concerning the revolutionary overthrow of the capitalistic superstructure by the oppressed classes, a great many social scientists have been keenly interested in the economic basis of political activity. From the Marxist viewpoint there is good reason to suspect a positive relationship between income (or occupational status) and participation in traditional political institutions (those ostensibly supported by the capitalistic system), and a negative relationship between income and more radical or revolutionary political activity.

Evidence thus far indicates that at least the first of these speculations has validity. Bronfenbrenner (1960), examining general community participation, found a positive relationship between participation and income, as did Gelineaux and Kantor (1964) in their study of individuals involved in social work and Erbe (1964) and Milbrath (1965) in their work on general political participation.

However, when we turn to antiestablishment activism, we find little support for the Marxist viewpoint. Investigating antiwar activism, Keniston (1968) and Cowdry, Keniston, and Cabin (1970) found a positive correlation with income; most of their activists were from middle- to upper-middle-class homes. In their inspection of general student activism, Westby and Braungart (1966) revealed that 68% of their leftist activists had yearly family incomes greater than $12,200. Examinations of leftist student activism by Lipset (1966a), Keniston (1967), Crotty (1967), Flacks (1967, 1970), Peterson (1968), Block, Haan, and Smith (1968), Watts, Lynch, and Whittaker (1969), Astin (1970), Hendin (1970, 1971), and Bayer, Astin, and Boruch (1971) all sustain this link between leftist activism and high family income.

Yet we cannot hastily bring the matter to a close. Lipset's early inquiry into student activism (1965) and Soare's work on student activism in developing countries (1966) both suggest a negative correlation between activism and economic level. Geller and Howard (1972) found no difference in family income in their study of student antiwar activism, a result that has been replicated in research in Women's Liberation activism (Goldschmidt et al., 1974). Probes of the radical right also pose difficulties. One might speculate that such groups should draw from the more economically established population. Indeed, research by Wolfinger et al. (1969) on the Christian Anti-Communist Crusade, Lipset (1960) and Grupp (1969) on the John Birch Society, and Proshansky and Evans (1963) on general right-wing activism does indicate a positive link between radical rightism and high income levels. In contrast, Chesler and Schmuck's investigation of the Christian Anti-Communist Crusade (1963a, 1963b) disclosed that most of their rightist subjects were lower middle class, a finding supported in discussions of the sources of radical rightism by Lasswell (1947) (who focused on Hitlerism) and Lipset (1964). Yet Hofstadter (1964) has emphasized the varied economic backgrounds of rightists in his study of radical rightism. In sum, work on general political and leftist student activism shows a strong trend relating activism to high income levels, but there is much dispute in the literature over economic class membership of the radical right. One might argue that most of the left-wing political activity in this country is not actually opposed to the present economic establishment, or that through education the middle- and upper-middle-class youth have been "enlightened." In any case, the present pattern of results does not offer obvious support for the traditional Marxist view of social conflict.

PARENTAL POLITICAL PREFERENCES

Based on the assumption discussed above, that family socialization establishes in the offspring his or her basic dispositions, much interest has been
demonstrated in the relationship between family background and political activism. The importance of this factor is indicated by Braungart's multivariate
analysis of varying influences of student political identification (1971); he found
family political background to be the strongest of all the predictors examined
(including religion, ethnicity, and social class). Work on this variable points
almost uniformly to a similarity between mothers' political ideology and
daughters' sympathy for the Women's Liberation movement; increased
liberalism of the mothers' views was related to increased support of the movement, both in attitudes and actions (Goldschmidt et al., 1974). Middleton and
Putney (1963), examining student political beliefs, found that parents of rightists
were generally ideologically conservative while parents of leftists tended to be
liberal. Westby and Braungart's investigation of general student activism (1966)
revealed that 68% of the parents of leftist activists were Democrats, while 71% of
the parents of rightist activists were Republicans. Researchers probing leftist
student activism have been particularly interested in the relationship with parental politics. Inquiries by Fishman and Solomon (1946b), Flacks (1967, 1970),
Keniston (1967, 1968), Smith et al. (1967), Peterson (1968), Haan (1971), and
Mankoff and Flacks (1971) all report clear, positive links between parental
political position and student political identification. Inspections of the radical
right also support this trend. Grupp (1969), studying members of the John Birch
Society, disclosed that parents of these activists were predominantly Republican,
as did Wolfinger et al. (1969), in their examination of people involved in the
Christian Anti-Communist Crusade. Thus, at least one body of research suggests
a compatibility between parental political preferences and the political activity of
their offspring.

Yet a contrasting view is supportable. Both Feuer (1969, 1972) and Bettelheim (1969) have argued that activism among the youth is partially a product
of their conflict with their parents. Research results also lend support to this line
of thinking. Dunlap (1970), Block (1972), Braungart (1971), and Lewis and
Kraut (1971) all found that family conflict was positively related to leftist ideology. How far this position may be sustained is unclear. Cowdry, Keniston, and
Cabin (1970), Flacks (1967), and Thomas (1971) found no association between
family conflict and either political attitudes or activism. Others have also pin-
pointed conceptual and methodological difficulties in the research which call into
question the early findings (cf. Block, Haan, and Smith, 1970; Cowdry et al.,
1970; Lewis & Kraut, 1972; Lipset, 1968; Silvern & Nakamura, 1971). Perhaps
the most convincing study to date is that of Kraut and Lewis (1975) in which
undergraduates were followed through three years of college life. Using both
cross-lagged correlational analyses and path analysis, they found that both leftist
parental ideology and high family conflict were antecedent to leftist ideology in

the offspring. It is possible that a different theory may be required to understand left- versus right-wing activism.

Toward Methodological Improvement

Although the present review is selective, it does provide a reasonably accurate picture of the major research strategies used in the contemporary study of personality and political activism. As can be seen, by far the dominant strategy is one in which the investigator determines the degree of association between scores on a given personality (or individual difference) dimension and some measure of political activity. This approach is hardly unique to this particular domain of inquiry, and indeed represents the dominant research motif in the study of personality and social behavior more generally. While this method has much to recommend it in the early stages of research, continued reliance on the paradigm is without significant promise. We may usefully discuss several of the major shortcomings inherent in the strategy, along with several possible means of improving on future endeavors.

CAUSAL SEQUENCE

The most obvious difficulty with the dominant strategy is its inability to isolate causal direction in the relationship among variables. Almost all investigations tacitly assume that personal needs, motives, dispositions, or characteristics causally influence political behavior. The reverse possibility is seldom discussed. Yet in most cases the possibility that political participation may influence personal dispositions is not only plausible, but compelling: e.g., if a political movement emphasizes the use of aggression or is conflict prone, participation could well influence the participant's scores on an aggression indicator. Similarly, depending on the character of the movement, the individual could be moved toward greater optimism (or pessimism), affiliation, alienation, distrust, altruism, self-esteem, and the like. Encounter groups, Alcoholics Anonymous, therapy groups, and consciousness raising groups actively seek to produce such changes and there is ample evidence of their impact. Similarly, an immense social-psychological literature documents the effects of behavioral engagement or role playing on subsequent psychological dispositions. There is little reason to suspect that involvement in political groups is not similarly effective. The possibility is indeed unsettling that most of the uniformity encountered in our review stems from just such effects.

It seems quite clear that future research would be immensely benefited by the use of longitudinal as opposed to cross-sectional research designs. In his long-term study of the political socialization and activities of Bennington College women, Theodore Newcomb made a salutory first step in this direction (1943).

However, with the exception of the Kraut and Lewis (1975) study cited earlier, very little effort has been devoted to improving, sharpening, or extending this line of research. Until such work is undertaken the meaning of the present patterns of results will remain obscure.

THE LIMITS OF LINEARITY

The typical question asked by contemporary research is whether persons possessing a certain trait or quality are more or less likely than other people to engage in a designated type of political behavior. Implied both by the form of the question and the widespread reliance on the Pearson r in analyzing data is the assumption of a linear relationship between the variables. Very seldom have investigators explored the possibility of nonlinear relationships between personal disposition and political behavior. There is also good theoretical and empirical reason to suspect that such relations are likely. For most personality variables, people at the extreme ends of the continuum can be viewed as deviant or anomalous. Persons who are exceptionally high in self-esteem, especially bent on gaining power, who feel they control virtually all their outcomes, etc. would probably find most groups hostile to their participation. Although we generally expect people who are moderately high on these characteristics to be more politically active, the extreme scorer may be an undesirable compatriot and discouraged from participation. On the empirical level, the importance of searching for nonlinear relations is nicely demonstrated in a study (Goldschmidt et al., 1974) of Women's Liberation participation. One initial concern of the study was whether liberationists were more or less inclined toward heterosexual relationships. A linear analysis did not yield a significant correlation between the various indicators of heterosexuality and participation in the movement. Yet in a nonlinear analysis it was found that heterosexuality was related in nonlinear fashion to participation. Thus, women who showed least interest in members of the opposite sex were very likely to join, as were women who showed moderately high interest in heterosexual relations. In effect, the movement seemed to be drawing from two very distinct groups, and conflict within the movement seemed highly likely. Tests for linearity obscured the issue.

A variety of methods exist for testing nonlinear relations among variables. One of the best of these, from our experience, is the Multiple Classification Analysis (Andrews, Morgan, & Sonquist, 1967). Essentially, this particular form of regression analysis makes no assumptions of linearity, and is an excellent detector of nonlinear patterns.

MULTIPLE DETERMINATION

If it can be demonstrated that particular dispositions give rise to political participation, the next important question is whether they do so independent of other factors. This question can take a variety of forms but, given the almost exclusive dependence of the field on correlational techniques, the issue is to what extent emerging correlations are uncontaminated. Most findings we have cited are based on single assessments of the relationship between a given disposition and a given type of political behavior. Yet most measures of personality are heavily contaminated by other factors. In the case of authoritarianism, for example, the trenchant volume *Studies in the Scope and Method of the Authoritarian Personality* (Christie & Jahoda, 1954) showed that the *F*-scale was highly correlated with such factors as intelligence, education, economic class, agreement response sets, etc. Thus, all findings using the *F*-scale become subject to serious question. To what extent do differences in authoritarianism account for the variance as opposed to its correlates? Similar questions can be raised concerning most of the studies reviewed above. In very few instances is it possible to rule out the effects of a host of potential contaminating factors.

To some extent such problems can be overcome through the use of multiple regression techniques. Such techniques have been employed with increasing frequency in recent years, but are utilized in only a minority of the published studies. However, they represent a vast improvement over the single correlation, and a substantial gain over the two- or three-way cross-tabulation. In effect, the relationship of each independent variable with a dependent variable may be ascertained while all other variables are held constant.

Multiple regression techniques are additionally advantageous in isolating the *relative* importance of various predictors to account for variations in behavior. If multiple determination is accepted as the rule rather than the exception, one must ask not whether a particular personality variable accounts for a significant amount of variance in political behavior, but *how much* of the variance in comparison to other predictors. We may use the Gergen and Gergen (1970) study of antiwar demonstrators to illustrate the importance of this point. As we saw, much early research demonstrated a positive relationship between various forms of intelligence and participation in the movement. Whether measured by grade-point average, participation in honors programs, or intelligence tests, antiwar activists seemed to be more intelligent than their nonactivist counterparts. In this nationwide study of 2,500 students, grade-point average was used as one of a series of 25 predictors, and was entered into a multiple regression analysis along with the other variables. When the separate effects of all variables had been partialed out, it was found that the beta weight for grade-point average was only .02, and that GPA alone accounted for 5 times less variance than race (which variable had seldom figured in dimensions of antiwar activity), and some 15 times less than previous experience with activism. In effect, the single correlational results reported in the earlier literature vastly inflated the importance of intelligence.

The emphasis on multiple predictors raises additional issues that must be confronted if the field is to advance. For one, the issue of interaction among predictors has received virtually no attention in the literature to date. The continued search for independent causal factors obscures more complex effects stemming from various combinations of factors. Some advantage may be gained through multivariate procedures such as the Automatic Interaction Detector (Andrews, Morgan, and Sonquist, 1967), a statistical device that may be coupled with multiple regression techniques to form a powerful analytic tool.

A second needed development is in the clustering of variables. It seems safe to say that most political movements are composed of various heterogeneous subpopulations. Different types of people may participate in such movements for different reasons. Thus, the number of participants who score in the upper regions of a personality indicator may well form a minority of the movement. If mean value is computed for this personality variable for all members of the movement, this one distinct subpopulation would be obscured. Indeed, the mean for the entire movement could be low, while the one subgroup might have joined the movement precisely because of strong tendencies of this variety. This line of thinking *threatens the validity of all generalizations developed above*. Whether a relationship is found between a given personality variable and political activity depends not only on the relationship of one to the other, but on the proportion of the politically active for whom this is an important fact. Much needed, then, are cluster analyses (cf. Tryon & Bailey, 1970) which may separate out subclusters of activists (or nonactivists), describe their characteristics, and provide an indication of their relative proportions within the larger group.

Guiding Assumptions Revisited

Thus far we have spelled out a number of major assumptions underlying research in this domain, sampled heavily from research which derives from these assumptions, and examined important methodological shortcomings. It is now appropriate to return to the initial assumptions and examine them more closely. Data from the present review along with additional developments in related areas cast serious doubt on these initial assumptions, and strongly suggest that modifications are necessary on more than methodological grounds. Indeed, a fundamental reorientation in effort may be required. Space limitations prevent an extended discussion of these matters. However, three lines of argument are much in need of attention.

PERSONALITY: FIXED OR FLUCTUATING?

As we pointed out earlier, one of the major assumptions in this domain is that the individual possesses reasonably stable and enduring dispositions, which are acquired during the early developmental years and which manifest themselves in significant ways throughout the life cycle. It is this assumption which potentiates the search for stable relations between such dispositions as aggression, dominance, authoritarianism, etc., and political activism. However, within recent years this line of thinking has come under severe attack within psychology, and research on personality and political behavior has yet to demonstrate sensitivity to the issues. One line of attack has been ably mounted by Walter Mischel (1968). In his volume, *Personality and Assessment,* Mischel reviewed a host of studies in which personality indicators have been used to predict varying types of behavior. His review of the evidence suggests that personality variables seldom account for more than 10% of the variance in the observed behavior. Indeed, an examination of the correlation coefficients encountered in the present review yields very similar findings. Seldom do correlation coefficients exceed .40, and typically they fall a good deal short of this mark. Given the relative triviality of personality indicators in predicting behavior, it has seemed apparent to many that factors residing in the immediate situation may be far more powerful in determining behavior than whatever personal dispositions the individual carries about with him. In effect, political participation may be far better understood in terms of the immediate life circumstances facing the individual rather than in terms of his or her early background: e.g., the participation of close friends in the movement, the costs incurred at home, the convenience of committing oneself, the immediate promise of action or change, etc. may play by far the most important role in understanding political participation.

This view gains additional support from research indicating marked fluctuations in personal disposition as the individual moves from one situation to another: e.g., self-esteem is typically viewed as a major member of the family of enduring personality traits. Women are often said to be lower than men in self-esteem, patients in therapy are said to be suffering from chronically low opinions of themselves, and whether one reacts to social influence pressures is often said to be the result of his or her level of self-esteem (cf. Gergen and Marecek's review, 1976). As we have seen in the present review, self-esteem has also figured prominently in the search for personality correlates of political activism. Yet further research has shown that an individual's level of self-esteem fluctuates dramatically from one circumstance to the next. Self-esteem level may be influenced by social approval (Gergen, 1965), interacting with others who seem either inferior or superior to oneself (Morse & Gergen, 1970), experiences of success or failure on various tests of ability (Walster, 1965; Kiesler & Baral, 1970), the presentation one has made of oneself (Gergen & Gibbs, 1965), etc. There is little reason to suspect that differences in altruism, trust, dogmatism, alienation, and many other variables figuring prominently in research on personality and political behavior, do not undergo similar situational fluctuations. In sum, it is unsafe to assume that most people harbor strong dispositions that pervade their behavior from one situation to another. If this is the case, measures of personal dispositions are seldom likely to account for more than a mediocre amount of the variance in political behavior.

Given the widespread repercussions of this view, debate continues to be waged between its proponents and more traditionally oriented investigators (cf. Greenstein, 1969; Bem, 1972; Endler, 1973; Mischel, 1973; Wachtel, 1973). There is also a prevailing tendency to fall back on an interactionist model (cf. Bowers, 1973; Ekehammer, 1974; Smith, 1969) in which behavior is viewed as a joint function of personality and immediate situation. In this framework the question is how much variance can be accounted for by personality, the situation, and the interaction between the two. It is not likely that such a question will ever be solved in a clear and satisfying manner. Undoubtedly, the answer to the question of "how much variance" will depend on what personality variable and what situation are selected; some combinations will be formed favoring the personality position, some the situationist, and some the interactionist. Essentially, the debate cannot be settled on empirical grounds. However, in the meantime, if research on personality and political behavior is to survive situationist attacks, its methods must become more sophisticated and its findings more robust. The extent to which findings rest on "situated personality" must be given special attention.

DOES EARLY SOCIALIZATION REALLY COUNT?

The fact that personal dispositions can often be altered with relative ease raises questions not only with the notion of personality as an enduring "core," but with the associated assumption that early socialization is important in establishing this core in the first place. In his handbook review of political socialization, Niemi (1973) raises significant doubts concerning the longevity of early socialization practices. As he points out, "A few years ago it was reasonable to argue that almost all learning takes place during early childhood. It now seems clear that a significant amount of political learning continues well into adulthood" (p. 155). However, in order to salvage the early socialization literature which he reviewed, Niemi further cited several tangentially related studies which together suggested a continuity in personal styles over the adult years. Using such studies, Niemi concludes, "nonetheless, in spite of the need for additional research, the presently available evidence strongly suggests that socialization at one point in time does have long-term effects" (p. 136). It is on the basis of just such a conclusion that the entire line of research reviewed in the present chapter rests. If it was believed that "personality" could easily be modified through ongoing experiences, then one would place little faith in the results of the types of studies we have been reviewing here. Rather, one might expect to find variegated and evanescent patterns of findings, patterns that would reflect the shifting "characterology" of the society.

Yet if a more thorough inspection had been made of the extensive body of literature relevant to these issues, a conclusion such as that of Niemi could scarcely have been drawn. In the most extensive longitudinal study conducted to date, Kagan and Moss (1962) examined the relationship between indicators of personality obtained during the first six years of life and similar indicators administered to the same individuals some 25 years later. Virtually no significant relationships between these periods emerged. Continuity was found between assessments of adolescent personality and similar assessments made during the early adult years. However, even in this case the average magnitude of correlation did not exceed .30 (see Gergen's 1973 analysis). Studies tracing the effects of early childhood experience into adulthood have reached similar conclusions. In his early review of the massive empirical literature stemming from the psychoanalytic tradition, Orlansky (1949) concluded that there was virtually no support for the notion that infant and child care influences adult personality. Even the Harlows' (1965) impressive research on rhesus monkeys no longer adds weight to the traditional assumption. This work indicated that the social isolation of the monkey had devastating effects on the behavior of the animal in adulthood. As followup work by Suomi and Harlow (1972) has shown, however, all such effects can be obliterated by a benign treatment of 6 months' duration.

Not only is there very little evidence supporting the notion that early socialization is primarily responsible for fashioning adult character, additional evidence from a variety of sources strongly suggests that the adult personality is highly malleable in nature. Of all the habits developed in the early years, surely among the most powerful must be those of language. One's language is practiced during virtually all one's waking hours from the age of approximately 2 onward. Yet if the individual is taken from his initial linguistic environment and placed in an entirely different environment (as in the case of emigrating to a new country), it is typically found that the initial language is all but forgotten within a relatively brief span (Gergen, 1974). Work on life span development and old age furnishes further evidence supporting the notion that normal human beings are highly plastic in character. Literature demonstrating marked changes in political behavior is reviewed by Niemi (1973); personality changes have been described in a variety of other accounts (cf. Riley & Foner, 1968). Recent advances in psychotherapy lend further support to the case. Using behavior modification techniques, hundreds of cases are now documented in which habits of 20 or more years' duration have been changed within a matter of months (cf. Lazarus, 1963). In light of these and other findings, it no longer seems reasonable to assume that early socialization engenders indelible life styles. To be sure, the individual may carry with him or her habits that are learned at an early age. However, the persistence of these habits may be due primarily to the fact that they have not met resistance or the environment has not encouraged change. Essentially, this line of thinking suggests that the characteristics of personality examined in research on adult political behavior may be of recent vintage and highly subject to further modification. It is just this unreliability in social patterning that has been so in evidence in the present review. As we have seen, the relationship between such factors as power needs, altruism, authoritarianism, affiliation tendencies, etc., and political activism was highly irregular. If people are capable of highly variegated and often contradictory feelings, attitudes, values, and associated behavior, we might anticipate just such desultory patterning.

THE PROBLEM OF HISTORICAL PERISHABILITY

Earlier we described the essential linkage of the field to the positivistic conception of science. From this standpoint, the aim of the science is to build general principles through systematic observation. With careful attention to the behavioral facts and their causal antecedents and through the testing of hypotheses against empirical fact, our theoretical knowledge should undergo continuous improvement. Eventually, it should be possible to construct a truly integrated, highly generalized, and empirically valid theory of political behavior. As we saw, much of the literature reviewed in the present chapter is carried out with just such aims in mind.

Unfortunately, this line of thinking is also subject to serious question. Results from a single empirical study set the stage for the attack. We have reviewed a great deal of research exploring predictors of antiwar activism. Much of this research has revealed similar patterns of results. The data were such that one might not only draw conclusions regarding the personal basis of antiwar activism but of left-wing activism in general. However, late in the period of "generalized revolution," Mankoff and Flacks (1971) replicated a number of the earlier explorations. They found, interestingly enough, that many of the earlier predictors no longer accounted for variability. Predictors that failed to prove important in earlier studies now loomed as significant. As they argued, the social basis of the American student movement had changed markedly. These findings strongly indicate that the correlates of political activism may not remain stable over time. In many respects, such alterations in the functional relationship between variables do not seem surprising. After all, the character of various political movements does not remain constant throughout history (cf. Mathews, 1954), and at various times given movements may appeal to or provide an expressive outlet for differing types of persons. However, such shifts in the data base pose a major threat to the positivistic assumption of a cumulative science.

In major degree the success of the natural sciences can be traced to the relative stability of events over extended periods of time. The velocity of falling bodies in a vacuum and the boiling point of water at sea level are highly stable events. Because they are stable, it is possible to build theories of broad predictive validity and which lend themselves to mathematical formalization. However, in the social sciences matters are far more difficult. Particularly in societies marked by rapid change and complex interdependencies, the character of social behavior may undergo constant modification. And, too, if our behavior is not dictated by genetic necessity, virtually any relationship may hold between any two variables. Thus, dogmatism may predict to political activism at one point in history, but with shifts in public consciousness, in the definition of activism, in the content of dogmatic beliefs, etc., the opposite relationship may occur or no relationship at all. If any functional relationship between variables is possible in principle, then in a rapidly changing society it is virtually impossible to build transhistorically valid theory. All theories may be valid, at least during certain periods of history.

Again, space limitations prevent a thorough discussion of this line of argument and its potential shortcomings. More thorough elaborations can be found in articles by Gergen (1973), Schlenker (1974), and Cronbach (1975).

What There Is to Do

With the serious questioning of major suppositions in the field, we must ask about the value of continuing the traditional research paradigm in the study of personality and political behavior. If personality traits are seldom stable, if early socialization fails to have long-term impact, and if knowledge cannot generally be accumulated, how functional are our current endeavors? Is it reasonable to extend them indefinitely into the future? In our view, to the extent that these attacks can be sustained, significant alterations are necessary in the scope and method of further inquiry. Certainly, the continued attempt to test hypotheses relating single personality and individual difference variables to particular types of political action, in the hopes of developing general theory, seems unmerited. However, there are a variety of extremely important tasks ahead and these deserve attention.

FACTS IN THE SERVICE OF SOCIAL CHANGE

Earlier it was reasoned that if the data base of the science was under relatively continuous change, it would be virtually impossible to develop theories of transhistoric generality. Yet we may view the potential instability of social facts in a more optimistic light. If social patterns remained perfectly stable, if they were built in genetically, there would be little hope for social change. However, if social patterns are malleable, it may be possible to use the science as a means of producing change. Rather than building knowledge, the field might be used to reshape the character of society. Such motives have not been absent from the literature. Particularly in the case of antiwar activism, many researchers were far less interested in the theoretical value of their findings than they were in their social import. Evidence that intelligence, altruism, nonconformity, and the like were characteristic of the antiwar demonstrator was used far less in constructing theories of activism than it was to demonstrate the positive qualities of such groups to the general public. Through the data, false stereotypes might be broken down and a better understanding of the demonstrators fostered. In effect, the hope was that attitudes toward the demonstrators and the war might be changed. If the findings were to have maximal impact, it was to be hoped that the ranks of the demonstrators would be swollen. However, in this case the character of the average demonstrator would be altered and the initial findings invalidated. No longer would the average demonstrator be more intelligent, altruistic, noncon-formist, and the like. He or she would approximate the population average.

REGENERATING UNDERSTANDING

From our earlier analysis it follows that virtually any individual may have reason to join any movement at any time. Knowledge of past behavior may have limited value. In this light, our present review is a documentation of past history. However, the fact that generalization from past events is hazardous only makes it more imperative that research continue on these matters. If we are to understand present-day events, it is important that research be conducted in the present day. Although facts about political activists may break down our stereotypes and create veridical perception, they also set the stage for creating new stereotypes. If the character of a given movement is changed as a result of the knowledge initially generated, this knowledge becomes misinformation. The validity of any finding is thus placed in continuous jeopardy by the changing character of social facts. In this sense it is important that knowledge be under a continuous state of regeneration.

Although the common notion that the aim of science is prediction and control is denigrated by this line of argument, such aims should not be cast aside altogether. If one must make decisions about the composition of various political groups when no immediate information is at hand, it is probably better to rely on earlier findings than on random guessing. Increasingly better predictions should also be made the more recent the data. Further strengthening of predictions may be achieved through time series analysis. If we can assess the composition of various groups through various historical periods, it is possible to determine the relative stability of certain characteristics over time and to extrapolate from trend lines developed over time. As a rule of thumb, however, the greater the public accessibility to the research findings, the more hazardous prediction becomes.

THEORETICAL SENSITIZATION

Thus far we have spoken only of the part to be played by future research. We have said nothing about the utility of theory and the use of research to test hypotheses stemming from such theory. Given the historical shifts in the nature of political behavior, and the discontinuity in personality over time, empirical tests of general theory seem of limited value. Validating data can undoubtedly be obtained for all plausible theories; all plausible theories probably have truth value for some groups of persons at some period of history. However, this is not to say that general theories have no place in the science. On the contrary, general theories can provide a retrospective integration of disparate facts; they can replace chaos with a "sense of understanding." Theories also act as excellent sensitizing devices; they may point to factors or processes not heretofore considered. As all theories are restrictive in certain respects, there is a particularly high premium to be placed on those which challenge our existing viewpoints of broad acceptance. Theories are much in need, but their data base may be furnished by common observation more often than by systematic test.

Summary

In this chapter we have attempted to review a broad number of significant contributions relating personal dispositions to political activity. In most cases we have found that it is extremely difficult to draw generalized conclusions from the data base. Conflicting findings and failures to replicate a given pattern of findings under slightly different circumstances cast serious doubts on the positivistic conception of the social sciences. When we further consider evidence suggesting that personal dispositions themselves are tenuous and highly malleable, and when we take into consideration the changing patterns of social behavior through history, we are given reason to reconsider our potential. Much needed is research for the purpose of producing change, research with immediate practical value, and theories for the purposes of broad integration and challenge.

PART FOUR

POSSIBILITIES

15

Political Socialization as a Policy Science

Harold D. Lasswell

Introduction

A REVIEW OF RESEARCH ON POLITICAL SOCIALIZATION confirms the view that this line of inquiry has undergone phenomenal expansion in recent years.[1] This proposition is true whether we consider the scope of the subject or the methods employed in its investigation. The field has attained cross-disciplinary importance in historical, social, behavioral, and biological studies.

It is no surprise to find that political socialization research has developed disproportionately. Flourishing new lines of investigation usually display an irregular profile. Growth is especially affected by the conceptions and examples provided by the pioneers. Once initiated, intellectual evolution tends to follow paths that are determined by internal as well as external factors. One self-correcting tendency, e.g., is to identify and to fill in gaps in research and also in possible influence on socialization policies. If early studies of socialization give prominence to psychocultural mechanisms in the formation of personality, it is plausible to anticipate that subsequent research will move (1) toward connecting these mechanisms with sociopolitical structures, and (2) toward anchoring the mechanisms in genetic predispositions. If early investigators seek to account for the emergence of eminent figures, the trend will presently move toward studying mid-elites and members of the rank and file. When pioneers emphasize a policy ("manipulative") perspective, later researchers will look for ways of strengthening the scientific ("contemplative") foundation for civic training.

[1] The literature cited and used in the present symposium provides ample confirmation of this statement. (I will not cross-reference to specific chapters in this article.)

The present is a strategic moment in the evolution of research on political socialization. Enough effort has been successfully expended to mark out the many dimensions of the field and to warrant the inference that the productive future lies in working out the implications of a policy science approach that is at once knowledge-wide and worldwide.

Policy science approaches can be characterized as contextual, problem oriented, and multimethod (Lasswell, 1971; Brewer & Brunner, 1975). To assert that a method is *contextual* is to recognize that every significant aspect of any social process is actually or potentially affected by the contexts of which it is part and with which it interacts. Political socialization unquestionably meets the criterion of significance inasmuch as it is an important feature of every past, present, or future body politic. Every community transmits with varying degrees of success the mature practices of its culture to the immature. Every stable subculture engages in a parallel process, since it also distinguishes between participation by the mature and the immature. Hence, American society not only socializes Americans; it includes a myriad of pluralized socialization activities. "Americans" are shaped by the society; and special relations between leaders and led are shaped in every sector. A generalized socialization model:

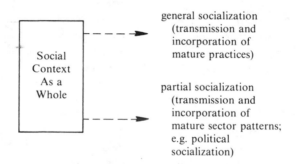

The social process is conveniently characterized as follows:

> *Participants* pursue *Values* (preferred outcomes)
> through *Institutions* affecting *Resources*.

The following concise set of categories for the classification of values has developed from the comparative study of the mature activities in past and present societies, whether tribes or civilizations:

Power. The giving and receiving of support in connection with important
(*P*)   decisions (authoritative commitments enforceable if challenged by the use of severe deprivations against challengers). Institutions: e.g., government, law.

Enlightenment. The giving and receiving of news or scientific information.
(*E*)   Institutions: e.g., mass media, scientific publications.
Wealth. The giving and receiving of the services of resources. Institutions:
(*W*)   e.g., industry, money and credit.
Well-being. Giving or receiving opportunity for safety, health, and comfort.
(*B*)   Institutions: e.g., nutrition, Medicare.
Skill. Giving or receiving opportunity to discover and perfect latent capa-
(*S*)   bilities. Institutions: e.g., occupations, professions, arts.
Affection. Giving and receiving opportunity for love and loyalty. Institu-
(*A*)   tions: e.g., families, larger identities.
Respect. Giving and receiving opportunity for recognition. Institutions: e.g.,
(*R*)   classes, ranks, castes.
Rectitude. Giving and receiving opportunity to facilitate and apply norms of
(*D*)   responsible conduct. Institutions: e.g., ecclesiastical or ethical or-
        ganizations.

To assert that a policy sciences approach is *problem oriented* is to emphasize the relevance of the five features of every problem-solving task: the clarification of *goals;* the description of *trends;* the analysis of *conditions;* the *projection* of futures; the invention, evaluation, and selection of policy *alternatives.* Although many specialists on political socialization do not much concern themselves with recommending value priorities and specifications, some specialists focus on these issues. Similarly, many specialists give little heed to the history and contemporary distribution of political socialization practices. There is, however, an increasing number whose principal concern is with ''The History of Child-hood.''[2] The most numerous fraction of political socializers concentrates on ''conditioning factors,'' pursuing scientific models or modes of data gathering and processing. A few specialists seek to chart the probable course of coming developments in political socialization, and they find it necessary to widen their vision to encompass the interacting world community. Many specialists are absorbed in perfecting the strategic alternatives available within a given socialization context. Whatever the intellectual task, we can be sure that some specialists at least will continue to find it necessary for their personal satisfaction to attempt to grasp the pertinence of their own operations, and those of colleagues, to the flow of past, present, and prospective events.

When we refer to the policy science approach as *multimethod,* the implication is that a specialist is free to use whatever procedures of theory building or data gathering and processing offer promise. We are accustomed to classify methods according to several criteria. One fundamental distinction emphasizes the basic components of every interaction, and refers to the operational indicators appropriate to these component elements: e.g., we postulate that the universal manifold of events in any social process is composed of: (1) subjective (sym-

[2]Greatly stimulated by a magazine of that title founded in 1973 by Lloyd DeMause.

bolic) events, which are the moods and images experienced by individuals; and (2) nonsymbolic events, which are signs, deeds, and resource manipulations. Symbolic events *refer;* and some of these references initiate or register *messages,* or mediated symbolic references, involving *sign* sequences. Signs are resources specialized to intersymbolic mediation (e.g., spoken or written words and word equivalents, such as gestures). *Deeds* are not specialized to communication, and involve nonsign movements and resource manipulations.

We distinguish among observational standpoints according to *intensity* and *extensity.* The former are relatively prolonged and technical modes of observing and recording. The second are relatively brief and less technical. (Contrast intensive psychoanalytic interviews and complex laboratory experiments with polling or traffic counts.)

Research Opportunities

Our present purpose is to suggest some implications of the policy sciences approach for the professional development of political socialization research. In the comments that are offered on future events attention is given to possible developments that, so far as the writer is concerned, may be preferred or unpreferred, and of varying degrees of probability. The treatment is necessarily brief and suggestive rather than prolonged and systematic. Socialization is discussed as a social process. Our most generalized social process model, it will be recalled, referred to participants, values, institutions, and resources. For present purposes it is convenient to expand the categories of social process dimensions:

Participants ⟶ Perspectives ⟶ Situations ⟶
Base Values ⟶ Strategies ⟶ Outcomes ⟶ Effects
(The arrows may run the other way and connect all categories)

PARTICIPANTS

Having defined political socialization as the transmission to, and incorporation by, the immature of mature participatory roles in the decision process (of the body politic as a whole or of any component context), it is apparent that participants in socialization fall into two broad categories:

Political ⟷ Political
Socializers *(SR)*   Socializees *(SE)*

The political socializers *(SR)* are the members of a political context whose status is that of an "adult" (defined as a mature participant) in the making and execution of important decisions. The socializees *(SE)* at any cross-section are the "preadult" (by definition immature) targets of socialization. It is not necessary to assume that the socializers or the socializees are aware of the process or the particular parts that they play in it.

Political socializers are *specialized* or *nonspecialized* participants in the process. Among us the most obvious examples of socializers are the educators and the scientists who study what goes on. It is apparent that specialized socializers do not necessarily take the most influential roles in socialization: e.g., political leaders provide models at the focus of general attention, which may exert the most important influence on maturing community members. The most potent impact of all may be made by persons who are relatively inactive in politics and whose effects are achieved in the nonpolitical sectors. The point is obvious in the case of families.

It is perhaps worth noting that what is defined as a mature status does not necessarily imply that affirmative action is the only mode of acceptable participation in a decision process. Prevailing expectations may include *apolitical* or *antipolitical* roles. Nonactivity is participation, since it provisionally removes some potentially affirmative act-completions from the calculation of activists.

Besides the family environment, referred to in the social process model as affection, other nonpower sectors exercise varying degrees of influence on political socialization. For instance: controllers of mass media (enlightenment) *(E);* merchandisers (wealth) *(W);* members of upper middle or lower classes (respect) *(R);* religionists (rectitude) *(D);* teachers of nonspecialized business subjects (skill) *(S);* health care personnel (well-being) *(B).*

It is not to be assumed that those individuals who at any given time are primarily to be described as socializees *(SE)* are entirely without influence on those who are mainly to be described as among the socializers *(SD).* However, when we look into the future and consider probable changes in population, it would appear that an *aging* population will alter the priorities given to specialized socialization policies.[3] We anticipate that, as the relative weight of preadults declines, the traditional stress on socializing the young will die down (after a transition period of concern about the situation). In a technoscientific society new differentiations will continue to appear and as a result the socialization of adults will if anything gain in relative and perhaps in absolute importance. The role of socialization specialists, though altered, need not diminish.

PERSPECTIVES

When we consider the perspectives of future socializers, a critical question is whether our divided and militant world continues. Repugnant as the prospect is, the factors that support collective violence seem to be of sufficient importance to

[3]How to think about aging or any other characteristic of population is outlined in Ilchman, Lasswell, Montgomery, and Weiner (1975), especially in part 1.

sustain the threat of continuing wars and revolutions (Lasswell, 1962). We do not regard this or any other "construct" of the future as "inevitable," and we do not overlook the opportunities and challenges that a militant globe poses for socializers, notably for educators and scientists. Political and other elites will provide constituencies of conflicting ideology; and the result will presumably be to continue the ideological cleavages that have been characteristic of the actual behavior of educators and scientists.

Regardless of ideological differences there will be increasing concern for problems of *effective* identity, particularly with political groups. Research results will be welcome (or unwelcome) in such matters as how *traditional loyalties* (e.g., national identity) can be transmitted in an interdependent and interactive world; and how these loyalties can be integrated with, or separated from, demands to maintain a significant military presence in the arena of world affairs. Some elites will hope to head off the consolidation of garrison police states by encouraging *effective identity with the common interests of mankind* (Lasswell, 1948). Thus political socializers will continue to have a choice of supporters for research on quite different practices and policies of socialization.

Alienation will continue to be perceived as a problem by elites who are committed to one or another established identity. For instance, it will be relevant to investigate the impact of upper-class mothering on alienation (e.g., the hypothesis that the use of bribery as a means of evading direct confrontation with children deprives the developing personality of the experience of subordinating the ego to the norms of a loving surrogate who stands for social order [Mitscherlich, 1967]).

Controversy will be sharpened between the devotees of *discipline* and those of *permissiveness*. It may be possible for specialists to isolate the characteristic features of a "disciplinary" or "permissive" program that sacrifices originality, though these results may be achieved by quite different means. (One program may block creativity by generating anxiety; the other program may accomplish this by cultivating lack of persistence.) The policy problem of "payoff" may be clarified as a result of this research.

One of the most sweeping challenges to older attitudes toward socialization will appear *when the relationship of women to the process is drastically altered*. The change is related to the scientific and technical innovations that will progressively eliminate dependence on the female body as an incubator. To an increasing extent, fertilization and fetal growth will be conducted outside the body.[4] What, then, will be the transitional consequences for female perspectives? Will motivations be changed? If discomfort and pain are eliminated, will substitute gratifications of the same kind be sought? Will these substitutes affect the nature of participation, e.g., by over- or undercompensation against inflicting or enduring pain and discomfort?

[4]On potentials see Amitai Etzione (1973).

The most far-reaching change in the role of women and of other primary socializers will occur if some of the more radical predictions are verified that refer to cell repair and genetic engineering. We do not ignore the possibility that *cell repair may eliminate death*[5] *while genetic engineering enables us to produce a limited number of progeny for needed or old models, or to introduce new designs. If children are made largely redundant, how can women be resocialized to other than their traditional involvements?* In principle, this can be accomplished by overcoming the barriers that presently circumscribe the scope of women's activities. It will be impossible to alter the role of females without changing the role of males.

It requires no great sagacity to foresee that socialization policies will become among the most serious and divisive issues in the public policy of tomorrow. If the creative potentials of genetic engineering are utilized, how much emphasis will be put on the further improvement of abstract intellectual capabilities? Will the possibilities of selective breeding mean that permanent castes can be evolved to perform routine operations with sophisticated computer equipment?

Assuming that technoscientific development continues, *how can "useless" (formerly useful) elements of the population (e.g., low-intelligence groups) be dealt with?* Can ways be found of resocializing them to satisfactory activities until population policies have diminished the likelihood of their reappearance?

Future socialization research will wisely include studies of the past that are deliberately selected to throw light on significant features of upcoming problems. Consider past circumstances in which relatively rapid change made a substantial fraction of the population at least temporarily redundant.[6] There may be more historical instances of this than current scholarship has emphasized. Recall, e.g., in the evolution of Great Britain, the enclosure movement that substituted sheep-raising for more labor-intensive rural production, and displaced throngs of agricultural laborers and small farmers, driving them to commercial and industrial towns, and disrupting lives on a huge scale. Is it possible to trace the impact on children and child rearing among those directly affected? And what of the "hardening" effects on members of society who reasserted their ego interests in the presence of widespread misery?

The phenomenon of at least temporary superfluity has occurred in connection with the expansion of western civilization and the obsolescing of agricultural skills, the crafts of artisans, and the traditional knowledge of elders. Past transitions—perhaps future transitions as well—range from wars of extermination (e.g., the fate of the North American Indian) to partial incorporation of the universalizing civilization, followed by eventual wars of colonial secession and liberation. Falling and rising groups play distinctive roles and provide resocialization opportunities for educators and scientists alike.

[5]A recent characterization of the cell is by Lewis Thomas (1974).
[6]John R. Montgomery (1974) draws on the history of Western Europe's industrial development.

SITUATIONS

Further consideration must be given to world changes in the zones of interaction. When reference is made to an increasingly interactive globe, it should be understood that the allusion is not necessarily to expanded exchanges of people or objects. The fundamental dimension is *the taking of the world environment into account in the making and execution of public and private policies.*[7] Whatever the vicissitudes of material exchange, it will be necessary to take the world environment into consideration in every sector of every component community.

The most widely extended areas of interaction are *attention zones,* which include the population whose attention is focused on common referents, such as images of the earth and the celestial environment. Members of every locality are part of world attention zones to the degree that they share images and sentiments.

It will be important to examine the socialization role of the principal channels of communication whose signs convey the messages that provide parallel experiences among members of global attention zones. It will be appropriate to describe the changing content of the channels and to connect trends with changing identities, demands, and expectations; and also to link trends with cooperative or antagonistic acts in the arenas of politics, in transnational markets, or in other situations.

In particular, it will be pertinent to discover to what extent, if at all, exposure to "nonpolitical" activities (e.g., music and sports) goes beyond interpenetrating attention zones to the formation of *zones of common knowledge and feeling.* Is the balance favorable or unfavorable to restraint of political antagonism?

The fundamental significance of such questions is suggested when we reflect on the selective function of communication media in the mobilization of public capabilities for action, whether in the expression of opinion, the assertion of sentiment, or the financing and implementation of joint activities. This selectivity gives especially crucial guidance to socialization. It is, in fact, remarkable to realize that millions of words or word equivalents, and of subjective events, are in perpetual flux; and yet out of this vast sea a process of convergence leads to concentration *on a small number of key symbols* of leaders, groups, and institutional myths and operating techniques. The manipulation of this modest array of key symbols provides the means by which the mature members of any context act together, and by which immature members are inducted into decision processes.

Research can be expected to find progressively more satisfactory ways of explaining how the evocativeness of target symbols changes. It is not necessary to assume that the process, though comprehensible, routinely follows more than the most tenuous path. Widely shared common moods may, e.g., be linked with economic prosperity or depression, political victory or defeat, rising or falling resentment against acts of perceived disrespect, rising or falling corruption; and

[7]An influential summary and interpretation of research is by Herbert Kelman (1965).

these overlapping moods may be partially displaced toward public figures as a result of largely accidental exposure.[8]

In this connection, a promising line of investigation is to compare the fluctuating moods and public symbol displacements of youth and of older age groups. *Widening or narrowing differences are probably related to changing dispositions toward civic action.*

The relations described above are relevant to *the fundamental hypothesis that connects the dynamic dimension of political action with the displacement of private affects on public objects (and justification in terms of inclusive common interest).* It will continue to be important to examine the degree to which symbols of the larger environment are continuations or reversals of the sign of the sentiment entertained toward figures in the primary family environment. Unrecognized attitudes (e.g., unacknowledged love or hate) may determine the nature of the sign (e.g., intense unrecognized doubt of parental love may dispose toward negative images of public leaders).[9]

BASE VALUES

Another dimension of an interaction process refers to base values, or the values available to each participant at a given time for affecting results. Consider, e.g., the significance of the socializee *(SE)* to the socializer *(SR)*. A recognizable example is the relationship of a child to the mother. It is conventional to assume that the mother perceives her infant as a target of affection *(A)*, and as a potential source of affectionate behavior (value indulgence). This is not universally true, of course, as in the case of the mother who sees the child as a value deprivation (actual or potential). If the infant is "conceived in sin" by an intensely religious person whose conscience is a source of continuing internal condemnation (guilt, which is a form of negative rectitude *[D]* in the model we have outlined), impulses to love may be overridden. Or if the infant is physically deformed and is perceived as an extension of the self, infant and self may be primarily evaluated in terms of negative well-being *(B)*. A positive or negative evaluation of an infant may depend on its significance in terms of power *(P)*, especially where a queen is permitted to remain a queen only if she produces a crown prince. Usually the birth of a child is welcomed by the mother as an enormously gratifying source of respect *(R)* for having fulfilled her destiny as a woman. Among those who demand family planning, however, an extra child may be seen, even by the mother, as disgraceful (negative respect). Where generous arrangements are made by family or government for the financial

---

[8]See the forthcoming publications by Ronald Brunner and by Steven Brown and colleagues.
[9]Important articles are by Steven R. Brown (1974) and Larry R. Baas and Steven R. Brown (1973).

support of children, the infant may be welcomed as an immediate wealth *(W)* asset. For the mother who possesses an active curiosity, the infant is a source of basic knowledge about "human nature" (positive enlightenment) *(E)*. Contrariwise, a mother may see the child as an obstacle to continuing a scientific career, hence a liability in terms of enlightenment. For most mothers, the infant represents an immediate and an eventual (actual and potential) source of skill *(S)*, indulgences or deprivations. As an indulgence, the child responds positively to nurturing skills. As a deprivation, a child may interact in ways that expose the clumsiness of the nurturing person.

It is clear on reflection that the value map can be employed as an instrument for comparing the significance of a socializee *(SE)* to a socializer *(SR)* at successive time periods, and for comparing group patterns with one another (by culture, class, interest, personality). Contextual analysis will demonstrate that any specific trait of a child (or of any participant in a social process) is linked with every value category; hence, the utility of a contextual map in describing these linkages. A representative example: If a child is the "wrong" sex to enable the mother to retain her power position, the deprivation of power will also elicit deprivations in all the other categories (e.g., she will probably be deprived of some wealth, respect, etc.). That comprehensive assessments must sample all relevant situations is evident: e.g., the loss of wealth that is attributable to the loss of power may be more than compensated by involvement in private economic activities. Such considerations underline the point that the scientific observer must carefully delimit the time-space-figure dimensions of the setting that is being taken into account. The scientific observer must also specify whether an observation is presumably made from the value perspective of the participants who are interacting, or from a standpoint for which the scientist takes responsibility. The mothers in one culture may perceive an epileptic seizure as a grave physical defect, or as an indication of supertalent (a potential medicine man who obtains enlightenment from transempirical forces). A scientific observer may adopt a category for descriptive purposes that coincides with, though it is nondependent on, the participant's evaluation. We know also that the scientist's "functional" definition may or may not coincide with evaluations in his culture of origin. The requirements of the scientific observer are met when the references of the scientist's terms are made explicit.

The base values *(SE)* of the socializee are as relevant to socialization research as the base values at the disposal of socializers *(SR)*. The changing base values of a socializee *(SE)* can be usefully described as approximations of the mature patterns of the relevant context. In general socialization research, the early interactions of the socializee *(SE)* with the social and physical environment are most readily described in terms of selected indicators of well-being (vocalization, gesture, and whole body movements defined as presumptive indulgences or deprivations) *(B)*. Early power indicators may include, e.g., "movement storms" elicited by the decisions of socializers (such as efforts to maintain a schedule) *(P)*. Some exploratory eye movements may serve as indicators of enlightenment *(E)*. Early wealth indicators may be efforts to grasp and hold objects (toys) *(W)*. Skills include the manipulation of people and things *(S)*. (As a rule, skills are acquired as base values rather than as scope values. The timing of a smile may be a "random" act completion that is indulged by "affectionate" body stimulation [A]. The obtaining of a smile from others may be sufficiently differentiated as an act completion to be considered as an "end" or "scope" value in an observed context.) Respect indicators may include shouting to gain the attention of those figures in the environment who are more numerous than those from whom affection is anticipated *(R)*. The first internalizations of a rectitude norm (as in food and toy sharing) are eligible indicators of a "conscience" that is not entirely a function of well-being (physical) deprivation.

It is not assumed that the socialization process is a straight-line sequence that enables the indicators of a value at T^1 to predict the value orientation at T^2. The cross-sections at T^1, T^2...make it feasible to follow the trends in socialization, and to search for the cluster of conditioning factors that enable dependable predictions and explanations to be made.

As socialization activities, especially in particular value-institution settings, receive higher priority in the future, the expectation is that more values will be made accessible to those who are involved in socialization science or policy. Possibly it may be useful to specify some indicators of the asset categories.

The power *(P)* assets include prescriptions (e.g., statutes, treaties, ordinances) authorizing socialization activities to be carried on, and allocating resources to administrative programs. Power indicators include the number of prescriptions that relate to socialization (e.g., statutes pertaining to all forms of education). Measures also include survey data about favorable, unfavorable, or indifferent perspectives toward public education.

Pertinent indicators of enlightenment *(E)* include the number of scientific publications on socialization, the number of active researchers, and the magnitude of available facilities.

The wealth *(W)* assets put at the disposal of public and private socializers are measurable as a fraction of annual budgets of organizations, and as a percentage of gross national (or other community) product.

Among the well-being *(B)* values available to socializers will be specialized protection (physical safety) services, services for physical and mental care, and recreational facilities.

Changes in socialization skills *(S)* are indicated by the years of training and experience of the socializers (such as teachers) who are active at any given time. Similar indicators assess the capabilities of the current targets of socialization.

The popularity of the socializers who are directly active in socialization can be assessed with the aid of survey interviews. There are common sense as well as scientific grounds for asserting that targets of positive sentiment (affection) *(A)* are likely to be among the most influential leaders of socializees.

Similarly, socializers who are respected in the appropriate community contexts (upper, middle, lower class) are positive assets. Convenient indicators of respect *(R)* are also obtainable by interviewing (and other procedures).

If socializers are perceived as incorruptible *(D)*, rectitude is an asset unless community demands for moral commitment have themselves become confused, contradictory, and slack.

It is not to go unnoticed that particular socialization activities may conflict with rather than strengthen general socialization within the body politic as a whole: e.g., the incorporation of individuals into provincial and metropolitan loyalties, or into one branch of the armed services, may weaken the larger decision process. Intensive research will be needed to uncover such trends and to explain ways of coping with them.

STRATEGIES

Participants in socialization employ the base values at their command by strategies intended to affect value outcomes. In a world civilization of scientific technology, political division, and mutual threat, the expectation is that anxiety-producing tensions will continue and even accelerate. Therefore, a sharper conflict is likely to divide socializers who favor the use of *drugs* for the management of themselves or others, and socializers who insist on meditation or other forms of symbol management *(communication)*. Continuing investigation will be necessary to provide increasingly satisfactory answers to such questions as these: To what extent does the use of particular drugs, in specific ways, by particular persons, produce discernible consequences over short or long time periods for sensory activity, creative imagination, realistic judgment, assertive or acquiescent value orientation, or egocentricity? Similar questions are appropriate for those who are trained to depend on the management of symbols.

The comparative study of human societies lends support to the proposition that *symbolic processes are relatively unstable means of maintaining the stability of established systems of public order*. No matter how conspicuous the physical strategies of terror or of economic inducement, detailed investigations indicate that these instruments fail or succeed as they affect the ideological unity of elites and the acquiescent perspectives and operations of mid-elites and the rank and file. Direct communication *between* the mature and the immature (as well as *among* the mature or the immature) propagate the selective symbols that coordinate or disrupt the body politic. Symbol structures are in perpetual flux, not only because of the side effects of activities that are not primarily communicative, but as a result of changes in the intensity and direction of mood and image commitment. It is not entirely a wisecrack to say that the world has been saved from tyrannical rule by virtue of bad pedagogy. The active socializers of tyranny have been unable to foster the incorporation of unquestioned loyalty and acquiescence.

It is not difficult to understand why ambitious oligarchs are tantalized by the new instruments that modern science and technology seem to put at their disposal. In coming years there will doubtless be more determined attempts to achieve automatic and perpetual compliance by means of *physical and biological procedures that eliminate the instability of symbolic means*.

OUTCOMES

The first step in examining outcomes is to postulate the objectives of socialization and to specify the indicators to be used in establishing the degree to which these preferred outcomes are realized in the relevant context. No matter how drastically indicators must be changed in future years, it will be possible to describe the equivalencies by the use of appropriate procedures: e.g., the hours and minutes of attention to political news are presently indicated by the content analysis of media and by interviewing or direct observation of audiences. If brain-to-brain transmission is eventually introduced, indicators will be needed which can be interpreted to show the content of these transmissions and the time devoted by recipients to the signs and messages involved.

Since we live in a body politic whose stated and in some degree actual operations involve "participation" in the shaping and sharing of values, it is appropriate to specify some of the problems that arise in any attempt to specify detailed indicators of power shaping and sharing. We referred to power assets above. For the study of outcomes a more differentiated map is necessary.

INTELLIGENCE

Intelligence decisions refer to the gathering, processing, and dissemination of information for the use of participants in the entire process of making and executing decisions. Those who are socialized participants in intelligence functions and structures demand of themselves and others that plans are made and carried out for the shaping (gathering, processing, and making available of relevant information) and sharing (the search for and exposure to relevant information). To suggest a few potential indicators of objectives related to shaping: number of words (and word equivalents) conveying messages from reliable sources that articulate the long-range goals and the actual or potential shorter range objectives of the body politic, plus the trends, conditions, projections, and alternatives related thereto; the number of the above statements that are made available to pertinent audiences in clear, vivid, and timely messages. Some possible indicators of sharing: the size of audiences that focus on the messages with an acceptable degree of comprehension.

PROMOTION

Promotional decisions refer to the shaping and sharing of activities that are intended to gain support for or to weaken policy alternatives. Hence promotion adds intensity to the alternatives formulated at the intelligence phase of decision. Socialized participants in the shaping and sharing of promotional functions and structures demand of themselves and others that commitments are made and executed for shaping (initiating, mobilizing, and employing promotional operations) and for sharing (serving as targets of promotional activities). Some potential indicators of shaping: per capita time spent in organizing and maintaining political parties and pressure groups. Sharing: per capita time spent as an audience of promotional messages.

PRESCRIPTION

Prescribing is the crystallization of general norms and sanctions as authoritative. Socialized participants demand of themselves and others that they engage in the shaping and sharing of prescriptions. Indicators of shaping: the number of specialized legislators, treaty negotiators, and regulators in various jurisdictions. Sharing: The number who familiarize themselves with prescriptions.

INVOCATION

Invoking decisions refer to the shaping and sharing of activities that begin to put prescriptions into effect. Socialized participants demand of themselves and others that initiating steps be taken. Shaping: e.g., devoting time to investigating claims that prescriptions are ignored which authorize official agencies to grant housing or other forms of assistance to the poor. Sharing: rank-and-file participation in the claiming activities referred to in the preceding.

APPLICATION

Decisions of application refer to the later phase of administering prescriptions that have been invoked. Socialized participants demand of themselves and others that applications are shaped and shared. Some indicators of shaping: the number of administrators involved in completing administrative tasks. A few indicators of sharing: rank-and-file participation in observing or encouraging application activities.

TERMINATION

Termination decisions put an end to prescriptions and provide compensation for those with legitimate claims that their expectations are violated. Socialized participants demand of themselves and others that they shape and share decisions to terminate. A few indicators of shaping: the percentage of prescriptions that are canceled and the number of compensation cases considered. Some indicators of sharing: amount of community support given to structures and functions of termination.

APPRAISAL

Decisions of appraisal judge the degree to which policy objectives are realized. Socialized participants demand of themselves and others that they shape and share these decisions. Some sharing indicators: official reports of successes or failures of policies relating to any sphere of activities. Sharing indicators include: expressions of community support for appraisal structures and functions.

The analysis of outcomes requires distinctions to be drawn between general and particular socialization activities. The former refers to the pattern of preferred participation in the decision processes of the body politic as a whole. A particular socialization is a subclass of decision, a choice in a nonpower sector. (With suitable changes in the indicators, it is relevant in all settings to follow the seven-term categories outlined in the decision map.)

Problems arise from the overlapping patterns involved in socialization activities. How much of a particular objective or practice should be included in the objectives or practices of general socialization? Consider, e.g., the overlap between a policy such as "a people in arms" and the particular requirements appropriately made for volunteer members of armed forces. Obviously, the latter must be specified in more detail than the former. General socialization must generate demands to volunteer in sufficient numbers to provide for national security. Those who present themselves for training in a security service must acquire detailed competences.[10]

EFFECTS

During any period of time specific socialization outcomes interact with the social context as a whole. Some pertinent questions are: How can any known discrepancy between socialization objectives and realized outcomes be explained? What is the probable impact of current socialization practices on future socialization outcomes? What are the future consequences of current socialization practices on the shaping and sharing of values in the relevant social contexts and on the initiation, diffusion, and restriction of institutional practices in these contexts?

As a means of obtaining an inclusive frame of reference, consider the following highly generalized conceptual map of socialization practices in social process:

$$\text{socialization} \longleftrightarrow \text{net value}$$
$$\text{practices} \qquad \text{indulgences}$$
$$\text{(over deprivations)}$$

Interpreted in reference to socialization practices during periods T^1, the model affirms that the pattern of socialization practices can be accounted for by

---

[10]Consider such questions in the context of a particular case, such as Herbert Goldhamer (1975).

examining the net value realizations by socializers and socializees. (T^1 is a time interval of any duration that is convenient for scientific purposes of the observer.)

The flow of significant value indulgences or deprivations is *not necessarily* supplied by the socializers *(SR)* or the socializees *(SE)* to one another: e.g., the socializers may maintain a socialization practice by rewarding one another, rather than by being immediately affected by the socializees. Thus the body politic may provide funds to continue schools for an extra month of compulsory military training. Instructors may welcome what they perceive as relative gain: extra pay *(W)*, more political influence *(P)* with the established regime, added popularity *(A)* and respect *(R)* in the mass media, heightened sense of duty well performed (rectitude [*D*], skill [*S*]), inside briefing on the diplomatic situation (enlightenment) *(E)*, special vacation facilities (well-being) *(B)*. The students *(SE)* may offer many deprivations to the teachers *(SD)* without any immediate impact on public policy. More specifically, they may be negligent learners (reflecting on the professional skill [*S*] of the staff), occasional rebels (deprivers of established authority and control arrangements [*P*]), frequently aloof and sullen reactors (negative affection [*A*] and respect [*R*]), careless destroyers of equipment (negative wealth [*W*]), physically assaultive (negative well-being [*B*]), secretive (negative enlightenment), and initiators of denunciations for allegedly immoral practices (negative rectitude [*D*]).

These examples are evaluated from the standpoint of the socializers *(SR)*. When we consider the net value position of students *(SE)* in a given setting the question may be why a student conforms as much as he or she does. The hypothesis is that more obvious acts of resistance are perceived as augmenting the deprivations to which students are liable: e.g., removal from the academic council *(P)*, chastisement *(B)*, fines *(W)*, denial of freedom of movement *(R)*, parental disapproval *(A)*, denial of admission to technical and higher education *(S) (E)*, and sense of guilt *(D)*.

Our projections of the future have emphasized both the changing net value expectations and realizations of participants, and the vast changes that are to be anticipated in the innovation, diffusion, and restriction of specific socialization practices. (Note once more, e.g., the net improvement imputed to the future role of specialized socializers; the persistence of a divisive, militant, and power-emphasizing world; the potential advantages to power groups of biological and chemical rather than communicative practices.)

Socialization outcomes can be partially described and explained by concentrating on the political perspectives and overt participations of the *newcomers* in the general or particular situations being studied. Suppose that T^{-10} is the 10-year period during which a particular socialization process occurs, and T^{+25} is the 25-year period of activity as mature participants in relevant operations. It is apparent that, in addition to the "graduates" of the past year, the record of inductees during the previous nine years must be analyzed. Since the predispositions of current inductees can only be fully visible in coming years, estimates must be made at any given cross-section in time.

Although it is important to maintain continuing scrutiny of current activities, in theory a supplementary method can provide important data for estimating future possibilities without waiting for longitudinal studies to be completed. The method of *interlapping observation* (Lasswell, 1937) calls for samples to be described in the following diagram:

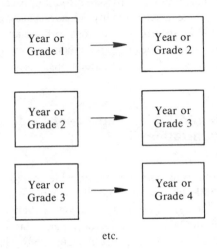

etc.

The procedure is to observe a group through the first and second year (period) or grade of induction into the decision process while a matched group of second-year participants is followed through its second and third year. The developmental model for the entire future of those involved can be obtained by substituting the overlapping samples. It is clear that the results are open to continuing recheck as the cohorts of a particular year or grade live through the calendar.

When the samples are large, it is possible to explore the latent responses of any given cohort by exposing it to a chosen environment. If the chosen environment is an innovation this becomes a convenient means not only of studying latencies, but of estimating the effectiveness of alterations in the decision process.

The appropriate method for exploring innovative practices is *prototyping*, which can usefully be distinguished from *experimentation* or *intervention* (Lasswell, 1963; Lasswell & Rubenstein, 1966). (A practice is an institutional component which is a pattern of perspectives and of operational behaviors.) Among the many socialization practices—in the military or people-in-arms arenas—are voluntary or compulsory training programs that provide for short full-time programs or part-time programs that run through the year; programs with heavy emphasis on strategic and tactical theory or with emphasis on obtaining experience with weapons (Goldhamer, 1975). The indicators of a practice are somewhat approximate, which affords a contrast to the rather precise indexes that are used in tightly controlled laboratory studies of such homogeneous variables as "time of exposure to text," "intensity of illuminated text," and "time of response." The management of political institutions is the management of practices. Therefore, the procedures of prototyping are particularly close to the problems with which participants must deal. A political "intervention" is an official change that is not primarily directed for scientific purposes. (It should be noted that officials may cooperate in scientific investigations and agree to procedures of appraisal that allow rather specific conclusions to be reached in regard to costs and gains. A true intervention does not give much priority to scientific purposes and typically fails to provide for control situations.)

Future Research and Policy Impacts of Professionals and of Professional Organizations

We have considered some possible and probable developments of research on political socialization. Future projections, it must be reiterated, are not inevitable. Rather, they are means of affecting decisions and choices in the succession of "presents" as we step into future history. Particular subjective events are inseparably interactive with other subjective and nonsubjective events in the social process. By applying a contextual, problem-oriented, and multimethod approach to the emerging future of specialists on socialization, it may be feasible to affect the future in ways that harmonize with preferred goals. (So far as I am concerned, the preferred goal is the realization of human dignity [*not* indignity] on the widest possible scale.)

It is not assumed that every specialist on political socialization concurs with this overriding goal or that, if the objective is acceptable, specific definitions and operational indicators will be identical. Nor, of course, is it taken for granted—especially in view of likely future conditions—that programs will necessarily succeed.

An advantage of cooperation among specialists who endorse the same policy goal is that much research can be directly aimed at the task of plugging gaps that exist in the currently available knowledge bearing directly on scientific hypotheses and policy judgments most relevant to the realization of fundamental objectives.

If studies of political socialization are to be more comprehensive, better grounded, and more influential, the structures specialized to obtaining knowledge in this field must be more adequate in terms of global coverage and coordination of the tasks of a problem-solving methodology. Specialists on political socialization will work closely with specialists on other sectors and subsectors. They will cultivate connections with specialists in the physical, biological, and cultural realms. Existing professional societies will be multiplied and diversified, and universities will be drawn into formal and informal networks of collaboration.

As they step into the future, the students of political socialization will plan to obtain *continuing feedback* of the data called for by the theoretical hypotheses and models that guide research. They will also plan for *intermittent revision* of theoretical formulations. Whether theories are stated in prose, in graphics, or in mathematics, they will be reconsidered according to the problem-solving task that they are intended to expedite (whether pertinent to goals, trends, conditions, projections, or alternatives). As models change, policy recommendations change, and the influence of professional investigators will change.

A body politic that moves toward the realization of human dignity continually adapts its institutions to the task of achieving and maintaining general participation in the shaping and sharing of values (preferred outcomes in all sectors of society). A partial statement of what is implied has received authoritative acceptance in the Universal Declaration of Human Rights, and in cognate documents. The obvious challenge is to improve these formulations and to strengthen a decision process capable of delivering a stream of decisions realistically compatible with articulated objectives.

It is well understood that professional societies and professional persons may participate in official and nonofficial activities relevant to decision processes. No doubt, the careers of professionals in socialization will show every conceivable combination of part-time or full-time participation in the decision process of bodies politic at every level of jurisdiction. In terms of our decision model:

Intelligence, or the gathering, processing, and distributing of the information relevant to the problems confronting decision makers (specialized structures include, e.g., libraries, computer storage centers, covert and overt intelligence agencies, planning boards).

Promotion, or the advocacy of policy (specialized structures include, e.g., political parties, pressure organizations, public relations firms).

Prescription, or the official formulation of norms, contingencies, and sanctions (e.g., legislatures, treaty negotiating agencies, top regulatory bodies).

Invocation, or the initial phase of an administrative process (e.g., allocation of resources or organizational adaptations by chief executives or cabinets).

Termination, or canceling a prescription and arranging compensations (e.g., reviewing and revisory commissions; compensation bureaus).

Appraisal, or estimating the execution of policy (e.g., commissions on aggregate efficiency or legality).

It has long been apparent to students of government, law, and politics that a dynamic interplay continually occurs between the structures and functions of power institutions and the personality (or character) structures and functions. A fundamental proposition affirms that the stability of political instituting varies inversely with the internalization of the perspectives and operational routines compatible with these institutions.

Stability is not to be confounded with rigid repetitiveness. On the contrary, stability implies capacity for innovating and adopting practices that *maintain* value-institution patterns in harmony with formulated goals, and that also *modify* these patterns toward more perfect goal realization.

In the context of a relatively democratic body politic, political socialization seeks appropriate strategies for ensuring that all members of the body politic: (1) are capable of contributing to the common life; (2) receive and provide opportunities to discover and develop potentialities; (3) receive and provide opportunities to exercise capabilities and to be equitably rewarded in terms of all values; and (4) participate in operations designed to direct public and private policy toward realizing the postulated goals.

The policy sciences approach is not necessarily grasped in much detail by all those who specialize in some aspect of political socialization. Individual specialists may choose to focus on a limited task with an intensive method. They may make little effort to diversify their roles in research or in relation to policy. However, the policy sciences provide an essential conceptual map for the making of research and policy decisions. Among the innovations that have been proposed and partially exemplified as means of perceiving the social and the socialization process as a whole are decision seminars and the social planetarium. Decision seminars on socialization adapt agendas and display procedures to the approach. The social planetarium is designed to provide an orienting environment suitable to both the mature and the immature participants in the policy processes.

If political socializers are to assist in guiding social change toward the realization of policy processes in the public and civic order that maintain and improve institutions, in harmony with democratic values, socializers must continually improve their knowledge of the policies that are most effective in the formation of democratic character.

Initially, it may be useful to examine a working conception of political character. Recall the distinction between "conventional" and "functional" definitions of "politics." In conventional usage, politics is often limited to the "official" or "governmental." Functionally, however, the term refers to the whole social context, and means that the most important decisions are political whether they are made by individuals in or out of what is locally called government.

In some communities a sharp contrast can be discerned between conventional structures of government and the effective pattern of power. In the United States, e.g., observers are well aware that such differences exist at many levels, especially in local communities, where disproportionate power is often exercised by the owners and managers, or the union leaders, in a factory or mining town *(W);* by the top executives of a college *(E,S),* hospital *(B),* or monastic village *(D),* or by the old families or a "feudal" estate *(A,R)*. In the USSR, where power is highly concentrated in a monopoly political party (or "order"), the disparity between conventional and functional structures is less striking.

Great disparities are found in all large bodies politic where the conventional language implies that power is "equal." Such self-serving claims do not stand up when confronted with the results of functionally oriented research (e.g., the USSR or the U.S.A.).

For socialization research the chief implication of the distinction between the conventional and the functional is that research is most revealing when two types of studies are conducted concurrently. Conventional usage is necessary for communication purposes, and functional research is indispensable if ordinary images of reality are to be appraised in realistic terms.

If political power is to be usefully defined for socialization studies and policies, a functional conception must be available that can be applied with minimal distortion to the most extreme figures known to us (like Genghis Khan or Alexander the Great), and to much less distinctive decision makers. Inclusiveness can be achieved if specifications of the "extreme" are related to the range of roles in each culture. If the range is from the nomadic conqueror to subserviency in one culture, we may find that less distinctive differences occur in another setting. For exploratory purposes the working definition of political characters may include *ambition to impose their will on others, and a ready resort to strategies of ruthlessness*. In some bodies politic the socialization process produces, not nomadic world shakers, but persons whose power potentials are adapted to strategies of persuasive accommodation. In any case the developmental sequence for leaders and led presumably runs from the primary circle provided by the family (or family equivalent), the peer group, and the neighborhood to the numerous settings of mature life. Schematically, the study of political socialization is focused on power in the developmental profiles of any selected context:

Emphasis on power in primary circles + playing political roles	(leads to)	Emphasis on power in secondary circles + playing political roles

In a democratic polity, decisions are made through a process of joint shaping and sharing. A demand to impose one's preferences on others must be kept under control so that democratic structures of decision can operate with minimal coercion (imposition). *A democratic character* (Lasswell, 1951) *incorporates the demand on the self and others to adhere to decision practices that put reliance on persuasion well ahead of coercion*. The implication is that *demands on the self and on others go beyond the protection of democratic forms to the cultivation of decision outcomes that foster the realization of goals in harmony with human dignity:* e.g., a democratic majority in a functional sense does not oppress—even as it outvotes—minorities.

Observations suggest several detailed components of democratic character. *Self-restraint in the pursuit of power outcomes is more likely when the person is concerned with a more diversified set of significant value outcomes and effects than power alone.* The multi-value-oriented person can subordinate and integrate power with other values, and empathize with a society in which general rather than narrow participation is preferred.

An inference from the democratic model is that if the primary value is not power but wealth (or some other outcome) the pursuit of the primary value, unless kept within moderate limits, predisposes the individual to suborn public policy for special purposes. Further, the person may be unwilling to bear some of the responsibility for forming and executing public policy. In extreme situations the body politic is left as a power vacuum filled by individuals and groups who are minimally concerned with the clarification and pursuit of common interests.

The democratic character calls for a *self system that includes demands on the primary ego and the several components of the self (family, nation, etc.) that seeks to integrate interests with one another in a noncoercive policy process.*

The conception of democratic character outlined above is a revision of some of the earliest recommendations in the history of political thought. Although the Greek thinkers operated within a society where "equality" was confined to a limited group, the specifications can be plausibly generalized to an inclusive context.

In a changing world it is to be taken for granted that the indicators of the preferred models of general or particular socialization must continually change. To some extent, these indicator changes will be made to keep in close touch with the shifting patterns of public and civic order.

It is pertinent to include some reminders of the direction in which democratic institutions (hence socialization indicators) are likely to be modified. The analysis of experience with governmental institutions has led to the generalization of principles of considerable importance for democratic decision making and execution. Consider the *principle of representation,* or the use of selected agents to look after details that community members are not willing to take the time to think about. The invention of the computer and the technique of modeling have provided instruments that will probably reduce without eliminating the use of representatives in decision processes.

The division and separation of powers (official authority and control) are principles that emphasize the importance of allocating the decision process among structures that are essentially equal, not hierarchical. The new instruments of information may be effectively used to counterbalance tendencies to substitute hierarchy for coarchy (e.g., to prevent domination by the executive over legislative and judicial structures).

A further principle distinguishes *the realm of public order and the realm of civic order,* or the domain of official decision from that of private choice. In the differentiated world of today and tomorrow, a major task is to improve the procedures by which the civic order is able to make realistic appraisals of the successes and failures of public order in the achievement of common goals. We have emphasized how specialists on political socialization can combine roles in civic and public order on behalf of democratic character and commonwealth.

For the fulfillment of the projected programs it is pertinent to direct attention to two research strategies which, though they take off from different starting points, promise to supplement and to correct one another. *Procedure A is the longitudinal study of individual career lines.* The starting point is birth or conception. Research proceeds by listing the physiological structures and behavioral predispositions of the embryo or newborn infant, and by describing the subsequent interaction of the individual with the cultural and physical environment.

Procedure B begins at the ''adult'' or mature end of the development process and moves backward. Democratic characters may be approximated among the role players in relatively democratic societies. (Other characters are likely to be found at the same time.) The explanatory problem is to account for the democratic character by examining the successive interactions between predisposition and environment. For convenient reference:

$$
\begin{array}{lll}
T^{-2} & T^{-1} & T^{0} \text{ (present)} \\
P - & P - & R\ (P) - \\
E - & E - & E -
\end{array}
$$

R refers to the ''response'' or state of the person so far as socialization is concerned at T^0 (present). P at T^{-1} is the R at an earlier cross-section in time. E is the environment at the times indicated. If we think of the socialization state of a person or group at any cross-section, the explanatory problem is to demonstrate the impact of environmental factors on predispositions (and, reversed, the impact of responses on relevant environing conditions) (Lasswell, 1954).

By beginning at the adult phase and thinking backward, the scientist's focus of attention is selectively guided to the values and practices of the social process model. Hypotheses about original ''instincts,'' ''reflexes,'' or what not are not eliminated. On the contrary, they are introduced as they become relevant. Note how ''inborn'' predispositions of the infant were related to the value indulgence-deprivation exchange between infant and mother (pp. 17–18).

''Thinking backward'' is, of course, a preparation for moving forward as well. The interlapping model (above, pp. 32–33) can be used to guide future as well as past data-gathering and theory revision operations.

We conclude by mentioning once more the profound shift that is occurring in the evolution of man as the living form endowed with the most complex intellectual equipment. From the earliest years of the human species man's evolution proceeded blindly, i.e., without conscious purpose or policy plan. With the advent of genetic and computer engineering, it is becoming feasible to live up to the dream of taking evolution into our own hands.

Bibliography

ABEL, T. *The Nazi movement*. New York: Atherton Press, 1938.

ABRAMOWITZ, S. I. *The comparative competence-adjustment of student left social-political activists*. Unpublished doctoral dissertation, University of Colorado, 1972.

ABRAMSON, P. R. The differential political socialization of English secondary school students. *Sociology of Education*, 1967, *40*, 246–269.

ABRAMSON, P. R. Social and political change in Western Europe. *Comparative Political Studies*, 1971, *4*, 131–155.

ABRAMSON, P. R. Intergenerational social mobility and partisan choice. *American Political Science Review*, 1972, *66*, 1291–1294

ABRAMSON, P. R. Generational changes in American electoral behavior. *American Political Science Review*. 1974, *68*, 93–105.

ABRAMSON, P. R. *Generational change in American politics*. Lexington, Mass.: Lexington Books, D. C. Heath, 1975.

ABRAMSON, P. R. Generational change and the decline of party identification in America: 1952–1974. *American Political Science Review*, 1976, *70*, 469–478.

ABRAMSON, P. R., & Inglehart, R. The development of systemic support in four Western democracies. *Comparative Political Studies*, 1970, *2*, 419–442.

ADAMS, B. *The theory of social revolutions*. New York: Macmillan, 1913.

ADELSON, J. The political imagination of the young adolescent. *Daedalus*, Spring 1971, 100.

ADELSON, J., GREEN, B., & O'NEIL, R. P. Growth of the idea of law in adolescence. *Developmental Psychology*, 1969, *1*, 327–332.

ADELSON, J., & O'NEIL, R. P. Growth of political ideas in adolescence: The sense of community. *Journal of Personality and Social Psychology*, 1966, *4*, 295–306.

ADELSON, N. C., & CROSBY, S. G. *The American government information unit: Curriculum alternatives for secondary schools*. Berkeley: Far West Laboratory for Educational Research Development, 1971.

ADLER, N., & HARRINGTON, C. Concluding essay. In N. Adler & C. Harrington (Eds.), *The learning of political behavior*. Glenview, Ill.: Scott, Foresman, 1970.

ADORNO, T. W., FRENKEL-BRUNSWICK, E., LEVINSON, E. J., & SANFORD, R. N. *The authoritarian personality*. New York: Harper, 1950.

AGGER, R., GOLDSTEIN, M. N., & PEARL, S. A. Political cynicism: Measurement and meaning. *Journal of Politics*, 1961, *23*, 477–506.

AGNELLO, T. Aging and the sense of political powerlessness. *Public Opinion Quarterly*, 1973, *37*, 251–259.

ALBERT, E. M., & KLUCKHOHN, C. *A selected bibliography on values, ethics, and esthetics*. Glencoe, Ill.: Free Press, 1959.

ALFORD, R. *Party and society: The Anglo-American democracies*. Chicago: Rand Mc-Nally, 1963.

ALGER, C. The multinational corporation and the future of the international system. *Annals*, September 1972, 104–115.

ALLAND, A. *The human imperative*. New York: Columbia University Press, 1972.

ALLEE, W. C. *The social life of animals*. Boston: Beacon Press, 1958.

ALLEN, I. L., & COLFAX, J. D. The diffusion of news of LBJ's March 31 decision. *Journalism Quarterly*, 1968, *45*, 321–324.

ALLEN, V. L. Situational factors in conformity. In L. Berkowitz (Ed.), *Advances in experimental social psychology* (Vol. 2). New York: Academic Press, 1965.

ALLEN, V. L., & LEVINE, J. M. Consensus and conformity. *Journal of Experimental Social Psychology*, 1969, *5*, 389–399.

ALLEN, V. L., & NEWTSON, D. Development of conformity and independence. *Journal of Personality and Social Psychology*, 1972, *22*, 18–30.

ALLPORT, F. H., & HARTMAN, D. A. The measurement and motivation of atypical opinion in a certain group. *American Political Science Review*, 1925, *19*, 735–760.

ALLPORT, G. The composition of political attitudes. *American Journal of Sociology*, 1929, *35*, 220–238.

ALLPORT, G. The psychology of participation. *Psychological Review*, 1945, *58*, 117–132.

ALLPORT, G. The historical background of modern social-psychology. In G. Lindzey & E. Aronson (Eds.), *Handbook of social psychology* (Vol. 1). Reading, Mass.: Addison-Wesley, 1968.

ALLPORT, G. W., VERNON, P. E., & LINDZEY, G. *A study of values*. Boston: Houghton Mifflin, 1960.

ALMOND, G. A. Comparative political systems. *Journal of Politics*, 1956, *18*, 391–409.

ALMOND, G. A. Introduction: A functional approach to comparative politics. In G. A. Almond & J. S. Coleman (Eds.), *The politics of the developing areas*. Princeton: Princeton University Press, 1960.

ALMOND, G. A., & COLEMAN, J. S. *The politics of the developing areas*. Princeton: Princeton University Press, 1960.

ALMOND, G., & POWELL, G. B., Jr. *Comparative politics: A developmental approach*. Boston: Little, Brown, 1966.

470   BIBLIOGRAPHY

ALMOND, G., & VERBA, S. *The civic culture.* Boston: Little, Brown, 1963.

ALVIK, T. The development of views on conflict, war and peace among school children. *Journal of Peace Research,* 1968, *5,* 171–195.

American Political Science Association Committee on Pre-Collegiate Education. Political education in the public schools: The challenge for political science. PS, *Newsletter of the American Political Science Association,* Summer, 1971, *4.*

ANCHOR, K., & CROSS, H. J. Maladaptive aggression, moral perspective and the socialization process. *Journal of Personality and Social Psychology,* 1974, *30,* 163–168.

ANDREAS, C. War toys and the peace movement. *Journal of Social Issues,* 1969, *5,* 83–99.

ANDREWS, F., MORGAN, J., & SONQUIST, T. *Multiple classification analysis.* Ann Arbor: University of Michigan, Institute for Social Research, 1967.

ANDRIAN, C. *Children and civic awareness.* Columbus, Ohio: Merrill, 1971.

APTER, D. *Politics of modernization.* Chicago: University of Chicago Press, 1965.

ARDREY, R. The territorial imperative. New York: Atheneum, 1966.

ARGYLE, M., & DELIN, P. Non-universal laws of socialization. *Human Relations,* 1965, *18,* 77–85.

ARGYRIS, C. *Organization and innovation.* Homewood, Ill.: Dorsey, 1965.

ARIES, P. *Centuries of childhood.* New York: Vantage, 1965.

ARMSBY, R. E. A reexamination of the development of moral judgment in children. *Child Development,* 1971, *48,* 1241–1248.

ARONFREED, J. *Conduct and conscience.* New York: Academic Press, 1968.

ARONFREED, J. The socialization of altruistic and sympathetic behavior: Some theoretical and experimental analyses. In J. Macaulay & L. Berkowitz (Eds.), *Altruism and helping behavior.* New York: Academic Press, 1970.

ARONFREED, J. Discussion: Developmental gains in moral conduct. *American Journal of Mental Deficiency,* 1974, *79,* 154–155.

ARROW, K. *Social choice and individual values.* New Haven: Yale University Press, 1970.

ARTERTON, C. F. The impact of Watergate on children's attitudes toward political authority. *Political Science Quarterly,* 1974, *89,* 259–288.

ASCH, S. E. Studies of Independence and conformity: A minority of one against a unanimous majority. *Psychological Monographs,* 1956, *70,* Whole.

ASHER, H. B. The learning of legislative norms. *American Political Science Review,* 1973, *67,* 499–513.

ASHMORE, R. D. Prejudice. In B. E. Collins (Ed.), *Social psychology.* Reading, Mass: Addison-Wesley, 1970.

ASTIN, A. Determinants of student activism. In J. Foster & D. Long (Eds.), *Protest! Student activism in America.* New York: Morrow, 1970.

ATKIN, C. K. Anticipated communication and mass media information-seeking. *Public Opinion Quarterly,* 1972, *36,* 188–199.

ATKIN, C. K., & Gantz, W. *The role of television news in the political socialization of children.* Paper presented to International Communication Association, Chicago, April 1975.

ATKINSON, J. (Ed.), *Motives in fantasy, action, and society.* Princeton: Van Nostrand, 1958.

AUSUBEL, D. The transition from concrete to abstract cognitive functioning: Theoretical issues and implications. In I. Athey & D. Rubadeau (Eds.), *Educational implications of Piaget's theory.* Waltham, Mass.: Ginn-Blaisdell, 1970.

AUSUBEL, D. Motivational issues in cognitive development: Comments on Mischel's article. In T. Mischel (Ed.), *Cognitive development and epistemology.* New York: Academic Press, 1971.

AZRAEL, J. Soviet Union. In J. Coleman (Ed.), *Educational and political development.* Princeton: Princeton University Press, 1965.

BAAS, L. R., & BROWN, S. R. Generating rules for intensive analysis: The study of transformations. *Psychiatry,* 1973, *36,* 172–183.

BACHMAN, J., & VAN DUINEN, E. *Youth looks at national problems.* Ann Arbor: Institute for Social Research, 1971.

BACHRACH, P. *The theory of democratic elitism.* Boston: Little, Brown, 1967.

BAIRD, L. L. Who protests: A study of student activism. In J. Foster & D. Long (Eds.), *Protest! Student activism in America.* New York: Morrow, 1970.

BAKER, D. Political socialization: Parameters and dispositions. *Polity,* 1971, *3,* 586–600.

BAKKE, E. W. Roote and soil of student activism. *Comparative Education Review,* 1966, *10,* 163–174.

BALCH, G. *Political trust and style of political involvement among American college students.* Paper presented at annual meeting of Midwest Political Science Association. Chicago, 1971.

BALCH, G. Political alienation and political involvement: Some perspectives from social learning theory. Paper presented at annual meeting of American Political Science Association, Washington, D.C., 1972.

BALES, R. The equilibrium problem in small groups. In Talcott Parsons, R. Bales, & E. Shils (Eds.), *Working papers in the theory of action.* New York: Free Press, 1953.

BALTES, P. B. Longitudinal and cross-sectional sequences in the study of age and generation effects. *Human Development,* 1968, *11,* 145–171.

BALTES, P. B., & NESSELROADE, J. R. Multi-variate longitudinal and cross-sectional sequences for analyzing ontogenetic and generational change: A methodological note. *Developmental Psychology,* 1970, *2,* 163–168.

BALTES, P. B., & NESSELROADE, J. R. Cultural change and adolescent personality development: An application of longitudinal sequences. *Developmental Psychology,* 1972, *7,* 244–256.

BALTES, P. B., & REINERT, G. Cohort effects in cognitive development of children as revealed by cross-sectional sequences. *Developmental Psychology,* 1969, *1,* 169–177.

BALTES, P. B., BALTES, M. M., & REINERT, G. The relationship between time of measurement and age in cognitive development in children: An application of cross-sectional sequences. *Human Development,* 1970, *13,* 258–268.

BANDURA, A. *Principles of behavior modification.* New York: Holt, Rinehart & Winston, 1969. (a)

BANDURA, A. Social learning of moral judgments. *Journal of Personality and Social Psychology,* 1969, *11,* 275–279. (b)

BANDURA, A. Social-learning theory of identifactory processes. In D. A. Goslin (Ed.), *Handbook of socialization theory and research.* Chicago: Rand McNally, 1969. (c)

BANDURA, A., & HUSTON, A. C. Identification as a process of, incidental learning. *Journal of Abnormal and Social Psychology,* 1961, *63,* 311–318.

BANDURA, A., & MCDONALD, F. J. The influence of social reinforcement and the behavior of models in shaping children's moral judgments. *Journal of Abnormal and Social Psychology,* 1963, *67,* 274–281.

BANDURA, A., ROSS, D., & ROSS, S. A. Transmission of aggression through imitation of aggressive models. *Journal of Abnormal and Social Psychology,* 1961, *62,* 575–582.

BANDURA, A., ROSS, D., & ROSS, S. A vicarious reinforcement and initiation. *Journal of Abnormal and Social Psychology,* 1963, *67,* 601–607.

BANDURA, A., & WALTERS, R. H. *Adolescent aggression.* New York: Ronald Press, 1959.

BANDURA, A., & WALTERS, F. H. The generality of moral behavior. In R. C. Johnson, P. R. Dokecki, & O. H. Mowrer (Eds.), *Conscience, contract, and social reality.* New York: Holt, Rinehart & Winston, 1972.

BANKS, O. *The sociology of education.* New York: Schocken, 1972

BARBER, J. D. *Presidential character.* Englewood Cliffs, N.J.: Prentice-Hall, 1972.

BARBER, J. D. *The lawmakers: Recruitment and adaptation to legislative life.* New Haven: Yale University Press, 1965.

BARBER, J. D. *Power in committees.* Chicago: Rand McNally, 1966.

BARBER, J. D. *Social mobility and voting behavior.* Chicago: Rand McNally, 1970.

BARKER, E. N. Authoritarianism of the political right, center, and left. *Journal of Social Issues,* 1963, *19* (2), 63–74.

BARKLEY, K. L. Attitudes of civilian females toward war as developed and held during peace and during war. *Journal of Social Psychology,* 1953, *38,* 241–252.

BARRY, H., CHILD, I., & BACON, M. Relation of child training to subsistence economy. *American Anthropologist,* 1959, *61,* 51–63.

BAUMRIND, D. Effects of authoritative parental control on child behavior. *Child Development,* September-December 1966, *37,* part 2, 887–907.

BAY, C. *The structure of freedom.* Stanford: Stanford University Press, 1958.

BAY, C. Political and apolitical students: Facts in search of a theory. *Journal of Social Issues,* 1967, *23,* 76–91.

BAY, C. Thoughts on the purposes of political science education. In G. J. Graham, Jr., & G. W. Carey (Eds.), *The post-behavioral era: Perspectives on political science.* New York: McKay, 1972.

BAYER, A. E., ASTIN, A. W., & BORUCH, R. F. College students' attitudes toward social issues: 1967–1970. *Educational Record,* Winter, 1971, 52–59.

BEALS, K., & KELSO, A. J. Genetic variation and cultural evolution. *American Anthropologist,* 1975, *3,* 566–579.

BECK, P. A. A socialization theory of partisan realignment. In R. G. Niemi (Ed.), *The politics of future citizens*. San Francisco: Jossey-Bass, 1974.

BECK, P. A., DOBSON, D., & BRUNER, J. *Political socialization across the generations*. Washington, D.C.: American Political Science Association, 1975.

BECK, P. A., & JENNINGS, M. K. Parents as "middle persons" in political socialization. *Journal of Politics*, 1975, *37*, 83–107.

BECKER, H. Personal change in adult life. *Sociometry*, 1964, *27*, 40–56.

BECKER, H., HUGHES, E. C. GEER, B., & STRAUSS, A. L. *Boys in white*. Chicago: University of Chicago Press, 1961.

BEHAR, M. Prevalence of malnutrition among preschool children of developing countries. In N. S. Scrimshaw & J. E. Gordon (Eds.), *Malnutrition, learning, and behavior*. Cambridge: MIT Press, 1968.

BELL, D. *Work and its discontents*. Boston: Beacon Press, 1956.

BELL, D. The dispossessed. In D. Bell (Ed.), *The radical right*. New York: Doubleday, 1964.

BELL, R. A reinterpretation of the direction of effects in studies of socialization. *Psychological Review*, 1968, *75*, 81–95.

BELLISFIELD, G. What attitudes toward racial integration in the urban riots of the 1960's. *Public Opinion Quarterly*, 1972, *36*, 579–584.

BEM, J. *Beliefs, attitudes, and human affairs*. Belmont, Calif.: Brooks/Cole, 1970.

BEM, D. J. Constructing cross-situational consistencies in behavior: Some thoughts on Alker's critique of Mischel. *Journal of Personality*, 1972, *40*, 17–26.

BENDER, L., & FROSCH, J. Children's reactions to the war. *American Journal of Ortho-psychiatry*, 1942, *22*, 571–587.

BENDIX, R. *Work and authority in industry*. New York: Wiley, 1956.

BENEDICT, R. *The chrysanthemum and the sword: Patterns of Japanese culture*. Boston: Houghton Mifflin, 1946.

BENGTSON, V. L. The generation gap: A review and typology of social-psychological perspectives. *Youth and Society*, 1970, *2*, 7–31.

BENGTSON, V. L. *The social psychology of aging*. New York: Bobbs-Merrill, 1973.

BENGTSON, V. L., & BLACK, K. D. Intergenerational relations and continuities in so-cialization. Reprinted from *Life-span developmental psychology: Personality and socialization*. New York: Academic Press, 1973.

BENGTSON, V. L., & CUTLER, N. E. Generations and inter-generational relations: Perspectives on age groups and social change. In R. Binstock & E. Shanas (Eds.), *Handbook of aging and the social sciences*. New York: Van Nostrand, 1976, 130–159.

BENGTSON, V. L., FURLONG, M. J., & LAUFER, R. S. Times, aging, and the continuity of social structure: Themes and issues in generational analysis. *Journal of Social Issues*, 1974, *30*, 1–30.

BENGTSON, V. L., & KUEYPERS, J. A. Generational difference and the developmental stake. *Aging and human Development*, 1971, *2*, 249–260.

BENNIS, W. G. *Changing organizations*. New York: McGraw-Hill, 1966.

BERELSON, B. R., LAZARSFELD, P. F., & McPHEE, W. N. *Voting*. Chicago: University of Chicago Press, 1954.

BERGER, B. M. How long is a generation? *British Journal of Sociology*, 1960, *2*, 10–23.

BERNSTEIN, M. H. The political ideas of selected American business journals. *Public Opinion Quarterly*, 1953, *17*, 258–267.

BERRY, J. W. Independence and conformity in subsistence level societies. *Journal of Personality and Social Psychology*, 1967, *7*, 415–418.

BERSCHIED, E., & WALSTER, E. *Interpersonal attraction*. Reading, Mass.: Addison-Wesley, 1970.

BETTELHEIM, B. *The children of the dream*. New York: Avon, 1969. (a)

BETTELHEIM, B. Obsolete youth. *Encounter*, 1969, *23*, 29–42. (b)

BETTELHEIM, B., & JANOWITZ, M. Dynamics of prejudice. Harper, 1950.

BEVER, T. G., MEHLER, J., & EPSTEIN, J. What children do in spite of what they know. *Science*, 1968, *152*, 921–924.

BIBER, B., & MINUCHIN, P. The impact of school philosophy and practice on child development. In N. V. Overly (Ed.), *The unstudied curriculum*. Washington, D.C.: Association for Supervision and Curriculum Development, 1970.

BINDER, L. Egypt: The integrative revolution. In L. W. Pye & S. Verba (Eds.), *Political culture and political development*. Princeton: Princeton University Press, 1965.

BINSTOCK, R., & LOHMAN, R. Identity and power: The case of the aged. Paper presented at Annual Meeting of American Political Science Association, 1971.

BIRDWHISTELL, R. *Kinesics and context*. Philadelphia: University of Pennsylvania Press, 1970.

BITTNER, E. Radicalism and the organization of radical movements. In B. McLaughlin (Ed.), *Studies in social movements*. New York: Free Press, 1969.

BLANCHARD, E. B., & Price, K. C. A developmental study of cognitive balance. *Developmental Psychology*, 1971, *5*, 344–348.

BLATT, M., & KOHLBERG, L. The effects of a classroom discussion program upon the moral level of preadolescents. *Merrill Palmer Quarterly*, 1969.

BLAU, P., & DUNCAN, O. *The American occupational structure*. New York: Wiley, 1967.

BLOCK, J. H. Generational continuity and discontinuity in the understanding of societal rejection. *Journal of Personality and Social Psychology*, 1972, *23*, 333–345.

BLOCK, J. H., HAAN, N. H., & SMITH, M. B. The moral reasoning of young adults: Political-social behavior, family background and personality correlates. *Journal of Personality and Social Psychology*, 1968, *10*, 183–201.

BLOCK, J. H., HAAN, N. H., & SMITH, M. B. Socialization correlates of student activism. *Journal of Social Issues*, 1969, *25*, 143–177.

BLOCK, J. H., HAAN, N. H., & SMITH, M. B. Activism and apathy in contemporary adolescents. In J. F. Adams (Ed.), *Understanding adolescence: Current developments in adolescent psychology*. Boston: Allyn & Bacon, 1973.

BLOOM, B. S. *Stability and change in human characteristics*. New York: Wiley, 1964.

BLUHM, W. T. *Ideologies and attitudes: Modern political culture*. Englewood Cliffs, N.J.: Prentice-Hall, 1974.

BLUMBERG, P. *Industrial democracy: The sociology of participation*. New York: Schocken, 1969.

BLUMENTHAL, M. D., KAHN, R. L., & ANDREWS, F. M. Attitudes toward violence. Mimeo. Ann Arbor: Institute for Social Research, 1971.

BLUMER, H. Social movements. In B. McLaughlin (Ed.), *Studies in social movements.* New York: Free Press, 1969. (Original publishing date 1951.)

BLUMLER, J. G., & KATZ, E. *The uses of mass communications: Current perspectives on gratifications research.* Beverly Hills: Sage Publications, 1974.

BOBROW, D. B. Organization of American national security opinions. *Public Opinion Quarterly,* 1969, *33,* 223–239.

BOBROW, D. B., & CUTLER, N. E. Time-oriented explanations of national security beliefs: Cohort, life-state and situation. *Peace Research Society (International)* Papers, 1967, *8,* 31–57.

BOEHM, L. The development of conscience: A comparison of American children of different mental and socio-economic levels. *Child Development,* 1962, *33,* 575–590.

BOEHM, L. The development of conscience: A comparison of students in Catholic parochial schools and in public schools. *Child Development,* 1962, *33,* 591–602.

BOEHM, L., & NASS, M. L. Social class differences in conscience development. *Child Development,* 1962, *33,* 565–574.

BONE, H. A., & RANNEY, A. *Politics and voters* (4th ed.). New York: McGraw-Hill, 1976.

BOOCOCK, S. S. *An introduction to the sociology of learning.* Boston: Houghton Mifflin, 1972.

BOULDING, K. Education for the spaceship Earth. *Social Education,* 1968, 648–649.

BOWERMAN, C. E., & KINCH, J. W. Changes in family and peer orientation of children between the 4th and 10th grades. *Social Forces,* 1959, *37,* 206–211.

BOWERS, K. S. Situationalism in psychology: An analysis and a critique. *Psychological Review,* 1973, *80,* 307–336.

BOWLBY, J. *Attachment and loss: I. Attachment.* New York: Basic Books, 1969.

BOWLBY, J. *Attachment and loss: II. Separation.* New York: Basic Books, 1973.

BRADY, D. & RAPPOPORT, L. Violence and Vietnam: A comparison between attitudes of civilians and veterans. *Human Relations,* 1973, *26,* 735–752.

BRAIBANTI, R. (Ed). *Political and administrative development.* Durham, N.C.: Duke University Press, 1969.

BRAINERD, C. J. Judgments and explanations as criteria for the presence of cognitive structures. *Psychological Bulletin,* 1973, *79,* 172–179.

BRAMSON, L., & GOETHALS, G. *War: Studies from psychology, sociology, anthropology.* New York: Basic Books, 1964.

BRAUNGART, R. G. Family status, socialization, and student politics: A multivariate analysis. *American Journal of Sociology,* 1971, *77,* 108–130.

BRENNER, C. *An elementary textbook of psychoanalysis* (rev. ed.) New York: International Universities Press, 1974.

BREWER, G. D., & BRUNNER, R. D. (Eds.). *Political development and change: A policy approach.* New York: Free Press, 1975.

BRIM, O. G., Jr. Socialization through the life cycle. In O. G. Brim & S. Wheeler (Eds.), *Socialization after childhood: Two essays.* New York: Wiley, 1966.

BRITTAIN, C. V. Adolescent choices and parent-peer pressures. *American Sociological Review,* 1963, *28,* 385–391.

BRODERSEN, A. National character: An old problem reexamined. *Diogenes,* Winter 1957, *20,* 468–486.

BRONFENBRENNER, U. Socialization and social class through time and space. In E. E. Maccoby, T. M. Newcomb, & E. L. Hartley (Eds.), *Readings in social psychology.* New York: Holt, Rinehart & Winston, 1958.

BRONFENBRENNER, U. Freudian theories of identification and their derivatives. *Child Development,* 1960, *31,* 15–40. (a)

BRONFENBRENNER, U. Personality and participation: The case of the vanishing variables. *Journal of Social Issues,* 1960, *16,* 54–63. (b)

BRONFENBRENNER, U. The role of age, sex, class and culture in studies of moral development. *Religious Education,* 1962, *57,* 3–17.

BRONFENBRENNER, U. Response to pressure from peers vs. adults among Soviet and American school children. *International Journal of Psychology,* 1967, *2,* 199–207.

BRONFENBRENNER, U. Reaction to social pressure from adults versus peers among Soviet day school and boarding school pupils in perspective of an American sample. *Journal of Personality and Social Psychology,* 1970, *15,* 179–189. (a)

BRONFENBRENNER, U. *Two worlds of childhood: U.S. and USSR.* New York: Russell Sage Foundation, 1970. (b)

BRONFENBRENNER, U. Developmental research, public policy and the ecology of childhood. *Child Development,* 1974, *45,* 1–5.

BRONSON, F. H., & DESJARDINS, C. Aggression in adult mice: Modification by neonatal injection of gonadal hormones. *Science,* August 1968, *161,* 705–706.

BRONTE, E., & MUSGROVE, M. Influence of war in children's play. *Child Development,* 1943, 129–200.

BROOKES, M., & SIGEL, R. S. Governmental performance and political involvement. Presented at annual meeting of Midwest Political Science Association, 1974.

BROWN, R. The authoritarian personality and the organization of attitudes. In R. Brown, *Social psychology.* New York: Free Press, 1965.

BROWN, S. R. Intensive analysis in political research. *Political Methodology,* 1974, *3,* 1–25.

BROWN, W. *Exploration in management.* New York: Wiley, 1960.

BROWNING, R. P., & JACOB, H. Power motivation and political personality. *Public Opinion Quarterly,* 1964, *28,* 75–90.

BROYLES, J. A. The John Birch Society: A movement of social protest of the radical right. *Journal of Social Issues,* 1963, *19,* 51–62.

BROZEK, J. Semi-starvation of nutritional rehabilitation. A qualitative case study. *Journal of Clinical Nutrition,* 107–118.

BRYAN, J. H. Why children help: A review. *Journal of Social Issues,* 1972, *28,* 87–104.

BRYAN, J. H., & LONDON, P. Altruistic behavior by children. *Psychological Bulletin,* 1970, *73,* 200–211.

BRYAN, J. H., & WALBEK, N. Preaching and practicing generosity: Children's actions and reactions. *Child Development,* 1970, *41,* 329–353.

BRZEZINSKI, Z., & HUNTINGTON, S. P. *Political power: U.S.A./U.S.S.R.* New York: Viking, 1963.

BUCKLEY, W. *Sociology and modern systems theory.* Englewood Cliffs, N.J.: Prentice-Hall, 1967.

BUDGE, I. Support for national and government among English children: A comment. *British Journal of Politics,* 1971, *6,* 389–392.

BUDNER, S. Intolerance of ambiguity as a personality variable. *Journal of Personality,* 1962, *30,* 29–50.

BULLOCK, C. S., III, & RODGERS, H. R., JR. *Black political attitudes.* Chicago: Markham, 1972.

BURLINGHAM, D., & FREUD, A. *Young children in wartime.* London: Allen & Unwin, 1942.

BURTON, J. W. *Word society.* Cambridge, Eng.: Cambridge University Press, 1972.

BURTON, R. The generality of honesty reconsidered. *Psychological Review,* 1963, *70,* 481–499.

BURTON, W. *Children's civic information,* 1924–1935. Los Angeles: University of Southern California Press, 1936.

BUSS, A., & PLOMIN, R. *A temperament theory of personality development.* New York: Wiley, 1975.

BUTLER, D., & STOKES, D. *Political change in Britain.* New York: St. Martin's, 1969.

BUTTON, J. Youth and foreign affairs: The school as a socializing agent. *Theory into Practice,* 1971, 346–352.

CALDWELL, B. M., & HERSLER, L. Mother-infant interaction during the first year. *Merrill-Palmer Quarterly,* 1964, *10,* 119–128.

CAMPBELL, A. Social and psychological determinants of voting behavior. In W. Donahue (Ed.), *The politics of age.* Ann Arbor: University of Michigan Press, 1963.

CAMPBELL, A. Politics through the life cycle. *The Gerontologist,* 1971, *11,* 112–117.

CAMPBELL, A., CONVERSE, P. E., MILLER, W. E., & STOKES, D. E. *The American voter.* New York: Wiley, 1960.

CAMPBELL, A., GURIN, G., & MILLER, W. E. *The voter decides,* New York: Harper & Row, 1954.

CAMPBELL, A., & SCHUMANN, H. Racial attitudes in fifteen American cities. In *Supplement Studies for the National Advisory Commission on Civil Disorders.* Washington, D.C.: U.S. Government Printing Office, 1968.

CAMPBELL, A., & VALEN, H. Party identification in Norway and the United States. *Public Opinion Quarterly,* 1961, *25,* 505–525.

CANDEE, D. *Watergate as a moral issue.* Paper presented at APA convention, New Orleans, 1974.

CANTRIL, H. *Public opinion, 1935–1946.* Princeton: Princeton University Press, 1951.

CARLIN, J. *Lawyers' ethics: A survey of the New York City bar.* New York: Russell Sage Foundation, 1966.

CARLSSON, G., & KARLSSON, K. Age cohorts and the generation of generations. *American Sociological Review,* August 1970, *35,* 710–718.

CARRIGAN, W. C., & JULIAN, J. W. Sex and the birth order differences in conformity as a function of need affiliation arousal. *Journal of Personality and Social Psychology,* 1966, *3,* 479–483.

CARROLL, J. B. The nature of data, or how to choose a correlation coefficient. *Psychometrika,* 1961, *26,* 347–372.

CARR-SAUNDERS, A. M., & WILSON, P. *The professions.* Oxford, Eng.: Clarendon Press, 1933.

CARTWRIGHT, D., & ZANDER, A. (Eds.). *Group dynamics.* Evanston, Ill.: Row & Peterson, 1953.

CENTERS, R. *The psychology of social class.* Princeton, N.J.: Princeton University Press, 1949.

CHAFFEE, S. H. (Ed.). *Political communication: Issues and strategies for research.* Beverly Hills: Sage Publications, 1975.

CHAFFEE, S. H., & BECKER, L. Young voters' reactions to early Watergate issues. *American Politics Quarterly,* 1975, *3,* 360–385.

CHAFFEE, S. H., & IZCARAY, F. Mass communication functions in a media-rich developing society. *Communication Research,* 1975, *2,* 367–395.

CHAFFEE, S. H., & McLEOD, J. M. Individual vs. social predictors of information seeking. *Journalism Quarterly,* 1973, *50,* 237–245.

CHAFFEE, S. H., McLEOD, J. M., & ATKIN, C. K. Parental influences on adolescent media use. *American Behavioral Scientist,* 1971, *14,* 323–340.

CHAFFEE, S. H. McLEOD, J. M., & WACKMAN, D. B. Family communication patterns and adolescent political participation. In J. Dennis (Ed.), *Socialization to politics: A reader.* New York: Wiley, 1973.

CHAFFEE, S. H., WARD, L. S., & TIPTON, L. P. Mass communication and political socialization. *Journalism Quarterly,* 1970, *47,* 647–659.

CHAFFEE, S. H., & WILSON, D. Adult life cycle changes in mass media use. Paper presented to Association for Education in Journalism, Ottawa, August 1975.

CHAIKIN, A. L., & DARLEY, J. M. Victim or perpetrator?: Defensive attribution of responsibility and the need for order and justice. *Journal of Personality,* 1973, *25,* 268–275.

CHAZAN, B. I., & SOLTIS, J. F. (Eds.). *Moral education.* New York: Teachers College Press, 1973.

CHESLER, M., & SCHMUCK, R. On super-patriotism: A definition and analysis. *Journal of Social Issues,* 1963, *19,* 31–50. (b)

CHESLER, M., & SCHMUCK, R. Participant observation in a super-patriot discussion group. *Journal of Social Issues,* 1963, *19,* 18–30. (a)

CHRISTIE, R., HAVEL, J., & SEIDENBERG, B. Is the f-scale irreversible? *Journal of Abnormal and Social Psychology,* 1958, *56,* 143–159.

CHRISTIE, R., & JAHODA, M. (Eds.). *Studies in the cope and method of "the authoritarian personality."* Glencoe, Ill.: Free Press, 1954.

CHRISTIE, R., & MERTON, R. K. Procedures for the sociological study of the value climate of medical schools. *Journal of Medical Education,* Part 1, 1958, *18,* 125–153.

CLEARY, R. E. *Political education in the American democracy.* Scranton, Pa.: Educational Publishers, 1971.

COBB, R. W. The belief-system perspective: An assessment of a framework. *Journal of Politics*, 1973, *35*, 121–153.

COHN, R. On interpretation of cohort and period analyses: A mathematical note. In M. W. Riley, M. Johnson, & A. Foner, (Eds.), *Aging and society: A sociology of age stratification* (Vol. 3). New York: Russell Sage, 1968.

COLDEVIN, G. The effects of mass media upon the development of transnational orientations. Unpublished doctoral dissertation, University of Washington, 1971.

COLE, G. D. H. *The future of local government*. London: Cassell, 1921.

COLE, M., & BRUNNER, J. S. Preliminaries to a theory of cultural differences. *Early childhood education*, 71st Yearbook of National Society for the Study of Education, 1972.

COLE, M., GAY, J., GLICK, J. A., & SHARP, D. W. *The cultural context of learning and thinking*. New York: Basic Books, 1971.

COLEMAN, J. S., *The adolescent society*. New York: Free Press, 1961

COLEMAN, J. S., CAMPBELL, E. Q., HOBSON, C. J., McPARTLAND, J., MOOD, A. M., WEINFELD, F. D., & YORK, R. L. *Equality of educational opportunity*. Washington, D.C.: U.S. Government Printing Office, 1966.

COLES, R. Social struggle and weariness. *Psychiatry*, 1964, *27*, 305–315.

Committee on Pre-Collegiate Education-Political Education in Political Science, *P.S.*, Summer, 1971, *3*.

COMREY, A., & NEWMEYER, J. Measurement of radicalism-conservatism. *Journal of Social Psychology*, 1965, *67*, 357–369.

COMSTOCK, G., & LINDSEY, G. Television and human behavior: The research horizon, future and present. Santa Monica, Calif.: Rand, 1975.

COMSTOCK, G. et al. *The fifth season: How television influences human behavior* (in preparation).

CONNELL, R. W. *The child's construction of politics*. Carlton, Australia: Melbourne University Press, 1971.

CONNELL, R. W. Political socialization in the American family: The evidence re-examined. *Public Opinion Quarterly*, Fall 1972, *36*, 323–333.

CONNELL, R. W., & GOOT, M. Science and ideology in American political socialization research. *Berkeley Journal of Sociology*, 1972–1973, *27*, 166–193.

CONVERSE, P. E. The nature of belief systems in mass publics. In D. Apter (Ed.), *Ideology and discontent*. Glencoe: Free Press, 1964.

CONVERSE, P. E. The concept of the normal vote. In A. Campbell et al., *Elections and the political order*. New York: Wiley, 1966.

CONVERSE, P. E. Comment: The status of non-attitudes. *American Political Science Review*, 1974, *68*, 650–660.

CONVERSE, P. E., & DUPEUX, G. Politicization of the electorate in France and the United States. *Public Opinion Quarterly*, Spring, 1962, 1–23.

CONVERSE, P. E., & SCHUMANN, H. Silent majorities and the Vietnam war. *Scientific American*, 1970, *222*, 17–25.

CONWAY, M. M., Stevens, A. J., & SMITH, R. G. The relation between media use and children's civil awareness. *Journalism Quarterly*, 1975, *52*, 531–538.

COOK, H., & JACKSON, D. Moral development of the concept of war: A cross-cultural test of a theory. Unpublished manuscript, Teacher's College, 1973.

COOK, T. J., & SCIOLI, F. P., Jr. A critique of the learning concept in political socialization research. *Social Science Quarterly, 1972, 52,* 949–962.

COOPER, P. The development of the concept of war. *Journal of Peace Research,* 1965.

COOPERSMITH, S. *The antecedents of self-esteem.* San Francisco: Freedman, 1967.

COORSIN, D. Nutrition and brain development. *Merrill-Palmer Quarterly, 1972, 18,* 177–202.

COTTRELL, F. Aging and the political system. In J. C. McKinney, (Ed.), *Aging and social policy.* New York: Appleton-Century-Crofts, 1966.

COUCH, A., & KENISTON, K. Yeasayers and naysayers, agreeing response set as a personality variable. *Journal of Abnormal and Social Psychology, 1960, 60,* 151–174.

COWAN, P. A., LANGER, J., HEAVENRICH, J., & NATHANSON, M. Social learning and Piaget's cognitive theory of moral development. *Journal of Personality and Social Psychology, 1969, 2,* 261–274.

COWDRY, R. W., KENISTON, K., & CABIN, S. The war and military obligation: Private attitudes and public action. *Journal of Personality, 1970, 38,* 529–549.

COX, H. *The feast of fools.* Cambridge: Harvard University Press, 1969.

CRAGG, B. G. The development of cortical synapses during starvation in the rat. *Brain, 1972, 95,* 143–150.

CRESPI, I. Structural sources of the George Wallace constituency. *Social Science Quarterly, 1971, 52,* 115–132.

CRITTENDEN, J. A. Aging and party affiliation. *Public Opinion Quarterly, 1962, 26,* 648–657.

CRONBACH, L. Response sets and test validity. *Educational and Psychological Measurement, 1946, 6,* 151–174.

CRONIN, J. N., DANIELS, A., HURLEY, A., KROCH, A., & WEBER, R. Race, class and intelligence: A critical look at the I.Q. controversy. *International Journal of Mental Health, 1975, 3,* 46–132.

CROTLY, W. J. Democratic consensual norms and the college student. *Sociology of Education, 1967, 40,* 200–218.

CROWLEY, P. M. Effect of training upon objectivity of moral judgment in grade school children. In R. C. Johnson, P. R. Dokecki, & O. H. Mowrer (Eds.), *Conscience, contract and social reality.* New York: Holt, Rinehart & Winston, 1972.

CUMMING, E. Further thoughts on the theory of disengagement. *International Social Science, 1963, 15,* 377–393.

CUMMING, E., & HENRY, W. *Growing old.* New York: Basic Books, 1961.

CUNDY, D. T. *Partisanship and political attitude formation: A social-learning model.* Unpublished doctoral dissertation in Political Science Department, Eugene, Oreg., 1975.

CUTLER, N. E. *The alternative effects of generations and aging upon political behavior: A cohort analysis of American attitudes toward foreign policy, 1946–1966.* Oak Ridge: Oak Ridge National Laboratory, ORNL-4321, 1968.

CUTLER, N. E. Generation, maturation, and party affiliation: A cohort analysis. *Public Opinion Quarterly,* 1970, 33, 583–588. (a)

CUTLER, N. E. Generational succession as a source of foreign policy attitudes: A cohort analysis of American opinion, 1946–1966. *Journal of Peace Research,* 1970, 7, 33–47. (b)

CUTLER, N. E. Aging and generations in politics: The conflict of explanations and inference. In A. R. Wilcox (Ed.), *Public opinion and political attitudes: A reader.* New York: Wiley, 1974. (a)

CUTLER, N. E. The effects of subjective age identification among old and young: A nation-wide study of political, economic, and social attitudes. Paper presented at 27th annual meeting of Gerontological Society, Portland, Ore., 1974. (b)

CUTLER, N. E. Toward a political generations conception of political socialization. In D. C. Schwartz & S. K. Schwartz (Eds.), *New directions in political socialization.* New York: Free Press, 1975. (a)

CUTLER, N. E. Review of M. Kent Jennings and Richard G. Niemi, The political character of adolescence: The influence of families and schools. *Journal of Politics,* 1975, 37, 600–601. (b)

CUTLER, N. E. Chronological age, subjective age, and social welfare orientations: The organization of attitudes toward society, economics, and politics. Paper delivered at 10th International Congress of Gerontology, Jerusalem, Israel, June 22–27, 1975. (c)

CUTLER, N. E. Demographic, social psychological, and political factors in the politics of age: A call for research in political gerontology. *American Political Science Review,* 1977, 71.

CUTLER, N. E., & BENGTSON, V. L. Age and political alienation: Maturation, generation, and period effects. *Annals of the American Academy of Political and Social Science,* 1974, 415, 160–175.

CUTLER, N. E., & DANOWSKI, J. A. Process gratification vs. content gratification in mass communication behavior: A cohort analysis of age changes in political information-seeking. Paper presented at annual meeting of Pacific Chapter of American Association for Public Opinion research, Los Angeles, 1975.

CUTLER, N. E., & SCHMIDHAUSER, J. R. Age and political behavior. In D. Woodruff & J. Birren (Eds.), *Aging: Scientific perspectives and social issues.* New York: D. Van Nostrand, 1975.

CUTLER, S. J., & KAUFMAN, R. L. Cohort changes in political attitudes: Tolerance of ideological nonconformity. *Public Opinion Quarterly,* 1975, 39, 69–81.

DAHL, R. The behavioral approach in political science: Epitaph for a monument to a successful protest. *American Political Science Review,* 1961, 55, 763–772. (a)

DAHL, R. *Who governs?* New Haven: Yale University Press, 1961. (b)

DAHL, R. *After the revolution.* New Haven: Yale University Press, 1970.

DANOWSKI, J. A., & CUTLER, N. E. "Political Information, Mass Media Use in Early Adulthood, and Political Socialization: Seeking Clarity Through Cohort Curves," in F. Gerald Kline (ed.), *Time Series Research in Communication.* Beverly Hills: Sage Publications, 1977 (forthcoming).

DANZIGER, K. *Socialization.* Baltimore: Penguin, 1971.

DAVIES, J. C. Toward a theory of revolution. *American Sociological Review,* 1962, *27,* 5–19.

DAVIES, J. C. *Human nature in politics.* New York: Wiley, 1963.

DAVIES, J. C. The family's role in political socialization. *Annals of the American Academy of Political and Social Science,* September 1965, *361.*

DAVIES, J. C. The priority of human needs and the stages of political development. In J. R. Pennock (Ed.), *Human nature and politics.* New York: Lieber-Atherton, 1976.

DAVIS, K. The myth of functional analysis as a special method in sociology and anthropology. *American Sociological Review,* 1959, *24,* 757–773.

DAVIS, M., & VERBA, S. Party affiliation and international opinions in Britain and France, 1947–1956. *Public Opinion Quarterly,* Winter 1960, *24,* 590–604.

DAWSON, R. E., & PREWITT, K. *Political socialization.* Boston: Little, Brown, 1969.

DAY, D. D. A scale of militarism-pacifism. *Journal of Educational Psychology,* 1931, *22,* 96–111.

DAY, D. D., & QUACKENBUSH, O. F. Attitudes toward defensive, cooperative and aggressive war. *Journal of Social Psychology,* 1942, *14,* 11–20.

DELIUS, J. D. The ontogeny of behavior. In F. O. Schmitt et al. (Eds.), *The neurosciences: Second study program.* New York: Rockefeller University Press, 1970.

DEMBER, W. N. Response by the rat to environmental change. *Journal of Comparative Physiological Psychology,* 1956, *49,* 93–95.

DENHARDT, R. B. The organization as a political system. *Western Political Science Quarterly,* December 1971, *14*(4).

DENNIS, J. Major problems of political socialization research. *Midwest Journal of Political Science,* 1968, *12,* 85–114.

DENNIS, J. Political learning in childhood and adolescence. Technical report No. 98. Madison: University of Wisconsin Research and Development Center for Cognitive Learning, 1969.

DENNIS, J. Future work on political socialization. In J. Dennis (Ed.), *Socialization to politics.* New York: Wiley, 1973. (c)

DENNIS, J. Political socialization research: A bibliography. *Sage professional papers in politics* (Vol. 1), Series No. 04-002 (Beverly Hills, 1973). (b)

DENNIS, J. (Ed.). *Socialization to politics.* New York: Wiley, 1973. (a)

DENNIS, J., LINDBERG, L., & McCRONE, D. Support for nation and government among English children. *British Journal of Political Science,* 1971, *1,* 25–48.

DENNIS, J., LINDBERG, L., McCRONE, D., & STIEFBOLD, R. Political socialization to democratic orientations in four western systems. *Comparative Political Studies,* 1968, *1,* 71–101.

DENNIS, J., & McCRONE, D. Preadult development of political party identification in western democracies. *Comparative Political Studies,* 1970, *3,* 243–263.

DENNIS, J., & WEBSTER, C. Children's images of the President and of government in 1962 and 1974. *American Politics Quarterly,* 1975, *3,* 386–405.

DERVIN, B., & GREENBERG, B. The communication environment of the urban poor. In F. G. Kline & P. J. Tichenor (Eds.), *Current Perspectives in Mass Communication Research.* Beverly Hills: Sage Publications, 1972.

DESHEN, S. A. *Immigrant voters in Israel*. North Manchester, Eng.: Manchester University Press, 1970.

DE SOLA POOL, I., KELLER, S., & BAUER, R. A. The influence of foreign travel on political attitudes of American businessmen. *Public Opinion Quarterly,* 1956, *20,* 161–175.

DEUTSCH, M. Conflicts: Productive or destructive. *Journal of Social Issues,* 1969, *25,* 7–41.

DEUTSCH, M., & GERARD, H. A study of normative and informational social influences upon individual judgment. *Journal of Abnormal and Social Psychology,* 1955, *51,* 629–136.

DEVOS, G. A. National character. In David Sills (Ed.), *International encyclopedia of the social sciences,* Vol. 11. New York: Macmillan-Free Press, 1968.

DEVOS, G. A., & HIPPLES, A. E. Cultural psychology: Comparative studies of human behavior. In G. Lindzey & E. Aronson (Eds.), *Handbook of social psychology* (Vol. 4). (2nd ed.). Reading, Mass.: Addison-Wesley, 1969.

DEWEY, J. *Moral principles in education*. New York: Houghton Mifflin, 1909.

DIPALMA, G., & MCCLOSKY, H. Personality and conformity: The learning of political attitudes. *American Political Science Review,* 1970, *64,* 1054–1073.

DIRENZO, G. J. Professional politicians and personality structures. *American Journal of Sociology,* 1967, *73,* 217–225.

DIRENZO, G. J. Dogmatism and presidential preferences in the 1964 elections. *Psychological Reports,* 1968, *22,* 1197–1202.

DOBZHANSKY, T. *Genetic diversity and human equality*. New York: Basic Books, 1973.

DODGE, R., & UYEKI, E. Political affiliation and imagery across two related generations. *Midwest Journal of Political Science,* 1962, *7,* 277–276.

DOLLARD, J. *Caste and class in a southern town* (3rd ed.). Garden City, N.Y.: Doubleday, 1957.

DOMINICK, J. R. Television and political socialization. *Educational Broadcasting Review,* 1972, *6,* 48–56.

DONLEY, R. E., & WINTER, D. G. Measuring the motives of public officials at a distance: An exploratory study of American Presidents. *Behavioral Science,* 1970, *15,* 227–236.

DOUGLASS, E. B., CLEVELAND, W. P., & MADDOX, G. L. Political attitudes, age, and aging: A cohort analysis of archival data. *Journal of Gerontology,* 1974, *29,* (6), 666–675.

DREEBEN, R. *On what is learned in school*. Reading, Mass.: Addison-Wesley, 1968.

DREEBEN, R. Schooling and authority: Comments on the unstudied curriculum. In. N. V. Overly (Ed.), *The unstudied curriculum*. Washington, D. C.: Association for Supervision & Curriculum Development, 1970.

DREITZEL, H. Introduction. In H. Dreitzel (Ed.), *Childhood and socialization*. New York: Macmillan, 1973.

DUNLAP, R. A comment on "Multiversity, university size, university quality, and student protest: An empirical study." *American Sociological Review,* 1970, *35,* 525–528.

DURBIN, E. F. M., & BOWLBY, J. *Personal aggressiveness and war*. New York: Columbia University Press, 1950.

DURKHEIM, E. *Moral education*. New York: Free Press, 1961.

EAGLY, A. H., & MANIS, M. Evaluation of message and communicator as a function of involvement. *Journal of Personality and Social Psychology*, 1966, *3*, 483–485.

EASTON, D. Harold Lasswell: Policy scientist for a democratic society. *Journal of Politics*, 1950, *12*, 450–477.

EASTON, D. *The political system*. New York: Knopf, 1953.

EASTON, D. *A system analysis of political life*. New York: Wiley, 1965.

EASTON, D. The theoretical relevance of political socialization. *Canadian Journal of Political Science*, 1968, *1*, 125–146.

EASTON, D., & DENNIS, J. The child's image of government. *Annals of the American Academy of Political and Social Science*, September 1965, *361*, 40–57.

EASTON, D., & DENNIS, J. *Children in the political system*. New York: McGraw-Hill, 1969.

EASTON, D., & HESS, R. The child's political world. *Midwest Journal of Political Science*, 1962, *6*, 229–246.

ECKSTEIN, H. Authority structures: A structural basis for political inquiry. *American Political Science Review*, 1973, *67*, 1142–1161.

ECKSTEIN, R. Psychoanalysis and education for the facilitation of positive human qualities. *Journal of Social Issues*, 1972, *28*, 71–86.

EDDY, E. M. Attitudes toward desegregation among southern students on a northern campus. *Journal of Social Psychology*, 1964, *62*, 285–301.

EDEL, A. Scientific research and moral judgment: A philosophical perspective. Paper presented at Conference on Studies on the Acquisition and Development Values, Boston, May 1968.

EDELSTEIN, A. S., & TEFFT, D. P. Media credibility and respondent credulity with respect to Watergate. *Communication Research*, 1974, *1*, 426–439.

Education Commission of the States. *National assessment of educational progress: Citizenship*. Washington, D.C.: U. S. Government Printing Office, 1970.

Education Commission of the States. *National assessment of educational progress: Political knowledge and attitudes*. Washington, D.C.: U.S. Government Printing Office, 1973.

Education on war, peace, conflict and change. *Intercom*, Fall 1970.

EDWARDS, L. P. *The natural history of revolutions*. Chicago: University of Chicago Press, 1927.

EDWARDS, W. The theory of decision-making. *Psychological Bulletin*, 1954, *5*, 380–417.

EHMAN, L. H. An analysis of the relationship of selected educational variables with the political socialization of high school students. *American Educational Research Journal*, November 1969, *4*, 559–580.

EISENBERG, L. The human nature of human nature. In A. Montagu (Ed.), *Man and aggression*. New York: Oxford, 1973.

EISENSTADT, S. N. The process of absorption of immigrants in Israel. *Human Relations*, 1952, *5*, 223–246.

EISENSTADT, S. N. *From generation to generation*. New York: Free Press, 1956.

EISENSTADT, S. N., WEINTRAUB, D., & TOREN, N. *Analysis of processes of role change*. Jerusalem: Israel University Press, 1967.

EKEHAMMER, B. Interactionism in personality from a historical perspective. *Psychological Bulletin*, 1974, *81*, 1026–1048.

ELDER, G. H. Democratic parent-youth relations in cross-national perspective. *Social Science Quarterly*, September 1968, *54* (42), 216–228.

ELDER, G. H. *Children of the Great Depression*. Chicago: University of Chicago Press, 1974.

ELKINS, S. *Slavery*. Chicago: University of Chicago Press, 1968.

ELMS, A. C. Psychological factors in right-wing extremism. In R. Schoenberger (Ed.), *The American right wing*. New York: Holt, Rinehart, & Winston, 1969.

ENDLER, N. S. The person versus the situation—a pseudo issue? A response to Alker. *Journal of Personality*, 1973, *41*, 287–303.

ENGELS, F. *The origin of the family*. Chicago: Kerr, 1902.

ENGLE, S. H., MEHLINGER H. D., & PATRICK, J. J. *Final report of the High School Curriculum Center in Government*. Washington, D.C.: USOE, 1972.

ENGSTROM, R. L. Race and compliance: Differential political socialization. *Polity*, 1970, *3*, 100–111.

ENTWISTLE, H. *Political education in a democracy*. London: Routledge & Kegan Paul, 1971.

ERBE, W. Social involvement and political activity: A replication and elaboration. *American Sociological Review*, 1964, *29*, 198–215.

ERIKSON, E. H. *Young man Luther*. New York: Norton, 1958.

ERIKSON, E. H. *Childhood and society* (2nd ed.) New York: Norton, 1963.

ERIKSON, E. H. *Identity, youth and crisis*. New York: Vintage, 1968.

ERIKSON, E. H. *Gandhi's truth*. New York: Norton, 1969.

ESCALONA, S. K. Children and the threat of nuclear war. In M. Schwebel (Ed.), *Behavioral science and human survival*. Palo Alto, Calif.: Science & Behavioral Books, 1965.

ETZIONI, A. *Complex organizations*. New York: Holt, Rinehart & Winston, 1961.

ETZIONI, A. *The active society*. New York: Free Press, 1968.

ETZIONI, A. *The genetic fix*. New York: Macmillan, 1973.

EULAU, H. Skill specialization and consultative commonwealth. *American Political Science Review*, 1973, *67*, 169–191.

EULAU, H., & QUINLEY, H. *State officials and higher education*. New York: McGraw-Hill, 1970.

EULAU, H., & SCHNEIDER, P. The dimensions of political involvement. *Public Opinion Quarterly*, 1956, *20*, 128–142.

EULAU, H., & SPRAGUE, J. *Lawyers in politics*. Indianapolis: Bobbs-Merrill, 1964.

EVAN, W. M. Cohort analysis of survey data: A procedure for studying longterm opinion change. *Public Opinion Quarterly*, 1959, *23*, 63–72.

EWING, D. *The managerial mind*. Glencoe, Ill.: Free Press, 1964.

EYSENCK, H. J. *The psychology of politics*. London: Routledge & Kegan Paul, 1954.

EYSENCK, H. J. The inheritance of extroversion-introversion. *Acta Psychologica*, 1956, *12*, 95–110.

FAIA, M. Alienation, structural strain, and political deviancy: A test of Merton's hypothesis. *Social Problems,* 1967, *14,* 389–413.

FANON, F. *Wretched of the earth.* New York: Grove Press, 1968.

FEATHER, N. T. Educational choice and student attitudes in relation to terminal and instrumental values. *Australian Journal of Psychology,* 1970, *22,* 127–144.

FEILLEN, A. The functions of informal groups in legislative institutions. *Journal of Politics,* 1962, *24,* 72–91.

FEIN, L. G. *The changing school scene: Challenge to psychology.* New York: Wiley, 1974.

FELDMAN, K., & NEWCOMB, T. *The impact of college on students: An analysis of four decades of research.* San Francisco: Jossey-Bass, 1971.

FENNO, R. F., JR. The House Appropriations Committee as a political system, *American Political Science Review,* 1962, *56,* 310–324.

FENTON, E. *Teaching the new social studies in secondary schools.* New York: Holt, Rinehart & Winston, 1966.

FENTON, E., PENNA, A. N., & SCHULTZ, M. *Comparative political systems: An inquiry approach.* New York: Holt, Rinehart & Winston, 1973.

FESTINGER, L. *A theory of cognitive dissonance.* Stanford: Stanford University Press, 1957.

FESTINGER, L., RIECKEN, H. W., & SCHACHTER, S. S. *When prophecy fails* (2nd ed.), reprint from 1956. New York: Harper & Row, 1964.

FEUER, L. *The conflict of generations.* New York: Basic Books, 1969.

FEUER, L. Student unrest in the United States, *Annals of the American Academy of Political Science,* 1972, 170–182.

FINER, S. *The man on horseback.* New York: Praeger, 1962.

FINIFTER, A. W. Dimensions of political alienation. *American Political Science Review,* 1970, *64,* 389–410.

FINIFTER, A. W. Emigration from the United States: An exploratory analysis. Paper presented at Conference on Public Support, Madison, 1973.

FINIFTER, A. W. The friendship group as a protective environment for political deviants. *American Political Science Review,* June 1974, *68,* 607–625.

FISHKIN, J., KENNISTON, K., & MACKINNON, C. Moral reasoning and political ideology. *Journal of Personality and Social Psychology,* 1973, *27,* 109–119.

FISHMAN, J. R., & SOLOMON, F. Youth and peace: A psychological study of student peace demonstrators in Washington, D.C. *Journal of Social Issues,* 1964, *20* (4), 54–73. (a)

FISHMAN, J. R., & SOLOMON, F. Youth and social action: An introduction. *Journal of Social Issues,* 1964, *20* (4), 1–27. (b)

FLACKS, R. The liberated generation: An exploration of the roots of student protest. *Journal of Social Issues,* 1969, *23,* 52–75.

FLACKS, R. The revolt of the advantaged: Explorations of the roots of student protest. In R. S. Sigel (Ed.), *Learning about politics: A reader in political socialization.* New York: Random House, 1970. (a)

FLACKS, R. Who protests: The social bases of the student movement. In J. Foster & D.

Long (Eds.), Protest! Student activism in America. New York: Morrow, 1970. (b)

FLAVELL, J. H. *The developmental psychology of Jean Piaget.* Princeton: Van Nostrand, 1963.

FLUGEL, J. C. *Man, morals and society: A psychoanalytic study.* New York: International Universities Press, 1945.

FONER, A. Age stratification and age conflict in political life. *American Sociological Review,* 1974, *39,* 187–196.

FONTANA, A. F., & NOEL, B. Moral reasoning in the university. *Journal of Personality and Social Psychology,* 1973, *27,* 419–429.

FOOTE, N. The old generation and the new. In E. Ginzberg (Ed.), *The nation's children* (Vol. 3). New York: Columbia University Press, 1960.

FRANK, J. D. *Sanity and survival: Psychological aspects of war and peace.* New York: Random House, 1967.

FREEDMAN, D. G. An ethological approach to the genetic study of human behavior. In S. Vandenberg (Ed.), *Method and goals in human behavior genetics.* New York: Academic Press, 1965.

FREEDMAN, J. L., & SEARS, D. O. Selective exposure. In L. Berkowitz (ed.), *Advances in social psychology* (Vol. 2). New York: Academic Press, 1965.

FREIDENBERG, E. Z. Current patterns of a generational conflict. *Journal of Social Issues,* 1969, *25,* 21–48.

FREUD, A., & BURLINGHAM, D. *War and children.* New York: Medical War Books, 1944.

FREUD, S. *Group psychology and the analysis of the ego.* London: Hogarth Press, 1948.

FREUD, S. *Civilization and its discontents.* New York: Norton, 1961. (a)

FREUD, S. The ego and the super-ego. 1923–1925. In *The complete psychological works of Sigmund Freud* (Vol. 19). London: Hogarth Press, 1961. (b)

FREUD, S. Anxiety and instinctual life. 1932–1936. In *The complete psychological works of Sigmund Freud* (Vol. 22). London: Hogarth Press, 1964.

FREUD, S. Why war? 1932–1936. In *The complete psychological works of Sigmund Freud* (Vol. 22). London: Hogarth Press, 1964.

FREUD, S. *New introductory lectures on psychoanalysis,* trans, by W.J.H. Sprott. New York: Wiley, 1968 (originally published 1933).

FRIEDMAN, D. *A comparison of children's moral judgments of the President, adults, and children.* In preparation.

FRIEDSON, E. *The profession of medicine.* New York: Dodd Mead, 1970.

FROMAN, L. A. Personality and political socialization. *Journal of Politics,* 1961, *23,* 341–352.

FROMAN, L. A. Learning political attitudes. *Western Political Quarterly,* 1962, *15,* 304–313. (a)

FROMAN, L. A., JR. *People and politics.* Englewood Cliffs, N.J.: Prentice-Hall, 1962. (b)

FROMM, E. *Escape from freedom.* New York: Holt, Rinehart & Winston, 1941.

FUCHS, L. H. American Jews and the presidential vote. In L. H. Fuchs (Ed.), *American ethnic politics.* New York: Harper Torchbooks, 1968.

GAGNE, R. M. *The conditions of learning.* New York: Holt, Rinehart & Winston, 1965.

GAGNE, R. M., & BRIGGS, L. J. *Principles of instructional design.* New York: Holt, Rinehart & Winston, 1974.

GALBRAITH, R. E., & JONES, T. M. Teaching strategies for moral dilemmas. *Social Education,* January 1975, *39.*

GALENSON, W. *The Danish system of labor relations.* Cambridge: Harvard University Press, 1952.

GALLATIN, J., & ADELSON, J. Individual rights and the public good: A cross-national study of adolescents. *Comparative Political Studies,* 1970, *3,* 226–243.

GALLATIN, J., & ADELSON, J. Legal guarantees of individual freedom: A cross-national study of the development of political thought. *Journal of Social Issues,* 1971, *27* (2).

GAMSON, W. *Power and discontent.* Homewood, Ill.: Dorsey, 1968.

GANONG, W. F., *Review of medical physiology* (4th ed.). Los Altos, Calif.: Lange, 1969.

GARCEAU, O. *The political life of the American Medical Association.* Cambridge: Harvard University Press, 1941.

GARCIA, F. C. Orientations of Mexican-American and Anglo children toward the U.S. political community. *Social Science Quarterly,* 1973, *53,* 814–829.

GARDNER, B. B. *Human relations in industry.* Chicago: Irwin, 1945.

GARDNER, G. Child behavior in a nation at war. *Mental Hygiene,* 1943, *27,* 353–369.

GEBER, M. L'environment et le développement des enfants africains. *Enfance* (Paris), June–October 1973, 3–4, 145–174.

GEBER, M., & DEAN, R. F. A. Psychological factors in the etiology of kwashiorkor. *Bulletin of the World Health Organization,* 1955, *12* (3), 471–475.

GEERTZ, C. *Old societies and new states.* Chicago: University of Chicago Press, 1963.

GEIGER, K. Changing political attitudes in a totalitarian society: A case study of the role of the family. *World Politics,* January 1956, *8,* 187–205.

GELINEAUX, V. A., & KANTOR, D. Pro-social commitment among college students. *Journal of Social Issues,* 1964, *20,* 112–130.

GELLER, J. D., & HOWARD, G. Some sociophysical characteristics of student political activists. *Journal of Applied Social Psychology,* 1972, *2,* 114–137.

GEORGE, A., & GEORGE, J. *Woodrow Wilson and Colonel House.* New York: Dover, 1956.

GERARD, H. B., Wilhelmy, R. A., & CONOLLEY, E. S. Conformity and group size. *Journal of Personality and Social Psychology,* 1965, *1,* 413–424.

GERGEN, K. J. The effects of interaction goals and personalistic feedback on the presentation of self. *Journal of Personality and Social Psychology,* 1968, *8,* 79–82.

GERGEN, K. J. Social psychology as history. *Journal of Personality and Social Psychology,* 1973, *26,* 309–320.

GERGEN, K. J. The decline of character: Socialization and self-consistency. In G. Di-Renzo (Ed.), *Social Change and Social Character.* Westport, Conn.: Greenwood Press, 1977.

GERGEN, K. J. & GERGEN, M. M. Higher education: Missing in action. *College Student Personnel Abstracts,* Summer, 1971.

GERGEN, K. J., & GIBBS, M. S. Role playing and modifying the self-concept. Paper presented at annual meetings of American Psychological Association, Chicago, 1965.

GERGEN, K. J., & MARACEK, J. *The psychology of self-esteem*. General Learning Corporation Module. Morristown, N.J.: General Learning Press, 1976.

GERGEN, K. J., & MORSE, S. J. Self-consistency: Measurement and validation. *Proceedings, 75th Annual Convention of American Psychological Association*, Washington, D.C., 1967, 207–208.

GERWIRTZ, J. L. Mechanisms of social learning: Some roles of stimulation and behavior in early development. In D. A. Goslin (Ed.), *Handbook of socialization theory and research*. Chicago: Rand McNally, 1969.

GESCHWENDER, J. Status discrepancy and prejudice reconsidered. *American Journal of Sociology*, 1970, *75*, 863–865.

GIBSON, Q. *The logic of social enquiry*. London: Routledge & Kegan Paul, 1961.

GILLESPIE, J. A. Relationships between high school and college instruction. *Teaching Political Science*, July 1975, *2*.

GILLESPIE, J. A., & PATRICK, J. J. *Comparing political experiences*. Washington, D.C.: American Political Science Association, 1974.

GLASER, B. *Organizational scientists: Their professional careers*. Indianapolis: Bobbs-Merrill, 1964.

GLASER, W. The family and voting turnout. *Public Opinion Quarterly*, 1959, *23*, 563–569.

GLASER, W. Doctors and politics. *American Journal of Sociology*, 1960, *66*, 230–245.

GLAZER, N., & MOYNIHAN, D. P. *Beyond the melting pot*. Cambridge: MIT Press, 1963.

GLENN, N. D. Aging, disengagement, and opinionation. *Public Opinion Quarterly*, 1969.

GLENN, N. D. Problems of comparability in trend studies with opinion poll data. *Public Opinion Quarterly*, 1970, *34*, 82–91.

GLENN, N. D. Sources of the shift to political independence: Some evidence from a cohort analysis. *Social Science Quarterly*, 1972, *53*, 494–519.

GLENN, N.D. Cohort analysts' futile quest: Statistical attempts to separate age, period, and cohort effects. *American Sociological Review*, 1976, *41*, 900–904.

GLENN, N. D., & GRIMES, M. Aging, voting, and political interest. *American Sociological Review*, 1968, *33*, 563–575.

GLENN, N. D., & HEFNER, T. Further evidence on aging and party identification. *Public Opinion Quarterly*, 1972, *36*, 31–47.

GLENN, N. D., & ZODY, R. E. Cohort analysis with national survey data. *Gerontologist*, 1970, *10*, Part 1, 233–240.

GLIDEWELL, J. C., KANTOR, M. C., SMITH, L. M., & STRINGER, L. A. Socialization and social structure in the classroom. In M. L. Hoffman & L. S. Hoffman (Eds.), *Review of child development research* (Vol. 2). New York: Russell Sage Foundation, 1966.

GODWIN, W. F., & RESTLE, F. The road to agreement, subgroup pressures in small group consensus processes. *Journal of Personality and Social Psychology*, 1974, *30*, 500–501.

GOFFMAN, E. *Frame analysis*. New York: Colophon, 1974.

GOLDBERG, A. Discerning a causal pattern among data on voting behavior. *American Political Science Review*, 1966, *60*, 913–922.

GOLDBERG, A. Social determinism and rationality as bases of party identification. *American Political Science Review*, 1969, *63*, 5–25.

GOLDHAMER, H. *The Soviet soldier: Soviet military management at the troop level.* New York: Crane, Russak, 1975.

GOLDMAN-EISLER, F. *Psycholinguistics: Experiments in spontaneous speech.* New York: Academic Press, 1968.

GOLDRICH, D. Political organization and the politicization of the Poblador. *Comparative Political Studies*, July 1970, *3*, 176–202.

GOLDSCHMIDT, J., GERGEN, M., QUIGLEY, K., & GERGEN, K. J. The women's liberation movement: Attitudes and action. *Journal of Personality*, 1974, *42*, 601–617.

GORDON, M. *Assimilation in American life.* Oxford, Eng.: Oxford University Press, 1963.

GORDON, R. Moral values and analytic insights. *British Journal of Medical Psychology*, 1973, *46*, 1–11.

GORE, P. M., & ROTTER, J. B. A personality correlate of social action. *Journal of Personality*, 1963, *31*, 58–64.

GORER, G., & RICKMAN, J. *The people of Great Russia.* London: Cresset Press, 1949.

GOSLIN, D. A. *The search for ability: Standardized testing in social perspective.* New York: Russell Sage, 1963.

GOSLIN, D. A. Introduction. In D. A. Goslin (Ed.), *Handbook of socialization theory and practice.* Chicago: Rand McNally, 1969.

GOSNELL, H. P. *Getting out the vote.* Chicago: University of Chicago Press, 1927.

GOUGH, H. G. A sociological theory of psychopathy. *American Journal of Sociology*, 1949, *53*, 359–366.

GOUGH, H. G., & PETTERSON, D. R. The identification and measure of predispositional factors in crime and delinquency. *Journal of Consulting Psychology*, 1960, *24*, 23–30.

GOY, R. W. Early hormonal influences on the development of sexual and sex-related behavior. In F. O. Schmitt et al. (Eds.), *The neurosciences: Second study program.* New York: Rockefeller University Press, 1970.

GOY, R. W., & GOLDFOOT, D. A. Experiential and hormonal factors influencing development of sexual behavior in the male rhesus monkey. In F. O. Schmitt & F. G. Worden (Eds.), *The neurosciences: Third study program.* Cambridge: MIT Press, 1974.

GRAHAM, D. *Moral learning and development: Theory and research.* New York: Wiley-Interscience, 1972.

GREELEY, A. M. *Ethnicity in the United States.* New York: Wiley, 1974.

GREENBERG, D. S. Venturing into politics: Scientists and engineers in election campaigns. In W. Nelson (Ed.), *The politics of science.* Oxford, Eng.: Oxford University Press, 1968.

GREENBERG, E. S. *Political socialization.* New York: Atherton, 1970.

GREENBERG, E. S. Children and government: A comparison across racial lines. *Midwest Journal of Political Science*, 1970, *14*, 249–279.

GREENFIELD, P. M., & BRUNER, J. S. Culture and cognitive growth. *International Journal of Psychology*, 1966, *1*, 89–107.

GREENSTEIN, F. I. The benevolent leader: Children's images of political authority. *American Political Science Review*, 1960, *54*, 934–943.

GREENSTEIN, F. I. More on children's images of the President. *Public Opinion Quarterly*, 1961, *25*, 648–654. (b)

GREENSTEIN, F. I. Sex-related political differences in childhood. *Journal of Politics*, 1961, *23*, 353–371. (a)

GREENSTEIN, F. I. *Children and politics*. New Haven: Yale University Press, 1965. (b)

GREENSTEIN, F. I. Personality and political socialization: The theories of authoritarian and democratic character. *Annals of the American Academy of Political and Social Science*, 1965, *361*, 81–95. (a)

GREENSTEIN, F. I. Political socialization. In D. L. Sills (Ed.), *International encyclopedia of the social sciences*. New York: Macmillan and Free Press, 1968.

GREENSTEIN, F. I. *Personality and politics*. Chicago: Markham, 1969.

GREENSTEIN, F. I. French, British, and American child's images of government and politics. Paper prepared for delivery at meeting of Northeast Political Science Association, November 13–14, 1970. (b)

GREENSTEIN, F. I. A note on the ambiguity of "political socialization": Definitions, criticisms, and strategies of inquiry. *Journal of Politics*, 1970, 32, 969–978. (a)

GREENSTEIN, F. I. Children's images of political leaders in three democracies: The benevolent leader revisited. Paper prepared for delivery at 1973 annual meeting of American Political Science Association, New Orleans, La., 1973.

GREENSTEIN, F. I. Letter to the Editor, *American Political Science Review*, 1974, *68*, 720–722.

GREENSTEIN, F. I. The benevolent leader revisited: Children's images in three democracies. *American Political Science Review*, 1975, *64*, 1371–1398.

GREENSTEIN, F. I., & TARROW, S. An approach to the study of comparative political socialization: The use of a semi-projective technique. Paper prepared for delivery at 65th meeting of American Political Science Association, New York, September 2–6, 1969.

GREENSTEIN, F. I., & TARROW, S. Children and politics in Britain, France and the United States. *Youth and Society*, 1970, 2. (b)

GREENSTEIN, F. I., & TARROW, S. Political orientations of children: The use of a semi-projective technique in three nations. Beverly Hills: Sage Publications, 1970. (a)

GREGOR, A. J. *An introduction to meta-politcs: A brief inquiry into the conceptual language of political science*. New York: Free Press, 1971.

GRINDER, R. Relations between behavioral and cognitive dimensions of conscience in middle childhood. *Child Development*, 1964, *35*, 381–392.

GROSS N., MASON, W. S., & MCEACHERN, A. W. *Explorations in role analysis*. New York: Wiley, 1958.

GRUPP, F. W., JR. The political perspectives of Birch society members. In R. Schoenberger (Ed.), *The American right wing*. New York: Holt, Rinehart & Winston, 1969.

GRUPP, F. W., JR. Personal satisfaction derived from membership in the John Birch Society. *Western Political Quarterly*, 1971, *24*, 79–83.

GUETZKOW, H. *Multiple loyalties: Theoretical approach to a problem in international organization*. Princeton: Center for Research on World Political Institutions, Woodrow Wilson School, 1955.

Guilford, J. P. The structure of intellect. *Psychological Bulletin,* 1956, *53,* 267–293.

Guilford, J. P. Three faces of intellect. *American Psychologist,* 1959, *14,* 469–479.

Guilford, J. P. *The nature of human intelligence.* New York: McGraw-Hill, 1967.

Guilford, J. P. *Intelligence, creativity and their educational implications.* San Diego: Robert Knopf, 1968.

Guitar, M. We're teaching our children that violence is fun. In O. Larsen (Ed.), *Violence and the mass media.* New York: Harper & Row, 1968.

Guskin, A. E., & Guskin, S. *A social psychology of education.* Reading, Mass.: Addison-Wesley, 1970.

Gutkin, D. C. The effect of systematic story changes on intentionality in children's moral judgments. *Child Development,* 1972, *43,* 187–196.

Haan, N. Moral redefinition in families as the critical aspect of the generational gap. *Youth and Society,* 1971, *2,* 259–282.

Haan, N., Smith, M. B., & Block, J. Moral reasoning of young adults: Political-social behavior, family background, and personality correlates. *Journal of Personality and Social Psychology,* 1968, *10,* 183–201.

Haan, N., Straud, J., & Holstein, C. Moral and ego stages in relationship to ego processes: A study of "hippies." *Journal of Personality,* 1973, *41,* 596–612.

Haavelsrud, M. Views on war and peace among students in West German public schools. *Journal of Peace Research,* 1970, *7,* 99–120.

Haavelsrud, M. Development of concepts related to war and peace: Impact of informational environment. Unpublished paper presented at Pacific University World Order Workshop, Pacific Grove, Oreg., 1971. (a)

Haavelsrud, M. Impact of informational environment in the development of concepts related to peace and war. Paper presented at annual convention of American Psychological Association, Washington, D.C., 1971. (c)

Haavelsrud, M. Impact of the communication structure on American and Canadian pre-adults orientations to war and peace. Paper presented at National Council for Social Studies meeting, Denver, 1971. (b)

Hagstrom, W. *The scientific community.* New York: Basic Books, 1965.

Hall, C. S. *A primer of Freudian psychology.* New York: Mentor Books, 1954.

Hall, R. *Occupations and the social structure.* Englewood Cliffs, N.J.: Prentice-Hall, 1969.

Halpern, S. *Police association and department leaders.* Lexington, Mass.: Lexington Books, 1974.

Hampden-Turner, C. *Radical man: The process of psycho-social development.* Cambridge: Schenkman, 1970.

Hancock, A., & Willmot, P. (Eds.) *The social workers.* London: BBC Press, 1965.

Handlin, O. *The uprooted: The epic story of the great migrations that made the American people.* Boston: Atlantic-Little, Brown, 1951.

Harlow, H. F. The nature of love. *American Psychologist,* December 1958, *13,* 673–685.

Harlow, H. F., & Harlow, M. K. Social deprivation in monkeys. *Scientific American,* November 1962, *207* (5), 136–146.

Harlow, H. F., & Harlow, M. K. The affectational systems. In A. M. Schier, H. F.

Harlow, & F. Stollnitz (Eds.), *Behavior of nonhuman primates: Modern research trends* (Vol. 2). New York: Academic Press, 1965.

HARLOW, H. F., & SUOMI, S. J. Induced psychopathology in monkeys. *Engineering and Science* (California Institute of Technology), April 1970, 33 (6), 8–14.

HARLOW, H. F., & SUOMI, S. J. Social recovery by isolation-reared monkeys. *Proceedings of the National Academy of Science, U.S.A.,* July 1971, *68* (7), 1534–1538.

HARLOW, R. What war does to the minds of children. *The World Tomorrow,* 1930, *13,* 488–490.

HARNED, L. Authoritarian attitudes and party activity. *Public Opinion Quarterly,* 1961, *25, 393–399.*

HARRINGTON, C. Pupils, peers and politics. In C. Harrington (Ed.), *Cross cultural approaches to learning.* New York: MSS Information Corp., 1973.

HARRIS, L. *The anguish of change.* New York: Norton, 1973. (b)

HARRIS, L. *Confidence and concern: Citizens view American government.* Washington, D.C.: U.S. Government Printing Office, 1973. (a)

HARTLEY, W. H., & VINCENT, W. S. *American civics.* New York: Harcourt, Brace, Jovanovich, 1974.

HARTMANN, H. *Psychoanalysis and moral values.* New York: International Universities Press, 1960.

HARTSHORNE, H., & MAY, M. A. *Studies in the nature of character: Studies in deceit* (Vol. 1); *Studies in self-control* (Vol. 2); *Studies in the organization of character* (Vol. 3). New York: Macmillan, 1928–1930.

HARTSHORNE, H., MAY, M. A., & SHUTTLEWORTH, F. K. *Studies in service and self-control.* New York: Macmillan, 1929.

HARTSHORNE, H., MAY, M. A., & SHUTTLEWORTH, F. K. *Studies in the organization of character.* New York: Macmillan, 1930.

HARVEY, J., & RUTHERFORD, J. M. Status in the informal group: Influence and influencibility at different age levels. *Child Development,* 1960, *31,* 377–385.

HARVEY, O. J., HUNT, D. E., & SCHRODER, H. H. *Conceptual System and Personality Organization.* New York: Wiley, 1961.

HARVEY, O. J., PRATHER, M., WHITE, B. J., & HOFFMEISTER, J. K. Teachers' beliefs, classroom atmosphere, and student behavior. In M. M. Miles & W. W. Charters, Jr. (Eds.), *Learning in social settings.* Boston: Allyn & Bacon, 1970.

HARVEY, S. K., & HARVEY, T. G. Adolescent political outlooks: The effects of intelligence as an independent variable. *Midwest Journal of Political Science,* 1970, *14,* 565–694.

HAVIGHURST, R., & NEUGARTEN, B. *American Indian and white children.* Chicago: University of Chicago Press, 1955.

HAWKINS, R. P., PINGREE, S., & ROBERTS, D. Watergate and political socialization: The inescapable event. *American Politics Quarterly,* 1975, *3,* 406–422.

HEBB, D. O. *The organization of behavior.* New York: Wiley, 1949.

HEBERLE, R. *Social movements: An introduction to political sociology.* New York: Appleton-Century-Crofts, 1951.

HEIDER, F. Attitude and cognitive organization. *Journal of Psychology,* 1946, *21,* 107–112.

HEIDER, F. *The psychology of interpersonal relations.* New York: Wiley, 1958.

HEILBRONER, R. L. *An inquiry into the human prospect.* New York: Norton, 1974.

HEIST, P. Intellect and commitment: The faces of discontent. In O. W. Knorr & W. J. Minter (Eds.), *Order and freedom on the campus.* Boulder, Colo.: Western Interstate Commission for Higher Education, 1965.

HEIST, P. Dynamics of student discontent and protest. Paper read at meeting of American Psychological Association, New York, September 1966.

HELFANT, K. Parents' attitudes versus adolescent hostility in the determination of adolescents' sociopolitical attitudes. *Psychological Monographs,* 1952, *66* (345).

HENDIN, H. A psychoanalyst looks at student revolutionaries. *New York Times Magazine,* January 17, 1971, 16.

HENNESSEY, B. C. Politicals and apoliticals. *Midwest Journal of Political Science,* 1959, *3,* 336–355.

HENNESSEY, B. C. *Public opinion* (2nd ed.). Belmont, Calif.: Wadsworth, 1970.

HENSCHEL, A. M. The relationship between values and behavior: A developmental hypothesis. *Child Development,* 1971, *42,* 1997–2007.

HENSLER, C. The structure of orientations toward government. Presented at annual meeting of American Political Science Association, Chicago, 1971.

HESS, E. H. *Imprinting: Early experience and the developmental psychobiology of attachment.* New York: Van Nostrand Reinhold, 1973.

HESS, R. D. Social class and ethnic influences upon socialization. In P. M. Mussen (Ed.), *Carmichael's manual of child psychology* (Vol. 2) (3rd ed.). New York: Wiley, 1970.

HESS, R. D. The system maintenance function of social development in the schools. *Proceedings of the 1971 Invitational Conference on Testing Problems.* Princeton: Educational Testing Service, 1972.

HESS, R. D. Socialization of attitudes toward political authority. *International Social Science Journal,* 1963 (15), 542–559; reprinted in N. Bowman & G. R. Boynton (Eds.), *Political behavior and public opinion.* Englewood Cliffs, N.J.: Prentice-Hall, 1974.

HESS, R. D., & EASTON, D. The child's changing image of the president. *Public Opinion Quarterly,* 1960, *24,* 632–644.

HESS, R. D., & TAPP, J. L. *Authority, rules, and aggression: A cross-national study of the socialization of children into compliance systems* (Part 1). Washington, D.C.: U.S. Department of Health, Education, and Welfare, 1969.

HESS, R. D. & TORNEY, J. V. *The development of basic attitudes and values towards government and citizenship during the elementary school years* (part I). Chicago: University of Chicago Press, 1965.

HESS, R. D., & TORNEY, J. V. *The development of political attitudes in children.* Chicago: Aldine, 1967. (Anchor Edition, 1968).

HETZLER, S. A. Radicalism-conservatism and social mobility. *Social Forces,* 1954, *33,* 161–166.

HILL, R. J., & BONJEAN, C. M. News diffusion: A test of the regularity hypothesis. *Journalism Quarterly,* 1964, *41,* 336–342.

HILL, W. Learning theory and acquisition of values. In R. Johnson, P. Dokecki, and O.

H. Mowrer (Eds.), *Conscience, contract and social reality*. New York: Holt, Rinehart & Winston, 1972.

HIMMELWEIT, H. T. *Television and the child*. New York: London University Press, 1958.

HIRSCH, H. *Poverty and politicization*. New York: Free Press, 1971.

HIRSCH, W. *Scientists in American society*. New York: Random House, 1968.

HIRSCHMAN, A. O. *Development projects observed*. Washington, D.C.: Brookings Institution, 1967.

HOCHRIEICH, D., & ROTTER, J. B. Have college students become less trusting? *Journal of Personality and Social Psychology*, 1970, *15*, 211–214.

HOFFER, E. *The true believer*. New York: Harper & Row, 1951.

HOFFMAN, M. L., & SALTZSTEIN, H. D. Parent discipline and the child's moral development. *Journal of Personality and Social Psychology*, 1967, *5*, 45–57.

HOFSTADTER, R. The pseudo-conservative revolt. In D. Bell (Ed.), *The radical right*. New York: Doubleday, 1964.

HOGAN, R. A dimension of moral judgment. *Journal of Consulting and Clinical Psychology*, 1970, *35*, 205–212.

HOGAN, R. Study of Values. In Q. Buros (Ed.), *Seventh mental measurements yearbook* (Vol. 1). Highland Park, N.J.: Dryphon Press, 1972.

HOGAN, R. Moral conduct—a psychological perspective. *Psychological Bulletin*, 1973, *79*, 217–232.

HOGAN, R. Dialectical aspects of moral development. *Human Development*, 1974, *17*, 107–117.

HOLLANDER, E. P., JULIAN, J. W., & HAALAND, G. A. Conformity process and prior group support. *Journal of Personality and Social Psychology*, 1965, *1*, 852–858.

HOLLANDER, N. Adolescents and the war: The sources of socialization. *Journalism Quarterly*, 1971, *48*, 472–479. (b)

HOLLANDER, N. Adolescents' perceptions of sources of orientations to war. Unpublished doctoral dissertation, University of Washington, 1971. (a)

HORN, J. Organization of data on life-span development of human abilities. In L. R. Goulet & P. Baltes (Eds.), *Life span developmental psychology: Research and theory*. New York: Academic Press, 1970.

HOROWITZ, E. L. Some aspects of the development of patriotism in children. *Sociometry*, 1940, *3*, 329–341.

HORST, P. *Psychological measurement and prediction*. Belmont, Calif.: Wadsworth, 1966.

HOUSE, J. S., & MASON, W. M. Political alienation in America, 1952–1968. *American Sociological Review*, 1975, *40*, 123–147.

HOUT, M., & KNOKE, D. Change in voting turnout, 1952–1972. *Public Opinion Quarterly*, 1975, *39*, 52–68.

HOVLAND, C. I. Effects of the mass media on communication. In G. Lindzey (Ed.), *Handbook of social psychology* (Vol. 2) (1st ed.). Cambridge: Addison-Wesley, 1954.

HOWE, I. (Ed.). *The world of the blue collar worker*. New York: Quadrangle, 1972.

HUDGINS, W., & PRENTICE, N. Moral judgment in delinquents and non-delinquents and their mothers. *Journal of Abnormal Psychology*, 1973, *82*, 145–152.

HUDSON, W. D. *Modern moral philosophy*. New York: Anchor Books, 1970.

HUITT, R. The Morse Committee assignment controversy: A study in Senate norms. *American Political Science Review*, 1957, *51*, 313–329.

HUITT, R. The outsider in the Senate: An alternative role. *American Political Science Review*, 1961, *55*, 566–575.

HUNTINGTON, S. P. The Marasmus of the ICC. *Yale Law Journal*, 1952, *61*, 470–509.

HUNTINGTON, S. P. *The soldier and the state*. Cambridge: Harvard University Press, 1967.

HYMAN, H. *Political socialization*. Glencoe, Ill.: Free Press, 1959.

HYMAN, H. Mass media and political socialization: The role of patterns of communication. In Lucian Pye (Ed.), *Communications and political development*. Princeton: Princeton University Press, 1963.

HYMAN, H. Mass communication and socialization. *Public Opinion Quarterly*, 1973, *37*, 524–540.

HYMAN, H. Cohort analysis. In H. H. Hyman (Ed.), *Secondary analysis of sample surveys: Principles, procedures, and potentialities*. New York: Wiley, 1972.

IGLITZEN, L. Sex-typing and politicization in children's attitudes: Reflections on studies done and undone. Paper presented at annual meeting of American Political Science Association, Washington, D.C., 1972.

ILCHMAN, W. F., LASSWELL, H. D. MONTGOMERY, J. D., & WEINER, M. (Eds.), *Policy sciences and population*. Lexington, Mass.: Lexington Books, Heath, 1975.

ILCHMAN, W. F., & UPHOFF, N. T. *The political economy of change*. Berkeley: University of California Press, 1971.

INGLEHART, R. An end to European integration? *American Political Science Review*, 1967, *61* (1), 91–105.

INGLEHART, R. The silent generation: Intergenerational change in post-industrial societies. *American Political Science Review*, 1971, *65*, 991–1017

INHELDER, B., & PIAGET, J. *The growth of logical thinking from childhood to adolescence*. New York: Basic Books, 1958.

INKELES, A. Social change and social character: The role of parental mediators. *Journal of Social Issues*, 1955, *11*, 12–23.

INKELES, A. Participant citizenship in six developing countries. *American Political Science Review*, 1969, *63*, 1120–1141.

INKELES, A., HAUFMANN, E., & BLIER, H. Modal personality and adjustment to the Soviet political system. *Human Relations*, 1958, *2*, 3–22.

INKELES, A., & LEVINSON, D. J. National character: The study of modal personality and socio-cultural systems. In G. Lindzey and E. Aronson (Eds.), *Handbook of social psychology* (Vol. 4). (2nd ed.). Reading, Massachusetts: Addison Wesley, 1969.

INKELES, A., & SMITH, D. *Becoming modern—individual change in six developing countries*. Cambridge: Harvard University Press, 1974.

IPPOLITO, D. S., WALKER, T. G., & KOLSON, K. L. *Public opinion and responsible democracy*. Englewood Cliffs, N.J.: Prentice-Hall, 1976.

ISAACS, H. *The new world of Negro Americans*. New York: Day, 1963.

ISAACS, H. *India's ex-Untouchables*. New York: Day, 1965.

ISAACS, H. *American Jews in Israel*. New York: Day, 1967.

ISAACS, H. Group identity and political change: The houses of Mumbi. Paper presented at annual meeting of American Political Science Association, Chicago, 1971.

ISEN, A. H., HORN, N., & ROSENHAN, D. L. Effects of success and failure on children's generosity. *Journal of Personality and Social Psychology*, 1973, *27*, 239–247.

JACKMEN, R. A note on intelligence, social class and political efficacy in children. *Journal of Politics*, 1970, *32*, 984–988.

JACKSON, D., & COOK, H. Moral development and the development of the concept of war: A cross cultural test of a theory. Paper presented at NATO International Conference on Determinants and Origins of Aggressive Behavior, Monte Carlo, 1973.

JACKSON-BEECK, M. Family communication and differential political socialization. M. A. thesis, University of Wisconsin, 1974.

JACKSON-BEECK, M., & CHAFFEE, S. H. Family communication, mass communication, and differential political socialization. Paper presented at International Communication Association, Chicago, April 1975.

JACOB, P. E. *Values and the active community*. New York: Free Press, 1971.

JACOB, P. E., & LANDAU, S. *The new radicals*. New York: Random House, 1966.

JACQUETTE, J. (Ed.). *Women in politics*. New York: Wiley, 1974.

JAHODA, G. The development of children's ideas about country and nationality. *British Journal of Educational Psychology*, 1963, *33*, 47–60, 143–153.

JAHODA, G. Children's concepts of nationality: A critical study of Piaget's stages. *Child Development*, 1964, *35*, 1081–1092.

JAHODA-LAZARSFELD, M., & ZEISEL, H. *Die Arbeitslosen von Marienthal*. Leipzig: Hirzel, 1933.

JANIS, I. L. *Victims of groupthink*. Boston: Houghton Mifflin, 1972.

JANOWITZ, M. *The professional soldier*. Glencoe, Ill.: Free Press, 1960.

JANOWITZ, M. *The military in the political development of new states*. Chicago: University of Chicago Press, 1964.

JANOWITZ, M., & MARVICK, D. Authoritarianism and political behavior. *Public Opinion Quarterly*, 1953, *17*, 185–201.

JAROS, D. Children's orientations to the president: Some additional considerations. *Journal of Politics*, 1967, *29*, 368–387.

JAROS, D. Biochemical desocialization: Depressants and political behavior. Paper presented at American Political Science Association, Los Angeles, 1970. (b)

JAROS, D. Political response to new skills. *Social Science Quarterly*, 1970, *51*, 522–560. (a)

JAROS, D., HIRSCH, H., & FELRON, F. J. Malevolent leader: Political socialization in an American sub-culture. *American Political Science Review*, 1968, *62*, 564–575.

JAROS, D., & KOLSON, K. L. The multivarious leader: Political socialization of Amish, "Yanks," and Blacks. In R. G. Niemi (Ed.), *The Politics of Future Citizens*. San Francisco: Jossey-Bass, 1974.

JENNINGS, M. K. Observations on the study of political values among pre-adults. Paper presented at Center for Research and Education in American Liberties, Los Angeles, 1966.

JENNINGS, M. K. Pre-adult orientations to multiple systems of government. *Midwest Journal of Political Science,* April 1967, 291–317.

JENNINGS, M. K., EHMAN, L. H., & NIEMI, R. G. Social studies teachers and their pupils. In M. K. Jennings & R. G. Niemi, *The political character of adolescence.* Princeton: Princeton University Press, 1974.

JENNINGS, M. K., & LANGTON, K. P. Mothers versus fathers: The formation of political orientations among young Americans. *Journal of Politics,* 1969, *31,* 329–358.

JENNINGS, M. K., LANGTON, K. P., & NIEMI, R. G. Effects of the high school civics curriculum. In M. K. Jennings & R. G. Niemi, *The political character of adolescence.* Princeton: Princeton University Press, 1974.

JENNINGS, M. K. & MARKUS, G. B. The effect of military service on political attitudes: A panel study. *American Political Science Review,* Vol. LXXI, 1977.

JENNINGS, M. K., & NIEMI, R. G. The transmission of political values from parent to child. *American Political Science Review,* 1968, *62,* 169–184. (b)

JENNINGS, M. K., & NIEMI, R. G. The division of political labor between fathers and mothers. *American Political Science Review,* 1971, *65,* 69–82.

JENNINGS, M. K., & NIEMI, R. G. *The political character of adolescence: The influence of families and schools.* Princeton: Princeton University Press, 1974.

JENNINGS, M. K., & NIEMI, R. G. Continuity and change in political orientations: A longitudinal study of two generations. *American Political Science Review,* 1975, *69,* 1316–1335.

JENSEN, J. Political participation: A survey in Evanston, Illinois. Unpublished master's thesis, Northwestern University, 1960.

JENSEN, L. C., & HAFEN, G. E. The effect of training children to consider intentions when making moral judgments. *Journal of Genetic Psychology,* 1973, *122,* 223–233.

JERSILD, A. T., & MEIGS, M. F. Children and war. *Psychological Bulletin,* 1943, *40,* 541–573.

JOHNSON, D. W., & JOHNSON, R. T. Instructional goal structure: Cooperative, competitive, or individualistic. *Review of Educational Research,* 1974, *44,* 213–240.

JOHNSON, N. What do children learn from war comics? *New Society,* 1966, *11.*

JOHNSON, N. R. Television and politicization: A test of competing models. *Journalism Quarterly,* 1973, *50,* 447–455, 474.

JOHNSON, R. C. A study of children's moral judgme ts. *Child Development,* 1962, *33,* 327–354.

JOHNSON, R. C., Dokecki, P. R., & Mowrer, O. H. (F s.). *Conscience, contract, and social reality.* New York: Holt, Rinehart & Winston, 1972.

JONES, H. E., & JONES, M. C. Attitudes of youth toward war and peace. *California Journal of Secondary Education,* 1941, *16,* 427–430.

KAGAN, J. Three faces of continuity in human development. In D. A. Goslin (Ed.), *Handbook of socialization theory and research.* Chicago: Rand McNally, 1969.

KAGAN, J., & MOSS, H. *From birth to maturity.* New York: Wiley, 1962.

KAMII, C. C., & RADIN, N. L. A framework for a pre-school curriculum based on some Piagetian concepts. In I. Athey & D. Rubadeau (Eds.), *Educational implications of Piaget's theory.* Waltham, Mass.: Ginn-Blaisdell, 1970.

KANDEL, D. B., & LESSER, G. S. *Youth in two worlds: United States and Denmark.* San Francisco: Jossey-Bass, 1972.

KAPLAN, A. *The conduct of inquiry.* San Francisco: Chandler, 1964.

KAPLAN, M. A. *System and process in international politics.* New York: Wiley, 1957.

KARLSSON, K., & CARLSSON, G. Age, cohorts, and the generation of generations. *American Sociological Review,* 1970, *35,* 710–717.

KATZ, E. The two-step flow of communication. An up to date report on an hypothesis. *Public Opinion Quarterly,* 1957, *21,* 61–78.

KATZ, E., & LAZARSFELD, P. A. *Personal influence: The part played by people in the flow of mass communications.* Glencoe, Ill.: Free Press, 1955.

KEASEY, C. T., & KEASEY, C. B. The mediating role of cognitive development in moral judgment. *Child Development,* 1974, *45,* 291–298.

KELMAN, H. C. (Ed.), *International behavior: A social psychological analysis.* New York: Holt, Rinehart & Winston, 1964.

KELMAN, H. C., & LAWRENCE, L. H. Assignment of responsibility in the case of Lt. Calley: Preliminary report on a national survey. *Journal of Social Issues,* 1972, *28,* 177–212.

KENISTON, K. *The uncommitted: Alienated youth in American society.* New York: Dell, 1965.

KENISTON, K. The sources of student dissent. *Journal of Social Issues,* 1967, *23,* (3), 108–137.

KENISTON, K. *Young radicals: Notes on committed youth.* New York: Harcourt, Brace & World, 1968.

KERPELMAN, L. C. Student political activism and ideology: Comparative characteristics of activists and nonactivists. *Journal of Counseling Psychology,* 1969, *16,* 8–13.

KERPELMAN, L. C. *Activists and nonactivists.* New York: Behavioral Publications, 1972.

KERR, W. A. *Manual of instruction for Tulane factors of liberalism-conservatism.* Chicago: Psychometric Affiliates, 1955.

KEY, V. O. *Public opinion and American democracy.* New York: Knopf, 1961.

KEYS, M., BROZEK, J., HENSCHEL, A., MICKELSON, O., & TAYLOR, H. L. *The biology of human starvation* (Vol. 2). Minneapolis: University of Minnesota Press, 1950.

KHRUSHCHEV, N. *Khrushchev remembers,* S. Talbott, ed. & trans. Boston: Little, Brown, 1970.

KIDD, J. Social influence phenomena in a task-oriented group situation. *Journal of Abnormal and Social Psychology,* 1958, *56,* 13–17.

KIESLER, C. A., ZANNA, M., & DESALVO, J. Deviation and conformity: Opinion change as function of commitment, attraction and presence of a deviate. *Journal of Personality and Social Psychology,* 1966, *3,* 458–467.

KIESLER, S. B., & BARAL, R. L. The search for a romantic partner: The effects of self esteem and physical attractiveness on romantic behavior. In K. J. Gergen & D. Marlowe (Eds.), *Personality and social behavior.* Reading, Mass.: Addison-Wesley, 1970.

KILLIAN, L. M. Social movements. In R. E. L. Faris (Ed.), *Handbook of modern sociology.* Chicago: Rand McNally, 1964.

KIRKHAM, J., LEVY, S., & CROTTY, W. J. *Assassination and political violence.* Washington, D.C.: U.S. Government Printing Office, 1969.

KIRKPATRICK, S. A. *Quantitative analysis of political data.* Columbus, Ohio: Merrill, 1974.

KIRKPATRICK, S. Aging effects and generational differences in social welfare attitude constraint in the mass public. *Western Political Quarterly,* 1976, *29,* 43–58.

KLAPPER, J. *The effects of mass communication.* New York: Free Press, 1960.

KLECKA, W. R. Applying political generations to the study of political behavior: A cohort analysis. *Public Opinion Quarterly,* 1971, *35,* 358–373.

KLINE, F. G., MILLER, P. S., & MORRISON, A. Adolescents and family planning information: An exploration of audience needs and media effects. In J. Blumler & E. Katz (Eds.), *The uses of mass communications: Current perspectives on gratifications research.* Beverly Hills: Sage Publications, 1974.

KLINGER, E. *Structure and functions of fantasy.* New York: Wiley-Interscience, 1971.

KLUCKHOHN, C. Values and value orientations in the theory of action. In T. Parsons & E. A. Shils (Eds.), *Toward a general theory of action.* Cambridge: Harvard University Press, 1951.

KLUCKHOHN, F., & STRODTBECK, F. *Variations in value orientations.* Evanston, Ill.: Row, Peterson, 1961.

KNOKE, D. Community and consistency: The ethnic factor in status inconsistency. *Social Forces,* 1952, *51,* 23–33.

KNOKE, D., & HOUT, M. Social and demographic factors in American political party affiliations, 1952–1972. *American Sociological Review,* 1974, *39,* 700–713.

KNUTSON, J. N. *The human basis of the polity.* New York: Aldine-Atherton, 1972.

KNUTSON, J. N. Pre-political ideologies: The basis for political learning. In R. Niemi (Ed.), *The politics of future citizens.* San Francisco: Jossey-Bass, 1974.

KNUTSON, J. N. *Personality stability and political beliefs.* San Francisco: Jossey-Bass, forthcoming.

KOEPPEN, S. R. The radical right and the politics of consensus. In R. Schoenberger (Ed.). *The American right wing.* New York: Holt, Rinehart & Winston, 1969.

KOESTLER, A. *Darkness at noon.* New York: Macmillan, 1941.

KOFF, D., & VON DER MUHL, G. Political socialization in Kenya and Tanzania. *Journal of Modern African Studies,* 1967, *5* (1), 13–51.

KOFF, D., VON DER MUHL, G., & PREWITT, K. Political socializations in three East African countries: A comparative analysis. In J. Dennis (Ed.), *Socialization to politics.* New York: Wiley, 1973.

KOHLBERG, L. Moral development and identification. In H. W. Stevenson (Ed.), *Child psychology, 62nd Yearbook of the National Society for the Study of Education.* Chicago: University of Chicago Press, 1963.

KOHLBERG, L. Development of moral character and moral ideology. In M. L. Hoffman & L. W. Hoffman (Eds.), *Review of child development research.* New York: Russell Sage Foundation, 1964.

KOHLBERG, L. Stage and sequence: The cognitive developmental approach to socialization. In D. A. Goslin (Ed.), *The handbook of socialization theory and research.* Chicago: Rand McNally, 1969.

KOHLBERG, L. The moral atmosphere of the school. In N. V. Overly (Ed.), *The unstudied curriculum.* Washington, D.C.: Association for Supervision and Curriculum Development, 1970.

KOHLBERG, L. From is to ought: How to commit the naturalistic fallacy and get away with it in the study of moral development. In T. Mischel (Ed.), *Cognitive development and epistemology*. New York: Academic Press, 1971. (b)

KOHLBERG, L. Stages of moral development as a basis for moral education. In C. H. Beck, B. S. Crittenden, & E. V. Sullivan (Eds.), *Moral education: Interdisciplinary approaches*. Toronto: University of Toronto Press, 1971. (a)

KOHLBERG, L. Discussion: Developmental gains in moral judgment. *American Journal of Mental Deficiency*, 1974, *79*, 142–146. (b)

KOHLBERG, L. Lessons of Watergate. APA comments, 1974. (a)

KOHLBERG, L. Reply to Bereiter's statement on Kohlberg's cognitive development. *Interchange*, 1974, *1*, 40–48. (c)

KOHLBERG, L. The cognitive-development approach to moral education. *Phi Delta Kappan*, June 1975, *56*.

KOHLBERG, L., & LOCKWOOD, A. Cognitive-developmental psychology and political education: Progress in the sixties. Harvard Moral Development Project. Mimeo, 1970.

KOHN, M. *Class and conformity*. Homewood, Ill.: Dorsey, 1969.

KOLSON, J. K., & GREEN, J. Response set bias and political socialization research. *Social Science Quarterly*, 1970, *51*, 527–538.

KORNBERG, A. The rules of the game in the Canadian House of Commons. *Journal of Politics*, 1964, *26*, 358–380.

KORNHAUSER, A. *The mental health of the industrial worker*. New York: Wiley, 1965.

KORNHAUSER, A., SHEPPARD, H., & MAYER, A. *When labor votes*. New York: University Books, 1956.

KORNHAUSER, W. *The politics of mass society*. Glencoe, Ill.: Free Press, 1959.

KRAUS, S., & DAVIS, D. *The effects of mass communication on political behavior*. University Park, Pa.: Pennsylvania State University Press, 1976.

KRAUS, S., & LEE, J. W. Mass communication and political socialization among adolescents in a presidential primary. Unpublished manuscript, Department of Communication, Cleveland State University, 1975.

KRAUT, R. E., & LEWIS, S. H. Alternate models of family influence on student political ideology. *Journal of Personality and Social Psychology*, 1975, *31*, 791–800.

KRECH, D. The chemistry of learning. *Saturday Review*, January 1968, *20*, 48–50 ff.

KROUT, M. H., & STAGNER, R. Personality development in radicals. *Sociometry*, 1939, *2*, 31–46.

KUBOTA, A., & WARD, R. E. Family influence and political socialization in Japan: Some preliminary findings in comparative perspective. In J. Dennis & M. K. Jennings (Eds.), *Comparative political socialization*. Beverly Hills: Sage Publications, 1970.

KUHLEN, R. (Ed.). *Psychological background of adult education*. Chicago: Center for Study of Liberal Education for Adults, 1963.

KUHN, T. S. *The structure of scientific revolutions*. Chicago: University of Chicago Press, 1962.

KURODA, Y. Agencies of political socialization and political change: Political orientation of Japanese law students. *Human Organization*, 1965, *24*, 328–331.

KURTINES, W., & GRIEF, E. The development of moral thought: Review and evaluation of Kohlberg's approach. *Psychological Bulletin,* 1974, *81,* 453–470.

LADD, E., & LIPSET, S. M. The politics of academic natural engineers. *Science,* 1972, *176,* 1091–1099.

LAMBERT, W. E., & KLINEBERG, O. A pilot study of the origin and development of national stereotypes. *International Social Science Journal,* 1959, *2,* 221–238.

LAMBERT, W. E., & KLINEBERG, O. *Children's views of foreign peoples.* New York: Appleton-Century-Crofts, 1967.

LANDAU, M. On the use of metaphor in political analysis. *Social Research,* 1962, *28,* 331–354.

LANE, R. A. Fathers and sons: Foundations of political belief. *American Sociological Review,* 1959, *24,* 502–511.

LANE, R. A. Political education in the midst of life's struggles. *Harvard Educational Review,* 1968, *38,* 468–494.

LANE, R. E. Political personality and electoral choice. *American Political Science Review,* 1955, *49,* 173–190.

LANE, R. E. *Political life.* Glencoe, Ill.: Free Press, 1959.

LANE, R. E. *Political ideology.* New York: Free Press, 1962.

LANE, R. E. The need to be liked and the anxious college liberal. *The Annals,* 1965, *361,* 71–80.

LANE, R. E. *Political thinking and consciousness.* Chicago: Markham, 1969.

LANE, R. E., & SEARS, D. *Public opinion.* Englewood Cliffs, N.J.: Prentice-Hall, 1964.

LANGTON, K. P. Peer group and school and the political socialization process. *American Political Science Review,* 1967, *61,* 751–758.

LANGTON, K. P. *Political socialization.* London: Oxford University Press, 1969.

LANGTON, K. P., & JENNINGS, M. K. Political socialization and the high school civics curriculum in the United States. *American Political Science Review,* 1968, *62,* 852–867.

LANGTON, K. P., & KARNS, D. A. The relative influence of the family, peer group, and school in the development of political efficacy. *Western Political Quarterly,* 1969, *22,* 813–826.

LA NOUE, G. R., & ADLER, N. Political systems, public schools, and political socialization. Paper prepared for Center for Research and Education in American Liberties Conference, Tarryton, N. Y., 1968.

LARSEN, O. (Ed.). *Violence and the mass media.* New York: Harper & Row, 1968.

LASCH, C. *The new radicalism in America, 1889–1963.* New York: Knopf, 1966.

LASSWELL, H. D. *Psychopathology and politics.* Chicago: University of Chicago Press, 1930.

LASSWELL, H. D. *Politics: Who gets what, when, how.* New York: McGraw-Hill, 1936.

LASSWELL, H. D. A method of interlapping observation in the study of personality in culture. *Journal of Abnormal Psychology,* 1937, *32,* 240–243.

LASSWELL, H. D. Person, personality, group, culture. *Psychiatry,* 1939, *2,* 533–561.

LASSWELL, H. D. *The analysis of political behavior.* New York: Oxford University Press, 1947.

LASSWELL, H. D. *Power and personality*. New York: Norton, 1948. (a)

LASSWELL, H. D. World loyalty. In W. Quincy (Ed.), *The world community*. Chicago: University of Chicago Press, 1948. (b)

LASSWELL, H. D. *The political writings of Harold D. Lasswell*. New York: Free Press, 1951.

LASSWELL, H. D. The selective effect of personality on political participation. In R. Christie & M. Jahoda (Eds.), *Studies in the scope and method of "the authoritarian personality."* New York: Free Press, 1954.

LASSWELL, H. D. The garrison state hypothesis today. In S. D. Huntington (Ed.), *Changing patterns of military politics*. New York: Free Press of Glencoe, 1962.

LASSWELL, H. D. *The future of political science*. New York: Atherton, 1963.

LASSWELL, H. D. Civic education in the technoscientific age. In C. H. Faust & J. Feingold (Eds.), *Approaches to education for character: Strategies for change in higher education*. New York: Columbia University Press, 1969.

LASSWELL, H. D. *A pre-view of policy sciences*. New York: Elsevier, 1971.

LASSWELL, H. D., & RUBENSTEIN, R. *The sharing of power in a psychiatric hospital*. New Haven: Yale University Press, 1966.

LAULICHT, J. Canadian foreign policy attitudes: Some major conclusions. *International Social Science Journal*, 1965, *1*, 472–486.

Law in American Society Project Staff. *Teacher's guide, Justice in Urban America series*. Boston: Houghton Mifflin, 1970.

LAW, N. Children and war. *Changing Education*, 1973, 12–17.

LAWSON, E. D. Development of patriotism in children: A second look. In N. Adler & C. Harrington (Eds.), *The learning of political behavior*. Glenview, Ill.: Scott, Foresman, 1970.

LAZARSFELD, P. F., BERLESON, B., & GAUDET, H. *The people's choice*. New York: Duell, Sloan & Pearce, 1944.

LAZARUS, A. A. The results of behavior therapy in 126 cases of severe neurosis. *Behavior Research and Therapy*, 1963, *1*, 69–79.

LEATHERMAN, D. R. The political socialization of students in the Mennonite secondary schools. *Mennonite Quarterly Review*, 1962, *36*, 89–90.

LEBON, G. *The psychology of revolution*. New York: Putnam's, 1913.

LENSKI, G. Status inconsistency and the vote. *American Sociological Review*, 1967, *32*, 298–301.

LEPPER, M. R., GREENE, D., & NISBETT, R. E. Undermining children's intrinsic interest with extrinsic reward: A test of the "overjustification" hypothesis. *Journal of Personality and Social Psychology*, 1973, *23*, 129–137.

LERNER, D. *The passing of traditional society*. Glencoe, Ill.: Free Press, 1958.

LERNER, M. J. The observer's evaluation of a victim: Justice, guilt and veridical perception. *Journal of Personality and Social Psychology*, 1971, *20*, 127–135.

LERNER, M. J. The justice motive: "Levity" and "parity" among children. *Journal of Personality and Social Psychology*, 1974, *29*, 539–550.

LERNER, M. J., & SIMMONS, C. H. Observer's reaction to the "innocent victim": Compassion or rejection? *Journal of Personality and Social Psychology*, 1966, *4*, 203–210.

LeVine, R. A. Socialization, social structure, and intersocietal images. In H. Kelman (Ed.), *International behavior*. New York: Holt, Rinehart & Winston, 1964.

LeVine, R. A. The internationalization of political values in stateless societies. In R. Hunt (Ed.), *Personalities and culture*. New York: Natural History Press, 1967.

LeVine, R. A. The role of the family in authority systems: A cross-cultural application of stimulus-generalization theory. In J. C. Pierce & R. A. Pride (Eds.), *Cross-national micro-analysis: Procedures and problems*. Beverly Hills: Sage Publications, 1972.

Levinger, G., & Breedlove, J. Interpersonal attraction and agreement: A study of marriage partners. *Journal of Personality and Social Psychology*, 1966, *4*, 367–372.

Levinson, D. J. Politico-economic ideology and group membership in relation to ethnocentrism. In T. W. Aderno et al., *The authoritarian personality*. New York: Harper, 1950.

Levinson, D. J. Conservatism and radicalism. In D. L. Sills (Ed.), *International encyclopedia of the social sciences*. New York: Macmillan and Free Press, 1968.

Levitin, R. Values. In J. P. Robinson & P. R. Shaver (Eds.), *Measures of social psychological attitudes*. Ann Arbor: Institute for Social Research, 1970.

Levy, M. J. *The structure of society*. Princeton: Princeton University Press, 1952.

Lewis, O. *Five families*. New York: Basic Books, 1959.

Lewis, O. *La Vida: A Puerto Rican family in the culture of poverty—San Juan and New York*. New York: Random House, 1966.

Lewis, R., & Stewart, R. *The managers*. New York: Mentor Books, 1961.

Lewis, S., & Kraut, R. Correlates of student political activism and ideology. *Journal of Social Issues*, 1972, *28*, 131–149.

Lewis, S. A., Langan, D. J., & Hollander, E. P. Expectations of future interaction and the choice of less desirable alternatives in conformity. *Sociometry*, 1972, *35*, 444–447.

Lickona, T. Piaget misunderstood: A critique of the criticisms of his theory of moral development. *Merrill-Palmer Quarterly*, 1969, *15*, 337–350.

Lifton, R. J. *Thought reform and the psychology of totalism*. New York: Norton, 1963.

Lifton, R. J. Thought reform of Chinese intellectuals. In M. Jahoda & N. Warren (Eds.), *Attitudes*. Baltimore: Penguin Books, 1966.

Lifton, R. J. *Revolutionary immortality*. New York: Random House, 1968.

Lifton, R. J. *History and human survival*. New York: Random House, 1970.

Lifton, R. J. *Home from the war*. New York: Random House, 1973.

Lightfoot, S. L. Politics and reasoning: Through the eyes of teachers and children. *Harvard Educational Review*, 1973, *43*, 197–244.

Limbert, P. M. What children think about war. *Progressive Education*, 1933, *10*, 67–71.

Lin, N. The McIntire march: A study of recruitment and commitment. *Public Opinion Quarterly*, 1974–1975, *381*, 562–573.

Lippit, R., & Zander, A. Boys' attitudes toward war. *Journal of Social Psychology*, 1943, 309–325.

Lipscomb, F. M. German concentration camps: Diseases encountered at Belsen. In H. L. Tidy & J. M. B. Kutschbach (Eds.), *Inter-allied conferences on war medicine*. London: Staples Press, 1947.

LIPSET, S. M. *Agrarian socialism: The Cooperative Commonwealth Federation in Saskatchewan: A study in political sociology.* Berkeley: University of California Press, 1950.

LIPSET, S. M. *Political man.* Garden City, N.Y.: Doubleday, 1960.

LIPSET, S. M. Three decades of the radical right. In D. Bell (Ed.), *The radical right.* Garden City, N.Y.: Doubleday, 1962.

LIPSET, S. M. The sources of the "radical right." In D. Bell (Ed.), *The radical right.* New York: Doubleday, 1964.

LIPSET, S. M. University student politics. In S. M. Lipset & S. Wolin (Eds.), *The Berkeley student revolt.* Garden City, N.Y.: Doubleday, Anchor Books, 1965.

LIPSET, S. M. Doves, hawks and polls. *Encounter,* 1966, *27,* 38–45. (a)

LIPSET, S. M. Student opposition in the U. S. *Government and Opposition,* 1966, *1,* 351–374. (b)

LIPSET, S. M. Students and politics in a comparative perspective. *Daedalus,* Winter 1968.

LIPSET, S. M., & LADD, E. C. College generations—from the 1930's to the 1960's. *Public Interest,* 1971, *25,* 99–113.

LIPSET, S. M., & SCHWARZ, M. A. The politics of the professionals. In H. Vollmer (Ed.), *Professionalism.* Englewood Cliffs, N.J.: Prentice-Hall, 1966.

LIPSETZ, L. Work life and political attitudes: A study of manual workers. *American Political Science Review,* February 1963, *28,* 69–75.

LITT, E. Civic education, community norms and political indoctrination. *American Sociological Review,* February 1963, *28,* 69–75.

LITT, E. Review of *Political Socialization* by Richard Dawson and Kenneth Prewitt. *American Political Science Review,* December 1969, *63.*

LOEHLIN, J. C. Psychological genetics. In R. B. Cattell (Ed.), *Handbook of modern personality theory.* Chicago: Aldine, 1969.

LOEVINGER, J., & WESSLER, R. *Measuring ego development* (Vols. 1, 2). San Francisco: Jossey-Bass, 1970.

LOFLAND, J., & STARK, R. Becoming a world saver. In B. McLaughlin (Ed.), *Studies in social movements.* New York: Free Press, 1969.

LONDON, P. *Behavior control.* New York: Harper & Row, 1969.

LONG-STEVENS, J. The effect of behavioral context on some aspects of adult disciplinary practice and affect. *Child Development,* 1973, *44,* 476–484.

LOPREATO, J. Upward social mobility and political orientations. *American Sociological Review,* 1967, *32,* 586–592.

LORENZ, K. *On aggression.* New York: Harcourt Brace, 1966.

LORINSKAS, R. A., HAWKINS, B. W., & EDWARDS, S. D. The persistence of ethnic voting in urban and rural areas: Results from the controlled election method. *Social Science Quarterly,* 1969, *49,* 891–899.

LOSCIUTO, L., & KARLIN, R. Correlates of the generation gap. *Journal of Psychology,* 1972, *81,* 253–263.

LUCE, R. D., & RAIFFA, H. *Games and decisions.* New York: Wiley, 1957.

LUPFER, M., & KENNY, C. *Children's reactions to the President: Pre- and post-Watergate findings.* Paper delivered at APSA convention, Chicago, 1974.

LYNN, K. (Ed.). *The professions in America*. Boston: Beacon Press, 1965.

LYONS, S. L. The political socialization of ghetto children: Efficacy and cynicism. *Journal of Politics*, 1970, 288–304.

MACAULAY, J., & BERKOWTIZ, L. (Eds.), *Altruism and helping behavior*. New York: Academic Press, 1970.

MACCOBY, E. E. (Ed.). *Development of sex differences*. Stanford: Stanford University Press, 1966.

MACCOBY, E. E. The development of moral values and behavior in childhood. In J. A. Clausen (Ed.), *Socialization and society*. Boston: Little, Brown, 1968.

MACCOBY, E. E., & JACKLIN, C. *Psychology of sex differences*. Stanford: Stanford University Press, 1974.

MACRAE, D. A test of Piaget's theories of moral development. *Journal of Abnormal and Social Psychology*, 1954, *49*, 14–18.

MADDOX, G. L., & WILEY, J. Scope, methods and concepts in the study of aging. In R. Binstock & E. Shanas (Eds.), *Handbook of aging and the social sciences*. New York: Van Nostrand, 1976, Chapter 1, 3–34.

MADDI, S. R. Exploratory behavior and variation-seeking in man. In D. W. Fiske & S. R. Maddi (Eds.), *Functions of varied experience*. Homewood, Ill: Dorsey, 1961.

MAITLAND, K. A., & GOLDMAN, J. R. Moral judgment as a function of peer group interaction. *Journal of Personality and Social Psychology*, 1974, *30*, 699–704.

MALINOWSKI, B. War—past, present, and future. In J. D. Clarkson & T. Cochran (Eds.), *War as a social institution*. New York: A. M. Press, 1966.

MANASTER, G. J., & HAVIGHURST, R. J. *Cross-national research: Social psychological methods and problems*. Boston: Houghton Mifflin, 1972.

MANKOFF, M., & FLACKS, R. The changing social base of the American student movement. *Annals of the American Academy of Political and Social Science*, 1971, 395, 54–67.

MANLEY, J. F. The House Committee on Ways and Means: Conflict management in a congressional committee. *American Political Science Review*, 1965, *59*, 927–939.

MANNHEIM, K. *Ideology and utopia*. New York: Harcourt, Brace & World. (First published in 1936.)

MANNHEIM, K. The problem of generations. In P. Kleckemeti (Ed.), *Essays on the sociology of knowledge by Karl Mannheim*. London: Routledge & Kegan Paul, 1952.

MARCH, J. G. Husband-wife interaction over political issues. *Public Opinion Quarterly*, 1953–1954, *17*, 461–470.

MARCUSE, H. *One-dimensional man*. Boston: Beacon Press, 1964.

MARCUSE, H. Repressive tolerance. In R. P. Wolff, B. Moore, Jr., & H. Marcuse (Eds.), *A critique of pure tolerance*. Boston: Beacon Press, 1969.

MARIÁS, J. Generations—the concept. In *International encyclopedia of the social sciences*. New York: Macmillan and Free Press, 1968.

MARKS, F. R., et al., *The lawyer, the public, and professional responsibility*. Chicago: American Bar Foundation, 1972.

MARSH, D. Political socialization: The implicit assumptions examined. *British Journal of Political Science*, October 1971, *1*, 453–465.

MARSH, D. Beliefs about democracy among English adolescents: What significance have they? *British Journal of Political Science,* 1972, *2,* 255–259.

MARSHALL, T. H. *Citizenship and social class.* London: Cambridge University Press, 1950.

MARTIN, J. G., & WESTIE, F. R. The tolerant personality. *American Sociology Review,* 1959, *24,* 521–529.

MASLOW, A. *Motivation and personality.* New York: Harper & Row, 1954.

MASON, K., MASON, W., WINSBOROUGH, H. H., & POOLE, W. K. Some methodological issues in cohort analysis of archival data. *American Sociological Review,* 1973, *38,* 242–258.

MASSIALAS, B. G. American government. In C. B. Cox & B. G. Massialas (Eds.), *Social studies in the United States: A critical appraisal.* New York: Harcourt, Brace & World, 1967.

MASSIALAS, B. G. (Ed.). *Political youth, traditional schools: National and international perspectives.* Englewood Cliffs, N.J.: Prentice-Hall, 1972.

MATRAS, J. *Social change in Israel.* Chicago: Aldine, 1965.

MATTHEWS, D. R. *The social background of political decision-makers.* Garden City, N.Y.: Doubleday, 1954.

MATTHEWS, D. R. *U.S. senators and their world.* Chapel Hill: University of North Carolina Press, 1960.

MAY, H. The student movement at Berkeley: Some impressions. In S. M. Lipset & S. Wolin (Eds.), *The Berkeley student revolt.* Garden City, N.Y.: Doubleday, Anchor Books, 1965.

MAY, M. A. Peace and social learning. In L. Bramson & G. Goethals (Eds.), *War: Studies from psychology, sociology, anthropology.* New York: Basic Books, 1964.

McCANN, D. C., & PRENTICE, M. N. The facilitating effects of money and moral set on the moral judgment of adolescent delinquents. *Journal of Abnormal Psychology,* 1973, *82,* 81–84.

McCLELLAND, D. C. *Power: The inner experience.* New York: Irvington, 1975.

McCLOSKY, H. Conservatism and personality. *American Political Science Review,* 1958, *52,* 27–45.

McCLOSKY, H., & DAHLGREN, L. Primary group influence on party loyalty. *American Political Science Review,* 1959, *53,* 757–776.

McCOMBS, M., & WEAVER, D. Voters need for orientation and use of mass media. Paper presented to International Communication Association, Montreal, 1973.

McCONAUGHY, J. B. Certain personality factors of state legislators in South Carolina. *American Political Science Review,* 1950, *44,* 897–903.

McDOUGALL, W. *An introduction to social psychology.* London: Methuen, 1908.

McEWEN, B. S. The brain as a target organ of endocrine hormones. *Hospital Practice,* May 1975, 95–104.

McLAUGHLIN, J. A., & STEPHANS, B. Interrelationships among reasoning, moral judgment and moral conduct. *American Journal of Mental Deficiency,* 1974, *79,* 156–161.

McLEOD, J., & BECKER, L. Testing the validity of gratification measures through political effects analysis. In J. Blumler & E. Katz (Eds.), *The uses of mass communication: Current perspectives on gratifications research.* Beverly Hills: Sage Publications, 1974.

McLEOD, J., BECKER, L., & BYRNES, J. Another look at the agenda-setting function of the press. *Communication Research,* 1974, *1,* 131–166.

McLEOD, J., & CHAFFEE, S. H. The construction of social reality. In J. T. Tedeschi (Ed.), *The social influence processes.* Chicago: Aldine Atherton, 1972.

McLUHAN, M. *Understanding media.* New York: McGraw-Hill, 1964.

MEAD, M. War need not mar our children. *Journal of Educational Sociology,* 1942, *16,* 195–201.

MEAD, M., & METRAUX, R. *The study of culture at a distance.* Chicago: University of Chicago Press, 1953.

MEEHAN, E. *The theory and method of political analysis.* Homewood, Ill.: Dorsey, 1965.

MEHLINGER, H. D., & PATRICK, J. J. *Teacher's guide for American political behavior.* Lexington, Mass.: Ginn, 1972.

MELTZER, H. Attitudes of American children toward peaceful and warlike nations in 1934 and 1938. *Journal of Psychology,* 1939, *7,* 369–334.

MERELMAN, R. M. Learning and legitimacy. *American Political Science Review,* 1966, *60,* 548–561.

MERELMAN, R. M. Intimate environments and political behavior. *Midwest Journal of Political Science,* 1968, *12,* 382–400.

MERELMAN, R. M. The development of political ideology: A framework for the analysis of political socialization. *American Political Science Review,* 1969, *63,* 750–767.

MERELMAN, R. M. The development of policy thinking in adolescence. *American Political Science Review,* 1971, *65,* 1033–1047. (a)

MERELMAN, R. M. *Political socialization and educational climates.* New York: Holt, Rinehart & Winston, 1971. (b)

MERELMAN, R. M. The adolescence of political socialization. *Sociology of Education,* 1972, *45,* 134–166.

MERELMAN, R. M., & McCABE, A. E. Evolving orientations towards policy choice in adolescence. *American Journal of Political Science,* 1974, *18,* 4.

MERESKO, R., RUBIN, M., SHONTZ, F. C., & MORROW, W. R. Rigidity of attitudes regarding personal habits and its ideological correlates. *Journal of Abnormal and Social Psychology,* 1954, *49,* 84–93.

MERTON, R. *Social theory and social structure* (rev. ed.). New York: Free Press, 1968.

METCALF, L. An interdisciplinary approach to peace and world order. *Media and Methods,* 1969, *36.*

MIDDLETON, R., & PUTNEY, S. Political expression of adolescent rebellion. *American Journal of Sociology,* 1963, *65,* 527–535. (b)

MIDDLETON, R., & PUTNEY, S. Student rebellion against parental political beliefs. *Social Forces,* 1963, *41,* 377–383. (a)

MIDDLETON, M., TAJFEL, H., & JOHNSON, N. P. Cognitive and affective aspects of children's national attitudes. *British Journal of Social and Clinical Psychology,* 1970, *9,* 122–134. (a)

MIDDLETON, M., TAJFEL, H., & JOHNSON, N. P. Relationship between children's preferences for and knowledge about other nations. *British Journal of Social and Clinical Psychology*, 1970, *9*, 232–240. (b)

MIDLARSKY, E., BRYAN, J. H., & BRICKMAN, P. Aversive approval: Interactive effects of modeling and reinforcement on altruistic behavior. *Child Development*, 1973, *44*, 321–328.

MILBRATH, L. W. Predispositions toward political contention. *Western Political Quarterly*, 1960, *13*, 5–18.

MILBRATH, L. W. *Political participation*. Chicago: Rand McNally, 1965.

MILBRATH, L. W., & KLEIN, W. W. Personality correlates of political participation. *Acta Sociologica*, 1962, *6*, 53–66.

MILGRAM, S. *Television and anti-social behavior*. New York: Academic Press, 1973.

MILLER, D. C. A research note on mass communication. *American Sociological Review*, 1954, *19*, 426–433.

MILLER, D. R., & SWANSON, G. E. *The changing American parent*. New York: Wiley, 1958.

MILLER, N. E., & DOLLARD, J. *Social learning and imitation*. New Haven: Yale University Press, 1941.

MINAR, D. *Ideas and politics: The American experience*. Homewood, Ill.: Dorsey, 1964.

MINTURN, L., & TAPP, J. L. *Authority, rules, and aggression: A cross-national study of children's judgments of the justice of aggressive confrontations*, part 2. Washington, D.C.: U.S. Department of Health, Education, and Welfare, 1969.

MISCHEL, T. Piaget: Cognitive conflict and motivation of thought. In T. Mischel (Ed.), *Cognitive development and epistemology*. New York: Academic Press, 1971.

MISCHEL, W. On the empirical dilemmas of psychodynamics approaches: Issues and alternatives. *Journal of Abnormal Psychology*, 1968, *73*, 49–61. (b)

MISCHEL, W. *Personality and assessment*. New York: Wiley, 1968. (a)

MISCHEL, W. Toward a cognitive social learning reconceptualization of personality. *Psychological Review*, 1973, *80*, 252–283.

MITSCHERLICH, A. Changing patterns of political authority. In L. J. Edinger (Ed.), *Political leadership in industrializing societies: Studies in comparative analysis*. New York: Wiley, 1967.

MONTAGU, A. *Man and aggression*. New York: Oxford University Press, 1968.

MONTGOMERY, J. R. *Technology and civic life: Making and implementing development decisions*. Cambridge: MIT Press, 1974.

MOORE, J. T. A systematic approach to teaching about war and peace. Bibliography prepared for National Council for the Social Studies Convention, San Francisco, 1973.

MOORE, W. E. Occupational socialization. In D. A. Goslin (Ed.), *Handbook of socialization theory and research*. Chicago: Rand McNally, 1969.

MOORE, W. E. *The professions: Roles and rules*. New York: Russell Sage Foundation, 1970.

MORRIS, C. W. *Paths of life*. New York: Harper & Row, 1942.

MORRIS, C. W. *Varieties of human value*. Chicago: University of Chicago Press, 1956.

MORRIS, D. *The naked ape*. London: Corgibooks, 1967.

MORRIS, W. Houston's superpatriots. *Harper's*, October 1961, *56*.

MORRISON, A. Attitudes of children toward international affairs. *Educational Research,* 1967, *9,* 197–202.

MORSE, S. J., & GERGEN, K. J. Social comparison, self-consistency and the presentation of self. *Journal of Personality and Social Psychology,* 1970, *16,* 148–156.

MURPHY, R., FRIED, M., & HARRIS, M. *War: The anthropology of armed conflict and aggression.* Garden City, N.Y.: Natural History Press, 1968.

MUSSEN, P., & WYSZYNSKI, A. Personality and political participation. *Human Relations,* 1952, *5,* 65–82.

MYERS, D. G., & BECK, P. J. Discussion effects on militarism pacifism: A test of group polarization processes. *Journal of Personality and Social Psychology,* 1974, *30,* 741–749.

NELSON, W. *The politics of science.* Oxford, Eng.: Oxford University Press, 1968.

NESBITT, W. Teaching about war and its control. A selected annotated bibliography. New York State Education Department, 1973.

NESBITT, W., ABRAMOWITZ, N., & BLOOMSTEIN, C. *Teaching youth about conflict and war.* Washington, D.C.: National Council for the Social Studies, 1973.

NESSELROADE, J. R., & BALTES, P. B. Adolescent personality development and historical change: 1970–1972. *Monographs of the Society for Research in Child Development,* Serial No. 154, May 1974, *39* (1).

NESSELROADE, J. R., SCHAIE, K. W., & BALTES, P. B. Ontogenetic and generational components of structural and quantitative change in adult behavior. *Journal of Gerontology,* 1972, *27,* 222–228.

NETTLER, G., & HUFFMAN, J. Political opinion and personal security. *Sociometry,* 1957, *20,* 51–66.

NEUBAUER, D. E. Value achievement in the schools. Mimeo, 1972.

NEUGARTEN, B. Personality changes during the adult years. In R. G. Kuhlen (Ed.), *Psychological backgrounds of adult education.* Chicago: Center for Adults, 1963.

NEUMANN, G. *A study of international attitudes of high school students.* New York: Teachers College Press, 1926.

NEWCOMB, T. M. *Personality and social change: Attitude formation in a student community.* New York: Dryden Press, 1943.

NEWCOMB, T. M. An approach to the study of communicative acts. *Psychological Review,* 1953, *60,* 393–404.

NEWCOMB, T. M. *The acquaintance process.* New York: Holt, Rinehart & Winston, 1961.

NEWCOMB, T. M. Persistence and regression of changed attitudes: Long range studies. In J. Dennis (Ed.), *Socialization to politics.* New York: Wiley, 1973.

NEWCOMB, T. M., KOENIG, K., FLACKS, R., & WARWICK, D. *Persistence and change: Bennington College and its students after twenty-five years.* New York: Wiley, 1967.

NEWCOMB, T., & WILSON, E. *College peer groups.* Chicago: Aldine, 1966.

NEWMANN, F. M. *Education for citizen action.* Berkeley: McCutchan, 1975.

NIEBUHR, R. *Moral man and immoral society.* New York: Scribner, 1932.

NIEMI, R. G. Political socialization. In J. N. Knutson (Ed.), *Handbook of political psychology.* San Francisco: Jossey-Bass, 1973.

NIEMI, R. G. *How family members perceive each other.* New Haven: Yale University Press, 1974. (a)

NIEMI, R. G. (Ed.). *The politics of future citizens.* San Francisco: Jossey-Bass, 1974. (b)

NIMMO, D., & UNGS, T. D. *American political patterns* (3rd ed.). Boston: Little, Brown, 1973.

NORDHOLM, L. A. Effects of group size and stimulus ambiguity on conformity. *Journal of Social Psychology,* 1975, *97,* 123–130.

NORTH, C. C., & HATT, P. Occupational ratings. In J. P. Robinson, R. Athanasiore, & K. B. Head (Eds.), *Measures of occupational attitudes and occupational characteristics.* Ann Arbor: Institute for Social Research, 1969.

O'CONNOR, R. E. Political activism and moral reasoning: Political and apolitical students in Great Britain and France. *British Journal of Political Science,* 1974, *4,* 53–78.

O'KANE, J. Economic and non-economic liberalism, upward mobility potential, and Catholic working class youth. *Social Forces,* 1970, *48,* 499–503.

OLIVER, D. W., & SHAVER, J. P. *Teaching public issues in the high school.* Boston: Houghton Mifflin, 1966.

OPPENHEIM, F. G. *Moral principles in political philosophy.* New York: Random House, 1968.

ORLANSKY, H. Infant care and personality. *Psychological Bulletin,* 1949, *46.*

ORREN, K., & PETTERSOM, P. Presidential assassination: A case study in the dynamics of political socialization. *Journal of Politics,* 1967, *29,* 388–404.

OSADA, A. *Children of the A-Bomb.* New York: Putman's, 1963.

OSGOOD, C. E., SUCI, G. J., & TANNENBAUM, P. H. *The measurement of meaning.* Urbana: University of Illinois Press, 1957.

OSGOOD, C. E., & TANNENBAUM, P. H. The principle of congruity in the prediction of attitude change. *Psychological Review,* 1955, *62,* 42–45.

OSTLUND, L. E., Interpersonal communication following McGovern's Eagleton decision. *Public Opinion Quarterly,* 1973, *37,* 601–610.

PAIGE, J. M. Changing patterns of anti-white attitudes among blacks. *Journal of Social Issues,* 1970, *26,* 69–86.

PARENTI, M. Ethnic politics and the persistence of ethnic identification. *American Political Science Review,* 1967, *61,* 717–726.

PATEMAN, C. *Participation and democratic theory.* London: Cambridge Press, 1970.

PATEMAN, C. A contribution to the political theory of organizational democracy. *Administration and Society,* 1975, *7,* 5–26.

PATRICK, J. J. The impact of an experimental course, "American Political Behavior," on the knowledge, skills, and attitudes of secondary school students. *Social Education,* February 1972, *36.*

PAVLOV, D. V. *Leningrad 1941: The blockade.* Chicago: University of Chicago Press, 1965.

PELTASON, J. W. *Fifty-eight lonely men: Southern federal judges and school desegregation.* New York: Harcourt, Brace & World, 1961.

PETERSON, R. E. The student left in American higher education. *Daedalus,* 1968, *97,* 293–317.

PETTIGREW, T. F. Personality and socio-cultural factors in intergroup attitudes: A cross-national comparison. *Journal of Conflict Resolutions,* 1958, *2,* 29–42.

PETTIGREW, T. F. *A profile of the Negro American.* Princeton: Princeton University Press, 1964.

PETTIGREW, T. F. Race and equal opportunity. Paper presented at Symposium on the Implications of the Coleman Report on Equality of Educational Opportunity at annual convention of American Psychology Association, Washington, D.C., 1967.

PETTIGREW, T. F. Racially separate or together? *Journal of Social Issues,* 1969, *25,* 43–69.

PHILLIPS, J. L., JR. *The origins of intellect: Piaget's theory.* San Francisco: Freeman, 1969.

PIAGET, J. *The psychology of intelligence.* New York: Harcourt, Brace, 1950.

PIAGET, J. *The moral judgment of the child.* New York: Free Press, 1965.

PIAGET, J. *Six psychological studies.* New York: Random House, 1968.

PIAGET, J. Piaget's theory. In P. H. Mussen (Ed.), *Carmichael's manual of child psychology* (3rd ed.). New York: Wiley, 1970. (a)

PIAGET, J. *Structuralism.* New York: Basic Books, 1970. (b)

PIAGET, J. *Genetic epistemology.* New York: Norton, 1971.

PIAGET, J., & WEIL, A. M. The development of the idea of the homeland and of relations with other countries. *International Social Science Bulletin,* 1951, *3,* 561–573.

PIERCE, B. L. *Civic attitudes in American school textbooks.* Chicago: University of Chicago Press, 1930.

PINNER, F. A. Parental overprotection and political distrust. *The Annals of the American Academy of Political and Social Science,* 1965, *361,* 58–70.

PINNER, F. A., et al. *Old age and political behavior.* Berkeley: University of California Press, 1959.

PITTEL, S. M., & MENDELSOHN, G. A. Measurement of moral values: A review and critique. *Psychological Bulletin,* 1966, *66,* 22–35.

PLOMIN, R. A temperament theory of personality development: Parent–child interactions. Unpublished doctoral dissertation, University of Texas, 1974.

POLLOCK, J. C., WHITE, D., & GOLD, F. When soldiers return: Combat and political alienation among white Vietnam veterans. In D. & S. Schwartz (Eds.), *New directions in political socialization.* New York: Free Press, 1975.

POLSBY, N. W. Political science and the press: Notes on coverage of a public opinion survey on the Vietnam war. *Western Political Quarterly,* 1969, *22,* 47–60.

PRANGER, R. J. *The eclipse of citizenship: Power and participation in contemporary politics.* New York: Holt, Rinehart & Winston, 1968.

PRANGER, R. J. Experience as a form of political education. Paper presented at annual meeting of American Political Science Association, Chicago, 1971.

PRESTON, R. C. *Children's reactions to a contemporary war situation.* New York: Teachers College, 1942.

PREWITT, K. Political socialization and leadership selection. *Annals of the American Academy of Political and Social Science,* 1965, *361,* 96–111.

PREWITT, K., EULAU, H., & ZISK, B. Political socialization and political roles. *Public Opinion Quarterly,* 1966–1967, *30,* 569–582.

PRICE, C. M., & BELL, C. G. The rules of the game: Political fact or academic fallacy. *Journal of Politics,* 1970, *32,* 839–855.

PRICE, D. *The scientific estate.* Oxford, Eng.: Oxford University Press, 1965.

PROSHANSKY, H. M., & EVANS, R. I. The radical right: A threat to the behavioral sciences. *Journal of Social Issues,* 1963, *19* (2), 86–106.

PROTHRO, J. W., CAMPBELL, E. Q., & GRIGG, C. M. Two-party voting in the South: Class vs. party identification. *American Political Science Review,* 1958, *52,* 131–139.

PROTHRO, J. W., & Grigg, C. M. Fundamental principles of democracy: Bases of agreement and disagreement. In C. Cnudde & D. E. Neubauer (Eds.), *Empirical democratic theory.* Chicago: Markham, 1969.

PUTNEY, S. & MIDDLETON, R. Some factors associated with student acceptance or rejection of war. *American Sociological Review,* 1962, *27,* 655–667.

QUAY, W. B., BENNETT, E. L., ROSENWEIG, M. R., & KRECH, D. Effects of isolation and environmental complexity on brain and pineal organ. *Physiology and Behavior,* 1969, *4,* 489–494.

RAFKY, D. Phenomenology and socialization: Some comments on the assumptions underlying socialization. In H. P. Dreitzel (Ed.), *Childhood and socialization.* New York: Macmillan, 1973.

RANSFORD, H. E. Blue collar anger: Reactions to student and black protest. *American Sociological Review,* 1972, *37,* 333–346.

RATHS, L. E., HARMIN, H., & SIMON, S. B. *Values and teaching: Working with values in the classroom.* Columbus, Ohio: Merrill, 1966.

RAUTMAN, A. L. Children's play in wartime. *Mental Hygiene,* 1943, 549–553.

RAUTMAN, A. L. War themes in children's stories six years later. *Journal of Psychology,* 1951, *31,* 263–270.

RAUTMAN, A. L., & BROWER, E. War themes in children's stories. *Journal of Psychology,* 1945, *25,* 191–202.

READING, R. R. Political socialization in Colombia and the United States: An exploratory study. In C. Pierce & R. A. Pride (Eds.), *Cross-national micro-analysis: Procedures and problems.* Beverly Hills: Sage Publications, 1972. (a)

READING, R. R. Is Easton's systems-persistence framework useful? A research note. *Journal of Politics,* 1972, *34,* 258–267. (b)

REAGAN, M. D. *The managed economy.* New York: Oxford University Press, 1963.

REARDON, B. The human person and the war system. *Intercom.* New York: Center for War/Peace Studies, 1971.

REARDON, B. A unit on peace and world order, *Media and Methods,* October 1969, 33–36.

REED, E. F. Does the individual tend to be consistently a progressive or a conservative? *Social Forces,* 1925, *6,* 49–52.

REHFISCH, J. M. A scale for personality rigidity. *Journal of Consulting Psychology,* 1958, *22,* 10–15.

REICKEN, H. W. Primary groups and political party choice. In E. Burdick & A. Brodbeck (Eds.), *American voting behavior.* New York: Free Press, 1959.

REISCHAUER, E. O. *Toward the 21st century, education for a changing world.* New York: Knopf, 1973.

REISS, A. *Occupations and social status*. New York: Free Press, 1961.

REISS, A. *The police and the public*. New Haven: Yale University Press, 1971.

REMMERS, H. H. (Ed.). *Anti-democratic attitudes in American schools*. Evanston, Ill.: Northwestern University Press, 1963.

REMMERS, H. H., & RADLER, D. H. *The American teenager*. New York: Bobbs-Merrill, 1957.

REMY, R. C. *International socialization*. Unpublished doctoral dissertation. Evanston, Ill.: Northwestern University, 1972.

REMY, R. C., & NATHAN, J. A. The future of political systems: What young people think. *Futures,* December 1974, *6,* 463–476.

REMY, R. C., NATHAN, J. A., BECKER, J., & TORNEY, J. *International learning and international education in a global age*. Washington, D.C.: National Council for the Social Studies, 1975.

RENSHON, S. A. *Psychological needs and political behavior: A theory of personality and political efficacy*. New York: Free Press, 1974.

RENSHON, S. A. Birth order and political socialization. In D. Schwartz & S. Schwartz (Eds.), *New directions in political socialization*. New York: Free Press, 1975. (c)

RENSHON, S. A. Personality and family dynamics in the political socialization process. *American Journal of Political Science,* February 1975, *19,* 63–80. (a)

RENSHON, S. A. Psychological needs, personal control and political participation. *Canadian Journal of Political Science,* 1975, *8,* 107–116. (d)

RENSHON, S. A. The role of personality development in the political socialization process. In D. Schwartz & S. Schwartz (Eds.), *New directions in political socialization*. New York: Free Press, 1975. (b)

RENSHON, S. A. *Personality theories and political analysis*. New York: Free Press, forthcoming.

Report of the National Advisory Commission on Civil Disorders (Kerner Commission). Washington, D.C.: U.S. Government Printing Office, 1968.

RESCHER, N. *Introduction to value theory*. Englewood Cliffs, N.J.: Prentice-Hall, 1968.

RESCHER, N. What is value change? A framework for research. In K. Baier & N. Rescher (Eds.), *Values and the future*. New York: Free Press, 1969.

REST, J. The hierarchical nature of moral judgment: A study of patterns of comprehension and preference of moral stages. *Journal of Personality,* 1973, *41,* 86–109.

REST, J. Developmental psychology as a guide to value education: A review of "Kohlbergian" programs. *Review of Educational Research,* 1974, *44,* 241–259.

REYMERT, M. L. The place of war toys in the present emergency. *Pedagogical Seminary,* 1944, *64,* 317–322.

RICCARDS, M. P. *The making of the American citizenry*. San Francisco: Chandler, 1973.

RICHAN, W., & MENDELSOHN, A. *Social work: The unloved profession*. New York: New Viewpoints, 1973.

RICHET, C. Experiences of a medical prisoner in Buchenwald. In H. L. Tidy & J. M. B. Kitschbach (Eds.), *Inter-allied conferences on war medicine*. London: Staples Press, 1947.

RIESMAN, D. *Faces in the crowd.* New Haven: Yale University Press, 1952.

RIESMAN, D., GLAZER, N., & DENNEY, R. *The lonely crowd.* New Haven: Yale University Press, 1950.

RILEY, M. W. Aging and cohort succession: Interpretations and misinterpretations. *Public Opinion Quarterly,* 1973, *37,* 35–49.

RILEY, M. W., & FONER, A. *Aging and society.* New York: Russell Sage Foundation, 1968.

RILEY, M. W., FONER, A., HESS, B., & TOBY, M. L. Socialization for the middle and later years. In D. A. Goslin (Ed.), *Handbook of socialization theory and research.* Chicago: Rand McNally, 1969.

RILEY, M. W., JOHNSON, M., & FONER, A. *Aging and society: A sociology of age stratification* (Vol. 3). New York: Russell Sage Foundation, 1972.

RIM, Y. Values and attitudes. *Personality: An International Journal,* 1970, *1,* 243–250.

RINTALA, M. Political generations. In D. L. Sills (Ed.), *International encyclopedia of the social sciences.* New York: Macmillan and Free Press, 1968.

ROBACK, T. Occupational and political attitudes: The case of professional groups. In A. Wilcox (Ed.), *Public Opinion and political attitudes.* New York: Wiley, 1974.

ROBERTS, D. Communication and children: A developmental approach. In I. de Sola Pool, Frey, F., Schramm, W., Maccoby, N., & Parker, E. (Eds.), *Handbook of communication.* Chicago: Rand McNally, 1973.

ROBERTS, D., PINGREE, S., & HAWKINS, R. Do the mass media play a role in political socialization? *Australian and New Zealand Journal of Sociology,* 1974, *11,* 37–43.

ROBINSON, J. P., RUSK, J. G., & HEAD, K. B. *Measures of political attitudes.* Ann Arbor: Survey Research Center Institute for Social Research, 1968.

ROBINSON, J. P., & SHAVER, P. R. *Measures of social psychological attitudes: Appendix B to measures of political attitudes.* Ann Arbor: Survey Research Center Institute for Social Research, 1969.

ROBINSON, W. S. The statistical measure of agreement. *American Sociological Review,* 1957, *22,* 17–25.

ROBINSON, W. S. The geometric interpretation of agreement. *American Sociological Review,* 1959, *24,* 338–345.

RODGERS, H. R., & LEWIS, E. B. Student attitudes toward Mr. Nixon: The consequences of negative attitudes toward a President for political system support. *American Politics Quarterly,* 1975, *3,* 423–436.

ROGERS, C. *On becoming a person.* Boston: Houghton-Mifflin, 1961.

ROGERS, E. M., with SHOEMAKER, F. F. *Communication of innovations: A cross-cultural approach* (2nd ed.). New York: Free Press, 1971.

ROGERS, V. Ethnocentrism and the social studies. *Phi Delta Kappan,* 1967, *49,* 209.

ROHTER, I. S. Social and psychological determinants of radical rightism. In R. Schoenberger (Ed.), *The American right wing.* New York: Holt, Rinehart & Winston, 1969.

ROHTER, I. S. A social-learning approach to political socialization. In D. Schwartz & S. Schwartz (Eds.), *New directions in political socialization.* New York: Free Press, 1975.

ROKEACH, M. *The open and closed mind.* New York: Basic Books, 1960.

ROKEACH, M. *Beliefs, attitudes, and values.* San Francisco: Jossey-Bass, 1968.

ROKEACH, M. Long-range experimental modification of values, attitudes, and behavior. *American Psychologist,* 1971, *26,* 453–459.

ROKEACH, M. *The nature of human values.* New York: Free Press, 1973.

ROSE, A. M. Alienation and participation: A comparison of group leaders and the "mass." *American Sociological Review,* 1962, *27,* 834–838.

ROSELL, L. Children's views of war and peace. *Journal of Peace Research,* 1968, *5,* 268–276.

ROSENAU, J. Foreign policy as an issue area. In J. Rosenau (Ed.), *Domestic sources of foreign policy.* New York: Free Press, 1967.

ROSENBERG, L. A. Group size, prior experience and conformity. *Journal of Abnormal and Social Psychology,* 1961, *63,* 436–447.

ROSENBERG, M. The meaning of politics in mass society. *Public Opinion Quarterly.* 1951, *15,* 5–15.

ROSENBERG, M. Some determinants of political apathy. *Public Opinion Quarterly,* 1954, *18,* 349–366.

ROSENBERG, M. Misanthropy and political ideology. *American Sociological Review,* 1956, *21,* 690–695.

ROSENBERG, M., VERBA, S., & CONVERSE, P. *Vietnam and the silent majority.* New York: Harper & Row, 1970.

ROSENBLUM, G. *Immigrant workers: Their impact on American labor radicalism.* New York: Basic Books, 1973.

ROSENHAM, D. L. Learning theory and pro-social behavior. *Journal of Social Issues,* 1972, *28,* 151–164.

ROSENTHAL, R. *Experimental effects in behavioral research.* New York: Appleton-Century-Crofts, 1966.

ROSZAK, T. *The making of a counterculture.* Garden City, N.Y.: Doubleday, Anchor Books, 1968.

ROTHLISBERGER, F. J., & DICKSON, W. J. *Management and the worker.* Cambridge: Harvard University Press, 1939.

ROTHSCHILD, E. G.M. in more trouble. *New York Review of Books,* March 1972.

ROTHSCHILD, M. L., & RAY, M. L. Involvement and political advertising effectiveness. Paper presented to American Association for Public Opinion Research, 1973.

ROURKE, F. *Bureaucracy, politics, and public policy.* Boston: Little, Brown, 1969.

ROZELLE, R. M., & CAMPBELL, D. T. More plausible rival hypotheses in the cross-lagged panel correlation technique. *Psychological Bulletin,* 1969, *71,* 74–80.

RUBIN, K. H., & SCHNEIDER, F. The relationship between moral judgment, ego-centrism and altruistic behavior. *Child Development,* 1973, *44,* 661–665.

RULE, B. G., & DUKER, P. Effects of intentions and consequences on children's evaluations of aggressors. *Journal of Personality and Social Psychology,* 1973, *27,* 184–189.

RUMA, E. H., & MOSHER, D. L. Relationship between moral judgment and guilt in delinquent boys. *Journal of Abnormal Psychology,* 1967, *72,* 122–127.

RUTTER, M. *Maternal deprivation reassessed.* Harmondsworth, Middlesex, Eng.: Penguin Books, 1972.

RYDER, N. B. The cohort as a concept in the study of social change. *American Sociological Review,* 1965, *30,* 843–861.

SAENGER, G. H. Social status and political behavior. *American Journal of Sociology,* 1945, *51,* 103–113.

SALES, S. M. Need for stimulation as a factor in social behavior. *Journal of Personality and Social Psychology,* 1971, *19,* 124–131.

SALISBURY, H. *The 900 days: The siege of Leningrad.* New York: Avon Books, 1969–1970.

SALTZSTEIN, H. D., DIAMOND, R., & BELENKY, M. Moral judgment level and conformity behavior. *Developmental Psychology,* 1972, *7,* 327–336.

SAMPSON, R. *The psychology of power.* New York: Vintage Books, 1968.

SANFORD, F. H. *Authoritarianism and leadership.* Philadelphia: Stephenson, 1950.

SANFORD, N. Authoritarian personality in contemporary perspective. In J. N. Knutson (Ed.), *Handbook of political psychology.* San Francisco: Jossey-Bass, 1973.

SCAMMON, R., & WATTENBERG, B. J. *The real majority.* New York: Coward, McCann, & Geoghegan, 1970.

SCARR, S. Social introversion-extraversion as a meritable response. *Child Development,* 1969, *40,* 823–832.

SCHAFFNER, B. *Fatherland: A study of authoritarianism in the German family.* New York: Columbia University Press, 1948.

SCHAIE, K. W. A general model for the study of developmental problems. *Psychological Bulletin,* 1965, *64,* 92–107.

SCHAIE, K. W. A reinterpretation of age-related changes in cognitive structure and functioning. In L. R. Goulet & Paul Baltes (Eds.), *Life span developmental psychology: Research and theory.* New York: Academic Press, 1970.

SCHAIE, K. W. Can the longitudinal method be applied to psychological studies of human development? *Determinants of Behavioral Development,* 1972, 3–22.

SCHAIE, K. W. Methodological problems in descriptive developmental research on adulthood and aging. In J. R. Nesselroade & H. W. Reese (Eds.), *Life-span developmental psychology: Methodological issues.* New York: Academic Press, 1973.

SCHAIE, K. W. Quasi-experimental research design in the psychology of ageing. In J. E. Birren (Ed.), *Handbook of the psychology of ageing.* New York: Rineholt, 1977.

SCHAIE, K. W., & STROTHER, C. R. A cross-sequential study of age changes in cognitive behavior. *Psychological Bulletin,* 1968, 70 (6), 671–680.

SCHARF, P., HICKEY, J. E., & MORIARTY, T. Moral conflict and change in correctional settings. *Personnel and Guidance Journal,* 1973, *51,* 660–663.

SCHEFLEN, A. *Human territories.* Englewood Cliffs, N.J.: Prentice-Hall, 1976.

SCHEIN, H. H. The Chinese indoctrination program for prisoners of war: A study of attempted "brainwashing." *Psychiatry,* 1956, *19,* 149–172.

SCHICK, M., & SOMIT, A. The failure to teach political activity. *American Behavioral Scientist,* 1963, *6,* 5–8.

SCHIFF, L. F. The obedient rebels: A study of conversions to conservatism. *Journal of Social Issues,* 1964, *20,* 74–95.

SCHILLER, H. *Mass communications and American empire.* Boston: Beacon Press, 1971.

SCHLEIFER, M., & DOUGLAS, V. I. Effects of training on the moral judgment of young children. *Journal of Personality and Social Psychology,* 1973, *28,* 62–68.

SCHLENKER, B. R. Social psychology and science. *Journal of Personality and Social Psychology,* 1974, *29,* 1–15.

SHONFELD, W. The focus of political socialization research: An evaluation. *World Politics,* 1971, *22,* 544–578.

SCHRAMM, W., LYLE, J., & PARKER, E. B. *Television in the lives of our children.* Stanford: Stanford University Press, 1961.

SCHREIBER, E. M., & MARSDEN, L. R. Age and opinions on a government program of medical aid. *Journal of Gerontology,* 1972, *27,* 95–101.

SCHUMAN, H., & HARDING, J. Sympathetic identification with the underdog. *Public Opinion Quarterly,* 1963, *27,* 230–232.

SCHWARTZ, D. C. A theory of revolutionary behavior. In J. C. Davies (Ed.), *When men revolt.* New York: Free Press, 1970.

SCHWARTZ, D. C. Health processes and body images as predictors of political attitudes and behavior: A study in political socialization. Paper presented at Congress of International Political Science Association, Montreal, 1973.

SCHWARTZ, D. C., & SCHWARTZ, S. (Eds.), *New directions in political socialization.* New York: Free Press, 1975.

SCRIMSHAW, N. S., & GORDON, J. E. (Eds.), *Malnutrition, learning, and behavior.* Cambridge: MIT Press, 1965.

SEARING, D. D., SCHWARTZ, J. J., & LIND, A. E. The structuring principle: Political socialization and belief systems. *American Political Science Review,* June 1973, *67,* 415–542.

SEARS, D. O. Political behavior. In G. Lindzey & E. Aronson (Eds.), *The handbook of social psychology* (Vol. 5). Reading, Mass.: Addison-Wesley, 1969.

SEARS, D. O. Political socialization. In F. I. Greenstein & N. W. Polsby (Eds.), The *handbook of political science: Micropolitical theory* (Vol. 2). Reading, Mass.: Addison-Wesley, 1975. (a)

SEARS, D. O. The problem of generations: A social psychologist's perspective. Paper delivered at annual meeting of American Political Science Association, San Francisco, 1975. (b)

SEARS, D. O. & McCONAHAY, J. B. *The politics of violence: The new urban blacks and the Watts riot.* Boston: Houghton Mifflin, 1973.

SEARS, D. O., & WHITNEY, R. E. *Political persuasion.* Morristown: General Learning Press, 1973.

SEARS, R. R., MACCOBY, E. E., & LEVIN, H. *Patterns of child rearing.* Evanston, Ill.: Row, Peterson, 1957.

SEBERT, S. K., JENNINGS, M. K., & NIEMI, R. The political texture of peer groups. In Jennings & Niemi, *The political character of adolescence.* Princeton: Princeton University Press, 1974.

SEEMAN, M. On the meaning of alienation. *American Sociological Review,* 1959, *25,* 783–791.

SEEMAN, M. Alienation, membership, and political knowledge: A comparative study. *Public Opinion Quarterly,* 1966, *30,* 353–367.

SEGAL, J. Correlates of collaborations and resistance behavior among U. S. Army POW's in Korea. *Journal of Social Issues,* 1957, *13,* 31–40.

SEIDLER, M. B., & RAVITZ, J. A Jewish peer group. *American Journal of Sociology,* 1955, *63,* 11–15.

SELMAN, R. The importance of reciprocal role-taking for the development of conventional moral thought. Unpublished mimeograph. Harvard Moral Development Project, n. d.

SELVIN, H., & HAGSTROM, W. Determinants of support for civil liberties. In S. M. Lipset & S. Wolin (Eds.), *The Berkeley student revolt.* Garden City, N.Y.: Doubleday, Anchor Books, 1965.

SENNET, R. *The uses of disorder: Personal identity and city life.* New York: Knopf, 1970.

SERRIN, W. *The company and the union.* New York: Knopf, 1972.

SEWELL, W. H. Some recent developments in socialization theory and research. *Annals of the American Academy of Political and Social Science,* 1963, 349, 163–181.

SEXTON, P. C. *The American school.* Englewood Cliffs, N.J.: Prentice-Hall, 1967.

SEXTON, P. C., & SEXTON, B. *Blue collars and hard hats.* New York: Random House, 1971.

SHAPIRO, M. J. Reflections on the politics of education. Paper delivered at Conference on Social Education and the Sociology of Education, East Lansing, Michigan, 1974.

SHAPIRO, M. J. Foucault: A political analysis. Paper delivered at annual meeting of American Political Science Association, San Francisco, 1975.

SHAVER, J. P., & LARKINS, A. G. *The analysis of public issues: Instructor's manual.* Boston: Houghton Mifflin, 1973.

SHEINKOPF, K. Family communication patterns and anticipatory socialization. *Journalism Quarterly,* 1973, *50,* 24–30.

SHERIF, C. W., SHERIF, M., & NEBERGALL, R. E. *Attitude and attitude change.* Philadelphia: Sanders, 1965.

SHILS, E. Authoritarianism "right" and "left." In R. Christie & M. Jahoda (Eds.), *Studies in the scope and method of "the authoritarian personality."* New York: Free Press, 1954.

SHILS, E. Primordial, personal, sacred, and civil ties. *British Journal of Sociology,* 1957, *8,* 130–145.

SHOKEID, M. *The dual heritage: Immigrants from the Atlas Mountains in an Israeli village.* Manchester, Eng.: Manchester University Press, 1971.

SHOUVAL, R., VENAKI, S. K., BRONFENBRENNER, U., DEVEREUX, E. C., & KIELY, E. Anomalous reactions to social pressure of Israeli and Soviet children raised in family versus collective settings. *Journal of Personality and Social Psychology,* 1975, *32,* 477–489.

SHUVAL, J. *Immigrants on the threshold.* New York: Atherton, 1963.

SIEVERT, W., & LANGER, H. The postwar pursuit of peace studies. *Saturday Review of Education,* 1973, 38–39.

SIGEL, R. S. Assumptions about the learning of political values. *Annals of the American Academy of Social and Political Science,* 1965, *361,* 165, 1–9.

SIGEL, R. S. Political socialization: Some reactions to current approaches and concep- tualizations. Paper read at annual meeting of American Political Science Association, New York City, 1966.

SIGEL, R. S. (Ed.). *Learning about politics: A reader in political socialization.* New York: Random House, 1970.

SIGEL, R. S. *Adolescent political involvement in a small town.* North Scituate, Mass.: Duxbury Press, 1975.

SIGEL, R. S., & BROOKES, M. Becoming critical about politics. In R. Niemi (Ed.), *The politics of future citizens.* San Francisco: Jossey-Bass, 1974.

SIGEL, R. S., & HOSKIN, M. Satisfaction and dissatisfaction with government output: American adolescents in the 70's. Paper prepared for annual meeting of Midwest Political Sicence Association, Chicago, 1975.

SILBIGER, S. L. Information sources and the development of political attitudes in children: The case of Watergate. Unpublished manuscript, 1975.

SILVER, B. Social mobilization and the Russification of Soviet nationalities. *American Political Science Review,* 1974, *68,* 45–66.

SILVERN, L., & NAKAMURA, C. Powerlessness, social-political action, social-political views: Their interrelations among college students. *Journal of Social Issues,* 1971, *27,* 137–158.

SIMON, H. *Models of man.* New York: Wiley, 1957.

SIMPSON, E. L. *Democracy's stepchildren: A study of need and belief.* San Francisco: Jossey-Bass, 1971.

SIMPSON, E. L. Moral development research: A case study of scientific cultural bias. *Human Development,* 1974, *17* (2), 81–106.

SIMPSON, E. L. A holistic view of moral development and behavior. In T. Lickona (Ed.), *Moral development and behavior.* New York: Holt, Rinehart, & Winston, 1976.

SISTRUNCK, F., & MCDAVID, J. Sex variable in conforming behavior. *Journal of Person- ality and Social Psychology,* 1971, *17,* 200–207.

SKARD, A. Children and war. *Delta Kappa Gamma Bulletin,* 1972, 33–38.

SKLAR, R. L. Political science and national integration—a radical approach. *Journal of Modern African Studies,* 1967, *5* (1), 1–11.

SLATER, P. *The pursuit of loneliness.* Boston: Beacon Press, 1970.

SMITH, C., & PROTHRO, J. W., Ethnic differences in authoritarian personality. *Social Force,* 1957, *35,* 334–338.

SMITH, F. R., & PATRICK, J. J. Civics: Relating social study to social reality. In C. B. Cox & B. G. Massialas (Eds.), *Social studies in the United States: A critical ap- praisal.* New York: Harcourt, Brace & World, 1967.

SMITH, M. Educational research and statistics: Spontaneous change of attitude toward war. *School and Society,* 1937, 30–32.

SMITH, M. B. Competence and socialization. In J. A. Clausen (Ed.), *Socialization and society.* Boston: Little, Brown, 1968. (a)

SMITH, M. B. A map for the analysis of personality and politics. *Journal of Social Issues,* 1968, *24,* (3), 15–28. (b)

SMITH, M. B. *Social psychology and human values.* Chicago: Aldine, 1969.

SMITH, M. B., BRUNER, J. S., & WHITE, R. W. *Opinions and personality.* New York: Wiley, 1956.

SMITH, M. B., HAAN, N., & BLOCK, J. Social-psychological aspects of student activism. Paper presented at meeting of American Sociological Association, San Francisco, September 1967.

SNIDERMAN, P. *Personality and democratic politics.* Berkeley: University of California Press, 1975.

SNOW, C. P. *The two cultures.* Cambridge, Eng.: Cambridge University Press, 1964.

SNYDER, M., & MONSON, T. Persons, situations and the control of social behavior. *Journal of Personality and Social Psychology,* 1975, *32,* 637–644.

SOARES, G. The active few: Student ideology and participation in developing countries. *Comparative Education Review,* 1966, *10,* 205–219.

Social Science Education Consortium Staff. Analysis of 26 projects. *Social Education,* November 1972, *36.*

SOLOMON, P., KUBZANSKY, P. E., LEIDERMAN, P. H., MENDELSON, J. H., TRUMBULL, R., & WEXLER, D. (Eds.), *Sensory deprivation.* Cambridge: Harvard University Press, 1961.

SOLOMON, R. L. Preliminary report on temptation and guilt in young boys. In R. C. Johnson, P. R. Dokecki, & O. H. Mowrer (Eds.), *Conscience, contract and social reality.* New York: Holt, Rinehart & Winston, 1972.

SOMERS, R. The mainsprings of the rebellion: A survey of Berkeley students. In S. M. Lipset & S. S. Wolin (Eds.), *The Berkeley student revolt.* Garden City, N.Y.: Doubleday, Anchor Books, 1965.

SOMIT, A., TANENHAUS, J., WILKE, W. H., & COOLEY, R. W. The effect of the introductory political science course on student attitudes toward personal political participation. *American Political Science Review,* 1958, *52,* 1129–1132.

SOREL, G. *Reflections on violence.* London: Collier-Macmillan, 1961. (Originally published 1908).

SOROKIN, P. *Ways and power of love.* Boston: Beacon Press, 1954.

SPIRO, M. Is the family universal? *American Anthropologist,* 1954, *56,* 839–846.

SPIRO, M. *Kibbutz.* New York: Schocken, 1970.

SPITZ, R. A. The role of sociological factors in emotional development in infancy. *Child Development,* 1949, *2,* 145–155.

SPITZ, R. A. *The first year of life: A psychoanalytic study of normal and deviant development of object relations.* New York: International Universities Press, 1965.

SPITZER, A. B. The historical problem of generations. *American Historical Review,* 1973, *78* (5), 1353–1385.

SPRECHT, H. The deprofessionalization of social work. *Social Work,* 1972, *17,* 3–15.

STAGNER, R. Some factors related to attitude toward war, 1938. *Journal of Social Psychology,* 1942, *16,* 131–143.

STAGNER, R. Studies of aggressive social attitudes II: Changes from peace to war. *Journal of Social Psychology,* 1944, *21,* 121–123.

STAGNER, R. Attitudes toward authority: An exploratory study. *Journal of Social Psychology,* 1954, *40,* 197–210.

STAGNER, R., BROWN, J. F., GUNDLACH, R. H., & WHITE, R. A survey of public opinion on the prevention of war. *Journal of Social Psychology*, SPSSI Bulletin, 1942, *16*, 109–130.

STAPLES, F. R., & WALTERS, R. H. Anxiety, birth order and susceptibility to social influence. *Journal of Abnormal and Social Psychology*, 1961, *62*, 716–719.

STARR, P. *The discharged army: Veterans after Vietnam*. New York: Charter House, 1973.

STAUB, E. Helping a person in distress: The influence of implicit and explicit "rules" of conduct on children and adults. *Journal of Personality and Social Psychology*, 1971, *17*, 137–144.

STAUFFER, R. B. The biopolitics of underdevelopment. *Comparative Political Studies*, October 1969, *2* (3), 361–387.

STEIN, G. M. Children's reactions to innocent victims. *Child Development*, 1973, *44*, 805–810.

STEPHENS, R. Schools and war. *Teachers College Journal*, 1967, 256–274.

STEVENS, R. *American medicine and the public interest*. New Haven: Yale University Press, 1971.

STONE, V., & CHAFFEE, S. H. Family communication patterns and source-message orientation. *Journalism Quarterly*, 1970, *47*, 239–246.

STORR, A. *Human aggression*. New York: Atheneum, 1968.

STOUFFER, S. A. *Communism, conformity, and civil liberties*. Garden City, N.Y.: Doubleday, 1955.

STRACHEY, A. *The unconscious motives of war*. London: Allan & Unwin, 1957.

SULEIMAN, E. *Political power and bureaucracy in France*. Princeton: Princeton University Press, 1974.

SULLIVAN, E., & QUARTER, J. Psychological correlates of certain postconventional moral types: A perspective on hybrid types. *Journal of Personality*, 1972, *40*, 149–161.

SULLIVAN, E. V., McCULLOUGH, G., & STAGER, M. A developmental study of the relationship between conceptual, ego, and moral development. *Child Development*, 1970, *41*, 399–411.

SULLIVAN, H. S. *Conceptions of modern psychiatry*. New York: Norton, 1953.

SUMMERS, R. S., CAMPBELL, A. B., & HUBBARD, G. F. *Teacher's guide to the American legal system*. Lexington, Mass.: Ginn, 1974.

SUOMI, S. J., & HARLOW, H. F. Social rehabilitation of isolate-reared monkeys. *Developmental Psychology*, 1972, *6*, 487–496.

SUTTON, F. X. Education and the making of modern nations. In J. S. Coleman (Ed.), *Education and political development*. Princeton: Princeton University Press, 1965.

TAPP, J. L. A child's garden of law and order. *Psychology Today*, December 1970, *54*.

TAPP, J. L. Developing sense of law and legal justice. *Journal of Social Issues*, Spring 1971, *27*.

TAPP, J. L., & LEVINE, F. J. Persuasion to virtue: A preliminary statement. *Law and Society Review*, 1970, *4*, 565–582.

TARG, H. Impacts of an elementary school inter-nation simulation on developing orientations to international politics. Unpublished doctoral dissertation, Northwestern University, 1967.

TARG, H. Children's developing orientations to international politics. *Journal of Peace Research*, 1970, *1*, 80–93.

Teaching about war, peace, conflict and change. *Intercom*, 1971.

TEDIN, K. L. The influence of parents on the political attitudes of adolescents. *American Political Science Review*, 1974, *68*, 1579–1592.

THIBAUT, J. W., & KELLEY, H. H. *The social psychology of groups*. New York: Wiley, 1959.

THOMAS, E. L. The I-E scale, ideological bias and political participation. *Journal of Personality*, 1970, *3*, 38.

THOMAS, E. L. Family correlates of student political activism. *Developmental Psychology*, 1971, *4*, 206–214.

THOMAS, L. E. *The lives of a cell*. New York: Viking, 1974.

THOMAS, W. L. The initial development of the differential value profile. Unpublished doctoral dissertation, University of Tulsa, 1970.

THOMAS, W. L., & ZNANIECKI, F. *The Polish peasant in America and Europe*. New York: Dover, 1958.

THOMPSON, D. *The democratic citizen*. London: Cambridge University Press, 1970.

THOMPSON, K. A cross-national analysis of intergenerational social mobility and political orientation. *Comparative Political Studies*, 1971, *4*, 3–20.

THOMPSON, K. Upward social mobility and political orientation: A reinterpretation of the evidence. *American Sociological Review*, 1971, *36*, 223–234.

THOMPSON, V. *Bureaucracy and innovation*. University: Alabama University Press, 1969.

THORSON, T. L. *Biopolitics*. New York: Holt, Rinehart & Winston, 1970.

THORPE, G. L. *A suggested procedure for teaching a 12-week unit on problems of peace and war in the modern world*. New York: World Law Fund, 1968.

THURSTONE, L. L. Primary mental abilities. *Psychological Monographs*, 1938, *1*.

TICHENOR, P. J., RODENKIRCHEN, J. M., OLIEN, C. N., & DONOHUE, G. A. Community issues, conflict, and public affairs knowledge. In P. Clarke (Ed.), *New models for mass communication research*. Beverly Hills: Sage Publications, 1973.

TIPTON, L. P. Effects of writing tasks on utility of information and order of seeking. *Journalism Quarterly*, 1970, *47*, 309–317.

TISDALE, J. R. Psychological value theory and research: 1930–1960. Unpublished doctoral dissertation, Boston University, 1961.

TOCH, H. *The social psychology of social movements*. Indianapolis: Bobbs-Merrill, 1965.

TOLLEY, H., JR. *Children and war*. New York: Teachers College Press, 1973.

TOMKINS, S. Left and right: A basic dimension of ideology and personality. In R. W. White (Ed.), *The study of lives*. New York: Atherton Press, 1963.

TOREN, N. *Social work*. Beverly Hills: Sage Publications, 1972.

TORNEY, J. Research in the development of international orientations during childhood and adolescence. Paper presented at 65th annual meeting of American Political Science Association, New York, 1969.

TORNEY, J. Conceptions of peace and war in children. Paper presented at Peace Research Society, Midwest, East Lansing, 1970.

TORNEY, J. Implications of the IEA cross national civic education data for understanding the international socialization of American adolescents. Paper presented at 70th meeting of American Political Science Association, Chicago, 1974.

TORNEY, J. Civic education in ten nations: An empirical study. *DEA News.* Washington, D.C.: American Political Science Association, 1975.

TORNEY, J., & MORRIS, D. *Global dimensions in U.S. education: The elementary school.* New York: Center for War/Peace Studies, 1972.

TORRANCE, E. P. *Guiding creative talent.* Englewood Cliffs, N.J.: Prentice-Hall, 1962.

TORRANCE, E. P. *Torrance tests of creative thinking norms—technical manual.* Princeton: Personnel Press, 1966.

TREIMAN, D. Status discrepancy and prejudice reconsidered. *American Journal of Sociology,* 1970, *71,* 651–664.

TRELA, J. Age structure of voluntary associations and political self-interest among the aged. *Sociological Quarterly,* 1972, *13,* 244–252.

TRENT, J., & CRAISE, J. Commitment and conformity in the American college. *Journal of Social Issues,* 1967, *23,* 34–51.

TROLDAHL, V. C. A field test of a modified "two-step flow of communication" model. *Public Opinion Quarterly,* 1966, *30,* 609–623.

TROLL, L. E. Issues in the study of generations. *Aging and Human Development,* 1970, *1,* 199–218.

TRYON, R. C., & BAILEY, D. E. *Cluster analysis.* New York: McGraw-Hill, 1970.

TURIEL, E. Developmental processes in the child's moral thinking. In P. Mussen, J. Langer, & M. Covington (Eds.), *Trends and issues in developmental psychology.* New York: Holt, Rinehart & Winston, 1969.

TURIEL, E. An experimental test of the sequentiality of developmental stages in the child's moral judgments. In R. C. Johnson, P. R. Dokecki, & O. H. Mowrer (Eds.), *Conscience, contract and social reality.* New York: Holt, Rinehart & Winston, 1972.

TURIEL, E. Conflict and transition in adolescent moral development. *Child Development,* 1974, *45,* 14–29.

TURIEL, E. The development of social concepts: Mores, customs and conventions. In D. J. DePalma & J. M. Foley (Eds.), *Moral development: Current research and theory.* Hillsdale, N. J.: Erlbaum Association, 1975.

TURNBULL, C. M. *The mountain people.* New York: Simon & Schuster Touchstone paperback, 1972.

TURNER, F. J. Quoted in J. Schafer. The microscopic method applied to history. *Minnesota History Bulletin,* 1921, *4,* 19.

TURNER, M. J., & HALEY, F. *Utilization of new social studies curriculum programs.* Boulder, Colo.: Social Science Educations Consortium, 1975.

U. S. Government, Department of Health, Education and Welfare. *Work in America.* Washington, D.C.: U.S. Government Printing Office, 1972.

VAILLANCOURT, P. M. Stability of children's survey responses. *Public Opinion Quarterly,* 1973, *37,* 373–387.

VAILLANCOURT, P. M., & NIEMI, R. G. Children's party choices. In R. G. Niemi (Ed.), *The politics of future citizens.* San Francisco: Jossey-Bass, 1974.

VANDENBERG, S. Heredity factors in normal personality traits (as measured by inventories). In J. Wortis (Ed.), *Recent advances in biological psychiatry* (Vol. 9). New York: Plenum, 1967.

VANDENBERG, S. What do we know today about the inheritance of intelligence and how do we know it? In R. Cancro (Ed.), *Intelligence: Genetic and environmental influences*. New York: Grune & Stratton, 1971.

VAN DEN DAELE, L. A developmental study of ego-ideals. *Genetic Psychology Monographs*, 1968, *78*, 191–256.

VANEK, J. *The participatory economy*. Ithaca, N.Y.: Cornell University Press, 1971.

VAN SLYCK, P. *Peace: The control of national power*. Boston: Beacon Press, 1963.

VELDMAN, D. J. *Fortran programming for the behavioral sciences*. New York: Holt, Rinehart & Winston, 1967.

VERBA, S. Conclusion: Comparative political culture. In L. W. Pye & S. Verba (Eds.), *Political culture and political development*. Princeton: Princeton University Press, 1965.

VERBA, S., BRODY, R. A., PARKER, E. B., NIE, N. H., POLSBY, N. W., EKMAN, P., & BLACK, G. S. Public opinion and the war in Vietnam. *American Political Science Review*, 1967, 317–333.

VERBA, S., & NIE, N. H. *Participation in America*. New York: Harper & Row, 1972.

VOGEL, E. *Japan's new middle class*. Berkeley: California University Press, 1968.

WACHTEL, P. L. Psychodynamics, behavior therapy and the implacable experimenter: An inquiry into the consistency of personality. *Journal of Abnormal Psychology*, 1973, *82*, 324–334.

WAHLKE, J., EULEAU, H., BUCHANAN, W., & FERGUSON, L. C. *The legislative system*. New York: Wiley, 1962.

WAHLKE, J., & LODGE, M. Psychophysiological measures of political attitudes and behaviors. *Midwest Journal of Political Science*, 1972, *4*, 505–537.

WALDMAN, S. *A theory of political exchange*. Boston: Little, Brown, 1973.

WALKER, J. A critique of the elitist theory of democracy. *American Political Science Review*, 1966, *60*, 285–295.

WALLAS, G. *Human nature in politics*. New York: A. Knopf, 1921.

WALLINGTON, S. A. Consequences of transgression. *Journal of Personality and Social Psychology*, 1973, *28*, 1–17.

WALSTER, E. The effect of self-esteem on romantic liking. *Journal of Experimental Social Psychology*, 1965, *1*, 184–197.

WALSTER, E. Assignment of responsibility for an accident. *Journal of Personality and Social Psychology*, 1966, *3*, 73–79.

WALSTER, E., BERCHEID, E., & WALSTER, G. W. New directions in equity research. *Journal of Personality and Social Psychology*, 1973, *25*, 151–176.

WASHBURN, M. Peace education is alive but unsure of itself. *War/Peace Report*, 1971, 14–18.

WATSON, N., & STERLING, J. *Police and their opinions*. Washington, D.C.: International Association of Police Chiefs, 1969.

WATTS, W. A., LYNCH, S., & WHITTAKER, K. Alienation and activism in today's college-age youth: Socialization patterns and current family relationships. *Journal of Counseling Psychology,* 1969, *16,* 1–7.

WATTS, W., & WHITTAKER, D. Free speech advocates at Berkeley. *Journal of Applied Behavioral Science,* 1966, *2,* 41–62.

WEAVER, D., MCCOMBS, M., & SPELLMAN, C. Watergate and the media: A case study of agenda-setting. *American Politics Quarterly,* 1975, *3,* 458–472.

WEBER, M. *The Protestant ethic and the spirit of capitalism.* New York: Scribner's, 1930.

WEISBORD, M. R. *The school and the democratic environment.* New York: Columbia University Press, 1970.

WEISS, W. Effects of the mass media on communication. In G. Lindzey & E. Aronson (Eds.), *Handbook of social psychology* (Vol. 5) (2nd ed.). Reading Mass.: Addison-Wesley, 1969.

WEISSBERG, R. *Political learning, political choice and democratic citizenship.* Englewood Cliffs, N.J.: Prentice-Hall, 1974.

WELTMAN, J. J. *Systems theory in international relations.* Lexington, Mass.: Lexington Books, 1973.

WERTHAM, F. *A sign for Cain.* New York: Macmillan, 1966.

WEST, J. *Plainville, U.S.A.* New York: Columbia University Press, 1945.

WESTBY, D., & BRAUNGART, R. Class and politics in the family backgrounds of student political activists. *American Sociological Review,* 1966, *31,* 690–692.

WESTIN, A. The John Birch Society: "Radical right" and "extreme left" in the political context of post World War II. In D. Bell (Ed.), *The radical right.* New York: Doubleday, 1964.

WHEELER, S. The structure of formally organized socialization settings. In O. Brim & S. Wheeler (Eds.), *Socialization after childhood.* New York: Wiley, 1966.

WHITE, E. S. Intelligence and the sense of political efficacy in children. *Journal of Politics,* 1968, *3,* 710–731.

WHITE, E. S. Intelligence, individual differences and learning: An approach to political socialization. *British Journal of Sociology,* 1969, *20,* 50–66.

WHITE, R. W. Competence and the psychosexual stages of development. In M. R. Jones (Ed.), *Nebraska Symposium on Motivation.* Lincoln: University of Nebraska Press, 1960.

WHITTAKER, D., & WATTS, W. A. Personality characteristics of a nonconformist youth subculture. *Journal of Social Issues,* 1969, *25,* 65–89.

WHITTAKER, D., & WATTS, W. A. Personality characteristics associated with activism and disaffiliation in today's college-age youth. *Journal of Counseling Psychology,* 1971, *18,* 200–206.

WHYTE, W. *The organization man.* Garden City, N.Y.: Doubleday, 1956.

WICK, J. W. Final evaluation report of the Law in American Society Project. Unpublished paper. Chicago: Law in American Society Project, 1973.

WIDICK, B. J. Black city, black unions. In I. Howe (Ed.), *The world of the blue collar worker.* New York: Quadrangle, 1972.

WILENSKY, H. L. The professionalization of everyone? *American Journal of Sociology,* 1964, *70,* 137–158.

WILLERMAN, L. Activity level and hyperactivity in twins. *Child Development,* 1973, *44,* 288–293.

WILLERMAN, L., & PLOMIN, R. Activity levels in children and their parents. *Child Development,* 1973, *44,* 854–858.

WILSON, C. M. Children and war films. *League of Nations Education Survey,* 1929, *1,* 12–64.

WILSON, J. Q. *Varieties of police behavior.* Cambridge: Harvard University Press, 1968.

WILSON, J. Q., & BANFIELD, E. Public-regardingness as a value premise in voting behavior. *American Political Science Review,* 1964, *58,* 876–887.

WILSON, P. R. *Immigrants and politics.* Canberra: Australian National University Press, 1973.

WINICK, M. Malnutrition and the developing brain. In F. Plum (Ed.), *Brain dysfunction in metabolic disorders* (Vol. 53 of Research Publications of the Association for Research in Nervous and Mental Disease). New York: Raven Press, 1974.

WINTER, D. G. *The power motive.* New York: Free Press, 1973.

WITHEY, S. B. Public opinion on war and shelters. *New University Thought,* 1962, 6–19.

WOLFE, A. B. The motivation of radicalism. *Psychological Review,* 1921, 28.

WOLFENSTEIN, E. V. *The revolutionary personality: Lenin, Trotsky and Gandhi.* Princeton: Princeton University Press, 1967.

WOLFENSTEIN, M., & KLIMAN, G. (Eds.), *Children and the death of a President: Multi-disciplinary studies.* Garden City, N.Y.: Doubleday, 1965.

WOLFINGER, R. E. The development and persistence of ethnic voting. *American Political Science Review,* 1965, *59,* 896–908.

WOLFINGER, R. E., WOLFINGER, B. K., PREWITT, K., & ROSENHACK, S. America's radical right: Politics and Ideology. In R. Schoenberger (Ed.), *The American right wing.* New York: Holt, Rinehart & Winston, 1969.

WOLIN, S., & SCHAAR, J. *The Berkeley rebellion and beyond.* New York: Vintage Books, 1970.

WOOD, R. Scientists and politics: The rise of an apolitical elite. In R. Gilpin & C. Wright (Eds.), *Scientists and national policy making.* New York: Columbia University Press, 1964.

WOODRUFF, D. S. The usefulness of the life-span approach for the psychophysiology of aging. *Gerontologist,* 1973, *13,* 467–472.

WOODRUFF, D. S. A physiological perspective of the psychology of aging. In D. S. Woodruff & J. E. Birren (Eds.), *Aging: Scientific perspectives and social issues.* New York: Van Nostrand, 1975.

WOODRUFF, D. S., & BIRREN, J. E. Age changes and cohort differences in personality. *Developmental Psychology,* 1972, *6,* 252–259.

WRIGHT, D. *The psychology of moral behavior.* Baltimore: Penguin Books, 1971.

WRIGHT, Q. *A study of war.* Chicago: University of Chicago Press, 1942.

WRIGHTSMAN, L. S. Measurement of philosophies of human nature. *Psychological Reports,* 1964, *14,* 743–751.

WRIGHTSMAN, L. S. Parental attitudes and behaviors as determinants of children's responses to the threat of nuclear war. In R. Sigel (Ed.), *Learning about politics.* New York: Random House, 1970.

WRIGHTSMAN, L. S., & COOK, S. Factor analysis and attitude change. *Peabody Papers in Human Development* (Vol. 3). Nashville: George Peabody College for Teachers, 1965.

WYLIE, L. *Village in the Vaucluse*. Cambridge: Harvard University Press, 1957.

X., MALCOLM. *The autobiography of Malcolm X*. New York: Grove Press, 1964.

YANKELOVICH, D., & BARRETT, W. *Ego and instinct*. New York: Random House, 1970.

YINGER, J. M. Anomie, alienation, and political behavior. In J. N. Knutson (Ed.), *Handbook of political psychology*. San Francisco: Jossey-Bass, 1973.

YOUNG, K. The psychology of war. In J. D. Clarkson & T. Cochran (Eds.), *War as a social institution*. New York: A. M. Press, 1966.

ZAJONC, R. The concepts of balance, congruity, and dissonance. *Public Opinion Quarterly*, 1960, *24*, 280–296.

ZAJONC, R. B. Cognitive theories in social psychology. In G. Lindzey & E. Aronson (Eds.), *Handbook of social psychology*. Reading, Mass.: Addison-Wesley, 1969.

ZAWADZKI, B., & LAZARSFELD, P. F. The psychological consequences of unemployment. *Journal of Social Psychology*, 1935, *6*, 224–257.

ZELLMAN, G. L., & SEARS, D. O. Childhood origins of tolerance for dissent. *Journal of Social Issues*, 1971, *27*, 109–136.

ZIBLATT, D. High school extracurricular activities and political socialization. *Annals of the American Academy of Political and Social Science*, 1965, *361*, 20–31.

ZIEGLER, L. H. *The political world of the high school teacher*. Eugene, Oreg.: Center for the Advanced Study of Educational Administration, University of Oregon, 1966.

ZIEGLER, L. H. *The political life of American teachers*. Englewood Cliffs, N.J.: Prentice-Hall, 1967.

ZODY, R. E. Cohort analysis: Some applicatory problems in the study of social and political behavior. *Social Science Quarterly*, 1969, *50*, 374–380.

Index of Names

Index of Subjects

Activity levels, 18–19

Adult political socialization, 259–293
  age and, 263, 264–271, 289–290
  constant change model, 262
  environmental changes and, 263, 285–289
  generational model, 262, 265, 290
  occupation and, 263, 271–284, 289
  persistence-beyond-childhood model, 262, 265, 269, 270, 290
  status and, 282–284
  theoretical perspectives, 261–263

Age
  adult political socialization and, 263, 264–271, 289–290
  ambiguity of chronological, 298–300
  cross-sectional research designs and, 306–308
  generational analysis and, 296, 298–302
  media use and, 251–253
  of peers, 173–174

Agents of political socialization, 115–141
  church as, 136
  college as, 135–136, 140
  communication and, 118
  epistemological considerations, 121–122
  exposure to, 117–118
  family as, 122–127, 139
  influence, measurement of, 118–121, 124–125
  mass media as: see Mass communication, political socialization and
  methodological considerations, 118–121

military as, 136
  peers as: see Peers, political socialization and
  receptivity and, 118
  relative influence of, 137–138
  schools as: see Schools, political socialization and
  siblings as, 136
  spouse as, 136, 178–179
  theoretical considerations, 116–118
  youth organizations as, 136

Aggression, 49, 365–366; see also War, childhood learning about
  origins of, 390–393
  political activism and, 415–416

Alienation, 273, 274, 280, 315–317, 450
  political activism and, 420–421

Altruism, political activism and, 426

Amish people, 73

Androgens, 152–154, 398

Animism, 354

Antiwar movement, 395, 416, 417, 421, 434, 439, 440–441

Appalachians, 73

Application, decisions of, 458

Appraisal, decisions of, 459, 463

Artificialism, 354

Attention zones, 452

Attractiveness of peer group, 176

Australia, 101, 278, 379

Authoritarianism, 162, 166–168
  political activism and, 418–419
  working-class, 281